# Ybor City

## The Making of a Landmark Town

*La Sétima, Ybor City. From a painting by Arnold Martinez.*

# Ybor City
## The Making of a Landmark Town

**Frank Trebín Lastra**

EDITED BY RICHARD MATHEWS

FOREWORD BY E. J. SALCINES

AFTERWORD BY RAFAEL MARTINEZ YBOR

**UNIVERSITY OF TAMPA PRESS**
**TAMPA, FLORIDA**

Manufactured in the United States of America
Printed on acid free paper
First Edition


The University of Tampa Press
401 West Kennedy Boulevard
Tampa, Florida 33606

ISBN-13: 978-1-59732-002-3 (hbk); ISBN-10: 1-59732-002-1 (hbk)
ISBN-13: 978 -1-59732-003-0 (pbk); ISBN-10: 1-59732-003-X (pbk)



**Library of Congress Cataloging-in-Publication Data**

Lastra, Frank Trebín, 1922-
   Ybor City : the making of a landmark town / Frank Trebín Lastra ; edited by Richard Mathews.— 1st ed.
        p. cm.
   Includes bibliographical references and index.
   ISBN-13: 978-1-59732-002-3 (hbk : alk. paper)
   ISBN-10: 1-59732-002-1 (hbk : alk. paper)
   1. Ybor City (Tampa, Fla.)—History. 2. Tampa (Fla.)—History.  I. Mathews, Richard, 1944-
II. Title.

F319.T2Y36 2006
975.9'65—dc2                       2005027946

# Dedication

This work is dedicated to *los tabaqueros*—the cigar workers of Ybor City, Palmetto Beach, and West Tampa—and to the *patrones*, the factory owners. Together they made Ybor City happen.

We are also deeply grateful to Don Vicente Martínez Ybor for his crucial role in founding this town for which we feel such pride. His leadership in inviting other tobacco industrialists to locate here soon propelled the primitive village of Tampa to become the "Clear Tobacco Capital of the Country." Making that a reality were the members of our diverse yet cohesive Latin society—Spaniards, Cubans, and Italians—together with supporting Romanian Jews and limited numbers of Germans in the Ybor City area.

The Latins in Ybor City molded a distinctive history, one shaped by a superb social fabric, strong medical institutions, and a rich overall quality of life, much of it sustained by enviable European values transferred and adapted to life here across the ocean. These include their love of family; devotion to hard work and self-sufficiency; determination; moderation; respect for their forebears, elders, and their fellow men, women, and children; their belief in the need for higher education; their love of America and freedom; and their need to be thankful for their blessings and beliefs. These were substantially the values that the town enjoyed through good and bad days alike.

The remarkable accomplishments of these shapers of Ybor City brought vitality, affection, and a kind of splendor to this place, and ultimately earned it the rare and highly coveted recognition as a National Historic Landmark District.

# Table of Contents

# ACKNOWLEDGMENTS

This book could not have come into being without the untiring support of many friends and family members, and a list too long to print of individuals and groups who supplied information, encouragement, photographs, letters, papers, and wonderful stories of the old days. Thank you all.

*S*pecial thanks and recognition to Frank García, Estevan Orestano, Agustine Fernández, Joe Benito, Joe Busciglio (recently deceased), Dominick Maggio, El Nene, Sam Williams, Benny Frisco, La Nena, cousins Tess, Ann, and sister Lola, Al Fernández, past president of Ybor City Chamber of Commerce (YCCC), for his having asked me to join the Ybor Chamber some twenty-four years ago. In his presence I always feel the beat of the town we both knew.

Much thanks to Victor Dimaio Sr., past president of YCCC, a very respected political activist and a leader in the Latin community, for editing much earlier historical material and giving his "amen," so typical of his style. Victor is one of the most informed sons of Ybor City on day-to-day events. And to Emmett Clary, long-term Director of YCCC and the Ybor Museum Society, who also reviewed much of this writer's work.. He has much knowledge of the Latin world of Ybor City of the last three decades and speaks Spanish fluently.

Special thanks to Roland Manteiga and his son, Patrick, eminent publishers of the incomparable tri-lingual newspaper, *La Gaceta*, for technical assistance, opening up the *Gaceta* files and supplying needed photos. Thanks also to Patrick's wife, Angela, and the *Gaceta* staff for much help and advice. (Thank you, Roland and Patrick, for publishing my articles.)

My thanks to Stephanie Ferrell and David Rigny (now deceased), former members of the Preservation Board; David Alderman, Ranger at the Ybor State Museum, Joan Jennewein and Rebecca Gagalis, both past presidents of YCCC, Jill Wax, Henry Woodruff, Ken Ferlita, Sam Leto, Vince Pardo, Kris Fernández, Gil Hernández, Sara Romeo, and Jack Shiver, respected business people all, for knowledgeable facts on recent happenings. Thanks to Steve Lester for Alcalde Association and Round Table material; and again to Ken Ferlita, who as incoming YCCC president had asked this writer to write several articles on the "old days." One title he suggested, "The Way it Was," became the name for that lengthy series of features that was a forerunner to this work.

Thanks to the various Social Clubs for lists of presidents, photographs, and other details, with my special appreciation to the staffs of L'Unione Italiana, Centro Asturiano, Círculo Cubano, and Union Martí Maceo for their helpful input. And special thanks to Margarita Pellon for two very wonderful photos from the early days. Margarita is the daughter of Estevan Pellon, "El Polaco," a historical personality connected with the oldtime picnic trips to Rocky Point, where he distributed supplies.

I wish also to thank Cookie Ellis, past YCCC Executive Director, and Lisa Harris, Editor/Art Director of *La Sétima Newsletter*, for the support they provided me towards the historical series, "The Way it Was," some of which I used in the preparation of this book; and to Annette DeLisle, Editer/Designer Rosalie Guarino Simms, Ana and computer whiz, Scot, of the YCCC staff.

Thanks to Angel Bustelo for verification of much Ybor city informational detail. Long ago Angel also supplied the name *La Sétimato* for the YCCC newsletter when this writer, as the president, appointed him to head the effort to create a newsletter, and to his wife, Alice Bustelo, fountain of knowledge and of much detail on Ybor City.

Heartfelt thanks to the University of South Florida Library, particularly the Special Collection Department's Tom Kemp, Paul Camp, and all the staff for their invaluable assistance; and to the John F. Germany Tampa-Hillsborough County Public Library, History and Geneaology department (especially Jean and the second-floor staff), and Patrick Grace for the help given me. My thanks also to Lois Latimer and the Tampa Historical Society for friendly and invaluable help.

Thanks also to Mary Alvarez and Sonya Ziegler, both presidents of the Ybor City Museum Society, Delia Sanchez, Eva Ciaccio, Rosann Garcia, and Yolanda Fernández, Adrienne García, Donna Parrino, and Violet Lombardia, all distinguished members of the Latin Community. And without a doubt to that grand lady, Providence Velasco, of the Ybor Museum Volunteers.

My thanks go to Rene Gonzalez, Founder and Director of the Spanish Lyric theater. He has contributed a wealth of culture to our town. What would Ybor City have been without the Zarzuelas which he directed for the last four decades?

I especially wish to thank Dr. Henry J. Fernandez, very eminent *Yborciteño*, for the use of his papers which he so graciously let me borrow, and which I passed to others so they would be aware of his real accomplishments for Ybor City. Henry, how easy it is to forget yesterday!

I also want to thank Cesar Gonzmart Jr. for both his official papers and his written, detailed summary covering some nine years of his timely, original, and crucial work on the Ybor City State Museum. It led to the opening of the Ybor City State Museum building and garden. His was the essential work that had to be done to give meaning to the other steps, concurrent or ahead.

I also want to thank Dr. L. Glenn Westfall, the consulting historian hired by the Division of Archives, History and Records Management, Bureau of Historic Sites and Properties, which resulted in his *Research Study for the Development of the Ybor City State Museum*. Dr. Westfall alerted this writer to the existence of this work, which was utilized by the State Division of Archives, History and Records as the basis for the Ybor State Museum's thematic historical and folkloric displays and photos.

Thanks, Bettie Nelson, first president of the Ybor Museum Society, for heading the committee to report the facts on the Ybor City State Museum building founding and planning, on which this writer served. The papers and reports submitted to me by her, and Cesar Jr. before her, form the basis for my coverage of the Ybor City State Museum building, patio, artifacts and Museum Society itself. They also led to the museum article by this writer, which cited the Founders: the above, plus Stanford Newman and Ney Landrum. This, too, will be recounted in this book. Modest Bettie Nelson is a member of the Daughters of the American Revolution and other historical societies one feels must be mentioned.

My thanks to Harris Mullen, author, for his detailed and friendly letter to this writer on correct writing techniques, which this writer still hasn't mastered. Harris developed Ybor Square, formerly the Don Vicente Martínez Ybor's *Principe de Gales* factory. It was an honor for this writer to have worked with Harris in several organizations geared to Ybor's growth. His wish and work for the creation of a "critical mass" of festive, historic and other sane venues for Ybor City influenced much of my writings.

I must thank Tampa and Hillsborough County's official historian, Tony Pizzo, now deceased, for his encouragement over the years and for the times we discussed and pinned down certain events. One was the years embraced by the "Golden Years of Ybor City," which we concluded were the years 1900-1950, and for much other information and advice he gave me. Thank you also, Josephine! Tony, much has been built on your writings, historical markers, plaques, oral histories, and kindnesses. What would we have done without these? May you rest in peace.

I want to thank my friend, now also deceased, Adela Gonzmart—Ybor's "First Lady" and owner of the Columbia Restaurant, an Ybor Institution—for her many views offered over two decades. She once told me, "Frank, if it happened, write it exactly like that!" She knew many behind-scene doings on many of Ybor City's activities. In fact, she spawned a great number of ideas that led to innumerable festivities, civic actions, ceremonies, and to the continuation of Ybor City's folklore. Adela provided and confirmed much information about happenings in the town that are included in this work.

x

**Ybor City: The Making of a Landmark Town**

I want to extend my thanks to former Florida Governor and Tampa Mayor Bob Martínez for his personal and political support on behalf of efforts to preserve and revitalize Ybor City, including one appointment I could not accept because of a potential conflict of interest he was not aware of. And special thanks to Bob Morrison—then Mayor Martínez's very able staff aide —for his many courtesies.

I must thank my close friend Rafael Martínez-Ybor, retired Vice President for International Banking for the Bank of Tampa, for much encouragement to proceed with the history of Ybor City, particularly during the composition of shorter, monthly versions which appeared in the Chamber newsletter, *La Sétima*. Rafael Martínez-Ybor is a key protector of the history his great grandfather, founder Don Vicente, bequeathed this town. Rafael, thank you for the copy of the picture of Don Vicente's country home, *la Quinta*, in Ybor City, as well as other notes on your great grandmother, and her role in the Cuban Revolutionary party in Ybor City. And thank you, Rafael, for writing the beautiful Epilogue for this work.

Also, my thanks to Emiliano José Salcines, prominent Tampa judge, for his many kind words with respect to this book. He is generally recognized as the unofficial senior member of the general Latin community of greater Tampa, and Tampa's most respected representative of the Spanish culture and tradition. He has also represented the broad Latin community magnificently.

For more recent and valuable information I wish to thank Harry Moradiello of the Lion's Club and Rolando Pérez Pedrero, president of the Circulo Cubano club, Jack Rodríquez, past president of YCDC, and Urban Planner Maricela Medrano de Fakhri and his staff for effective historic district boundary information. Special thanks are due to Leland Hawes, *Tampa Tribune* history columnist, Elizabeth L. Dunham, Director of Collections and Exhibitions for the Tampa Bay History Center, and Gary R. Mormino, Frank F. Duckwall Professor of Florida History at the University of South Florida and official Hillsborough County Historian, for reading and editing the manuscript. They were tremendously helpful in catching many of my mistakes. I thank them for this great assistance and apologize for the errors that remain, which I can assure readers are unintentional and for which I take full responsibility. Please know that I invite your comments and corrections to be mailed to me in care of my publisher so that I can correct and improve any subsequent printings.

I want to especially recognize my father's old, close Spanish friends, now all deceased. They played a big role in my young life. I often sat and listened to them on those many evenings when they sat with father under his Sycamore tree and talked of the happenings of the day. I learned much about the ways of the town, the cigar factory, the Spanish Civil War and of Spain itself from them. These are José, Andres, Braña, Alfonso, and López. In influencing my life they all inspired my desire to write this book, and to convey as accurately as possible the world of that time.

I also want to say "thank you" to the many individuals I have forgotten to mention, and to Ellen White, Sean Donnelly, and Richard Mathews at the University of Tampa Press for transforming my manuscript into the book you are reading.

*Finally, my love, thanks, and apologies to my wife and family for the many months and years I have devoted to this project, much to my neglect of them.*



**Acknowledgements**

# EDITOR'S PREFACE

Frank Lastra's extraordinary contribution to Ybor City history has been a labor of love and a work of many years. His conception was large and comprehensive; his goal was to collect in one place virtually everything that he could find and record about the history and heritage of his town. For a project of such scope to be carried out by someone with no formal training in scholarly research and no academic degree in history makes it all the more remarkable. Yet a lifelong knowledge of the town where he was born, a breadth of cultural and historical interests, college training in industrial engineering at M.I.T. and Georgia Tech, and personal involvement in Ybor City's preservation and revitalization have uniquely qualified him to tell this story of the immigrants, industrialists, residents, and visionaries who created a National Landmark town.

It has been a great pleasure to work with Frank as he sought out missing photographs, prodded and cajoled friends and acquaintances for information, always revising, correcting, and supplementing the details in a story he had assembled into multiple notebooks full of letters, typed recollections, newsletters, newspaper clippings, and multiple revisions of a complete manuscript. The book had already gone through at least four or five drafts when we met, and since that time he has rewritten, photocopied, and had professionally bound into covers several different revisions of his typescript, which numbers more than 300 pages—excluding all the photographs and captions.

My goal in editing his manuscript has been to preserve his voice and his wide-ranging vision while helping to clarify areas of confusion, provide connections and transitions, draw together loose ends, carry forward the process of coordinating text, photographs, and captions, and complete the notes, bibliography, and index. It is my hope that you will find very little of an English professor's hand in this book, but the unmistakable style and sensibility of the author. Similarly, I determined from the start to trust Frank's instincts for what is important and not to second-guess his history. My favorite parts are those in which he writes directly from his own experience—especially his years growing up in Ybor City and his accounts of childhood and family experiences. It also strikes me that his effort to record as much as he could discover about the determined efforts to move Ybor City beyond the catastrophe of Urban Renewal and toward genuine historic renewal is both useful and unique. As far as I know, there is no other history in print that tells this complex story and records the individual contributions of dedicated citizens since the 1950s who have made Ybor City the National Historic Landmark District that it is today.

I am deeply indebted to all those who have helped, but most especially to Ellen White, whose enthusiasm and commitment to this book are responsible for bringing it to the University of Tampa Press to begin with; to Gary Mormino and Elizabeth Dunham, who read and commented on the book in its earliest galleys; to Leland Hawes, whose knowledge and support through many drafts have been invaluable; to E. J. Salcines for sharing his expertise and contributing his Foreword; and to Ana Montalvo and Sean Donnelly, my colleagues at the press, without whom this book would not exist.

As we finally deliver the book to the printer, both Frank and I are acutely aware of its rough edges and of how much remains to be done. Yet, having worked together toward completion of this project since 1998, we determined that we could not allow another year to pass before the book saw print. We present it now in the spirit of a work-in-progress, with apologies for its shortcomings and with the hope that it will contribute to a growing appreciation for a very special place under the sun.

– Richard Mathews

# $\mathcal{F}$oreword

It's finally here! After years—decades to be exact—of writing, researching, reviewing, and documenting, "the Rambling Wreck from Georgia Tech" has exceeded our expectations. Frank Lastra is a professional industrial engineer, successful businessman, and exemplary citizen whose love and devotion to Ybor City history is well known. For years he has been patiently researching, collecting, and archiving volumes of historical data, maps, photographs, and artifacts on the people who built this great mosaic of cultures, languages, and traditions. It inspired him to put together this one-volume encyclopedia of Latino presence in this region of Florida. *Ybor City: The Making of a Landmark Town* is a book that everyone interested in Tampa history should read and pass on together with family heirlooms. It is full of treasures of our past.

In one single volume, neatly presented in chronological sequence and conveniently indexed, the development of Ybor City, Palmetto Beach, and West Tampa is superbly reviewed.

Frank is a native of Ybor City and the product of a Sicilian mother and a father from northern Spain. He grew up in this multilingual enclave observing, understanding, and remembering events and details of the past. He has documented very well the Latin community before and after the Spanish Civil War (1936-1939), the Second World War (1941-1945), Urban Renewal, the crisscrossing of the interstate systems, and the impact that these had on the unique area of Florida and the diaspora of its people as a result of these different events. Our Latins dispersed all over!

Throughout his lifetime, Frank has made serious inquiries and research. He studied articles, reports, and books about our rich history and collected thousands of oral histories from the old-timers who had lived the experiences. As years pass and memories become fuzzy and fade away, unless they are documented, retained, and preserved for posterity, they're lost.

For many years, we've known that Frank understood the historical importance of our unique community. Many of us urged him to write this book. Over the last ten years, he has allowed us to proofread portions of drafts and manuscripts. He received our helpful criticism and suggestions very well. We couldn't convince him to spell "La Septima" with a "p"—but he overwhelmed us with a listing of early cafés, restaurants, and bakeries, let alone pioneer cigar factories and "chinchales" (small cigar factories) up to World War II, plus clubs, hospitals and clinics, names of presidents of all of our mutual aid societies, civic clubs, Ybor City Chamber of Commerce, alcaldes and alcaldesas, identified unions, major strikes and devastating fires, biographical data of leading personalities, and splendid photographs—old and new, many of which have never been published before—even popular names and expressions. Then when he had put all of this information together, he sought and got the help of an outstanding professional team that Dr. Richard Mathews supervises at the University of Tampa Press.

This is Frank's first "big book," but not his first. He published a paperback titled *The Knife Sharpener* that he and his dear friend and C.P.A., the late Manuel Blanco, co-authored. He also wrote *Games and Pastimes in the Golden Years of Ybor City* as well as a book of poems entitled in Spanish *Recuerdos de Ybor* (Memories of Ybor). Many of his articles and short stories have appeared in *La Gaceta*—Tampa's trilingual newspaper published since 1922. Also, we've all learned a lot from his articles on Ybor City history titled "The Way It Was."

Significantly, *Ybor City: The Making of a Landmark Town* contains materials presented in an easily accessible format that we trust will help and supplement future publications about the hard-working, loyal, and visionary people—remarkable men and women of different nationalities, languages, customs, races, and religions. We feel certain that this book will spark new inquiries, research, articles, exhibits, publications, and greater appreciation of this heritage that has strengthened the foundation upon which our unusual, fascinating, diverse, and dynamic cosmopolitan community has developed. This history must be told and not forgotten. This past—is prologue!


E. J. Salcines
Vice President
Tampa Historical Society

# Introduction

*Ybor City: The Making of a Landmark Town* has been a long time in the making. The thought of writing a thorough history of the town has often been high on my list of projects. Increasing this desire has been my personal observation that the old Ybor that many remember is fast fading away. In fact, it is only in conversation among today's "originals"—the sons and daughters who eagerly wear their parents' more authentic crowns—that the town comes alive in all the majesty which memories can conjure. It is none too soon to record these recollections, as the number who justly claim the title of "originals" grows smaller with the passing years.

I hasten, thus, to write this history, lest the remaining intrinsic pieces fall apart and cannot be sewn together to bring back the town as Cubans, Spaniards, and Italians remember it. This work, certainly in the coverage of the period before 1930, relies heavily on the reporting of others whose accounts were published by such respected newspapers as *La Gaceta*, the *Tampa Tribune*, the old *Tampa Times*, the *St. Petersburg Times*, and other media. I am especially thankful to the many dedicated authors, both in our area and out of it, many now deceased, who passed down a legacy of historical detail and anecdote.

My work is based on research using primary materials at the various major libraries in Tampa, including Special Collections at the University of South Florida and at the downtown John F. Germany Library. I have also read the existing books on the town's history. All this is necessary to reconstruct the past.

However, at the heart of the story I have included my personal observations from the mid-1920s through 1940—those early, vigorous years of Ybor City—after which I headed to college and Army service. And I will quickly add that whatever I have written is in consonance with the street talk I heard in those happy years. My account also benefits from later observations and conclusions drawn during my engineering years away from home and from what I could assimilate during regular return visits. This was much like taking snapshots of the town several times a year, for many years. Changes were easier to detect and understand because of the distance. The continuing trips to the cafés with my father on those visits home did much to enlighten the gaps. And my "return" to the area, beginning in 1960 to Clearwater, and then to the Tampa area from 1967 to the present, afforded me a full view of happenings in the town. Thus I have been able to draw from some six decades of knowing this place.

Today, Ybor City is still blessed with a fair number of active sons and daughters. They are still involved in its theatrical, musical, and social activities. The Ybor City Chamber of Commerce, the Ybor City State Museum Society, and the various social clubs—The Centro Asturiano, L'Unione Italiana, El Círculo Cubano, and Centro Español—make strong attempts to keep the Latin culture alive. However, to the town's great loss, as these sons and daughters become fewer, the preservation of its cultural roots appears increasingly uncertain.

This book tries to nourish Ybor City's historic roots by recording some of the personal stories, as well as the larger sagas of cigar industry unionism, ideological struggles, and worker reactions and responses—for the town's story is the story of those who lived and labored long and hard. These workers' minds were coveted by all manner of militant forces existing in the first and early second quarter of the twentieth century. Their thoughts were shared in coffeehouse talk and chatter. And always at the forefront of conversation were the doings of the *capatáz*—the *tabaqueros'* (rollers') floor boss—the *encargados* (supervisor), and the *patrón* (factory owner). Add to this the Reading Committee and its *Presidente de Lectura*, which were so often penetrated by militant forces. They controlled the material the *lector* would read. This, obviously, was a most effective tool used to influence the workers' minds. Early unions and foreign ideologies competed for the right to represent the *tabaqueros* and understand their minds.

The attitudes of workers and residents alike in these formative years were strongly rooted in firm, positive underpinnings of Peninsular Spanish mores. A solid sense of propriety, correct manners, law and order, and the ethic of hard work were hallmarks of the times. Moreover, the existence of Castilian as a common language made for easy communication. Italians spoke it very well.

These Spanish values that I speak of are the ones we learned at home and which I saw and felt in operation in the town. Coupled with my Sicilian mother's strong love of family and all the other positive cultural values Sicilians possess, they form the human perspective I bring to this book, together with an inclination toward systematic analysis that stems from my engineering background. I have written my account in an attempt to leave a record of the town in which I grew. It is, factually, a fascinating human saga—the story of a town that an industrialist created, one virtually destroyed by outside forces, and in the end resuscitated. Its final breath of life was instilled with "Anglo" and other American drives and initiatives within the warmth of the wonderful Latin ambiance. The human spirit seems indomitable.

The path to Ybor City's new vitality has led it to affirm its history. The special attributes of the old Centro Español building—its dating from the early period, its historic leadership role, its exemplary activities and cradle-to-grave medical services—compelled the government to award it the National Historic Landmark classification. And due to the existence of this and many other National Historic buildings and organizations embodying the Latin mores and qualities of self-sufficiency which shaped the history, the federal government has seen fit to award the town the National Historic Landmark District classification. Little wonder, then, that much needs to be said of the values that shaped Ybor City, founded and anchored in those human qualities that historically have moved men and women to greater heights.

History records that the town's pulse still vibrates strongly in the civic and social activities that Latin sons and daughters continue to maintain. The entire twentieth century pulsed to a Latin beat—

and today a new century begins with a growing segment of Ybor City activity introducing a more eclectic lifestyle, built heavily on evening, night, and weekend drinking and festive entertainment. In the last quarter of the century, there is much to be said about the heavy contribution made by non-Latins, or "Anglos," as the street jargon referred to typical Americans. Their accommodation into the mainstream of Ybor City was gradual and guarded, but finally recognized and appreciated. Today much of the investment in Ybor City is being made by Latin and non-Latin interests, with enormous funding coming from statewide or national enterprises. Still, the Latin pulse throbs underneath.

Why have I written this book? The answer is simply pride and fear. Pride in the town's heritage—the heritage of today's remaining "originals"—and the lives and sagas of the fathers and mothers who bequeathed the town to us. And fear that time will eventually leave this heritage behind, forgotten, or, perhaps, inadvertently destroyed. Each writer has his own agendas. Mine has been to record the manner and quality of life as it was, or at least as I knew it.

I hope that my choice to follow a chronological approach, rather than a discussion "by subject" will provide easy access to general readers and students alike. In order to offer more than just historical narrative, I have included many tables at the end of the book. These record such things as officers of civic, social, and medical clubs year by year; major strikes; historical newspapers; the proposed street car line; major fires; popular Spanish sayings; special exhibits; and other materials of interest. Although I am not a professional scholar, I have also gathered and presented footnotes and annotations to document my sources as much as possible. Dr. Richard Mathews and the staff of the University of Tampa Press have helped with this, but I should state in advance that in some cases we have simply had to leave the references incomplete; when I began this work I never thought I would need to document my research so thoroughly, and often my notes simply do not contain complete source information for every fact, despite my having literally tracked down each and every one. What you will find here has been cross-checked and documented as thoroughly as I could manage, given the constraints on my time and my limited notes. I also have included photographic acknowledgments and an index of important names and topics that I believe will help complete this picture of this unique community. Still, there is much left to be said, and it is my sincere hope that there will be a surge of fresh writing on the subject—a boom, if you will—and that this book may contribute to it. If so, history will be served.

With complex historical facts, interwoven social fabric, wide scope of ambition and idealism, and intensity of activity, the people established and maintained a special place on this earth. Yes, Ybor City earned its National Historic Landmark District classification. It was—and is—no ordinary town.

*–Frank Trebín Lastra*
Tampa, 2002

# Ybor City
## The Making of a Landmark Town

*Don Vicente Martínez Ybor, founder of Ybor City.* Rafael Martinez Ybor.

# The Founding of Ybor City: 1492-1824

## Destiny

Destiny must have played a part in Spain's link to America and particularly to Florida.

It began with Christopher Columbus in 1492 and his alliance with the Catholic monarchs Isabella and Ferdinand.[1]

Destiny figured again in 1513 when Juan Ponce de León set foot on a desolate stretch of land on an Easter morning in the season known to the Spanish as the Festival of Flowers or "flowery paschal," *Pascua Florida*, a phrase that resonated long enough to give the state its name.[2]

The period 1539 through 1567 saw three more Spanish explorers come to Tampa Bay, then sometimes referred to as *La Bahía de Espíritu Santo* (The Bay of the Holy Spirit). Among these were Hernando de Soto, Panfilo de Narváez, and Pedro Menéndez de Avilés.

And it was destiny, also—although intense design and imperial power played a heavy hand—that through a succession of twenty-four Spanish governors *La Florida* remained under Spanish control, with only brief periods of interruption. It was destiny for Spain to establish St. Augustine, the first permanent European settlement in the continental U.S. (which would later become Florida's first National Historic Landmark town); hold the first Mass on the American continent there; construct an impregnable fortress that still stands; build scores of missions in Florida to Christianize the Indians; and give us pigs, sheep, hardy Cracker cows, oranges, waterways, paths and byways, names, and countless other invaluable resources.[3]

Once again, in 1783, Spain's presence in Florida proved beneficial to America. The Spanish Captain General Bernardo de Galvez contributed greatly to the American colonies' war of independence. He seized Mobile and Pensacola from the British and held them both for the duration of the conflict; Americans repaid him later by naming Galveston in his honor. And as a further recognition of Spain's contribution to the thirteen American colonies and their fight for independence, the victorious colonial government gave both East and West Florida back to Spain.[4]

Spaniards made many contributions to the people of the Tampa Bay region through their fishing *ranchos*, although knowledge of them seems to have faded over time. Still, traces can be seen in the presence of the large number of Cuban and Spanish fishermen and oystermen who first settled in what is now Tampa's Old Hyde Park. In the first third of the 19th century, the area was referred to as *Spanish Town*.

*The culture and romance of Spain are part of Ybor City's heritage. The connection was often expressed in cigar label art such as this one for El Tipo brand made at the Arguelles, Lopez, and Brothers factory in Ybor City.*

*Vicente Martínez Ybor first left Spain for Cuba in 1832 at the age of 14. In 1854 he began to manufacture the cigar he called "El Principe de Gales" ("The Prince of Wales") in a large Havana factory. It remained his most popular cigar after he moved his factory to Key West, New York, back to Key West, and then to Ybor City.*

## Don Vicente Martínez Ybor: His Early Life

Spanish dominion over Cuba created the conditions that caused Don Vicente Martínez Ybor, a native of Valencia, Spain, to flee the island. In Spain, Valencianos are known to have great business acumen, and Vicente did not let his countrymen down in this respect. The son of a prominent family, he had gone to Cuba in 1832, when he was just fourteen. The cigar industry there was in its formative years, and he first worked as a clerk, then became a broker, and soon he was a cigar manufacturer himself when he opened his first factory, "El Principe de Gales" (Prince of Wales), in Havana in 1853. The brand name was an interesting choice in many ways—affirming an association with the highest circles of status and wealth; embracing the royal family of England in the language of Spain; looking toward the future with a princely title that claimed to be "heir apparent," the new-born brand that would one day truly be "King of Havana Cigars." It was a bold step for this Spanish immigrant, yet his ambitious choice of name was not mistaken. The firm soon became a distinguished one, earning international awards for the excellence of its cigars.[8]

Many remaining inhabitants claim to be of Spanish ancestry, descendants of families who lived on the site for hundreds of years.[5] However, after 1824, when the U.S. Army established Fort Brooke, the fishing grounds were disturbed by the Army settlement, and many of the original residents along Spanishtown Creek moved away.[6]

Destiny had seemingly run its course some seven decades after the U.S. bought Florida from Spain in 1821, and in a sense it had. In the latter part of the century it was not Spain itself, but a "Spaniard with Cuban sympathies," who assumed a position of leadership in the destiny of a primitive little town in the middle of mangroves, palmettos, alligators, and bay water.

This influx of Spanish entrepreneurial invaders brought a new, exciting, and vigorous industry to Florida, and this time, the economic pioneers were not alone. They were joined by Cubans, both white and black, other Spaniards, and soon, by Italians. All these shared heritage and opportunities through a common language—Castilian. And they, in turn, quickly formed alliances with two crucial supporting groups—Jewish merchants and German craftsmen, mostly—who played a necessary and memorable role in the commerce of the town. [7]

However, social unrest and revolutionary activities in colonial Cuba began creating difficulties for Spain, which had by then occupied the island for more than three centuries. A Spanish tax was levied on tobacco to help raise the revenues needed to finance the country's struggle in Cuba. The effect was similar to that of colonial patriots in Boston when an English tax resulted in the Boston Tea Party, with its revolutionary consequences. In 1868 a rebellion at Yara marked the beginning of the ill-fated Ten Years War in Cuba.

With a temperament that instinctively defended independence and a practical businessman's resentment of tobacco taxation, Ybor found himself attracted to the

Cuban cause, and soon enough Spain realized he had Cuban sympathies. Advised by a friend that he was about to be arrested, Ybor disguised himself and shipped off to Key West in 1869. In so doing, he first transplanted his cigar manufacturing expertise to the little island at the tip of Florida.

In Key West, Don Vicente rented a cluster of buildings and began manufacturing his *Principe de Gales* (Prince of Wales) brand on U.S. soil. In time he became Key West's second largest manufacturer of cigars. By 1875 there were twenty-one cigar factories on that last Florida key, and Don Vicente's factory had produced 10,200,000 cigars. In Key West, "Don Vicente accumulated sufficient wealth to loan money to other manufacturers, and by 1873 he had reinvested profits in Key West."[9]

While Key West as a manufacturing site was considered ideal, due to its proximity to Havana and the tobacco fields in Piñar del Rio, there were some unsettling situations. Louis A. Pérez Jr. described the situation in *La Gaceta* newspaper in a story on "Cuban Cigar Workers in Tampa" in 1972. Pérez reported that the labor relations issues which formed the work environment for the cigar workers defined the essential quality of the Cuban community in Florida. Their attitudes included strong Marxist influences and a highly developed proletarian consciousness with a long tradition of trade union militancy. These were attitudes the Cuban tobacco workers brought with them to the United States, and they flourished in Florida.

The growing labor ferment and rumblings of unionization in Key West, as well as a need for steady expansion at a location where both the land and the laborers were limited, caused Ybor to consider an alternative to Key West manufacturing. With his successful business booming, he had the necessary capital to move, and he first branched out to New York, where he constructed a factory characterized as "mammoth." He named it *El Coloso* (The Colossus). It was five stories high and employed five hundred workers. However, here, too, the labor situation was dominated by union militancy, and with years of entrenched organizing, these Northern unions were experienced and well-positioned. In 1876 and 1877 his New York factory was crippled by strikes. Don Vicente returned to Key West. Perhaps the only consolation was the balmy weather and the moisture content in the air, far superior for tobacco than the drier climate in New York City.[10]

Many Cubans in Key West were active in worker activities and constantly sought increased wages and other benefits, to the dismay of the *patrones* (factory owners). Many also had at least a passing interest in the militant ideologies gaining ground throughout the industrial world. Additionally, the desire for a free Cuba consumed the passions of Cuban workers, and their spirits were lifted by the Cuban *lectores* (factory readers) of the day, so that their donations to the revolutionaries became of great concern to the Spaniards. In fact, revolutionary leaders on the island often lent their services at promoting peace between *patrones* and *tabaqueros* in order that donations to the cause of Cuban liberation would not be diminished.[11]

Despite these concerns, cigar manufacturing in Key West through 1886 increased dramatically as Northern manufacturers also opened factories there. But in the great fire of 1886 some fifty buildings, including eleven of the major factories—*El Principe de Gales* among them—went up in flames. At the time of the fire it was widely believed that Spanish *voluntarios* (volunteers) had torched the factories, because a substantial amount of worker income was now aiding the revolutionaries. Whether or not there is any truth to the suspicion, the fire prompted workers whose factories had been destroyed to look beyond the Keys for work. And it prompted Ybor, whose Key West interests were reduced to ashes,

to turn his full attention to New York and to a distant town on the west coast of Florida where some interesting beliefs and discussions would soon lead to resolute decisions and actions.[12]

## Gavino Gutiérrez and Guavas

Who would have guessed that interest in the guava, an unusual and distinctive tropical fruit, would play a role in the history of Tampa?

This wrinkle of Tampa history relates to a trip Gavino Gutiérrez made to Tampa just two years before the Key West fire. One version goes as follows: In November of 1884, Gavino Gutiérrez, a young Spaniard who worked for a food brokerage firm in New York, came to the Tampa area with the firm's manager, Bernardino Gargol. The company was an importer and exporter of Spanish and American jelly, fruit, and paste. While working in New York, Gutiérrez had attended Columbia University and had become a civil engineer, a fact favorable to the future of Ybor City.

Gutiérrez, intrigued by the landscape, waterways, and climate, expressed his belief to Gargol that guavas grew abundantly in the Tampa area and that it would be a good location for their commercial cultivation. Traveling by land to a place called "Peru" (today's Riverview) on the Alafia River, Gargol and Gutiérrez explored the area but found no trace of guavas. Gargol returned to New York, while Gutiérrez went on to Key West. There he would visit his fellow Spaniard Vicente Martínez Ybor, who still operated his cigar factory in Key West at that time.[13]

Gutiérrez and Gargol were not the only people to consider the tropical fruit potential in the Tampa area. An 1885 publication by the Hillsborough Real Estate Agency in Tampa for the Board of Trade, issued the first year the Tampa Board of Trade (Chamber of Commerce) was formed, expressed great expectations for growing fruit commercially in the Tampa Bay area, observing, "The tropical and semitropical fruits which are grown in this county are of such great variety, and include so many different kinds, that we are pardonable if we omit to mention quite a number, and furthermore, if we only mention some which justly merit elaboration ... and without any reference either to their natural or logical order." Concerning the guava, the writer goes on: "The guava, a tree which is so numerous and so prodigal in its growth and

bearing that it almost impresses upon the mind the belief in spontaneous generation, gives us an abundance of its elegant fruit. While its shape and manner of growth resemble the peach more than anything else with which perhaps the reader is familiar, its fruit, in size and general appearance, is more similar to the pear. As yet experiment has devised no other way of utilizing the guava than converting it into jelly, marmalade and preserves; so superb are the three considered, by even the finest epicure, that if carried on to any considerable extent it would prove one of the best paying industries of Florida. Of course it is understood that the guava is considered one of the most desirable and palatable fruits we have when fresh from the tree."[14]

The promotional narrative introduces several questions yet to be answered about the connection between it and the Tampa visit of Gutiérrez and Gargol. Did the article come first? Did Gutiérrez and Gargol receive a copy which helped pique their interest? Since Gutiérrez reported that no commercial quantities of guava were found on his trip with Gargol, it seems likely that he simply missed talking to the right people. That guavas do grow in the Tampa area, perhaps the result of seeds being brought by early tabaqueros to Tampa, has long been known by the townspeople, for many grew them in their own yards. In the Lutz area an Italian farmer, Angelo Leto, my mother's uncle, had an acre in guavas in 1930 where I played as a very young boy, and the grove was not a new one.

But whatever the case with Tampa guavas, it did not interfere with Gutiérrez's historic trip to Key West—a most fortuitous one.

### The "Providential" Meeting

In his fruitless search for guavas, Gavino Gutiérrez had made several observations about the land that he was visiting just outside of Tampa. He observed that it was conveniently situated for commerce with Havana, and indeed, almost a straight shot to the tobacco-rich Vuelta Abajo region of Piñar del Rio Province in western Cuba. A friend of Don Vicente Martínez Ybor, Gutiérrez surely must have been aware that the *Principe de Gales* brand, which had earned Ybor's cigars such a reputation for superior quality, were handmade with leaves from that exclusive tobacco-producing area in western Cuba.

Gutiérrez had noticed that Tampa Bay had a fairly deep port and thus could accommodate ships in close proximity to potential factory locations. This would lower attendant transportation costs. He was aware of the tropical climate, and the fact that Tampa's humid air contained the necessary moisture for processing tobacco leaves. It was far superior to the dry New York climate that necessitated frequent spraying of the tobacco leaves to keep them moist. As a civil engineer, he certainly would have noticed the excellent drainage that most of the area possessed, in spite of the existence of some ditches and depressions next to the bay. In that period (before major construction began) a person standing some ten blocks north of the bay could easily notice the elevation of the land, with a definite slope as it lowered itself towards the bay.

*Vicente Martínez Ybor (left) and his friend Ignacio Haya looked for creative opportunities and competitive advantages to improve their cigar manufacturing operations.*
SAN CARLOS INSTITUTE; THOMAS VANCE/TAMPA BAY HISTORY.

**Chapter 1 • The Founding of Ybor City: 1492-1824**

*This drawing of an early Cuban tobacco plantation depicts the unique semi-tropical agriculture there, distinctly different from Florida but convenient to Key West and Tampa Bay.*

When Gutiérrez arrived at Key West he found that Vicente Martínez Ybor's friend, Ignacio Haya, was also visiting. He had gone there to rest and to discuss the serious labor problems they both were experiencing. Haya, a large cigar manufacturer in New York, was quite concerned at the growing demands of unionists and militant cigar workers in that giant northern industrial city. That, of course, was the reason Don Vicente had left New York.

The American labor movement took definite shape in the 1880s, culminating in the founding of the American Federation of Labor (AF of L, later AFL) in 1886 under the leadership of Samuel Gompers. Its "federalism of unions" rather quickly replaced the "one union for all labor" concept espoused by "The Knights," a 700,000-strong body which had collapsed in a few brief years. The organization of workers had serious business implications for cigar manufacturing. The cigar industry was ready-made, due to its classic manual manufacturing process, for unionists to try to penetrate. The fact that Samuel Gompers himself worked as a reader in a cigar factory in New York must not have escaped Don Vicente's and Don Ignacio's attention.

Moreover, growing proletarian ideologies spreading across the western world, stemming from the French Revolution and later reinforced by their German and Russian counterparts, were trying to tap into America's growing industrial might. While these were not yet strong, they posed an additional menace. Thus, one assumes that Haya had reasons to be concerned in New York, just as Ybor had earlier.

On the table was the fact that Ybor had received a sweet offer from Galveston's city fathers to locate his factory there.[15] However, it was just at this time that

*Included in the Florida State Archives is this image by pioneer Tampa photographer James C. Field of a street in Ybor City, circa 1885. FSA/TBHC.*

**Ybor City: The Making of a Landmark Town**

Gavino Gutiérrez tendered his thoughts about the attractive advantages in Tampa. Gutiérrez reported that not only was the soil suitable to build on, but there also was plenty of pine wood to construct with. Also, the recently constructed narrow gauge railroad that Gutiérrez had last traveled to Tampa on was fully operational. Moreover, the Tampa Bay area offered convenient access to Havana and to the tobacco fields of the Vuelta Abajo region of western Cuba. Add to this Tampa's semi-tropical climate favorable for tobacco leaves and its rather deep port for shipments to and from Cuba, and it was a most attractive location for his factory.

No doubt Gutiérrez also mentioned that the town's leaders were doing their best to improve economic prospects and the newly appointed members of the Board of Trade believed the factory would attract other new businesses. Additionally, the small town of Tampa had reportedly been chosen as the site of a new, large hotel by the railroad tycoon Henry B. Plant.

Evidently, with this promising intelligence, Don Vicente approved Tampa as his construction site, and was joined immediately in principle by Don Ignacio Haya.

Industrial America had, in recent decades, explored the idea of a company-owned worker town. Philadelphia tool and equipment industrial giant Hamilton Disston[16] had obtained good results with that concept. Don Vicente had heard and read of this and was interested. Undoubtedly the thought crossed his mind that even a primitive worker town constructed where there was no previous industrial activity and therefore no steady source of income, should be welcomed by the people of the area.

9

*Tampa and Ybor City surged to life in the 1880s.  One important improvement for Ybor City was the narrow-gauge railroad that Don Vicente Ybor constructed to link the burgeoning cigar town to the heart of downtown Tampa. The impressive building to the right of the engine is Ybor City's original Centro Español clubhouse.*

# The Early Years: 1824-1900

## Fort Brooke and Tampa Town

The little pioneer settlement which eventually grew to become Tampa arose from the establishment of Fort Brooke in 1824. The United States had taken possession of Florida from Spain in 1821, and the Seminoles became a problem for the U.S. to deal with as land speculators sated their appetite by appropriating attractive Indian territory. Col. George Mercer Brooke was ordered to establish an outpost on Tampa Bay as a means of maintaining a military presence to control the Indians in the west coast central area. Brooke selected a site originally 16 miles square (256 square miles) and established "Cantonment Brooke."

Dependent upon the fort from its inception, the town of Tampa literally wobbled into independent existence. Florida was admitted to the Union in June 1845, and the Secretary of War reduced the size of Fort Brooke to four miles square in 1847.[1] A year later the size was redefined again to include only the military quarters and their enclosures.[2] With these dramatically restricted boundaries imposed on the military post, public and commercial life increasingly assumed a separate identity. During the 1840s and 1850s new lines of trade and commerce opened, an identifiable Tampa business district emerged, and a small city grid evolved, bounded by Washington, Marion, Tampa, and Whiting Streets.

The town was incorporated in January 1849, having about 185 inhabitants at that time (though only fourteen men voted in the first election!), but its economy was precarious, and the first town administration voted to dissolve itself because of debt in 1852.[3] The Civil War brought new challenges and changes, and even an attack by Union gunboats in 1862.[4] Tampa reorganized at least twice more through 1878, but the decade of the 1870s brought little progress, and historian Hampton Dunn records it as the "dismal decade."[5] The town's stability was no doubt made worse by the eventual closing of Fort Brooke, in what is now southern downtown Tampa, in 1880.

For both Tampa and Ybor City, destiny held greater things in store. Historian Hampton Dunn declares that "one fine spring day in 1885 the sleepy village of Tampa woke up" and on May 7, 1885, "organized an enthusiastic Board of Trade which set about to transform the tiny fishing hamlet into a productive metropolis."[6]

Underlying the change was the fact that just a little over a year earlier, on January 22, 1884, the industrial tycoon Henry B. Plant had ex-

*Ignacio Haya was a close friend of Vicente Martínez Ybor, who was attracted to Tampa from New York City. His first wooden factory was "Factory No.1" because it produced the first cigar made in Ybor City. He called it "La Flor de Sanchez y Haya."*

tended his railroad to Tampa from earlier stops at Sanford and Lakeland. Train transportation offered an alternative for travellers and tradesmen alike, who previously could only reach the outside world by stage coach through Gainesville, or by boat from Key West or Cedar Key. The Tampa rail line also ran near the site where phosphate had been discovered, promising access to natural resources that could bring income to the town in the years ahead.[7]

The 1885 Tampa Board of Trade boasted the energies of the town's strongest and most progressive boosters, including as president the respected physician and *Sunland Tribune* editor, Dr. John P. Wall. The enterprising Henry B. Plant, in a bid to outdo his rival Henry Flagler on Florida's east coast, had agreed to build a truly great hotel for Tampa, far beyond the dreams of the early settlers. It would be constructed on the west bank of the Hillsborough River, just across from the emerging town center. The active Board of Trade gave Plant all the cooperation he desired. This included arranging to build a wooden bridge to access the planned hotel, establishing a city waterworks, constructing an ice plant, and introducing a host of other improvements.[8] At the time, the town could only offer limited attractions. The three existing small, wooden hotels could only accommodate some one hundred and fifty guests. Tampa's wooden "opera house" hosted many more political meetings, business deals, and dances than it did operas. Nonetheless, the Board of Trade (which had held its organizational meeting at Branch's Opera House, of course) perservered in its endeavors to improve the town, as demonstrated by the forthright manner with which it negotiated to attract new business and commercial ventures. It believed its actions would truly bring lasting wealth to the primitive village.

Despite the efforts of these civic leaders, Tampa was still a small and rowdy place. In the election of 1887 there were 895 registered voters, and, according to the *Tampa Journal* only 575 voted (64%).[9] The report of that election in the *Journal* conveys the flavor of the times, and also records the perspective of determined and responsible citizens looking toward a more civilized future for the town:

> The Journal would be derelict in its duty if it passed over some of the irregularities and disgraceful occurrences of Tuesday's election without calling attention to them. It was such an election as we hope never again to see in Tampa. Two or three days before the election, whiskey was dispensed free by some of the saloons. On election day the streets were lined with drunken men; the most obscene, vulgar and profane language could be heard, not only on the streets, but in the room in which the election was held. . . . and the Journal desires to place itself on record as being opposed to any such proceedings. We denounce the buying of votes by any man, whether with money or whiskey . . . and we call upon the respectable, law abiding, intelligent citizens of Tampa to see to it that the like does not happen again.[10]

### The Birth of Ybor City: 1885-1887

In September 1885, both Vicente Martínez Ybor and Ignacio Haya were back in Tampa to continue negotiations for potential factory locations with members of the Board of Trade. Several landowners proposed locations for the cigar industrialists. Not fully sold on Tampa, however, neither Don Vicente nor Don Ignacio would commit, and instead they announced they had decided to extend their "fact-finding" tour on to Galveston, where an attractive offer had been made earlier. Just before leaving Tampa, they visited the Miller & Henderson dry goods store owned by Capt. John Miller and William B. Henderson, the largest store south of Jacksonville. On this occasion Col. Henderson himself offered to sell them some valuable property he owned. W. C. Brown, at that time Clerk of the Circuit Court, who was with Col. Henderson, also offered to give up some of his land if the visitors would establish factories here. Apparently even these attractive overtures were not acceptable.

Faced with the prospective buyers' firmness, the members of the Board of Trade decided to improve the offers—arriving at a new proposal just as the two men were about to depart.

Fearful that Captain John Thomas Lesley's price of nine thousand dollars for forty prime acres that he owned northeast of town—the land stretching from the current Ybor commercial district to the bay, and the site with greatest appeal to the visitors — was too high and might be rejected, the Board of Trade passed several motions to guarantee Don Vicente that they would raise four thousand dollars in land or in money. (This would make his actual outlay for the land only five thousand dollars—just five hundred dollars more than Lesley had paid for the property a few months earlier). This last-minute offer, and the energy and commitment it conveyed, evidently tipped the scales in favor of Tampa as a site.

Once the choice was made, Don Vicente was in a hurry to begin construction. W. C. Brown, A. J. Knight, and W. B. Henderson had been appointed as a committee to raise the four thousand dollars that the Board had pledged, but Ybor acted decisively. He went ahead and purchased Lesley's land, and fifty more adjacent acres from S. P. Haddon, as well as additional parcels from Lesley, Stephen M. Sparkman, Thomas Spencer, and Gavino Gutiérrez, who had reserved some of the good property himself when he saw it.[11] That gave Ybor ownership of land extending all the way to Hillsborough Bay, some of which would soon become a desirable home site for the well-to-do (today called Tampa Heights).[12]

As soon as the purchase was made, Don Vicente sent word to his civil engineer, Gavino Gutiérrez, to hurry to Tampa. Gutiérrez would have the job of planning the town which would be called Ybor City.

The project moved quickly forward. The *Tampa Guardian* reported that work began within a month: "On the 8th of October 1885, the first tree was felled which covered the site on which Ybor City is now building."[13] In a nearby orange grove which he had also bought, Ybor erected his residence, *La Quinta* ("the country house"). It would be located just north of today's Hacienda de Ybor project, bordered, approximately, by Michigan Avenue (today's Columbus Drive).

Deciding to join his friend Don Vicente, Ignacio Haya also bought twenty acres of land and returned to New York.

**Chapter 2 • The Early Years: 1824-1900**

Later, when he received word from Don Vicente to come down, he moved to Tampa and began construction of a two-and-a-half-story building located on 15th Street and La Sétima. This was just over a block from where Don Vicente was building his first factory, between 12th and 13th Streets. Haya's partner, Serafín Sanchez, remained in charge of their New York City factory at 2 Liberty Street. In Tampa, meanwhile, Ignacio Haya named the new factory *La Flor de Sánchez y Haya* (The Flower of Sánchez and Haya).

Years later, Mrs. Fannie Haya, widow of Ignacio Haya, talked about the lack of business in Tampa at the time of Don Vicente and Don Ignacio's arrival: "Due to the shortage of business at the First National Bank, Mr. T. C. Taliaferro, banker, was preparing to leave Tampa and return all fixtures and equipment to the home office in Jacksonville. When Ignacio Haya learned that the only bank in Tampa was closing its doors, he at once called on Mr. Taliaferro and informed him of the decision of Mr. Ybor and himself to open factories here in Tampa. He told Mr. Taliaferro that it would be impossible to conduct these factories here without a bank to handle the payrolls . . . when Mr. Haya assured him that the initial payroll would be at least $10,000, without more ado, he commenced unpacking the bank's fixtures to remain in Tampa."[14]

Clearly Tampa Town's future growth had not been self-evident to the bank up to this point. However, the clear prospect of major cash transactions planned for Ybor City was enough to turn the tide.

Now, the local architect and contractor, C. E. Parcell, was awarded the contract for a two-story building to accommodate a cigar factory. Also, Don Vicente authorized him to build fifty houses for the cigar workers. To keep out animals and snakes, these wooden houses were to be built on brick pillars.

Both owners had agreed to finish their respective factories on the same day. But a slight hitch developed. The workers at Don Vicente's *El Principe de Gales* (The Prince of Wales) factory were Cubans—all but one. The Cuban employees, who resented the continuing colonial control of their country by Spain, refused to work at the factory as long as the non-Cuban Spanish bookkeeper remained employed there. They threatened to walk out, but Don Vicente interceded and arranged for the Spaniard to work for Ignacio Haya. In the meantime, the Haya factory was quickly up and running.

What doubtless helped Ignacio Haya to get Permit No. 1 and claim the credit for having manufactured the first cigars in Ybor City was the fact, as reported by Durwood Long in an article in the Journal of Southern History, that after Haya had built his frame structure on La Sétima, "Stripped tobacco, ready for rolling into cigars, was transported from the Sánchez and Haya warehouse in New York to Ybor City" at the same time that "Ybor shipped bales of unstripped tobacco from Key West. While both firms opened the same day, March 26, 1886, the Sánchez and Haya firm, beginning with stripped tobacco, had the first shipment to leave the new city."[15]

**Ybor City: The Making of a Landmark Town**

Still, it was obvious to all that Don Vicente's early decisiveness in purchasing land, and his astute leadership together with the resources he had brought into play had correctly earned him the title, "Founder of Ybor City."

With the city street grid already laid out by Gavino Gutiérrez (see map on page 52), Don Vicente and his partner Eduardo Manrara organized the Ybor City Land and Development Company. It immediately started construction of the fifty houses Ybor had authorized, as well as two large buildings, outhouses, and other amenities. Some wooden sidewalks were built. Additionally, Don Vicente built a narrow-gauge railroad from his factory to downtown Tampa. Narrow-gauge tracks connected all the larger factories. The small train was pulled by an equally small engine.

Both the scale and pace of development were unprecedented. Arthur Cawston's history of Hillsborough County reports:

> Within a year, the holdings of the Ybor company had been increased to one hundred and eleven acres, including the original block, and a tract of one thousand acres a short distance to the east of the scene of their operations. The total dwellings in Ybor City numbered one hundred and seventy-six, most of them two stories high, built to accommodate from two to three families, and ranging in cost from $300 to $3,500. The commodious three-story brick factory, which took the place of the temporary two-story frame building, afforded ample room for six hundred employees. The old factory was converted into four stores on the first floor, while the second floor was used as a theater and became known as El Liceo Cubano.[16]

Ybor City Land and Improvement Company soon established itself as the major real estate agency and developer, further adding to Ybor's claim as Ybor City founder. The company played a major role in arranging for other, similar businesses to locate in the area, offering not only a supportive climate, experienced construction crews, and a sympathetic business environment, but specific benefits

*The historic brick Ybor Cigar Factory dates from 1886. It was three stories high in the center portion and was known for its famous cigar brand El Príncipe de Gales.* RAFAEL MARTINEZ YBOR.

to appeal to both owners and workers. Cawston explains that

> in most cases, [when] a factory was built by the Ybor Land Company, one or two blocks of land were given, a residence for the manager was constructed—all rent free—for ten years upon the condition that the new business employ a stipulated number of workers and produce a certain quantity. Occasionally, the Tampa Board of Trade also contributed a cash bonus or other subsidy as a 'sweetener.' For example, Edward Manrara wrote the Board on March 17, 1888, that a certain company was willing to relocate in Tampa for a subsidy of $8,000, plus other things.[17]

At Don Vicente's invitation, many factories began to locate in the area. A waterworks was established as well as a fire station built across from Ybor's Principe de Gales factory. There was talk of setting up a system of gas lights to illuminate the town. Shade trees were planted on both sides of the streets, the dwellings were enclosed by picket fences, and wooden sidewalks were being laid.[18]

The first clear Havana cigar, the only type made in Tampa, was turned out on April 13, 1886, by the Haya factory, using the stripped tobacco they had brought from New York. By the end of the first year of operation, Don Vicente's factory was producing at the rate of 900,000 cigars per month. By 1890 the annual payroll was $1,909,730 on 88,000,000 cigars worth $5,500,000 (in 1890 dollars).

*The Sanchez y Haya Cigar Factory at the corner of 15th Street and La Sétima was completed in 1886.* THCPL.

*The original Ybor Cigar Factory was this wood frame building which became a recreational center for Cuban workers, with El Liceo Cubano located on the second floor.* USFSCL.

## Scenes of the time

When his three-story brick factory, *Principe de Gales*, was completed, Ybor turned over his first wooden frame factory to the Cubans as a recreational building. The *Liceo Cubano* (Cuban Lyceum) occupied the second floor. Here a drama was presented titled "For the Love of a Mother." Also presented there on November 25-26, 1891, was "José Martí, Cuban Patriot," an appearance by the radical champion of Cuban independence who had been invited to Tampa by sympathetic local revolutionaries. He observed that the chairs in the theater formed a circle and later commented "that the Liceo could well be called '*El Club Círculo Cubano*'."[19] It was a memorable and poetic turn of phrase, and today the name "*El Círculo Cubano*" graces the current, beautiful building.

During 1887 and 1888 Yellow Fever—thought to be due to mosquitoes—ravished Ybor City. "People were dying like flies," was a saying common in that period. Many workers relocated to Key West, Havana, and New York. Factories were hit hard.[20] Cubans formed one of the first groups for mutual medical assistance during this time, *Los Caballeros de la Luz, El Porvenir #7*, founded on July 18, 1888. Yet fevers and hardship took their toll. Missed by the Cuban *tabaqueros* was Manuel Garcia, a "king of the Cuban countryside" who mixed drinks at the bar on the bottom floor of El Liceo Cubano.[21]

Despite the assaults—or partly because of them—the town retained a rugged, pioneer spirit. It was an exciting place to live and work, despite its problems. Cuban feelings centered on the impending Cuban war of independence against Spain. The explosive feelings of Cubans towards Spaniards were stirred by the "faithful island's" struggles against its colonial bondage, and the common cause formed a solidarity among the Ybor City workers. However, the increasing militancy of the *tabaqueros* as they organized, coupled with the 1887 Yellow Fever outbreak which virtually closed the cigar industry for several months, made daily life in Ybor City difficult to bear. Complicating things further was a growing friction with the "Anglo" world in the small town of Tampa. "Anglos" could not understand Cuban militancy. Conditions in this mosquito-infested, feuding town were so formidable that many newcomers wanted no part of it and headed back to their place of origin. One case is known where a wife literally pleaded with her husband to go back home. It was probably not an isolated occurrence.

To the rear of the Ignacio Haya factory on 15th Street and *La Sétima* there

**Ybor City: The Making of a Landmark Town**

*This photo circa 1889 shows the new brick Ybor Cigar Factory designed by local architect C. E. Parcell before any additions were made. It was the tallest building in Tampa at the time of its construction. The observatory on top offered views of Tampa, Ybor City, Tampa Bay, and all the surrounding country-side. Railroad tracks ran just behind the fence in the foreground.*

*The rapid growth of the cigar industry in Ybor City attracted families as well as single male workers. This photograph by James C. Field, circa 1885-86, shows a cluster of family homes. In the enlarged detail (left), a youngster stands near his family on a porch rail, three ladies sit together on a porch, and in the background a woman walks in her yard with a parasol to shield her from the blazing sun. Conditions were harsh and uncom-fortable in many ways during these early years, and it was not unusual for immigrants to wonder why they had left home for this place. FSA/TBHC.*

**Chapter 2 • The Early Years: 1824-1900**

*The Ybor City Ice Works building at 5th Avenue and 13th Street provided ice for the Ybor City area starting in the 1890s. Behind it is the Florida Brewing Company building. The brewery, organized by Eduardo Manrara, was the first in Florida and one of America's finest. It opened February 24, 1897. The brewery enjoyed substantial sales in Florida and Georgia, but sold the most beer in Cuba. The building was based on the design of the Castle Brewery in Johannesburg, South Africa.* HILLSBOROUGH COUNTY HISTORICAL COMMISSION COLLECTION, TBHC.

*This view of the first railroad depot at 6th Avenue and 16th Street in Ybor City is not dated, but it is likely from the late 1890s. Henry Plant's rail line ran through Ybor City on its way to downtown Tampa.* HILLSBOROUGH COUNTY HISTORICAL COMMISSION COLLECTION, TBHC.

**Ybor City: The Making of a Landmark Town**

was a *cafetín*, a small café owned by Estevan Pellón, who was known as *el Polaco*. The *cafetín* abutted the rear of Don Haya's factory, La Flor de Sánchez y Haya. Often Spanish factory managers wearing shirts, ties, and elegant straw hats (*sombreros de pajita*); businessmen wearing dark suits and hats to match; early adventure-seekers; and an assortment of unlikely characters, could be found frequenting this locale. Some of those in the dark suits were enterprising Italians who comprised another growing ethnic presence in the Ybor community. Together the unlikely assembly could be seen sipping their Cuban café or eating their Cuban or Spanish fare and chatting away.[22] The furnishings were spare, but the customs timeless.

*El Inglesito* ("the Englishman") Mr. Clarkson ("the older one"), had a dairy on 2nd Avenue, and, along with a small Spanish dairy, supplied milk for the community. Later, Italians would also join in this occupation. People of different nationalities besides Spanish and Cuban opened cafes, bars, groceries, and shops on La Sétima. Also, Jewish merchants began opening stores.[23]

Merchants like Louis Wohl and Adam Katz established businesses that were conveniently located on the main strip of La Sétima. *El Café Europa* and *Café Anabál* had opened. In the late 1890s and early 1900s silent movie houses included *El Eden* (the building that housed it was a large twin-towered one, almost identical to the first *Centro Español*) and the Pathé. Gavino Gutiérrez himself owned the Pathé, located on La Sétima and 16th Street.[24]

DeSoto Park in Palmetto Beach attracted many Cubans to visit, and many

*The Cafetín owned by Estevan Pellón was located in back of the Sanchez y Haya Cigar Co., on the southwest corner of 15th Street and La Sétima. Pellón is shown here standing behind the counter between his daughter Margarita (with a goat at the left end of the bar) and his wife, who stands in front of the bar in the center of the photograph.*
MARGARITA PELLÓN.

*19*

settled there. The beach was clean by today's standards, and there were fiddler crabs, sand crabs, and horseshoe crabs in abundance. Mothers played with their children on the sands of McKay Bay. Spaniards lived there, also. At a *glorieta* (band stand) in the park a Cuban band played mostly Cuban *danzones*, with only an occasional Spanish *paso doble* mixed in. Though they lived and worked in close proximity, Spaniards and Cubans had to juggle civil coexistence while ill feelings between the two nationalities festered.[25]

On the bandstand at the park the famous Felipe Vázquez, known as the "King of the *Danzones*," played to the countless couples and oldsters who danced away the time. Nearby, children played on the *cachum-ban-beys* (see-saws)and swings, and they contrived a host of other games. One well-known personality of the day, Carbajál, a runner, bet that he could outrun a horse. When the wager was taken up, he beat the horse and won. From the corner of 16th and La Sétima, next to the original twin-towered Centro Español building, young men engaged in bike races that ended at Palmetto Beach.[26]

*Born in Scotland, Hugh C. Macfarlane immigrated to the United States with his parents in 1865. After practicing law in Boston and New Orleans, he moved to Tampa in 1883. He built the first cigar factory in West Tampa on the corner of Howard Avenue and Union Street in 1892.* USFSCL.

## V. M. *Ybor* - Cigars - Cubans - Spaniards: 1887-1892

The late 1800s were turbulent times in American social and industrial history. The flow of immigrants from Europe in the last half of the century was unrelenting. Few nationalities were spared a part in the historic battles between factory owners and their workers, and newly arrived laborers at the bottom of the heap were especially vulnerable to the radical ideologies so rapidly spawning at the century's end. Passionate socialists and anarchists strove to redefine capitalism as an oppressive system holding its own workers in bondage. In Tampa they found a perfect breeding ground in the immigrant factory environment. Many *tabaqueros* were still in their late teens. Some factory workers at the starting level were a mere twelve years old. Other more experienced laborers came from Key West and Havana, and they were already indoctrinated.

By 1892 factory construction in Ybor City had slowed. It was an interim period in which the birth of cigar manufacturing in West Tampa had begun its initial steps. At the time, Hugh C. Macfarlane, a lawyer by profession and an astute visionary, had become interested in developing land for new cigar factories. He observed that the cigar industry was growing fast and was seeking new sites to avoid labor problems. Moreover, it was a highly profitable industry.[27]

And so in 1892 the Scottish immigrant Macfarlane, who became city attorney and state's attorney in Tampa after practicing law in Boston and New Orleans, offered to construct buildings and donate land for cigar factories to proprietors who might want to establish their businesses in West Tampa. Just six years after Don Vicente Martínez Ybor opened his Principe de Gales factory in Ybor City, the Del Pino brothers opened their factory in West Tampa. It was located in a rather isolated section across the Hillsborough river, on



**Ybor City: The Making of a Landmark Town**

Howard Avenue and what is now Union Street. This factory was followed soon by a few others, among them the Fernandez O'Halloran Cigar Co., whose owners, the O'Halloran brothers, later played a small but key role in the Cuban Revolutionary Party's message to Cuba to begin the fight for freedom against Spain.[28]

The early growth of factories in West Tampa slowed up after the initial flurry. However, in time, Macfarlane and his associates built a few roads to the desolate West Tampa areas to increase accessibility. He also constructed a bridge across the river and streetcars to offer workers from Ybor and surrounding areas shorter routes to new factories. These strategies helped spur construction in the undeveloped outskirts, with many major factories making West Tampa their home. Following closely behind the movement of factories into West Tampa came the building of homes in the area. Soon the fact that West Tampa was beginning to rival Ybor City as a cigar manufacturing center became a topic at cafés and factories on both sides of the river.

West Tampa's early spurt of growth was slowed due to increasing numbers of cigar workers who did not wish to live so isolated in the primitive, undeveloped area. The Del Pino Brothers, Manuel and Fernando J., had been pioneers in West Tampa. They had opened their cigar factory there in 1892 in the heart of deserted scrub palmetto and pine lands, starting a little West Tampa enclave that was known as Pino City. But in 1893 they were forced to shut down when they couldn't keep enough employees. Julius Ellinger and Company from Key West opened a large factory in late 1892 on the west bank of the Hillsborough River, becoming the closest factory to the Tampa business district. Like Pino City, it drew almost exclusively from the Cuban population for its employees. The need for more trained workers prompted cigar factory owners to

*West Tampa was a flurry of construction in the 1890s. A Cuban social club, Céspedes Hall, is surrounded by scaffolding in this 1895 photograph. Macfarlane's first West Tampa cigar factory, built for A. Del Pino and Company in 1892, is visible in the background to its left.* USFSCL.

seek alternative sources of labor. Fortunately, at the same time, other Cuban workers in Key West continued to be frustrated by working conditions there, and many of them were willing to relocate to West Tampa in search of a better life. Gradually, West Tampa overcame its early obstacles and soon attained a heavy growth rate that propelled it rapidly into a very large cigar manufacturing center.[29] C. F. Arnsworth and Company opened there in March 1893, and it was soon joined by Cuesta, Rey and Company, A. Santaella, Pendas and Alvares, Morgan Cigar Company, and others.[30]

Against the background of sometimes spectacular financial prosperity for these early pioneering businessmen and the increasingly concentrated Cuban population of struggling workers, radical sentiments continued to thrive. During 1891 in Ybor City two new Cuban revolutionary clubs were formed: *Los Independientes* and *Ignacio Agramonte*. "The Independents of Tampa" were composed of members who had organized local anti-Spanish demonstrations, as an offshoot of efforts to support the four anarchists who had been executed in the aftermath of labor protests that had erupted into violence at Haymarket Square in Chicago. But demonstrations had taken a new twist in Ybor City due to anti-Cuban factions. As a result, the Ignacio Agramonte Cuban Revolutionary Club was formed in honor of Ignacio Agramonte y Loynaz, one of



**Chapter 2 · The Early Years: 1824-1900**

the six major Cuban patriots in the war to liberate Cuba. In Tampa, supporting the Agramonte club was Nestor Leonelo Carbonell, who had fought in the Ten Year War against Spain. He was an articulate, patriotic writer of poetry and prose, and his small bookstore in Ybor City, called The Literary Gallery, served as a cultural influence far greater than its small physical size would have indicated. His exemplary role in the defense of Cuba brought him many followers in Tampa. These backed him in the anti-Spanish efforts fostered by the Agramonte Revolutionary Club.[31]

To take care of the medical needs of their own, the Cubans formed La Benéfica (not to be confused with the later Spanish organization associated with the Centro Español), and the Spaniards established El Porvenír; both of these were mutual aid societies. By 1890 foreign-born Cubans in Hillsborough County numbered 2,424; foreign-born Spaniards numbered 233; and foreign-born Italians numbered 56. But the flow of Spaniards and Italians would accelerate greatly in the pre-Cuban Independence War years, with Spaniards soon numbering slightly below Italians. These two would tend to equalize in numbers in the succeeding decades, while the Cubans maintained a significantly greater number into the 1940s.[32]

Spaniards from Cuba and Spain continued to arrive. These were mostly single men, some as young as twelve years old. Many had been sent to the former colony of Cuba to escape overpopulated, small, Spanish farms that could not truly support them. The long winters and small mountain plots in Spain, made even less efficient by an inheritance system that over the years scattered the families' lands, made life for many young Spanish citizens demeaning and offered few prospects. Furthermore, the odds of being sent to the North African colonies to fight the eternal wars against the Moors were extremely high.

In view of conditions in the farms in Spain, a move to Cuba or to the former Spanish colonies further to the south in the New World made sense. Spanish being the language of the Cuban colony made it appealing. However, the situation in the last half of the decade had become increasingly hopeless in Cuba due to social and political unrest, and the economic and political conditions there seemed poised to collapse at any moment. When reports reached Cuba that in Tampa there was a great demand for cigar factory labor, many Spaniards and Cubans found the news irresistible. Word also had it that Spaniards were in particular demand there, so some young men from Spain found that Cuba became only a temporary stop on their way to Ybor City. In spite of the conditions brought by the war, it is remarkable that young Spaniards continued to be sent to the now-liberated Cuba for at least another decade—as was my father, Evaristo.[33] Spaniards, of course, still owned much of the property in Cuba, including warehouses where many young Spaniards were boarded on an in-kind basis, working in return for basic necessities.

Havana, Key West, and New York City each had become well-known for manufacturing cigars. By the mid-1850s the excellence of Cuban cigars was widely recognized, and there were major cigar-making workplaces in Havana. New York was a hub for profitable northeast and national American markets, and a logical factory location for Cuban entrepreneurs seeking access to abundant labor and efficient product distribution. Ignacio Haya was the co-owner of one of the largest New York City factories. In Florida, Key West had been the largest population center until the turn of the century. It had developed its own cigar industry at the start of the Ten Years War with Spain in 1868. Thousands of Cubans moved to Key West then, creating a huge population boom and a major industry producing handmade, clear Havana cigars. By the 1870s there were at least twenty-nine factories in Key West producing more than 62 million cigars each year.[34] Cuba was so close to this southernmost Florida city that in times of strike or adversity Cuban workers moved quickly from one place to the other. By the second half of the century all three cities had skilled cigar workers. New York City and Havana vied for the claim to greatest labor unrest. The upstart cigar-making center on Florida's west coast was too busy building, growing, and organizing to take part in the growing national battle between labor and big business.

On December 21, 1891, the Centro Español was formed in Ybor City as a teaching and recreation facility. Its first president was Ignacio Haya. The majority of its membership consisted of Galicians (from one of the four northwestern provinces of Spain), Asturians (from the northernmost province of Spain) and other *peninsulares* (from the Iberian peninsular). Some eleven years later, in 1902, Asturian members of the Centro Español, following the lead of the Centro Asturiano de La Habana, took steps that resulted in their own new Centro Asturiano in Ybor City. This was linked at first with the Havana senior branch, but it eventually achieved autonomy as an independent club. Leading and guiding that process was a dynamic personality, Antonio Gonzalez Prado, president of the committee to establish the Tampa branch. The Centro Español would also serve as model for L' Unione Italiana when it was founded in April 1894 with an original membership of 116 Italian and 8 Spanish immigrants.[35]

In the factories the *patrones* (owners) assigned the better jobs, such as foreman, bookkeeping, sales, and other positions crucial to quality, to the Spaniards, whose loyalty they felt they could trust in these turbulent times. This created an unofficial hierarchy, with the *patrón* at the top; the supervisor (*el encargado*) under him; the main factory floor foreman (*el capatáz*); the

*The original Centro Español Clubhouse, built in the 1890s. The shoeshine stand on the corner was a familiar feature. The building was located on La Setima at the corner of 16th Street, and it was replaced by a red brick clubhouse in 1912.*

select, highly skilled leaf and brand selector and issuer (*el rezagador* and *el escogedor* respectively); and finally the average cigar roller (*el torcedor*), the most numerous employee on the main floor. The factory staff— bookkeeper, salesmen, and the factory supervisor—reported directly to the *patron*. The cigar rollers answered to the foreman, the *capatáz*. This made the men chosen as *capatáz* powerful in the eyes of the cigar rollers, since they constituted the larger part of the total *tabáqueros* in the factories of Ybor City.

The *escogedores* (selectors), who were above the cigar roller level, also enjoyed great prestige and often took considerable pride in their position. This gave rise to the expression, *muy estirados*, meaning "very stuck-up!" The combination of being in high demand and having a highly touted and crucial factory job inflated many egos. But without question, they were indispensable to the industry. Espe-

cially during the war years *patrones* could count on the loyalties of the Spaniards who were dedicated to not disrupting the workplace and to insuring the high quality image of the factory.[36]

Cuban workers were mobile and appeared more interested in their own revolutionary activities than in working or settling down. Families would come later. Most of them were intent on finding the best and steadiest jobs to be found; the option of relocating to Key West, New York, or even Havana, was a choice they would take many times, whenever jobs were cut or production slowed or stopped. Even in Florida there were scattered cigar factories at Jacksonville, Ocala, Pensacola, St. Augustine, and elsewhere competing for workers. Cubans naturally preferred those places where many other Cubans worked, where Spanish was the spoken language, and where conviviality was more plentiful. Still, they would go where the work was to be found. When work would again become available in Ybor City, many returned.[37]

Though many Cubans were excellent cigar workers, their mobility reduced their dependability at the factory level, which is one reason that they were often let go instead of Spaniards. If the factory was on strike, leaving for the interim was one option. Cubans in large numbers were single in the early years. This, plus the choice to

live in boarding rooms, made instant mobility a way of life.

Many Italian cigar workers, on the other hand, were living with their families in Ybor City; for them, mobility was a much less desirable solution to factory strife. A small amount of movement on the part of the single Italians did take place, but for the most part the Italian workers were more rooted. And while many Spaniards had come to Ybor as single young men who might have moved if circumstances merited, they were in demand for key factory jobs, especially during times of labor unrest. This lessened their inclination to relocate. The great distance to Spain undoubtedly was a factor; like the Italians they would find it hard to return home. This also applied to Sicilians, their country of origin being yet more out of reach.

In Tampa, conversation among factory owners in closed circles must have focused on just such perceptions of the inclinations and loyalties of their workers and on new threats to labor relations. Inspired by new ideologies, workers demanded higher wages and other benefits. Factory owners' reactions to these influences were of utmost importance to the workers. The seeds of conflict were being sewn. Nonetheless, in 1894 the *Tampa Tribune* wrote, "the Cigar industry of our city is the leading factor in our phenomenal prosperity. Some $75,000 was paid out for wages last week."[38]

## Ybor City Street Scenes

Ybor City was rapidly developing a unique street scene and café culture. Within a few years, on the northwest corner of La Sétima and 15th Street, where the Las Novedades building is today, an open air *teatro* (theater) would be set up. There, with a curtain for a screen, a silent movie could be shown. Across the street on the second floor, over the bar and café owned by Sendoya, a band was led by Maestro Felipe Vazquez.[38] Most nights, people on



24

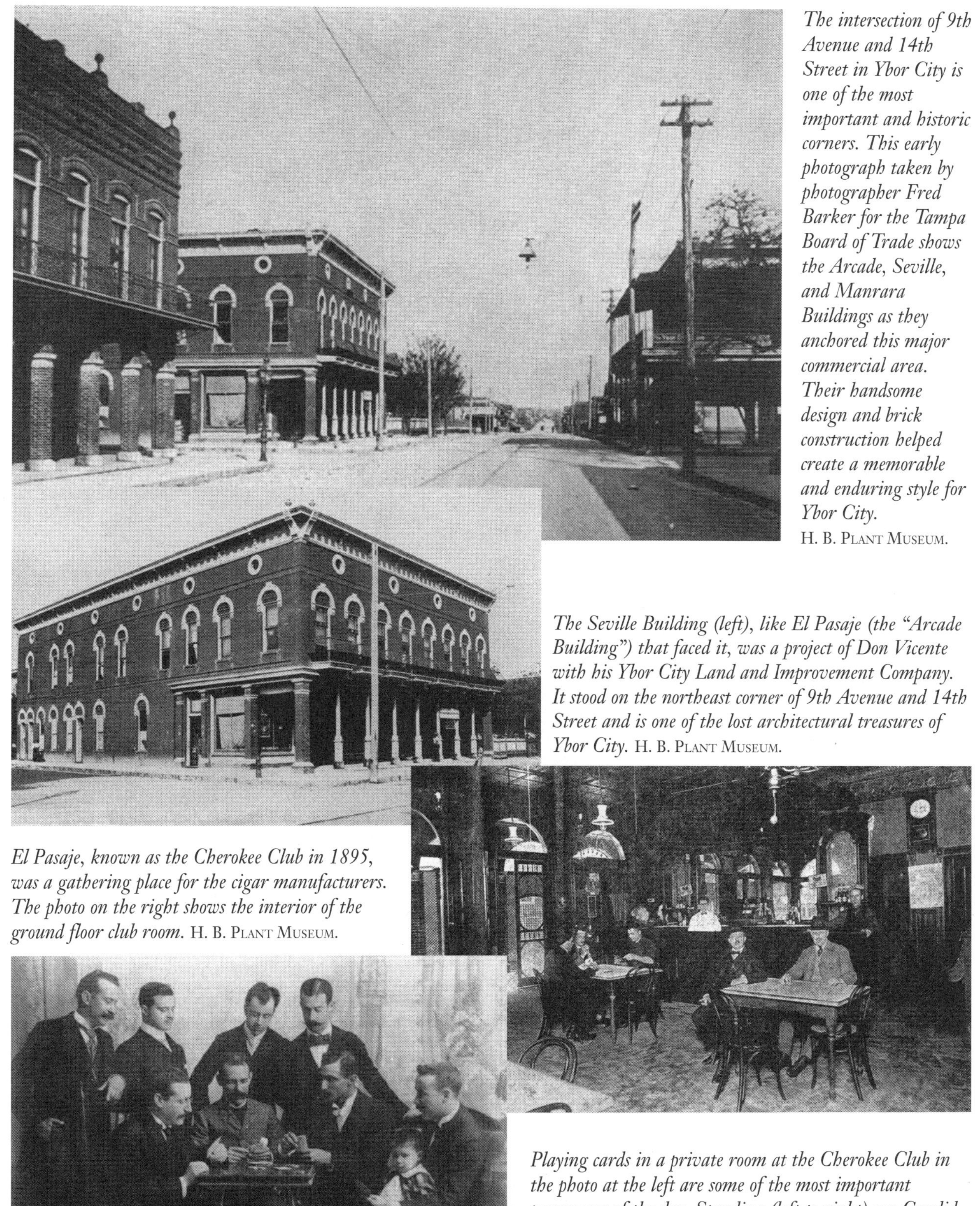

*The intersection of 9th Avenue and 14th Street in Ybor City is one of the most important and historic corners. This early photograph taken by photographer Fred Barker for the Tampa Board of Trade shows the Arcade, Seville, and Manrara Buildings as they anchored this major commercial area. Their handsome design and brick construction helped create a memorable and enduring style for Ybor City.* H. B. Plant Museum.

*The Seville Building (left), like El Pasaje (the "Arcade Building") that faced it, was a project of Don Vicente with his Ybor City Land and Improvement Company. It stood on the northeast corner of 9th Avenue and 14th Street and is one of the lost architectural treasures of Ybor City.* H. B. Plant Museum.

*El Pasaje, known as the Cherokee Club in 1895, was a gathering place for the cigar manufacturers. The photo on the right shows the interior of the ground floor club room.* H. B. Plant Museum.

*Playing cards in a private room at the Cherokee Club in the photo at the left are some of the most important personages of the day. Standing (left to right) are Candid M. Ybor (son of Vicente); Auturo and Oscar Manrara (sons of Eduardo); and M. Guonod. Seated (left to right) are William Kline; Emilio Pons; F. A. Solomonson; and an accountant holding a child.* THCPL.



**Chapter 2 • The Early Years: 1824-1900**

The Manrara Building (above) was the site of the second office of the Ybor City Land and Improvement Co. In 1925 it would be transformed by Dr. Jose Ramon Avellanal into El Publico Clinic. Still later, in 1939 it would be remodelled by Dr. A. A. Gonzalez to become a 45-bed hospital and clinic.

The Tampa Street Railway Company was established by Manrara and Ybor to run between Ybor City and Tampa. It provided a modern commercial link when this photograph of the steam engine "Hattie" was made in 1886. Eduardo Manrara, in suit and hat, stands beside the train. THCPL.

**Ybor City: The Making of a Landmark Town**

La Sétima would be gathered around, listening and talking—some under their breath.

José Martí, supreme Cuban patriot, had by now made his third trip to Tampa. Revolutionary activities were at fever pitch. In cafés all along La Sétima the talk was rife with patriotism, factory concerns, and revolution.

## José Martí, Ruperto and Paulina Pedroso, 1890-1895

Jose Martí had become an important presence in Ybor City by 1890, and his connections to the community were cemented through his friendship there with Ruperto and Paulina Pedroso. Today Martí is recognized as the principal national patriot of Cuba. He is the George Washington figure in the Cuban nation's struggle for freedom and independence. He was born in Havana on January 28, 1853, the son of retired Spanish army sergeant Mariano Martí Navarro of Valencia, Spain, and his wife, Leonor Perez Cabrera, a Cuban from the Canary Islands.

During his early teens Martí became active in the movement for Cuban independence from Spain. In 1869, when he was just 16, he was sentenced to six months of hard labor for revolutionary activities. Two years later he was banished to Spain. During his forced stay there he attended the university in Madrid, studying literature, politics, and history. He wrote and began to publish poetry and essays, eventually also earning a degree in law from the University of Saragossa in 1874. For the next four years he worked in France and Mexico as a journalist, and in Guatemala as a professor of literature. He tried to return to Cuba in 1878, but was ejected again for dissident political activity. He lived briefly in Spain, France, and Venzuela before moving to New York City, where he won international recognition as a columnist and correspondent for

Latin American newspapers. His literary fame also was on the rise, and his 1885 novel *Amistad Funesta* (*Ill-Omened Friendship*) is regarded by some critics as the first truly modernist novel written in Spanish. His most famous poem, *Guantanamera*, set to music, has become a popular international standard.

It is no wonder, then, that his visits and speeches in Ybor City were events to catalyze the community. His fame had not diminished his dedication to Cuban independence, but had only increased his abilities as a leader. His trips to Tampa helped him recruit the army of exiles he hoped would at last bring independence to his island home. The Cuban Revolutionary Party was established in Ybor City in 1892 as one result of his influence. After more than two years of careful planning and organizing, Martí landed in eastern Cuba on April 11, 1895, with an army of liberation, and just a few weeks later he was killed during an encounter with Spanish troops at Dos Ríos, Cuba, on May 19. He was 42 years old.[39]

José Martí was accustomed to sleeping at the Pedroso house when he came to visit Tampa and its Cuban Revolutionary Party. Paulina and husband, both Afro-Cubans, are today very much an integral part of the lore of that struggle to free Cuba from Spain's domination. In their

*This 1885 portrait of Martí shows him at the time of the publication of his novel* Amistad funesta. *The intensity and determination written on his face, the rousing idealism of his writing, and his stirring delivery as an orator found a sympathetic audience in Ybor City.*

home, José Martí was lovingly attended and guarded. There had even been an attempt to poison his wine during one of his visits to Tampa. The Pedrosos opened their home as a safe haven for him to recuperate as he prepared more of his revolutionary writings and speeches.[40]

Today the land where the José Martí Park is located is where Ruperto and Paulina Pedroso lived. I remember well the old, unpainted but historic wooden building there that had been their home. Later the building was removed due to its rundown condition. However, the park on the southeast corner of 8th Avenue and 14th Street remains to honor a spot where history was made. The park was created thanks in large part to the initiative of Tony Pizzo, with assistance of other city leaders and Cuban officials. In addition, the memory of Paulina Pedroso, the Black Cuban woman who befriended and protected Martí on his visits, is forever preserved in the Florida Women's Hall of Fame.

*The Pedroso Family (above) opened their hearts and home to the brilliant and charismatic leader José Martí. The photograph at the left shows the poor repair at the site of their modest wooden dwelling behind the brick cigar factory on 13th Street as I remember it in the 1950s. The buildings were destroyed, and today this is the site of José Martí Park.* Tony Pizzo Collection, USFSCL.



**Ybor City: The Making of a Landmark Town**

## Increasing Arrivals - Italians - Expectations - First Centro Español Building: 1892-1895

Italians, mostly Sicilians, were the last major group of immigrants to arrive in large numbers in Ybor City. Once they began settling in the area, the pace of new arrivals accelerated. Italian immigrants streamed in from Louisiana small towns like Bayou Goula (where Ybor City's Francesco Leto had lived) and from cities like New Orleans. Many came from St. Cloud, Florida, where they had worked at a sugar plantation. Others had worked on the railroads, until the work ended.

Tony Pizzo, Tampa's official historian, explained the St. Cloud exodus and the attractions of Ybor City in an article on "The Italians in Tampa."[41] The St. Cloud Sugar Plantation, near Kissimmee, paid its workers only seventy-five cents a day. With such low wages, news of greener pastures had nearly irresistible appeal, and Pizzo describes the story spreading statewide that "a Cuban boom town near Tampa had sprung up like a mushroom in the night."[42] Rumor had it that cigar workers there were being paid top dollar, and for unemployed railroad workers, "Mr. Plant, the railroad magnate, was offering one dollar and twenty-five cents per day for hands needed in the extension of his railroad to Port Tampa."[43]

The Italian influx not only contributed to the human and cultural resources available to the young community, it also brought a new perspective on ethnic identity. Many of the Italians had come from "the bleak hills of central Sicily," and their island had been under Spanish rule for more than four centuries. Like the Cubans, they had come from an island once an outpost of Spain. However, Pizzo explains that Spaniards were rarely treated as enemies or considered as foreign by the Sicilian population and that intermarriage was common. The official languages were Catalan and Castilian (the languages of Cataluña and Castilla, respectively) and according to Pizzo the *Spagnolismo* on the model of the Sicilian culture was extensive, so that "for these people, living in a Spanish environment would not be a totally new experience. . . . The Italians were a kindred culture coming to renew old bonds."[44]

The addition of Italian immigrants complicated what might otherwise have been an unalleviated and accelerating Cuban-Spanish conflict. In the longer term, it became an important factor in creating a unique multicultural atmosphere.

On arrival most Italians settled in the eastern fringe of Ybor City. Many had young families and they needed homes. Also, a good many bought land and farmed it. As the flow of Italians increased, there was pressure on the young Italian mothers and daughters to enter the factories.[45] Ironically, as mentioned earlier, the Cubans and a few Spaniards resisted their entry, passively, for a large pool of new labor would tilt the wage scales in favor of the *patrones*. In time, however, the Italian women worked their way in. Some had learned the rudiments of cigarmaking right at home in Ybor City from the fathers who did work in the factories. This was the case of Felice Leto and his daughter Ana.

Meanwhile, toward the center of town, an increasing number of Romanian and other Jewish merchants joined the few Spaniards and Cubans already operating their own businesses. Those early pioneers found Ybor City a friendly place, and word spread to other kinfolk and friends in Tampa and elsewhere. The news of diversity and opportunity in Ybor traveled quickly. Others would soon arrive and set up shop in Ybor. Among the newcomers were some German craftsmen, who found a tiny nucleus of other German immigrants already in the area. They were not numerous, but they could be found pursuing a variety of activities demanding high skills, such as precision craftsmanship in the local box factory south of La Sétima or re-markable lithographic work to produce the extraordinary labels and finely printed packaging prized by collectors today.

In Ybor City and West Tampa many radical publications were taking root with the help of Cuban, Italian, and Spanish so-cialists and anarchists. The factories and meeting rooms were filled with pamphlets. From Sicily's upper Maggazzolo River re-gion—an area operated under an absen-tee-landlord, semi-feudal system that ex-ploited workers and condemned large numbers of families to poverty from cradle to grave—came the intense "localized loy-alties" which grew from common geogra-phy and experience. About sixty percent of the Sicilian population of Tampa, includ-ing nearly all of the earliest settlers, came from the single little village of Santo Stefano Quisquina.[46] There, too, socialism found receptive prospects. It is no wonder then, when socialist dynamics surfaced in Ybor City, fueled by localized loyalties of the past, traces of semi-feudal labor rela-tions, and present resentments between wealthy factory owners and their workers, there were favorable conditions for the seeds of socialism to take root.

By now, also, unionism and proletariat philosophies from Europe and Russia had been introduced into the northern indus-trial fabric of America. Many leaders there considered Ybor City fertile ground for their efforts. All looked at the Latin *tabaqueros* as targets—so young, so naive, and so desirous of a life with hope for their children's future. Later, in the 1920s, even communists entered the contest for their minds—but with very limited success. There were ample mundane challenges at home and work that occupied their energy and attention.

Notwithstanding the vicissitudes of life these early Florida emigrants faced, the multicultural community in Ybor City re-mained surprisingly attuned to national and international trends. In this diverse and intense environment, the interna-tional workers' movement found receptive spirits. Following an important labor meeting in Cuba, *El Congreso Obrero de La Habana*, in 1892 there was an immediate increase in radicalism in Ybor. What the factory workers learned of the issues and principles debated there renewed and in-vigorated their sense of solidarity with their Cuban counterparts. The represen-tatives at the Havana Congress, with strong participation by the cigar workers in attendance, delivered a radical procla-mation calling for a general strike and an-nouncing proudly that *los obreros formamos una sola clase* —"the workers form a single class."[47] It sounded like a revolution of the proletariat.

Meanwhile, Cuban revolutionary fever ran rampant. In many ways this nationalis-tic devotion to Cuban independence con-flicted with an increasingly militant labor ideology that many Ybor workers had em-braced earlier in their lives in the factories of Key West. And while Ybor City grew, Key West had become the site of a declin-ing cigar industry, beset and to some extent doomed by this very militancy. Probably none of the workers could have articulated the irony that it had been labor unrest, to a large extent, that had motivated Don Vicente to establish their new home town of Ybor City in the first place.

The new factories at Tampa offered many laborers a better living wage, and the Ybor City founders had taken steps to im-prove conditions for workers and their families. Nonetheless, the sharp class dif-ferences between workers and owners re-mained, and the assertion that "the work-ers form a single class" was hard to shake off. Amidst labor tension and nationalistic fervor, the workers also faced the practical need to provide decent medical care for their families and themselves. There were no doctors in Ybor, so any Latins who were seriously ill would have to seek out



**Ybor City: The Making of a Landmark Town**

emergency care from an Anglo physician, or travel to Key West or Havana for more sympathetic treatment. Among Cubans, many tobacco workers were single men who were highly mobile. Lacking the benefits of a home or family, the availability of a medical center was imperative. In 1886 Cubans began *La Sociedad Benéfica*, a mutual aid organization to meet medical needs, and that same year Spanish workers established El Porvenir.[48] The groups combined individual resources to provide health support in Ybor City, and when necessary to help financially with the expense of extra care or travel.

*La Sociedad Benéfica* was only one of many Cuban mutual-aid societies to appear in Ybor City. Despite their dedication to the struggle for Cuban independence, they were conscious of immediate community needs for associations, newspapers, schools, and societies. Human services and care were essential in this small, primitive enclave. Early enlightened and motivated Cubans—some from Key West—included José Dolores Poyo, Carlos E. Balino, and Ramon River Rivero, whose efforts helped improve opportunities for all. Early newspapers such as *El Yara*, published by Poyo,

and *La Traducción*, which the *lectores* often read from in the factories, and a Lodge, *Orden Caballeros de la Luz*, were begun. Also, a Baltimore Cuban, Carlos Zequira, started the first school for Cubans. Today the unique flavor and accomplishments of the voluntary associations are regarded as among the most important cultural contributions of the Ybor community. However, the societies were not unique to Ybor. They were really patterned after the revolutionary clubs which for years had been competing for members and support in Key West, trying to undermine Spanish power in Cuba. Mutual aid was broadly combined with the quest for economic and political equality. In Key West the highest attainable "aid" which could be accomplished by the Cuban mutual aid groups was always thought of as the ability to complete the glorious fight for independence initiated in Oriente province by Cuban patriot Carlos Manuel de Céspedes on October 10, 1868, when his revolt began the Ten Years War. At one time the rebels controlled half the island before their defeat in 1878.[49]

At the same time that the forces advocating Cuban independence from Spain gathered strength, all during the late 1880s the Spaniards in Ybor City were becoming more patriotic towards their Spanish homeland, which only served to strain community relations. Nonetheless, despite fierce nationalistic allegiance, Spaniards in increasing numbers continued to arrive in Ybor City from Spain via Cuba. Many of them were very young, single boys and men, from twelve years old into their early twenties. They came from several provinces in Spain, but mostly from Galicia and Asturias, in the north and northwest regions of Spain. These areas are mountainous and the farms are small and primitive. Traditionally, the families are very large. Life there was demeaning, and it offered rather poor prospects. Historian John A. Crow reports that in 1929, just prior to the establishment of the Republic there, out of 1,026,412 landowners or tenants assessed in Spain, 847,548 were earning less than one peseta a day.[50]

Many Spaniards sought to escape from such poverty and from the threat of the time-honored wars against the Moors of North Africa by shipping off to the South American colonies. Many also went to Cuba, long considered *la isla fiel*, "the faithful island," because Cuba was the last of Spain's colonies to achieve its independence. Often, however, they stopped only briefly in Cuba before seeking their fortunes in Florida, where rumors had it there was high demand for labor in factories or in warehouses owned by Spaniards. Age was no stumbling block, as revealed in old photographs showing youngsters in their early teens at work in the Ybor City factories. Young Spanish workers were welcomed wholeheartedly by Spanish *patrons*, and the adaptable young people could live cheaply in one of the many small boarding houses. My father followed this same pattern. He left Galicia as an eleven-year-old boy, stayed three years in Cuba, and arrived in Tampa in 1908, where he quickly found work. My mother was working beside her father, Felice Leto, in the Corral Wodiska #8 factory by the age of fourteen or fifteen.[51]

In Ybor City the Spaniards had already opened *El Porvenír* center for their medical needs. Late in 1891 the Centro Español was formed as a teaching and recreational facility. Its twin-towered social club was built in early 1892. The magnificent edifice occupied one of the most important sites of the town at La Sétima and 16th Street. To the right and left of the entryway were towers that contained four floors each. There was a portico at the entrance, a large lobby, a theater with 500 chairs and a large game room, a convertible dance hall, and other features. A condition for membership read: "in order to belong to this organization it is necessary that the candidate be Spanish of race and sentiments and that he be sympathetic to Spain's prestige in America."[52] For Spaniards, this club served as home and entertainment for both Galician and Asturian immigrants, and it became a model for L' Unione Italiana (1894).[53]

The impulse toward mutual support based on heritage and national background helped to shape a strong sense of community for each immigrant group. Impending events would divert some of the community focus and redirect it toward patriotism for one's homeland.[54] Mutualism in Ybor City—contentious, but necesssary—would just have to wait.

## Fall-Out: The Cuban War of Independence and the Spanish-American War, 1895-1900

By the early years of the nineteenth century most of the Spanish colonies in the New World had obtained their independence. This thirst for independence had grown in many countries, especially after the French Revolution in the late 18th century. Cuba, the Philippines, and Puerto Rico remained as outposts of Spanish colonial rule. Cuba had suffered long in its

*Martí poses with some of his supporters, on the steps of the Ybor Cigar Factory after a speech in 1892. The iron staircase was later removed and shipped to Cuba, where it remains on display at the Martí Museum in Havana.*

efforts to shake free. Its Ten Year War against Spain had achieved only modest success, and eventually resulted in failure. But the thirst for independence remained.

In Cuba, the struggle for *Cuba Libre* brought to the forefront many genuine leaders: Carlos Manuel de Céspedes, Maximo Gomez, Calixto Garcia, Ignacio Agramonte, Antonio Macéo, and José Martí. All except Martí had personally faced the acrid smell of the field of battle. And all, including Martí, felt inexpressibly strong emotions for their *patria* (homeland). Martí, the Supreme Patriot, became the spirit and soul of the struggle against Spain.[55]

José Julian Martí y Pérez (known simply as José Martí) was born in Havana on January 28, 1853, the son of a father from Valencia, Spain, and a mother from the Canary Islands, both of humble birth. José Martí had witnessed mistreatment and persecution of Cubans at home at an early age, and from his youth was an activist with organizations that were regarded as suspect by Spanish authorities. He was twice banished to exile in Spain, which is where he received his university education, gradu-

ated as a lawyer from the University of Madrid, and later enrolled at the University of Zaragoza. While his love for his father's people in Spain was genuine, (he occasionally made reference to it), his deep-seated hatred of Spain's top-down institutions, colonial occupation, persecution of Cubans, and their part in promulgating the general European exploitation of the colonies, became universally known. His revolutionary activities at the intellectual level, and his increasing leadership at the grassroots level, left no question that he was the "purest" supreme leader of the heart and soul of the Cuban revolutionary efforts.[56]

Martí was in the midst of completing the formative stages of the Cuban Revolutionary Party when he was invited to Tampa in late 1891 by the members of the Ignacio Agramonte Cuban Revolutionary Club (*Club Revolucionario Cubano—Ignacio Agramonte*). This recently formed club was headed by Eligio Carbonell Malta and José Gomez Santoyo.[57]

The occasion is described well by Jose Rivero Muniz, author of one of the most readable early accounts of Ybor City history, and a witness to many of the events:



33

The news of the coming of Martí was given out by *El Crítico de Ybor City* (*The Ybor City Critic*), a newspaper that Ramon Rivero had begun to publish the year before he discontinued the *Revista de Florida*. . . . There was rejoicing in all the Cuban homes. In all the cigar factories nothing else was discussed. . . .

It was the night of November 25, 1891. Through the streets of Ybor City that were barely illuminated by a few street lights, groups of people were defying the rain which fell incessantly and were hurrying to reach the railway station situated on Sixth Avenue between Seventeenth and Eighteenth Streets. . . . The sandy soil of the streets hardened by the rains made walking easier for pedestrians. The small waiting room and the not very wide station platform were filled with people. Then at midnight sharp the train from Jacksonville stopped on one side of the small platform.[58]

In the morning Martí got an early start, accompanied by Rivero, Carbonell, Iznaga, and others, to look over "Cuban Tampa" and to visit the factory of Ybor and Manrara, the largest and best-known factory in the city, where he was greeted at the door by Manrara himself. There Martí found some eight hundred workers being read to by a *lector*, and Muñiz writes, "The reading stopped, and at the foot of the rostrum Ramon Rivero introduced Martí. The cigarmakers, rising from their stools, greeted the visitor with a noisy and prolongued banging of the blades of their tobacco leaf cutters on the hard wood boards of their tables."[60] The eloquent visitor made a short speech, and was "moved by such a spontaneous and kind reception."[61]

Martí met there briefly with Don Vicente before continuing with his followers to "Piño City," the new, rugged cigar factory site at the lower eastern end of what would become West Tampa. There the Cubans would not be slighted. At a vast reception room in Céspedes Hall, he once again addressed an enthusiastic crowd of faithful followers, in each case inviting all to attend his formal speech that evening at the Cuban Lyceum.

Muñiz also provides a vivid description of the main event:

Night had not yet fallen when already the premises of the Cuban Lyceum overflowed with people. The stairs, that from the outside of the building led to its second floor, were completely occupied . . . . The clock was striking eight when Eligio Carbonell, obeying a signal, announced with a loud, "Viva Jose Martí!" the arrival of the hero. A thunderous ovation greeted him the moment the curtain was pulled back and he was seen on the stage surrounded by the directors of the Cuban Lyceum and the Ignacio Agramonte Club. It seemed as if the building were coming down with the tremendous noise . . . . Suddenly, all the noise ceased. It was Martí, pale and full of emotion, with his hands crossed upon his chest, beginning to say, "For Cuba, who suffers, I have the first word . . ."[62]

Muñiz quotes the Cuban writer and biographer Jorge Mañach in praise of the speech as "a model of perfect public speaking." Muñiz then vividly describes the response:

The audience, surprised by this austere tone to which it was not accustomed, was moved by this masterful speech. Sometimes, as Martí finished some more patriotic sections, the ovation would result in an uncontrollable explosion of emotions, with multitudes weeping. The enthusiasm of the listeners reached its maximum, however, when . . . his vigorous speech vibrated like the battle call of a bugle . . . and the speaker closed his patriotic and unforgettable address: "Now let us form ranks! . . . enough of mere words. From our torn insides let us lift up an inextinguishable love for our country . . . . There she is; from there she calls us; one hears her moan; they raped her; they scoff her, and they cause her to have gangrene. Before our eyes, they corrupt us and they tear apart the mother of our heart. Well, let us rise once and for all, with one final charge from our heart. . . . Let us rise in behalf of the real republic. Those of us with our love for what is right and with our dedication to work will know how to keep it alive. Let us rise to offer a place to die to the heroes whose spirit wanders through the world ashamed and alone. Let us rise so that someday our children may have a place to die. And let us place around the star in the new flag this formula for triumphant love— *with the people and for the people.*"[63]



**Ybor City: The Making of a Landmark Town**

The response from the audience was overwhelming. They kept Martí for more than an hour, shaking his hand and pledging their support. Meanwhile, a stenographer's notes were quickly edited, typeset, and printed by *The Ybor City Critic* so that the speech could be more widely shared, and read aloud by *lectores* the next afternoon.[64] Meanwhile, the Ignacio Agramonte Club had held a meeting (Martí was too tired to attend ) at which Cuban patriot Carbonell of West Tampa suggested that José Martí be named president of The Cuban Patriotic League, and that, except for extreme extenuating circumstances, there never be another president elected.[65]

On November 27, 1891, Martí, still in Tampa, climbed the stage of the Liceo Cubano and delivered a second speech that was "a model of greatness."[66] Filled with the dream of his life, filled with inexpressible emotions and the profound need for a free Cuba, he began by saying, "Everything tonight lends itself more to a respectful silence than to words." Yet, he went on to cast into words the painful and inspiring yearnings for Cuban freedom. Taking to heart the execution of students, he declared that

It is not becoming of a Cuban, nor will it ever be, to get into blood up to the waist and to bring to life again the crimes of the world with a fagot of dead children . . . . Let the lamentations that are to accompany only the useless dead cease, since it is because of them that the fatherland is purer and more beautiful People live from heroic leavening.[67]

He concluded with images which had come to him during his train ride across the inhospitable plains as he approached Tampa:

I heard it yesterday from the very earth, when I was coming through the dark afternoon into this faithful town. The ground was damp and blackish, the marshy stream ran turbulently, the canes, few and withered, did not wave their green coloring . . . . All at once the sun suddenly broke over a clearing of the forest, and there, by the sparkling of the sudden light, I saw above the yellowish grass, around the black trunk of the fallen pines, the joyful bunches of new pines. That is what we are—new pines! [68]

That night Martí and the leaders of the Cuban community met again. They approved the draft of the resolutions he had written, in conformity with what the revolutionary organizations had agreed the day before, all of them uniting behind the common cause of liberation. The following day the resolution was presented at the Cuban Licéo to a great Cuban multitude, who also approved it. Then the Cubans—some four thousand strong—accompanied José Martí to the railroad station in Ybor City. The tune of "Hymn of Bayamo," played just as the locomotive departed.[69]

José Martí was in Tampa twenty documented times—perhaps twenty-two times—according to Emiliano J. Salcines, lawyer, judge, writer, and speaker, a total of "not less than 55 days, about the same number of days he spent in Key West."[70] Leland Hawes also quotes Salcines as having said that Martí later spent at least ten days in Martí City, a cigar town near Ocala in the 1890s.

During Martí's visit to Tampa in November 1892, there was the attempt on his life on the streets of Ybor City that led to his friendship with Ruperto and Paulina Pedroso. The poison in his glass, which he vomited instantly, did not have the in-

*After the threat on his life, Martí always felt a sense of safety and a sincere welcome at the home of Ruperto and Paulino Pedroso. For her courage and leadership, Paulina (below) was inducted into the Florida Women's Hall of Fame. The Pedroso home (bottom) is no longer standing, but was a well-known Ybor City landmark for many years. FSA/ DEL RIO.*

**Chapter 2 • The Early Years: 1824-1900**

ther inciting the Cubans and partisan Spaniards to rise up furiously.[71]

In New York City, on January 29, 1895, the Cuban Revolutionary Party Junta, with José Martí present, signed the order authorizing revolution in Cuba. The message carried the implication that the order should be issued simultaneously over different parts of the island. And that being accomplished, Marti wrote to his mother saying, "*para mi ya es hora*" (for me, the time has arrived).[72]

Tampa historian Tony Pizzo, writing in *La Gaceta* in a 1952 article titled "The Historic Cigar" completes this story, as he vividly relates how the declaration of revolution was successfully relayed to Cuba:

> With the message in hand that José Martí had handed to him, Gonzalo de Quesada departs to Tampa. At the station he is met by Fernando Figueredo, local party chief, and other Cuban patriots . . . . The Junta meets at the Blas O'Halloran Cigar factory (West Tampa), where Blas rolls five Panatelas—all identical. The one concealing the message is distinguished by two tiny yellow specks on the tobacco wrapper. A few days later, Gonzalo Quesada, with five Panatelas well concealed on his person, sails for Key West. There he is met by Miguel Angel Duque de Estrada, the man chosen to deliver the message to Juan Gualberto Gomez, the insurgent chief of the island of Cuba . . . . On a moonlit night on February 21, 1895, Estrada, with the cigars in his coat pocket, boards the *Mascotte* for the seething island. Arriving at the port of Havana, the courier calmly proceeds through routine customs inspection and passes out four cigars to the authorities. Then Estrada holds the 'loaded cigar' in his mouth and pretends to light it. He puffs several times. The cigar refuses to stay lit. He picks up his luggage . . . and walks into history![73]

On February 24, 1895, Cuban patriots proudly raised the flag of the Cuban Republic in the mountains of the province of Santiago in the eastern end of the island, in the town of Baire. The action reverberated like a great cry for liberty. It has been referred to by revolutionaries as "*el grito de Baire*" (the shout at the town of Baire).[74]

tended effect, and Martí only emerged as a stronger leader after the restorative care of Dr. Eduardo Barbarosa and the help given to him by the Pedrosos. Agents of the Spanish government were blamed for the attempt on his life, and the episode won him even greater sympathy.

On July 18, 1893, Martí arrived in Tampa for the third time. He was traveling throughout southern Florida with Jose Dolores Poyo and the Generals Serafín Sanchez and Carlos Roloff advancing the cause of the revolution. The following day, in his role as a delegate of the Cuban Revolutionary Party, he visited the main factories. In one of them, the Sanchez y Haya factory, the cigarmaker Pérez Molina, a Spaniard with progressive ideas, greeted the visitors and pleaded for the cause that they were presenting. The next day Martí attended an open-air meeting where not only thousands of enthusiastic Cubans were present, but also numerous Spaniards who supported the cause of Cuban independence. This last event enraged Spaniards who attempted to keep their dissenting countrymen from seeking work, furthermore...



**Ybor City: The Making of a Landmark Town**

Within three months—on May 19, 1895—José Martí, the supreme Cuban patriot, was killed on Cuban soil at *Dos Ríos* by a Spanish ambush, "facing the sun."[75] His loss was greatly felt by all Cubans in Tampa, as was, also, the death of Black Cuban patriot and military leader, Antonio Macéo, on December 14, 1896.[76] But the revolutionary struggle fathered by these Cuban leaders continued.

In an article written in all likelihood to commemorate the death of Vicente Martínez Ybor and titled (my translation), "That Cigarmaker, Friend of Martí," Nydia Sarabia quoted a certain Gaspar García Callo:

> Much has been written concerning the role that the cigar workers have played concerning the national independence, but there is something that has not been said . . . It is that José Martí was able to sell his concept and strategy concerning the revolution to the old chiefs, over a few months, by economic and ideological thoughts advanced by the cigar makers. Martí would have been, undoubtedly, a great leader, but with the cigar makers, with the organized cigar makers of the time, Martí was the indisputable national leader.[77]

While Martí was undoubtedly a catalyst, the Cuban revolution also sprang from the soil of Ybor City, and even to some extent directly from the Ybor family. Sarabia explains that

> Mercedes de la Revilla, Don Vicente's wife, was an honored member of the Association of Cuban Revolutionaries, and lent great service to the cause of Cuban liberty, not only in Key West but in Tampa. In her home and in her husband's factory, meetings were held with the assistance of Martí and other revolutionaries . . . When war . . . broke out, many workers of the factory elected to swap the cigar worker's *chaveta* (leaf cutter) for a *machete* (the long, heavy knife used to cut hard sugar cane) . . . and donated much money for the revolution . . . .[78]

Resources to support the revolution came from Ybor workers in the form of energy, enthusiasm, manpower, and cash. Sarabia notes that Mercedes de las Revillas de Martínez Ybor "was a member of the Cuban Revolutionary Party . . . she assisted all the meetings and the juntas that were presided by the Master [Jose Martí], who had his principal meetings at Vicente's factory." Sarabia makes it clear in marking the death of Ybor, that Don Vicente's idealism and patriotism should not be overlooked. Finally, Nydia Sarabia writes, "Vicente Martínez Ibor, [note her use of "I" instead of "Y" for Ybor; in his hometown in Spain that is the

correct usage] the good man from Valencia, just as Martí's father (also from Valencia ) had done, helped with all his heart, in an un-selfish manner, in the difficult but beautiful labor to liberate Cuba, and he motivated his workers to enlist in the future ranks of the Cuban liberating forces."

Don Vicente Martínez Ybor died on December 14, 1896. He had founded the town of Ybor City only ten years earlier. Moreover, just as José Martí and Antonio Macéo, Don Vicente had not lived to see Cuba's final liberation.

## The Death of Founder Don Vicente Martínez Ybor, 1818-1896

Many writers have attempted to capture the significance of the work of Don Vicente Martínez Ybor with respect to the town he founded. It seems as if his status and prestige are all that one reads about today, but a more immediate and personal sense of his impact as a person can be found in the responses to his death from his contemporaries. Two articles which appeared in the *Tampa Weekly Times* on December 17, 1896, give a clear view of his standing. One headline reports:

> **Don Vicente Martínez Ybor is Dead**
> **One of Tampa's Greatest Promoters**
> **and this Country's Most Prominent**
> **and Successful Business Man**

The anonymous reporter writes that "the venerable Don Vicente Martínez Ybor died at the residence of Hugo Schwab, his son-in-law, at 10 o'clock in the morning."[79] After summarizing Ybor's early life, the writer reports that

> in 1886 the firm removed their business to Tampa, having become convinced of superior advantages here. The success of the firm's business operation here has been phenomenal–greater than even the sagacious businessman at its head anticipated–and one important result was that many other large concerns followed it. Until now Tampa is the most important clear Havana cigar manufacturing center in the country.[80]

What seems noteworthy here is the direct sense of impact and importance the writer finds in Ybor's life. In effect he credits him with putting Tampa on the industrial map.

The reporter continues:

> The body has been embalmed and now rests in the family residence. . . . The body will be placed . . . in the receiving vaults at Oaklawn Cemetery, but later will be taken to Havana for interment [explained in a later article as meaning "after the war." The funeral services in Tampa were held under the direction]. . . . of Rev. Tyrrell, pastor of St. Louis church, at 10 o'clock. The full ritual of the Catholic services was given." In a later article, the casket was described as the "finest and most costly ever brought to this state."[81]

The headline of the second major Page One article in *The Tampa Weekly Times* read:

> **The Ybor Obsequies Today**
> **Impressive and Very Largely Attended**
> **The Whole People Joined in Showing**
> **Their Respect for the Honored Dead.**

Excerpts from the report show a profound and complex response from the citizens and reporter alike:

> There has never been in this state on any account a more impressive and general exhibition of feeling and a desire on the part of the people to prove their respect and esteem than was shown this morning at the funeral of the venerable Don Vicente Martínez Ybor, father and founder of Tampa's great cigar manufacturing industry, and most prominent promoter of the city's substantial growth and development. . . .
> The funeral procession was over a mile in length, there being in it ninety-nine vehicles besides the hundreds of pedestrians. . . .
> The procession was formed under the direction of L. G. Cone. Following the carriages containing Father Tyrrell and attendants were the family hearse, floral pieces, pallbearers, family, and Italian and Cuban Society representatives. According to the report, these were followed by the carriages and personalities below:
> Carriage of H. B. Plant and D. P. Hathaway . . . Carriage of Messrs. Oscar Manrara, Riquelme, Chamberlain, and Poujaud . . . Carriage of Mayor Gillett, Judge Phillips, P. O. Knight, and J. H. [not readable] . . . Carriage of the members of the Board of Public Works . . . Carriage of Capt. John T. Lesley, M. W. Carruth and E. R. Gunby . . . City Council and

other board and numerous city, county and state officials . . . hundreds of private citizens in carriages and buggies, many of whom carried magnificent floral decorations to be deposited on the tomb.

All of the cigar factories and many of the business houses in the city were closed during the morning and the Cherokee club building, the office of the Ybor City Land Improvement company and the V. M. Ybor and Manrara's factory was draped with black crepe. The various societies and other flags in the city were hung at half mast, and on every hand, was apparent evidence of the sincere sorrow of the people at the loss of their great benefactor.[82]

Revealing, then, is the great esteem that the full spectrum of the community —the city elitists, the founding fathers, the cigar manufacturers, leading personalities of the day, the judiciary, government, civic, and social leaders and the multitude of cigar workers and townspeople—had for him. The magnificence of the funeral and the documentation of the mourning of the town that lasted a week is a telling testimony to Tampa's most important historical personality, the founder of Ybor City, Don Vicente Martínez Ybor.

Until recently, only two modest monuments to Don Vicente existed in town: a

bust sculpture of him in the patio of the Ybor City State Museum, and the sizable Ybor mausoleum standing in lonely vigil at Oaklawn Cemetery. The Ybor City Museum Society sought ways and means of having an appropriate arm of government

This preliminary sketch for a statue of Vicente Martínez Ybor by sculptor Steve Dickey conveyed the vision of a more sizable monument in tribute to the founder of our National Landmark town. The Ybor City Museum Society helped to find the resources to commission an impressive larger-than-life sculpture as a permanent reminder of his role. It now stands at Centro Ybor.

RAFAEL MARTINEZ YBOR.

**Chapter 2 • The Early Years: 1824-1900**

assist with the task of erecting, within a reasonable time, a more substantial statue or monument befitting the man, who in a real sense was the economic and cultural founder of the prosperous and diverse modern city of Tampa, as well as the landmark town which bears his name.[83] He was buried with what was undoubtedly the state's most auspicious funeral ceremony ever, in manner and honor marking him as an industrial giant and Ybor City's founder. Yet, when I first wrote this chapter, there was still no permanent public tribute remotely worthy of this giant of a man: the founder of Ybor City, the man responsible for making Tampa the Clear Cigar Capital of the United States, and the single individual most deserving of recognition for propelling a small, remote town called Tampa, into a young, robust and fast-growing city in Florida, now known and respected by the entire nation. Perhaps the statue that now stands in Centro Ybor will help at last to celebrate and honor his achievements.

### The Spaniards in Ybor City and the War in Cuba

The story of Ybor City plays out against a global background from the start. Before continuing to focus on events within the town, a quick brush with Spanish history seems necessary.

Over two millennia of foreign invaders, vicious defense of their land, final victory, unity, and then ownership of the world's largest empire, Spaniards shaped a proud, distinctive nation. Additionally, the different geographic origins of the many peoples within its borders left an imprint on Spain, resulting in today's many autonomous regions, each with its own set of attributes. The impact of the sweeping political and intellectual changes in the Middle Ages, the Renaissance, the French Revolution; the earlier Masonic influence; the very brief, intermittent periods of enlightenment; and the long years of retrenchment and conservatism left further marks on the Spanish people.[84]

Add to this the religious, social, and intellectual impact of disciplined Jesuit initiatives and the political restrictions of the Carlist wars, followed by liberalization brought about by loss of the colonies, and the dynamic history becomes clearer. One product of the liberal Spanish mood swing was "the Generation of '98" that spawned so many liberal writers, known by their period of bloom at the century's end. This last mind-set we capture here in Ybor City after the latter part of the century, when Spain lost Cuba along with the Philippines and Puerto Rico in its war with America. Yet mountain Spaniards, including Asturians and Galicians, were generally too isolated to be in the mainstream of much history. They (with a few notable exceptions) were more influenced by the Spanish triumvirate—the Monarchy, Church, and Army. The strong, concerted influence of this powerful threesome kept the peasants isolated, uneducated, uninformed, close to the land—and impoverished. It strengthened the "Spanishness" of character that Miguel de Unamuno and others wrote about.

Spain's first attempt at democracy had ended with the failed First Republic (1870-1873). Alfonso XII had died at an early age, and his second wife, Maria Cristina of Austria, headed the nation as Regent. Her reign was characterized by internal military uprisings and a Carlist War fallout, a broken treasury, successions of governments within the realm, lack of forceful political leaders, bad agriculture, and an outdated and exhausted military. In the 1890s the small Spanish nation, with a population of only 16 million, its treasury totally depleted, its industrial assets virtually nonexistent, was ill-equipped to maintain overseas colonies. Its army in disarray, its navy antiquated and facing wars in two faraway corners of the world—Cuba and the Philippines (where trouble was brew-

**Ybor City: The Making of a Landmark Town**

ing)—the nation was torn apart by vestiges and remnants of an antiquated monarchy. It was no match for the revolutionary fervor sweeping its remaining colonies, or the growing power of a young, vigorous democracy. Monarchies were—in fact—anachronisms.

In the last years of the war, Spain resorted to shipping only very young recruits to Cuba; these were 15- to 17-year-old soldiers, ill-equipped and untrained. They were led by an uninspired officer corps to fight against determined Cubans and Americans, a situation that aroused considerable criticism in Spain. Economic conditions at home were so disastrous that the nation was unable to budget monies to support the Spanish-American War in Cuba. In the last year of that conflict, out of a force of 200,000 Spanish soldiers on the island only a very small fraction of soldiers were able to stand up to fight.[85]

Young Spanish soldiers went hungry for lack of pay. In 1898 some troops in Oriente Province had not been paid for close to a year, and most of them not for some six months. Some were forced to beg for food, while others had no choice but to steal food in the towns of Cuba. It was a prescription for total defeat. A significant percentage of the fighting force was ravaged by tropical diseases and received no medical care. The real situation during the final two years of the war was one that many in Spain were not even aware of, until the returning sick, hungry, and morally defeated young soldiers revealed the truth of the war to a tired nation.[86]

Such were conditions in Spain in the 1890s. Of course, it was not the loss of Cuba alone. As the great Spanish empire slipped away, the collapse of Spanish colonial control revealed the ineptness of the monarchy. The days of strong command from across the seas were over. This small nation, now with an antiquated form of government and greatly reduced income as a result of the loss of its colonies, could

not do battle with a young, vigorous, and growing power thousands of miles away. Nor could it simultaneously defend the Philippines on the far side of the world. It was a haunting cross for the Spanish psyche to bear. Nonetheless, Spain would retain its monarchy under Alfonso XIII for some three decades more, at which time in 1931, its Second Republic would be voted in—the election that was a prelude to the Spanish Civil War.[87]

In Ybor City, many factory owners, well-positioned employees, Spanish club leaders, and young Spaniards had strong nationalistic leanings toward Spain. The news they read and received from home most likely spoke of the war in Cuba from the Spanish perspective. Against a growing Cuban revolutionary spirit, news at the factories or cafés and early club cantinas at the old twin-towered Centro Español must have reeked with talk of the conflict. *Lectores* no doubt kept the cigar workers informed. One surmises that the news was often straightforward because of the occasional mixed sympathies of the workers listening—Cubans and Spaniards. Some factories hired mainly Cubans, while others hired mostly Spaniards.

In the factories, cantinas, boarding houses, and coffeehouses the talk was often passionate. It increased, no doubt, when souls were occasionally stirred by the sound of Spanish (Peninsular) music played on primitive Victrolas, or by a musical group or visiting artist from South America or Spain. What can fire the spirit more than a *Paso Doble* (with its martial airs), a regional *Jota*, or some select melodies from a Spanish light opera or Zarzuela. The Zarzuelas were then at their pinnacle in Spain, with stories based on the old barrio life in shows such as *El Barrio de Lavapies*. If today this music still stirs the passions and emotions and draws new generations of descendants to Spain, then one must understand that the hearts of Ybor City's young lads would have been yet more deeply stirred a hundred years ago.

Most of the young Spaniards in Ybor City had been originally sent by their parents to one of the few remaining Spanish colonies where it still seemed possible to seek a better life and to avoid the physical danger of having to fight in potential wars with Morocco in Africa or in defense of remaining colonies in Africa. Many Spanish sons never returned from the wars there. Those sent to colonial Cuba before the insurrection had come to Tampa for economic reasons, mostly. And those Spaniards who went to Cuba after the end of the war, imagining better economic conditions in a newly independent Cuba than in a defeated Spain, soon experienced its reality—a land in turmoil, unable to feed itself, caught between two imperial powers. That many Ybor Cubans who were deeply committed to the independence movement and passionate about their homeland, returned to Cuba and quickly elected to come back to Tampa gives strong witness to the turmoil and deep uncertainties that reigned in Cuba in the early post-war years.

Most Spaniards, however, had not freely elected to be in Ybor City. Economic reasons were usually their strongest motivation. Unlike many of the Cubans, and even other national groups, few Spanish workers had roots planted in North America in the late 19th century. Most of them remained rooted in Spain. Given these conditions, the aggressive stance of the Cuban revolutionaries in Tampa, understandably presented a dilemma for these young Spaniards in their everyday life in the workplace and on the streets of Ybor.

The Spaniards found themselves in a very delicate situation. On the one hand, they had been accepted into a great country, a gracious land full of opportunities they could not have found in Spain. They had come without families, mostly. Additionally, they were working in the same industry and town where Spanish-speaking Cuban patriots worked. The Cubans, while they were bitter in their resentment of Spanish colonial repression, were heavily endowed with Spanish heritage and blood—Galician and Asturian, primarily. They were enemies and brothers at the same time. Amidst this tension, America had officially taken Cuba's position against Spain. This was not a comfortable situation for the Spanish worker.

*This documentary photograph by Gilson Willets shows Cuban volunteers in their barracks during the Spanish Civil War. Many of these men were cigar makers in Tampa.* H. B. Plant Museum.



**Ybor City: The Making of a Landmark Town**

Given this environment in Ybor City, the Spanish leaders sought to steer a middle course. That is the path chosen by the early presidents of the few Spanish clubs, the Spanish Consul, the Spanish *patrones*, and the mature, well-placed Spanish employees, whose factory loyalties the *patrones* had always counted on during labor strife. They tried not to feed the flames of hostility, while never renouncing the patriotic fires of patriotism that was their cultural heritage. Nor was patriotism less prevalent among the large numbers of young Spaniards employed in the factories, where a few boys as young as twelve years old began work, though most were several years older.

The power structure in downtown Tampa had many business and social contacts with the *patrones* of the cigar factories. These venues included Tampa social club sites and the Cherokee Club, built in 1896, that catered to the elite factory owners. Teddy Roosevelt is said to have dined there during his brief time in Tampa before the troops departed for Cuba. But aside from the monetary interest, Tampa understood the law-abiding and orderly character of the cigar workers, though they didn't enjoy all aspects of their culture. Tampa, in those early years, had a vital monetary stake in the continued well-being of the cigar industry, which meant having to practice tolerance for both Cuban and Spanish ways of thinking.

Making feelings worse during the immediate prewar years was the very nature of labor in the factory. *Tampa Tribune* staff writer Archie Blount explained in a retrospective feature that "Spaniards monopolized the Sanchez y Haya factory while Cubans dominated the Martínez Ybor factory. Earlier, Cubans had stoned Ignacio Haya (the factory owner) and his American-born wife as they walked down Seventh Avenue." The national allegiances of Spanish and Cuban workers were also complicated by capitalist competition for reputation, market share, and overall economic success. Blount traced hostilities to the earliest days, and quoted Spanish pioneer Bautista M. Balbontín's recollections from a 1930 interview, "the Spanish at that time [1890s] were persecuted, abhorred, and were the target of Cuban hatred because of the Spanish government in Cuba. The Spanish-American War further crystallized these feelings of nationalism, radicalism and prejudice as thousands of troops massed in Tampa prior to embarking for Cuba to fight the colonial Spanish regime."[88]

The gathering of thousands of U.S. troops in Tampa in 1898 served as yet another divisive factor in the lives of the Spanish and Cuban workers of Ybor City. *Tampa Tribune* history columnist Leland Hawes reported an example for February 3, 1895, when "Tampa seethed with Cuban revolutionary activity" and "two intensely rival events—a rally for Cuban independence and a reception for the officers of a Spanish torpedo boat"—vied for front-page attention in the *Tampa Tribune* of that day.[89]

The 1895 *Tribune* questioned the visit of the Spanish naval vessel with a headline, "Does It Mean War?" In fact, these events did serve as prelude to full-scale warfare, but the reality of the situation was that both Spanish and Cuban interests were represented in the community, and were grappling with ways to live together.

Hawes pointed out that "a key figure in the Cuban rally was the man who became the first mayor of West Tampa, Fernando Figueredo Socarras, a native Cuban who had been involved in the independence movement since the abortive Ten Years War of 1868-78."[90] Spanish and Cuban residents had been living with their differences since the founding of the city and they certainly had abundant opportunities to struggle both publicly and privately with the conflicts during the Ten Year War and in its aftermath.

Figueredo, in fact, was a relative newcomer to the Tampa scene, but no stranger



**Chapter 2 · The Early Years: 1824-1900**

to the Cuban-Spanish conflict, having won recognition as a hero of the Ten Years War. In 1894 he, along with hundreds of other Cuban workers and factory owners, had left Key West for Tampa following the Cuban strike at the La Rosa Española factory, when the Spanish *patrones* there had brought in Spaniards from Cuba as strikebreakers. Figueredo's prominence in the Cuban Revolutionary Party placed him in close consultation with Jose Martí, who had met with Figueredo in West Tampa during his visit in May of 1894. Martí came to Figueredo's home during a subsequent visit and wrote the manifesto for the new Revolutionary Party while staying there.[91]

## The Last Year of the Cuban Uprising and The Rough Riders in Ybor City

In the 16th and 17th centuries the Spanish army was generally recognized as the most effective fighting force in Europe. This was the peak of the Spanish Empire period, when Charles I and Phillip II reigned not only in Spain, but, through inheritance, ruled much of Europe and its lands and colonies.[92] Years later, just after his defeat at Waterloo by Wellington, Napoleon was asked why his superb army had "met its Waterloo." He replied that he had lost the cream of his officer corps fighting the Spaniards years earlier, resulting in his defeat to Russia and the British.

By the 19th century, Spain's loss of most of its colonies had bankrupted the nation and its military forces. Approaching the end of that century there was grave concern in Spain for the effectiveness of its army in the defense of Cuba and the Philippines. When two newspapers vilified the easy, gentlemanly life of the Spanish military students in the Academies, the young cadets invaded the newspaper and destroyed its facilities to defend their honor. Several ministers resigned, but the incident demonstrated widespread reservations regarding national military preparedness.[93]

In fact, it was not just the competence of the military that was being challenged. The general lack of faith in the Spanish monarchy's government headed by the Regent, Queen Maria Christina—in the face of various contentious events—resulted in a request from the government head at that time, Praxedes Mateo Sagasta, that she resign. Spain had ceased to be a formidable opponent. It was a bankrupt nation. It was now up to foreign policy leaders to find an honorable way out of conflict, but that would take time.

In Cuba the Captain General of Spain on the island, Arsenio Martínez Campos, had been accused of following a very lenient and ineffective struggle against the Cuban revolutionaries and was given credit only for securing the death of Jose Martí at Dos Ríos. As a result of his overall ineffectiveness, on February 10, 1896, General Valeriano Weyler replaced Campos as Captain General of Cuba.[94]

Weyler took immediate forceful measures, precipitating a great exodus of Cubans. Many of them relocated in Ybor City. In May of 1896, General Weyler announced an edict prohibiting exportation of tobacco to Tampa, since Ybor City Cuban workers, through their donations to the revolutionary cause, were essentially using revenues from exported Cuban tobacco to buy arms to be used against Spain.[95] Meanwhile, in anticipation of the severe shortage of tobacco from Cuba, Don Vicente and other *patrones* sent two ships to Havana to bring back all the tobacco that could fit on board before the edict went into effect. This supplied the factories until new sources could be found.

In Spain the government had hoped to contain the Cuban uprising, possibly to install a semi-autonomous government and make concessions, looking for a way out. A very loosely affiliated government similar to the one Britain had used for Canada in 1867 was also considered. However, all initiatives were rejected by both Cuba and the United States.[96] Then on

**Ybor City: The Making of a Landmark Town**

*The U.S. Battleship Maine is shown in an 1898 photograph at the far left as it enters the harbor at Havana, Cuba. On the right is the result of the 1898 explosion that served as catalyst for the declaration of war by the United States: at the time the Maine was believed to have been sunk in Havana Harbor by Spain.* LC.

*A U.S. artillery battery at the wharf commands a sweep of Tampa Bay in 1898. Troop transport ships are assembled in the bay.* H. B. PLANT MUSEUM.

*Mounted troops conducted drills in fields near the encampments (left). Another 1898 photograph (below) captures Col. Theodore Roosevelt speaking with (left to right) journalist and novelist Richard Harding Davis, a correspondent for New York and London papers; journalist Stephen Bonsall of the New York Herald; and U.S. Major Dunn.* H. B. PLANT MUSEUM.

*Col. Theodore Roosevelt enjoyed the national attention he and his "Rough Riders" attracted. His famous charge up San Juan Hill put him on the road to the Presidency.* LC.

**Chapter 2 · The Early Years: 1824-1900**

Before leaving Tampa in 1898 (below, from left) are Unidentified [possibly Maj. Brodie], Allen Capran [possibly Maj. Dunn], Maj. Gen. Joseph Wheeler, Chaplain Brown, Col. Leonard Wood, Lt. Col. Theodore Roosevelt. FSA.

Many of the top officers stayed at the Tampa Bay Hotel. Photographed here on the southeast verandah in 1898 are General William Shafter and his staff. H. B. PLANT MUSEUM.

**Ybor City: The Making of a Landmark Town**

February 15, 1898, a tremendous explosion ripped through the U. S. Battleship *Maine*. The dead crewmen numbered two hundred and sixty. The "Yellow Press," as the rival newspaper empires of William Randolph Hearst and Joseph Pulitzer were labeled in the country, quickly accused Spain of this treacherous deed.[97]

On April 18, 1898, the U.S., citing "Our Manifest Destiny" and responding to the sinking of the battleship *Maine*, declared war on Spain.

The Cuban revolutionary movement quickly discovered that highly competitive American newspapers had an appetite for war stories. The scoop-happy news empires ruled by William Randolph Hearst and Joseph Pulitzer fought each other to position correspondents and artists to report sensational stories from the front.

"Atrocities of the most appalling kind perpetrated by the Spaniards began to appear upon nearly every American front page," wrote historian Walter Mills. "It shocked us profoundly—and it was extremely good reading."[98]

One of the most familiar journalistic anecdotes of the period concerns a famous exchange between Hearst and the artist Frederic Remington, who had been sent to Cuba to illustrate the news. When Remington telegraphed Hearst from Cuba in 1897 that little was happening and since war was unlikely he wanted to return home, Hearst responded: "Please remain. You furnish the pictures, I'll furnish the war!" In Tampa, an estimated thirty thousand U.S. troops were housed on some two hundred and fifty acres of land, under the command of General William Shafter. They were from all walks of life. By the time war was declared, the troops were ready. The Port of Tampa had been selected as the port of debarkation for armed convoys heading for Cuba, and as it turned out, Remington did provide pictures, including drawings of General Shafter and other officers, and a famous (but invented)

rendition of Teddy Roosevelt leading the charge to take San Juan Hill.

While camping in Tampa, the troops had enjoyed a warm reception from Cubans in Ybor and Americans in general, and there was much last minute preparation, letter writing, street visitation, and much carousing.

Some of the best-known soldiers were among the last to reach Tampa. Local historian Leland Hawes reports that the "last-minute arrivals included the Rough Riders, led by Col. Leonard Wood and his flamboyant sidekick, Lt. Col. Theodore Roosevelt. They were here only a week, but they camped not far from the Tampa Bay Hotel."[99] They found the city crowded and nearly gridlocked. "The confusion appeared to be utterly inextricable. . . . The sidings from the port . . . for perhaps 50 miles . . . were blocked with cars. Roosevelt hijacked a coal train to move his men nine miles to Port Tampa. . . . They mingled with the military mob at dockside or sampled Last Chance Street," where, Hawes quotes an individual as saying, "You could get a drink or a damsel, or both."[100]

"Teddy" Roosevelt, intrepid of character and action, made Ybor City history by having dinner at the Cherokee Club, then primarily an elitist club for cigar factory *patrones* and top Anglo personalities from Tampa. One of the often-told stories of the Rough Riders in Ybor City is referred to as "The Charge of the Yellow Rice Brigade," when the troop rode on horseback into the front door of Las Novedades Restaurant. Owner Manuel "Canuto" Menendez seems to have taken it in stride, and even offered the men a round of drinks on the house.[101]

The actual cause of the sinking of the *U.S.S. Maine* that had drawn the nation into the war remained obscure and controversial. In 1898 two inquiries into the incident were made, one of them by Spain, utilizing divers. Then, in 1911, after a cofferdam was built around the wreck, the

U.S. Board of Inspection's Report delivered inconclusive findings. Admiral Hyman Rickover eventually concluded that it had been destroyed by a blast inside its hull, "since the plates were blown inside out."[102] More recently, the *National Geographic* hired a marine engineering company to investigate using modern techniques and "determined either a mine or a coal fire could have blown up the Maine."[103] Whether or not the explosion was directly caused by an aggresive action by Spain has never been proven.

For the Cuban community in Ybor City, the war brought pride, excitement, and hope. Meanwhile, Spaniards in Tampa did not fare as well. Membership in Centro Español dropped to three hundred. "From May to August the Centro lost 193 members and its revenues were sharply reduced," Rivero Muñiz wrote. "The most prominent members of the Spanish colony held a reunion on the outskirts of the city, at the home of Ignacio Haya, who several times had been president of the Centro Español de Tampa. There they begged him to ask the city officials to extend protection to the lives and interests of his fellow countrymen . . . It wasn't necessary for Haya to go through the formalities . . . as soon as Figueredo [the most prominent Cuban patriot and civic leader] visited Haya in person . . . [he said] his greatest wish was that more cordial relations be established among members of the Spanish-speaking colony. . . . In turn Figueredo carried the understanding to his fellow Cubans, explaining the agreement, and obtaining their consent on cordial relations with the Spaniards."[104]

Many Spaniards had left Tampa in 1898 due to the impending conflict. Later, American troops occupied the Centro Español and its owners had to abandon the building. "Municipal authorities, realizing the deep disappointment of the Spaniards, approved a resolution praising the honest conduct of the Spaniards, supported in turn by the newspapers. Accompanied by Mayor Myron E. Gillett, President Adalberto Ramirez of the Centro Español and Bautista M. Balbontín (a wealthy founding member) visited General William Shafter and secured the retirement of the troops from the Centro Español, closing of the building under the custody of a special guard."[105]

In the military skirmishes through a sharp series of actions on land and sea, U.S. forces defeated the Spanish army and navy. The run-down, ill-equipped, and disease-ridden Spanish Army—a direct outcome of a bankrupt monarchy— yielded quick victories for American troops. In the naval battles of Manila Bay and Santiago, the stronger, more up-to-date U.S. Navy destroyed the outgunned Spanish fleets defending the Philippines and Cuba, cutting these colonies off from the motherland and making defeat of the Spanish land forces inevitable. On August 12, 1898, an armistice was declared, followed on December 10, 1898, by a treaty ending the war between Spain and the United States.

## Scenes of the Time

Some American troops were stationed near or on the outskirts of Ybor City. Cuban men and women performed support duties for the troops—and some were invited for meals. Troops with all manner of uniforms, hats, and belts took leisure on La Sétima.

 **April 1891:** Archie Blount reported in a *Tribune* story that "The strong ethnic and nationalistic feelings spilled over into the workplace. On April, 1891, a small body of artisans and businessmen in Ybor City gathered to discuss an alarming problem, the anti-social atmosphere prevailing against the Spanish."[106]

**Jan. 14, 1897:** "With Cuban and Spanish immigrants comprising a large percentage of the Tampa population, passion ran high with regards to events in

Cuba reported in the papers. Reports such as this in the Tribune only served to fuel the fire."[107]

**June 9, 1898:** "Fort Brooke and Ybor City were virtually in control of a mob Monday night and yesterday morning and the most disgraceful scenes were enacted, and, to their shame, be it said, the disorderly mob was composed almost the entire lot of soldiers of the U.S. army.

"The mob of white and black drunken soldiers started their wild acts in the saloon of Francisco Ysérn, and broke up everything in the place. They stole every bottle of whiskey and beer in the place and fired their pistols . . . Café Cantante was next visited and completely wrecked . . . house of ill repute was entered by force, and the white and black inmates [residents] were forced, at the point of pistols, to submit."[109]

**December 1898:** The returning American troops arrived in Tampa and were paid their owed salaries. The flush of this sudden wealth in the hands of soldiers created a flurry of commercial activities like this town had never seen before, as they waited to be transported home.[110]

**Circa mid-1898:** In his book *Cuba between Empires (1878-1902)*, Louis A. Pérez Jr. wrote, "James Boyle, [President] McKinley's private secretary, later recalled McKinley lamenting: that 'The Declaration of War Against Spain was an act which had been and will always be the greatest grief of my life. I never wanted to go to war with Spain . . . all I wanted was more time.'"[111]

Pérez suggests that both nations had come to the realization that colonialism was dead, but that it took time to shut down and dismantle a 400-year-old system of Spanish rule. On the American side, Congress and the military were anxious for an immediate resolution of the crisis. President McKinley wanted Spain—which was negotiating with America diplomatically and cooperating fully—to close up and leave.

A few years earlier, Grover Cleveland had wished for Spain simply to establish a Cuban autonomy. It would bring peace, he felt. (It had been offered, but refused.)

Meanwhile, Pérez described how the Cuban separatists, autonomists, volunteers, the wealthy sugar mill owners, the Creoles' upper layers—in fact, all the competing interests—were positioning themselves even as Cuban revolutionaries fought a sometimes invisible war on all sides. The revolutionaries complained constantly that they were being left out of the forthcoming peace and governing process. Their romantic and philosophical spirit did not square with American realism and needs—whether in the field or in government formation. The revolutionaries wanted independence—nothing else.

When months and years went by and American troops remained in Cuba, the spirit of the Cuban revolutionaries changed radically. American contact with or dependence on them, appreciated for their enthusiasm in the early months, lessened substantially. As more time passed, with some exceptions, contact with and dependence on them became virtually nil. And the press, both in New York and in Washington, spoke openly and negatively of the Cuban leaders at the time and the ability of the Cubans to fight.

To this, however, one must add that this was a serious misreading of the Cuban Patriots and their revolutionary fervor. Except for the early fighting, they remained mainly in the distant hills and marshy areas, maintaining their strength and integrity as a fighting unit until they could understand the happenings and believe that independence was, indeed, being planned between Spain and the U.S. Governing their actions was the need to maintain their strength should they again have to fight for their independence. A free Cuba had to be assured.

In the next several years until America removed its ships from Cuban waters,

Cuban revolutionary leaders wondered whether theirs was, indeed, a nation between two empires.[112]

Gil Klein quotes historian Irwin F. Gellman from his book *Roosevelt and Batista* as saying, "Ironically, the Roosevelt administration used Cuba as a model of Good Neighbor diplomacy.... The United States claimed truthfully that it had not landed troops on Cuban soil, and in early 1934, to strengthen its nonintervention declaration, the Roosevelt administration abrogated its Platt Amendment, which the United States had originally forced the Cubans to write into their Constitution of 1901, legalizing American military intervention on the island for the sake of stability." Klein adds, "It was, as one U.S. commentator called it, a 'splendid little war', that often is ignored in the study of American history. But in those 113 days, the United States fundamentally changed." He reminds us that this marked the country's emergence into international affairs. In the words of historian G. J. A. O'Toole,"It was a national rite of passage, transforming a former colony into a world power."[111]

In November 1908, Army General José Miguel Gomez was elected president of Cuba. On January 28 the U.S. turned over the Cuban government to Gomez.

In spite of the war, and of General Weyler's earlier embargo, some three million dollars were paid in wages in Tampa and under one hundred million cigars were sold in 1898. Moreover, there were now some twenty thousand people in Tampa.

With the end of the Spanish-American war, the subsequent assassination of president William McKinley, and great popularity stemming from the legendary story of his leading Rough Riders up San Juan Hill,[113] the pre-war Secretary of the Navy, Vice President Theodore "Teddy" Roosevelt, became President of the United States from 1901 to 1909.

*María Ruiz Martínez Ybor (center), the daughter-in-law of Vicente Martínez Ybor, holds her son Vicente, who is two years old in this 1905 photograph. He died in 1906 at the age of three. She is flanked by two maids, the one on the left holding Rafael (1904-1985), father of Rafael M. Ybor III. The photo shows a marked contrast between wealthy and working class women, such as those dressed in black standing to the right in the photograph below.* USFSCL.

*This photograph of Tampa cigarworkers posed in their workshop at the turn of the century conveys their social status by their attire and position. The group includes seated gentlemen in front, with a young boy standing behind a gentleman of higher status at the left, and plainly dressed women, standing rather than seated, at the right.* THCPL.

50

*This 1899 photo by the Burgerts shows many of the key features of Ybor City. To the right is a water tower providing an essential city utility for the growing number of residents. In the background to its left are some larger wooden boarding houses similar in style to those in the earlier photos (pages 8, 9, and 17). The large two-story home is that of cigar manufacturer Jose Arango, and to its left are some casitas that were homes for cigar workers.* HAMPTON DUNN.

*This turn-of-the-century photograph at the corner of 14th Street and 9th Avenue includes a glimpse of the El Pasaje Hotel with its wrought iron balcony on the far right. The gas street light on the corner has a step ladder leaning against it for lighting. Across from El Pasaje on the right is the Ybor Cigar Factory. On the other side of the street is the Gonzalez Clinic, formerly El Bien Publico.* CHARLES E. HARNER.

*For cigar makers, businessmen, and customers, the Ybor Cigar Factory remained a central feature of Ybor City at the end of the century. It would  become an important historic anchor for the town as it later helped regain economic vitality for a faltering community when a new generation of visionaries more than a century later would re-open it as Ybor Square.* HAMPTON DUNN.

51

**Chapter 2 • The Early Years: 1824-1900**

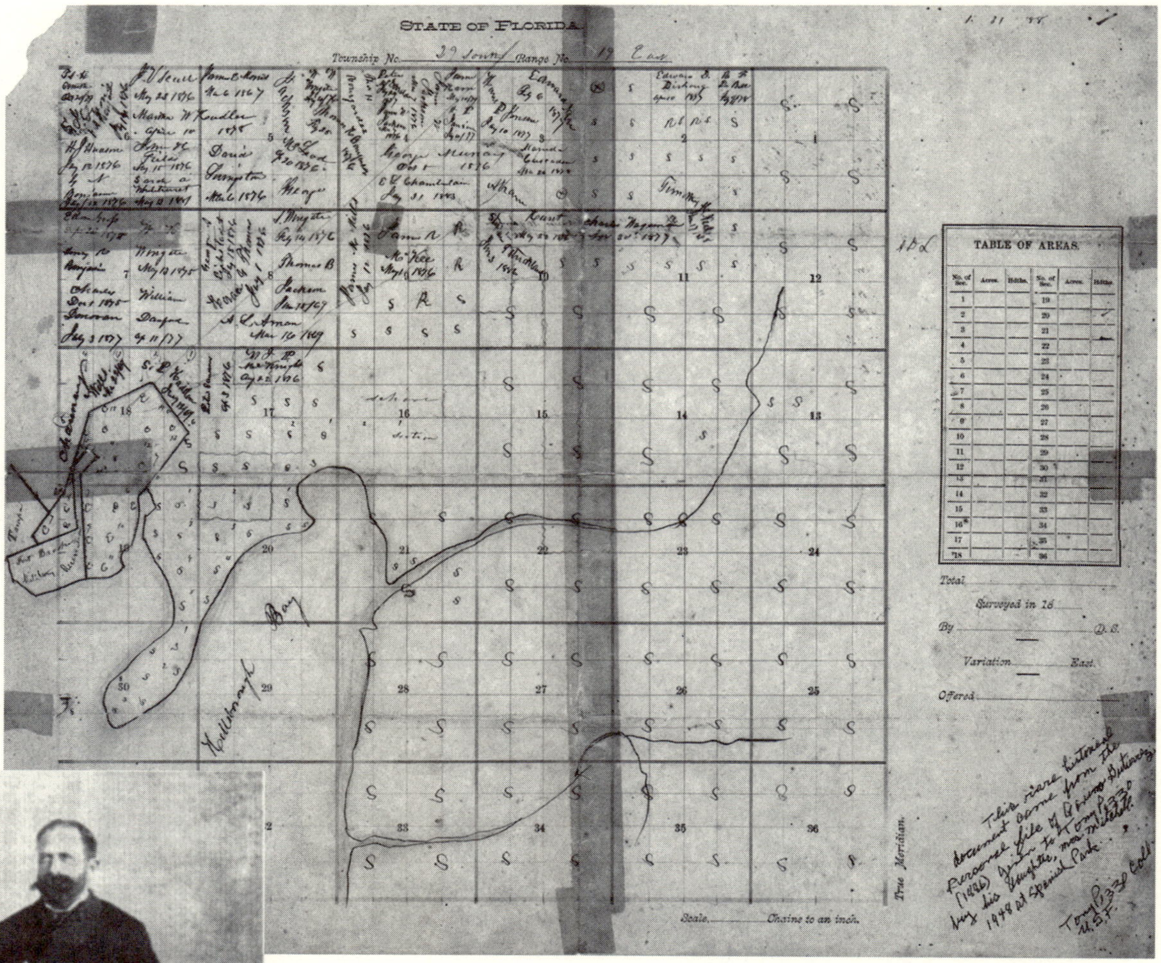

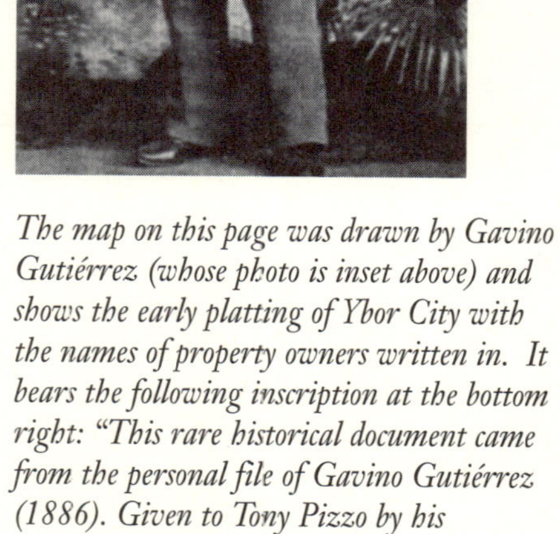

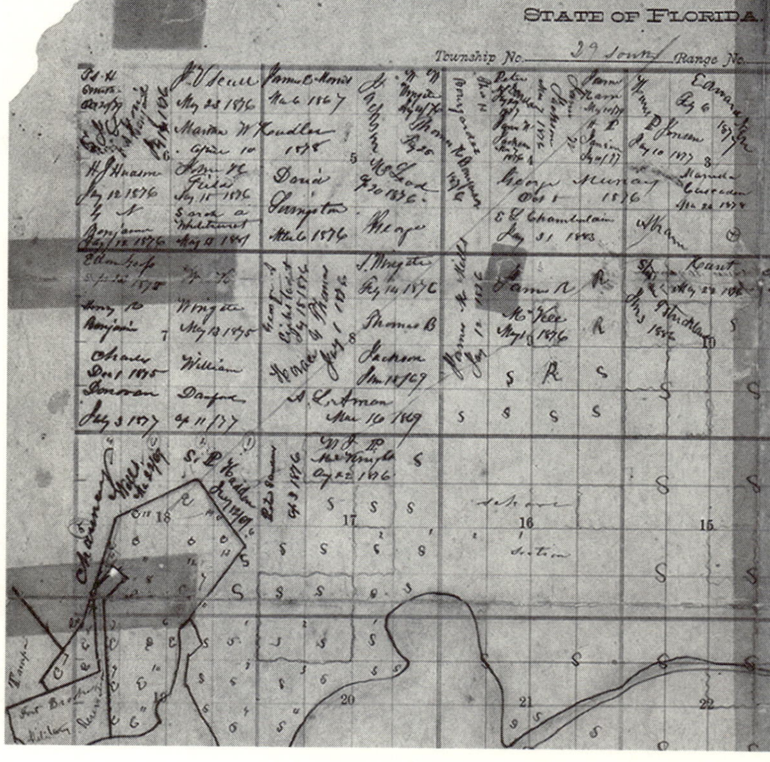

The map on this page was drawn by Gavino Gutiérrez (whose photo is inset above) and shows the early platting of Ybor City with the names of property owners written in. It bears the following inscription at the bottom right: "This rare historical document came from the personal file of Gavino Gutiérrez (1886). Given to Tony Pizzo by his daughter, Mrs. Mitchell, 1948 at Spanish Park." A detail from the map is enlarged at the right. USFSCL.

**Ybor City: The Making of a Landmark Town**

*Ybor City faced fire dangers from the start. This photo shows Fire Station No. 4 in 1899. It was located at 1801 9th Avenue and its captain was E. P. Symmes. Today's historic marker in Centennial Park is shown below.* TONY PIZZO/RM.

*Professional photographer H. Weimer was a tall, friendly German immigrant who spoke Spanish well and was known for his kind and friendly manner. He held a membership in the Photographers Association of America and his skills helped preserve a visual record of Ybor City in the early years. He had been a buffalo hunter in the west and bore a striking resemblance to "Buffalo Bill" Cody.* TONY PIZZO.

*Adalberto Ramirez, President of Centro Español in 1897, was part of an 1898 delegation to Gen. William Shafter at the Tampa Bay Hotel to assure him the club was not hostile. Once a superintendent in Ybor's Principe de Gales factory, he formed his own company in the early 1900s adopting the "Jules Verne" label in honor of Verne, who launched a rocket from Tampa in his 1865 novel From the Earth to the Moon.*

*This photograph of students at the Italian School in Ybor City in 1903 shows a healthy array of well-dressed youngsters. Tony Pizzo reports that at one time there were five such schools in Ybor City. They served as pre-schools for children before entering the small county school commonly known as the "Free School," located on 8th Avenue at the southwest corner of 14th Street. The photographer is H. Weimer.* TONY PIZZO.

53

*The Mortellaro Macaroni factory started on La Sétima and 19th Street. Success enabled it to move to this three-story building on the southeast corner of 11th Avenue and 20th Street.*

*Don Perfecto Garcia and his Westcott "Lighter Six" touring car in front of the Perfecto Garcia Cigar Company.* ANGEL GARCIA.

*Pietro C. Martino, one of the original nine Italian settlers in Ybor City, started the P. C. Martino Co. in 1906 to distribute feed and grain. The business was located at 1112 9th Avenue, moving later to a large brick warehouse at 1107 3rd Avenue. Eventually, in 1966, they expanded to a 13-acre site on Adamo Drive and Orient Road, having become one of the largest graineries in the state. In this photo, left to right, are Francisco Frisca, Pietro's son-in-law and partner; employee Francisco Traina; Pietro; and (on the wagon) Tom Martino, Pietro's son and also a partner who went on to serve many years as president of the firm.* TONY PIZZO.

*Street festivals seem to have been a natural part of Ybor City life from the earliest days. This 1905 Columbus Day celebration features a costumed Christopher Columbus at the control of one of the old open streetcars. Participants are dressed as sailors and Indians, perhaps in celebration of Columbus for leading the mostly Italian participants to their life in the New World.* TONY PIZZO.

54

**Ybor City: The Making of a Landmark Town**

*This photograph from about 1900 shows Pardo & Bros. bakery on 8th Avenue at 21st Street, one of the original sources for the "Cuban bread" so popular in Ybor City. Drivers are posed with their horse-drawn wagons that delivered fresh baked goods to merchants, cigar workers, and manufacturers. Also noteworthy in the photo are the stacks of bricks along the sidewalk. Soon they will be installed to pave the street. The bakery remained at the same location, later becoming Pardo & Gonzalez, and finally Casino Bakery. The four houses and the bakery building survived until Urban Renewal.*

*This 1907 photograph shows 5th Avenue (foreground) being occupied by homes and rooming houses. The Ybor factory stands in the background with its familiar water tower.* La Gaceta.

**Chapter 2 • The Early Years: 1824-1900**

The Cosmopolitan Drug Co. was an early business serving practical health needs for Ybor City residents.

This portrait of Ignacio Haya and his family is an emblem of high fashion and elegance. On the left is daughter Marina Haya and wife Fannie Haya is on the right. Ignacio and Fannie were married in 1872. After the death of her husband in 1906, Fannie became Tampa's first female executive of a large corporation.

The Florida Brewing Company building in Ybor City from an illustrated report in May 1899 (above) and as it appeared in 1903 from the Ybor City Ice Works side. Notice the street railway in the top photo. USFSCL.

**Ybor City: The Making of a Landmark Town**

Workers at the Haya factory in this photograph are dressed professionally, many wearing summery white. Notice that many of thhe men wear hats, and at the left of the porch, one worker seems to be waving a copy of a newspaper or leaflet. Bicycles like the one held by the worker at the bottom of the stairs offered a convenient form of transportation.

At the second annual convention of the Methodist Woman's Parsonage and Home Missionary Society, held in Nashville in October, 1894, a decision was made to establish two Cuban schools in Tampa. Mrs. M. A. Wolff of St. Louis was chosen to superintend the work. In November of that year, Mrs. Wolff rented a building in Ybor City and furnished it, using $200 of her own money. Two teachers who spoke Spanish were employed and the school began. Their second mission school was opened in West Tampa in December, 1894, in the home of two Spanish women from Key West, Mrs. Rosa and Miss Emelina Valdes. By 1895 construction on a new building started in Ybor City to be called the Wolff Mission Boarding School (pictured above). By 1903 it was valued at over $7,000, "well equipped in every department, kindergarten and industrial work being carried on, besides the teaching of the English branches of learning." Miss Lula Ford was its chief officer and it employed three teachers to teach 122 pupils.

"THE LIFE AND WORK OF LUCINDA B. HELM" BY ARABEL W. ALEXANDER (NASHVILLE: METHODIST EPISCOPAL CHURCH, SOUTH, 1904).

**Chapter 2 · The Early Years: 1824-1900**

*The Cafetín El Palacio at the corner of La Sétima and 15th Street was owned by Esteban Pellón, known as El Polaco. This popular coffee shop reflects the outdoor culture of Ybor City in the days before air conditioning. There was lively conversation in the open air, on porches, or through open windows and doors. In this photo Mrs. Pellón sits in front of the window with their daughter Margarita (they are also in the interior photo on page 19). Notice the hexagonal pavers of the sidewalk and the well-dressed customers, often wearing suits and hats.* MARGARITA PELLÓN.

# Clear Cigar Capital and the Start of the Golden Years: 1900-1925

## Cigar Industry Growth & Early Strikes

By 1900 Ybor City's socio-economic structure, which had initially coalesced around the twin poles of Cuban and Spanish culture, had accommodated a slow but steady influx of Italians. These mostly joined the white and black Cubans at the lower levels of the cigar industry. At the top of the ladder were the Spaniards, especially the factory owners and foremen, who were quickly able to overcome the negative Spanish stereotypes that arose during the Spanish-American War.[1]

*Vicente Martínez Ybor's sons produced cigars with this label in his honor in 1902.*

The "splendid little war" had ended in the loss of Spain's last remaining colony in the New World. American military forces occupied and governed Cuba from 1898 until 1902, when Cuba at last became a free and independent country. Revolutionary activities came to an abrupt end. After 1898 there was no need for revolutionary rallies or covert activities; the Cuban Revolutionary Party's activities ceased in Ybor City, West Tampa, and elsewhere. The victory in the war gave Americans and Cubans reason for satisfaction and rejoicing. In Ybor City, however, the Cuban cause of celebration could not be shared by the entire town's population. For the Spanish immigrants there was sorrow at their mother country's loss of one of its oldest colonies, and its defeat in battle was also deeply felt. The war for them was a painful ordeal that only time could heal.

At the end of the war, also, a heavy flow of young Spaniards came to Tampa from Cuba. They had originally left farms in Asturias and Galicia, sent to find a better life in Cuba or some other Spanish colony where the ambience was friendly and the Castillian language was spoken. The procedure of sending the youngsters to former Spanish Colonies would continue for decades, Cuba's independence notwithstanding. Cuba's economic infrastructure was still owned largely by Spaniards. Therefore, young Spaniards could find accommodation on the island granted or arranged by Spanish family friends or others willing to assist the transition.

This was the case with my Spanish father, Evaristo. He was born in 1894 in Pacios, Puente Nuevo, in the province of Lugo, one of the four provinces of Galicia in the northwestern Celtic part of Spain. When Evaristo was eleven years old, his father, seeking a better life for his son than that which awaited him in the crowded family farmhouse, arranged to get him aboard a trade ship anchored offshore. An older acquaintance also seeking new opportunity had agreed to watch over

him as they both shipped off for Cuba. On arrival, Evaristo was taken to a warehouse owned by a Spaniard who had previously agreed to accept him. He received free room and board in the warehouse, including medical service if needed. In return, he worked full-time in the warehouse, ate, and slept there at night. No pay was involved.

Evaristo worked in that warehouse three years, until one day he received word from a young Spanish friend who had struck out on his own for Tampa and who urged Evaristo to come join him. They had met in Cuba, and their common experiences and aspirations fed their mutual sympathy and understanding. The friend promised to pay Evaristo's fare from Cuba when the ship arrived at its Florida debarkation point. On the strength of that promise, Evaristo boarded the ship *Mascotte* in Cuba, and when it docked at Port Tampa, the friend threw him the money to pay his fare. My father made certain that he later repaid his friend. Spaniards received many courtesies from other, more established countrymen, which made it possible for newcomers to work their way into the mainstream quickly. On just his promise to pay the rent as soon as he began to work, Evaristo was accepted into a local boarding house.

Spanish cigar factory owners favored Spanish workers, and Evaristo was employed within a week at an entry-level job—sweeping, emptying trash, and such. He immediately applied for and received medical coverage in the newly opened Centro Español Hospital on Bayshore Boulevard. The medical services were "cradle to grave" in coverage. At the new Centro Español club house he enjoyed socializing at La Cantina with other young Spaniards and partaking of other amenities. In a short time he became an apprentice cigar maker, and he was on his way toward success. (Later he left the trade and became a Realtor). My father's case is typical of many young Spaniards coming to America.

The influx of Spaniards from Cuba picked up heavily after the war. Entry into Ybor City factories was easy, as jobs were vacated by patriotic Cubans returning home to share the fruits of independence. Demand for clear Havana cigars was

**Ybor City: The Making of a Landmark Town**

*Part of the Lastra family in Spain stand at the doorway to the old home in the 1950s. Left to right are (child) Anita, (standing) Venancio, Hortencia, Dora, and Arturo. After nine centuries, the "old" and "new" homes still remain in the Lastra family. Today, thanks to the parliamentary democracy in Spain, they are equipped with telephone, television, indoor plumbing, and other conveniences.*

*A 1950 family gathering in the "new house," under 400 years old, in Galicia, Spain, about five miles away from Asturias, near Les. My mother is at the left front and my father is on the left at the head of the table.*



**Chapter 3 · Clear Cigar Capital and the Start of the Golden Years: 1900-1950**

*Plaza de la Escandalera in Oviedo, capital of Asturias, Spain, and birthplace of many of the Spaniards who came to Ybor City.* MINISTER OF INFORMATION AND TOURISM, OVIEDO, SPAIN.

*La Gallega Boarding House on the northwest corner of 14th Avenue and 19th Street in this 1995 photograph looks much as it did when it was first built after the great fire of 1908. It housed mostly Spaniards, including my father. When he lived there it was home to many young Spanish workers like him (eight years and older) known as "Gallequitos" and "Asturianitos." The front and rear doors were left open all day and night to let the public use the only telephone in the area. It was shaded by oak trees in those days, and the dampness gave Pop bronchitis. Doctors both here and in Havana could offer no hope for a cure, other than suggesting he row a boat to strengthen his lungs. He rowed daily on the Hillsborough River for three years, and made a complete recovery.*

*The El Dorado at the corner of 8th Avenue and 14th Street offered clean and convenient accommodations for Latin workers on its second and third stories. In this photograph taken on August 12, 1925, the clean sheets drying in the summer heat on the balcony bear witness to a well-run establishment. On the ground floor was El Dorado Cafe, a fashionable "speakeasy" during the Prohibition era owned by Serafin Reina, descendant of an old Ybor cigar family, but widespread talk reported that his silent partner was Tampa racketeer Charlie Wall. The El Dorado had absolutely first-class gambling tables, including roulette wheels, baccarat tables, faro layouts, and, most popular of all, bolita cages. They say that many of the social elite of Tampa frequented the place, and that some of America's top mobsters could be found among the stylish men in fancy suits and hats, with women sporting elegant gowns and furs.* USFSCL.

*The Ficarrotta family in Santo Stefano Quisquina, Sicily, during sheep shearing season in the late 1880s. Rosario Ficarrotta first immigrated to St. Cloud, Florida, in the 1890s and later moved to Tampa. Today her descendants include many of Tampa's Ficarrottas, and through marriages, descendents with family names including Ferlita, Lo Res, Palermo, Pizzolato, and Valdes.* Fortune Bosco & La Gaceta.

*This Leto family photograph was taken in the early 1900s on a New York farm after picking cherries (note the baskets). Left to right (top row) the man with hat, unknown; Americo Leto; Nino Leto; (second row) Ana Cacciatore Leto (my mother, daughter of Felice Leto and Angelina Cacciatore, deceased; unknown New York Lady believed to be wife of man with hat; young Rosalie Leto; Joe Leto; Rosalie Leto, second wife and first cousin of Felice Leto; Felice Leto, son of Francisco Leto; (third row) Frank Leto (sitting); Angelo Leto (with tie, a lawyer); family patriarch Francisco Leto; Anna Alfieri Leto, his wife; babies Ann Leto and Pauline Leto with their mother, Zia Día Leto and father Joseph Leto (my aunt and uncle who returned to New York to live; (front row) lady is believed to be the first wife of Angelo Leto. In the early 1870s Francisco Leto was general foreman of a large Southern plantation in Bayou Goula, Louisiana. He rode the plantation on horseback, supervising many foremen. Great grandmother Ana Leto was the unofficial "banker" and kept the plantation workers' meager savings and medical ointments in her several petticoats. would produce these upon request with a great, quick whirl of her skirts. Many decades later, she dazzled me as a boy with her petticoat-whipping ability to produce pennies for candy and often the candy itself. She left many fond memories. Great grandfather "Nano," then very old, would take me to what were at that time swamps above Lake Avenue where he would pasture the family cow all day.*

**Chapter 3 · Clear Cigar Capital and the Start of the Golden Years: 1900-1950**

booming at the time. Reliable workers found themselves in demand. Some young Spaniards, thinking to increase their bargaining power, even joined the powerful local union, "La Resistencia." Unaware of its long association with the Cuban revolutionary movement, they found themselves working side by side with Cubans.

As for Cubans, many returned to their homeland only to find their country in disarray. Soon many of those came back, where they again found work in the productive Ybor City factories. Among these were smaller numbers of black Cubans. They found work in the *galerías* alongside the white Cubans, Italians, and Spanish men and women, young and old. Spanish *patrones* made no distinctions, a practice that was tolerated by the white power structure in Tampa only if kept within Ybor town boundaries. Nothing must interfere with the health of the cigar industry, Tampa's major claim to fame. The flow of Ybor City money into downtown banks became the basis for the city's vigorous growth.

Unlike most of the other arrivals, Italians, by and large, had their entire families with them when they came. Many of them moved to Ybor City from the sugarcane plantations in St. Cloud, near Kissimmee in central Florida. Most continued to settle on the eastern fringes of Ybor, gradually occupying the area from 18th Street east to approximately 26th Street. In time, also, the Italian enclave would stretch from 4th Avenue to Michigan Avenue (now Columbus Drive). The area was referred to as *La Pachata*. Tony Pizzo said it came to be called *Pachata* after a Cuban rent collector in that district who had that name. My Italian grandfather, Felice Leto, was a longtime cigar maker in both New York and Tampa, and shared his knowledge of the town with me. He and Paul Ferlita, who delivered bread for the Rosario Ferlita Bakery at 2516 15th Avenue, and Angelo and Americo Leto, mother's uncles, together with Joe Leto, mother's brother, carried on vivid, detailed discussions of the early days. They shared their stories, which I recall for their color and intensity, all during my youth and adulthood upon many visits home.

*La Pachata* was not entirely Italian. There were exceptions in this area, as for example between 16th and 21st Streets, along 12th Avenue, which gradually ac-

64

**Ybor City: The Making of a Landmark Town**

quired the name *La Pequeña Asturias* (Little Asturias) due to the many houses owned by Asturianos. My father became a Realtor during the Ybor City boom years and continued in real estate into the early years of the Depression. He often took me riding in his Ford through these and other areas of Ybor, West Tampa, and Palmetto Beach, sharing his knowledge of the neighborhoods and the people who had settled there. Even today these streets seem alive with the people and the stories of the old days, which I know mainly just from listening. I loved listening to father's friends, too, for with each new story, or each repetition of one that I had already heard many times before, I discovered and remembered something new.

Ybor City was not one place or one history, but many. The people formed a quilt of origins; the parts were somehow separate but connected by shared work and social lives. Partly this was due to the cigar factory environment and the common experience of emigration. And partly it was due to the unique social clubs and customs that grew up in the town.

For a time after the Spanish-American War and the deactivation of the Cuban revolutionary clubs, the direction of Ybor life just seemed to drift. Soon, however, the Centro Español picked up the mantle of leadership.

It was not a new role for this pioneering organization. After all, Centro Español had been the model and inspiration for community culture and concern ever since its incorporation in 1891. One of the best reviews of the importance of its leadership in Ybor City is preserved in a 1941 address by the prominent Tampa lawyer and businessman Peter O. Knight, during the celebration of Centro Español's fifty-year anniversary. Knight himself had been a member of the association almost from its inception. As a young, energetic attorney, he had served as legal representative for Ybor and Manrara and represented the Ybor Land and Development Company in dealings with the Anglo business community. He witnessed Centro Español's accomplishments first-hand, and he understood the remarkable social and cultural vitality the organization brought to the community:

It is indeed a rare and exceptional privilege to be able to address the officers and members of an association to which I have

*Looking east on La Sétima, circa 1912, Ybor City is a comfortable town for families. On the left side of the photograph, the new brick clubhouse of Centro Español anchors the corner of 16th Avenue. It was a social and cultural center, providing leadership in the community for many years.* FISHBAUGH PHOTO/H. B. PLANT MUSEUM.

65

**Chapter 3 · Clear Cigar Capital and the Start of the Golden Years: 1900-1950**

*Peter O. Knight*

had the honor of belonging for nearly half a century.... After the clear Havana industry had started, and brought of course with it the necessary people to carry it on, those who came here thought it wise, beneficial, and even necessary to organize some institution or association which could be the center of thought for their activities in connection with educational, recreational, and benevolent purposes generally.

And so, on October 22, 1891, the Centro Español was formally organized.

Its original name was "Centro Español de Recreo e Instrucción de Tampa"; and it had a membership at the time of its incorporation of sixty-two.

When Ybor and Manrara first brought the clear Havana industry to Tampa, it (Tampa) was a village of probably eight or nine hundred people. By reason of the development of the industry, by October, 1891, Tampa and Ybor City combined had grown to a population of about five thousand ....

Little did the original sixty-two incorporators and their friends think that the time would come when the membership of the organization would exceed in number the entire population at that time . . . but such has proved to be the case. . . . Centro Español now has a total number of members of six thousand one hundred and four, divided as follows: two thousand of the Centro Español proper and four thousand of "La Benéfica". . . . The organization owns four buildings: the Ybor City club house and theatre, located at the corner of Sixteenth street and Seventh avenue (the site on which the original building was erected); the West Tampa club house and theatre; the Bayshore hospital; and the Ybor City Clinic, "La Benéfica."

It has been an eleemosynary institution of the first rank, not only in Tampa or in Florida, but anywhere in the country. . . .

And what a wonderful influence Centro Español has had upon the children and the young people who have always been furnished magnificent ideals and inspiration from what the older members of the association were endeavoring to do.

If the association were to select today sites for its club house and its hospital, it could make no better choice than was made at the time by the original founders. Not any of the sites would be changed. Where is there a more beautiful location than the one of the Bayshore Hospital?



**Ybor City: The Making of a Landmark Town**

*The Centro Español of West Tampa was built in 1913, constructed within a year of the completion of the Ybor City Centro Español to accommodate the heavy demand for cultural and social services. This photograph (left) was taken in 1914.* THCPLS.

*The Board of Directors of the Centro Español in 1904 supervised the opening of the modern health care facility on Bayshore Boulevard and provided forward-looking leadership in all matters. Pictured are, left to right: (first row, seated) Frederico Arnavat, Adalberto Ramírez, Vicente Guerra (president), Fermín Souto, Eduardo Pividal; (second row) Claudio Alonso, Juan Méndez, Domingo Ruiseco, Santiago Fernández, Antonio Cueto, Pedro San Miguel, Constante Campo; (third row) Fermín Palacio, Enrique Vélez, Ramón Córces, Eugenio Valdés, Gervasio Díaz, and Isidoro Randazzo. The Sanatorio del Centro Español on Bayshore Boulevard (below) was completed in 1904, shown here just as construction ended.* CENTRO ESPAÑOL.

**Chapter 3 · Clear Cigar Capital and the Start of the Golden Years: 1900-1950**

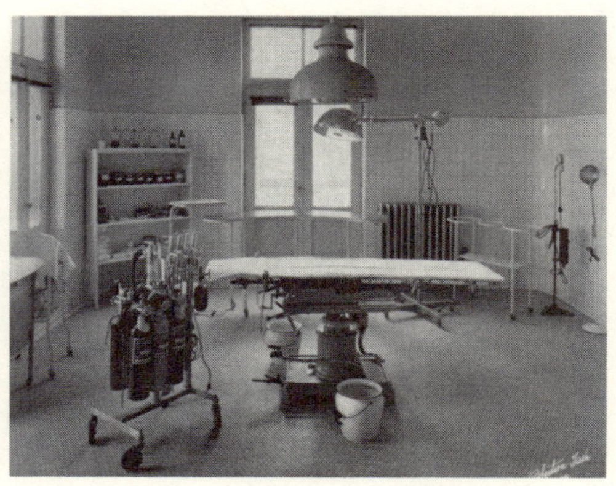

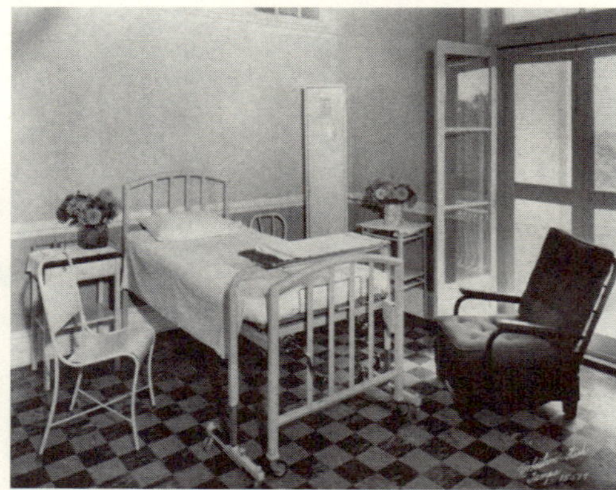

The operating room (above, top photo) and a private hospital room (above, bottom photo) were beautifully maintained and well-equipped. The nursing staff (left) poses for a photograph in front of the Sanatorio. They are (left to right) Oneida Diaz, Mary Jacoby, Dora Balseiro, Eloise Wilder, Justa Alpizar, Minnie Ola Sorrells, and Adelaide Morey. CENTRO ESPAÑOL.

**Ybor City: The Making of a Landmark Town**

Nothing has ever happened in the long history of the organization to cast a blot upon its magnificent reputation. It has always, in every respect, obeyed the laws of this country. Its history is spotless.

The founders and members of Centro Español set high standards for themselves and others in everything from architecture and cultural programming to insurance and health care. When there was a need for new leadership to inspire and revitalize the community as it entered a new century, Centro Español stood ready.

In his *Ybor City Story* Muñiz gives a specific date for the turning point: "On December 31, 1900, on the eve of the new year that would open a new century, the Centro Español club gave a grand ball at which the guests of honor were the local public officials and the most socially prominent Cubans. The event turned out to be a cordial celebration of fond memories which no doubt revived among the Cubans the desire to establish the great club cherished by all."[2] The inspiration born of that occasion led eventually to the

new Cuban Club of Tampa, but it also helped create a climate for the success of the Black Cuban club known as *Librepensadores De Martí y Maceo*, which had just been established on October 26, 1900, about a month before.

Then in 1902 the Centro Asturiano in Tampa began as a branch of the similar Havana organization. Since 1892 the founders had been members of the Centro Español Club located on La Sétima and 16th Street. While the war continued, loyalty to Spain was foremost in the minds of both Galicians and Asturians, but when it was over concerns about the need for medical services and facilities became a

*The beautiful Centro Asturiano Club House was built in 1915.* USFSCL.

point of contention. The decision by Asturians to have their own organization was precipitated by the fact that the 1899 and 1900 junta of the Centro Español had decided to forego any immediate efforts at mutual aid, a decision that did not fall on deaf or complacent ears.[3]

The Centro Español had confronted severe budgetary hardships in the face of a dwindling membership due to fallout from the Spanish-American War. The club, the junta felt, could thus not afford to provide all the medical facilities and benefits the Asturianos thought were needed. The leaders of Centro Español were still smarting from the drop in membership after the declaration of war by the U.S. against Spain, and they believed the club finances were insufficient to undertake a medical care program. Nor were the wealthier members of the club willing to undertake a heavier share of the funding, as had been the case in the early 1890s. Additionally, "El Porvenír," a separate, older mutual aid organization, had not accepted an offer to join forces with the Centro Español. The financial situation was indeed dismal. Centro Español, through lack of resources in money, membership, and vision in effect rejected the responsibility of mutual assistance. The result was "deep divergence in the heart of the Spanish colony."[4]

The success of the Spanish immigrants in Havana in forming separate Asturiano and Galician organizations offered strong appeal as a model for Ybor City. As historian Ana Varela-Lago suggests, patriotism had now relinquished its claim in favor of the need for mutualism.[5] Close cultural and social ties were strengthened at the same time that mutual health care needs were met.

The Asturianos were a very proper and tightknit segment of the Spanish membership. They had a distinct culture, with a different history than Galicians, though they both were Spaniards. The history of the Asturianos was enviable, and they were very proud of it. In about 722, King Pelayo, first king of Asturias, and his nobles began the reconquest of Spain after seven hundred years of Moorish rule. They were (and are) proud of the fact that Asturias itself had never been conquered. Independence, strength, and determination shown forth in their history. They had led their country to reclaim its national identity.

Such patriotic spirit found resonance in Cuba following its independence, and there were large numbers of residents now living there who claimed direct Asturian roots. In Havana there was a large and beautiful Centro Asturiano Club building, which served as architectural inspiration for Ybor

**Ybor City: The Making of a Landmark Town**

*The Centro Asturiano Sanatorium opened its doors in 1905 at the northwest corner of Ola Avenue and Jackson Avenue (now Gladys Street); the location was on the west side of the old Jefferson Senior High School north of Columbus Drive. The sanatorium was christened "Covadonga Clinic" in veneration of the patron saint of Asturias. The facility had a total of sixty beds, with one wing dedicated to general medicine and one reserved for surgery. This photo was taken August 19, 1925, shortly before construction began on a new hospital building.* THCPLS.

*When Centro Asturiano attempted to open a mutualistic health care system in Tampa, the medical establishment resisted it through its Medico-Latina Association that blocked any licensing of a new facility that might compete with existing practices. The problems were solved when Dr. G. H. Altree (right), a British philanthropist who looked upon medicine as a ministry rather than a business, stepped forward to cede his own licensed Florida Avenue sanatorium through arrangement with the original Centro de La Havana to render care to members of the new Tampa mutual benefit society.*

*A larger and more splendid Sanatorio del Centro Asturiano was completed in 1927. It stood in the center of a large Spanish community on 21st Avenue and 13th Street and offered medical and cemetery services to Spaniards, Cubans, and Italians. In 1975 aggressive management increased the hospital's size even further, but a decreasing Latin membership and spiraling medical costs took their toll during the 1980s. The facility was forced to close in the early 1990s. By 1998 all but the magnificent central part of the building was destroyed. It alone remained as testimony to seven decades of service offering the finest in medical care by a staff of Cuban doctors joined by Italian, Spanish, and American physicians and staff. Like the social club, the cemetery division still functions as planned, and is, indeed, growing as it fulfills its obligations to the remaining and incoming members.* CHARLES E. HARNER.



**Chapter 3  ·  Clear Cigar Capital and the Start of the Golden Years: 1900-1950**

My mother and father met while working in the Corral, Wodiska cigar factory. It is shown above in 1921 as the setting for M. M. Corral and his C-38 Wetscott automobile (left) and C. Sierra with his B-48 Westcott (right). The cigar firm was known for "the famous Julia Marlowe Cigars." The building was torn down in the late 1920s. HAMPTON DUNN.

City Asturianos. Now that the subject of Spanish patriotism was not a question, they favored going their own way and, especially, taking concrete steps to solve their mutual medical needs. Accordingly, an independent Centro Asturiano delegation was formed on May 6, 1906, to seek its own future, and an effusive and cordial letter was sent to the Centro Español in appreciation for past services.[6]

Meanwhile, as their savings allowed, Italians increased their purchases of property, buying single or multiple lots which they could cultivate. Most of these were located on the eastern side of Ybor, often spilling over to nearby areas. Many Italian men went into business with small dairies, vending, fishing, and other work. A few bought large acreage miles away, which was then relatively cheap. Decades later their sons would benefit greatly from these valuable lands. But in those days the land alone was not enough to get by on; it was necessary that the women also work to cover essential food costs. In the early years Italian women were still not universally accepted for employment, due to the feeling that their low entry-level pay hurt wages for all. This, however, finally disappeared, as they dutifully performed to expectations in the factories and proved their worth. My mother, Anna Cacciatore Leto, was able to begin work at the Corral Wodiska #8 factory with the foreman's approval in the 1920s by sitting next to her

father, Felice, who monitored her work. She quickly became proficient at her job and was soon regarded as a valuable asset by her coworkers and supervisors at the wooden factory located at the southwest corner of Michigan Avenue (Columbus Avenue) and 14th Street.

While Tampa in the early period was not exactly a hotbed of labor strife, factory owners always considered it important to be able to recruit new, trainable, entry-level workers. Between 1887 and 1894 there had been 23 walkouts, but no effective large organization claimed labor leadership. Hampering the formation of strong unions was the absence of time for debate and discussion among the workers, due to the more important Cuban revolutionary activities that existed. In that period *Cuba Libre* was foremost in the minds of Cubans, who formed the largest part of the work force. The number of Spaniards in Tampa was still relatively low. There was no surplus of middle-aged Spaniards in their prime to push campaigns of unionization. The Spanish population was heavily weighted toward young men. Daily activities in the old Centro Español club building absorbed a good part of the leadership of prominent or well-positioned Spaniards. And the existence of this early Centro Español engaged much of the after-factory and weekend hours. Passing away a few hours at the early cafés provided an escape valve particularly for the unmarried male segment of the population.

In addition, there was a new element in the town to command the eyes and attention of the single males. These were the young Italian girls, often seen out walking with their families, who watched their daughters carefully. By and large, Spaniards had no families at all. Some of the Cubans had small families, but nothing to match the extent of the Italians, many of whom had been in the United States for some two to three decades and who placed a high priority on family values.

**Ybor City: The Making of a Landmark Town**

But all of this would change.

With the return to Ybor City of Cubans who had found conditions too unstable on their island, the arrival of many young Spaniards, and the increased presence of Italians from Louisiana and the Kissimmee farm region, a record population filled the town, and the newcomers were eager for work. It created a faster pace to life and a more competitive environment for workers and employers alike.

Factory strikes during this period were common. The strike of 1899—*La Huelga de la Pesa* (the Weight Strike)—had been a costly one. It began over a relatively simple change in working conditions which the managers thought was necessary in order to keep track of production supplies. In the past, when a worker needed more *picadura* (filler) he simply got as much as he thought he would use. Believing that the *tabaqueros* always took more than they needed, in order to keep some to take home for extra *cherutos* (cigars) or other reasons, the *capatáz* (foreman), with the *patrón's* blessing, enforced a new rule. This required weighing out preassigned portions for the cigarmakers' needs.

To the workers, this was an insulting rule. Spaniards felt their integrity was being questioned. They valued their honor and integrity above all else. They could not allow the insult to stand. And to make matters worse, the *patrones* also wanted to apply a uniform wage scale in the factories— a *cartabon*. As a result, some four thousand *tabaqueros* went on strike. The *patrones* felt the pressure and dropped both the *cartabon* and the weight requirement, resulting in the workers going back to work.[7]

The Weight Strike was hardly forgotten when, in 1901, a huge general strike occurred. The feud between *La Resistencia*, the primary longtime local union, and the Cigar Makers International Union (CMIU) festered. *La Resistencia* declared its cause in the broadest social terms, "to resist the exploitation of labor by capital,"[8]

indicting the CMIU by comparison as being virtually a partner of the capitalists. The issues came to a head when the local union demanded that Cuesta-Rey and Company close its branch factory in Jacksonville, where the new wages were lower than those in Tampa. The company refused, causing the workers in the West Tampa factory, with the exception of some members of the CMIU, to walk out. *La Resistencia* faced with strikebreakers from a competing union, broadened its demands, insisting not only that the low-wage Jacksonville branch be closed and all members of the International Union working in the Tampa factories be fired, but also that owners increase the Tampa cigarmakers' wages. Otherwise, they threatened a general strike.[9]

The downtown establishment, almost totally dependent on the huge volume of banking done by the *patrones*, could not tolerate the drastic interruption of cash flow which a general strike would cause. A "Citizens' Committee" was formed and it "detained" thirteen workers who were thought to be strike leaders. After being held temporarily in several locales, these men were put aboard a schooner named the *Marie Cooper* and dropped off in Honduras. With an allusion to the inflammatory articles written by the local newspapers at the time, Ramon Piquero, one of the men kidnapped and removed to Honduras, referred to his group as, "thirteen defenseless men held captive on the high seas for six days," an account of the incident which seems likely closer to the truth than the *Tribune's* vague reference to them as "deported agitators."[10] The identities of all of the responsible parties are not known with certainty, but they were from the ranks of the pillars of the Tampa business establishment. D. B. McKay, the prominent native son of Tampa who became editor of the *Tampa Daily Times*, later acknowledged that he personally had a part in "deporting" the thirteen men, and his

newspaper's accounts would no doubt make interesting reading. Unfortunately, there appear to be no surviving copies of his paper from 1901.[11]

The forced disappearance did not put an end to the strike, as the armed Citizens' Committee vigilantes had hoped, but appeared to increase the resolve of the strikers. Given that *La Resistencia* claimed a membership of about 4,500, which was ninety percent of the cigar labor force, this was a crucial contest which could make or break the authority of the union shop.[12]

The Citizens' Committee vigilantes raised the stakes by ordering an additional seventeen strike leaders to leave the city. They even ordered the deportation of an editor of the union newspaper La Federación, and when that did not silence the paper they raided the office, broke apart its printing press, and hauled it away. Finally, anonymous vigilantes attacked and shut down the soup kitchens that La Resistencia had operated to feed the needy strikers.[13] With CMIU strikebreakers and others desiring to work being protected by armed members of the Citizens' Commit-

tee, the union's strength began to dissolve. The tactics of terror and deceit had worked. Desperate union members gradually began to return to work to feed their families, and La Resistencia was forced to declare the strike ended without achieving its aims.

Disquieting actions such as those employed by the Citizens' Committee may have broken the local union as an organization, but it did serve to bring individual Cubans, Spaniards, and Italians closer together. More and more they shared an awareness of their mutual needs and common circumstances. The more repressive and unethical the machinations of the establishment became (and incidents of this kind were to happen over and over again), the greater was the solidarity of the workers in resistance to the imposition of authority and control. As ethnic or national identity became less of a primary focus, intermarriages would eventually also become more common.

In the meantime, Black Cubans[14] moved ahead with plans and activities for the Libre Pensadores de Martí-Maceo as a recreation and instruction club whose

**Ybor City: The Making of a Landmark Town**

membership soon numbered just under a thousand. It was modeled after its counterpart in Cuba. High respect for José Martí and Antonio Maceo, the inspiring Cuban patriots whose names were part of Ybor City consciousness from the beginning, was a cornerstone of the club named after them in the early days. Both patriots had died on the battlefield. Their dedication to the cause of freedom and independence was celebrated and their heritage honored.

The club eventually changed its name to Sociedad La Unión Martí-Maceo. In 1908 it constructed a two-story building on 6th Avenue and 12th Street. Today the club is still active, with a location on La Sétima, between 12th and 13th Streets.

Black Cubans, from the time of their arrival in Ybor City, worked in the cigar factories side by side with white Cubans, Spaniards, and Italians. They accommodated easily, yet they also proved to have great mobility. Key West, Havana, New York, and other cigar-making cities also recognized their skills and offered them opportunities. Many had a thirst for knowledge, were respectful, and desired respect. They had an exuberant, friendly attitude which helped to shape the tone of Ybor City life. The great war of independence over, black Cubans continued to ponder their future. Some had been in America since the founding days of Ybor City. Work away from home had allowed them time to make many new acquaintances. To many, Ybor City, Palmetto Beach, and West Tampa were where Cuban history was made, where labor strikes evolved, and where their future lay. Love for Cuba but nearly equal love for their friendships, accomplishments, and history in Tampa fills these proud citizens today.[15]

In the early twentieth century Rafael Martínez Ybor, son of Don Vicente, was the Cuban Consul in Tampa. He published *Revista* magazine, and supported the construction of a Cuban Club building. Still, unlike the Spaniards and the Italians, the growth of a strong Tampa Cuban Club organization seemed stunted. For many, it would be almost a decade before they could make up their minds—whether they would return to Cuba once again, or commit to a future in Tampa.

The Spaniards and the Italians were not so fortunate to have that choice. The

*The founding members of Sociedad La Unión Martí-Maceo as photographed in 1904. Bruno Roig, the Afro-Cuban patriot who had a grocery store in Ybor City and who had helped arrange and host José Martí's visits, is seated at left in the first row, holding his Panama hat on his knee. The other founders have not yet been indentified. USFSCL.*

75

events in the motherland had not changed. In Sicily, the direction was still outward. As for Santo Stefano Quisquina and Allesandria della Rocca, a visit then would have found it all the same. These are the two cities where the largest number of Tampa Italians had originated from. But worse yet, the motherland was thousands of miles away. Quick communication was unknown. They would be fortunate to make one or two trips to the old motherland in their lifetime! Their children's motherland was America. Nothing would ever place that legacy in jeopardy!

Meanwhile, in 1905 some 220,400,000 cigars were produced here, and the Tampa population approached 25,000. Eyeing this robust and growing cigar industry were the many militant unions, anarchists, and socialists in America. Their local leaders were waiting in the wings.

## Radicalism and the Cigar Industry: 1905-1910

After the Cuban War of Independence, such important revolutionary newspapers as *El Yara*, *Heraldo de Tampa*, *Cuba*, *La Contienda*, and *El Patriota* disappeared from the town. In the years ahead other periodicals filled some of the needs. These were the mainstream downtown dailies, such as *The Tampa Morning Tribune*, the *Tampa Times*, and other less influential English-language newspapers. There were also Cuban, Spanish, and Italian papers. *La Traducción* translated English newspapers into Spanish.[16] In addition there were weeklies directed at worker interest. Some were pro-union; others fostered socialistic, anarchistic, or syndicalistic thinking. Even a listing of the titles of these publications reveals much about their followers and philosophies. Directed at Spanish-speaking workers were *El Obrero* (The Workman); *El Despertár* (The Awakening); *La Protesta Humana* (The Human Protest); and *La Defensa* (The Defense). Newspapers published out of town, directed at Italian workers, were *La Voce Della Colonia* (The Voice of the Colony); *Il Martire* (The Martyr); *L'Ora* (The Hour), from Palermo, Italy; *Il Proleterio* (The Proletariat), from New York; *Il Martello* (The Hammer), from New York; *La Parola dei Socialisti* (The Word of the Socialists), and others. There were also innumerable pamphlets, posters, and handouts in at least

La Traducción *newsboys gathered for a photograph on December 31, 1936, displaying papers with an illustration of Santa Claus and news of a devastating earthquake beneath the headline "200 Deaths in El Salvador."* La Traducción *was founded by Ramon Valdespino and José Gregory.*



**Ybor City: The Making of a Landmark Town**

three languages. Clearly, experienced organizations with imported philosophies aimed to sell and convince, were actively seeking the workers' minds.[17]

Meanwhile, Cuban labor militancy and socialistic thinking were transplanted to Ybor from Key West and Havana. Radical ideologies seemed to follow from the same ethnic and geographic roots as the citizens themselves. In turn, anarchism from northern Spain and socialism from the Magazzolo region of Sicily pressed local *tabaqueros* for converts.

Another important factor in a climate which seemed ripe for antiestablishment movements of all kinds was the existence here of many of the vital elements of a typical northern industrial town. Northern union leaders saw Ybor City, West Tampa, and Palmetto Beach, to the south of Ybor, as an industrial area that met their criteria perfectly. It had piecework, apprenticeships, and a fixed and regimented manufacturing methodology. Personal perks traditionally provided to the workers included coffee privileges and donation of three to five free cigars a day. Working in the *galería* was common. Mobility between towns that had similar cigar industries, such as Key West, New York, Jacksonville, and other sites was common, especially for younger and unattached workers.[18]

One somewhat unique characteristic of the Tampa factories was the specific limits on obtaining raw materials for their products. Most factories were heavily dependent on one source for their quality tobacco — the Vuelta Abajo region of the Pinar del Río province in Cuba. Certainly in Tampa, cigar quality was everything. From climate and physical location to the ethnic mix and attitudes of the workers, the large cigar culture in Tampa worked the way it did because of its dependence on those specific raw materials and the specific place from which they came.

Within each of the above major elements of industrial production and associated attributes there were scores of significant variables that could be manipulated or exploited by unions to their advantage. Organizers carefully considered timing and accessibility to workers as they looked for ways to win new members.

The factory hierarchy, so favorable to the *patrón* and to his ability to efficiently manage operations, was, in itself, antithetical to unions. The entrenched management included the *patrón* and his salesmen, bookkeeper, and office staff. In charge of the factory were the general foreman; the main cigar-making floor foreman—*el capatáz*; strippers; bunchers; banders; and lesser factory employees.

The *patrónes* utilized their management hierarchy to control every aspect of the process and that could impact a factory's reputation and the quality of its cigars. They were concerned that unions would could be detrimental to quality control. On the positive side for workers, *patrones* were careful to hire and retain top-level employees. Yet, despite the tolerance for diversity fostered in daily life, Spanish *patrones* remained partial to hiring and retaining Spaniards for top jobs. The loyalty of Spanish employees during Cuba's War of Independence had proven indispensable. Commonality of origin and culture heightened the bonds, and common language assured perfect understanding of what was expected of them. The Spaniards' generally more serious demeanor and orderliness of conduct were further assets at the workplace. In short, Spaniards were the preferred workers, and their status carried into the daily life of the town. That having been said, it is also important to record that Cubans were widely known and valued for their skillfulness at all aspects of cigarmaking.

Among the many factors that union leaders took note of were the existence of a very young work force and the country's growing demand for cigars that assured more factories being opened as well as numerous *chinchales*, (small cigar-making businesses, referred to as "Buckeyes" in English). Further, the ability of the *patron* to change wages as his factory required, especially due to the impact of competition, was a heavy point of interest to union leaders, who sought every available opportunity to increase their role in the industry's life—restricting, in so doing, the ability of the factory management to have sole and clear communication with the *tabaqueros*.

What the *patrones* needed above all else was consistency in cigar quality. Nothing must mar the brand's reputation. Loyalty at crucial levels of the factory and flexibility to meet competition were vital. All this needed to be managed within an atmosphere of orderliness and good will.

In turn, unions needed mentalities they could control, an industry with preferably largely manual processes, a product whose many variables they and the workers could alter to force the *patrones* to submit to their wishes in favor of the workers. They also wanted a strong national affiliation to provide local workers the funds that might be needed in times of long struggles. Small unions could not compete with nationally affiliated unions. *Tabaqueros* largely preferred a non-ideological union organization dedicated to economic benefits. That could allow them a way to improve their quality of life — to marry and to raise a happy and healthy family. That, by and large, was what they worked for. And they wished for a good environment for their children.

Like the trade unionists, the ideologists needed pliable minds, an industry heavy in manual work, a largely immigrant work force, friendly newspapers, and factory accessibility. The *comité de lectura* (the reader's committee), and the *lector* (reader), provided that opportunity, even as it did for the unions. A volatile atmosphere of unrest suited the more militant forces. These were the socialists, anarchists, syndicalists, and the communists.

The factory environment of these Cuban, Spanish, and Italian *tabaqueros* held enough elements to appeal to each movement in one way or another. Rapidly the mix of competing organizers and ideologies became a fact of life in the community and strongly held loyalities led to passionate debates.

*The first building constructed by the Círculo Cubano was completed in 1907 and stood at 14th Street and 9th Avenue. The mayor, city council, and three foreign consuls attended the opening ceremonies. Its facilities included a 1,500-seat theater, a library, classrooms, billiard room, and a cantina. Unfortunately, it was destroyed by fire just nine years later, in 1916.*

**Ybor City: The Making of a Landmark Town**

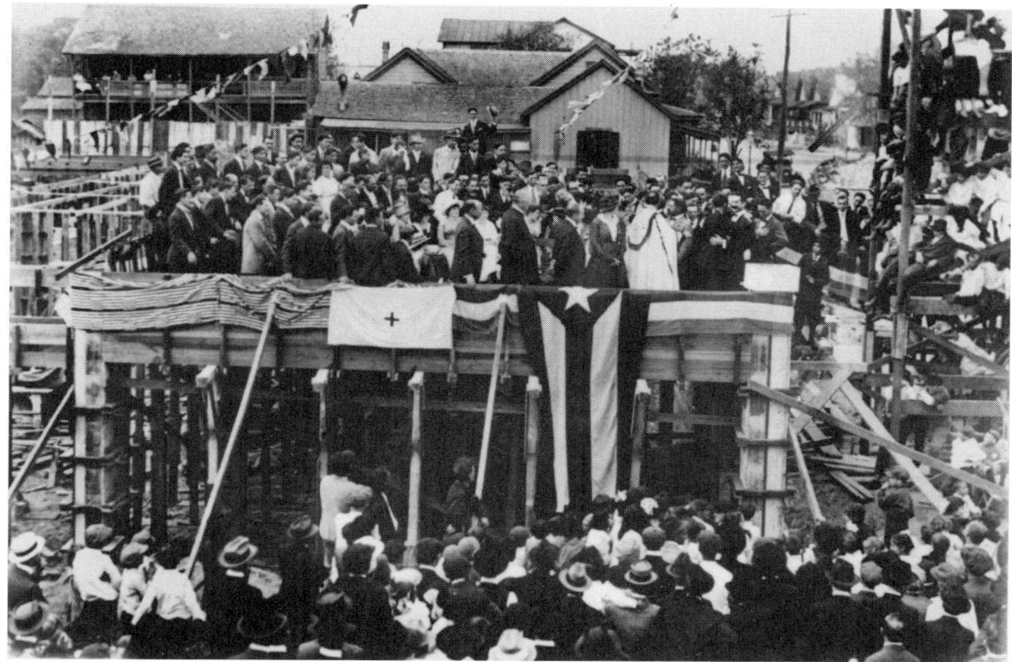



## New Buildings and Devastating Fires

In the early years of the new century, on the top floor of a reconstructed brick building, site of the old Liceo Cubano, the Cuban Sans Souci Theater had its home. Here traveling stock companies from Havana came and put on many light comedies. An occasional Spanish *zarzuela* was shown.

Music and performances had been important cultural activities for the Cubans from the early years. Their organization dates from the charter of *El Club Nacional Cubano* on October 10, 1899, when it began as a recreational group. Early leaders included Rafael and Salvador Martínez Ybor, sons of Vicente Martínez Ybor. The name was changed in 1902 to *El Círculo Cubano*, but they continued to meet in a two-story building on the corner of 14th Street and 9th Avenue (where Hillsborough Community College now stands), which had been the location of the Cuban National Club.

As the membership grew, the club was able to plan to construct its own building, and the ceremony for the laying of its cornerstone was held on October 31, 1905. It was a grand event, attended by the consuls of Cuba, Spain, and Italy.

The two-story brick building included a theater seating 1,500 and was completed in 1907. The Cubans finally had their first social club house at 14th Street and 10th Avenue. This first building was a step greatly needed to provide unity and purpose to the Cubans who were uncertain as to whether they really wanted to grow roots in Ybor or return to Cuba. The very existence of the building, and the services it rendered, did much to increase Cuban contentment with Ybor City. Cubans were a convivial sort and seemed to enjoy their

*Cuban Club dancers who performed in the original building are shown in a 1912 photo below.*

79

*Primary school students in this 1910 photograph are in costume for a Cuban Club play at DeSoto Park.* FSA.

*This photo, ca. 1917, was taken to promote a picnic outing to DeSoto Park sponsored by Círculo Cubano.* FSA.

*The Labor Day parade in 1912 included this cigar float sponsored by members of the Cigar Makers International Union. Here in front of the Labor Temple, notice how well-dressed everyone is—from boy apprentices through adults, complete with ties and hats.*

*This 1926 photograph by the Burgert Brothers shows the historic and impressive second Cuban Club building that was dedicated in 1918. It was designed by the architects Bonfoey & Elliott as a concrete, fire-proof building with three stories and a basement. The firm of McGucken and Hyer handled the actual construction. The historic building continues to serve the community today. THCPLS.*

**Ybor City: The Making of a Landmark Town**

*This photograph of the devastating Ybor City fire of 1908 was taken from the corner of 12th Avenue and 17th Street, looking north. At the end of the street is the La Trocha Cigar Factory. After the fire, the look of the town changed. Many of the wooden buildings were not rebuilt, and the disaster helped reinforce the advantages of brick construction over wood.*

life in the town. But the powerful force of their love for their homeland was difficult to contain or ignore.

By now the Italian community was growing rapidly and plans were underway to begin construction of its first major building. Italian women were entering the factories in greater numbers. Some of the men also took up factory work. Felice Leto, for example, was *"uno de los largos,"* a high producer. By 3 p.m. each day he was already proudly walking down *La Galería* on the way home. But many Italian men continued to resist a move into the factories. Possessed by the free enterprise spirit, most of them wished to work for themselves. These were the ones who began small dairies, went into commercial farming, sold produce and other provisions, or opened grocery or bakery shops. Success was by no means guaranteed, but they were willing to throw themselves into the work to get their enterprises off the ground. In the interim the women's paychecks would put food on the table.

Fires were not uncommon in the early years. Very many of the original, interim, and later factory buildings were made of wood, and given the limited natural materials Florida offered for construction, wood was also the usual choice for building homes and stores. Timber was in ample supply, but due to the hot and periodically dry Florida climate, it had its shortcomings. The use of lanterns and candles for light posed a daily danger, as did wood and kerosene stoves for cooking. But most important, the overwhelming use of matches in this cigar town in those early years posed a serious threat to all structures. Even the more permanent red brick buildings contained a fair amount of wood and were not totally immune to fires.

The smoking of several cigars a day by a typical *tabaquero* was not uncommon. The *patrones* allowed them some three to five per day as a job benefit. They could smoke in the factories, and the factory *buches* (sips of coffee) served at the work benches were often followed by another



**Chapter 3 · Clear Cigar Capital and the Start of the Golden Years: 1900-1950**

*The terrible Ybor City fire of March 1, 1908, was extremely hard to control with the limited capability of the horse-drawn firefighting equipment, especially as the wooden housing was so vulnerable. It is thought to have been set by a cigarette in the Antonio Diaz boarding house, located at 1914 12th Avenue. This is also the site of the Ybor City Branch Post Office, which was destroyed by fire on May 19, 2000, and once again rebuilt at this location.*

smoke. Then, at the cafés or club house *cantinas*, cards, dominoes, and pool playing were common. This, too, required a good cheroot for concentration. Thus, the possibility of misplacing a lit match was high, whether it was on the plate or discarded and stepped on. Disposal of the final cigar butt was also a large possible source of fire. Ybor City neighborhoods were always vulnerable to this ever-present danger—and, in fact, many fires broke out. In this period three of the early club houses burned down and were later replaced.

Tampa's worst fire ever occurred on March 1, 1908, evidently spreading from a boarding house at 19th Street and 12th Avenue to engulf 17 blocks over 55 acres.

*The 1908 fire destroyed much of Ybor City, leaving some 2500 residents without homes and many others without jobs. In all, fire destroyed seventeen city blocks, including five cigar factories and two hundred and forty homes.*

82

**Ybor City: The Making of a Landmark Town**

The damage included 171 cottages, 42 wood buildings, five brick stores, and five cigar factories.[19] Other townspeople reported it went from 12th Avenue to *La Míchiga* (today's Columbus Drive). Additionally, fifteen boarding houses were evidently destroyed. Property damage was set at $1,000,000 in 1908 dollars, a staggering sum. Many of the homes had been bought from Don Vicente and his partner, Eduardo Manrara. Cuban workers contributed considerable money to help the victims.

That year many Cubans built homes in Palmetto Beach, a growing community off 22nd Street, south of Ybor City. The fire had prompted the move away from the old town center. The Palmetto Beach area, with Desoto Park on McKay Bay as a magnet, had attracted both Cubans and Spaniards as a recreational destination since the founding of Ybor City.

Meanwhile, as the radical and legitimate organizations planned ahead toward medical benefits and mutual aid, the *tabaqueros* worked and went to picnics, club dances, fishing, or to the club cantinas. Activities on La Setima grew. Eclectic architecture was fast defining the style of the new buildings. Silent movie houses like Pathé, El San Soucí, La Plaza, the Broadway, and the Rívoli, as well as live theater at the various club houses were beginning to brighten the lives of the townspeople. Meanwhile, Jewish merchants increased their presence in Ybor City and supplied much of the growing demand for clothing, boots, shoes, and other wares shopped for at their stores.

Now it was time for a young tabaquero to look for a sweetheart, and soon a wife. Saturday night at La Sétima was a great time to be young. A simple evening stroll implied excitement and romance. Making it more challenging, however, was the chaperone institution, which remained a part of Latin life—and in spite of which new young families blossomed in due course.

## Non-Latin Ethnic Cultures

The multicultural atmosphere of Ybor City made room for diverse interests, talents, and traditions. In addition to the Italian strain of entrepreneurial free enterprise, there was a substantial Jewish merchant class, Romanian Jews primarily, who worked easily among the Latin population. Their main presence was seen along the principal spine of Ybor City, La Sétima. A brochure released in the early 1990s called "Florida Mosaic: Jewish Geography of Ybor City, 1920-1970" lists over 80 locations on La Sétima and an additional few perhaps a block away. The vast majority, however, were located between 14th Street and 20th Street.[20]

Their places of worship were the Rodeph Sholom (located just west of Jefferson south of Palm Avenue) and the Knesses Yisroale (Central and Oak Avenue and 8th Avenue) Synagogues. Many of the Jewish merchants lived in the Tampa Heights area, then a prosperous residential section that was also home to many Spanish cigar manufacturers. Most of the smaller Jewish retail or service stores were located from the Fenman Kosher Market just west of 14th Street to Ozias Meerovitz Men's Store between 20th and 21st Streets. The heavier service businesses were located past 22nd Street to 34th Street. These included Southern Iron and Bag, Peretzman Scrap Iron and Metal, and West Coast Salvage and Iron, to name but

*Congregation Rodeph Sholom was founded in 1903 at the home of J. L. Mairson. Meeting at first in a small building on Palm Avenue in Ybor City, the congregation grew into a larger structure built there in 1909. The Rodeph Sholom Temple at 309 East Palm Avenue is shown below as it was under construction on May 1, 1926, in the Burgert Brothers photograph. Other features of the neighborhood are also visible—the shady trees and wooden houses with open porches and balconies. THCPLS.*

*Silver's, also widely known as "La Casa Barata," was a variety store popular with youngsters and adults alike.*

*Max Argintar (center in photo below) opened his store in Ybor City in 1908 and became the first major Jewish merchant in town. In this photograph he poses with his brother Sender (right) and an unidentified cousin. The pawnshop portion of the business is underscored by the large loan safe on the right and the "Pawn Broker" sign. The cases are filled with watches and jewelry and the walls behind the counter are lined with musical instruments. Later the store concentrated on clothing and became known for quality menswear.*

a few. Jews also provided some of the dentists and lawyers on the main street.[21]

Some of the highly popular stores were Silver's (*La Casa Barata*), a five-and-ten-cent store; Max Argintar Men's Wear, still open and going strong in 1997; Louis Wohl Household Supplies; The Palace; Adam Katz Furnishing Family Clothing; Manuel Leibovitz & Sons; Modern Home Furnishings, owned by Louis Buchman and son "Booky" (now much expanded into an imposing multi-story office, showroom, and wholesale building); and the Sunshine Department Store, among others.

The above retailers serviced shoppers from far away "Cracker" country to the north, east, and south. A large part of the boots, overalls, shoes, cowboy-type clothing of the day, jeans, and much more were supplied by these merchants. Spaniards, of course, also owned many food and retail businesses in the early to middle periods. Italians in time began to open groceries, bakeries, fish markets, and other commercial ventures. The majority of businesses were located between 13th and 18th Streets along La Sétima. I often visited these stores myself, frequently on Saturday nights as a youngster with my parents. Spaniards had numerous businesses along the streets up to Michigan Avenue (Columbus Drive). Italian establishments were particularly heavy along 22nd Street (approaching Lake Avenue, on the east side of the street). Spanish businesses went all the way to Buffalo Avenue (now Martin Luther King Jr. Boulevard) along 15th Street. The Lopez feed store was located there, on the southeast corner, with a colorful chicken supply outlet store a few doors south. In fact, Latin retail businesses were scattered all over the "Golden Period" areas of Ybor (see Tables).

84

**Ybor City: The Making of a Landmark Town**

The relationship between Latins and Jewish merchants was excellent, though they had diverse cultural traditions and lifestyles. Jews were mostly seen in their shops or offices. I simply don't remember ever seeing or hearing of negative interactions or derogatory comments between the Latins and Jews.

Among the delights that today's remaining "originals" remember were the beautiful times on Saturday nights, when as children we hung onto Mother's skirts or Father's hands as they shopped the crowded Sétima, and particularly if they stopped at one of the popular *casas baratas* (five-and-ten-cent stores) such as Silver's and Kress. During the struggling 1970 to 1980 period, when many merchants had left the area, I remember the crucial role played by some of the Jewish merchants who did not leave Ybor City. Chief among these was the Max Argintar Men's Clothing Store, as well as the Louis Buchman and Son's Modern Home Furnishing businesses. Showing faith in the area's future, these last two survived to move into a greatly enlarged, major multi-story office and showroom after urban renewal in the mid-1970s.

In honor of the exemplary historic role played by the Jewish community in the city's development, the Ybor City State Museum Society in 1994, with Sonya Ziegler as president, honored them at a special event on the patio of the State Museum building and attended by many Jewish merchants, Museum Society members, and local citizens. Many new and especially older Ybor City residents were very much in evidence. The featured speaker was Rene Gonzalez, prominent director of the Spanish Lyric Theater. Rene's family owned a popular imported gifts and artifacts store in the heart of La Sétima, and Rene grew up there. A walking tour of Jewish heritage sites was published by the State of Florida in the *Florida Jewish Heritage Trail*, available from the Ybor City State Museum and on the Web at http://dhr.dos.state.fl.us/services/trails/jht/map.cfm. See an updated map at the back of this book, Exhibit 7.

## The Germans in Ybor City

The German presence in Ybor City history dates back almost a century. Today's remaining Latin "originals" can hardly recall the German influences on the Ybor City scene, for most of the German

*Katz's was one of the best places to buy clothing for the entire family. It was operated by Adam Katz, one of the early Jewish merchants in Ybor City. The open-sided streetcars played an important part in the success of the Ybor City shopping experience. Here "Old 700" moves along La Sétima at the corner of 15th Street.* HAMPTON DUNN.

85

activities in Ybor city formally ended about 1918. But, in fact, they remained in Tampa. They made their mark on Ybor City, and most certainly on Tampa.

Dr. L. Glenn Westfall, author of an exhaustive research study that provided the area's historical mosaic utilized in the founding of Ybor City State Museum, writes of the German presence:

> One of the least known elements of Ybor City's ethnic population were Germans who arrived in the area after the 1890s. Most German Americans in Tampa were enterprising businessmen who formed several important businesses. German cigar box art was considered the best of its kind in the world, and several early cigar box labels were made by German lithographers. . . . German Americans in the late 1890s decided to join their Latin counterparts in forming a health benefit association. On Dec. 8, 1901, they formed the Deutche Amerikanscher Verein (German Club) [the beautiful building was located on Nebraska and 11th Avenue and still stands]. It not only served as a social center for Tampa's German Americans, but also had a rathskeller and restaurant open to the public, offering German cuisine to the local population. It soon received the reputation as one of the finest German clubs in the South . . . and over 2,000 Americans of the South attended songfests, musical presentations, and banquets.[22]

When America finally abandoned its neutrality and declared war against Germany in 1917, Germans faced discrimination. This was somewhat similar to the case of Peninsular Spaniards during Cuba's War of Independence and the succeeding Spanish-American War. In the case of the Spanish-American War, federal troops occupied the Centro Español clubhouse, and then, after complaints about the action — in light of the exemplary conduct of the Spaniards — they were stationed outside the building for the duration of the war.

Julius J. Gordon, author of *German American Influence in Florida*, collected some revealing data on the German presence in Tampa. He found that in 1880 there were forty-seven Germans in Tampa out of a population of 5,532; by 1900 there were one hundred and sixty-two Germans in a population of 15,839. During the space of these twenty years, the percentage rose from well below one percent to slightly more than one percent of the population. Gordon indicates that from 1820 to 1920 about five million Germans entered the United States. In the last half of the 19th century, German immigration

*The Tampa Box Company provided essential packing for the cigars of Ybor City and employed highly skilled workers. It was located on 2nd Avenue between 20th and 21st Streets. This is where the author bought the sticks for his kites as a boy.* THCPLS.

**Ybor City: The Making of a Landmark Town**

to America exceeded that of any other country, and Tampa continued to add to its German population into the early twentieth century.[23]

"The cigar industry," Gordon writes, "already well established . . . employed the skilled laborers of the German-American community. Many served in the capacity of managers, bookkeepers, or supervisors of the large cigar warehouses . . . some union leaders came from Germany to organize the cigar factories in Tampa."[24]

Specifically mentioned by Gordon are certain lines of work pursued by Germans in Tampa, including occupations in commercial development, woodworking, cabinetry, real estate, pharmaceuticals, iron and mill work, printing and lithography, repairing office machinery (such as typewriters and adding machines), cigar box making, and teaching. Clearly, Germans possessed a useful range of strong organizational, commercial, and craft skills. The large factory on 2nd Avenue between 19th and 21st Streets that supplied delicate cigar boxes for the industry was German-owned.

The typical *tabaquero* was not consciously aware of the country of origin for many of the non-Latin citizens of Ybor City, and certainly remained unaware of the diversity in greater Tampa. Also, there was a tendency to lump all *Americano*-appearing types, especially since most also spoke English, as simply "Anglos" from greater Tampa.[25]

In my frequent visits to cafés, grocery stores, bakeries, playing fields, and even in my travels with my father during the late boom years and throughout the Great Depression in the Latin areas, I was aware of only one German family in Ybor City. They lived two doors from my great-grandmother on 18th Street, north of 19th Avenue, on the west side of the street. It was a very quiet and respectful family. I cannot remember any children from that house, but I recall they had a windmill, an object of much attention from people of all ages.

I was never aware of any German boys or girls playing games in the Ybor parks. In fact, Germans were not a topic of discussion in the twenty years from about 1920 to 1940, except where cigar boxes or kite sticks were involved. We simply didn't know them. Our talk was all in Spanish. Yet as I look back to the George Washington Junior High School days I remember that there were a few non-Latin-looking children who lived in nearby areas and attended school there. These included Jews, Germans, and "Anglos." We all got along beautifully. In fact, some of my friends existed in these categories. Many lived in Tampa Heights and areas between Nebraska and Florida Avenues, all the way to Robles Park to the north. A recent check with friends who lived with me during those years confirms my recollections.

The huge German-owned Tampa Box Company factory on 20th Street and 2nd Avenue produced thousands of high quality cigar boxes. In the process of making them, they generated excess thin sticks of light balsa wood, some two- to five-feet long. I remember buying a bundle of about one hundred and fifty sticks for fifteen cents, and later for a quarter. From these, and with *papel china* (fine-colored paper) from Papito's drugstore across from the Regensburg Cigar Factory, I made many Ybor City-type kites, some of which I sold. (See Exhibit 9 at the back of this book for more about kites and games.)

On the occasion of an Ybor City Museum Society event to honor the museum volunteers at the St. John's Presbyterian Church in West Tampa, someone mentioned the fact that they would be going to the German-American Club off Rome Avenue for some dancing after the church program. My wife and I joined friends and went along. It was one of the most enjoyable evenings we spent for a long time. The music included German, Latin, and

*This early 1900s photograph of the German-American Club, located on Nebraska Avenue, on the western fringes of Ybor City, shows its ironwork railings and expansive staircase. It was a center for social and cultural activities and hosted a number of important German dignitaries. It was disrupted during World War I, and various other organizations later occupied it, including the Young Men's Hebrew Association (YMHA) in the 1930s, later falling into disrepair.*

American selections—a reminder of how naturally the cultures and the people mixed in both the past and present. The host and hostess were delightfully pleasant and extended a warm return invitation.

More recently the German-American Club building has been renovated and restored. For the opening ceremony on December 29, 1997, at the club site on 2105 North Nebraska Avenue, Mayor Dick Greco's office sent out an invitation which included the following pertinent detail on this beautiful building:

> This magnificent structure was erected in 1908 as a social club for Tampa's German immigrants. An outbreak of anti-German feeling sparked by World War I caused the building to be sold in 1919 to the Young Men's Hebrew Association, who occupied it from 1925 to 1944. A Hispanic group, *Los Caballeros de la Luz*, acquired the building in 1962. As part of the Mayor's Heights Project, the Tampa Economic Development Corporation, in partnership with the City of Tampa, is restoring this historic structure into offices for City departments and non-profit organizations.

According to Fernando Noriega, Tampa's Director of Business and Community Services, renovation costs of about $300,000 for the project were paid by the Tampa Economic Development Corporation (TEDCO), which leased the building to the City of Tampa for 25 years. The City used it to house such groups as the Community Redevelopment Agency and the Economic Development Resource Center. After the lease is over, Noriega said, the City will buy the building from TEDCO for one dollar. The renovation was completed in February of 1998, and a handsome, substantial and historic building has been given new life.

## The Black Cubans in Ybor City

Today, the Sociedád La Union Martí-Maceo stands proudly as a reminder of the early days when a few of the leading Black Cubans in Ybor City shaped a community enterprise to meet their mutual needs. By pooling some of the wages they earned in the cigar factories they gathered the resources to establish their own club, and

*The restored building of the German-American Club is part of the renaissance of Ybor City. It is currently used for City of Tampa offices, including the utilities deparment.*

88

most Black Cuban workers joined it. The original group was founded by leaders including Ruperto Pedroso and Bruno Roig. They took as their model a Cuban organization called the Antonio Maceo Free Thinkers of Santa Clara. The Tampa group wanted to continue honoring the black Cuban General Antonio Maceo, who had been killed as a champion in the Spanish-American War, but they also wanted to reaffirm their solidarity with another hero and friend to black Cubans in Tampa, José Martí. They therefore decided to call themselves the Society of the Freethinkers of Martí and Maceo, and sought primarily to be a group for discussion and social interaction, "to meet outside the house in a way acceptable to men of dignity."[26] By the end of 1901 they had recruited 117 members, which Professor Susan Greenbaum discovered from the original membership lists and registries, represented "approximately one-third of the Afro-Cuban households in Tampa."[27]

After several years, some of the members who were particularly concerned about health care formed a separate group which they called *La Unión*. In 1904 they arranged through other Tampa mutual aid organizations to provide medical and prescription benefits for members. There were those who were skeptical at first about La Unión's ability able to make good on its health care arrangements and others who believed that health and medical problems were distractions from more essential social and cultural needs for any group to meet, so the Society and La Unión shared overlapping memberships, and each had some exclusive members, until in 1907, when they merged to form La Unión Martí-Maceo.[28]

The combined resources resulted in a stronger, more effective group which supported members with activities and services for both their minds and bodies. The construction of their ambitious two-story brick clubhouse in Ybor City took about two years. When it was completed it included meeting rooms, an auditorium, and a dance hall. In the years that followed, it was a reliable pillar of stability which could be counted on through strikes and layoffs, even during the Great Depression. After

*La Unión Martí-Maceo not only had a strong and active membership, but a dedicated and enterprising leadership. In this 1917 photograph of the directors, their poses, attire, and facial expressions communicate the intelligence, professionalism, and friendliness. They are (left to right) seated: José C. Rivas, Jacinto San Martin, Francisco Flores (president), Julio Pozo, Juan Franco; and standing are (standing, first row) Eladio Valdes, Emilio Carcanal, Alejandro Hernandez, Pablo Valdes, Juan Casellas, (standing, second row) Rogelio Pérez, and Gustavo [last name unknown].*

helping its members through those catastrophic economic times, it continued through the struggles of mid-century and into the Urban Renewal years. The organization seemed to embody the heart and soul of the community. When Urban Renewal claimed its building in the 1960s, the society proved its tenacity by surviving that crisis as it had so many before. Now it has its home across from the small park dedicated to José Martí. Not only is it appropriate in terms of the Cuban hero honored in La Unión's name, but the park itself is on the site of the Pedroso house in which the Society of the Freethinkers of Martí and Maceo was founded.

Looking back to April 12, 1886, when fifty Cuban cigar workers in Key West boarded the side-wheeler *Hutchinson* and sailed for Tampa, it is important to recall that they were a multicultural body from the first. Through that spring and summer, boatloads of Cubans and Spaniards continued to arrive, eventually totaling some 3,000. Of the Cubans, approximately 15 percent were black. Within the immigrant community there was wide support for liberal social doctrines, and much disagreement with southern views on labor unions and race relations. As Ybor City grew, there would be numerous clashes between militant multi-ethnic cigar workers and the local white "Citizen Committees." The deal that had been struck between Ybor and the Tampa Board of Trade was a marriage of convenience, the beginning of a relationship between Latin immigrants and native-born Southerners that profited both, but which has not always been congenial. In large degree the history of Tampa is a product of that relationship—a study in sharp contrast between cultures, beliefs, religions, and races. Nowhere are these contrasts more clearly drawn than in the unfolding development of Tampa's Black Cuban community.

The general lack of awareness by politicians regarding the original population and the importance of its diversity became evident during urban renewal. The loss of

*In the late 1960s the original Martí-Maceo building was bulldozed by Urban Renewal. The group moved to this structure next to the southwest corner of La Sétima and 14th Street, near José Martí Park. The iron grillwork links the bulding to past times, and though the membership has dwindled, it still remains active, providing medical and hospital benefits to its black Spanish-speaking membership.*

**Ybor City: The Making of a Landmark Town**

the original building led to worries that a new round of redevelopment could bring similar consequences. Black Cubans were struggling to preserve La Unión Martí-Maceo.

After many decades of low visibility in the local community, histories of the city and the Latin community rarely included more than a passing mention of Afro-Cubans or recognition of Sociedád La Unión Martí-Maceo as one of the important mutual aid societies, the forerunners of today's health maintenance organizations. Members identified and approached the different agencies and advisory boards involved in Ybor City planning, and advised them of their wish to be included in their deliberations.

Future roles envisioned for both the group and its structure are now aligned with the other heritage groups determined to accurately portray the unique aspects of the roots of Ybor City as a multi-ethnic, multi-racial community in the American Deep South. Sociedád La Unión Martí-Maceo members continue to restore their structure and work conscientiously and progressively in the preservation of their unique aspect of Tampa's ethnic heritage as part of the Heritage Club Consortium.[29]

I remember a number of Black Cubans from café visitations with my father in the late Twenties and Thirties. I remember them as noble in character, soft-spoken, and seemingly perpetually good-natured and respectful. They were active and mobile. They often fished off the 22nd Street bridge and crabbed in the waters of McKay Bay off DeSoto Park. They were often present at Ybor rooster fights in those days, sometimes selling artifacts. Most of them were excellent cigarmakers and proud of their work. They fell into conversation easily in the town cafés, exchanging stories about events in the factories or news of local happenings. They were easy with colorful words and expressions, many originating in the Cuban countryside. I recall they sometimes kept guinea hens. These made good "watch dogs," as most residents could agree. Street talk had it that the hens slept with one eye open. Indeed, the Black Cubans provided much area folklore. They delighted in stories flavored with humor, and they enjoyed many forms of games.[30]

The Ybor Museum Society sponsored several Folk Festivals in the 1980s. For the publicity in connection with the 1987 festival, Hipolito Arenas is shown in the event brochure, rolling handmade cigars. Joaquin Maldonado, in turn, is captured preparing an initial block of wood to be carved into a spinning top. And the 1989 brochure carries a half-page view of the *Septeto Floridano*, a seven-man musical group, in a photograph taken circa 1940.

In the period 1970 and forward I was privileged to meet many of the adult members of the black community at some of the civic events. They were well-educated and certainly those I spoke with were extremely well-informed concerning their proud heritage in Ybor City. Now as a new millennium has begun, there appears to be a reawakening of the leadership of the Sociedád La Unión Martí-Maceo. Undoubtedly this is a heroic effort, since the youngsters—as is true of Latins' children—are now American-born and -educated, and are virtually indistinguishable from any other part of the American mainstream. For the most part, they look to the future, rather than to the past.

## CMIU - Seven Months Strike - Tampa Cossacks: 1910-1915

Indicative of the chaotic nature of labor relations in the factories of the Cigar Capital was the fact that between 1887 and 1894 alone there had been twenty-three walkouts. However, despite the workers' unrest shown, no single organization emerged to give them a voice.[31] Clearly, the lack of an effective organization favored the radicals whose aims and philosophies went beyond the simple desire of the *tabaqueros* to improve their quality of life. Most of these radical workers were quite young. Some were recent arrivals in their mid to late teens, who listened to the older, more experienced, and more persuasive men in their groups. Whether it was through talking in the cafés, the social clubs, the streets, the boarding houses, or reading from the militant newspapers and pamphlets that circulated through the town, the *tabaqueros* were influenced to participate. Many enrolled in unions because they saw them as the only defense against forces of change—including new machines and cheaper labor—which threatened their factory jobs.

By now the three distinct cultures—the Cubans, the Spaniards and the Italians—had somewhat found their relative "place in the sun" in the *galería* (the main production floor) of the cigar factories. The extreme friction between the Cubans and Spaniards over a free Cuba was substantially put to rest. Indeed, following the end of the Cuban War of Independence, many Cubans quickly chose to return to the Cuban mainland, now run by Cubans, to savor the fruits of a land now supposedly a bountiful, orderly and equitable one. But alas! This was not the Garden of Eden they expected.

It is true that many jobs were available in the Spanish- or Cuban-owned factories in West Tampa and Ybor. Most of those who had been part of the postwar wave of immigrants had soon made friends and understood the way of life here. The chaotic conditions on their island were not at all comparable to the more orderly ways in Tampa. When nostalgia or idealism—or even family and friends—attracted Ybor immigrants to return to Cuba, they soon realized the blessings and the opportunities of their adopted home. So return to Tampa they did. The once stressful and tense working relationships with the Spaniards had begun to change. Cubans could now work more comfortably alongside them, though it would take a few years for the wounds to be healed. After all, many of the Cubans themselves shared a Spanish heritage—Galician or Asturian. Now that the war in Cuba was over, Spanish *patrones* were willing to hire Cubans as hand rollers of cigars. Many excelled at this work.

Italian women had found their niche in the factories. Starting usually as apprentices, they gradually established themselves as rollers in the main floor or *galería*. As the numbers of females in the *galería* increased, their jobs became relatively safe. For the younger women, in spite of parental objections, the chance to catch a husband in the workplace was high. The Spaniards were respectful, and treated women with courtesy. And slowly but surely, the increasing numbers of women in the *galería* changed the work environment. The tradition of *lectores* (readers) who read aloud to the workers had continued, and following the war there was even greater variety, with less emphasis on news and revolutionary politics and more tolerance for literature. With the number of women increasing, there was rising demand for more romantic novels in the afternoons. This was a wish that *lectores* often honored. Among the favorite books was *Marianela*, by Benito Pérez Galdos, an eminent Spanish writer of the "generation of writers of 1868." It was undoubtedly one of the most revered and popular selections.

The factory *galerías* offered something not found readily in other areas—certainly not in greater Tampa. They provided safe, sit-down jobs, where hand skill was all that was required to bring in a small but stable income. And coffee was served on the job, not to mention the free cigars men were allotted. Factory work guaranteed food on the table. In turn, the soft Castilian language spoken in the factory was relatively easy to learn. The heavy population of Spanish and Cubans on the floor offered ample opportunity for Italians to learn Spanish. The constant factory talk all around them encouraged the adoption of a second language. Spanish and Italian are both romance languages and have Latin roots in common; the linguistic similarities became yet one more inducement for factory workers to become bilingual.

Soon the problems in the factories no longer stemmed primarily from cultural antipathies. They arose from the increasing conflicts and jockeying for position between the Cigar Makers International Union (CMIU—a national AFL affiliate), the *patrones*, the Tampa Cigar Manufacturers Association, and the dozens of other organizations that stirred and upset an otherwise settled and friendly ambiance. In the early years much of the unsettling labor circumstances came from conflicting allegiances to mother countries and from influences filtering southward from the northern industrial centers. Each worker seemed to be following his dream. Some of them had sweethearts to court, homes to pay for, families to support, or just regular boarding house and meal payments to make. However visionary or mundane the purpose, local cigar factories offered worthy and dependable jobs to meet the need. They were the only significant industrial jobs in town.

But now, pushed by the more organized and experienced national CMIU, the local branch had grown to some 6,000 members. In previous strikes the CMIU had broken the back of the old *La Resistencia* worker's union. *La Resistencia* was simply no match for this national CMIU organization. In mere size and experience it posed a serious threat to the factory *patrones*, who were trying to remain competitive. On the employer side too, however, there was a centralization of power which added fuel to the fire. Three of the largest factories, including the original Ybor factory, had been purchased by the American Tobacco Company in 1901,

part of the Duke family tobacco trust that soon controlled job opportunities for fully twenty percent of the cigarworkers in the city.[32]

As the new century began, local labor leaders were concerned that many factories had not lived up to the uniform wage scale—*el Cartabón*—previously agreed to during the Weight Strike (*La Huelga de la Pesa*.). Their concern about salary levels increased as an undeclared price war commenced among the manufacturers. As the factories began cutting labor costs in order to cut prices, the cigarmakers were trapped. Eventually, they had to refuse wage rates below earlier agreements, but the owners in turn refused to pay more. In the end, the *patrones* simply shut down the factories and locked the workers out, hoping to force cigarmakers to work for less. It seems to have been almost the reverse of a strike by the workers; instead, the workers were shut out by the owners.[33]

By mid-1910 the demands from each side had reached a critical impasse. When factories of the Clear Havana Cigar Manufacturers Association "trust" began to dismiss *escogedores* (cigar selectors) belonging to CMIU Local 493 in June 1910, it was clear this was no mere skirmish but an outright labor war. By August 1910 more than 12,000 cigarmakers had walked out (or been shut out) of the workplace. A *Tampa Tribune* journalist covering a strike meeting of over 5,000 demonstrators reported "bevies of gaily dressed Spanish, Cuban, and Italian women waving their red bandannas."[34]

Workers without jobs tried to keep their spirits up, but there was no early end in sight. The situation deteriorated over the next weeks, until on the afternoon of Sept. 14, 1910, a crowd of striking cigar workers confronted a still-employed bookkeeper, John F. Easterling, as he tried to enter the Bustillo Brothers and Díaz factory in West Tampa. Someone fired several shots, hitting Easterling, who collapsed on the steps and later died. The war of economics and willpower had turned bloody.[35]

And the killing did not stop there. It was not clear who had done the shooting, but the next morning two Italians, Angelo Albano and Castrense Ficarrotta, who were said to have been responsible, were found hanging dead from an oak tree, their bodies riddled with bullets.[36]

This extreme action shook the city. The Italian community reacted strongly against the attack on its people, and in this they received sympathetic support from the large majority of Spaniards and Cubans. The underlying tensions between the Anglo establishment and the ethnically diverse work force began to surface.

Once again the strike of 1910 was at its core an action to establish the union's right to bargain for the workers. The movers and shakers of Tampa seemed equally determined to thwart the efforts of organized labor. With some 10,000 cigarworkers off the job, however, the city found the strike action difficult to ignore.

The Italian Vice Consul G. Maroni was brought in from New Orleans to investigate the vigilante execution, and concluded "the lynching itself was not the outcome of a temporary outburst of popular anger, but was rather planned, by some citizens of West Tampa with the tacit assent of a few police officers, and all with the intention of teaching an awful lesson to the strikers of the cigar factories."[37]

The intended lesson only seemed to intensify the conflict. The Balbin Brothers cigar factory in West Tampa, on the northeast corner of St. John and Howard Avenue, was destroyed by arson. There was even an unsuccessful effort made to set fire to the *Tampa Tribune* building. The business community responded rapidly. Led by Col. Hugh C. Macfarlane, the pioneering developer of West Tampa and a former prosecutor, more than four hundred businessmen and professionals signed a pledge to join the Citizens Committee to protect the cigar industry "to the fullest extent possible" in view of the fact that it "furnishes approximately sixty-five percent of the total income of the city and makes a basis for several other millions of dollars being paid in wages annually."[38]

Owners announced they would reopen their factories, which had been

94

**Ybor City: The Making of a Landmark Town**

closed for two months. More than two hundred Citizens Committee members armed with rifles patrolled the streets to stifle protest and to protect strikebreakers or workers willing to return to their jobs. However, the strike held. Only a few hundred workers returned, and the behavior of the Citizens Committee was vehemently attacked in the editorial columns of the local CMIU newspaper *El Internacional*, which declared that "the craving for money" had warped the hearts and morals of citizens willing "to disregard Freedom, Justice . . . and even the Constitution of their own country."[39] The editor was arrested for conspiracy, and when the editorial criticism continued unrelentingly, the Citizens Committee resorted to the more violent tactics which had helped break the *La Resistencia* strike: they beat up a printer and destroyed the paper's printing press.

The strike put a tremendous strain on the workers and the union. Some returned to Cuba, where they could still get jobs, as soon it became clear that the matter would drag out. Those who remained received financial help from fellow workers in Cuba and from the international union until its funds were exhausted. Finally, facing not only the violent and ruthless tactics of the Citizens Committee but the economic hardship of its members as well, labor leaders decided to take a vote to see whether or not workers favored a continuation of the strike. The majority voted to return to work. Before the seventh month was over, the factories were more or less back to normal. Many of the families who had fled to Cuba when the conflict started, returned to Tampa.[40]

The action became known as *La Huelga de los Siete Meses* (The Seven

*Even when no particular action or rally was underway, the Old Labor Temple building on 8th Avenue was a gathering place for Ybor City workers. Radical pamphlets and brochures were always in abundance and those who stopped by could catch up on the latest causes and issues of the day.*

**Chapter 3 · Clear Cigar Capital and the Start of the Golden Years: 1900-1950**

Months Strike). It was another victory for the Trust, the national Clear Havana Cigar Manufacturers Association, with support from the Anglos of the infamous Citizens Committee. It allowed the *patrones* to push ahead to assert other advantages over the workers, including elimination of the idea of the *Cartabón*, the uniform wage scale. Nonetheless, the Latin *tabaqueros* justifiably viewed their solidarity as exemplary. Even though they had chosen at last to return to the factories, they had held out for seven months, and the *patrones* knew the simple truth that without the workers, they had no cigar industry. They had felt the dramatic power of labor solidarity.

Retributions by many Spaniards, Italians, and Cubans against the strikebreakers in the factory were harsh. In retrospect, many today can understand the rationales of both the *tabaqueros* and the *patrones*. But those workers who had suffered through the strike could never cease to view the actions of the self-proclaimed "Citizens Committee" of Tampa—a mob of vigilantes—as anything but shameful and unworthy of a civilized people. The socialists, in turn, branded them "the Cossacks of Tampa."

Still, the cigar workers looked with hope to the future. The *Huelga de los Siete Meses* was one of the great episodes in the life of the industry. Decades later I would sit at the cafés with my father and hear his friends at the table talk about the strike as a historic catalyst in their lives. This event, and the talk about it, continued to unite the *tabaqueros*—Cubans, Italians, and Spaniards alike, for they were all impacted, from the factory *galería* to ordinary street life where they intermingled daily. There would be other major strikes. The *tabaqueros* were on one side; the *patrones* and the Anglos downtown and in South Tampa were on the other. The *patrones* wanted nothing to stand in the way of their cigar sales contracts, and the downtown Anglos wanted nothing to impede the flow of money into their banks. All were willing to defend their livelihood at any cost.

Following the Seven Months Strike, factory inventories were low. The owners increased their cigar output, quickly drawing workers back from Cuba, Key West, and New York. By 1915 production in Tampa had increased from 201.4 million cigars to 285.4, a forty-two percent increase. By the end of World War I in 1918,

**Ybor City: The Making of a Landmark Town**

production had risen a total of eighty-three percent above production in 1910, the year of the strike. Demand for quality cigars throughout the nation was booming, thanks, also, to the returned American doughboys. At the end of 1915, Tampa's population had jumped to 48,160—all this in spite of the strike of 1910, which had cost $15 million in lost orders.[41]

The resurgence in cigar production, the return of *tabaqueros* who had moved to other industrial centers, and the growing list of Cubans, Spaniards, and Italians flowing into the town, created a demand for more local services. It proved without a doubt that the existing Latin organizational facilities had to be enlarged. New merchants arrived on La Sétima, the main spine. Many Jewish merchants opened department stores. Spaniards opened restaurants, cafés, and groceries. Italians, also, began to go into the grocery and food provision business. Stores were still rather primitive but the town offered a surprising range of goods and services not previously enjoyed.

The social clubhouses had to be enlarged to accommodate the newest arrivals. Latins needed a place to hold meetings, and simply to sit, talk, and relax in an environment approximating that of a hometown *cantina*. It would be the sort of room where one would meet close friends to play cards or dominos, drink coffee and share stories. It would be a place to celebrate, a stage to present their popularly chosen theatrical line-up, a hall to dance in and to dream. The war that had pitted Spain against Cuba, and then against the United States was now virtually forgotten. The wave of Spanish patriotism had subsided, though it did not vanish. A major concern now was mutualism.[42] In 1911 the Centro Español demolished its first club building, a twin-towered one, in order to build a larger home in Ybor City, while simultaneously constructing a similar clubhouse in West Tampa. These new structures were immense and ambitious, befitting the ideals of mutual support and continuing success. The Centro Español vision of the grand mutual clubhouse was followed and extended by their construction of the first major hospital, at a location that at the time seemed far out on Bayshore Boulevard. It compared with the best in the state.

In 1911, also, the first Centro Asturiano Club building was destroyed by fire and the current beautiful building was constructed on the same site, at Nebraska and Palm Avenue. It had built its first hospital, then state-of-the-art and one of the best in the state, in 1905. Later, in 1925, the new Centro Asturiano Hospital, located conveniently on 21st Avenue and 13th Street, began construction. It offered service to their own Spanish members, and also to many other ethnic groups. Considerable emotion and pride were wrapped up with both the Centro Español and Centro Asturiano hospitals, for they offered very low-priced cradle-to-grave medical services. They supported families through crucial times of life and death, and sustained them through their more routine health needs as well. This was on the cutting edge of American HMO history.

In 1908 the Cuban club had built its first clubhouse on 10th Avenue and 14th Street. It was a two-story, red brick building with a veranda not unlike the buildings today on La Sétima. In 1916 this original clubhouse was destroyed by fire, and the beautiful Circulo Cubano, still standing today, was built on the same site in 1918. In 1918, also, the Italians built their elegant club building on La Sétima at 18th Street, across from their original home which had been constructed in 1911 and destroyed by fire in 1914. All of the early Latin club buildings have often been referred to as "palaces." Yet their grandeur was not built on elitism and inherited wealth, but on the promise of mutual assistance and the dream of a better life.

## Labor Peace - Spanish, Cuban and Italian Culture: 1915 - 1920

During the mid to late teens Ybor City was a town on the move. The effects of the *Huelga de los Siete Meses* were gone. Tampa cigar production was up forty-two percent, bringing new prosperity, and by 1915 Tampa had some 1,200 automobiles, selling at an average cost of $1,000 each.[43] Along La Sétima, *Fotingos* and *Chivolocos* (Fords and Chevrolets) were parked on each side. The very early cars had no doors or windows and were invariably black in color. In the late 1920s and early '30s four-door cars were often seen on La Sétima. Cars with rumble seats were still a novelty and a delight, especially to youngsters and teenagers. That feature soon became very popular.

In between parked autos yellow electric trolleys passed incoming ones. These were variously called *El Trole* or *El Carrito Electrico*. The slow trolley speeds easily accommodated the frequent stops required by the small street grid—a match seemingly made in heaven. Usually, within a few yards of a stop the trolley would come to a halt. Standing passengers in the vehicle hung on tight as the sudden slowing momentum carried them forward.

One would often see passengers run to catch the trolley, step on the running board and climb the steps, even as it began to move forward. When the trolley picked up speed it would sway side to side. The delicious, cool breezes through its open windows made the ride almost always enjoyable, except for a few days in winter or whenever it rained. Adults, youngsters,

98

**Ybor City: The Making of a Landmark Town**

*La Sétima in the 1920s was a neat and active business district. The ironwork balconies and globed streetlights are among the unique characteristics of the street. The banner in front of the shop at the far right verifies that the "Closing Out Sale" was not a feature reserved for more recent times when businesses left the area.* TECO ENERGY ARCHIVES COURTESY OF LA GACETA.

and the elderly all loved this unique trolley ride. It also allowed for unexpected greetings and exchanges with friends or acquaintances. Conversation often ensued. And many simply read the newspapers even as the trolley swayed gently back and forth at higher speeds. Often, it had no sooner speeded up from a given corner when it was time to slow down. Mothers and children would stream out of the front or rear doorways. It was a memorable experience.[44]

By 1913 the Tampa Electric Street Railway System connected Ybor City to most other important Tampa areas, including Seminole Heights, Sulphur Springs, Jackson Heights, Tampa Heights, West Tampa, Grand Central (Kennedy Boulevard), Port Tampa, Gary, Union Station, and Palmetto Beach.[45] There were fifty-three miles of trolley lines and sixty-seven coaches to travel them.[46] While the ride was relatively slow, the lines were very direct and car parking was not required, so the overall time might be reduced for the smaller distances.

In this period, anything and everything took root. Immigrants from many lands settled and thrived. The early industries of tourism, agriculture, and cigar manufacturing were blossoming. Services and goods of all kinds were sprouting up to meet the tastes and needs of diverse residents and visitors. Modern issues such as zoning restrictions, wetlands protection, parking problems, traffic flow, traffic jams, and late night curfews were more matters for personal initiative and responsibility than for regulation by legislative or judicial bodies. And space, of course, was not yet at a premium. In Florida there was a nearly ideal climate, plenty of cheap land, and confidence that the future held boundless opportunity. Anything seemed possible. Laws were simpler. Demand for goods was a common need that motivated merchants to sell more and to expand. Merchants responded to the steadily growing population and its increasing diversity with goods and services to adequately meet their needs. In turn, the number of merchants on La Sétima in-



**Chapter 3 · Clear Cigar Capital and the Start of the Golden Years: 1900-1950**

creased. As a growing number of marriages occurred, demand for everything
expanded, so it was largely family needs
that these merchants hurried to supply.
For periods of time it was possible to forget the strikes and all the ugly issues of
class and race, power and control they revealed; for brief periods of time at least,
Ybor City fairly smacked of vigorous and
healthy free enterprise. It staked its fair
claim to a portion of the American dream.

But if the town's hustle and bustle
seemed that of an unrestrained people, it
simply wasn't so. It was a town whose morals were heavily European-based, and
where the family was everything.
Rowdiness, bullying, disrespect of women
and the elderly, skimpy dresses—all that
was as intolerable as it was rare. The hallmarks of value were there. Even the merchants hailed the civil peace that existed.
Better yet, they took it for granted. One
could build in that climate. One could
plant roots and plan for the future.

Families loved to shop in Ybor City's
downtown stores. Saturday evenings were
delightful times for the whole family, and
particularly the children. Taken for
granted was the fact that most families
lived close by and simply walked a few
blocks from their homes to get downtown.
Many families lived above their businesses
and they just walked downstairs to shop.
This residential downtown base assured
the merchants all-day shopping. Bakeries,
cafés, groceries, and more were opened
early. Merchants didn't have to wait until
noon or later to see their first customers;
people stopped in on their way to and from
school or work, or in the course of pursuing the errands and routines of the day. Security, for businesses and individuals alike,
was taken for granted; many of the townspeople were owners of one sort or another,
and were neighbors if not friends. All had
a vested interest in an orderly town, and
unruliness was quickly erased by the mere
dynamics of the way of life.

While the diversity of national and racial backgrounds made for tolerance and
variety, Spanish influence was an unobtru-
sive but particularly strong force in daily

**Ybor City: The Making of a Landmark Town**

*La Sétima looking east from 16th Street. The signs for the popular Woolworth's and Kress stores are visible on the left side of the street.* THCPLS.

life. If the cigar factory was the economic engine that drove the town, then peninsular Spanish was its strongest underpinning — both in general cultural attributes and in the total use of Spanish as the town's language. Though the Cubans were the largest cultural group—and uninformed tourists referred to Ybor City as a Cuban town —their heavy involvement with the revolution, their inclination toward mobility, and their consequent unreliability at the factory, kept them in the lower echelons of society during those early years. More correctly, Ybor City was, in the early and middle years, a Latin town with strong peninsular Spanish underpinnings and leadership, and key Spanish social organizational fabric.

The Latin town—Cuban, Spanish, and Italian—was joined by the significant but far less widespread Romanian Jewish presence in the downtown area. Peninsular Spaniards addressed a new acquaintance —and certainly the elderly—with a formal and respectful, *usted* (you), and definitely not with the common or familiar, *tu*. Familiarity with new acquaintances had to be earned; only then was the *tu* deemed proper. Elderly always were addressed as *usted*. Those not following this unwritten code were instantly noted, then judged not to have proper upbringing. Yes, proper conduct at home and within the community was rock solid among Spaniards. Theirs was the town's norm that many sought to emulate. The situation of the Spaniards in Ybor City was similar to that of the English in America— sometimes admired, sometime envied, and yes, a few times despised. The term *muy estirado* (stiff; excessively distant or formal) was often used for those very few who seemingly put on airs. For the most part, Spaniards valued the qualities of hard work, great propriety, correctness of demeanor, stability but a desire to move forward, and belief in education, higher education, and advancement. Above all, strong family values and love were fundamental. Respect for the elders was ingrained. Spaniards looked to the past for values without forgetting the future.

*101*

Spanish newspapers, periodicals, social institutions and *lectores* reinforced the community's cultural pride, self-esteem, and hope for the future. They provided the continuing stream of information around which optimism could reinforce the desire to grow and work hard for a better Ybor City. This was echoed and supported by similar Cuban and Italian values. Weekly events at the clubhouses, theaters, dances, and club meetings reinforced the upbeat mood of these Latins. All this, to the consternation of a downtown Tampa society who did not view kindly many of the Latin social club activities, particularly on Sunday, nor the need for these huge buildings.

Actually, the large social club buildings provided much of the fabric of Latin culture. They housed beautiful theaters, dance halls, cantinas, exercise rooms, offices, conference or meeting rooms, and libraries. Latins were self-sufficient. They provided for their needs without asking for help from anyone. These buildings were well-maintained and sources of great pride. The Sunday Matinee dances in the afternoon were wonderfully chaperoned, and the dress was beautifully correct. Entertainment included performances by visiting troupes of singers, dancers, dramatic groups, Spanish *zarzuelas* (operettas or musicals) and opera soloists. Most importantly, the social clubs provided state-of-the-art hospitals, giving Latins exemplary "cradle to grave" medical services. These Spanish hospitals would be the envy of much of Tampa for many years.

The *lector* institution also did much to promote Spanish values. Aside from presenting readings assigned by the *Comité de Lectura*, the *lectores* read a variety of serious and romantic novels. Many of these stemmed from the Spanish writers of the "*generación de '68*," or the "*generación de '98*," popular terms designating writers of those middle to late years of the 19th century. These years were particularly rich for literature, including some of Spain's best contributions to world literature and letters, aside from those of the earlier Golden Age of Spanish literature of the 16th and 17th centuries. The *lectores* helped preserve and extend Spanish literary culture to the new generations in Ybor City. It also found an appreciative and receptive audience among Cuban workers.

*Seated on his specially constructed platform, a lector reads to workers in an Ybor City factory.* USFSCL.

**Ybor City: The Making of a Landmark Town**

The later arrival of the Italians, as well as the delayed entry of Italian women into the factories, required them to adjust to the town's ways. This entry into the factory *galerias* was a big factor in the Italian family's ability to cope and meet expenses as the men slowly found their own niches. Italians gradually merged into the mainstream and were soon speaking Spanish fluently. This was influenced much by factory lore and particularly listening to the Spanish novels recited by the *lectores*.

Italians held sacred their own family values and cultural ways. Fortunately, most Italians already had their families with them. Respect for the parents and elders was high. Italian women tended to gravitate to the cigar factories where they could earn steady income until the men found a niche. If the husband opened a business, he could count on much help from his resourceful wife. In turn, the husbands prized self-sufficiency and would improvise greatly in order to understand and fit into the order and social expectations of the town. They were great learners, especially at overcoming obstacles that impeded their progression up the economic ladder. They were high on creativity and adaptability. They possessed strong will and, most importantly, they were hard workers. In time their perseverance would advance their status.

The Cubans, meanwhile, were caught up in currents stirred by the Cuban War of Independence. Their passionate demand for independence spilled over into widespread local activism and militancy and led to vigorous support for unionism and socialism. Life for many of the Tampa Cubans must have seemed continuously unsettled. Buffeted by dangerous and powerful tides of idealism and confrontation, they found themselves in a situation unsuited to raising families, pursuing education, or setting down roots. This impeded the early growth of new Cuban families in Ybor City, and the concomitant affirmation of schools,

churches, and other family oriented cultural institutions so important to an improved quality of life. In the postwar years, Cuba itself experienced less than perfect democracy, as political maneuverings produced a succession of dictatorships and *coup d'etats*. Indeed, the traditional high mobility of the Cuban workers added to the above created many unstable situations in Tampa for them.

When one considers the circumstances, it is gratifying how well Cuban *tabaqueros* maintained their values.[47] The Cuban bloodline had a 400-year mixture of Spanish, with a heavy dose of it in the late 19th century, the years of growing turmoil notwithstanding. In many ways they shared similar values with the *Peninsulares*, but it was love of Cuban soil that kept their roots shallow in Ybor City in those early days. Perhaps their habit of maintaining job mobility, with attendant lower wages, fostered dependence on renting rather than home ownership in the early periods. This led to the creation of an area such as *El Bataclán*. This area, just north of the Cuban Club and west of 15th Street, was a less than desirable one. As a young boy, I often waited in a *Fotingo* (Ford), as father, then a Realtor, collected rent from tenants there.



*103*

It would take years for many Cubans to feel that this was home—that this was where the family would grow. It was not their lack of desire or disdain of work that held the Cubans back, though their indecisiveness in the early years occasionally gave other Latins that feeling. In a way, the very slow progress of the Círculo Cubano, rebuilt late in 1918, reflected this situation well.

When on April 30, 1916, the first Cuban Club burned, both the Italians and Spaniards put their clubs at the disposal of Cubans for the conduct of their affairs. Some eight months later they began construction of their new, elegant "palace," the current building, at the same site on Palm Avenue and 14th Street. Cubans then began to buy houses. In 1918, now more confident of their future, they celebrated the opening of their new club house. Factory wages were adequate, and at least for the near future were dependable. Production demand was still very strong, though the early 1920s would see a major struggle, before the Boom years set in, and in the Great Depression that followed the Boom Years.

With the construction of the new and splendid Círculo Cubano, the pioneering Cuban community in Ybor City at last set down its roots and blossomed for all to see and to share. The many events and community activities as well as the political and social ideals from the Cuban community that spun outward from this building were highly visible and influential. It defined and expressed the Cuban presence until the next major single wave of immigration expanded and reshaped it once again. The very fast arrival of Cuban exiles into Tampa in the late 1950s brought in a great number of businessmen and professionals. These by and large were highly educated and many were at the higher levels of Cuban society, though the majority of the most affluent went to Miami. The many who came to Ybor City, however, quickly adjusted, went into business, and rose to the highest levels of their society in Tampa. Many of them were already professionals when they arrived, and that expanded their work options. Today they rank at the very top of the Hispanic population in terms of income. Many of these have Spanish blood ties.

**Ybor City: The Making of a Landmark Town**

It was inevitable that intermarriages between Cubans, Italians, and Spaniards would occur. Still, marriages between Spanish men and Italian women were slow in evolving. It is known that many Italian fathers preferred that their daughters marry their own kind. Some fathers feared that the Spaniards might have wives in Spain. Still, young Spaniards were the object of many young Italian women. Parents notwithstanding, many Italian girls simply listened to their hearts. In turn, Spaniards admired the beauty and strong home values of these Italian girls. Time has only proven the wisdom of these marriages. Many Spaniards married their own kind, but these were not very plentiful. A few married Cuban women. And like other Latins, some went out of their own cultural group and married an "Americana."

In April 1995 I accidentally helped confirm some of the previous beliefs about the manners and customs of young Spaniards in Ybor City. I had been asked by *La Gaceta* publisher Roland Manteiga to investigate the possibility of writing an article on La Gallega boarding house—a historic building that still languished across from I-4 in Ybor City. Soon I was meeting with La Gallega owners at Ybor City's mecca of Cuban coffee, La Tropicana.

*La Gallega* signifies "the lady from Galicia." I knew it was the name given to a familiar and important boarding house that had served Spanish immigrants to Ybor City in the early years, and the purpose of my meeting with the owners was to obtain information on the status of the building in light of announced plans from the Department of Transportation for widening of the highway. When finally rebuilt, the highway would cause the removal of this historic building. In due course I asked Hilda Alchidiak and Ernesto Fernandez, descendants of Lucas and Ramona Fernandez, founders of the boarding house (Ramona was the first "*Gallega*"), about the character of the

Spaniards who once lived there. Hilda's response, reinforced by Ernesto's nods and gestures, was that "the Spaniards were very young and they seldom came out of the building without a coat and tie! They were very courteous and had excellent manners." This answer simply confirmed what most Spaniards already knew.[48]

These polite, well-dressed young Spaniards were desirable catches. And there were plenty. Some 45 percent were reported single in 1910. This compared with only just under 10 percent of the Italian girls being single. Marry a young Spanish bachelor and a young lady would surmount many economic and social impediments in this cigar town. In that year ninety single Spanish women were included in the U.S. Congress' "Immigrants in Industries" report.[49] Italian girls were viewed as a very desirable catch by the young Spaniards.

Nor were there biases against Cuban girls. While just under 30 percent were single, possibly the past struggles between the two countries hampered a more normal relationship between the young men and women of the day. A higher early Cuban mobility also had impaired this process.

Italian men, in turn, did their share in capturing Spanish girls, though these were relatively few. These were hampered by

*La Gallega boarding house at 1822 14th Avenue East was built after the Ybor City fire of 1908. In 1979, when this photo was taken by Walter Smalling Jr. for the Historic American Buildings Survey, it remained an eloquent brick monument to the lifestyles of young Spanish immigrants. The building was moved to the southeast corner of 13th Street and Columbus Drive to make room for the widening of I-4.* LOC.

the job situation at the factories. Many were unable to overcome the absence of "prospects" in an area with fewer available openings in the established job market. Here, too, early difficulties finding employment would propel many into better businesses and enterprises.

The existence of rather structured social club activities tended to offer bachelors few opportunities for meeting young women, other than those stemming from otherwise casual or school acquaintances. The strong chaperone culture practiced by all groups also contributed to slowing the process of getting acquainted with the opposite sex, but this beautiful custom improved the quality of marriages. Eventually changing times reduced many of the barriers, and more opportunities for meetings destroyed any remaining thought that real love could be corralled. Today, offspring of Ybor's originals are happily intermarried and number many. A common heritage of family experiences in Ybor City where the traditions and manners blended in unique and interesting ways cements their lives as couples and creates a shared social and cultural experience with others like themselves. And apart from the clubs and social mores, a common factory life was the rock-bottom unifier of the cultures in old Ybor. Factory folklore, and particularly the romantic novels recited by the *lectores*, must be credited with introducing a good deal of content and style into conversations.

In this gregarious but correct setting, a Saturday night (or day) trip to La Sétima was a joyful weekly promise young people counted on, and mothers and fathers could count on proper conduct prevailing. Young ladies were all escorted. Still, no amount of chaperoning kept the young people's eyes from exchanging glances. Thus the "Sétima walk" became a very important part of the courtship process.

In the decade beginning in 1910 the cultural and social activities of El Centro Español were developing strongly, having received a great boost by the very active factory owner Don Ignacio Haya who served five years as Centro Español president, from 1911 to 1915. Other highly dedicated factory *patrones* that followed in that leadership role were: Dons Enrique Pendás, Vicente Guerra, Angel Cuesta,

**Ybor City: The Making of a Landmark Town**

Vicente Pendâs, Celestino Vega, Ramon Fernandez Rey, and Alejandro Nistâl, among others. Between them, they employed a sizable number of *tabaqueros*.

As community leaders and individuals of culture and refinement, the officers of the clubs took their positions to heart and generally endeavored to enrich the lives of the membership. A glance at some of the events of the Club at that period as reported by *Tampa Ilustrado* illustrates the point: on February 10, 1913, Señora Emilia Rico, first soprano of the Compañia Opera appeared in "El Gran Teatro Español." Coverage, including pictures, appears on page 184 of *Tampa Ilustrado*. A reviewer writes, "Carmen Ramirez, the celebrated singer, was great in her role in the unforgettable 'Carmen.'" On March 12, 1913, it reports, "Five operas were presented—five marvelous presentations: Rigoleto, Aida, Lucia, La Traviata, and Il Travatore! . . . the Opera company . . . was an excellent group from Europe." And on April 28, 1913, *Tampa Ilustrado* reported that, "His Excellency Sr. Don Juan Riano Gayanos, the Spanish Ambassador to the United States, visited the Centro Español. Alicia, his wife, was given a tea party at the Club."[50] The Ybor City clubs were by nearly any standard state-of-the-art, world-class institutions that attracted political and cultural attention far beyond the reach of most communities of comparable size. Add to this the commercial clout of the cigar industry, and the result was a remarkable convergence of assets.

Of course, not everyone wished to enter the factories. It was true that factory work offered steady wages and strong job security. And relatively speaking, Spaniards enjoyed prestigious positions in the workplace. Nonetheless, not all Spaniards wanted to spend a lifetime in the factories. For some, the continuing turmoil brought about by unions, strikes, competitive counteractions by the *patrones*, and other factory related concerns all indicated an uncertain future. This especially applied to the Italian men who were obliged to send their wives to work in the factory so that the family could rely on a paycheck each week. Creativity and independent action dominated their spirit. The need for adjustment perhaps governed their movements around the periphery of the town. Inside the town, much of the activity seemed to be driven by or tailored for the strong Spanish presence.

Many Italians saw a future in land, cattle, and service occupations. They moved into distant locales as they started dairies, produce farms, fishing-related businesses, fruit importation, and other service businesses. And many turned to more modest or traditional pursuits—simply opening small groceries, pushing vending carts, and discovering ways to serve the needs and desires of the community. Some simply moved out to the country and struggled to pay for land today worth considerable money. For most, a few decades would have to make the difference.[51]

In the late 1890s *el Gallego*, Manuel Suarez, brought a game called *bolita* to Tampa from Key West. Here was yesteryear's Florida Lottery on a local scale. It quickly took hold, and *el Gallego* moved it to El Sevilla Building, on the northeast corner of 14th Street and 8th Avenue. The popularity of this simple and addictive game grew and grew until the downtown fathers became alarmed, a concern that led eventually to manipulation and cover-up as the gambling went underground. With substantial wealth and influence at stake, the bolita trade attracted outside interest, including the attention of Charlie Wall, son of a respected turn-of-

*This set of bolita balls now on display at the Ybor City Museum was made for Manuel Suarez in the early 1890s.*

*Charlie Wall became a wealthy bolita kingpen.*

the-century Tampa doctor and civic leader, and a reputed dabbler in organized crime. Wall seemed to have a way with people and a playboy sense of style and flair that helped him parlay his oldtime family connections into an underworld business network that won him the label "the brilliant gambling czar." Soon Wall had gained control of bolita in Tampa. In the end, he would be brutally murdered at his home in Ybor City.

Meantime, in 1919, the United States began its "noble experiment" with national Prohibition. It was an idea tailor-made for black market entrepreneurs like Wall, and it only helped to strengthen his enterprises and increase his revenues. The high-minded Prohibition experiment failed miserably, as moonshiners all over American made their mark. In Spanish one said, "*el problema se encona*" ("the problem festers"). Tampa soon became one of the wettest places in America. Italian bootlegging would be a major enterprise until the law was repealed in 1933. But Italians were certainly not alone in cashing-in on the opportunity.

World War I began in 1914, and America entered the war in 1917. New words and worries entered life at home in Ybor City as we sent our "doughboys" across the sea to help the Allies. It was the war to end all wars—to make our world safe for democracy. And they went there to the bewitching melodies of, "Over There," "Johnny Get Your Gun" and "Roses of Picardy."

Not many Latins fought in World War I, except for a relative few. Many of those who did were recent arrivals to America. Most Latins had come for economic reasons. Yet some, including my father, Evaristo, felt they "owed a debt of

*This painting by C. Caseza from the Ybor City Museum depicts some of the key elements in Bolita playing.* Ybor City Museum Society.

**Ybor City: The Making of a Landmark Town**

blood to the Spanish King, Alfonso XIII." Others simply were not yet into the mainstream of American life—married, rooted, house-broken—nor did they possess children who would be swept up by the wartime experience. It would take a couple of decades for them to establish themselves firmly enough to feel an American identity.

No—Latins in Ybor City, West Tampa, and Palmetto Beach, did not respond admirably to that war. Their war would be World War II, for then the participants would be American-born and well-rooted. Their record then would be enviable, with many serving as officers. Some would enter the nation's best military academies. And many would die for America.

## 1920-1925 — Nine Months Strike and The Roaring '20s

In early 1920, the Cigar Makers International Union (CMIU) considered it to be time to fight for a closed shop. The massive *Huelga de los Nueve meses* (the "Nine Month Strike") would soon follow. It would leave an indelible imprint. By this time finished cigars in Tampa had increased to 386 million units, a 35 percent increase over 1915. Ominously, the rate of cigarette smoking was by now outpacing that of cigars.[52]

Bolstered by successes in the two small strikes of 1916 and 1918, the Cigar Makers International Union (CMIU) pushed for concessions: more precisely, for a closed shop. The union wanted any new employee hired to be a member of the CMIU. In northern industrial America, closed shops reigned where unions had the upper hand. Wages, vacations, perks—any and every activity or wish of the factory owners, managers or presidents—had to be approved by the union, which had a strong say on the matter. Changes in factory operations would require votes, both locally and nationally. Once in the door, the union could dictate direction, even

though perhaps some individual employees were not in favor of the proposed action.

Among the union's wishes was a uniform wage rate for a given brand—one that would hold across Ybor, West Tampa, Palmetto Beach—and, ideally, one that would apply throughout the state and even the nation. Cigars were manufactured in six major cities in Florida and in forty-two other states. Additionally, the *uniform weight scale* had also been in contention, and much more. The threat would be the walkout with no employment, no production, and the threat of lost markets.

All the above was threatened by the union at a time when *patrones* were hard-pressed by competition. The current lower prices were brought about by the introduction of molds, then machinery; and, by the promotion of marketing techniques that clashed with the Spanish hand or the hand-mold methods of cigar production. The hand-mold was an improvement over the hand method. It introduced wooden molds that aided shape uniformity. Other aspects of increased competition included fancier cigar bands and wraps. Nor were the *patrones* assured that new factories would not open up. Available comparison data in 1936 indicated that on a national basis, the labor cost to make 1,000 long filler cigars with a four-operator machine was approximately half of the cost of making it by hand, all relevant costs having been included.[53]

Although the toal numbers of cigars manufactured in Tampa increased during the 1920s—with a peak of 504,753,265 in 1929—they decreased throughout the 1930s. Extrapolating from U.S. government data and personal reports, the production after 1920 went downward for large and handmade cigars, although small cigars went modestly up and helped account for the increasing totals, until they, too, declined after 1930. Demand for large, handmade cigars was seriously slipping, at a time that cigarette smoking was becoming the fashion.[54] The rise of cigar popularity was now history. Demand alone could not guarantee jobs. Moreover, innovations in cigarmaking machines increased the steady pressure on the *patrones* in the factories to watch their labor costs closely. Small manufacturers could not afford the massive machinery purchases, disruption of the workplace, or the change in skills and methodology that went with mechanization, nor could they afford to increase their labor costs by hiring more handmade cigar workers. In order to remain competitive, factories large and small had to let go numbers of the loyal workers who were the backbone of the quality handmade cigar. Thus, mechanization posed a significant threat to all factories using traditional hand and hand-mold methods. It was feared that fashion and commercial trends would result in a catastrophic lowering of demand for the handmade Cuban cigar brands, would endanger smaller factories, and would place added inducements on the larger firms to mechanize.

To the union's consternation, the larger factories added many cigar molds and brought in a few cigar-making machines. The mold method did not impact the quality of the cigar significantly. And, to assert their position, the Cigar Manufacturing Association acted to control the cigar box output to appease the factories.

Meanwhile, a national euphoria fueled by the end of World War I was in the making. The world was tired of the old ways and failed politics that resulted in a war with 8,500,000 soldiers killed and with 21,000,000 injured. Demand for exciting new technology was in the works. Change fueled a penchant for the better things of life. A Ford that cost $850 in 1914 sold for only $350 in 1926. Machines lowered costs dramatically. Italy's Marconi had invented the radio. Its production would soon make an evening at home seem very entertaining and would change American social life.

*This mass meeting in October 1920 celebrated the survival of the workers through the first seven months of the strike. The strike concluded when, at the end of nine months, the owners gave in to most of the workers' demands for change.*

**Ybor City: The Making of a Landmark Town**

Electricity, appliances, fur coats, and fancy, shorter dress styles were the rage. Grun's "Time Tables of History" records that in 1922 the "stock market boom began in America." Now, "Let the good times roll!" best explained the country's mood.[55]

But in Tampa, *tabaqueros* felt squeezed. Because of strong factory competition *patrones* watched their labor costs closely. On April 16, the CMIU ordered 6,400 workers to go on strike. *Patrones* in turn, responded with a lockout. They closed the and locked the doors of their factories. Tragically, other workers were already out of work. The early era of plentiful work for all Latins was over. Work availability would now ebb and flow according to laws of supply and demand.

By the end of the nine months strike in 1920, the Cigar Manufacturer International Union capitulated. The *patrones*, now organized into The Clear Havana Cigar Manufacturers Association (the Trust). Additionally, with the Tampa establishment's backing, *patrones* secured an open shop and forced work rules governed solely by the wishes of the cigar Trust. The installation of cigarmaking machines would now be brought in as needed. The machines, of course, replaced many of the "rollers." The Cartabón (Uniform Wage Scale) was out.

Also eliminated was the *lector* institution, which was so often accused of fostering radical ideas. Thus, *lectores* were no longer permitted in the factories, except for a few who were allowed back to read until finally dismissed in 1931, on the occasion of another major strike. Some, also, would actually enter the factory simply as ordinary *tabaqueros* and a few left for other cigar towns. Many Cubans went back to Havana, Key West, New York, or Philadelphia. *Tabaqueros* in Tampa were exhausted and dismayed.

In America, cigars were actually manufactured in most of the states, though some 60 to 65 percent were made in six states—New York, Pennsylvania, Illinois, Wisconsin, Massachusetts, and Florida. New York was the heaviest producer. Available data indicates that during 1929-1937, Florida had, by far, the fewest number of factories of the above stated six.[56] Florida was known for the quality of its cigars and not for the volume it produced, and quality, not quantity, was the standard for the Tampa Bay area as well. Utilizing tobacco from the Vuelta Abajo region of Pinar del Rio in Cuba, Tampa was considered the "fine cigar capital of the United States." This, too, Tampa owed to Don Vicente Martínez Ybor, for long ago in the nineteenth century he had elected, contrary to other Cuban manufacturers, to manufacture his cigars from the tobacco harvest of the above cited region. His quality cigars were suddenly in great demand in Cuba, as well as in America and Europe. When later he manufactured cigars in Key West, New York, Key West (again) and finally in Ybor City (in that order) he remained faithful to the Vuelta Abajo region of Pinar del Rio province in Cuba as his source.

With the arrival of the nine month strike, some *tabaqueros* left the industry altogether. Competition between the factories both here and in the rest of the states, the fast-increasing cigarette production, and the growing need for *patrones* to control labor production via machines, all caused many to elect other ways of earning a living aside from making cigars. Chief among these were Spaniards and many Italians. In looking for new alternatives, neither restricted themselves to Ybor, Palmetto, and West Tampa. Tampa, the distant suburbs, farmlands, nearby towns, and beaches were targets. The rush of Americans to the Bay area, the growth of the Hyde Park area, the forthcoming arrival in 1924 of a baron of land development, D. P. Davis, and other large developers opened up new centers of commerce and opportunities.

By now many well-positioned factory workers moved north, across *La Michiga*, now Columbus Drive. A greater Ybor was in the making. From Nebraska on the west and almost 22nd Street on the east, Ybor City was moving up to 19th Avenue, to 21st Avenue, then to 26th Avenue, and a few pioneers even up to Buffalo Avenue, now Martin Luther King Jr. Boulevard, along a thin 15th Street spine. By the Depression years the 15th Street spine would fill out coming south to *La Michiga*, roughly in a triangular manner. Mostly Spaniards built homes from Ybor Street to the west. To the east of Ybor Street, the neighborhoods were heavily Italian. Some Spanish and Italian families were interspersed in the center, and indeed, one could find Italians or Spaniards in any area, though this was not the norm. Often the scattered homes were families where Spaniards and Italians had intermarried, and intermarried Spaniards and Cubans were also sprinkled into all these areas, together with some Cuban households. But again, this did not change the essential cohesiveness of the respective areas. The area from 21st to 19th Avenue and from 15th east through Ybor Street was called "*el barrio Candamo*," because many of the residents in that area were from the Asturian villages of Aces, Granelos, and others.[57]

*Palm Avenue, shown above in the 1920s, was a well-kept, tree-lined street of largely Spanish residents near the Centro Asturiano. Another predominantly Spanish area, shown below, was near the Centro Asturiano Hospital between Michigan Avenue (now Columbus Drive) and the hospital to the north, and west of 14th Street to Nebraska. The homes fronted on paved streets with curbs and sidewalks on both sides. Alleys behind the houses provided convenient access. Groceries and cafés were within walking distance, and the streets were safe. Homes like these were also typical of the expanded Italian areas across Michigan Avenue to the north. The movement across Michigan Avenue began just prior to 1920 as the Ybor factories prospered.*
C. E. Harner.

The dynamics of the economy moved rapidly. In the cigar world of Tampa, with the defeat of the CMIU, labor peace returned to the cigar industry and workers returned to factories. Local stability and an exuberant post-World War I national economy meant that sales of quality cigars increased and Ybor again began to prosper. The demand for quality cigars boosted sales for the factories that utilized Cuban tobacco for handmade cigars. Suddenly, leaf selectors, binders, rollers, finished cigar selectors, banders, cellophane wrappers, and even unskilled laborers were again in demand. Not until the Depression would there be great concerns about unemployment in Ybor City, even though cigarette consumption per capita more than doubled from 1920 to 1930. The

**Ybor City: The Making of a Landmark Town**

The new homes were a substantial upgrade from the *cañon* (shotgun houses) and various other standard smaller designs of early worker housing in the central core. Many of the new wooden homes in the Spanish areas across *La Míchiga* were larger, single-story houses in the range of one thousand to fourteen hundred square feet, and they were similar in size and design to wooden homes in the Seminole Heights area of Tampa at the time. A few of the one-floor houses exceeded this size in square feet, and the occasional two-story home easily picked up more footage. Certainly, the area along a three- to four-block corridor east of Nebraska was exceptional in both design and quality. Of course, the amenities originally included in the Gavino Gutierrez platting of early Ybor (see page 52) were continued. These were curbs, paved streets, common alleys, and sidewalks. That Charlie Wall, wealthy and prominent Bolita kingpin, lived at the corner of 17th Avenue and 13th Street for years testifies to the quality of housing in that part of town, but his elected profession and sudden death degraded the exemplary character of this Spanish neighborhood.

The Spaniards' expansion across *La Míchiga* was inevitable. By the 1920s many new families were being formed. Many of the young Spaniards who had come from Cuba at the turn of the century already lived in the Spanish neighborhood. They were by now young married men. Their years of enjoying higher factory wages and their preferred status in key factory positions gave Spaniards a substantial advantage as to the future prospects, such as a young man could wish for. Most of the better housing was being constructed outside the original Ybor City area. The location on the east side of the river appealed to many. The drive along Palm Avenue west to the river and to Michigan Avenue became very popular, as was the Michigan strip from the Hillsborough River east to Florida Avenue.

Better housing was also sought out by others who could afford to "move up"—the office staff, salesmen, accountants, floor supervisors, manufacturing floor foremen, and the various selectors, all of whom enjoyed higher wages and stable jobs. High volume producers among the rollers — the final makers of the cigars — also earned substantially higher take-home pay than average rollers. This stable employment allowed many *tabaqueros* — whether Spanish, Italian, or Cuban — to show their new brides their aspirations for a better new or expected style of life in the future. These newer housing areas thus increased in density, and were the preferred ones in the early decades of the twentieth century.

While the Italians had arrived in Ybor City a few years later than the Spanish and Cubans, their dedication to work, their adaptability, and their early small business start-ups soon provided their families with a strong foothold for later growth. Many of the original Italians had, as stated earlier, located on the eastern and southern fringes of Ybor. This was referred to as "Little Italy," and extended from approximately 17th or 18th Street to perhaps 26th Street. From 23rd Street east, the homes thinned out quickly, since many families farmed from one to three vacant lots next to their homes. Italians also located south of La Sétima from approximately 18th Street to about 26th Street. Most were in neighborhoods south to about 4th Avenue. South of that, the residential areas gave way to industry, such as the German-owned cigar box factory along 2nd Avenue and 21st Street, Eagle Roofing, and other commercial operations that covered a good part of the section south to the railroad where Adamo Drive today is located. A popular Italian named Maraune farmed the tract from 22nd Street to the port waters (Ybor Channel) along the south side of today's Adamo. Many families walked over there to buy *giri, escarolla, cucuzza,* and other vegetables.

Many Italian families saw their futures across *La Michiga* in the early '20s. They also built modern houses in the area from 17th to 20th Streets. From *La Michiga* south to perhaps 12th Avenue and between 22nd and 24th Streets there were exceptionally attractive homes for several decades. On Michigan Avenue near 24th Street, Salvatore Greco had his first store. He was the founder of the huge Kash n' Karry supermarket chain.

The thin strip along 12th Avenue between 16th and 21st Streets also featured excellent housing. This was the area known as *La Pequeña Asturias*, "Little Asturias," perhaps the most central part of the old core residential area. Twelfth Avenue contained many two-story buildings that housed cafés, pharmacies, groceries, and other businesses. This was a very solid commercial area. On this avenue, between 16th and 17th Streets were well-built white frame houses, typical of homes constructed in the late 1910s and 1920s beyond Michigan Avenue. Across the street was the Wolff Mission School. Up to the Spanish Civil War, many fathers and mothers—my parents included—dropped their children off there during working hours. Parts of the school had once been within the grounds of Don Vicente Martínez Ybor's *Quinta* estate.

Another desirable area ran west on what is today Palm Avenue, leading to and surrounding Centro Asturiano west of Nebraska.[58] The area immediately north of Michigan Avenue, west of 17th Street and going all the way west to Nebraska was, with a few exceptions, Spanish. It extended north to 19th Avenue, then east and northeasterly to 12th Street. Some Cubans with stable roots in Ybor City also moved to the near north. A number of Cubans settled between 15th Street and Orange Grove School and concentrated in many other pockets as well. It must be remembered that many Cubans had elected to maintain job mobility in the early years. Those who stayed in Ybor and grew early roots had a more stable and prosperous life style, often reflected by their housing. Thus, gradually a number of Cuban families moved within some of the Spanish areas. Below (south) of *La Michiga*, Cubans had settled into some of the areas west of 15th Street going as far as Nebraska along 10th Avenue through 15th Avenue, sharing some areas with Spaniards. Within that large space one small area was known as *El Bataclán*. It included three Cuban-type concrete homes rented by low income tenants. Cubans also lived below Michigan Avenue to 19th Street, between 15th and 18th Streets.

By the mid '20s, the demand for housing increased and real estate activity throughout Tampa rose sharply. Suburbs like Temple Terrace were building up, and D. P. Davis in 1924 had just begun the development of Davis Islands from land mostly dredged from the surrounding bay. The boom that had "started and centered around Miami . . . had attracted swarms of tourists, speculators and investors. . . . a frenzied storm of buying and selling of land, that was accompanied by widespread land speculation, followed by surging prices and values in property. Miami had boomed into a real estate crazed metropolis."[59] The rest of Florida and much of the nation copied what they observed. Reporting on the 1924 annual convention of the National Association of Real Estate Guards in Washington, D.C., the *Tribune* wrote that "Tampa received more first class and desirable publicity than any other city represented at the gathering."[60]

Charles A. Brown and Mary J. Brown, in their book, *Bayshore, Boulevard of Dreams* explain that: "by late fall of 1921, the Florida boom was underway, and nothing could stop it—not even a hurricane. Businessmen were getting rich quick."[61]

On La Sétima, Jewish and Latin merchants again prospered. Ybor's shoppers didn't include only Latins. Rural "Americanos" or "Crackers" came for

miles from Dade City, Mango, the Lutz area, Gary and other places. Much country wear — overalls, heavy shoes, boots, dresses and much more were available in the Jewish shops on the eastern side of La Sétima. One easily remembers Louie's Department Store, Buchman's Department Store, Weissman clothing store, and others on the north side of the street past Cuervo's café on 18th Street.

In 1925 the beautiful Centro Asturiano broke ground for what, in that period, was undoubtedly the most elegant and up-to-date medical facility in Tampa and possibly in the state: *El Sanatorio del Centro Asturiano.* Located on 21st Avenue and 13th Street, next to a huge, community water tank, it faced a relatively new and upbeat Spanish community. The homes surrounding it were a step up from the inner town's older housing. Many had St. Augustine grass lawns, trimmed bushes, flowers, and some occasional fruit trees. The houses were relatively new and beautifully painted. This was now a solid middle income neighborhood, very orderly and safe.

The site selection for *El Sanatorio del Centro Asturiano* was no doubt made because of the outward move of Spaniards to that area. Another factor must have been the fact that a very fine institution, the Old Peoples Home, had been constructed just next door but a few years earlier. It catered to the finest of the old Anglo families of Tampa. This location, then, seemed to be ideal. And, in fact, it proved to be for the next six decades, until this beautiful Centro Asturiano Hospital closed. (As of February 1998, only the beautiful centerpiece of this historic building remained. The rest of the large facility had been bulldozed). The equally well-equipped and beautiful facility on Bayshore Boulevard, the Centro Español Hospital, would in time be the first to be closed and relocated to northern West Tampa.[62]

With factories recovering from the Nine Month Strike and employment growing fast, some of the better-off families sent what their first sons or daughters to college. Latins were great believers in higher education, but in the early '20s very few were of college age.

On a national level, cigar production for the first half of the decade had decreased 24 percent while cigarettes had increased 66 percent.[63] While this data was being observed by the Cigar Manufacturing Association, the average *tabaquero* was not necessarily conscious of it. In Ybor City local factories were again busy, now unimpeded by a defeated CMIU union. Jobs and disposable income grew overnight. The population of Tampa went from 51,608 in 1920 to 94,746 by the mid-decade, an increase of 83.5 percent. This percentage increase would not be equaled again.

The work of entrepreneurs like Alfred R. Swann and Eugene Holtsinger in developing the framework for construction of the early Bayshore Boulevard, the earlier work and influence of Chester Chapin, and the foresight of George Baldwin and attorney Peter O. Knight, both of the Tampa Electric Co., and others, set the pace for much of lower Tampa's development.[64] The underpinning—the cigar money banked in the downtown banks— was again growing stronger, and for the next few years would help the overall growth of Tampa. Still, the heavy increase in population, due to the draw of great climate, the wider grid being developed in South Tampa and to the near north, the 1924 commencement of Davis Islands, the emergence of Temple Terrace's desirable housing, and the increase in regional businesses such as agriculture, particularly citrus growing—all these—provided the basis for the good times ahead.

The "Roaring '20s" had arrived, and throughout the country people seemed content to "let the good times roll!" In Ybor City the illusions of the decade had begun to take hold.

By the turn of the century, Ybor City outpaced Tampa in population, employment opportunity, cultural activities, and economic development. This 1910 photograph shows the paving of its streets with brick. FSA.

This photo about 1900 shows water pipes being installed in Ybor City. The Ramirez Building (right) was built in 1898. Marcos Mesa Fruit and Vegetable Store is on the left. ARSENIO M. SANCHEZ.

Merchants Isidor Kaunitz and Max Argintar standing outside El Sombrero Blanco, circa 1903-1907. FSA.

A view from a balcony looking east on La Sétima. THCPLS.

This building on the southwest corner of 15th Street and 8th Avenue was taken in the 1920s. The familiar sight of laundry drying on the second story balcony is appropriate for a building that later housed El Encanto Cleaners. THCPLS.

In this photo from about 1915, Don Gavino Gutiérrez stands with friends at Spanish Park, which was known as "La Finea de Gutiérrez," prior to his leaving for a trip around the world. Left to right are Simon Gonzalez, general manager of the Sanchez & Haya Tobacco factory; George Stecker, president of the German Center and executive officer of Tampa Box Company; Gutiérrez; Mrs. Jesusa Torres, wife of Laureano Torres, general manager of the Regensberg Factory and for many years president of Centro Asturiano; and William H. Frecker, former mayor of Tampa. TONY PIZZO/LA GACETA.



**Ybor City: The Making of a Landmark Town**

*M. Perez Cigar Co. in Ybor City was located at 2411 19th Street. This photograph was taken in 1901.* THCPLS.

*Workers at the small La Flora Factory on 20th Street illustrate the mix of workers in a "buckeye" shop before the child labor law was enacted in 1916. Boys clearly under fourteen years old form a substantial part of the work force.*

**Chapter 3 • Clear Cigar Capital and the Start of the Golden Years: 1900-1925**

*The Gonzalez & Sanchez Company in Ybor City, 1915.* THCPLS.

*The Jose Arango factory building on 15th Street about 1933.*

*The southwest corner of La Sétima and La Calle Quince (15th Street) was once the site of Sanchez y Haya's first factory, with El Cafetín, a U.S. post office, and later the Blue Ribbon Grocery with other well-known venues on the other corners.*

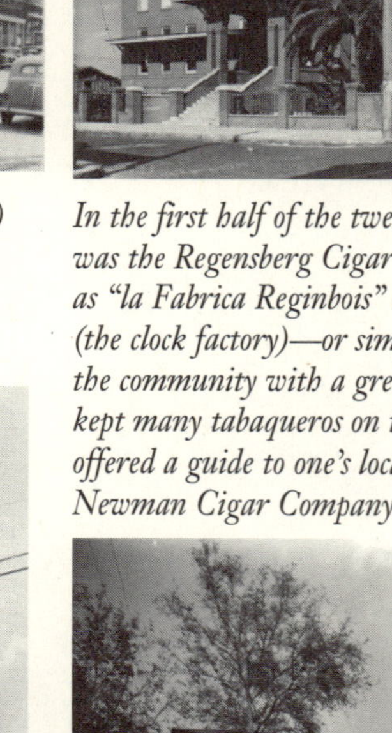

*In the first half of the twentieth century, this factory was the Regensberg Cigar Company. It was known as "la Fabrica Reginbois" or "la Fabrica del Reloj" (the clock factory)—or simply "El Reloj." It provided the community with a great service, since the clock kept many tabaqueros on time, and the tall tower offered a guide to one's location. Today it is the J. C. Newman Cigar Company.*

*In 1927-29 the Corral Wodiska factory relocated from its older wooden factory on 14th Street and Michigan Avenue to this new facility. The new building at 1306 19th Street was a modern brick structure and one of Ybor City's larger factories.*

*The factory of Arguelles, Lopez, and Company at 2511 21st Street was photographed by the Burgert Brothers about 1920.* USFSCL.



**Ybor City: The Making of a Landmark Town**

*The Perfecto Garcia Factory in 1915 (left) and in 1919 (right). The firm was established in 1904 by Garcia and his brothers.*

*Emilio Pons originally built this pioneer wooden factory building, later home to La Floridana cigars.*

*The F. Lozano Son & Co. factory at 4th Avenue and 21st Street.*

*L. Golovine Havana Cigars Factory in 1923.*

*The Haya Cigar Factory at 2311 18th Street.* USFSCL.

*The Hav-A-Tampa Cigar Factory in the 1920s.*

*The Charles the Great Factory building dates from 1895.*

*The Pancho Arango Cigar Factory in 1919. It has been renovated for use as offices for Corral Wodiska.*

*Three Friends Cigar Factory (Buckeye) with Mims Transfer Co. wagons at East Scott Street.*

*Wenger Cigar Factory in 1930.*

*The Cyrilla Cigar Factory was located on 15th Street and 11th Avenue. USFSCL.*

*The Cuesta Rey Cigar Company at 1901 North 13th Street. USFSCL.*

*The Celso Cigar Company in 1946 operated in the Manuel Katz Building at 2108 La Sétima.*

*The Carl Upmann Cigar Factory in 1936.*

*Corral Wodiska & Company (Bering Cigars) at 2612 14th Street. USFSCL.*

**Ybor City: The Making of a Landmark Town**

*A lector (on wall at right between the second and third windows from front) reads to cigar workers at the Corral Wodiska & Co. Factory #2 in this Burgert Brothers photograph taken on August 27, 1929. While lectores were laid off in 1921, some were eventually allowed back into factories until 1931, when the institution was finally discontinued. Notice that many of the employees are wearing the flat straw hats known as sombreros de pajita that were especially popular among the Spaniards, often worn with ties or bow ties. Black umbrellas and some straw hats are neatly hanging along the wall at left. Other workers here have caps or eyeshades, and all are well-dressed. The high-volume, quality cigar producers—known as "de los largos" or "de los buenos"—took great pride in their work of making fine cigars for a living, and they were highly respected in the larger community, Cubans, Spaniards, and Italians alike.*

*Cigarmakers are hand-rolling cigars in the Cuesta Rey Cigar Factory on North Howard Avenue in West Tampa in this photograph taken circa 1930. The lector is Jose Rubio. Standing to the right is the foreman, Ramon Fernandez Rey, who was also president of the Centro Español.* USFSCL.



**Chapter 3 · Clear Cigar Capital and the Start of the Golden Years: 1900-1925**

# The Making of Ybor City Cigars

*Ybor City became famous for the art of its handmade cigars. In the painting below, using tobacco pigments, artist Arnold Martinez shows how the leaf is rolled. A wooden cigar mold is at the worker's right. Other aspects of the process are illustrated on the next few pages.* ARNOLD MARTINEZ.

Cuban tobacco in bales from Havana.

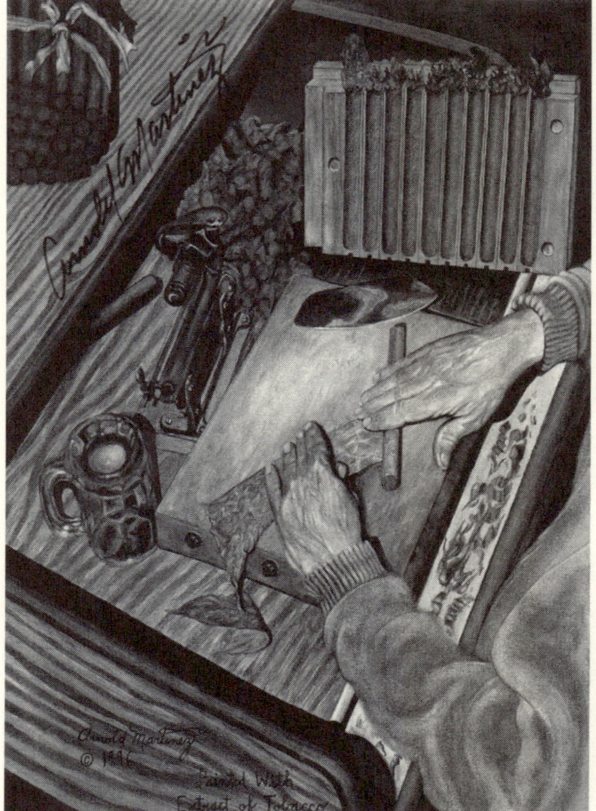

Drying tobacco.

Selectors sorting tobacco leaves for wrappers at the Cuesta Rey Factory.

This photograph shows the sorting process in a factory context. Good natural light from the numerous large windows provided favorable working conditions for inspecting the leaves.

**Ybor City: The Making of a Landmark Town**

*Selecting tobacco requires careful attention.*

*Preparing tobacco leaves*

*Sorting tobacco by color and quality.*

*A work station for a single cigar roller, used in "Buckeye" shops.*

*Sorting tobacco leaves on the main floor of a large factory.*

*Gathering tobacco for filler.*

**Chapter 3 · Clear Cigar Capital and the Start of the Golden Years: 1900-1925**

# The Process of Making Cigars in Ybor City

The secret of success for cigarmaking in Ybor City involved the careful execution of each stage in a process. Once strippers had removed the stems from tobacco leaves, selectors would sort the leaves by color, texture, and maturity. Each cigarmaker then would take the correct amount of filler in the palm of his hand and roll it into shape, placing it within a cigar press, where it remained for a half-hour or 45 minutes. Then the cigarmaker would place it within a final wrappper, shaping it with a chaveta, a blade in the shape of a half moon. A worker would average from 1,000 to 1,300 cigars per week.

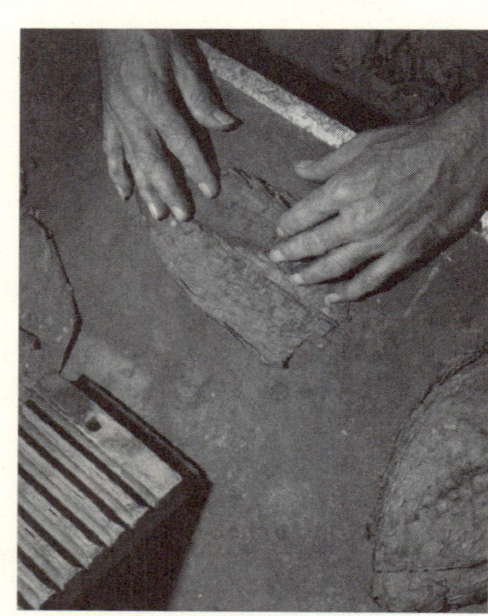

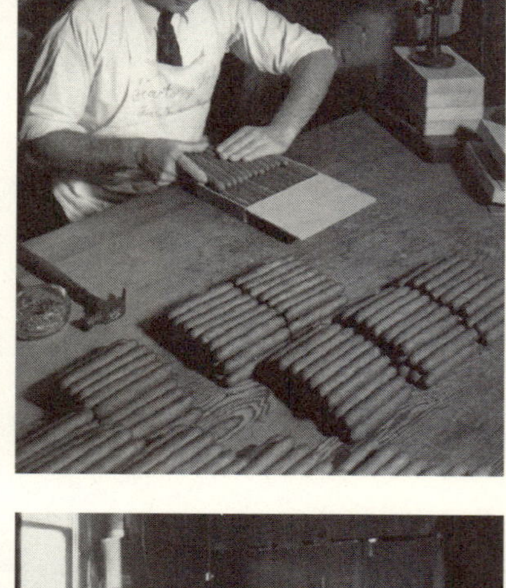

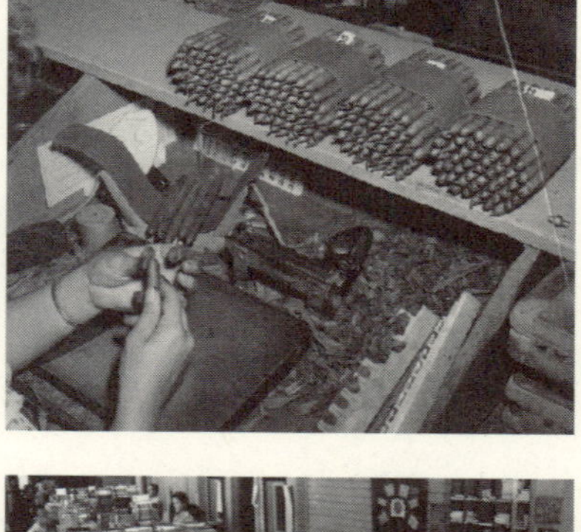

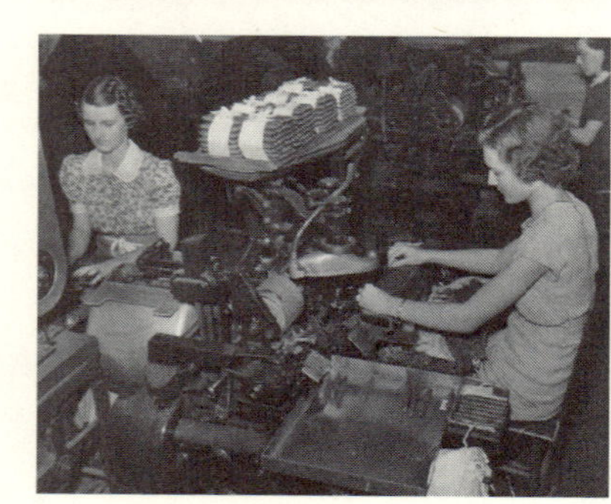

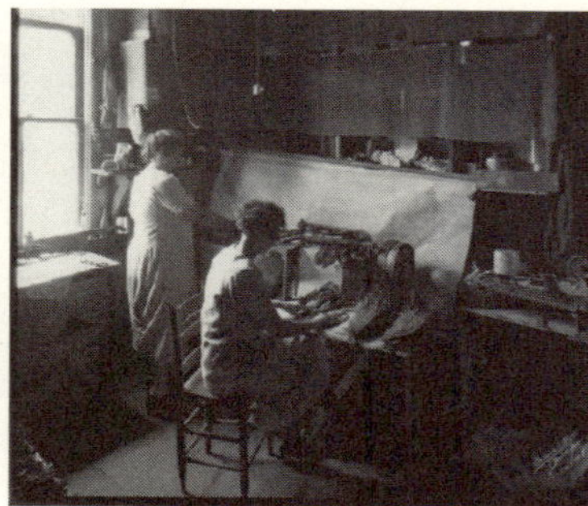

**Ybor City: The Making of a Landmark Town**

*Workers rolling cigars.*

*Women rolling cigars.*

*Finishing cigars.*

*Roller at bench.*

*Packing Rothschilds Extra Fine cigars.*

*Applying bands to cigars at Sanchez and Haya.*

**Chapter 3 • Clear Cigar Capital and the Start of the Golden Years: 1900-1925**

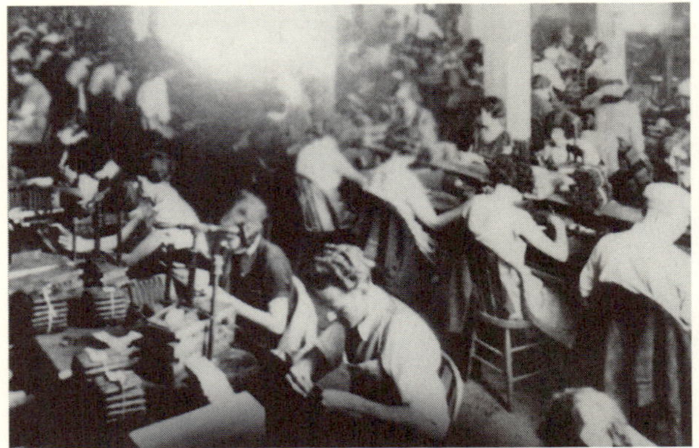

*Women rolling cigars.*

After each cigar is rolled into shape, it is sealed at the smoking end, or "head" end, with a little tobacco patch and vegetable glue. The cigarmaker then cuts the head to size with his cutter. A color grader sorts finished cigars by the shade of their tobacco, from light to dark, the darker leaves being considered the strongest and finest. Finally, packers place them in boxes, from left to right, with their best sides showing. Banders remove each cigar to put the company's band around its face and replace it carefully, showing it to best advantage. The boxes are sealed and stacked for shipment.

*Packing boxes with finished cigars*

*Sorting cigars by color*

*Packing boxes at Cuesta Rey.*

*Women packing Swann Cigars.*

**Ybor City: The Making of a Landmark Town**

*Women were increasingly operating machines as the handmade cigar factories experienced pressure from automated production methods.*

*Women making boxes inside the Jut Box Factory.*

*This worker stacking boxes begins to convey the monumental scale of Ybor City's productivity.*

**Chapter 3 · Clear Cigar Capital and the Start of the Golden Years: 1900-1925**

*The first Italian Club building opened October 11, 1912, built at a cost of $60,000. It stood across the street from the present building. It was destroyed by fire in 1914.* USFSCL, TONY PIZZO COLLECTION.

*The new L'Unione Italiana Club building, dedicated in 1918, was centrally located on 18th Street and La Sétima. Architects M. Leo Elliot and B. C. Bonfoey, who also designed the Cuban Club and the Tampa City Hall, planned it to include a theatre with an auditorium and balcony for opera performances, a library, cantina, bowling alley, recreational rooms, and even a large dance floor on the top story. Outside they used a neoclassical style with Corinthian columns, small balconies with railings, and arched as well as transom windows.* THCPLS.

*This early photo of the Italian Club Cantina was likely taken not too long after the building was completed in 1918. By the early 1920s a bar was installed along the back wall where the billiard tables stand in this photo, and the tile floor is not yet installed here.* L'UNIONE ITALIANA.

128

*During the 1930s and 1940s the Italian Club was home to a movie house called the Broadway Theatre, shown here in 1936.* USFSCL.

*On the stage of Centro Asturiano in 1923.*

*This 1919 Burgert Brothers photo (right) documents the great fire that destroyed much of Ybor City. The impact on electrical infrastructure is especially evident. The detail (above) draws attention to the apparell and expressions of police and spectators.* USFSCL.

*The town's resilience can be read in the dramatic contrasts a decade after the fire. Members and dancers at Centro Asturiano in 1928 (left) and on the steps of the club building in the 1930s.*

**Chapter 3 · Clear Cigar Capital and the Start of the Golden Years: 1900-1925**

*Ybor City Novelty Works in 1926.*

*El Malecon sold general merchandise at 1417 La Sétima. The interior is shown here in 1905 with (from left) Federico Toledo, Charlie Carrera, Prisciliano Carrera, and Pancho Carrera.* ERNIE CARRERA/LA GACETA.

*An exterior view of El Malecon, located in the 1300 block, facing La Sétima.*

*The interior of Las Novedades Café in 1929.*

*The Red Star Department Store.*

*La Tropical in 1936.*

*The Mecca Cafe at 1701 La Sétima in 1929 with a Panadaria la Joven Francesa bakery delivery truck parked in front.* THCPLS.

**Ybor City: The Making of a Landmark Town**

*Looking west on La Sétima between 16th and 17th Streets, the popular Kress store is on the right. The autos of the day, with smaller size and slower speeds, perfectly suited the scale and pace of the community. Trolleys would stop, pick up speed in mid-block, and slow again by block's end. There was rarely a fender scratch or accident. USFSCL.*

*This Burgert Brothers photo of La Sétima, circa 1930s, shows Bright's Shoe Store at 1614 and Demmi Napoli and Company at 1616 in the S. Dekle Building next door to Kress. USFSCL.*

*Cherry Blossoms and Orange Squeeze sodas were produced in Ybor City at the Angelo Puleo soda works, located on the southwest corner of 9th Avenue and 23rd Street. The most popular drink was "Gazosa," (or "Gasiosa") an early version of Sprite or 7-up that was especially popular with the Italian community. The Gasiosa bottles were capped with an old-fashioned wire and ceramic top. USFSCL.*

*The Burgert Studio was located on La Sétima between 15th and 16th Streets in 1919. The three-story Mayo Building can be seen on the left, with a movie house downstairs and apartments upstairs. On the right was the dry goods store of Isador Kaunitz, a Jewish merchant from Romania. Their sign proclaims "La Primera Fotografia de Ybor"—the first photographers of Ybor City. USFSCL.*

*The lively spirit of the era is captured in this Burgert Brothers photograph of diners eating outdoors along the colonnade of El Pasaje on October 20, 1928. The Great Depression would soon change the country's mood and the tempo of life in Ybor City.* USFSCL.

# CHAPTER 4
## Through Good Times, Depression, and War: 1925-1950

### The Boom Years: 1925-1929

The birth of new technologies from World War I fueled a great demand for better goods and services in the second half of the 1920s. Returning doughboys had had enough to do with war. They wished to find jobs, buy land, win brides, and have children. They simply wanted to get started with a better life. They had seen so much overseas. A song of the period said, "How're you gonna keep them down on the farm after they've seen Par-ee." Time was slipping away. Their savings and initial jobs created a new surge of demand for goods. It stirred the economy. America could feel the cycle of supply and demand change.[1]

Henry Ford's marvel, the assembly line, had caught on. It made the price of goods much more affordable. Prices were tumbling on high demand items. While still not very sophisticated, the industrial processes were changing. A new engineering and management discipline called "industrial engineering" was weaving its way through the labyrinth of industrial methodology and processes. Giants in this conversion were Henry L. Gantt, Frederick W. Taylor, and Frank and Lillian Gilbreth. (The 1950 movie *Cheaper by the Dozen* was based on the experiences of the Gilbreths, adapted from a book written by two of their twelve children). Early improvements in manufacturing efficiency and simplification were reducing factory costs.[2]

Automobiles, radios, talking movies, freezers, improved hardware and materials—all these and more were coming into existence. Heavy industry was "cranking out" goods. Factories were hiring more workers. Thanks to assembly lines, prices plummeted on goods previously out of the reach of the common man. In turn, with this came the good life, the easy life, the unfettered life. There was a national euphoria—a new beginning—even as many families grieved the loss of sons or daughters. It was all here: a few years of dreams . . . and much illusion.

The "Roaring '20s" was now in full swing "as a 'devil may care' era, complete with sheiks and flappers, bare legs and strapped bosoms, races (speed was king!), Ku Klux Klan chasing after militants and radicals spawned by the Bolshevik revolution, bathtub gin mooching—a spinoff of the 'Noble Experiment' against booze—Al Capone, rum running and bootlegging." All this and more marked the decade as garish and eccentric and brash.[3] In the Latin areas, the chic couples imitated what they saw in the movies: the Charleston, marathon dancing, short dresses, balloon popping, and more.

*This Tampa Times label includes a view of the H. B. Plant Hotel, now a National Historic Landmark building of the University of Tampa.*

Nor was Ybor City spared any of this. Elitists were occasionally seen in upscale locales with fur coats, fancy hats, and "devil may care" dresses. Some from the Anglo world frequented "El Dorado," a gambling club in the heart of Ybor City, just under a very respected boarding house on the top floor. From the outside it seemed as unexciting as a small, rectangular brick building could look (see the photos on the bottom of page 146). But inside, avant-garde women and style-setters puffed cigarettes at the ends of long, silver holders and whisked in and out at all hours of the night. Not to be passed over, cigar factory women in Ybor City sported Clara Bow haircuts, obtained at Paco Vinagre's salon on 15th Street. It was the rage! In a period photo taken on the steps the Centro Asturiano (below) one sees many of the young ladies sporting Clara Bow haircuts.[3a]

*Fotingos* (Fords), *Chivolocos* ("Crazy Goats"–Chevrolets), and Packards were now more affordable, and the narrow streets easily became congested, as on La Sétima at both 15th and 22nd Streets. Now distance was no object. Some families took early morning trips to "*La playa*," at Palmetto Beach, more than a mile beyond the Columbia Restaurant. Autos tooted and kids waved at sassy yellow trolleys loaded with *tabaqueros*, and continued to the beach,

*Nearly 200 young people of the "Juventud Entusiasta" gathered on the front steps of the Centro Asturiano building for this photo in March 1928. Those identified in the front row are Velia Cuervo Cueto, Clarita Cigarran Garcia, Violeta Alvarez Tamargo, Perla Alvarez Garcia, Raquel Cabla, Delores Nuñez, Violeta Fueyo Trafficante, and Evelyn Godinet. Second row: Grace Alvarez Cabeza, Graciela Fernandez, Dalia Gonzalez Fernandez, Gus Ayala, Ramiro Tamargo, Lizzie Noriega, Dalia Fueyo Reina, and Augusto Garcia. Third row: Ralph Godinet, Manuel Melendi, and Armando Blain. Standing on the step's left arm rest: Mañito (El Cubano) Fernandez, Dr. Carlos Barbas, Antonio Garcia, and Johnny Corces. Seated on step's left arm rest: Domingo Pasaron, Maximo Gonzalez, and Ceferino Fernandez. Standing in front of the window: Daniel Alvarez and Gonzalo Garcia. Standing on the step's right arm rest: Nino Bode. Holding onto the right lamp post: Victor Garcia, Armando Diaz, and Manuel (Pichueto) Fernandez. Seated in front of the window: Evi Lopez. Others who were identified in the photo include Willie Diaz, Lalo Fernandez, Albertico Reyes, Emilio Solares, Frank Felitas, Chaval, Pilar Lodos, Alicia Lopez Fernandez, Paquita Diaz, and Delores Castro.* Louis H. Garcia and La Gaceta.



**Ybor City: The Making of a Landmark Town**

*A Rocky Point picnic, circa 1920. Estevan Pellón, "El Polaco," owner of El Cafetín, was in charge of the Cuban Club picnics to Rocky Point.*
MARGARITA PELLÓN; FTL.

just past the 22nd Street bridge. One saw a beehive of bathers in 1920s long swimsuits! Some also wore snug rubber caps to protect their hair. They swam in the bay waters on both sides of the road, though the north side better suited the bathers' taste. The slight exposure of the body was eye-popping! It was the '20s! Families enjoyed a swim in the warm waters of McKay Bay and headed back. But first they took their Cuban *café con leche* and *pan con mantequilla* from the few venders in tiny makeshift booths. As an alternative, fathers and sons would stop at Cuervo's, Los Helados de Ybor, or El Buen Gusto for Cuban coffee and bread. Others took refreshment at the Columbia, or perhaps Las Novedades. They were all convenient! Who needed more? Much of this was done before the fathers would go to work, as did my father.

At night families often returned to the water to witness a strange phenomenon—phosphoric lights that glistened as the wave caps crashed over the surface or along the shore. These were more visible on breezy nights.

At last, small children in rear rumble seats of the late-1920s cars would doze off as their families returned from such outings. With these new cars one could now dare visit friends in nearby communities—West Tampa, Palmetto Beach, the early Bayshore Boulevard, and more. Again, a

night stop at Brana's Garage on 15th Street was a treat. There, under the shadows of the Regensberg Cigar Factory clock and the Latin American Dry Cleaners across the way, we breathed deeply of the exotic gasoline smell. And on other occasions we children chewed stick gum, blew balloons, and sang our giddy versions of "Amapola," "Constantinople," or "My Blue Heaven."[4]

The good times included unforgettable Sunday picnics to Ballast Point and Rocky Point and other parks. A very popular businessman, *El Polaco*, arranged many Sunday picnic trips to Rocky Point. There he supplied food and beverages from his small store on the primitive but popular and festive site. On Saturday afternoons crowds of young girls and boys walked La Sétima. An *Españolito* (young Spaniard) might see a pretty Italian girl and become infatuated by an illusive glance, a hint of interest, or a distinctive facial feature, perhaps—and suddenly a romance bloomed.[5]

At the social clubs family members dutifully chaperoned young ladies at Sunday matinee dances. Girls preferred brothers for chaperones—these were easily distracted. But more than likely they were saddled with *abuelita* (grandma).

Meanwhile, the beautiful sounds of "La Vereda Tropical" spilled over the walls of the open Cuban Club patio on Saturday nights. Late pedestrians heard these lovely

135

and romantic strains. There, too, the girls were dutifully chaperoned. The decibels were modest and the harmonies melodious. Those who lived nearby were not offended—indeed, children and elders looked forward to sitting on porches and listening to the music. Neighborhood children pranced around, anxious for the time when they would be old enough to go. While most songs were Latin ones, the new top Hollywood and Broadway songs were sometimes played after sheet music became available. But Latin music was what it was all about! Those who knew how also did the "Charleston," complete with hand and leg shuffles. And ever so slowly the hemlines of dresses went up a bit.

Hand-cranked Victor Victrolas brought music into the home. Before Marconi and his glass tube radios, Victrolas offered much home music entertainment. The old records—Argentina Carlos Gardel's *tangos*, the *paso dobles* of Conchita Piquer, "Katarina," "Muddy Waters" (not the '80s one), "I Found a Million Dollar Baby at the Five and Ten Cent Store"—were all very popular. One heard these at the popular *casas baratas*, the old 5- and 10-cent stores—Silver's, Woolworth, and Kress. The records were played there as mothers shopped. Early Italian emotional and dramatic records were also popular in this period. There was a beautiful, intensely dramatic Italian record of a feud. In it a shot is fired and one of the singers is killed. A few hillbilly records were also played.[6]

The family celebration on New Year's Eve, aside from Christmas Eve and Day, was perhaps the most important celebration of the year in Ybor City. Some preferred to get an early supper at home and then go to the New Year's Eve dances sponsored by the social clubs. Young couples without children generally attended their particular club, as did the older couples with married children. Eating grapes at midnight was a very old Spanish custom many enjoyed. Also, many families waited until approximately 9 or 10 p.m. to have supper. This was especially true of families that had young children and old family members. Not every family patronized the club dances, preferring to celebrate in the home. Nor did children stay up that late except for Christmas Eve and perhaps New Year's Eve to greet the new year. For those special nights, many families invited relatives and celebrated at home.

As midnight approached everyone began to look at the clocks, adjusting them as needed, for the timing was critical. The man of the house would go to the bedroom and grasp a pistol, revolver, or rifle, and head to the porch or yard. At exactly twelve o'clock they began to fire their weapons in the air, in celebration of the new year. The cigar factories, in turn, began to blow their whistles, so that dozens of factory whistles were ringing in the air. Everyone listened for the peculiar sound of his own factory's whistle. Most could recognize several whistles, and occasionally arguments would ensue as to which factory a particular sound belonged to. Gunshots gradually tapered off. Factory whistles did not last over fifteen minutes.[7]

Meanwhile, Marconi's radio created a revolution in entertainment. Now even Havana was next door! The popular Cuban stations, *La Cadena Suarito* and *La Cadena*

*Many young people met and became acquainted in the restrained and formal atmosphere of an afternoon tea dance, captured in this view of a Sunday tea dance at the Centro Asturiano ballroom in the 1930s. Here young couples were properly chaperoned.* TONY PIZZO COLLECTION, USFSCL.



**Ybor City: The Making of a Landmark Town**

For lively dancing in the Roaring Twenties, the basement of Centro Asturiano clubhouse had a handsome lounge featuring what was thought to be the longest onyx (Mexican marble) bar in the world. It ran a full fifty feet along one wall. This 1927 photo shows a tango contest with a portion of the bar visible beneath the mirrors at the back. The basement also was equipped with a gymnasium and sauna baths. TONY PIZZO COLLECTION, USFSCL.

*Azul*, filled the homes with *danzones*, *boleros*, and even *décimas guajiras*—all types of Cuban music. Many were already familiar with *Diario de la Marina*, a conservative Cuban newspaper, or *La Bohemia*, a popular magazine,[8] but the radio brought the island closer for all of us.

After two to three years of work, the Centro Asturiano completed its brand new Sanatorium on Oct. 2, 1927. It was a very modern hospital incorporating nearly all the latest advances in medical treatment. The medical staff relied heavily on Cuban doctors from Havana and elsewhere. After some contentious situations involving the local medical association, Cuban doctors were allowed to practice at the Latin club hospitals. A few Italian, American, and Spanish doctors also practiced there. Soon, locals observed many tuberculosis patients in red robes sitting at the outdoor benches, sunning themselves. In the evenings one would hear the excruciating sounds of the mental patients coming out of the eastern, front windows of the building. Children enjoyed an evening walk to see *los locos* (the crazy ones). On occasion a very young child would run across the street, scared stiff by the sight and sound of a particular *loco*. (I grew up in the shadows of the hospital and watched them often.)

Movie houses were plentiful in Ybor by this time. Among these were the Rivoli, later followed by the Ritz Theatre; the Casino, on the main floor of the Centro Español; the Broadway at L'Unione Italiana; and the Garden Theater, at the southeast corner of 19th Avenue and Nebraska. Farther away, there was a theater on Nebraska, three doors north of Buffalo Avenue (now Martin Luther King Jr. Boulevard). For those whose family owned a *Fotingo* or a *Chivoloco* there was the Seminole Theater on Florida, almost due west of Hillsborough High School, where one saw such movies as the later *Blockade*, with Henry Fonda, about a simple peasant forced to take up arms during the Spanish Civil War.[9]

In greater Tampa, the pace of real estate activity was rapidly increasing. Thomas H. Meyer, in a *Sunland Tribune* article on Davis Islands, wrote: "Bolstering Tampa's fame was its booming economy. After its 'most successful winter' 1923-1924, Tampa ushered in the 'biggest and busiest six months' in its entire history . . . Bank clearings for the third quarter of 1924 were 33% greater than for the same quarter of 1923 . . . and September showed a 51 percent increase." Meyer describes pedestrians crowding the side-

*137*

Florida was experiencing a banner year in tourism. Miami and Tampa were both enjoying land booms. Tampa was blessed with relatively cheap land and it seemed that the area was ready and willing to excel in growth and prosperity. One lot that appeared on the tax roll for $300 in 1924 sold for $2,600 just a few years later. Property value increases of ten-fold or more were not unusual.[11]

What was happening on Davis Islands was, to some extent, happening elsewhere in Tampa, including the Latin areas. Loans were relatively easy to get. One bought land on credit and stocks on margin—little down—pay later! Speculators, investors, Realtors, and much of the general public invested in properties on both sides of Lafayette Street. People were reaching out for low cost land, which they would, in turn, rapidly resell. Much of this property was bought with a small down payment in expectation of quickly turning it over for a profit. A mountain of debts rested on a small layer of cash.

Soon, however, danger signs appeared; the very large Temple Terrace subdivision collapsed. It was situated far to the northeast of Tampa, bordered by the Hillsborough River on the east and south, at the extension of what is today Busch Boulevard. I was then all of about six years old, and I specifically remember riding out there with my father and asking him why all the weeds were so high by the recently paved streets, just past some new houses. He told me that something bad had happened to the project. That was late in 1927.

And on famed Davis Islands, the unflappable tycoon, Mr. Davis, who had worked so hard at the shaping of what was truly a magnificent subdivision for that period, must have concluded it was time to reevaluate his situation. His project was not completed and he was seriously in debt. With sales suddenly drastically reduced, he contemplated closing either his planned St. Augustine enterprise, Davis

*Davis Islands (above) were empty little clumps of land in Tampa Bay when D. P. Davis planned to ride the Florida land boom and develop them in 1924. By 1927 (below) he had dredged, cleared, and subdivided the land, but he and his plans disappeared. Soon weeds reclaimed many of the lots.* USFSCL.

walks of Tampa, and autos having to circle blocks several times to find a parking space.[10]

And in 1924, D. P. Davis filled the offshore mud flats of Hillsborough Bay with the help of five huge dredges, and converted that marshy mud into coveted real estate. It ranked as the most noteworthy island project in Florida and possibly in the country. Tampans marveled at his daring vision and his dynamic personality. His undaunted and rapid fire promotion of the Davis Islands project kept Tampa at the forefront of the local and national press.

138

Shores, or Davis Islands in Tampa, to be able to complete one of the two. He unexpectedly sold Davis Islands in September 1926 and left on a cruise to Europe the following month. However, Davis never disembarked at his destination, having apparently gone overboard during the trip, and was never seen again. The exact circumstances remain a mystery.[12]

In Tampa, the speculation in land and stocks continued unabated while the nation buried an idol, Rudolph Valentino. His glamorous lover, the silent film star Pola Negri, made a grand entrance at his funeral as she mourned. But who cared? Feel-good slogans were on everyone's lips: just "keep cool with Coolidge" or " let Herbert Hoover do it!" We hummed cheery and comforting songs: "You're the Cream in My Coffee" and "Button up Your Overcoat."

On that murky sea of illusions and false hopes the nation—and Ybor City—approached 1929.[13]

**Early Depression Years: 1929-1943**

The 1927 early "bust" due to land speculation had already revealed itself in Tampa as the two large subdivisions at Temple Terrace and Davis Islands went bankrupt. Still, much speculation continued. The public sneezed but continued frolicking. However, in October of 1929 the great stock market crash shattered any remaining illusions. Billions of dollars were lost. Depositors raced to take out their savings. Not all banks could cope with the great number of withdrawals.

In Tampa the Citizens Bank and Trust Co. and affiliate banks closed their doors. Others teetered. In Ybor City only John Grimaldi's Columbia Bank remained open. Expensive properties were suddenly worthless, but buyers had to continue making payments on them at a time when many were out of work. Bankruptcies and foreclosures multiplied and businesses closed. Suicide rates went up. The bitter 1929-30

*The Hav-A-Tampa factory was quick to take advantage of the new machines that could produce cigars cheaper and faster. As this photograph shows, they also changed the look of the workers, employing large numbers of non-Latin women who lacked expertise and experience, but who could be trained to perform the steps necessary to keep up with the pace of machines.* THCPLS.

winter quickly dissipated the unfettered optimism of the Boom years. The "Roaring '20s" were over, replaced by a Great Depression. Ready money could get you nearly anything at a bargain—but no one had much of it to spend. The Depression's fury would persist for years. In the cafés there were rumors of an occasional local suicide. To make matters worse, in Ybor City thousands were out of work. The country could not afford expensive, quality cigars.

Having defeated workers in the great strikes of 1920 and 1931, factory owners began to mechanize. Not all could convert overnight. They simply could not pay for expensive machines, train employees, and find ways to market the resulting lower quality products. Machine-made cigars were already normal fare for the great number of factories in six major producing states, not to speak of some forty other states with small production. Our factories could not easily adapt in the face of the sharp drop in demand and stiff competition from the other established cigar and the cigarette industries using machine production.

The Hav-A-Tampa Cigar Company factory on 22nd Street already made their cigars with machines. They were heavily

into it. Additionally, they employed non-Latin women, a further blow to Ybor City households. Mechanization proceeded feverishly, and by the beginning of the depression years this resulted in great job loss. Cheap cigars hurt the sales of better cigars. Thousands of *tabaqueros* were laid off. Between 1929 and 1931 seventeen of the larger factories closed their doors.

*La Sétima* was soon but a shadow of itself! Gone were the heavy family crowds vying for walking space on the avenue. Merchants faced very lean times. Store owners saw a huge drop in business. They watched their income and outlay closely, and reduced their stock levels. Belt tightening was the only recourse. In the confusion and misery of the economy, the coffee houses were the places to exchange information and learn of the latest factory happenings. However, even attendance at those institutions was down considerably.

*Tabaqueros*, with rare exceptions, paid their bills on payday each week. This was common practice. Interim daily purchases were customarily charged: "*Pongamelo en la lista* [place it on the charge list], *por favor*." Generally an ironclad agreement

sealed by word of honor, this custom wavered in the first few years of the Great Depression—particularly during the early months. A few grocery store owners came close to losing their stores on that account.

There were instances where single men just disappeared for Key West, New York, or other cities, especially during strikes or heavy layoffs. They were unable to pay. Yes, one heard of store owners complaining about such events. But there were many cases where, months later, the borrower would return, begin paying the bills, and resume normal trading. A few never returned.

Nationally, demand for quality handmade cigars had plummeted. In turn, demand for cheap nickel cigars rose. Chewing tobacco demand skyrocketed. In Ybor City brand names of chewing tobacco had been virtually unknown. But in the early Depression years, new brand names became as common as *cherutos*, *panetelas*, and *queens*. Non-smoked tobacco had been rare for Latin *tabaqueros*, but necessity fostered it. Some craftsmen, laborers, lower managers, and others resorted to chewing tobacco. Still, some tried it and reneged—



**Ybor City: The Making of a Landmark Town**

*These typical homes of cigar workers along 12th Avenue in the early 1930s show that the Depression years held little glamor and a good deal of grit for many ordinary families in Ybor City.*

a matter of pride. Many began to roll their own cigars at home.

The sale stands in Tampa were loaded with assorted varieties of cheap cigars, often made at *chinchales* (buckeyes). In Ybor City many *tabaqueros* switched to these low quality cigars.

I remember Father rolling an occasional cigar at home. The ones he made were not quite up to the standard smooth look, but they seemed to smoke well enough. There was no quality leaf wrapper to finish them off professionally. But necessity is the mother of invention, and during the Depression it was necessary to find ways of making do. Father once tried a box of chewing tobacco, thinking he would attempt to savor it as a less expensive alternative to cigars, but he ended up throwing the box away. This ugly mass between the teeth was disgusting—to him and to Mother.

Ominously, also, the demand for cigarettes had increased heavily almost overnight, though their encroachment on the cigar market had started over a decade earlier. Among the most popular brands were Camel, Chesterfield, Old Gold, and Lucky Strike. A major reason for the very depressed cigar market was the sudden, dramatic increase in the smoking of these cigarettes. The depression years had an impact on everyone. Cigarette packs were seen all over Ybor. Even Father now began to smoke cigarettes.[15]

In early 1930 some boys and girls took sandwiches to school that had only sugar between the slices of bread. Others sprinkled salt, vinegar, and pepper on the bread, and nothing else! I did this myself at Orange Grove Grammar School in the early, worst months of the Depression. Still others bought *mata hambres* ("hunger killers") from a baker's leftover dough and jellies. In the 1934 to 1935 period at George Washington Jr. High School, I threw up many times from eating them. "*Ahi va el Neno!*" ("There goes *el Neno!*" ["the writer"]), they would say as I ran desperately to the rear of the building to vomit. With only a nickel in my pocket, this was often all I could buy. The availability of *mata hambres* lasted until about 1936.[16]

A woman was known to have cried coming back from the Del Monte grapefruit factory. Her hands were red from knife wounds and the severe winter cold. Her net wages after the cost of the knife



**Chapter 4 · Through Good Times, Depression, and War: 1925-1950**

were approximately thirty-five cents. Her husband vowed she would not return and multiplied his efforts at working the land.[16]

The sudden, intense, and unexpected depression caught many families by surprise. Many were not prepared for the intensity of the layoffs that eventually lasted many years.

Many area fathers and mothers showed great resourcefulness and drew on their parents' old country ways in order to keep food on the table. From Cuscaden Park to Buffalo Avenue, the open fields filled up with cows. Cuscaden Park suddenly had a surprising number of cows pasturing on it. Many Spaniards and Italians across Michigan Avenue (Columbus Drive) also acquired family cows. From these came milk, butter, *"leche cortada,"*

which was nothing else than yogurt, and a homemade cheese that resembled ricotta. This cheese was made in a large cheese cloth that very gradually filtered the liquids through the woven fabric and formed a layer of greenish looking scum surrounding the cheese cloth. In weeks the sour milk coagulated and turned to cheese. Mother made all of these dairy products herself.

Among our neighbors who owned cows in the area near 21st Avenue and 14th Street were Señores José Fernandez, Andres Lopez, La Señora Montañesa (a woman from Santander in the northern mountainous region of Spain), Señora Regina Garcia, Señores José Blanco, Jesus Lopez, and my father.

Having been a Realtor, Father managed to buy three houses and three extra lots on Lake Avenue, at the very depressed price of $1,000 for the total property. Soon we milked a cow and grew vegetables where St. Augustine grass had grown just two years earlier, in the Sanatorio del Centro Asturiano area. The extra lots on Lake Avenue now were filled with seedbeds and vegetable plots. After the first two months of planting, the garden supplied lettuce, tomatoes, carrots, escarole, green peppers, and collard greens for Spanish soups. Mango, avocado, lemon, and orange trees yielded considerable fruit. Chickens and turkeys supplied eggs and meat. And soon the land included six honey bee boxes and a haystack for the family cow, which produced milk from which came the butter, sour milk (yogurt), and ricotta-type cheese mentioned above. This is how Father and Mother coped. Spaniards in Ybor City remembered their families' farm ways of living and many put these practices into play. Except for the first few months, things improved rapidly.[17]

Each ethnic background offered something unique. A large number of Italians had ovens in their back yards for their daily bread, and, of course, pasta was a staple of their diets. Both Spaniards and Italians



142

*Here my father is making a haystack from hay cut from the overgrown fields on Davis Islands a year or so after Mr. Davis abandoned the project and sailed to Europe. The ground below the stack had just been turned over to prepare it for planting vegetables and fruit trees. This was just after we moved to Lake Avenue, between 15th and 16th Streets, from our house at 21st Avenue and 14th Street.*

*Mother waves to the camera (above) as my father displays a harvest of fresh honey. The blossoms from our citrus trees were ready made to help our bees thrive. We kept hives that supplied honey for sweet treats. Italians in the community also showed talent for growing, but in addition they had small bread ovens, made their own pasta, and even made wine. Cubans fished, grew tropical fruits, root plants, kept guineas (Guinea Hens), chickens, and other domestic animals. The Depression years had met their match in these Latins.*

*In this photograph, Mother displays a prize orange from one of our trees. After we moved to Lake Avenue we had some forty lime and orange trees with plenty of fruit for marketing. There were also mango and avocado trees.*

**Chapter 4 · Through Good Times, Depression, and War: 1925-1950**

were also known to hunt for meat. Americo Leto hunted rabbit or quail every Sunday morning, assuring his family more than just a plate of spaghetti, vegetables, eggs, milk, and fruit.

The Cubans raised chickens for eggs and also kept guinea hens. Some planted potatoes and yucca (a Cuban potato-like root vegetable). Many fished and crabbed in the bay. The 22nd Street Bridge over McKay Bay where we fished was often filled with people out to catch yellowtails, and others crabbed in boats or from the shore. An uncle and I once caught some one hundred and twenty-five yellowtails at the bridge on McKay Bay—all in just under two hours. Some peddled fish, vegetables, fruits, and delicacies. A few of the Cubans were known to have cows. Margarita's family on Lake Avenue, between 17th and 18th Streets, milked five cows and sold milk. Café con leche was a standby for all Latins, which soothed the early hungry moments.

Mango and avocado trees were particularly common in Cuban yards, as, indeed, they were in Spanish and Italian yards. Some Cubans returned to Key West or Havana or moved to New York or Philadelphia, where some cigar factories were still open.

Spaniards were known to make haystacks from grass in the southern end of Davis Islands, using long scythes. This grass grew on the land abandoned by Mr. Davis, whose project had folded up earlier. There was one person in greater Ybor City who planted forty lime trees and sold some of his fruit to restaurants and bars.

Spaniards also expanded the number of cooperative stores, such as *El Recurso* (The Recourse), which offered low prices to members and regular prices to others. *El Recurso* was a very popular place to chat. It was located on the corner of 15th Street at 21st Avenue, across from Cuscaden Park. These stores abounded in the late Twenties and early Thirties.[18]

In 1931, a move by *patrones* to lower wages resulted in a call to strike by the Tobacco Workers International Union (TWIU), widely regarded as a Communist-dominated union. Inspired by the Bolshevik revolution and winning a foothold in the northern industrial towns of America, Communists had wormed their way into the national labor movement. In Tampa, the TWIU had elbowed the Cigar Makers International Union (CMIU) out of the area. The CMIU was a more traditional unionist organization with fewer radical political dimensions. However, by the 1930s most *tabaqueros* were at TWIU's mercy. Many didn't understand the political subtleties. Still others were more in tune with the revolutionary spirit. Hunger often changes one's mind.[19]

Throughout the country socialism and communism were making inroads into America's labor organizations. The severe Depression, coupled with stagnating industrial cities, greatly aided this phenomenon. Communist support of existing union organizations and their committees was a way to win over workers' hearts. Ybor City, with its strong industrial base, was well-suited for the contests ahead. It had an ideal structure for union penetration—similar manufacturing methodol-

144

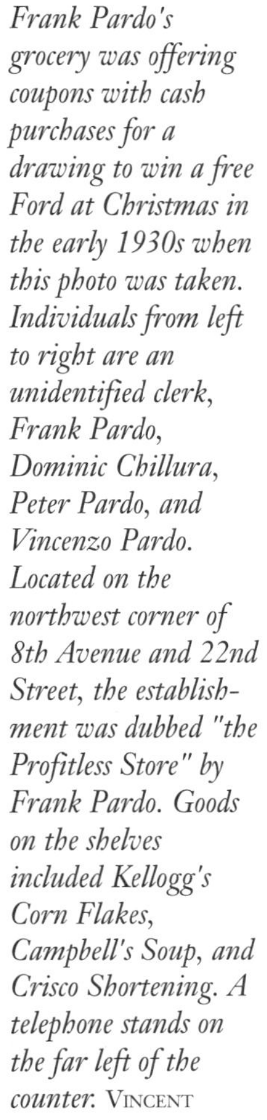

Frank Pardo's grocery was offering coupons with cash purchases for a drawing to win a free Ford at Christmas in the early 1930s when this photo was taken. Individuals from left to right are an unidentified clerk, Frank Pardo, Dominic Chillura, Peter Pardo, and Vincenzo Pardo. Located on the northwest corner of 8th Avenue and 22nd Street, the establishment was dubbed "the Profitless Store" by Frank Pardo. Goods on the shelves included Kellogg's Corn Flakes, Campbell's Soup, and Crisco Shortening. A telephone stands on the far left of the counter. VINCENT PARDO AND LA GACETA.

This photograph of the Rodriguez Grocery shows commonplace features of even the most ordinary building styles. The balconies, with covered sidewalks beneath them, and the proximity of shops to residences made the community a convenient place to live and work. THCPLS.

The Cuban Market in Ybor City, shown here circa 1930, was popular for its inexpensive produce and Cuban specialties. The building also provided a covered sidewalk. USFSCL.

The Martinez Building, nestled near modest residences, featured a corner café in the 1930s. THCPLS.

Centro Asturiano was the location for Tampa's part in the WPA Music Project. During the trying times of the Great Depression, elaborate musical productions like this offered entertainment and culture to the community—and it provided work for singers and actors. YBOR CITY STATE MUSEUM.

**Chapter 4 • Through Good Times, Depression, and War: 1925-1950**

The Gutiérrez Building in 1921 remained home to one of the popular drugstores in Ybor City. THCPLS.

The Tampa Gas Company plant in Ybor City began in 1896 led by the energetic Eduardo Manrara as president. It quickly became a major operation, as can be seen in this July 1, 1915, photograph. THCPLS.

The bustling streets of Ybor City in the 1920s held appeal for all ages, as can be seen in this photograph featuring the popular Café El Central on the left corner.

By contrast, this scene at a different time of day off the main street of the town reveals the peaceful village side of Ybor City. Railroad tracks cross this deserted Ybor street in 1921. THCPLS.

As the 1930s neared an end, cigars were no longer quite as strong an engine for the Ybor economy, but this 1937 poster (above) shows that the town continued to celebrate its most famous product. USFSCL.

The El Dorado Lounge on 8th Avenue is easily recognized by its painted white brick in these 1934 photos (left and above). Its token Art Deco facade and billboard look out of place on the old building, but it was a fashionable gambling spot.



**Ybor City: The Making of a Landmark Town**

ogy, a *lector* institution, volume production pressures, worker-intensive inter-factory competitiveness, an established factory hierarchy, and a strong immigrant base of young, impressionable workers of both sexes—and all this made it very promising terrain to introduce new ideologies. In Ybor one saw Communist pamphlets at the Labor Temple.[20] A Communist meeting was known to have taken place in a farmhouse near Tampa. There was also a case where a mother pinned red ties on her sons and his friends prior to their walking to grammar school. These were, in fact, trying and dangerous times for America.[21] But by the end of the decade many of these ideologies had faded from the scene.

With the importance of cigars to Tampa's overall economy now minimal and often in jeopardy, the power of the *patrones* waned. Suddenly, Tampa's power structure, not the factory *patrones*, felt strong enough to exert its wish. Business leaders and politicians signaled the end of dependence on cigars, and now began to court a new handmaiden—tourism. In turn, the *Tribune* called for a "silence by all" environment. A new Tampa image was sought. These were new times. Vigilantes kidnapped a Communist organizer, and KKK members with guns entered the Labor Temple seeking to break up a meeting. Radios at home eventually replaced *lectores* who earlier, in 1921, had been removed as the chief source of information for the *tabaqueros*. Allowed back in 1927, the *lectores* were discontinued permanently in 1931. By now radio and newspapers provided most of the news.

Though it had been played on a small-scale in Tampa since the 1880s, during the Depression years *bolita* ("little ball'), which Tony Pizzo characterized as "throwing numbers," became immensely popular, it was brought in from Key West by a Spaniard, Manuel Suarez, known as *El Gallego*.

Bolita appeared first in Paris over two centuries ago and spread to Spain from France. Spaniards brought the game to the colonies, where it became popular in Cuba and Key West. According to *Tribune* writer Lee Landenberger:

> Generally considered a harmless game of chance, most bets were a nickel, dime or quarter. The payoff was in the thousands of dollars, modest by today's lottery. Pizzo estimates that bolita was thrown in about 300 places across the city in 1927, while more than 1,000 runners crisscrossed the city collecting bets.[22]

Bolita soon flourished in the back rooms of saloons, and in time it entered many small businesses such as cafés, groceries, small general stores, tobacco stores, a few restaurants, gambling joints, and individual vendors. They all handled bolita sales. Very many *tabaqueros* played bolita once or twice a week. They regarded it as a casual amusement; in downtown Tampa the amounts played were much higher.[23]

Large saloons featured it daily. Frank Alduino, in the 1991 Fall/Winter issue of *Tampa Bay History*, writes, "The El Dorado Gambling Casino, located at the southeast corner of 8th Avenue and 14th Street in Ybor City, featured dice tables, a roulette wheel, and a lounge where guests played faro. Customers gathered there nightly for the bolita throw." The owner was Rafael Reina, a Spaniard. [24]

The popularity of bolita "throwing" induced Charlie Wall, the free-wheeling son of distinguished physician and Tampa civic leader John P. Wall, to enter the bolita racket. A known gambling kingpin, Charlie Wall had the organizational skills, the city and state connections, and the money to buy legislators' support. With Wall, bolita entered the bigtime. Outlawed by the city, the game continued to be played, often with the knowledge of city officials, some of whom turned their heads the other way or faked police enforcement, which generally missed its targets. Typical of the treatment is an investigation in the late 1930s described by Hampton Dunn, then a reporter for the *Tampa Daily Times*, that resulted in "a grand jury indictment of the owners of 22 bolita shops." However, the charges did not stick. "One week later," he noted, "the shops were open again doing a brisk trade."[25]

After a struggle for control in the 1930s, Wall lost his supremacy. The appetite for bolita gambling was an opportunity too good to pass up for an Italian underground that had thrived on bootlegging profits during Prohibition. By the end of the 1930s Italians had more or less completely taken over from Wall and the Cubans. They continued to run bolita in Tampa and Ybor City through the 1940s.

Finally, in 1950 the crusading journalist Virgil M. "Red" Newton, managing editor of the *Tampa Tribune*, took on the racket once and for all. His crusade "marked the end of the bolita era in Tampa."[26] A hearing by a U.S. Senate committee headed by Estes Kefauver in December 1950 sounded the death knell for organized rackets in Tampa. In 1955, Charlie Wall was found murdered in the bedroom of his home in Ybor City.

In an article on "Organized Crime," in *La Gaceta*'s 70th Anniversary issue, Gary R. Mormino and George Pozzetta explained that

> Bolita with its Latin and American consumers, soon became a fixture of the Tampa scene. It existed because the public wanted it, but also because certain Anglo civic leaders permitted it because the industry funneled massive amounts of money into the pockets of politicians and police.

Earlier, the authors state:

> Bolita became part of Ybor City's Latin culture, as Cubans, Spaniards and ultimately Italians came to regard it as an accepted fixture. On paydays at the cigar factory, workers routinely paid *el cafetero, el lector* and *el bolitero* . . . Tied to mobsters, the game once started by Spaniards and Cubans ultimately passed to Italians.[27]

Bolita playing was the Lottery of Ybor City. Spain and pre-Castro Havana offered it using its own format. Now Florida and many other states conduct their legal versions of it as money-raising games to support causes including education and budgetary deficiencies.

Despite its illegality, bolita remains part of the history and folklore of Ybor City. Today, the respected Ybor City Rotary Club occasionally uses bolita throwing as a fundraiser at its annual celebration at the Hyatt Hotel or other venues. Past prizes have included free trips to Spain, new cars, and other premiums to the winning ticket holder. It is a festive and enjoyable event, of which the historic procedure for selecting the winning ball is, in itself, a thoroughly attention-getting spectacle. Bolita's importance for the folklore of the *tabaqueros* of Ybor City and the people of greater Tampa is confirmed by its appearance in works by the area's favorite artists, Arnold Martinez, Mario Sanchez, and Ferdie Pacheco.

Indicative of the mood of large regions of America, in 1916 advocates of Prohibition achieved a milestone as twenty-four states voted against alcoholic beverages. Then, in 1919 a Prohibition Amendment to the U.S. Constitution was ratified on January 16, becoming the eighteenth amendment and the law of the land. In 1920 the prohibition of alcoholic beverages went into effect throughout America, beginning a new era.[28]

Mormino and Pozzetta in *The Immigrant World of Ybor City* describe its impact on Italians in Ybor City:

> Prohibition provided Italian immigrants, among others, with unforeseen opportunities to capitalize upon the American public's disdain for the Volstead Act. For Italians, singularly left out of the *bolita* bonanza, the prohibition era enabled them to carve a niche in organized crime. The timing was propitious. By 1920 the Italians had gained a familiarity with the urban economy and its marketplaces.[29]

Many things favored bootleggers at the time; supply and demand were not the least of these. The Depression had wiped out the local economy, but the "Roaring Twenties" had created habits and a de-

*Rural parts of Hillsborough County provided prime locations for the operation of moonshine stills during Prohibition. This photograph from 1920 shows a productive operation. The law against legal purchase of alcoholic beverages created an opportunity for economic success in the black market. And because of the widespread tacit approval of "bathtub gin" and the consumption of alcoholic beverages regardless of the law, it offered an opportunity for organized crime and underground enterprises to flourish in a climate of substantial public approval.* THCPLS.

*This photograph shows the Tampa Smokers baseball team in 1924. They were a source of pride and pleasure for many Ybor City residents.* THCPLS.

*Jose Luis Avellanal seems the perfect image of a dapper young man of the 1920s. He was the son of a respected physician, Jose Ramon Avellanal, born in Spain and educated in Cuba, who was the first medical director of the Centro Español sanitorium. The son was a flamboyant "Great Pretender" who claimed many unearned titles and degrees, and even sold fake degrees and diplomas.* LELAND HAWES, TAMPA TRIBUNE.

*The Imperial Theatre and Cafe on 15th Street south of La Setima was a "swinging place" where practically anything could happen. It was operated by Louis Athanasaw. People came to Ybor City for its lively night life, and three important modes of transportation for getting there are evident in this 1920s photo: horse, car, and train. The Ybor City trolley is not to be seen, but it became a beloved feature of the town.* HAMPTON DUNN, USFSCL.

mand for light alcoholic beverages and hard liquor. To the suppliers, perhaps this way of life invited inventiveness and creativity. Public thirst didn't dry up. The need and desire for saloons and restaurants to have available what the market wanted—beer, hard liquor, brandy, and fine wines—was still here. Italian men, in turn, had the creativity and daring to take charge in filling these needs. Those who managed to get alcohol, in whatever form, could sell it quietly and pick up additional income. Houses or barns in farm areas were potential sites for stills—as were some homes in Ybor City, though this was risky. Winds carried the smell easily. But in the distant hinterlands and in town, moonshine stills were erected, and then patronized. They supplied the demand.

The town was not unaware of the bootleggers. At the cafés one heard that this or that person had stopped for a quick café looking very tired; it was said to be because the person had run moonshine all night long. Or a story would go around that a bootlegger's car had gotten stuck in the dirt because it was overloaded with gallons of moonshine. In family homes the comings and goings of the men were interesting to the youngsters, who knew little of such activities, but were intrigued by the impression that mysterious things were going on.[30]

In 1933, the twenty-first Amendment to the United States Constitution repealed Prohibition. The romantic notions of moonshine stills and moonshine brewing persisted in many areas of America. This period, after 1933, saw the opening of many legal liquor outlets in greater Tampa. Still, in some states, such as Kentucky, the practice of making moonshine continued until at least the early 1940s. When I was a college student at Georgia Tech, a visit to a roommate's home in Kentucky revealed that, indeed, the family made moonshine, as the roommate had often mentioned. For with the opening of

the front door, the smell of moonshine enveloped me. Also, during World War II a few soldiers made potato moonshine on the Island of Adak, in the Aleutians. Soldiers often spoke of moonshine operations in their towns.[31] No doubt this skill at Adak came from a hometown experience.

Winemaking was desirable for many average families. Prohibition was over, but the Depression years remained for another five to seven years. There was still no money to buy Rioja wine, a Marques de Riscál or a Brillante, or for that matter a Chianti or other Spanish or Italian wines. But wine drinking, even with a heavy Sunday meal, was a necessity. For many Latins, one glass of wine, only, was a part of the way of life. Drunkenness was not tolerated by the great majority of Latin families. Many children had never seen a drunk person until they saw one in the movies. The term *borracho* (drunk) was used, nonetheless, but in disdain. If some of the out-of-reach saloons attracted out-of-town people, children saw little of that. Those, generally, were on the south or eastern end of town, though two or three were close to Ybor's main spine. But one small glass of wine at the family table, particularly with a heavy meal, was a gift from heaven!

Many mixed families of Italians and Spaniards made wine together. California grapes were easily available. Much experimentation took place, as these amateur family winemakers mixed a certain out-of-state grape with perhaps a Scuppernong grape grown easily in the Tampa suburbs. The result made for much enjoyment and conversation.[32]

During the Depression years, many Spaniards and Italians left the cigar industry to open new businesses in greater Tampa. They worked primarily for themselves, and their intiative and perseverance over time translated into sizable operations employing many. Some turned toward the local waters, and fishing and selling raw sea products became a way of life. Some went

150

deep into the surrounding countryside, bought very large tracts of land, and moved there. Decades later their sons would be land barons. Others went into dairying, insurance, pharmaceuticals, real estate, trucking, restaurants, groceries, bread making, warehousing, and many other endeavors where individual effort was everything. Latins, certainly at this stage, were not highly educated, with rare exception, and their foreign accents made them less than desirable employees for office work dealing with the public or the corporate world. But in the long run, these early businessmen would be employers themselves.

During this trying period, El Centro Asturiano, El Centro Español, and the clinics continued to supply quality medical services. Grocery stores at times extended credit. Debts were paid back. Hardy Jewish merchants tightened their belts and waited it out. Meanwhile, Tampa soup lines were busy and Roosevelt's early Federal WPA projects helped to pay bills.

## Some local Depression-era scenes

The Depression taught the children of that time many lessons. They had experienced the good times of the 1920s, extravagant and unrealistic as they were and had lived through rapid reversal into a time of deprivation. The early years saw parents struggling to survive, retrench, and adapt quickly to dispose of all the unreal values only recently experienced.

There was no money for new socks, dresses, pants, or shoes. Holes in socks were solved easily: simply pull the socks down a notch. Pants or dresses too short? Mothers now had sewing machines. Seams were redone. If one ran out of handkerchiefs, part of a white shirt was the answer. The seams were sewn by hand needle or sewing machine. Young girls learned to imitate their mothers at these machines. One knew the thread's roll numbers when buying more. Wearing homemade jumpers for girls was not new. And getting a haircut was often done at home, whether for girls or boys, in the early 1930s.

Boys milked family cows, pastured them, and took them water in the fields after school. Often they would re-pasture them in the late evening hours before bringing them to the barn. The process repeated itself on the morrow. Some delivered milk. Others churned butter. Bicycles came in handy, but hazardous falls occurred. Bicycle repair shops kept very busy.

Smudge pots had to be refilled for winter and relocated close to the citrus trees, then fired and watched over at three in the morning in anticipation of a freeze below 30 degrees lasting over two hours. When that happened they had to be lit to protect the citrus from the hated freeze. Later they had to be cleaned and refilled for another cold spell, and the procedure was repeated. Vegetables and fruit trees had to be watered and fertilized. Each family did what it needed to do to survive. Father had planted forty lime trees that he and I maintained.

Henry Ayo, Frank Garcia, and I also worked paper routes. We met at Leon's corner service station on Lake Avenue and 15th Street at 3:30 a.m. We then pedaled to the pickup site on 29th Street and 21st Avenue. Here we got the newspapers, made small packs of them, and slung them from our bike baskets, delivering some 150 to 200 papers each. On returning home, we slept about an hour; then it was milk time, after which the cow had to be taken to the nearby field and staked out until we came home from school. At that time the cow had to be watered and re-staked until milk time at 6 p.m. Riding a bike to Hillsborough High School in the morning sometimes became a chore, depending on the weather.

Of course, it must be pointed out that some of the well-positioned *tabaqueros* did not lose their jobs. Most of these were Spaniards. Among these were the *rezagador* (who allocated leaves according to brand, and approved count for wage purposes) and the *escogedor* (who selected cigars and grouped them by appearance, shading, etc., for boxing). Naturally *tabaqueros* who were blessed with being *de los largos*, or, *de los buenos* (a high-volume producer or one whose quality is very good), enjoyed much better job security. These exceptional *torcedores* (rollers) were at "the top of the heap" among cigar workers.

School and the play field allowed much camaraderie. There we learned of one another's experiences. To children all the work seemed natural, as though it was no great thing. As long as Father and Mother were present and working, everything seemed proper. Everyone was more or less in the same situation. In their daily school life, the Cubans, Italians and Spanish intermingled. This would later lead some of them to marriages; others would develop lifetime friendships. All of us shared many of the same experiences. The town, out-wardly, was all the same. Spanish was still the common language. The aspirations were about the same. And when we were able to hit the playing fields—and there were over thirty games that we played in the fields of Ybor City—this too, brought our lives together.

Families living side by side respected and helped each other as needed. Assistance was volunteered and never requested. A case in point is our family's move to Lake Avenue. As a Realtor, Father had lost virtually everything in the years following the stock market crash. Property had lost its value. Overnight he was out of a job. He had lost a fortune. Looking ahead, he had bought the land and three houses previously mentioned at faraway Lake Avenue for a total of $1,000, but he could not begin farming there without a fence. For two weeks in the winter of 1931, three of my

*During the 1930s the Works Progress Administration (WPA) offered jobs to writers, artists, and actors. This 1937 photograph of employees with the WPA Federal Theater Project in Tampa was taken at the old Florida State Fairgrounds (now on the campus of the University of Tampa). The stage backdrop promoted Tampa industries and celebrated the opening of the Davis Causeway between Tampa and Clearwater. From left in the first row are Sergio De Meza, Joseph Salinas, Onelio Velasco, Agnes Mitchell, Peggy Foster, Lorraine Ayres, Rosetta Sampson, J. A. Burt, Humberto Leon, and Joe Cueto. Standing are A. D. Juran, ____ Villafañes, Charles D. Cooley, Fernando R. Mesa, art director "Syl," A. Junior Chapin, Scott Morris, Alberto Acosta, Eugene Green, Raleigh Sappe, and Frank Hewlitt.* FERNANDO RODRIGUEZ MESA.

**Ybor City: The Making of a Landmark Town**

father's friends, whom I knew only as José, Lopez, and Andres, all well-positioned and employed Asturian cigarmakers, walked a mile after work to help Father put up a fence around the empty lots next to the house.

It was a bitterly cold winter. Their assistance was completely volunteered. They insisted that they wanted to help father, a next door neighbor at the Centro Asturiano Hospital site. The fence took a whole week of work in the late afternoons to complete. They also helped Father frame the barn. Mother made them hot Cuban coffee and bread. A firm handshake was the only payment required.

I often marvel at the values of our fathers. Up until I went away to college, Father often took me to see these friends. He never missed visiting them during Christmas holidays when he presented Spanish confections, pastries, and a bottle of Marques de Riscal to each. Now I treasure the memories of those special days. The beauty and correctness of these Spaniards' ways I will never forget.[33]

By 1938 the heaviest part of the Great Depression was over! But for many it would continue through 1943, the official end of the depression, for in that wartime year the nation discontinued the WPA. For others, the recovery took a little longer. Nonetheless, the Latins lived this saga together. Their children, now elderly, share this common experience. The period had a very trying beginning and a beautiful ending. It was a great epic journey that further unified the Latin families.

Hardly noticed by many struggling with the burdens of the Depression years, in 1931 the Ybor City Chamber of Commerce had formed. Despite the chilling economic climate, this invaluable community resource took root and grew.

Another milestone Latins would face during these years surfaced by mid-decade. In 1935, Spaniards suddenly found themselves glued to the Madrid short-wave radio stations. A tragic Civil War was about to erupt in Spain.[34]

## Spanish Civil War (1936-1939)

Much has been written concerning the Spanish Civil War. In Ybor City, newspaper accounts, detailed historical brochures, oral histories, and other means have produced much detailed information about the real impact of the Spanish Civil War on Spaniards and other Latins in living there. My discussion here is intended to review briefly Spain's past, to offer a short history of the Second Republic, to expound on the complexities the new government faced, and to describe its final defeat at the hands of the Nationalist forces under General Francisco Franco. In writing this, I am especially thankful for the invaluable information collected by the authors cited in my notes who have devoted years to research, visiting historic locations in Spain, scrutinizing leading newspapers, and distilling original documents, references, and interviews, both national and international, concerning this major historical event.

Apart from the two world wars, the Spanish Civil War was the bloodiest conflict in the first half of the 20th century. A total of approximately 640,000 people died in battle—or from malnutrition, disease, or execution. Some 240,000 political prisoners were jailed. The effects of this combined loss of life and the extensive destruction of property were widespread and long-lasting. Hugh Thomas, author of *The Spanish Civil War*, appropriately concludes that it was a vicious war, and, as was the case with our own civil war, it would take the better part of a century for the lingering passions to be ameliorated.[35]

### Background

Spain is an old nation. Its history is diverse and difficult to grasp or convey. However, it will be helpful to call to mind the country's governance following the

Middle Ages, at a time when its great explorers had extended the nation's global reach. The Catholic monarchs King Ferdinand and Queen Isabela in the second half of the 15th and early 16th century had ruled under the symbol of national unity. Yet with the exception of those kings who closely followed them—Carlos I and Philip II—all other successors to the throne gradually let the empire slip away. Throughout these centuries Spain's countryside remained extremely backwards, a situation closely related to the ruling elite's disregard for the peasantry.[36]

Castilla and Extremadura, two important regions in Spain, furnished what were at the time the world's best soldiers and shipped much farm produce, animals, and by-products to its colonies overseas. To work the soil, deliver its produce, and send its sons in support of the kingdom were the peasant's burdens.

Little of the gold that the Spanish took out of South America stayed in Spain; certainly very little of it benefited the peasants, who were, in fact, taxed heavily to finance more empire-building. Gold was shipped to Seville to be accounted for, and then sent to the Netherlands, financial center for Carlos V, Emperor of the German empire, the Austrian empire, and the remains of the Holy Roman empire, who

was also Carlos I of Spain through family connection.

Spanish colonial gold helped finance the Christian Crusade against the Turks as well as other imperial ventures, while Spanish peasants lingered in poverty and ignorance. Nor did Carlos's son, King Philip II of Spain, lessen the plight of the peasants, though he was an effective king in affairs of the empire. And aside from Carlos III ("the enlightened one," who, coincidentally, helped America in its fight for independence) all other kings, whether of Hapsburg or Bourbon lineage, cared little about improving the quality of life for the peasants, who occupied over 90 percent of the land.[37]

In Spain's vast countryside, particularly in Castilla and Leon, life never changed. There could be no change. Supporting it were three fixed pillars of power—the Monarchy, the Church, and the Army. The *Latifundistas* (land barons), an extension of the monarchy, came equipped with titles. They were nobility and entitled to a portion of wealth. The odds were stacked high against the villagers, small farmers, and laborers in the fields. The triumvirate worked together. It was best to keep the masses subdued, backward, and largely uneducated. The army assured this.

The French Revolution, the authors who spread its impact through inspiring emotional and ideological writings, and the great Spanish authors of the Generation of 1868 and of 1898, and those now called the Generation of 1925, just before the advent of the Spanish Second Republic—all these were instrumental in stirring the souls and imaginations of Spaniards to the point that they became aware of their poor conditions. Likewise, the Industrial Revolution that began in Europe, slowly worked its way to the doorsteps of Spain's large cities—Bilbao, Barcelona, Valencia, and into Madrid. With it came militant modern ideologies—anarchism, syndicalism, radicalism, and the milder socialism—already

*Miguel de Unamuno (left photo) was a strong advocate for education as Rector of the University of Salamanca and a conservative voice for preserving the deeply rooted "Spanishness" of Spain. José Ortega y Gasset (right photo) in 1929 looked his part as a progressive, modern "European" author advocating revitalization through the latest scientific advancements and progressive education.*

present in Spain, including many offshoot political organizations. From Russia came communist ideology, with its proletariat mentality that probed for openings in this militant labyrinth.[38]

All the while, the affairs of the court—titles, inheritance, successions, lavish displays and socials—all these wasted Spain's grassroots potential and its best minds.

Among the most widely read authors and philosophers of Spain—genuine men of letters—were Miguel de Unamuno and José Ortega y Gasset. Their views influenced the people as few ever did, particularly as the nation approached its terrible Civil War.

Unamuno was rector of the University of Salamanca and served the Second Republic as a deputy in the Constituent Cortes of 1931. The world of Unamuno was the Spain of small, almost medieval, towns and the peasants' countryside; it was a nation steered by a triumvirate—the monarchy, the Catholic Church (though he had philosophical problems with immortality), and the Army. Unamuno was a rebellious spirit who attacked alike the king, the dictator, Marxism, fascism, and even the Republic, which he had at first

celebrated. He was strongly conservative and protective of the spirit of "eternal Spain" which he feared was endangered.

Historian John A. Crow writes that "Unamuno believed firmly in the substance of 'Spanishness,' and his philosophy was permeated with the Spanish Catholic tradition." He believed in fate, in death, and in the Spanish individualism; he was against the European mentality and of progress brought by the French Revolution "distrustful of science and rationalism."[39]

At the opposite pole was José Ortega y Gasset. He was labeled "the European," by friends and opposition, for he believed in science, progress, and light, in justice and in education. "He wanted to regenerate, to re-invigorate, and to resuscitate his country, by revealing and revitalizing its best values. He also "feared the masses, particularly the Spanish masses with their semi-education, and upheld the rule of a select minority."[40] Ortega y Gasset, too, was as Spanish as the windmills!

Spain, in 1931, was a place torn apart by the conflicting values articulated by Unamuno and Ortega y Gasset: the Spanishness of Spain versus the Europeanizing of Spain; the State, Church, Army, and land barons versus progress, education, science, and dynamic change brought by the new European mentality.

Unfortunately, the two separate world views articulated by Unamuno and Ortega y Gasset did not allow compromise. Little did Spain realize that only a fusion of these opposing views could alleviate its dilemma, for each side had its virtues. No, it would take a massive and bloody civil war followed by thirty-six years of dictatorship before the Spanish people would have what they wanted: a democratic environment where ordinary people could see progress, get an education, secure a future for the family, and enjoy the freedom to practice one's own faith or simply till the land, but with means to achieve a reasonable quality of life, with modern equipment to soothe their backs and dignity.

This was the situation Spain faced, as Alfonso XIII abdicated his throne in 1931. He was accused of making wrong and costly decisions. His approval of dictator Primo de Rivera's decision to send heavy forces to fight Morocco, all of which were wiped out, was a tremendous embarrassment to him and to the nation. His abdication was a last-ditch effort to avoid civil war, but it precipitated a series of rapidfire events.

On April 12, 1931, in the wake of Alfonso XIII's abdication, Spain held municipal elections nationwide. Just under 90 percent of the electorate voted. The municipal councilors elected gave the victory to the Republicans in the large cities. In turn, the greatest number of the councilors voting throughout Spain's countryside favored the monarchy. After adjusting for some falsification of voting scores by those loyal to the monarchy, the republican vote of 53.7 percent carried the day. The socialist vote was under 7 percent and the communist vote considerably less than 1 percent (sixty-seven out of the approximate 73,492 total adjusted councilors from throughout Spain).[41]

*Results in June 1931.* Based on the above election results, the total left wing (Republicans, socialists, and communists) numbered 282 elected deputies, and the extreme right numbered 172 deputies.

*Election of 1933.* In this election the Republic moved far to the right. Gil Robles took the helm of the Second Republic. The socialists, who in the 1931 election had won 115 seats in the Cortes, now held only 59, whereas the total left-leaning deputies that had numbered 282 dropped to 99. In turn, the total rightist vote climbed from 60 to 207.

*Election of 1936.* This election apparently gave a strong victory to the coalition of the left, the Popular Front, within the framework of the Second Republic. However, the center, with 54 deputies, could swing votes in the Cortes by voting with the right. The communists, who had not previously elected a member to the Cortes, had now won 14 seats (3 percent of the total Cortes deputies). The vote totals were: Popular Front, 256 deputies (56.5 percent); center, 54 deputies (11.9 percent); and the right, 143 deputies (31.6 percent).

The left claimed an overwhelming victory, but considering the delicate balance of votes, the claim was exaggerated. Still, based on frightened concerns by the right, in March 1936 the Spanish Military Union decided to rise against the Republic. On July 17, 1936, General Francisco Franco brought troops from Morocco and, joined by many rebellious army troops, attacked cities and towns in Spain. The Spanish Civil War had begun. It lasted three years, ending in the total defeat of the Second Republic in 1939.[42]

## The Republican Struggle to Survive

Some well-known and respected names of the Second Republic and, five years later, of the Popular Front (elected within the Second Republic framework) were the Second Republic's conservative

*The Spanish consul in Tampa was Pablo de Ubarri, shown on July 20, 1936, reading news of the war in Spain reported by the* Tampa Tribune. *He resigned three months later to return to Spain for work with Franco's National Movement.* TBH.

first President, Niceto Alcalá Zamora (1931-36); socialist ministers Indalecio Prieto, Largo Caballero, Fernando de los Ríos, and Republican Marcelino Domingo; and Popular Front president and respected national politician, Manuel Azaña (1936-39). Their presence among many others in Spain's ruling government was believed to guarantee a moderate cabinet that nullified the extreme left.[43] Fernando de los Ríos and Marcelino Domingo both visited Tampa, and were well-known and admired here. All the others in this group were respected in Ybor City, and mention of their names at the cafés brought much attention.

When the truculent Archbishop of Toledo cast suspicion on the new Republican regime and praised the abdicated Alfonso XIII, mobs responded and began to burn churches three days later, even though more moderate bishops and hundreds of priests had voted for the Republic in 1931. As churches burned, red flags appeared.[44]

Some historians suggest that the nobility, who in the final moments had done nothing to defend the monarchy, resisted taking sides because any new social reform would run against its economic interests. Agrarian reform by the incoming Popular Front later would validate these fears, for land barons would suffer from it. It was in the cities that people heatedly exchanged views and quickly took sides. Still, in the years of the moderate republic, 1931 to 1933, there were needed reforms. The first Minister of Education created three thousand new schools, and then Minister of Education Fernando de los Ríos, himself a historian and professor of law (later the Republic's ambassador to Washington), added seven thousand more (the world José Ortega y Gasset also envisioned). Hundreds of reform laws were passed.

However, approximately two thousand of the planned schools were never completed, nor could the hundreds of laws that were passed be rapidly enforced. Aside from a relatively few that were promptly and successfully implemented, much legislation lay dormant. Not understanding the democratic time-consuming processes of government, the masses wanted immediate action. Thus, they became easy targets of the left. In turn, the leftist politicians exalted and exploited the confusion. They pushed for a totally new direction. An ill-prepared and uneducated citizenry inundated by laws and edicts could not cope. Now, the masses in the cities also wanted immediate results and couldn't understand why things didn't change. Meanwhile, opposition from Spain's triumvirate increased. These placed many roadblocks, since they had the resources, the wealth, the well-equipped armed units and networks. There could be no compromise.[45] Spain, now, was torn apart. It could not be fixed. It festered.

By this time in Spain there were six center and right wing parties, which included nationalists—and which carried the seeds of some of the future autonomies; five extreme right wings included elements of the fascist Falange and Officer's Military Union; ten left wing parties which included left wing militant groups; four extreme left wing groups included communist elements and a workers-and-peasants bloc; nine trade unions had both university and trade union elements; and then

*Jose Martinez (left), president of the Committee for the Defense of the Spanish Popular Front, collects donations in 1936 in front of Ybor City's Labor Temple. Volunteer Victoriano Manteiga is seated at right, while Blanca Valls makes a donation. Within two weeks of its establishment, the group had raised $2,000 to send to support Republican Spain. Over the three years of the war they gathered and sent almost $200,000 to the Spanish Red Cross. The photograph was published in the* Tampa Tribune *on August 21, 1936.* TBH.

there were six youth organizations as well as separate communists, socialist Catholics, and other blocs.[46] When in 1936 the moderate Second Republic became ungovernable, the leftist Popular Front assumed power within the framework of the Republic. Behaving much like a democratic entity at first, it increasingly leaned far left as the worldwide communist influence and the internal cooperating elements revealed their presence—to the dismay of the Republicans.

Crow writes bluntly that Barcelonians were "out and out anarchists," the Basques were generally the religious and conservative elements on the Republican side, while the masses of the Republican forces, who belonged to neither of these camps, were left to struggle to understand the best ways to defend the Republic.

Areas voting for the Popular Front in February of 1936 were Andalucia, Galicia, Asturias, Vizcaya, Cataluña, Valencia, Extremadura, and Madrid. Voting for the Popular Front, also, were entrenched enclaves of anarchists, socialists, and many varied ideologies. Alarmed by these events, General Francisco Franco's (Nationalist) forces attacked the Republic in the early days of the Popular Front.[47]

## The Loyalists in Tampa

In Ybor City and West Tampa, Spaniards followed the events in Spain closely. The vast majority of Spanish *tabaqueros* favored the 1931 democratically elected Second Republic. They were imbued with the ideals of freedom, equality, honest work, and social justice. They desired a democratic government for their countrymen. Most Loyalists in Tampa were just that—loyal to the officially elected Second Republic. Five years of the Republic had filled them with passion and expectations, though the first two years' work is what they praised. A certain percentage were more idealistic and leaned left. Only a relatively few Nationalists who sided with General Franco and the triumvirate were recognizable in Tampa. Most kept quiet and avoided conversation of the war, almost revealing their real interest in so doing. The cafés and *fondas* (small eating houses adjoining cigar factories), meetings, short wave radio and the local press provided the daily fodder that kept emotions high.[48]

In Tampa, strong moral support came from Italians and Cubans. These Italians—Sicilian, mostly—had no stomach for Mussolini's Fascists. They favored the Loyalists, as did the working Cubans.

158

*General Santiago J. Philemore, General Inspector of the Spanish Red Cross, and his wife, Olga, were photographed in Ybor City in front of the Labor Temple with members of the Democratic Popular Committee to Aid Spain. This photograph is dated August 7, 1938. USFSCL.*

Many also contributed money and supplies to the Loyalists. Thus, the majority of the Latins favored the Loyalists in Ybor City. They were Loyalists—loyal to the Republic. It was substantially the overwhelming sentiment of the town.[49]

In the rare instance that a person siding with the Nationalists—the rebels or *Franquistas*—was seen walking the street, that person crossed to the other side, to keep from being ridiculed or cursed at. Many fights and beatings actually took place. Some vicious fights occurred in school areas, as children sought to defend their families' beliefs. In cafés, *fondas*, Spanish social clubs, and hospitals one saw animated discussion of the war in Spain. To Spaniards it was a very personal matter and a matter of great passion.[50]

During the civil war years, the café at the Columbia Restaurant saw Spaniards at night waiting for the appearance of the early morning edition of the *Tampa Tribune* received there at approximately 10 p.m. Las Novedades, Cuervo, Los Helados, and others saw much the same routine. At night, Spaniards with a short wave radio listened to *La Voz de Madrid* (The Voice of Madrid) to get the very latest news from the war front. When a Loyalist victory oc-

curred, the results soon circulated through the cafés, though the cafés in those days were still not as full, due to the impact of the Great Depression and the fact that any extra money often went for donations to the Loyalists.

Italians and Cubans joined the pro-Loyalist conversations, but the real involvement was from Spaniards. They remained very much attached to their native soil. Spanish, of course, was the language spoken. Generally, Spaniards talked about much of the war news heard on *La Voz de Madrid*, the Madrid short-wave radio. It was more detailed and covered the total war front. It was food for conversation—sometimes passionate. While these meetings were casual, one usually found the same friends present. One counted on seeing the same friends. It was a ritual.[51]

Meanwhile, volunteers collected money for Spain outside the factories. *Patrones* wanted to stay neutral, because that was the official U.S. position. Collections, therefore, were made outdoors at the foot of the factory steps. Much money was donated. A dollar in those depression years was a lot of money. Some gave that much, while most gave according to their abilities, an amount that often varied.[52]



**Chapter 4 · Through Good Times, Depression, and War: 1925-1950**

A song that hit Ybor City and West Tampa in the early war years was titled "No Pasarán" (They Shall Not Pass). The song was written by Leopoldo Gonzalez, a Tampa cigarmaker. Peter N. Carroll, author of the book, *The Odyssey of the Abraham Lincoln Brigade*, states that, "From the Communist leader Dolores Ibarruri (known because of her fiery oratory as '*La Pasionaria*'), these blue-clad urban workers had adopted the rallying cry: 'No Pasarán!'" She was known by the moniker "*La Pasionaria.*" The song itself was passionate, and it wrenched the souls of those who believed in the Second Republic and wished the Popular Front to defeat Franco's well-armed military. It was, undoubtedly, the song that best represented the Spanish Civil War effort for the Popular Front in Ybor City.[53]

At this time there were also communist, socialist, and anarchist influences in Ybor City. In fact, the communist influence was here even before the early period of the Spanish Republic and was related to factory worker militancy, receiving a sudden boost when the Great Depression hit. We knew of the anarchist who delivered literature on his bike, of the free Russian magazines stacked alongside the old Labor Temple for people to pick up, of the presence of a card-carrying communist, of a terrible fight that occurred in school that was believed to have been Spanish Civil War related, and other

events. Leftist ideologies in Tampa in that period came from northern Spain, Sicily, Cuba, Key West, and our northern industrial centers in America.

There could be no doubt. The Tampa cigar industry—so heavily dependent on the Spanish handroll or hand-and-mold method, with similar methodology in factories in Key West, Cuba, and the North—was ready made for American unionism—and for foreign ideologies.

But whether related to the earlier depression period or to the Popular Front period, communist influence in Ybor City was *mucho ruido y pocas nueces* (a lot more noise than the actual quantity of nuts in the bag). I know that at least one card-carrying communist did visit Tampa and made real attempts at spreading the doctrine. Also aiding the work of the small communist cliques were the trash peddlers. The ideologies needed the peddler's work, for confusion and subtle misinformation are the allies of doctrinaires.

During the last major factory strike in Tampa in 1931, *patrones* had broken the back of factory unions in Tampa. Unfortunately, it was also the end of the *lector* institution in the factories, a tradition that had brought much culture to the cigar workers, in spite of its control by ideologues in the *Comité de Lectura*. Loss of this institution was a tragedy in itself. This bit of Ybor lore is one of the most valued parts of its history.[54]

## A Reflection of the War Years: 1936-1939

Spaniards in the countryside were too individualistic to be controlled or indoctrinated. But communist influence had penetrated heavily into the Popular Front government and its tentacles reached deep into the countryside. Except for a few regions of Spain, the countryside peasants were too individualistic to change. The confusion that reigned is beyond simple description due to the myriad

**Ybor City: The Making of a Landmark Town**

*The Democratic Popular Committee to Aid Spain regularly prepared shipments of supplies to help war victims. Here members of the Tampa Committee to Aid Spanish War Sufferers prepare boxes of clothing and other goods in 1937 for the Spanish Red Cross. More than twenty tons of relief supplies were gathered and shipped by the Tampa Committee during the war.* TBH.

views, reactions to national directives, hidden agendas, and much more. Also, specific traditional regions of Spain carried hidden passions and agendas. Catalonia, for example, had long aspired to again win independence from Spain, and Crow reports that the Cata-lonians "pompously declared their region to be the 'Republic of Catalonia.'" This, however, was never allowed. They continued to support the Spanish Republic.

Finally, to the joy of the masses in the large cities as well as pockets in the countryside, Russia sent military help to the beleaguered Popular Front. When Asturian coal miners had rebelled during the conservative period of the Second Republic, Gill Robles, then the conservative Republican president, had called on the Commandant of the General Military Academy, a certain General Francisco Franco, to quell the revolt. In response, Franco had gathered Spanish and Moorish troops to crush the uprising. Crow points out that "the appearance of these troops in Asturias had a terrible effect on the populace, for this seemed to be a deliberate affront to their honor and to their legendary history." The revolt was crushed, but at a cost of over a thousand lives and many thousands of wounded.

In Tampa, Loyalists were thankful for that Russian aid, though it is certain that most did not understand that country's agenda. Loyalists here backed the Popular Front. The full implications of the Front's strong shift to the left were not fully understood by most Loyalists. What prevailed in Ybor City was the aura and passion of the Second Republic and its original ideals.[55]

Russia's communist inroads in Spain were enhanced greatly by the failure of America, England, and France, to support Spain, particularly in the early and mid years of the Republic. They had five years of the Second Republic to act before the Popular Front arrived, though by that time it was well nigh too late. By then their worst fears were indeed approaching realization. The Republic had to continue to defend itself. It gladly accepted aid from Russia.

By contrast, the U.S. froze the Second Republic's $120 million (equivalent to just under a billion dollars today) reserve in New York banks, denying the Republic the ability to buy arms for its own defense. The U.S. concluded a non-intervention accord, followed by an embargo of arms to the Spanish Republic.



**Chapter 4 · Through Good Times, Depression, and War: 1925-1950**

*A Labor Day march through Ybor City in 1938 featured children carrying signs and placards for the Tampa Democratic Popular Committee to Aid Spain.* TBH.

Aid to Spain would now come only from Russia and Mexico. This was done through France, based on a mutual agreement between Russia and France. Small arms only were allowed to cross the borders, even though France was a member of the non-intervention accord. This was greatly appreciated, and the Loyalists often expressed it.

At the time the situation represented a tremendous opportunity for Russia. Spain occupied a strategic location in Europe. A strong foothold there was of great importance to them. Where Russian arms went, their ideology followed. Russian political baggage thus soon found its way into the cities, towns, and countryside of Spain. There were even some communes begun, particularly in the northern part of Spain. All this increasingly undermined the democratic ideals of the Republic, since the main tenets of communism are simply not in tune with the democratic ideals of liberty, personal rights, freedom of religion, and the pursuit of happiness. These were the ideals won by the Second Republic elected in Spain in 1931. But these fine points were not really understood as the mystique, passion, and loyalty to the Popular Front progressed. Loyalists continued to believe strongly in an idealized Popular Front. Constant and well-conceived propaganda insured that. And that was the case here in Ybor City. Faith in the Second Republic was an integral part of the mix.

When in 1937 German planes bombed and killed or wounded 1,654 Spaniards at Guernica, provoking Picasso's famous painting and pulverizing the town, Ybor Spaniards felt the pain deeply. A *Tribune* editorial titled "Savagery in Spain" precipitated widespread local reaction. Looking back, in a *Tribune* history feature on July 29, 1990, Leland Hawes wrote, "On Thursday, May 6, 1937, the women workers left their work tables at 3 p.m. to assemble at the labor temple . . . six abreast . . . arm-in-arm, as sisters, holding hands and showing a fine composure. . . . The numbers ranged from 5,000 to 7,000. . . . They were headed to city hall to protest the killing of innocent civilians." Hawes reported that "Editor Victoriano Manteiga of *La Gaceta* presented a petition to the Mayor, R. E. L. Chancey, expressing the horror of Tampa's Latin population at the beastly acts of slaughter of defenseless women and children in Spain."[56]

Aided by the detailed coverage of Victoriano Manteiga's *La Gaceta*, and his resolute posture, opinions and feelings crystallized on the side of the Popular Front, the need for locals to send aid to Spain was hastened. *La Gaceta* in those days was the main source that Spaniards, Cubans, and Italians relied on for news and views of Spain. A widely attended mass meeting at the Labor Temple facilitated the formation of the Committee for the Defense of the Popular Front. José Martinez became president of the Tampa Democratic Popular Committee to Aid Spain. Franco's attack on the Popular Front had polarized the town.

The military campaign that General Francisco Franco followed was essentially a counterclockwise action that captured Granada, Sevilla, Galicia, Castilla, Leon, Vizcaya, Navarra, and then Catalonia and Valencia, according to Ronald Fraser, au-

thor of *Blood of Spain*. Due to the heavy resistance from Asturias and Castilla La Nueva, the Nationalists were delayed, and protracted battles ensued. Asturias was eventually isolated and captured. Madrid was also attacked early on with Mussolini's Fascist Divisions, but they failed to take Guadalajara, crucial to the defense of Madrid from the north. This was repulsed and the Madrid front was firmed up. It allowed time for the Loyalists to organize.

The International Brigade, composed of volunteers from over sixty countries, made its first major contribution of the war not only by stopping Mussolini's forces but by exerting a tremendous impact by their presence. Madrid's citizens were overcome emotionally by the fact that so many volunteers from all over the world would risk their lives to fight for Spain's Second Republic. The presence of the International Brigade aroused passion, camaraderie, and determination.

In America, the volunteers who fought in Spain were of battalion strength—some 2,800 strong. This included some twenty-four volunteers from Tampa. They at first called themselves the Abraham Lincoln Battalion, but in time, through affiliation and service with the 15th International Brigade. The Americans in the war referred to themselves as the Abraham Lincoln Brigade.

Though they were widely believed to have been inspired and directed by communists, a good many volunteers were prompted by noble motives to join and defend the Second Republic and its democratic ideals. They also fought to prevent the rampant forces of Hitler and Mussolini from destroying this young democratic nation. Many of them were appalled at the fact that America, England, and France had turned their backs on the legitimately elected Spanish Republic. Their great passion to fight for democratic freedom and their heroic warfront sacrifices are still, today, celebrated by those who lived

*This photo from the Abraham Lincoln Brigade Archives shows a group of American volunteers in Spain in April 1938.* TBH.

through the period and also cared. These are glorious and noble reasons in any war.[57]

Peter N. Carroll, a key American member of the Brigade, opens his book *The Odyssey of the Abraham Lincoln Brigade* with the following words: " The history of the Spanish Civil war is consumed by mythology and legend, so much so, that it is difficult to separate fact from fiction." In Ybor City, most Loyalists believed in the beauty and nobility of the Brigade's mission—that is, to defend the Second Republic—to defend the Spanish nation. That was this writer's impression then and is today.

It is what the majority of the fathers in Ybor City believed in.[58]

In late March 1939, General Francisco Franco overran Madrid, assuring the fall of the Second Republic. On April 1, 1939, he declared the end of the war.[59]

In Tampa, Spaniards, bolstered by Italian and Cuban participation, had donated a substantial amount of money to help the Loyalists. Ambulances, medical supplies, and huge numbers of cigarettes were paid for by the Ybor City workers, collected at the factory steps and sent to Spain. Additionally, wrappers from cigarette packs in Tampa were opened, the metallic foil salvaged, and boiled. The resulting soft metal was shaped into fishing weights. In turn, these were sold to collect money for the Loyalist war effort.

A Second Republic party leader, Marcelino Domingo, stopped in Tampa

and talked at all of the Spanish clubs and hospitals, at the Cuban and Italian clubs, and at the Labor Temple. The essence of his message was to thank Tampa for its contributions to the Loyalists.[60] In addition, Fernando de los Ríos, Spanish Ambassador to the United States, was in Tampa at least two times. He spoke at the Labor Temple accompanied by Isabel Cyarzbal de Palencia, who appealed to the women delegates of the AFL.

"I am not a communist," she told the crowd. "At the time the rebellion broke out, there was not a single Socialist or Communist in the Cabinet, and only fifteen out of four hundred and seventy-two members of parliament were communists."

Speaking to the cheering crowd at the Labor Temple, Don Fernando de los Ríos said that it was better for Spaniards to die fighting for the Popular Front government than to live under the Fascist rebels. During the first four years of the Spanish Republic, Socialist de los Ríos, then Minister of Education, was responsible for many of the more than eight thousand schools that the republic had built before the advent of the Popular Front.[61]

In late 1938, Don Fernando de los Ríos returned again to Tampa, where among other events, he spoke to a overflow crawd at the theater in the Centro Asturiano Club building (I was a 16-year-old teenager, attended with father, and was greatly impressed by the passion of his message and the eloquence of his well-spoken Castilian language). The Ambassador thanked the Committee for the Defense of the Spanish Republic and presented a gold Red Cross medal to the Popular Democratic Committee for its contributions. When the contributions were tallied, Tampa Spaniards, with help from Italians and Cubans, had donated at least two ambulances, millions of cigarettes, tons of beans, clothing, and medical supplies, and much-needed cash to the republic.[62]



**Ybor City: The Making of a Landmark Town**

The Spanish Civil War made a lasting impact on Latins. During and after the war—for years—church attendance and baptisms dropped considerably. Reaction by churches to events in Ybor City in early years had been trying at best. There was criticism of Spaniards for their practice of sending excessive help to the war front, since they noted that local needs for donations should come first. A Catholic Ybor church was known to have been watched by Loyalist sympathizers to verify those who were on the side of Nationalists.

Church weddings also dropped. Previous modest progress by Latins toward church attendance was drastically set back by the reported role of priests actively fighting and killing Loyalists. Both Spanish and Italian experiences with priests in their old country had been very negative. The generation that remembered those events was still living at the time of the war.[63]

Yes, many fathers and mothers removed their children from church attendance and from early children's institutions such as the Wolff Mission School on 17th Avenue, across from the old Michigan Avenue. Later Father dropped this young writer and his sister after school, at the Methodist church located between 12th and 13th Avenue on 16th Street (razed by Urban Renewal). When the war started, Father removed us from its activities. This was a typical of reaction by many Latin fathers to the reported role of priests in their actions in Spain and their support of the Nationalists.[64]

Leland Hawes, quotes Lisa Tignor, a University of South Florida graduate student, as follows:

> Italians, Spaniards and Cubans in Tampa derived some of their anticlericalism from radical ideologies and some from personal experiences . . . but whatever the source of this attitude, the anti-catholicism of Tampa's Latins mirrored the sentiments of Spanish Republicans.

In answer to a line from a *Tribune* editorial generalizing that Spaniards were

"acting as their fathers and grandfathers before them—courageous, cruel and proud," Hawes also quotes Tignor: "Manteiga said the *Tribune* editorial writer was 'not only discourteous to the Latins who helped build Tampa, but naive about the situation in Spain,'"[65]

The Spaniards in Tampa suffered greatly at the loss of the Spanish Republic. For months after the end of the war in 1939, the post office, (then at 15th and La Sétima) often had lines of Spaniards waiting to send packages to families in Galicia and Asturias.

When many years later Spaniards in Ybor finally condescended to visit Franco's Spain, many truths became apparent—some validating the reports received from Spain in wartime and others turning out to be erroneous propaganda.[66]

*The Wolff Mission School provided educational opportunities in Ybor City.*

*These boys from the Wolff Mission School are at work in the school's garden.*

*Don Fernando de los Ríos was Spain's ambassador to the United States during the Spanish Civil War of 1937-39. At the Centro Asturiano Club and other venues in Ybor City he gave thanks to Tampa's Loyalists who backed the duly elected Spanish Second Republic of 1931 for donations of money, ambulances, cigarettes, and other practical items. Tabaqueros donated money weekly on the factory steps. In 1931, as Spanish minister of education for the Second Republic, Don Fernando had overseen the construction of 8,000 schools to help overcome Spain's backwardness. He made a lasting impression in Ybor City with his message, his intellectual bearing, and his beautiful, impeccable use of the Spanish language.* La Gaceta.

## A Look Back at the Spanish Civil War

No, between the Spanish Triumverate and the Second Republic there was no compromise. It was too far gone for discussion. The republicans wished for legitimate representative democracy. It wanted to educate—it had to educate. As mentioned earlier, in the first two years of the Second Republic (before the Popular Front) more than eight thousand new schools had been built. But this was not acceptable to the Triumverate. The republic had to be derailed. On a visit to Galicia in 1975, the year of Dictator Franco's death, I noticed that less-than-acceptable bathroom facilities were the norm. Many farms did not even have outdoor bathrooms. Could this be true? In a bus station in Puente Nuevo, the men's room facility was truly medieval and will not be described here. Nonetheless, I experienced it. This, incidentally, was General Francisco Franco's own province. His home was in El Ferrol, Galicia. In 1929, two years before the republic, 83 percent of the farmers were earning *under one peseta per day*! This was the Spain of the tril-

ogy. Is it any wonder their young sons were sent overseas for reasons other than the desire to avoid being sent to fight the Moors? Those who could pay to keep their sons in Spain, did just that.[67]

Most peculiarly, the man who crushed the Second Republic, General Franco, in the last months of his 36-year rule, had set in motion a set of political actions that, by design or in spite of him, became a powerful move toward today's democracy: a parliamentary monarchy. Even the mountains suffer erosion. Did Spain need to see nearly a million of its people killed or injured in a savage civil war to learn that the people's desire for freedom of expression, for equality, for education and progress could not be contained?

The interim government under Carlos Arias Navarro was followed by Adolfo Suarez, the pragmatist. Under pressure from all of the political forces in Spain, the first democratic election in four decades was held. It recognized that Spain's civil war proved that the country needed wide representation. It was greeted by a young Juan Carlos, now King, with understanding.

Indeed, in this election even the communist *La Pasionaria* was allowed to vote. Voting, also, was José Ortega y Gasset's son, José Ortega, legislator and originator of *El Pais* newspaper. Today it vies with the conservative newspaper *ABC* to claim credit as the country's largest paper. The election was a triumph of democracy. Some 87 percent of the voters had elected the new parliamentary monarchy. The youthful King Juan Carlos made reference to the effect that *all* recognized the sovereignty of the Spanish people, and that democracy in Spain had now begun. As of today in the year 2000, twenty-five years after Franco's death in 1975, this parliamentary democracy is representing the Spanish people well.[68]

In 1995 I visited Spain again and went to Castilla, to Oviedo in Asturias, and to Galicia. While the mountains never

**Ybor City: The Making of a Landmark Town**

change, a close-up look and contact with the people revealed a new revival. People were happy. One noticed the difference quickly in Oviedo. The people were spirited and the cafés packed. Visiting one of the cafes, I was thoroughly delighted at these Asturianos playing cards and dominos at the side, each sipping a timeless café con leche, while a fairly packed central space kept the waiters busy. It was a vision of old Ybor City come true. This was a free world they lived in. It was written all over the men, women, and children present. Similarly, the new four-star Oviedo Hotel, spoke of economic progress and of a new vitality. And in El Parque de San Francisco, couples and families were leisurely walking, happiness written on their faces, so very different from the somber faces I had seen in 1975. Franco had died shortly after that visit.

Indeed, modern home conveniences and means of communications were now possible. Making a big impression on me was the fact that the family farmhouse in Galicia, which in 1975 lacked an indoor bathroom, by 1995 featured modern facilities. The house enjoyed a television set, telephone, radio, inside commode, a bidet, and other facilities. These were not luxurious, but very adequate. The two hand-milked cows had been increased by seven, now machine milked, with the milk refrigerated for distributor pickup. The century old meager plantings for income, aside from a minor field for house use, had been abandoned. Income from the milk was adequate for the family's needs. A small, national retirement income system had lifted the burdens, and the spirits flowed. Now the youngsters worked away from the farm and drove small modern cars. This pattern of hopeful improvement was repeated by family members in the nearby 950-year-old ancestral farm where Father was born. (Readers may recall the "new" farmhouse is not yet quite 400 years old.)

Responding to these encouraging changes, children who lived overseas planned frequent returns to Galicia. This held the promise that others would continue to experience the sense of renewal and connection I did during my trip—perhaps nowhere more powerful than my visit to the old church on the distant bluff where, as a young boy, my father rang the church bells.

The Parliamentary Monarchy government since 1977 has allowed for much progress, industrial growth, education, and optimism in Spain. Church life continues uneventfully. This was the compromise that fit Spain's anatomy, the compromise secured from a combination of Unamuno's and Ortega y Gasset's worlds. They were both patriots and great men of letters. At the time of the Parliamentary Monarchy's arrival they were both dead.[69]

**Personal Note**

The Spanish Civil War left an indelible imprint on Spaniards in Tampa. To a great majority of the Spaniards who lived through those days, talk of the Republic, of the fathers' and mothers' passions at the time—which many of their children vividly remember today—is unquestionably the deepest emotional legacy bequeathed them by these parents.

I am able to make this observation as one who lived through this period myself—intensely—as a boy between the ages of nine through sixteen years old. I visited the Columbia Restaurant with father every night to get the early edition of the Tribune to read detailed war news. After a coffee we returned home to listen to La Voz de Madrid to pick up the latest frontline reports. In late afternoons, father and his friends José, Andrés, López, and Braña sat under the Sycamore tree by our fence—there, in the shadows of the Sanatorio del Centro Asturianos—and talked about all aspects of the war. Their

love of the Second Republic was a beautiful and passionate thing. What filtered though the passing months, aside from local events and farm talk back in Spain, was belief in freedom, equality, education, a future for the children, though it was not spelled out as such. What truly haunts my memory are the sounds and rhythms of their voices and the many cuss words so typical of northern Spaniards—and perhaps typical of male conversation everywhere. Hearing them talk this way among themselves made me feel a part of their conversation, and almost acknowledged as an adult myself because I was allowed to listen. I cherished their values. They are my values today. That is what I received from these Gallegos and Asturianos. Those moments with father and his dear friends I always carry close to me.[70]

## World War II—The Early Home Front Years: 1940-1945

After the Spanish Civil War ended in 1939, lines formed at the post office at 15th Street and La Sétima as Spaniards sent aid packages to their families in a devastated Spain. Spaniards in Ybor City continued to send family packages for many years. The Loyalist defeat was a bitter pill to swallow for local Spaniards.

Trips to Spain were out of the question. One did not know to what extent Franco exacted his form of justice.[71] In other cases there were severe family conflicts, the war often having pitted brothers against brothers. In some cases Ybor Loyalist leanings of a kinfolk here might not square with the side the family's region had allied with. In such a case, real inner leanings of the visited family placed the visiting kinfolk in a very undesirable situation. Real feelings were hard to fathom. The absence of family news to kinfolk in Tampa often gave indication of opposing sentiments. The reverse was also true. (America lived these hard times during the aftermath of the Civil War here )

Thus, only after many years did some Loyalists in Tampa condescend to visit their loved ones in a land dominated by the dictator, General Francisco Franco. Personal family calamity such as the death of parents or close relative caused a small number to visit the old homeland. Most put off visits for decades.

With the passage of years, however, a modicum of merit was allowed to Franco's rule. Slowly some old Loyalists acknowledged the return of law and order, security, and clean cities. Still, the lack of enlightened progress was condemned. Much sentiment was simply due to seeing the land of their mothers and fathers. But most decried the controls, lack of free speech, cultural censorship, and the absence of opportunity.[72]

Towards the end of the Republic, many of Spain's top newspaper publishers had escaped to South America. "Almost the entire publishing industry left, along with the best writers, university professors, artists and scientists."[73] There they opened newspapers in the largest cities. However, in South America, during subsequent decades, the source of most of the free world news from Franco's Spain was obtained from England's BBC.

With the advent of the Parliamentary Monarchy, Spain's new open society had allowed uncensored newspapers to operate and grow. By the early 1990's Spain had replaced the BBC as the principle exporter of Spanish and European news to South America.[74] The passing away of Franco's Spain and the advent of the present Parliamentary democracy had allowed a free press and free enterprise. This, too, was what the Second Republic wanted and what the *tabaqueros* in Tampa struggled for. However, by that time most Spanish *tabaqueros* had passed away or were simply too old to care.

Looking back, by 1936 Roosevelt's WPA program had employed approximately 5,000 on projects in Tampa. These included the Peter O. Knight Airport on Davis Islands, Fort Homer Hesterly Armory, the Bayshore sea wall and balustrade, Drew Field, and many others accomplishments. Its end marked the technical end of the depression era in the country. Actually, much of the doldrums days had already evaporated by the late 1930s.

In the early '30s over 13 million were out of work in the country. This was down considerably by the late 30s. But in the mid part of that decade a mini-depression had appeared due to the lack of free enterprise and other factors. A rebellious congress was accused of fostering Roosevelt's so called "mini-depression" that added two additional millions to the six million still unemployed.[75]

Nonetheless, by the early 1940s stability returned to the cigar industry. Better and regular earnings allowed the men the luxury of buying more quality cigars. As a result, some workers reentered the factory. However, the mix of workers was now different. While Spaniards still occupied key jobs more Cubans and American women from the northern and eastern suburbs were also employed. Employing many "crackers" from the suburbs was the Hav-A-Tampa Cigar Co. The wooden factory was located on 22nd Street, just south of

*The famous 9A1 class at George Washington Junior High poses for a class picture in 1937. The worst of the Great Depression was over, but some still ordered the five-cent "mata hambre" (hunger killer pastry). Now we were aware of the Spanish Civil War and the various opinions and support activities in Ybor City. The intensity of the Depression and Civil War years deeply affected our values and perspectives as young people. This class includes many successful business people, a prominent cartoonist, a West Pointer, several WWII officers and pilots, an engineer, civic leader, government administrator, clothiers, general contractors, and other successful members of the community. This was a great group of family-oriented Americans, and over the years it has reunited many times. Left to right, starting with the front row: Josephine Arcuri, Amelia Pedrero, Carmela Reale, Nadine Gonzalez, Obdulia Nuñez, Isabel Garcia, Rose Martinez; second row: Joe Benito, Joe Busciglio, Frank Lastra, David Jordan, Irene DeGuzman, Ida Americh, Mary Jordan, Helen Peretzmon, Alice Miguel; third row: Joe Martinez, Joe Pianna, Raymon Alvarez, Ben Llano, Frank Sarabia, Rudy Granda, Norberto Beiro, Lionel Diaz; back row: Nestor Cueto, Julian Fernandez, Manuel Fernandez, Gonzalo Fernandez, Junior Gay, and Adrian Ynclan.*



**Chapter 4 • Through Good Times, Depression, and War: 1925-1950**

*The committee leading Centro Español in 1941, when its membership had climbed above 13,000, included celebrated "dons" of the time who owned some of the large cigar factories and were financial and cultural leaders in Ybor City. In the front row, from left, are Mariano Alvarez, Celestino Vega Sr., and Francisco Escalante; standing are Ramon Fernandez Rey, Alfredo Gonzales, and Moises Bustillo.* La Gaceta.

*This meeting of the Ybor City Optimist Club took place on April 12, 1942, at Las Novedades Restaurant. The photograph is noteworthy not only because it offers an early look at a constructive organization, but also because it includes so many young people as well as adults at the tables.* USFSCL.

*Members of the Cuban Club Board of Directors posed for this picture after a meeting on Sept. 22, 1937. From left to right, in front are Luis "El Chino" Collado, [unidentified], Manuel Santos Pau, and [unidentified]; middle row, Juan Burrea, Manuel Garcia Talavera, [unidentified], [unidentified], Johnny Díaz (treasurer), Francisco "Paco" García (president), José Fuentes Rosa (secretary general), José Vega, Juan Quesada, César Benítez, [unidentified]; and in the back row, Pasqual Garbalosa, Gustavo A. Corces, Andrés González, Rogelio Rodriguez, [unidentified], José Rodríguez, Elodio Mesquida, José Manuel Rodríguez, Luis Sánchez, [unidentified], Alberto Álvarez, Luis Menéndez, Raúl Lavín, Eduardo Pedrero, and Juan Pérez Acosta.* Rolando Pedrero/La Gaceta.

**Ybor City: The Making of a Landmark Town**

*The Chili Bowl Restaurant on La Sétima (photo far left) was owned and operated by Stella James Bennett (left) from 1945-49. She later managed a rooming house in Ybor City until the 1960s.* YBOR CITY STATE MUSEUM.

*These two views of La Sétima, circa 1949—the year the Ingrid Bergman film showing at the Ritz Theatre was released—show Ybor City's main artery as the decade of the '40s was ending. In the left photo, Miller's Outlet Store at 1515 East 7th Avenue is a "modern" merchant anchoring the middle of the block. In the corner building of the 1500 block, sharing the bill with the venerable Ritz Theatre, are Royal Jewelers, the Adorable Hat Shop, and the W. T. Grant Company, which occupies its own building at 1507.* USFSCL.

*Rogelio "Roy" Berdeal served as President of the Circulo Cubano and was a pioneer for Ybor City historic preservation. In 1940 he founded the original Ybor City Round Table, La Mesa Redonda de Ybor.*

*With an up-to-date Art Deco style, the Fernandez & Garcia clothing store brought a futuristic look to Ybor City when this photograph was made in 1948.* USFSCL.

| 71 |

10th Avenue, and looked east away from Ybor City. It was a very unseemly four story building. Still, its production was a welcome boost that helped Tampa out of the remains of the Great Depression. It pumped out streams of low cost, machine made cigars. In the second half of the century it moved east of Tampa to modern facilities. In 1997 the corporation was purchased by a Spanish firm.

With a world in turmoil, Tampa opened four shipyards. Skilled workers came from several southern states as news of jobs got around a hungry land. Twenty-second Street from Sligh Avenue to the shipyards was crowded every morning and evening, helping many businesses along the route to survive and others to grow. Restaurants like the Columbia literally filled up overnight. Also, the costs of living skyrocketed. At Lake and 22nd Street the pumps at the Midway General Store served out record amounts of gasoline, and there was much euphoria.[76]

An empty cigar factory, La Flor de Cuba, now housed some 400 "sewing ladies." Somewhat less than 50 percent of these were Latins. These ladies worked for the Red Cross, Boy Scouts of America, Clara Frye Negro Hospital, and other community agencies. The WPA projects provided Tampa's women a chance to earn a living during this trying period, which lasted until 1943, when it ended. The invasion of Poland and Czechoslovakia by Hitler in 1940 had brought in a rash of orders for goods and services. Demand for cigar smoking increased, thus impacting the factories. It was a welcome boost that, along with general demand for products made scarce by the war, helped Tampa out of the tail end of the Great Depression.

By the time of the Japanese attack at Pearl Harbor on December 7, 1941, there were hundreds of sons and daughters in uniform in Ybor City. Some had volunteered and others were conscripted into wartime service. Many Latin young people had entered southern colleges.

Long before, many Latins had not personally heeded or felt the demands of WWI. Those were different years. Genuine patriotism takes time to grow. In the intervening decades, new families had formed, and the children were American-born. This was home. Children enrolled in high schools and colleges. Feelings for the American way grew by leaps and bounds. Martial music and America's patriotic and national songs were the rave. These and movies and radios softened the road overseas. There was a land to defend. Patriotism was real and it ran deep, though at times it carried a Latin flavor. Just don't mess with the land and its institutions. These new soldiers—men and women alike—were native born. They were as American as apple pie with, of course, a little addition of black beans and rice, garbanzos, pasta, and certainly Cuban *café con leche*. These last remnants of the culture would also pass to their grandchildren.[77]

The years 1942 through 1945 saw a crescendo of activity. Suddenly soldiers, sailors, and airmen were coming and going to the four corners of the earth. Patriotism and emotion filled our home front. Everyone helped in any possible way to win the war. In World War II, America's unity and determination were powerful forces to behold! And in Ybor City, pride in the nation's heritage knew no limits.

The home front was left to the parents, grandfolks, young children, and those relatively few patriotic Americans who could not serve due to physical problems. Most of the departing GIs, Wacs, and Waves had grandparents. These originals were still around when their sons, daughters, and grandchildren were going to war. The younger generation was going off to fight for the land that received their parents and grandparents years earlier. Now it was their own land.

At home, fathers often milked the cows while the wives pastured and watered them in the daylight hours. The work situation away from home had much to do with who did that chore. The depression years had accustomed the women to make butter, cheese, and clabber milk or plain yogurt, while the men did the outside work, such as tending the gardens, fruit trees, chickens, and even bee hives. But in the war years the practice of keeping a family cow was reduced somewhat. It would have completely slipped away, but with rationing it still made sense to keep the cows around, even if the son was not home to assist with the barn chores, including the milking.

On the home front, mothers were constantly preoccupied with the varying availability or shortages of foods and supplies due to wartime disruptions. In Ybor City, fortunately, avocado and mango trees were as plentiful as citrus trees are today. Some homes grew large, yellow lemons and a few even had peaches. Except for the war news coming from the radio, for some families, the nights at home were long and lonesome. Not having to feed big, hungry boys, mothers and fathers found the opportunity on occasion to eat out at the local, inexpensive restaurants. Los Helados de Ybor, El Buen Gusto, Barcelona, and Cuervo's were quite popular for common fare.

In addition to their inexpensive outings, for special occasions they went to the the Spanish Park, the Columbia, or to Las Novedades. When they ate at the Columbia, the locals preferred the first dining room beyond the café room known as *La Fonda* from earlier days. At the Spanish Park, locals in those days seemed to favor the eastern side of the large central dining room. It was beyond the café and bar area. At Las Novedades, the café and adjoining room were favorites.[78]

The absence or whereabouts of the sons or daughters in the armed forces was usually the prime topic of conversation. The occasional news that this or that mem-

*Many young men from Ybor City fought in World War II. Gathered at the Spanish Park Restaurant in 1942, just before going into military service are: (front row, left to right) Raymond Alea, Al Fernandez, Frank (Paco) Diaz, and Mario Garcia; (back row, left to right) Oscar Molina, Joe Rodriguez, Cesario Alvarez, Rene Rego, Rudolfo Alvarez (Cuti), Julio Fernandez, and Alfredo Fernandez.* La Gaceta.

ber of the family had been killed in battle brought much lament and sadness. And both mothers and fathers spoke of their longing for the war to end, and their desire to see their sons and daughters again.

Meanwhile, all the above, plus the myriad daily routines, including a daily walk to the grocery store, or to La Sétima, gave mothers plenty to do to keep the home fires going at home. Perhaps one of the most popular personalities of the wartime years was the mailman. "*Creo que tienes noticia del barón*" (I think you have news from the boy), the mailman would sometimes say, as he handed the mail to the mothers. The moment was one of rejoicing!

Mothers' efforts to occasionally send some favorite delicacies to their sons or daughters, received a heavy boost when Tampa Electric Company arranged for mothers to can some of their home made soups and other specialties. The services, dates, and times were well publicized. These canned goods were then sent to the men and women overseas. For those who experienced the powdered milk, powdered



**Chapter 4 · Through Good Times, Depression, and War: 1925-1950**

*Sammie Argintar was just 21 when he enlisted in the Navy in 1941. He later served aboard the destroyer escort USS Slater, a ship built and launched in Tampa in 1944. After the war he returned to Ybor City, where he ran the successful and historic Max Argintar Men's Wear store on La Sétima.* SAM ARGINTAR.

eggs, and reliable peanut butter syndrome in the mess halls, there was no matching the wonders of a food package received from home.[79]

Entertaining both the troops overseas and the mothers and fathers in Ybor City were the many wartime songs. Worth mentioning are "Lili Marlene," "God Bless America," "I'll Never Smile Again," "The Last Time I Saw Paris," "A Foggy Day in London Town," "Coming in on a Wing and a Prayer," "Praise the Lord and Pass the Ammunition," and "White Christmas." These made many cry—not to speak of the wealth of other truly beautiful, romantic songs of the wartime period.[80]

The sacrifices of the war years were many. Fortunately, neighbors could converse about these. Some felt the war more than others. But these sentiments evaporated briefly when letters from the front arrived. The war years were like that. And as Ybor parents sent their sons and daughters to war and they listened to the radio—the commentaries and wartime melodies, they felt the heartbeat of America. These fathers had been too young to experience World War I. Some had arrived just prior to that period.

Then, they looked to their homelands, and were unaffected by a call to arms by America. Now it was different. Their hearts and allegiance were with their children and their country. They were proud to see them wear the nation's uniform, even as they prayed for their safety.[81]

## World War II—Return of the Sons and Daughters: 1945-1950

By the time of the Normandy landing by the Allies on June 6, 1944, Tampa was the center of consderable military troop movement. Airmen, soldiers, and sailors arrived and waited here until they were processed to their final destination. MacDill Army Air Field was seething with plane flights at all hours of the day or night. Overhead, periodically, one watched squadrons of large aircraft. Onlookers searched the skies for them and heard the loud roar of engines becoming distant hums. Long convoys of army troop trucks to and from MacDill jammed our few highways. The increased traffic necessitated the construction of Dale Mabry Highway to alleviate congestion. On U.S. 41, long convoys of army trucks, jeeps, and other equipment rolled to or away from MacDill or Drew Fields.

Harry Crumpacker, a *Tribune* correspondent, referred to "a plane a day in Tampa Bay," as he described the scene: "By the tens of thousands, servicemen and workers poured into Tampa and the drumbeat of war picked up—shipyards, USO halls, bars, and bombers. When they left, the city had been transformed."[82]

Tampa at night was a sea of bars, eateries, drive-ins, and movie houses loaded with young warriors attempting to get a last taste of America before shipping out. Jitterbugging was in. Due to a Korean War freeze on new channels, TV would not hit the area until 1952, though prospective engineers at Georgia Tech, where I studied at the time, experienced it at the adjoining Varsity fast food eatery in 1948.

174

But in Tampa, radio served well enough, and locals in Ybor City picked up patriotic fever from its broadcasts.[83]

"Downtown Tampa was packed at night, full of servicemen who headed into town with money in their pockets. Strains of Glenn Miller's 'Chattanooga Choo Choo' and 'In the Mood' floated out of juke joints and elegant restaurants."[84]

Meanwhile, German subs menaced our Atlantic and lower Gulf waters. In Ybor City, La Sétima's restaurants and retail stores reflected the times. New moneys from wartime, such as 400 ships built in Tampa's shipyards, invigorated a previous depression-weary Tampa. Yet with the youngsters eating in army mess halls, in army camps, or on foreign lands, a thirst for wartime news was insatiable. Movie theaters like the Tampa, Rialto, or the Ritz on La Sétima, put on many wartime movies. On the radio Walter Winchell still opened his radio program with, "Good morning, Mr. And Mrs. America and all ships at sea." And the afternoon serial, "Ma Perkins," captured many a mother's ear in Ybor City. It was possibly as popular as listening to Cuba's *La Cadena Suaritos* (the Suarito channel) in Havana. Al Jolson still sang "Mammy," and "Don't Fence Me In" had hit the airwaves. "Rum and Coca Cola" was popular.

Tampa again resembled a boom town, and Ybor City was along for the ride. The government had invested huge amounts for the war effort. The improved wartime economy had a positive impact on Tampa and Ybor City, and many families came and went as though all was right. Then, soon, many of the early returning GIs were intent on marriage. They invested in small homes or bought land in West Tampa and began a slow expansion of the housing market, which in reality helped greater Tampa more than Ybor City. West Tampa was particularly appealing, for much land remained uncleared at the time.

The battlefields claimed many Latins.

Mothers and fathers awaited in fear of receiving a telegram from the War Department. Many escaped death by inches, including those left to die in the Pacific islands. Friend Dominick Maggio was shot by the Japanese on a lonely island and left to die. Miraculously, he is still with us today. In the far Pacific, Col. Frank Adamo (a physician) saved many lives and limbs utilizing leeches and roots, in the absence of modern medicine. Captured, he spent two years in prison on Bataan. Today, Adamo Drive honors his name.

Tommy Gomez, one of the great boxers of Tampa, received the Purple Heart for his heroic deeds in Germany.

Among the officers from Ybor City serving gallantly were Captain Augustine (Chunchi) Fernandez; Captain Joe Benito; Lt. Julian Fernandez; Captain Marcelino Huerta; Naval officer Tony Fernandez and brother Buck Fernandez, Colonel (West Pointer) and Naval officer Joe Aizpuru. All these lived within a three-block radius of the Centro Asturiano Hospital, an indication of the heavy participation of the area's sons and daughters in the armed forces.[85]

The first session of the 96th Congress published a list of Congressional Medal of Honor Recipients, dated from 1863 to 1978. Among these was Tampa's Baldomero López, First Lieutenant, US Marine Corps, 1st Battalion—1st Marine Division (Rein). He received this highly coveted metal posthumously.

During the Korean War, Baldomero López, a graduate of the Naval Academy, entered the Marine Corps. He died during America's Inchon invasion, smothering a live grenade to protect his Marine comrades. An American flag watches over him at the Centro Asturiano cemetery located just past 56th Street and Martin Luther King Jr. Blvd. The 46th anniversary of his death was celebrated in September 1996. The speakers were a Marine lieutenant general and Judge E. J. Salcines. Lt. Baldomero López, son of a Spaniard from

Asturias and a Sicilian mother from Tampa, received truly rare honor for his courageous action at saving his men from a grenade he was about to throw at the enemy defenses. Hit in the chest and shoulder and unable to hold the grenade fimly, he chose to cover it with his own body to protect his men. He took the full impact of the explosion.[86] The Baldomero López Veterans Nursing home in Pasco County was named in his honor in 1999.

By 1945 Hitler and Mussolini were defeated in Europe, Russia, Sicily, and North Africa. Germany capitulated on May 8, 1945, V. E. Day. Japan surrendered on August 14, 1945. Although millions were killed or wounded in World War II, the defeat of Japan "following the bombing of Hiroshima saw millions of Americans coming back home, of which many thousands were from Tampa."[87]

Many, regretfully, did not return. They died honorably in defense of America.

"More than 55 million human beings perished from the face of this earth, during World War II"[88] The majority did return to Tampa and Ybor City. And Ybor was still here—looking and feeling much as it had in their memories when thousands of miles away in trenches and battlefields. Families were reunited again. What a glorious feeling! And after they rejoiced, mothers filled their bellies with their favorite home-cooked foods. There was much visiting, sightseeing, strolling along La Sétima, and sitting for that authentic *café con leche* and *pan con mantequilla*.

The days and weeks of homecoming prompted much talk and endless questions by friends and family members, all trying to find out all the exciting situations that our soldiers experienced. But most important, for the returned soldiers and college graduates of the GI Bill era, it was a chance to see the object of their many dreams, a noble and friendly world, a world where the sound of Spanish and Italian made it unique, warm, and emotional. "What a feeling to be home, to see the town and meet our life-long friends again!" I remember many saying similar words. Firing the spirits was the warm and melodic Caribbean music from the Cuban stations—*La Cadena Azul* and *La Cadena Suaritos*—or a *paso doble*, or martial air songs from bullrings in Spain, so stirring and reminiscent of the past. Life in a beautifully friendly Cuban, Spanish, and Italian motif, one dreamed of that while overseas.

As the young soldiers returned home, the social clubs saw an increase in attendance. The Sunday matinee at the Centro Español was the place to be and to look for a sweetheart, a future wife. Or was it at the Casino, the Ritz or the Broadway theaters? And what about the Cuban Club patio dances, or the L'Unione Italiana and Centro Asturiano Club socials. These were all respectable places. Utterly respectable! Mothers and family members were still around to chaperone. It was the Latin way.

Unquestionably, the young men and women who returned home had somehow changed. They had seen America at war and working together in times of stress and peace, and they had seen the world, with all its idiosyncrasies, diverse people, and varied landscapes. They had seen other cultures, heard other tongues, understood other values, and seen people of many shades of color and facial appearances. Many had fallen in love with young girls in other parts of America or with girls overseas. These ties would most assuredly take many local soldiers away from home again. Many had already married girls from different cultures. Love had hastened and softened the transition.

For many, the war years had changed the course of their lives. A few would not return to live in Ybor or Palmetto. To those who loved their culture, moving to West Tampa, where there was more room for growth, was an option many preferred and executed. For West Tampa, this more than made up for the outflow of its own natives due to similar loss of the cigar industry and evolving demographic patterns.

Throughout the town, grocery stores were filled with mothers who simply walked around the corner, a few blocks at the most, to shop for favorite foods. La Sétima still offered a wide array of merchants, and a goodly number of residents still shopped it, especially on Saturday night, as in years past. The bakeries and coffee roasting outlets, such as La Norma and Naviera, filled the town with Ybor's smells and flavors. An occasional wind would blow in the smell of tobacco, reminding one that somehow things were about the same. But this didn't last long, and the breezes sometimes blew in vain.

In the Ybor City cafés, the presence of returned GIs fostered talk of yesteryears, which then shifted to the larger world that is America, and to the transitions and relocations that were underway throughout the world. For the parents, the arrival of sons and daughters was a memorable event. Often the highlight was a trip to a favorite coffee house to reflect on old times—to leave again, this time to return the following day. Many could count this as the beautiful arrival to a place of dreams, and a sober departure from the many places one's wartime fate had taken one. A simple thing like seeing once again a mango or avocado tree waving in the breeze was a great joy, as were the sounds of the *piruli* candy man, or the whistle (*el pito*) of a knife sharpener.

Children playing marbles on the sandy earth, men playing dominoes in the local Cantina, or the muted sound of music from the social clubs in the evenings, especially from the Cuban Club patio, all these and more made coming home a blessing.[89]

And when all the greetings were over, when all the favorite foods were savored and the postponed visitations and café gossip sessions were fulfilled, the slow realities of life began to emerge. What now,

Son? What now? Much heavy thinking and decision-making took place in those early weeks after returning from overseas. These would impact the whole future lives of these returning heroes.

The country was experiencing great readjustments in the workplace and in the social demands on returning GIs. These found the nation still segregated. But many remembered that black Americans fought alongside them with distinction. This contradiction was quite apparent in Tampa. Our sons and daughters had acquired new standards. Their views were highly idealistic. They had fought to make this a better world. Indeed, these were more mature young Americans who returned.[90] This was true of the nation as a whole, but with some entrenched exceptions.

Meanwhile, in 1948 a new civic club, Ybor City Rotary, was initiated. At its Charter presentation in the beautiful patio of the Círculo Cubano, Tony Pizzo, its first president, unleashed a whirlwind of proposed activities. These would eventually include trips to Havana to foster trade and understanding, fiestas, parades, citywide historic plaques, initiation of the Pan American Commission, promotion of Latin culture, and the writing down of Ybor City and Tampa history. The José Martí Park opposite Ybor Square is one tangible result of these activities.[91] And in the years to come, these and other works would help assure that the culture and the history of this formative place of dreams, though they might dim, would still have means to shine.

*This 1925 view of the corner of La Sétima and 22nd Street gives a glimpse of the Columbia Restaurant building in the right foreground, with the 22nd Street Drug Store across the street and Senour Hardware Company at the diagonal corner.* USFSCL.

*Long a meeting place for community organizations, the Columbia Restaurant's tiled banquet room shows up to good advantage at this Rotary Club banquet March 21, 1946.* THCPLS.

*The social clubs were important outlets during every era. This Burgert Brothers photograph (left) taken in 1926 shows the interior of Centro Español with members playing cards at the tables and in the background at the upper left.*

*An early photo (above) shows Las Novedades Café in its original location on the left side of La Sétima. The new Las Novedades Restaurant in 1946 (left) enjoyed great popularity at its corner location. The interior is shown below (right).* USFSCL/THCPLS.

**Ybor City: The Making of a Landmark Town**

*The Colon Saloon, a popular local pub on La Sétima at 12th Street, ran this ad in a local publication showing enough "regulars" in the photograph to appeal to friends and neighbors.*

*The dedication of Cuscaden Park on Sunday, April 12, 1938. Rafael M. Ybor stands with the flag. The small boy next to him is today's Rafael Martínez Ybor. At the microphone is Harry Wilderman, chairman of the dedication committee. Rev. Walter B. Passiglia stands behind the microphone and Joseph E. Chamoun, president of the Ybor City Chamber of Commerce stands at the far right.*
ROBERTSON AND FRESH/RAFAEL MARTÍNEZ YBOR.

*This class photo from Our Lady of Perpetual Help School in Ybor City was taken in 1937. In the front row (left to right) are Albert Fernandes, Tony Alvarez, John Foy, Joe Bowers, Manuel Garcia, Bernard Clark, and Henry Garcia; in the second row are Virginia Rodriguez, Violet Garcia, Grace Mascuñana, _______ Garcia, Gloria Juan, Rose Echevarria, Aida _______, and Grace Barcelo; and in the back row are Olga Menendez, Dolores _______, Tony Villavicenzo, Albert Velasco, Mike Blanco, Albert Castillo, Frank Gonzalez, Gloria Caruso, and Mildred Gutierrez.* FRANK GONZALEZ/LA GACETA.

**Chapter 4 • Through Good Times, Depression, and War: 1925-1950**

*Early site of La Benefica Clinic in 1931 at La Sétima and 15th Street (later the U. S. Post Office site).*

*El Pasaje in 1941.*

*The main location of La Benéfica Clinic of Centro Español at 10th Avenue and 15th Street, southeast corner.*

*La Benefica Clinic in the 1940s was a model of modern health care. The building (top) and waiting room (above). The staff of La Benefica Español in 1941 included, left to right: (seated) Sra. Carlos Barbas, nurse; Dr. J. R. Porta, pharmacist; Dr. Carlos Barbas, medical intern; Srta. Manuela Failde, bacteriologist; Sr. Eloy Vergara, secretary, and Srta. Julia Marchín, nurse; (standing) Emilio Gonzáles, student pharmacist; Manuel Llera, assistant secretary; and Mateo Gómez, student pharmacist.*



**Ybor City: The Making of a Landmark Town**

This Burgert Brothers photograph on the left, reproduced in the 1930 almanac printed by La Traducción *newspaper shows the Clinica Dr. Trelles that was located on 8th Avenue between 15th and 16th Streets. The clinic of Dr. Sueiras Miralles is shown on the right.*

The Centro Asturiano Hospital was located on 21st Avenue facing 13th Street. This photo taken in the early 1930s includes many of the highly qualified staff. From left to right, beginning on the first row: are Dr. Luís Barreras, Nibia Santana, Marie N. Humphrey, Annie M. Lino, Angie Coniglio, Rosalie M. Fojaco, Superindent Lucy Mae Hobby, Fannie Mae Rawls, Mildred Russell, X-ray Technician Mary Militello, Dietician Emilia Díaz, Elizabeth Swett, and Dr. José O. Afanador, Intern; second row: Pharmacist Florentino Saldaña, Dr. A. P. Perzia, Dr. H. M. Faver, Dr. J. A. Más, Dr. I. Angulo, Dr. R. Ortega, Dr. M. R. Winton, Dr. J. A. Domínguez, Dr. Luís J. Garcia, Dr. R. Roque, and Dr. C. R. de Armas, Radiologist; third row: Dr. Kenneth Berno, Director Dr. P. M. García, and Juan Bernardo; fourth row: Ignacio Noguez, Francisco Rodríguez, Félix Bernaldo, Antonio León, Jesús Villanueva, Manuel Miranda, Severino La Fuente, Administrator Félix García, Angel García, Leonardo García, Vicente Ojea, Joe Lolina, Rafael Montaño, and Severino Fernández. CENTRO ASTURIANO.



**Chapter 4 · Through Good Times, Depression, and War: 1925-1950**

The Ladies Auxiliary of Centro Español (La Seccion de Damas del Centro Español) posed for this group portrait in 1934. Seated at the table are officers: (from left) Amelia Escalante Gonzales, president; Angelita Gonzales Alvarez; Elena Lastra; Julia Escalante Cigarran, and Katie Scaglione. Others in the picture are Rose Bonis, Manuela Fernandez, Benigna Llano, Mayita Limia Gonzalez, Delfina Alonso Crow, Joaquina Garcia, Sarita Morales, Margarita Fernandez, Josefina Corrales Sanchez, Josefina Garcia, Rose Chiaramonte, Eulalia Paniello, Conchita Gijon, and Lizzie Noriega. AMELIA ESCALANTE GONZALEZ/LA GACETA.

Many large enterprises have small beginnings. Kash n' Karry, a widely known supermarket chain, is no exception. Founder of this well-known enterprise is Salvatore Greco, seen here wearing a dark hat, photographed with members of his support team, his dedicated family. The market was located on busy Michigan Avenue (Columbus Drive), crossed many times daily by a typical yellow electric trolley car.

This photograph of Los Helados de Ybor Spanish Restaurant was taken circa 1933 when the restaurant was located on the southwest corner of 14th Street and 8th Avenue. One of the owners, José Faza, is standing behind the bar at the left. Francisco Faza first opened Los Helados in downtown Tampa, but he moved the business to Ybor City in 1925. His three sons—José, Aniceto, and Ralph—assumed responsibility for the business in the 1930s. On the wall in the dark corner at the far right of the photo is a slot machine, a reminder of the time when gambling was commonplace in Ybor City. José Faza passed away in 1990. ANDRES FAZA.

**Ybor City: The Making of a Landmark Town**

*The Columbus Day Dinner at the L'Unione Italiana Club Ballroom in 1949.*
Mary Anastasi.

*The original Centro Asturiano building (above) and a view of its dining room (below).*

*Centro Asturiano dining area.*

*Centro Asturiano Hospital lobby.*



**Chapter 4 • Through Good Times, Depression, and War: 1925-1950**

*Joe Guagliardo helped his family dairy grow from two cows into one of the largest dairy distributors in the state of Florida. Founded by his grandfather, Giuseppi Guagliardo, the dairy was called G. Guagliardo and Son, and started operation on 40th Street in 1922, when the cigar factories where Giuseppi worked were closed on strike. Originally from Santo Stefano in Sicily, Giuseppi and his wife Vicenta had five children. Joe's father, Nelson, had also worked in the cigar factories, but quit in 1923 to work at the family dairy, which soon grew to 4,000 cows, eventually moving to a 2,000-acre farm in Brandon in 1928. Joe started working at the dairy himself full time in 1942, after graduating from Hillsborough High School. He met his wife, Lily Favata, at a dance in Ybor City during WWII.*

*The Cantina Room on the first floor of Centro Español.*

*The Centro Español club building in 1941. It was declared a National Historic Landmark Building as of 1988.*

*The Marcelino Perez factory at 19th Street and 10th Avenue served as the backdrop for this family photograph taken in the early 1930s. While the homes in this neighborhood were demolished during Urban Renewal, the wooden factory building continued to be used as a tobacco warehouse. Standing are Henry Cagnina, Angelo Cacciatore, Giovanino Canzoneri, Rosina Canzoneri, Maria Cagnina, Mary Cansoneri Tognella, Joseph Cagnina, Antonia Cagnina, Mary Canzoneri Brombiela, Assunta Canzoneri, and Rose Canzoneri. The seated children are, from left, unidentified, Frances Canzoneri Militello, and Josie Friscia. LA GACETA.*

**Ybor City: The Making of a Landmark Town**

*A banquet at the Columbia Restaurant in 1937.* THCPLS.

*Columbia Restaurant entrance to El Patio.*

*Photographers Robertson and Fresh captured a bumper crop of youngsters attending Vacation Bible School at the Ybor City Presbyterian Mission Assembly Hall in 1950. The Rev. Walter Passiglia stands at the far left. The church was located at 953 11th Avenue.* USFSCL.

*These 1937-38 graduates of the Wolff Settlement mission school include future Tampa Mayor Dick Greco (front row, fourth from left) as well as Roy Cotarbo, Bette Rose ("Saba"), Henry DiStefano, and Donald L. Re. The building seen here, located at 2801 N. 17th Street, was built in 1932 and more recently served as the home for the Tampa United Methodist Centers.* Mary Capitano/La Gaceta.

**Chapter 4 • Through Good Times, Depression, and War: 1925-1950**

*La Sétima looking east in 1952. The once famous Las Novedades restaurant is on the left and Fernandez & Garcia, Ybor City's largest clothing store, stands on the corner across from it on the same side of the street. On the right side of the street is the Ybor branch of Maas Brothers, which remained only briefly.* © LEWIS ELLSWORTH.

# Mixed Years and a Withering Town: 1950-1965

## Sports, Social Clubs, and Zarzuelas: 1950-1955

With the defeat of the Axis Powers in 1945, America found itself virtually master of a war-weary world. Now, its armed forces began to scale back. It would take a few years for America to plan and accomplish the return home of most of its worldwide military forces and to assert its dominance without the haughtiness some expected. It did, in fact, display the benevolence of a truly great victor. The late 1940s and 1950s saw the initiation of the Marshall Plan in Europe and of General MacArthur's rebuilding of Japan.

Tampa in these years was constructing a new, sprawling air terminal building on Columbus Drive. This was an important step forward and very much needed. It was the forerunner of the current Tampa International Airport. The old airport, assisted by the small south field on Davis Islands and the St. Petersburg airport on the other side of the bay, clearly could not provide the capacity that the fast-growing Tampa metropolitan region required. Tampa's population had just hit 124,000 and plans for expansion of the city limits were underway. Moreover, the purchasing power of thousands of returning GIs continued to increase, adding fuel to an already buoyant urban economy.

In turn, expectations for a continued resilient Ybor City were heightened by the seemingly robust shopping on La Sétima. A photograph provided by Lewis Ellsworth, a photographer for the *Tampa Tribune*, shows the town's main street in 1952 decked out in overhead flags to celebrate a festive event. Clearly displayed are the Las Novedades restaurant and the Fernandez and García retail store, the largest retail establishment in Ybor. Both were located on the corner of 15th Street and La Sétima, the heart of Ybor City. Also to be seen in the photograph are many new automobiles in a variety of colors parked or moving on the Avenue.

And if one squints an eye carefully at this photo, he will see the newly added Ybor City branch of Maas Brothers, a spit of its downtown size, but apparently geared for limited, special-access service. Maas Brothers was the largest quality retail department store in the Tampa Bay area, and its opening of an Ybor branch was in synch with the upbeat tempo of the time. Unfortunately, it did not last long. But most reassuringly, the Max Argintar Men's Clothing Store was still

*The Donna Tampa brand was a stock label used by various factories. This one is from Don Alvarez y Cia.*

there. In the early 1950s there were no big shopping malls in greater Tampa. Heavy shopping was done either in downtown Tampa or in Ybor City. But the continuing diaspora to the suburbs, the loss of the trolleys, the introduction of bus service, and the increase in auto use all slowly shifted shopping patterns toward downtown Tampa.

During the 1950s the parks in Ybor City were filled with activities. This included Cuscaden Park on 15th Street, Ragan Park on Lake Avenue, and Desoto Park in Palmetto Beach. In the '40s the Tampa Smokers baseball team had brought new life to Cuscaden, but soon it had suffered the loss of young men going off to war. Now, inspired by the early 1950s baseball craze sweeping the country in a period referred to as the "Golden Age of Sports," returning GIs again turned toward baseball. In Tampa, Tom Spicola rejuvenated the Tampa Smokers as a Florida International League (FIL) team, but sold the

team in 1952. Today I still remember stars like Benny Fernandez, Charlie Cuellar, and Tony "Cooch" Cuccinello, who died in Tampa in 1995. Cooch had previously coached three major-league teams, and he came back to coach in Ybor City. With no television yet in town, they could count on a full house nearly every night.

The Tampa Smokers are probably best remembered for their strong performance in 1947. After winning three games against Havana and 102 games out of 154 overall, they fell just a little short of the FIL championship. They were a strong source of community pride and interest. However, taken over several decades, the mainstays of baseball at Cuscaden were not the professional games, but those played by the Inter-Social League. Players such as Joe Benito, an outstanding second baseman, were such attractions that the league filled the grandstand at most games.

The return of the young warriors from the service also rekindled the local inter-

**Ybor City: The Making of a Landmark Town**

est in football. University of Florida football star Marcelino "Chelo" Huerta was a local standout who later became coach of the University of Tampa team. He also coached in Wichita, Kansas, and at Parsons College in Fairfield, Iowa. Huerta had flown a B-24 bomber during the war. His son, Marcelino Huerta Jr., who is an attorney, says that during a newspaper interview once his father told *Tribune* reporter Doug Carlson that after the ordeal of the war, "playing football now is a piece of cake!"[1]

A young man from Ybor City who made weekly headlines playing at the University of Florida was Frank Lorenzo. He later became coach of Plant Senior High School. And in a less common sport, a local boy who was called "Tampa's young gunner," Dick Greco, was named to the All-American Junior Skeet and Trap Shooting team. Also, in Tampa, Tommy Gómez kept the city's boxing world on its toes with his fights at Benjamin Field (now the Armory) until his loss much later to Jersey Joe Walcott. When I talked with Gómez in February 1997 at the funeral of Joe Busciglio, a sorely missed, mutual friend and great professional artist, Tommy Gómez still thoroughly looked the part of a great fighter. He said he had been within a short breath of winning the Heavy Weight Title of the World at the time he lost to Jersey Joe Walcott.

Yes, sports in the early post-war period had picked up where it left in the pre-war years. Now, however, it had been accelerated by a strong, national thirst for physical recreation, the return of the town's sons and daughters, and the past history of athletics in Cuscaden and Ragan Parks. Two of the other popular teams that played in Cuscaden Park were the Optimist Baseball Team of Tampa and the Silver Bar Brewing Company team. Undoubtedly, the decade of the '50s is remembered as the Golden Age of Sports, not only of the nation, but of Ybor City.

*An Ybor City sports standout was Marcelino Huerta, who coached the University of Tampa and the Wichita, Kansas, football teams. During the war he was an Air Force captain and led a B-24 crew. For over a decade he was director of the MacDonald Training Center for the handicapped in Tampa.*

In Ybor City the following names are still discussed among the old timers, though the names and events gradually fade away, as do the memories of the shouting and cheering. The corroding effect of time erases them from one's mind. But here they are again: Charlie Cuellar, pitcher; Joe Benito, second baseman; Chelo Huerta, local boxer for a limited career, better known for his exploits at UF football and many years coaching at the

*From the 1920s through the 1940s Tampa's boxing clubs produced a string of contenders for the world championship. Shown together here in a 1977 photograph are (left to right) Tommy Gomez, Oscar "Chino" Alvarez, Carl "Red" Guggino, Manuel Quintero, and Jimmy Leto. Alvarez is holding the plaque honoring him as a new member of the Hall of Fame of the Florida West Coast Veterans Boxers Association. He was inducted at Ring 50's annual banquet at Bartke's Dinner Theater on Rocky Point, January 17, 1977.* LA GACETA.



**Chapter 5 · Mixed Years and a Withering Town: 1950-1965**

*Captain Joe Benito (left) flew his P-47 Thunderbolt "Sack Time" on ninety-three missions over Europe during the war. He received a Distinguished Flying Cross in 1944. Cadet Bombardier Augustine "Chunchi" Fernandez (right) was captain of his B-17 crew and flew with them over Germany. He was later shot down and held prisoner until the war ended. Promoted to Major, he served his country again in the Korean War.*

*These are two of at least five officers I know of who were raised in the vicinity of the Centro Asturiano Hospital and Cuscaden Park. Others include naval officers Tony Fernandez and Joe Aizpuru, and Tony's brother Col. Buck Fernandez, a West Point graduate. All of them attained success in post-war civilian or military life. Ybor City had many other distinguished sons and daughters in the military, such as Col. Frank Adamo, a doctor, for whom Adamo Drive is named, and Marine 1st Lt. Baldomero López, recipient of the Congressional Medal of Honor.* Joe Benito & Augustine Fernandez.

university level; Al Lopez, Hall-of-Famer, catcher, and coach of two major leagues; Tony Cuccinello, who coached three major league ball teams; Tommy Gómez, heavyweight contender and knockout artist, who won a Purple Heart in the war; Chino Alvarez, a much-admired boxer of the Cuban Club and of all Tampa's Latin community. Not quite yet forgotten also are Benny Fernandez, of Tampa Smokers fame; Charlie Grannel, who in the mid-1930s captured everyone's admiration playing baseball at Cuscaden and Ragan Park; and Albert de la Torre and Reggie Fernandez of the Silver Bar team.[2]

In the ongoing life of Ybor City in 1953, a young man whose family had lived in town and run a store on La Sétima for over a half century, Rene Gonzalez, organized the Spanish Little Theater, which became better known as the Spanish Lyric Theater. This brought back to life *la zarzuela*, a type of Spanish musical entertainment resembling light opera, which more and more at that time was slipping away. Thanks to this new performance company, the *zarzuela* would, in the next three decades, become monthly fare for many deep-rooted Spaniards and other Latins from Ybor City and West Tampa. It was a style long admired in the community, and by performing it, the Spanish Lyric Theater preserved a significant portion of our cultural heritage.

Spain is not generally known for grand operas, though some of its artists such as Placido Domingo, Jose Carreras, and others have attained the very pinnacle of international acclaim in the opera world. In place of opera the Spanish populace has embraced the more light-hearted form known as the *zarzuela*, incorporating music, dance, and dialog with flair and popular appeal in a form that somewhat resembles the shows of Gilbert and Sullivan. When the famous novelist James Michener was in Madrid writing *Iberia*, he was taken by a friend to a zarzuela performance and discovered a theatrical form he had never known existed. He praised it in his book as one of the highlights of his stay in Spain. It is not surprising, then, that the Latins in Tampa felt themselves fortunate to be able to attend live performances in their community.

The name *zarzuela* is derived from the Spanish palace where the shows were frequently presented, *La Zarzuela*, built in Madrid by Felipe II of Spain. Over the course of the years two recognizable types developed: full three-act zarzuelas, referred to as *genero grande* or "large genre," such as *Luisa Fernanda* and *Los Gavilanes* (*"The Hawks"*); and shorter one-act shows with several scenes, known as *El Genero Chico* (*"small genre"*), such as *La Verbena de La Paloma* (*"The Festival of the Lady of the Dove"*), *La Revoltosa* (*"The Unruly One"*),

**Ybor City: The Making of a Landmark Town**

*In the 1940s the Centro Asturiano had a young theatrical company. They entertained in plays and presented Spanish folk dances. The group here is dressed as* Manolas y Chavales *("Gals and Guys"), in costumes typical of the dress in many* zarsuelas, *a musical genre which ranged from Broadway musicals to light operas.* Zarzuelas *became very popular toward the end of the 19th century, when Spaniards grew tired of long and heavy dramas. Many of the plots for the Spanish* zarzuelas *centered on life in the lower barrios of Madrid, such as the famous* Lavapies. *The musical shows remained popular with Ybor City residents and in the 1950s the Spanish Lyric Theater made them a permanent Ybor City cultural institution.* CENTRO ASURIANOS DE TAMPA INC. AND USFSCL.

and *Agua, Azucarillo y Agua Ardientê* ("*Water, Rock Candy, and Brandy*") among others. Rene Gonzalez and his company put on all of these and many, many more.

At about the same time that this engaging live-performance company was drawing crowds to its theater, a new technological communications form was enticing people to stay home. Introduced elsewhere in 1946, black and white TVs became more widely available to Tampa citizens in the early 1950s. This brought great relief to parents' monotony and loneliness created as their children were drawn away by war and college years, and, eventually, by marriages of their own which took them permanently away from home. For cigarworkers' families, television helped soften the impact of an increasingly uncertain future. The radio slowly moved to second place in homes throughout the city, but would assume a new popularity and importance inside our autos.

In 1951, the songs of the '30s and '40s and early '50s were rapidly being replaced by newer, faster-paced music. Country music was also gaining new popularity. The world seemed to be changing quickly at mid-century. The new British Queen Elizabeth succeeded her father, King George VI, after his death in 1952, and that was the year Ernest Hemingway wrote *The Old Man and the Sea*. By 1955 Stalin had died; and here at home the price controls that had been imposed on goods and wages to halt the spiraling rates between 1951 and 1953 were finally removed. In 1954 the Supreme Court rejected segregation in public schools. Some slower and more melodic new songs like "Love is a Many Splendored Thing" also became very popular, and the songs and music of the war years would still captivate both the country and Ybor City for many decades.

And early in 1953, ushering in a change with consequences no one imagined or intended, General Dwight Eisenhower, wartime hero and recently inaugurated President, approved new legislation intended to improve the nation's deteriorat-



**Chapter 5 · Mixed Years and a Withering Town: 1950-1965**

ing inner cities. It was the forerunner of Ybor City's calamitous "Urban Renewal."

## The Last Privileged Years: 1955-1960

The last half of the decade of the '50s brought privileged years, but they were evaporating ever so quickly. They were the last few years for Ybor's sons and daughters to live in and remember their town before hungry bulldozers devoured it—a possibility certainly not even entertained by the residents of the core area at the time. True, the cigar industry had folded up around them, but in 1955 Ybor City was still much more than a dying industrial town. It had a special appeal, a continuing vibrancy that foretold its strong potential as a major tourist attraction.

Ybor City still had the allure of the fascinating Latin community it had become—one where the homes and the families that made the town were still intact. They defined the community, interweaving business with social life both in the core area and in the far suburbs up to Buffalo Avenue, now Martin Luther King Boulevard. While many of the sons and daughters were gone, mothers and fathers and young grandchildren were always to be found at work or play. Cuban, Spanish, and Italian households were being maintained with pride that passed along the cultural traditions. Unfortunately, the condition of housing in the core area was beginning to slip. Many of the *tabaqueros* with lower wages lived there. Nonetheless, it retained the beautiful prospect of its well-laid township grid with sidewalks, tropical bushes, and mature trees—many of them mangos and avocados—spilling over the walkways and streets.

Castilian was still the town's language, and Italian was often heard as well. A Spanish or Italian greeting in town, followed with a matching smile and a handshake, or in some cases a hug, quickly sent the spirit soaring! On far-out Lake Avenue and 15th Street, Leon Hernandez, service station and auto repair owner, still could be seen leisurely sitting down on the corner bench. Here, also, my father Evaristo joined Leon, Pachin, and other friends to while away the time, interrupted regularly by cars gassing up. From their bench they could clearly see a new hardware, lumber, and building supply venture started by a young Spaniard, Al Fernandez, with his wife Yolanda. That long bench calls up many memories and scenes from decades earlier—scenes of yesteryear in a part of distant Ybor City that pulsed to its own heartbeat. Most traces of that past have blown away in the winds of time, surviving only in the stories of a few "originals" who now seldom meet. Where did these memories go?

The town's special ambience was noticed by strangers who walked La Sétima and its environs, drawn by the warmth of the red brick pavements. For visitors from the rising urban center of downtown Tampa, the reduced architectural scale of Ybor City imparted an intimate and more human feeling. Many shop owners still lived above their stores or just a few blocks away. Businesses like Kress's, Raul Vega, Max Argintar, La France, and others were still open. Who needed special security, when owners and families lived and moved on the streets and the people who carried on this culture thrived on orderliness and respect for one another? The women walked everywhere with never a concern for their safety. Indeed, personal worry about security was never a factor in daily life. In the town, mothers and children relaxed and talked on the balconies, while the men socialized in the cafés and clubhouse cantinas. There they played their games of cards and dominoes as they sipped *café con leche* as they had year after year.

While many people still knew or at least recognized each other, the faces and paces on *La Sétima* were brisk with a different sort of speed now — faster, more directed, more often involving people coming from

*An ordinary scene at the famous Columbia "Café on the Corner," circa 1950. The man with his elbow resting on the counter at the end of the bar (right rear) is Bebe Menendez, later owner of La Tropicana Café. The grey-haired man facing the camera at the front table is my father having coffee with Joe Dominguez (left) and friends.*

*These Latin American Fiesta Association members, queen, and court visited the Bacardi company offices in Havana, Cuba, in January 1959, as part of their annual good-will trip. Among those in this photo are Mrs. Leon Cazin, Paco Vinagre, Albert Knapp, Louis and Delia Salazar, Mario and Helen Cabrera, Hector and Olga Jimenez, Sam Rodante, Pete Sones, Sam Marino, Al Cazin, Nancy Sierra, Sylvia Sears, Cookie Salazar, Sylvia Jimenez, Ann Fernandez, and Lucille Cabrera.* LOUIS SALAZAR/LA GACETA.



**Chapter 5 · Mixed Years and a Withering Town: 1950-1965**

The familiar Ybor City afilador is captured with charm and affection in this sketch by Mario Sanchez. MARIO SANCHEZ.

A Galician afilador demonstrates his trade for a young boy. The wheel took hold in Galicia in the early 19th century and from there its use spread in both Spain and the colonies. Experienced afiladores were essential to the cigar industry for sharpening "las chavetas," the cutting blades used to cut the wrapper leaves of the cigars. MANUEL BLANCO.

José Ramos, a visiting knife sharpener from northern Spain (left) is seated with the author (center) across from Manuel Blanco, son of Ybor City's foremost knife sharpener at the Columbia Restaurant. The craftsmanship involved in such a simple yet essential activity as knife sharpening has a long history of respect in the Ybor community. E. J. SALCINES.

Manuel Blanco, a C.P.A. by profession, demonstrates the mobility of an afilador's wheel similar to one used by his father and uncles in Ybor City. It is an easily portable and all-weather wheel (when an umbrella is attached to the frame). Afiladores went door-to-door in Ybor City announcing themselves with a unique whistle or "pito." They sharpened factory cigar blades, household knives and scissors, and even repaired umbrellas. SANDRA MELENDEZ.

**Ybor City: The Making of a Landmark Town**

or going somewhere¡ else. Automobiles from the late forties and early fifties driven by Ybor's suburbanites zipped by or circled looking for a place to park. Noticeably absent, however, were the people-friendly yellow trolleys, *carritos eléctricos*. These colorful, popular vehicles had been removed for nearly a decade, and their absence had contributed to the change of pace. When the trolleys were running, wives could see retail goods and services offered, read store hours, and even scan for ongoing sales as they rode by. The shoppers came and went easily and regularly from Palmetto Beach, Belmont Heights, Gary, West Tampa, and other locales. Children could point to this or that new store display, or read the latest movie marquee, or wave at friends. There was time to ask a question or exchange a comment in quite a different way with a parent or adult escort who was not driving. Undoubtedly, the absence of the trolleys hurt the commerce as well as altering the speed and focus of life along *La Sétima* and removing much of the warmth and quaintness.

In the town, the aroma of dark-roasted coffee beans from the Naviera and La Norma coffee mills, the rich smell of seasoned Cuban tobacco leaves emanating from a few remaining cigar factories, and the seducing smell of Cuban and Italian breads and pastries still wafted through the air. Indeed, in the 1950s the Cuban, Spanish, and Italian cultures remained strong in the town. In the 1950s *café con leche y pan con mantequilla* and Castilian voices all along the way, were the pinnacles of the remaining Latin culture in Ybor City — and these were still present in abundance.

*El Manicero* and *El Pirulero* (peanut and stick candy vendors) fascinated the children. Fish, fruit, vegetable, and deviled crab vendors plied their wares, as did the ice cream vendor! Julio the *afilador* signaled his coming with a burst of his *pito*— a mouth whistle—and sharpened the housewives' knives and scissors. House-

wives still paid their *recibos* (hospital receipts) for "cradle to grave coverage." This, of course, included a doctor's home visit if needed, as well as hospital and cemetery coverage. Also delivered to each home daily or weekly was fresh Cuban and Italian bread as well as milk, coffee, and laundry. Refrigerators had long put an end to the practice of home delivery of block ice. But in the late '50s most remembered Luigi Frisco and his open truck loaded with block ice that he would cut to any size that would fit the demands of each housewife's particular icebox. And visible still was the huge water tower by the Centro Asturiano Hospital, where many years earlier we children had played marbles and flown kites.

Saturday nights were still fairly busy on *La Sétima*, and weekly shopping on that main spine continued. It was hard to imagine things had begun to move in completely new directions. "Crackers" from the rural eastern and northern outskirts

*Francisco Sanchez (right) was known as* El Pirulero *or the "piruli man" and sold the popular penny candy known as "piruli" on the streets of Ybor City for more than 25 years. The hard candy was shaped into pointed sticks and carried by the vendor on a special staff. Each vendor had a call or whistle, and Sanchez was especially known for the tone of his whistle. This photograph is from a brochure published by the Ybor City Chamber of Commerce.* LELAND HAWES.

still shopped the Avenue at Louis Buchman, Louis Wohl, Raul Vega, Rophies Men's Wear, and Little Katz. Windows of Jewish stores on eastern *La Sétima* displayed the latest rugged boots and farm clothing which appealed to these types of customers. Youngsters promenaded on Saturday afternoons, doing the *Sétima walk*, from which many courtships evolved. The *casas baratas* (five- and ten-cent stores)—especially Silver's, Kress, and Woolworth's—attracted shoppers inside with their soda counters, where banana splits, milk shakes, and sandwiches were a must.

Social clubs still promoted their weekly dances. Single former soldiers, GI Bill college students, and other young people crowded the dance floors, some now seriously looking for future wives. Proper conduct and dress were monitored by the ever-vigilant chaperones at the tables. These reminded the young people of the area's traditions, social customs, and high expectations, so different from many other customs soldiers had experienced overseas. Evidence of both the new and the old mentalities could be observed in the cafes, where young veterans and students mixed with the older ex-*tabaqueros*.

Women crowded Moré's Segunda Central on the corner of 12th Avenue and 15th Street. As mothers ordered bread, children eagerly looked at the pastries below, begging that they buy this one or that one. A sweet *señorita* (pastry) was a delight.

The old Methodist church on 12th Avenue between 16th and 17th Streets was still there, where fathers and mothers before the Spanish Civil War days had often dropped their children off for day school while they conducted business. Already sights and customs were vanishing, or their former uses becoming only part of memory, like the hulking, staring factories where *lectores* once had informed the public and shaped opinion.

There were a few remaining active cigar factories, among which were Perfecto Garcia on 16th Street and 18th Avenue, Corral Wodiska on 2nd Avenue and 19th Street, and Hav-A-Tampa on 22nd Street. Also "El Regenbois" (the Regensberg factory) was there. Its community clock on top of its tower could still be seen from faraway Lake Avenue. On 11th Avenue and 19th Street was Maximo Diaz's drug company, a wooden building. It, too, was majestic in an odd sort of way. Its old tower at the top easily caught the eye.

Many *fondas* fed the *tabaqueros* at noontime. Among these were *el Paraíso*, *Máximo's* (not the drug store cited above), *Barcelona*, *Cuervos*, *El Buen Gusto*, *Los Helados de Ybor*, and others. The old fire station on 16th Street, running 8th to 9th Avenue, still functioned. The fire stations in the last days of old Ybor City lacked for excitement. The huge fires of old were not occurring. Not only was cigar-lighting with its attendant fire dangers dropping drastically, but the large wooden stick matches of old were being replaced with match packs filled with "safety matches" which were, honestly, considerably safer, even if very clumsy. Electric stoves were also safer.

La Benéfica, perhaps Ybor City's most handsome building, was quite active in these days. It was associated with the Centro Español Hospital and was the town locale where members could see their doctors for local care or have themselves referred to the equally handsome



**Ybor City: The Making of a Landmark Town**

La Benefica Clinic at 15th Street and Palm Avenue was the town's medical office of the Centro Espanol Sanatorium. It served as a clinic for doctors who provided HMO-type services to members of all Latin clubs. La Gaceta was housed in this building until the late 1970s when it moved to La Sétima two blocks west of the Spanish Park Restaurant. This was considered one of the most handsome buildings built by the Spanish, and was still in excellent condition when this photograph was taken in March 1993.

Fernando R. Mesa celebrated with an annual birthday party on a grand scale, like this one on Saturday, November 1, 1958. Given at the home of his parents, Mr. and Mrs. Eladio Mesa, at 210 East Ross Avenue, the decorations carried out as a theme of the "Space Age" included satellites, space men, a miniature rocket on a launching platform, and a rocket cake. Signing the guest book in the photo are (left to right)  Mr. and Mrs. Max and Hortense Echegaray, Mr. and Mrs. Ramon and Helen Alvarez, Fernando Mesa, Mr. and Mrs. Eladio and Stella R. Mesa, and Ms. Socorro A. Ruiz (with the guest book). In the front is Ruiz's son.

The Wolfson Building (left), dating from 1922, was home to Poller's and the Wolfson's clothing store, marked here by "Haberdashery." In a 1953 Burgert Brothers photograph (right) the camera is positioned for a pedestrian's point of view along La Sétima. The overhanging canopies and balconies shade the sidewalks made of hexangonal pavers. Garcia Brothers Jewelry is on the left, with the Broadway Theatre at 1731 East La Sétima is showing recent films across the street and adjoins L'Unione Italiana  at 1725. USFSCL.

*Candidates for the title of Queen of the Tampa Cigar Festival in 1958 are, left to right (front row) Earlene Corrales and Donna Caruso; (middle row) Lynda Castellano, Frances Eileen Ferraro, and Margaret Fernandez; (back row) Cecelia Fernandez, Marie Ausley, Pat Rodriguez, Laura Scaglione, and Alice Gonzalez.* JEROME SIERRA/LA GACETA.

*Ybor City's largest clothier, Fernandez & Garcia, on the northeast corner of La Quince (15th Street) and La Sétima, was bought by Belk Lindsey in the 1950s and a Dollar Department Store opened nearby. The street had traffic, but it was losing its history and charm.* USFSCL.

*The view from 17th Street looking west along La Sétima on June 18, 1964, shows the styles and cars have changed, but Ybor City's business area remains active. Many of these businesses would soon find themselves closing their doors.* TOM JOHNSON AND LA GACETA.

**Ybor City: The Making of a Landmark Town**

Centro Español Sanatarium on faraway Bayshore Boulevard.

Hair stylist Francisco "Paco" Vinagre, located at 2202 1/2 15th Street in the '30s, had women waiting for a Clara Bow haircut. In those years women thought he was king of that style. Later, in the post World War II period he had moved to 1402 11th Avenue. Meanwhile, on 14th Street and 26th Avenue, Joe's Barber Shop was going strong, carrying on a tradition which his father had started when he began cutting hair there before 1926. Joe's father had placed me on a wooden box perched on the rectangular seat of the barber chair when he gave me my first haircut in the mid-1920s, and other generations of children received similar treatment. *La Casa Cune*, which had specialized in turkish baths, also lingered on. It was located on 10th Avenue, between 14th and 15th streets. In earlier years it had restored life to tired *tabaqueros* whose work was indoors and sedentary. And in the far northeast — the Italian area between 17th and 22nd streets just south of 21st Avenue — youngsters waded the sudden swamps that formed after heavy summer showers, and a few old-timers remember it as "*La Playa de Maria*," "Maria's Beach," named after Maria Leto, wife of Mother's uncle Americo Leto.

In the 1950s, greater Ybor City extended, broadly speaking, from 2nd Avenue to Buffalo Avenue, which is Martin Luther King Boulevard today, and from Nebraska to 24th Street. Make no mistake about it, greater Ybor was still functioning as a strong community in those years. Life in the suburban areas still had a law-and-order underpinning, a bedrock assumption that people were honest and the neighborhood safe. One could still sleep with only the screen door closed — no great event in Ybor City's law-and-order ambience — which helped, since air conditioning was still not available.

The Fernandez & Garcia clothing store business on the corner of *La Sétima* and 15th Street, built in 1922, still operated as a private business in the first half of the 1950s, but was sold to Belk Lindsey near the middle of the decade. This had meant a change in that the local ownership was gone, but it was a commercial sale, not a closing-down. The three large Spanish restaurants—the Columbia, the Spanish Park, and Las Novedades—all on *La Sétima*, continued to serve their famous Spanish dishes to mixed crowds.

The Spanish areas to the northwest and middle north still looked well-kept and inviting, as did most of the Italian areas to the north and northeast. El Centro Asturiano Hospital in this period was quite popular. Its location was convenient; its services enjoyed an outstanding reputation for quality and friendliness. The Cuban homes likewise looked very friendly, distinguished by the mango and avocado trees in many yards and abundant tropical flowers. The demise of the exquisite small Ybor City mango would closely correlate with the exodus of Cubans in years ahead, and to Italians and Spaniards who grew them. Cuscaden Park, undoubtedly the best sports and recreation field in Ybor City, continued to thrive, and in this period frequent Inter-Social League ballgames were held there. The large field saw many youngsters fly *papalotes* and play *el Ríquiti, los Prisioneros*, and *el Palito*, which were a few of the recreational activities popular with young people in Ybor City.

Yet while the external appearances of the town seemed almost normal, for the most part it was somewhat of an illusion. The image of health and vitality was reinforced by the strength of the culture and folklore of the area, but it was not the cigar industry that produced much of the commerce. The impact of World War II on the town was still visible. Some five hundred ships had been built only a few years earlier, and the income generated from the effort did not immediately disappear. The small income from WPA



**Chapter 5 · Mixed Years and a Withering Town: 1950-1965**

projects had also helped the community adjust to changing economic conditions and the loss of cigar factory employment. There had been the WPA's art and history projects of the late '30s and '40s in greater Tampa, the "sewing ladies" at a converted cigar factory, the Bayshore seawall and balustrade, the Armory, and the MacDill highway project. None of these hurt the town. In fact, they kept the citizens busy and helped create a sense that there was still ample work to be done. But now all these side projects were gone.

When many of the thousands of GIs who flooded home returned to the greater Tampa area to invest their small but significant wartime savings, they also attracted and spent some GI Bill funding. This infusion of cash helped to keep the Tampa economy afloat, and some of that money spilled over into Ybor City. Then, too, many Spanish and Italian businessmen raised their sights toward greater Tampa, and some opened establishments there. A few retained their old residences; they were paid for. Others relocated for better value or convenience. Most of them, however, like most of the rest of the town, returned to Ybor for shopping.[3] The grocery stores — Castellano and Pizzo, Santo's Market, Pardo's, Demmi's, and Agliano's fish market — drew them in with service, quality, and tradition. Raul Vega, Sam Argintar, and others continued to provide a stable, traditional business base for the community.

In addition, this was a time when some of the fathers of today's well-known Italian and Spanish families began large businesses or owned considerable land. This included the Guagliardo Dairy, with a distribution center on 40th Street; the large Lopez Feed Store that backed onto the railroad, just past The Spanish Park; Greco's early grocery, precursor to today's Kash n' Karry chain of stores; Garcia's Dairy, with a few thousand acres of land between today's Livingston and Tampa Palms; the Geracis's many thousands of acres far out on north Dale Mabry Highway, which their fathers had bought in early Ybor City days; and the Cabreras, who ended up in a national trucking business. Spaniards were dairying in the far-out West Tampa areas. The Valentis were energetically building their banana import and distribution enterprise.

Leadership in the town was changing. It no longer included the originals — the countless founders who had led and inspired the town, its industry, and its social life. Others of a slightly later era made history in enterprises of one sort or another, such as Casimiro Hernandez II of the Columbia Restaurant; John Grimaldi of the Columbia Bank; "King Greco" Sr. of King Greco Hardware; Raul Vega Sr., famous clothier; Manuel Garcia of Las Novedades; Charlie Spicola Sr., owner of Spicola and Sons Hardware Wholesaler; and Fernandez and Garcia, Ybor's largest clothiers. The social clubs, whose presidents in the early years had included cigar factory *patrones*, now were directed by more current personalities who had to cope not with growth but with a declining membership. Among these were Raul Vega Sr., Severino Quintanilla, Jose Colmenares, Ramon Alvarez, Bautista M. Balbontín, Angel de la Riva, Angel Alonso of the Centro Español, and many others.

There were also Justo Rodriguez Fernandez, Prudencio M. Gonzalez, Joe Moran, Jorge Trelles, Manuel Alonso y San Miguel, and José Martinez Martinez



**Ybor City: The Making of a Landmark Town**

of the Centro Asturiano Club, to mention only a few of the Spanish club leadership. Some of the Italian leaders of the day were Joe P. Maniscalco, Phil LoCicero, Tom Castiglia, Phillip Licata, Jimmy Pardo, Frank Settecasi, Philip Valenti, and others. The Cuban Club leaders were Armando Dorta, Francisco Fernandez de la Nuez, Emilio Almendares, Santos Rodriguez, and Evelio Alvarez. Many of these capable, responsible citizens served with distinction. Unfortunately, only a very few remained to assist the difficult moments the town experienced.

This is but a brief review of the last, privileged years of Ybor City. The sense of confidence, tradition, and citizen-support one could still sense during this period were never to return. This was Ybor City in the period just before Urban Renewal, that ill-fated, nationally initiated program that would soon shake the town and its history to the very heart.

But something had to be done. With the passage of each year it became clearer that the core merchants were not thriving. When Fernandez and Garcia sold their shop to Belk Lindsey, at first it seemed good to have a major department store chain investing in the old neighborhood, but the company soon closed the Ybor branch, and with that the locals lost the largest retail store in Ybor City. It was part of an increasingly ominous commercial atmosphere. Many business owners were making plans to move out of the area. Latin civic leaders, conscious of the shaken confidence being felt by local entrepreneurs, foresaw the need to do something. They decided they had to introduce new concepts and encourage new ventures that could sustain the town and counteract the impulse for other residents and companies to follow the example of the cigar factories and abandon the community. They needed to do something, *anything*, to keep the town afloat. A new manner of provid-

*In this view of 18th Street in Ybor City in 1953, Cuervo's Restaurant (on the corner) and Garcia Brothers Clothing are two of the favorite spots still to be seen.* USFSCL.

ing livelihood for the thousands of aging *tabaqueros* was necessary.

By the late '50s and early '60s Ybor City was in desperate need of new direction. The old leaders who had pioneered the town were either dead or too old to lead. And the well-to-do who had gone into major businesses in greater Tampa had no inclination to come back to Ybor City, much less lead the town in civic ways. Successful businessmen are realists.

It would take other leaders—leaders of the total community—to reverse the fortunes of the town. These would not necessarily be found among the social club officers, individuals identified with particular ethnic groups or causes, who for the most part were already preoccupied with the difficult problems posed by declining memberships. It would take civic leaders in the broadest sense, knowledgeable in entrepreneurial and political ways, to identify and promote new ventures. Even more importantly, it would take individuals with an abiding love of Ybor City and an equal portion of inspiration.

### The Columbia Restaurant – Early Years

Born in Matanzas, Cuba, into a war-ravished land where he was conscripted into the Spanish navy, Casimiro Hernandez I jumped ship, and later, with his wife and two children, found his way to a small spit of a town called Tampa. Restlessness and rumors of opportunity in a cigar town where spoken Spanish was the

*Following his father's death just before the stock market crash in 1929, Casimiro Hernandez II became owner of the Columbia Restaurant with his Uncle Lawrence. He proved to be an astute and aggressive businessman who carried the Columbia to great heights of national and international renown. By 1936 he oversaw four dining areas— the Café, Fonda, Don Quixote, and El Patio. He brought in Pijuan as chef, a master cook from the kitchen of King Alfonso XIII of Spain. Casimiro II success- fully built the restaurant into a Ybor City landmark known throughout the world.* LA GACETA.

norm attracted him here. Possessed of strong personal attributes from his Spanish forebears and with great love of the new land that took him in, he opened a small café at 22nd Street and La Sétima. The year of its founding was 1905. He called it the Columbia Restaurant, and added the subtitle, "The Gem of Spanish Restaurants." This boast expressed much of the man's aspirations.

Business at the tiny café grew, propelled by the menu: *sopa de garbanzo* (garbanzo bean soup), the Cuban sandwich, and *arroz con pollo* (chicken with yellow rice). In this primitive town called Ybor City, the taste and smell of the items on his menu, topped off by a Spanish *flan* (custard) and a Cuban "solo" (a tiny cup of black Cuban coffee with sugar) blessed the town with a cuisine much sought-after by the *tabaqueros* and early businessmen. Casimiro I superimposed on the tempting selection and tastes the classy demeanor of waiters with a continental service style previously unknown in these parts. He had a formula that would catapult the Columbia Restaurant forward to enduring acclaim. In spite of the town's ideological conflicts, the wiles of the day, the struggles of unionism, and the strong up-and-down flares of the local economy,

he stuck to his dream—so much so that Casimiro I took in a partner, Manuel Garcia, who had already been operating a café and later achieved a separate fame for his own restaurant, Las Novedades. With Garcia came his next-door *fonda*, which was incorporated into a single, impressive Columbia Restaurant complex.

In late March of 1929 Casimiro I passed away just months before the stock market crash. His son Casimiro II and his uncle Lawrence took over the restaurant. Author Ferdie Pacheco, in his book with Adela Gonzmart, *The Columbia Restaurant Spanish Cookbook*, states that "part of what Casimiro II inherited was a mountain of debt, an apparently insurmountable sum, and an unstable economy."[4] When the town soon suffered economic hard times due to factory layoffs of just under 10,000 cigar workers, the restaurant staggered. Dismayed, Casimiro II ordered a loyal employee known as "El Rey" to board up the main door — instructions which were, fortunately, never carried out.

As the cigar industry very slowly took back employees, the local economy improved and the Columbia gained in vitality. By 1935, a determined Casimiro II borrowed $35,000 on a handshake with an officer of Grimaldi's Columbia Bank. By 1936 the addition of the Don Quixote and El Patio dining areas—which with the café and the *fonda* gave the restaurant four beautiful and distinctive dining options—the Columbia gained considerable stature. And now, also, a former employee in the kitchen of King Alfonso XIII of Spain, a man called "Pijuan," took over the top chef's position at the restaurant and further distinguished this now-famous institution.

In the meantime, Casamiro II's uncle, Lawrence Hernandez, had won increasing political clout—locally, statewide, and in Washington, D.C.—and an irreversible and continuous path of growth for the restaurant took hold. Nor did the restaurant lack for a distinguished band: it had the



**Ybor City: The Making of a Landmark Town**

*The Columbia Restaurant, Columbia Coffee Company, and Jones Barber Shop occupied the buildings at 2110-2117 La Sétima when this photo was taken in 1935.* THCPLS.

*A view from the corner of La Sétima and 22nd Street in 1935 shows a popular but modest Columbia Restaurant in need of repair and revitalization.* THCPLS.

*Architect Ivo A. de Minicis (left) and Casimiro II (center) dine with a friend in one of the improved and comfortable dining rooms of the Columbia Restaurant in the late 1930s.* USFSCL.

*A tile scene from the adventures of Don Quixote on the wall of the Columbia Restaurant taken by the Burgert Brothers on February 8, 1936.* THCPLS.

*The Don Quixote dining room at the Columbia Restaurant ready and waiting for the restaurant to open in 1937.* THCPLS.

203

*The tile patio of the Columbia Restaurant was conceived by Casimiro Hernandez, whose daughter Adela is the lovely señorita in this photograph. The Italian architect Ivo A. de Minicis designed the patio, including a retractable roof that could be drawn back in good weather so that dinners could be served beneath the stars. THCPLS.*

*Cesar Gonzmart enjoyed success as a concert violinist. La Gaceta.*

*Architect Ivo A. de Minicis.*

*This view of El Patio in the late 1930s shows how the atmospheric dining area takes advantage of the Ybor City climate as well as its Latin heritage. THCPLS.*

*Painted tiles and decorative iron work created a unique and impressive entrance to the Columbia Restaurant.*

*A photo from the wedding of Adela and Cesar Gonzmart, Dec. 30, 1946. La Gaceta.*

**Ybor City: The Making of a Landmark Town**

Don Quixote Orchestra. It was a very proud and happy Casimiro II who, with his wife Carmen, saw their daughter Adelita, a Julliard School of Music graduate, perform regularly in the Columbia's famous musical entertainment room. The opening of the Tampa shipyards and the pre-World War II economic upswing in Tampa propelled the Columbia Restaurant into greater national fame, as senators, national boxers, musicians and even a distinguished Mafia gentleman frequented the café.

The Columbia Restaurant of Casimiro II was tightly run. He was stern, determined, and taciturn. Under his direction the restaurant grew in stature, sales, inventory of fine dishware, artifacts, and indoor and external trimmings. Its wide fame was additionally assured as it garnered many national awards. It was by now the nation's largest Spanish restaurant and soon its most distinguished one.[5]

## Columbia Restaurant— The Coming of Cesar Gonzmart

The fortuitous wedding of Adelita Hernandez to a young, long-haired musician did much to carry forward the aging Casimiro II's famous Columbia Restaurant. However, during the short musical interlude before and after he entered the restaurant, there was much skepticism by cigar workers who frequented the café as to the future of the restaurant due to this tall, elegantly attired newcomer. The sight of him usually elicited a low murmur of whispers around the café. As a youngster I often heard from *tabaqueros* at the café tables words like, "there he is, the pretty boy that will ruin Casimiro." But in time the forecasts by many began slowly to change. *Tabaqueros* had not been privy to the many personal talents this young man brought with him. In addition to his musical abilities, this accomplished violinist possessed many qualities of imagination, determination, leadership, and common

sense, which were surely among the traits that had attracted Adelita to him in the first place.

If inspiration is what was needed to draw the best of the town's young men into action, the individual who could convey it was present in Ybor City. He was one who inspired and brought out the latent potential of those who knew him. He could gather a young, pivotal group around him, communicate a vision, draw out their own talents, and bond them into common action. The man possessed of these envious attributes was the tall, courtly, debonair import from Havana, Cuba: Cesar Gonzmart—upon whom Adelita had settled her affections. When she first came to know him, she heard mostly of his Spanish forbears and saw him as a young but experienced and developing musician. He had spent much of his youth in Tampa at local schools, though eventually his credentials included a doctorate in music from the Municipal Conservatory of Music in Havana. He had graduated from Stetson University, then continued his studies at the University of Havana. He soon became concert master of the Havana Symphony under the world-renowned composer Ernesto Lecuona.

Cesar formed an orchestra and traveled Central and South America for four years where he rubbed shoulders and shared billing with some of the leading personalities in American show business. He later had interviews with Spain's highest leaders, including General Francisco Franco and Don Fraga Iribarne, who later became president of the Galician autonomy and then Minister of Tourism and Information. All of these interviews were in the interest of promoting the Columbia and the town of Ybor. Cesar must have charmed General Franco, because he and his wife Adela were given a six-hour interview, including dinner with the General. Never was Cesar's magnetic and charming personality more tested.

*Adela and Cesar Gonzmart in those early flowering years—years full of dreams and expectations for the future growth of the Columbia Restaurant and Ybor City.*
RICHARD AND CASEY GONZMART.

His beautiful violin playing, coupled with his captivating charm and his ability to bring out the best in future leaders, would in years to come help ensure the survival of the remaining Latin culture in Ybor City in the late '50s and continuing through the mid-'80s—his efforts complementing those of the diminished social clubs. That he married Adela, the talented pianist and daughter of a well-entrenched restaurant owner, Casimiro II, would prove crucial to ensuring that Ybor City did not simply evaporate.

Cesar's unique position, personal drive, and action-oriented agenda soon catapulted him into the presidency of the Ybor City Chamber of Commerce. Also, while he worked miracles in the evolution of the Columbia Restaurant, building its national reputation into an international one, he also brought into the fold key personalities, themselves already inspired. Among this group were Dr. Henry Fernandez, Joe Lopez, Raul Vega Jr., Manuel Ballota, Daniel Martinez, and Joseph Granda, all presidents of the Ybor City Chamber of Commerce in those years. Working closely with them was banker Eddie Spoto, president of the Broadway Bank. All of them were possessed of great appreciation and pride for the Spanish, Cuban, and Italian legacies bequeathed them by their fa-

thers, and by the beautifully correct and self-sufficient Latin world they had lived in. They were fully motivated to push the town forward, to stop its bleeding, and redirect its energies as needed.

Like most busy businessmen, Cesar gave his time primarily to high-impact ideas or proposals. Personally acquainted with most civic leaders in Ybor City, as well as Tampa's political leaders, the Hillsborough County commisioners, state representatives, and some key national politicians, he was wonderfully equipped to bend their ears or get needed backing. Many of his political contacts dined at the Columbia. Yes, he was a person with dynamic qualities, wonderful resources, and the grace to use them. Cesar would often drop by a Chamber meeting in the Columbia, and upon recognition, would often make a point and slip out to tend the restaurant, leaving others to follow suit. He meant what he proposed, and often pursued it doggedly. He had access to politicians at all levels who kept him ahead of the day-to-day civic agenda.

Cesar was a man for the times, a man to have on one's side. He thought in terms of solutions. He was adequate to the task. Many civic leaders sought his friendship and backing. He was not a man to oppose. His connections could run circles around the issues. Yet, despite the influence he wielded, Cesar did not respect "yes-men." I worked with him often enough to see that he respected those who fought for a point, even when it might be different from his own. As a president of the Ybor City Chamber of Commerce, my service there overlapped with Cesar's during his later years. I experienced firsthand his magnetism, charm, wrath, and support. Many accomplishments of others were undertaken and pursued due to Cesar's inspiring qualities.

Aside from his own astuteness and drive, Cesar could bring Adela's family resources to bear on problems or issues he

**Ybor City: The Making of a Landmark Town**

became convinced needed attention. These, to be sure, were substantial. It was a formidable base from which to maneuver, but Cesar's focus and energy seemed to be magnetic to family, friends, and even adversaries. His qualities fostered the growth of clientele and reputation for the restaurant. It was under Cesar's leadership that the Columbia became such a powerful institution that in many ways it could influence attempts at Ybor City redevelopment.

However, not everything that Cesar dreamed of and then started was completed, though by and large these failings were not of his doings. The climate, the miserly economy, the changing politics, the international events (including, for example, the Mariel Boat Lift), and other factors certainly derailed some of his dreams.

Nonetheless, Cesar remained involved with Ybor City issues and problems during three decades, up until the late 1980s. Sometimes it would be direct involvement, and other times he participated as an observer, often giving a nod of sorts. These three decades that followed his arrival at the Columbia Restaurant would feel both his presence and his shadow — both hostage to his magnetic qualities.[6]

## The Latin Plaza

It is something of a paradox that the general condition of Ybor City should have deteriorated so steadily at the same time that the Columbia sustained and enlarged its reputation. However, history seems to be filled with unexplained swings of fortune and contradictory events. In the decade following the end of the war, the ethnic identity of Ybor City was eroded as large numbers of the sons and daughters moved away to West Tampa or more distant suburbs. Mormino and Pozzetta attribute it to three main factors: the GI Bill, which paid for young veterans to attend public universities when there *was* no public university near Ybor; Veterans Administration loans for housing, which helped veterans buy homes, but which only offered mortgage support for *new* homes at a time when there were no new homes being built in Ybor City; and the dynamics of "urban ecology," which meant that as soon as ethnic families vacated inexpensive property in Ybor City, African Americans tended to move in, taking advantage of the low-cost housing and at the same time contributing to the breakup of the Latin ethnic identity of the community. It was becoming clear that the solid foundations of tradition were being eroded.

*Today the decorative tiles, ornate arches, and the statues and fountains in front of the Columbia Restaurant are icons of Ybor City's history and vitality.* RM.

207

At the same time, in another odd contradiction, political leaders with Ybor City roots were gaining influence in the politics of Tampa. Nick Nuccio, who was the son of Sicilian immigrants in Ybor, is credited with being the first Latin politician to challenge and win against the Anglo establishment.[5] He was elected as a city alderman from Ybor City in 1929, moved on to the Hillsborough County Commission in 1936, and finally challenged Tampa Mayor Curtis Hixon in the mayoral election of 1955. Although he lost the 1955 election, Nuccio ultimately won the office just a year later when Hixon died unexpectedly and Nuccio defeated interim mayor J. L. Young to become Hixon's successor as mayor of Tampa in 1956.[7]

Nuccio's election placed an immigrant from Ybor City at the head of Tampa municipal government and gave old-time Ybor residents reason to hope that their deteriorating neighborhood and economy might receive assistance in revitalization efforts. Leaders in the community had been seeking the means to create a new economic engine for the community, and in a state which boasted tourism as its major industry, some of them began to think that the unique history of Ybor City might have tourist appeal.

Of course, leaders in Ybor City had known that for a long time. From their belief in their beloved town came the idea that with the help of new government investment, a Latin Plaza could be built restoring and remodeling a core of empty or derelict buildings. It could not only attract investors and tourists into the area, but draw especially from Cuban, South American, and Latin visitors and businesses. It might serve as a Tampa embassy reaching out to an international Latin community for trade, tourism, and cultural exchange.

A letter written in 1957 by Dr. Henry J. Fernandez, president of the Ybor City Chamber of Commerce, on the Chamber's letterhead, was directed at many local organizations as well as city and county governments. It suggests the strong leadership of Dr. Fernandez and outlines the vision he had for the ambitious undertaking:

> The proposed Plaza that is to be built in Ybor is of vital importance, not only to Ybor City but to Tampa, which has in the past few years made great strides towards becoming a great industrial city. The economy of our city has been greatly improved due to the influx of new industries, but we have lost sight of the fact that Tampa is in the State of Florida, the greatest tourist state in the Nation.
>
> We have made no plans whereby our city can share the tourist dollar as we should share it. What does Tampa have to offer the northern visitor? Very little, compared to other cities in Florida. Much credit should go to the officials of Gasparilla, the Tarpon Tournament, and Spring Training of the Major Leagues, but little more has been done towards making our city attractive to the visitors from out of State. We have the sunshine but no beach to go with it, and not many more attractions that would attract visitors to our city.
>
> We have one great attraction that has gone unnoticed and undeveloped for these many years, and that is Ybor City. The Chamber of Commerce, Civic Clubs and the Alcalde Association . . . have succeeded . . . in bringing much valuable publicity to Tampa and Ybor City without having at their disposal the facilities needed for a program of this type. We have run into one stone wall after another in trying to develop Ybor City into the attraction that we know it can be. We know that the building of this Latin Plaza could overnight turn Ybor into a beehive of community activity for self-improvement such as this City has never seen . . . and the building of the Latin Plaza would more than increase this interest."[8]

Dr. Fernandez, an optometrist by profession, was a dedicated community leader with a deep affection for Ybor City and a contagious appreciation for its cultural and historic heritage. He would go on to serve as president of the Ybor City Chamber five terms by 1981.

Over the next months, the idea for a Latin Plaza seemed to be picking up support. Ruben Fabelo, host of the local radio program "Fiesta in Tampa," had been campaigning strongly for the adoption by the City of Tampa of a plan to support the

*Celebrating the inauguration of Dr. Henry J. Fernandez are (left to right) Molly Ferrara, Mac Traina, Johnny Diaz, Dr. Fernandez, and Tony Pizzo, July 25, 1955.* "WALDO" DIAZ/ H. J. FERNANDEZ.

Latin Plaza. In the period October 5-10, 1958, he received a flurry of positive letters in support of the initiative from Joe Fernandez, Carlos Sureda, and others whose names cannot be read on the surviving photocopies. The success as well as the political controversy arising from the grassroots effort to build support can be gauged from an October 8, 1958, letter to Ybor City Chamber of Commerce President Fernandez from Louis de la Parte Jr., an attorney who later was elected to the Florida senate, eventually going on to become its president:

> I want to congratulate you for the work you are doing to keep the Latin Plaza alive. I want to assure you if I can be of help to you in this matter, please call on me.
>
> For many years, Ybor City has been neglected only because it was an area that could be offended without political repercussion [this phrase was highlighted by the author]. I think that Doug West's statement wherein he threatened the Ybor City Chamber with possible withholding of city funds was in extremely poor taste. I believe, also, that the important thing now is to present a sound program to the city, and to sell it as a source of future revenue to the city as a tourist attraction.

> Thanks again for the fine work you are doing on behalf of that 'forgotten part of town.'
>
> Cordially yours,
> Louis de la Parte, Jr.[9]

Mayor Nuccio had promised in his 1956 election campaign, "I can pave the way by my conduct and my performance for all Latin people."[10] For a little while the Latin Plaza project looked as though it might be happening. Some $1.2 million in bond funds were obtained for financing. West and others, combined with budget limits caused the ambitious project to be rejected.

In an article headlined "Hopes Go on Dream for Plaza," *Tampa Times* journalist Bob Turner reported:

> The Latin Plaza death knell tolled louder today as city representatives headed down the homestretch to balance the new budget with the bob-tailed mileage. Doug West said, 'There is no way you can back off from the Board's plan to drain off some $1,200,000 in Plaza bond funds to help balance the budget submitted by Mayor Nuccio . . .
>
> The seven-man Board became pretty well unified behind diverting the bulk of Plaza money into the budget on the heels of repre-



**Chapter 5 · Mixed Years and a Withering Town: 1950-1965**

sentatives rejection of Nuccio's hotly contested seven mill increase proposal . . .

Protests still rumble from a number of Ybor Citizens, angry about the plaza project getting the axe . . .

But West today dispelled any doubt that the venture is dead, at least in the foreseeable future. 'There is no way possible to balance that budget without diverting part of the Latin Plaza bond money,' the Chairman said. He said this was the only way to obtain needed funds without diverting part of the Latin Plaza bond money . . . The chairman reiterated the theory behind reallocating the Plaza bond funds. He said this money itself will go only for capital improvement . . .' The action the board took in . . . last year's 23.3 operating mileage definitely ties down part of the bond money,' West said.[11]

No sooner was the original Latin Plaza concept defeated by the Tampa government, than Fernandez was imagining it anew. He presented a scaled-back version, which he conceived as at least a first step, and suggested it should begin with the appointment of a group to direct the architectural approval of remodelling and construction accompanying the ambitious rebirth of the community. In a *Tampa Times* article dated December 8, 1958, editorial page editor C. W. Johnson applauded his efforts:

> Orchids and a rousing *olé!* to Dr. Henry Fernandez, president, and other members of the Ybor City Chamber of Commerce on their new proposal for vitalizing Ybor City and pushing the long-discussed Latin Plaza project . . . the Ybor City program is directed at fundamentals . . . Certainly the plan for a commission to oversee building design in the area is basic . . . The group will also campaign . . . to get the Latin Plaza started on an abbreviated, town block basis with the money remaining from bond funds originally designated for the project . . . Much of the charm of the French Quarter in New Orleans stems from the fact that a commission there has insisted either on retention of the unique homes and other structures or restoration of buildings in keeping with the architectural style of the area . . . members of the proposed commission should also insist that new structures conform to an agreed on [Ybor city] style of architecture. One such building could house Tampa's consular corps and offices [as was proposed] and agencies . . .

concerned with trade and other relations with Latin American countries. It could be the center to spark the construction of more buildings, sidewalk cafes, art galleries, museums displaying materials from our neighboring countries to the south, handicraft shops, libraries and auditoriums for indoor and outdoor concerts and other entertainment.[14]

By December 10, 1958, Spanish groups were writing letters to complain about city officials acting to kill the Plaza Latino Plan. This brief excerpt, originally written in Spanish and translated to English, will convey the serious and professional tone of their objections:

> Honorable Nick C. Nuccio, Mayor
> Honorable Members
>     of the Board of Representatives
> City of Tampa
>
> Gentlemen:
>
> We, the below signers, citizens of the great City of Tampa, very respectfully ask that you reconsider the following deed, before you finally decide to eliminate the Latin Plaza project funds that have been already appropriated by you. You will remember that the study and the recommendations for this grand and commendable project was made by a select committee of twenty outstanding citizens, and that you had approved of this Latin Plaza on various occasions . . .[12]

The above letter went on to cite the many resources of Ybor city such as the hospitals, clinics, social clubs, its beautiful Spanish restaurants, Masonic Lodges, and La Sicilia. It pointed out that all of these assets, and the widespread affection for Latin culture, would foster better commerce and economic exchange with Latin America, including tourism from those countries Ybor maintained its ambiance.

The letter stated, also, that on October 23, 1958, L'Unione Italiana had passed a one-page resolution in support of the Latin Plaza supported by a brief, but pertinent history of the organization since its founding on April 4, 1894, summarizing its contribution to its membership of three thousand active members, its savings to the community of substantial costs that

without the organization would have been required in public assistance and other welfare dollars, and it detailed many proud accomplishments. It concluded:

> Whereas, the Italian club considers the erection of the Latin Plaza a step forward in averting the eminent danger of Ybor City becoming a slum area, and . . . Whereas, the Italian club vigorously opposes the use of bond money for the regular operation of city affairs instead of for its original intended purpose; . . . Be it resolved: That the Italian Club is 100% in favor of building the Latin Plaza, and irrevocably against the use of Bond money earmarked for this worthy project, and . . . Be it further resolved: That the Italian club requests your consideration in not diverting this money to be used for other purposes . . .
>
> Phil LoCicero
> President, Italian Club[13]

The determined Ybor City leaders knew the courage of their convictions and did not give up on their cause. There was hope that some of the $1.5 million originally earmarked for the project would be available to support a more modest project. Ybor political and business leader Charles Spicola reported confidence that the City of Tampa could provide at least $600,000 from city bond money for the Latin project. That would be enough to develop a small plaza, two blocks in size — a far cry for the dream of a thirteen-block plaza for which the land alone would have cost more than the $1.5 million, but still a dramatic and tangible step forward. Ybor spokesmen urged that the $600,000 in bond money be set aside for the plaza and released as soon as Ybor City leaders, Mayor Nuccio, and the City Board of Representatives had selected a proper site and worked out an exact design.[15]

Unfortunately, Nuccio was forced to cover his city budget problems by reallocating of some of the funds originally earmarked for Latin Plaza. On Nuccio's watch, however, the scaled-back Fernandez alternative received a nod of approval.

## The Barrio Latino Commission and the Vieux Carre Commission

Journalist Bob Turner of the *Tampa Times* was soon reporting new initiatives in Ybor City. Advocates for the revived plan to develop a strictly controlled Ybor City Latin Plaza were taking their case to the State Legislature. As president of the YCCC, Fernandez stated that a plaza study committee would be ready to lay its program on the table by January 1959. He explained that the Ybor Chamber had been studying the operation of the Vieux Carre Commission in New Orleans, the designated group that governs the French Quarter, and planned to send a committee for a firsthand look at how they functioned. Based on their findings, they would put together a proposal to establish a similar Ybor City Commission. They intended to have a specific proposal read for incorporation into a bill to go before the state legislature by the start of the new year. State Senator Sam Gibbons had told Fernandez, "We would like to have a specific proposal in the form of a bill in January."[16]

A *Tampa Times* story on December 19, 1958, describes the delegation:

> A group of Ybor City leaders traveled to New Orleans today to make a firsthand study of the French quarter with a view to drawing up similar control legislation for Tampa's Latin Quarter. Dr. Henry J. Fernandez, president of the YCCC, Gus Ayala and Sam P. Ferlita left Tampa this morning. They will be joined in New Orleans by Dr. Anthony Martino to confer with the city's chamber of commerce officials and with members of the Vieux Carre Commission.
>
> The commission is the body which has broad powers to regulate all construction, demolition and building modification in the French Quarter. The commission's basic authority was granted through an amendment to the Louisiana state constitution.
>
> Dr. Fernandez has said that his group intends to have similar legislation drawn up for presentation to the next session of the Florida Legislature in January. He envisions a five-man commission, with authority over architectural

design in a wide area of Ybor City, ultimately creating a harmonious Latin style in structures there.[17]

The visit to New Orleans proved to be extremely valuable. The group returned with a sense of energy and hope—and with specific models to assist in drafting the laws necessary for a similar commission structure in Ybor City. Subsequent notes by Dr. Fernandez, scribbled on his copy of Vieux Carre Commission organizational documents, summarize its purposes and functions, and describe how the Ybor City Commission legislative draft was completed:

> After we came back from New Orleans, I copied the Vieux Carre commission law and changed their street names and boundaries to correspond to Ybor City . . . .
> Sam Gibbons who was then our state representative, agreed to sponsor the enabling legislation. We went to Tallahassee and Paul Danahy, Sam's aide, who is now Judge Danahy, prepared the act in April 1959. It passed through Sam's efforts and we came to the City council who prepared and passed the ordinance in August 1959 to create the Barrio Latino Commission. The Mayor (Nick Nuccio) then named the first members to serve: Dr. Henry J. Fernandez (Chairman), Eliot C. Fletcher, Mark G. Hampton, Mrs. Jim Quinn, Fred C. Billing, Joseph R. Lopez, Mrs. Harry L Weedon, Dr. James W. Covington, and William J. Webber.

The notes are accompanied by a snapshot of New Orleans Mayor deLesseps Morrison presenting certificates to Ayala, Ferlita, and Fernandez. They and the other members of the committee were made Honorary Citizens of New Orleans.[18]

Over the next few weeks the Barrio Latino Commission concept was transformed from the abstract to the concrete. It happened in surprisingly short order. Within eight months the commission legislation had cleared both state and local hurdles. At last Ybor City's future would be guided by a unifying, long-range vision.

And on a notepad, Dr. Fernandez scribbled the following after attending a meeting of the Redevelopment Committee on which he served:

> Aug. 4, 1959, should become a historical date in the history of Tampa and Ybor City . . . today the 'Barrio Latino Commission' was officially made law of the city of Tampa. [19]

By late 1959, the local community was beginning to understand that a redevelopment vision for a true Barrio Latino would have major economic implications for local residents and tourists alike. Using the New Orleans French Quarter as a model had been not only efficient in saving time drafting complicated legislation, but it had also been an excellent way to communicate the possibilities and approaches that could be successful in Tampa. When Fernandez, in his role as chairman of the Barrio Latino Commission, predicted that the redevelopment of Ybor City along Mediterranean architectural lines would eventually bring $425 million per year to Tampa in tourist trade, business leaders and citizens could simply look at the New Orleans French Quarter and see how it would work.[20]

The commission concept was key to making the dream a reality. At a Rotary Club meeting, where he was introduced by the eminent Ybor City doctor Mariano Paniello, Fernandez himself clarified the structure and purpose of the Barrio Latino Commission Act passed by the 1959 State Legislature and approved by the Tampa City Council.

> This act sets up a nine-member "authority" to regulate building and remodeling in a large part of the area known as Ybor City in an effort to reestablish the predominantly Latin section of Tampa as a "Latin Quarter" similar to the French Quarter's Vieux Carre area of New Orleans. . . .
> Under the act, the commission has the power to approve building permits in an area bounded by Nebraska Avenue, 22nd Street, Columbus Drive, and 4th Avenue. Anyone wishing to remodel or construct new building in the Ybor area, would [be required to] have his plans approved by the commission before

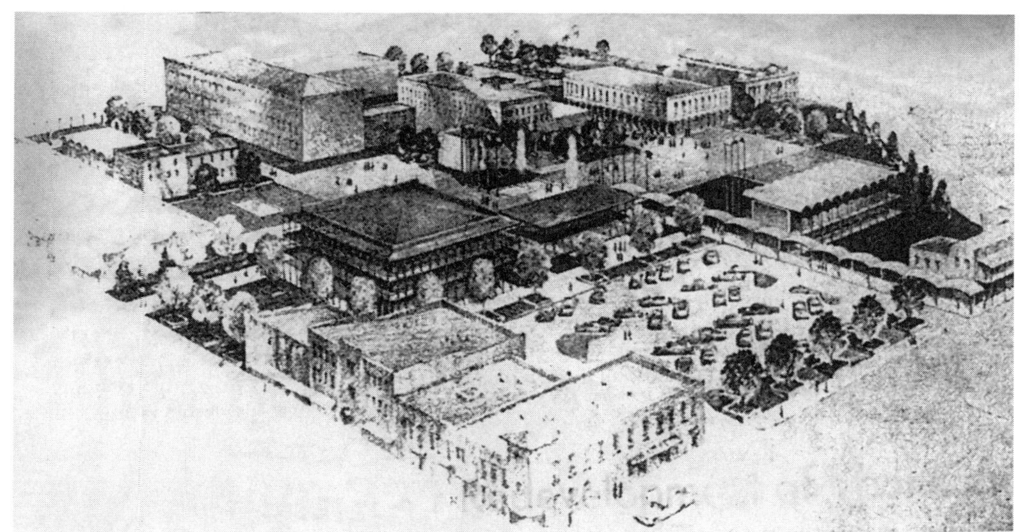

*This 1960 artist's conception of the new Latin Plaza included offstreet parking, pools, covered walks, and pavillions.* TAMPA TIMES.

receiving a city building permit. All remodeling would capture a "Latin Quarter" flavor by using wrought iron, tile and balconies in accordance with the act.

On this occasion and others, Fernandez reminded his audience that the commission was patterned after the similar organization in New Orleans which turned their French Quarter into a $90 million annual tourist attraction.[21]

In the election of 1959 Nuccio was defeated by Julian Lane, who had been supported by the *Tribune* and armed with a background sure to appeal to middle-class Tampans. He had been a baseball star at Hillsborough High School, football captain at the University of Florida, and had built and run a successful dairy farm. Lane was the man in the mayor's seat when the council finally set plans in motion that Nuccio had supported but had been unable to see through to the end. In a *Tampa Times* article on April 8, 1960, a picture of the New Latin Plaza Proposal appeared with the headline, "Mayor Gets Plans for Redevelopment of Ybor City." Many of the details were set forth:

> Plans for a major long-range development program for Ybor City were laid before the Mayor today and it was agreed that off-street parking there required priority. The program explained by Ybor City leaders in the plan proposes step by step creation of a Barrio Latino .

> . . that would tie with the overall redevelopment . . . the planned Latin Plaza had 2.5 million dollars earmarked in bond money, but this subsequently was trimmed to $600,000. Lane said he thought this would stretch a long way with help that would come from federal participation in the two proposed urban renewal projects . . . Dr. Henry Fernandez, chairman of the newly established Barrio Latino Commission [which Fernandez had personally gotten established in Tallahassee and Tampa, with the help of his friend Sam Gibbons, [then senator in Tallahassee] said merchants in Ybor City have signed pledges to show their desire to tie in with the plaza theme . . . [and demonstrate] that the broad plan . . . has the united enthusiasm of merchants, civic clubs, the YCCC and other groups.[22]

The development group reconstituted itself to include the newly formed Urban Renewal Commission with its director A. R. Ragsdale.

In the months and years that followed, Fernandez, the Ybor City Chamber of Commerce, and various other organizations and commissions continued the crusade to protect Latin architectural heritage. As a recognizable leader of the effort as well as a former Alcalde of Ybor City, Fernandez was appointed by Mayor Lane to Tampa's Ybor City Redevelopment committee, and that placed him in an excellent position to coordinate ideas and plans.

By September 10, 1962, Raul Vega Sr., chairman of the Property Owners Committee, Ybor City Redevelopment Project, and then also president of the YCCC, reported another step forward. He announced he had received a reply from a local architectural firm in which the firm agreed to prepare a schematic preliminary design with a cost analysis for the two blocks last considered for the Latin Plaza.

However, just as these initiatives seemed to be bearing fruit, in the early '60s the coming of a new, federally inspired program began to muddy the concept of a Latin Plaza—or at least that is one explanation for the new setbacks that began to slow the implementation of plans. In the cafes in Ybor one heard the rumor that the downtown Tampa establishment did not favor a rebirth of Ybor City. In fact, the incoming Urban Renewal program would level the core of Ybor City. In the wake of that heavy blow, the community's dream of a revitalized Barrio Latino would lie dormant for three decades—until rigorous support from a new mayor with Ybor City roots, Dick Greco, and his director of business and community relations, Fernando Noriega, would once again lift the hearts and hopes of the dreamers, the visionaries, and the faithful.

## The Optimist Club of Ybor City

Interspersed with the difficult politics and planning there were lighter events going on in Ybor City. Many of these were directed at marketing the town, with or without new redevelopment. On December 19, 1958, in the middle of logistical planning for the major forthcoming initiatives on the Latin Plaza, the Optimist Club of Ybor City had visited its sister club in Havana. Among the many enjoyable festivities, the Ybor City delegation handed out a *"Bienvenido a Tampa"* brochure that was written in Spanish. It carried interesting information about the area and included a strong message intended to encourage them to visit Ybor City, which I offer here in my translation:

> A cordial welcome . . . Here [in Ybor City] you can enjoy . . . fairs, fiestas and carnivals . . . from here you can visit many of the nearby Florida attractions . . . Here you also have a great variety of stores and establishments such as clothing and department stores, theaters with English and Spanish movies, famous Spanish restaurants, and a world of other things . . . And don't be concerned with cultural differences, for you will feel at home here among the Latin colony.[23]

A photograph of the group taken at Rancho Boyero airport in Havana receiving a farewell from the Havana Optimist delegation is graphic evidence that members in both countries were living up to the name of their club. A central figure near Optimist Club insignia is an energetic-looking man in a white suit—Dr. Henry Fernandez.[24]

It would have been easy to lose the spirit of optimism in Ybor City as the erosion of Latin culture gathered momentum. Many of the returning GIs after the war had moved to outer West Tampa, and more than made up for that region's own diaspora. By the late '50s, some 25 percent of the Latin population had moved from the greater Ybor areas. As Latins left, Black American families moved into the low-cost housing being vacated, creating a cultural influx that matched the outflow of the Latins. An example of this was the gradual change in the Ponce de Leon Housing Project on 26th Avenue. A large number of good African American families moved in, but it changed the Latin image of the area. It greatly thinned-out the Latin density. La Sétima suffered as local Latins, most of whom now owned automobiles, began to shop at North Gate Shopping Center and Sears Roebuck, located far to the north.

Without a doubt, the late '50s saw the end of the kind of Ybor City that had enjoyed a continuous Latin history back to the turn of the century, when Cuba had at last obtained its independence from Spain. Then, those that taunted the Spaniards be-

gan to acquiesce, for by and large the Spaniards controlled the purse strings and supplied the dominant culture. The end of the Cuban war years had ushered in the beginning of the fabled Golden Years, complete with industrial struggles. Cemented by the job security offered by the massive cigar industry and by a common struggle which unified the cultures, the Golden Years were years of great pride. Many children who lived through those fabled years are today in the 1990s now mothers, fathers, and grandparents themselves.

But as the '60s began, a physical and cultural vacuum sucked the remaining cultural atmosphere from the surviving enclave—the federally sponsored Urban Renewal program was at hand.

## The Anxious Years—I-4 and the Battle of the Balconies: 1960-1965

In the 1960s Ybor's economy was under assault. The city merchants were besieged by powerful forces from all sides. The opening of the mall at North Gate above Busch Boulevard, the new Sears Roebuck store on Hillsborough and 22nd Street, the increase in the number of small stores on far-out 40th to 50th Street, and the disturbing numbers of people who had moved out of the community—all of these took life-sustaining business from the remaining merchants on La Sétima. The closing of Belk Lindsey was a disturbing omen not long after the respected chain had bought the hometown Ybor City firm of Fernandez and Garcia in 1955. The surviving merchants debated their future. A few were positive on Ybor City. Others reacted to the cash register intake and to the townspeople's mood. Some looked toward the political, social, and commercial leadership in the community, and at this time most civic leaders were hopeful that Urban Renewal still had the potential to revive the core area.

In the meantime, the uncertainties created property bargains and an fluid commercial atmosphere ripe for speculation. Some existing owner were ready to modify and modernize properties; some outside investors saw a chance to buy cheap and adapt inexpensively. During this period, the question of whether certain building modifications were legal or not arose before the Barrio Latino Commission had been empowered. The situation underscored the importance of developing a clear and fair process for evaluating and passing judgment on proposed architectural additions and modifications. As the discussion and debate moved forward without such a process yet firmly in place, the result was a battle to determine whether the City of Tampa or the Barrio Latino would prevail in decisions that involved Ybor City architectural matters.

In the early years of the decade, a *Tampa Times* article describes the Tampa city council's action with regard to a fracas over balconies in the Latin Quarter. Tampa statutes specifically prohibited construction that resulted in a projection over city property, including streets and sidewalks. This made balconies in Ybor City illegal, but the *Times* reporter cut to the heart of the good news in his story when he wrote:

> Balconies are legal. Or rather, ornamental balconies, canopies or awnings may now be part of the architectural design of new or remodeled buildings in Tampa's Barrio Latino.
>
> Tampa City Council last week clarified what had been jocularly dubbed "the battle of the balconies," by adopting an ordinance exempting the Barrio Latino area from the provisions of Chapter 10 of the City of Tampa Code, particularly Section 1061 and ordinance 2612A. These provisions banned erection of projections over City of Tampa property . . . including streets and sidewalks.
>
> Since ornamental balconies and canopies are an integral part of Spanish and Mediterranean style architecture, which the Barrio Latino Commission sponsored, building contractors found themselves in a quandary. Balconies and canopies were added in plans at the creation of the Barrio Commission, but the city building inspector's office refused to issue a

building permit because of the projections.

Such roof-like projections are now permitted under Amendment Ordinance no 2692A, in the Barrio Latino area . . . in the effort to revitalize Ybor City by renewal of its 'quaint and distinctive' Latin atmosphere.[25]

The controversy had a happy ending in a sense, but it was one of relatively few moments when common sense and sound architectural or cultural judgment prevailed. For the most part, these were years of worry and uncertainty. Storms of change had unleashed strong winds and heavy weather on the town, and the future remained cloudy and unsettled.

## Urban Renewal—The Beginning

By now, less affluent Latin families, sensing the dismal future of the cigar industry and experiencing much lower incomes, began to put off repairs to their homes. Most of the inner core homes were between fifty and seventy years old at the time. New and more complex electrical requirements in the 1960s would mean higher costs for upgrading these homes to keep up with changing demands. Air conditioners, television sets, hot water heat-

ers, refrigerators, telephones, and rising taxes were creating additional expenses for homeowners throughout the country. Here in Ybor City, the future for the cigar economy was very uncertain. Still, for many, the cost of electrical and utility repairs, including wall or roof repairs and paint, would be a bearable price to pay for the peaceful, friendly, and respectful Latin way of life. The home improvements and repairs, within a prearranged low-interest plan worked out with the city's leadership and cooperating banks, would be a way to rejuvenate the core area.

Unfortunately, increasing expectations for what might be accomplished by the federal Urban Renewal program that was just being implemented diverted attention from the Plaza Latino concept. Confusion developed due to the similarity in objectives and physical areas that each project proposed to cover. Somewhat parallel efforts by leading personalities did appear to compound the confusion about the course that should be taken. Some suspected that personal political agendas accounted for the public differences of opinion about what ought to be done. Other motives, including capital

gains, were also very apparent. These factors as well as others muddied initiatives and confused the town's needs.

Meanwhile, apparently unnoticed during discussions by local civic leaders as they reflected on the news of the time, was a 1958 law passed in Tallahassee that enabled Urban Renewal in the State of Florida. This had come about as a result of the Eisenhower inner city rehabilitation program passed in Washington. However, the state law authorizing Florida's participation would stay on the books for months before a newly motivated Tampa seized an opportunity to solve a growing problem.

Finally, as the decade ended, politicians and civic leaders put two and two together. In December 1959, the city created the Urban Renewal Agency of the City of Tampa. It had a seven-man board, an administrative staff, and a board Chairman—on paper. The local program worked in conjunction with the Federal Housing and Urban Development program. The HUD initiatives were an outgrowth of the Great Society program in the Kennedy and Lyndon Johnson years, tying back in turn to the Eisenhower inner-city rehabilitation legislation.

Although Tampa's agency was created on paper in December 1959, it was a full three years—late 1962—before the agency was actually staffed and operational. This delay proved to be very costly!

The way Urban Renewal in Ybor City would work was to offer the people in the inner city temporary housing elsewhere, while the program administration took care of dismantling old houses, clearing the land, and arranging the financing for 50-year loans at 3-percent interest. They also would assist in the negotiation and moving of families into newer, modern homes.[26]

Utilizing primarily federal HUD moneys, the agency began to rehabilitate areas of Tampa in two phases:

The first phase—designated "R-1"—included the old Maryland Avenue African American area known as "the Scrub," which had been a kind of buffer between Ybor and downtown Tampa; the second—labeled "R-13"—was the 70-acre heart of Ybor City. The plan was to publicize the program, inventory the housing and deter-



**Chapter 5 · Mixed Years and a Withering Town: 1950-1965**

*Ybor City streets were often closed to traffic during the construction of I-4. Here in 1962 a worker places a detour sign in position at 15th Street and 12th Avenue. The only streets offering access through Ybor City at this time were 14th, 19th, and 22nd Streets.*

It struck a dagger at the heart of Ybor City, carving a swath from east to west along 13th Avenue, displacing houses and some businesses. Residents in some of the small, frame homes in the core area found themselves facing a noisy, automobile-clogged, exhaust-filled major highway. Their air was polluted. Their privacy was gone. Children no longer could play on the streets. In addition, the town had been dissected. The only connections between the two parts now were through 14th, 15th, 19th, and 22nd Streets. Two of these, 14th and 15th Streets, became one-way. Unless they had cars, people on the north side of I-4 could shop the town only with great inconvenience. Once again, merchants on both the main spines, La Sétima and 15th Street, suffered a substantial loss of business.[29]

mine its condition, advise those residents of the intent to buy them out, move them to sites in greater Tampa, and then, eventually, move them back into new housing.

In Ybor City the plan was to proceed through the "moving out" phase, while gradually working up the resources for the "rebuilding phase." At first, this did not seem as though it would be difficult. Money for the agency's proposed low-cost housing programs seemed readily available in the mid-1960s. One example of the atmosphere was an elaborate display at a local bank showing the Ybor City subject area with the promised buildings included. It was presented with the assumption that all the new construction would be financed by HUD money. For most civic leaders that assumption was a given.[27]

Finally, in 1962, three years after it was created, the Urban Renewal Program office in Tampa was actually staffed. It was set up as an independent agency not reporting directly to any department of city government. Its executive director, Tom Fox, was only asked to report the agency's activities to the city council regularly for its approval.[28]

The change was dispiriting, and it caught residents and business people by surprise. Of course, they had known this was coming, but the reality of the I-4 intrusion was something impossible to imagine in advance. A sample of the effects of the change and the malaise soon to afflict the Ybor City core area is found in a an article by Keith Coulbourn of the *Tampa Tribune* that ran on June 3, 1962, accompanied by a photograph taken at the intersection of 15th Street and 12th Avenue:

> Ybor City has never been so divided. . . . The colorful Latin section of Tampa is practically bisected by a two block strip of desolation, site of future spans making up Interstate Hwy. I-4 . . . most of the north-south roads are cut off by the plowed right-of-ways .
>
> "I have lived here many years and I'm glad I was not moved," [one local resident said]. "Many of those who were moved had lived here many years, too. Some were my friends. And some of them said they were not paid as much as they thought they should be . . . But also many others said they didn't receive enough to buy another house somewhere else . . ."
>
> The grocer who runs the store at the corner came out to watch, joining the six or so others . . . "I lost many customers who used to live out there," he said . . . . [My] customers come

## The Construction of I-4

Meanwhile, the new Interstate Highway I-4 opened October 4, 1963, with construction having started in early 1962.

in every day and buy something. They buy on credit. And they come from within a block away, do you see?"[30]

The painful reality of the grocer's loss as he described his customers could be seen in the photograph that showed that everything within the nearby block had been leveled.

Seldom has a town suffered so completely from the ravages of poor planning. The impact of decisions by the Department of Transportation and the city only compounded the troubles. They reversed the direction of traffic on 15th Street and altered the access of Latin shoppers from the heart of the northern part of greater Ybor. The idea was to bring them in on 14th Street. But the southern flow was stopped at 10th Avenue, and then traffic was shunted onto Nuccio Parkway, headed to Tampa. Yes, they could decide to take a left, but that was inconvenient—almost like a detour. The natural flow of Ybor life was gone. Add to that the previous discontinuation of the little yellow streetcars in the late 1940s, and the encroaching shadows of a new mall at North Gate and a new Sears Roebuck on Hillsborough, and one is left to ponder what Latins had done to deserve this treatment. In addition, the traffic planners created their east-west corridor right through the center of Ybor City, so that the remaining autoless townspeople could no longer walk conveniently to the town's center. Clearly, the destruction of the core area could scarcely have been more complete if it had been intentionally plotted step-by-step.[31]

The deterioration process, once begun, had predictable results. As the Latins left, good African American families needing housing increased their ongoing migration into Ybor City, raising their proportion by approximately 38 percent, especially in the northern suburbs. Aiding this process were real estate agents and speculators. Street talk held that the real estate firms were

*Looking west from 26th Street, the roadbed is being prepared for the Interstate in this 1962 photograph. In the distance an automobile tries to make its way across.*

entirely insensitive to the needs for Latin cohesiveness. Moreover, the unpredictable future of the area and the changing demographics scared Tampa's banks. All of these factors worked to accelerate the vulnerability of central core and together they created a situation that made Urban Renewal marketable.

Local Ybor leaders now also came to view the federal Urban Renewal program as the only practical solution to this morass. They supported the early efforts while working to insure that the town's displaced people would be returned, and the Latin architecture, historic buildings, and Latin culture would be protected. In time, an Urban Renewal report would recommend "that 92.9 percent of the housing be cleared in Ybor's 70 acre plot of land . . . to preserve and strengthen the distinctive qualities . . . of Tampa's Latin heritage and present day Latin community." The people who were displaced were supposed to be brought back towards the end of Phase 2, when, supposedly, new housing constructed with a view toward preserving a Latin style would be available. At least, that is how the renewal effort was touted, and that is what the displaced citizens understood.[32]

Against a mountain of bureaucracy—HUD, a host of state and city agencies, and complicated Urban Renewal program



**Chapter 5 · Mixed Years and a Withering Town: 1950-1965**

*This aerial photograph taken in 1963 shows a portion of the residential area of Ybor City. The street running diagonally nearest the bottom is 6th Avenue, interesected with 13th Streeet at the far left. La Sétima runs parallel to 6th Street one block up from the bottom. To the far right is 15th Street. The large building near the left center is now Ybor Square.* LA GACETA.

*An aerial view of Ybor City after Urban Renewal, 1967. The arrow indicates a proposed site for an Environmental Protection Commission building.* MORRIS OF SELBYPIC.

guidelines—the Tampa office completed the Maryland Avenue project first, the "Scrub" land area southwest of Ybor. Then the Riverfront project was essentially completed. In 1966, some seven-plus years after Tampa had taken up the cause of Urban Renewal in late 1958, the bulldozing of Ybor's core began. Soon they had leveled some seven hundred sites and related businesses. The area from I-4 to 8th and Nebraska to 22nd Street (with a very few exceptions) was decimated.

Late in the HUD era Ybor City was in total remission. On La Sétima, ex-*tabaqueros* and townspeople in the suburbs huddled, shook their heads, hurled epithets, and talked in disbelief at the apparent faithlessness towards the "contract with the people." They pointed to Washington, to Anglo power-brokers in Tampa, whom they felt didn't want a rebuilt Latin town, and to the conspicuously non-Latin staff of the Urban Renewal organization who pushed other projects ahead while Ybor stagnated. They hurled epithets, also, at the DOT and I-4 contractors for slicing the town in half. It did not exclude the earlier incumbent politicians who allowed the changes in direction of 14th, 15th, 19th 21st, and 22nd Streets, some leading to Tampa and not Ybor. They despised the decision that allowed heavy trucking on some of our main roads, such as 22nd Street. All these actions accumulated their effects to virtually wipe out the merchants.

All honest, self-respecting men and women rebelled in their hearts at this rap-



**Ybor City: The Making of a Landmark Town**

*An aerial photograph of Ybor City in 1960 shows the area before Urban Renewal cleared many of the historic homes and neighborhoods.*

ing of their town! At La Norma Coffee Mill the townspeople talked for hours each day. One heard comments like *"Tienen cojones!"* A very mild translation might be: "they had a hell of a lot of gall!"[33]

With the exception of two initiatives that had arisen from the Ybor City Latins themselves—Haciendas de Ybor and the Barrio Latino Commission—the renewal efforts had merely led to destruction and confusion. Fortunately, both of the Ybor initiatives were still in place. The point man for both was Dr. Henry J. Fernandez, a highly motivated civic leader. This local optometrist would eventually serve five terms as president of YCCC. The power of the Barrio Latino Commission concerning protection of its Latin architecture has been challenged, but today as the 21st century begins it endures as a strong and valiant arm of the community.[34] The story of the Haciendas de Ybor project will be told more fully in the next chapter. It reached completion in the later years of the decade.

By mid-century, however, the prospects were not encouraging. Countless Ybor civic leaders, including many Chamber presidents, had wrenched their imaginations attempting to find the means to reinvigorate the town. People like Cesar Gonzmart, Dr. Henry Fernandez, aging Victoriano Manteiga, Eddie Spoto, "King" Greco, Joe Lopez, Daniel Martinez, Charles Spicola, Raul Vega, Manuel Ballota, Max Argintar, Anthony Grimaldi, Joe Granda, active merchants, and others, promoted and sometimes tried to implement ideas. Some of them were visionary, but without the cigar industry, a near miracle was needed. There did not seem to be the critical mass of grass roots activists nor visionary private investors with deep pockets, nor the flash of inspiration needed for success.

The Columbia Restaurant, again, was a hotbed of talk, concern, and planning. There, in the Siboney Room, or in the old Cafe Room, and at the many social dinners, countless ideas were discarded and



**Chapter 5 · Mixed Years and a Withering Town: 1950–1965**

others solidified; acceptance and support were solicited. The facility for interchanging ideas with the town's leaders spawned many suggestions. There was considerable concern for the changing demographics and the march of other forces, especially to increasing amounts of outside governance and influences not in consonance with the area's Latin culture. In these years, the townspeople had some expectations, but more often they had fear.

The future of the social clubs that had been pillars of support for Latin culture was also bleak in the doldrums of this Urban Renewal period. Their memberships dwindled. Many Latins had moved away, and although autos had come into wide use, some Latins were too old to drive. Many had never needed a car and had never learned to drive. Many sons and daughters would drive their fathers to the club cantinas, and would later have to drive back to pick them up. Even the life left in the clubs was often bought at great inconvenience to the family. To add a final lethal blow to wide club attendance was the fact that, except for the Centro Asturiano, the clubs lacked parking space. This was a big factor in the club members opting to quit attending the Centro Español, and to turn, reluctantly, to some much less-esteemed pastime in greater Tampa. In turn, movie houses like the El Casino, Ritz, Broadway, and Garden theaters experienced declining attendance. The cycle of entropy, once begun, ran ruthlessly downhill.[35]

To compensate for the lack of local jobs, the town's more flexible citizens began to spread out and find work in the greater Tampa area. Many continued to open small businesses throughout Tampa. Some pursued food importing and distribution, wholesaling, large-scale fishing, taxi and delivery services, and small manufacturing. Others continued in phases of the cigar industry in Caribbean countries. Frank Garcia imported and distributed ceramic tiles. Today he is one of the very top state wholesalers of this product, with warehouses over many Florida cities. Obviously, these were free enterprise sons of

*In the early 1960s when this photograph was taken, attendance at the Ritz and other Ybor City theaters was on the decline. There were also noticeably fewer shoppers on the streets. Residents were being relocated and traffic diverted by detour signs and road closings.*

222

**Ybor City: The Making of a Landmark Town**

the town. A few began to enter city politics or took jobs with city or county government. Some recent graduates of American colleges and universities became doctors, lawyers, engineers, accountants, Realtors, or educators. Higher education was, indeed, one of the great legacies many Latins bestowed on their children.

In the 1960s Belk Lindsey, a branch of a national chain of clothing store, left Ybor City's most central corner, 15th Street and La Sétima, where the Fernandez and Garcia clothing store had been a city landmark for many years. Its vacated space brought fear to many merchants, even as others increased their commitment to modernize and improve their service. Needing much more office and manufacturing space, partners Ramon Diaz and Cesar Medina, expanded their bread operation from Ybor, where it had adjoined the Columbia Restaurant, to a large, modern manufacturing building on Hillsborough and 22nd Street, where they made American-style Bambi bread. The company grew regionally and created jobs for many Latins. At the same time it left vacant the west corner of the Columbia property on La Sétima. Fortunately, that was soon filled by an expanding Columbia Restaurant.

The lack of income in the area helped create a deteriorating inner core. The view was expounded that the inner core was not fixable. The only solution advanced was that the core should be demolished, and then brought back to life. This further accelerated the exodus to the other Tampa areas. Ybor City in the mid-'60s was a town in distress.

Beyond the Ybor City neighborhoods in the first half of the 1960s, Tampa survived a battering by Hurricane Donna. Residents celebrated the opening of the Howard Frankland Bridge across Tampa Bay to St. Petersburg, and the University of South Florida was in its first decade offering new opportunities in higher educa-tion. The Cuban missile crisis assured the survival and strategic importance of MacDill Air Force Base, and President Kennedy visited Tampa four days before he was assassinated in Dallas in 1963. In 1965 the downtown Curtis Hixon Convention Center was dedicated.

The U.S. population at this time was 178.3 million, and the gross national product totaled $502.6 billion. Ybor City seemed disconnected from the national trends of growing population and increasing revenues, but the residents were very much involved in events at the heart of national political and military issues. In 1961, the Bay of Pigs invasion by Cuban exiles with U.S. support was a disaster, and the USSR agreed to respond with arms to Cuba—including those famous missile sites just ninety miles from U.S. soil. Our government blockade of the island and President Kennedy's forceful leadership in the showdown with the Soviets resulted with their withdrawal of the missiles.

This was the matrix of seemingly unrelated events that began the decade for a new generation. For the young men and women of Ybor's fast-eroding population most of these events further removed Ybor City from the spotlight. For a significant number, their vision was elsewhere in America. Still, for most who had grown up

*Derelict buildings were silent reminders of Ybor City's history as the town was cut in half by I-4 and steadily dismantled, building by building. This brick structure on the southwest corner of 12th Avenue and 16th Street was once the home of the Spanish language newspaper* El Heraldo Dominical. *USFSCL.*

**Chapter 5 · Mixed Years and a Withering Town: 1950-1965**

in Ybor City, the town still held their hearts hostage. Some broke the bonds. But for very many, whether now in Tampa or away, the bonds that pulled at the heartstrings never wavered. Of this there are many witnesses. One writer who quickly comes to mind is Jose Yglesias. Born and raised in Ybor City, a witness to much of the early factory militancy and folklore of the area, he left Ybor City and wrote his best works away from home. Today he is considered Ybor City's leading author, and his death in 1995 was mourned throughout the community. Of those Ybor City residents who scattered to the four corners of America, their Spanish language went with them, in most instances seldom to be used again. But in those instances that a friend, acquaintance or rare opportunity arrived, they found themselves uttering Castilian words that were part of their legacy. But it is certain that they passed to their children some choice, exclamatory words that sudden events would demand, and which they in turn, would pass on. These were likely to be the mountain farm words of Galicia, Asturias, Sicilia, and of the Cuban countryside.

Yes, the pull of a way of life so unique and exemplary, in spite of the occasional adversities of the period, has left an indelible imprint on many of the town's people. To most, no other living experience compares with this warm, emotional, and historic saga they shared in Ybor City.

Despite the heavy trend for longtime residents to move to distant parts of Tampa or beyond, a few decided to stay. These lingered on, particularly in the greater Ybor City areas. And in a few rare cases, their sons or daughters also remained, living in the old homestead, some of them in the very heart of the town. Today, for example, Señor Braña's daughter still lives on Columbus Drive and 15th Street. Here the town's residents once stopped for gasoline at Ybor City's most popular and centrally located service station; nearby were the town's largest laundry, the "Regenbois" factory clock, the V. M. Ybor Grammar School, and Cuscaden Park. In the late 1920s my sister Lola and I sat in the rear rumble seat of father's *fotingo* as he got gas there. Despite all the circumstances that combined to dispossess the original families, some roots held firm

224

As a new century begins, now more than a century since don Vicente Martinez Ybor founded this cigar town, it still retains the indelible feel of the place our fathers—Cubans, Spaniards, and Italians—first settled and defined. One must view with awe and respect these rare Ybor City citizens who in addition to having embraced the mores of their fathers and mothers and retained and passed along the town's ethnic lore, have elected to remain in their old homesteads. Are they the real patriots? Or must we look elsewhere—perhaps toward distant states or countries which for one reason or another lured the Ybor originals to seek new opportunities—to find those who now, though virtually unknown and forgotten, keep the flame of the town's authentic culture alive and close to their hearts—there, far away, in distant solitude, or in fresh companionship through stories they may be passing on to new generations of friends and family far from their old Ybor homes? Who, indeed, are the real patriots who carry the dying flame of the old Ybor City?

There is a strong argument that they all are.

*Nick C. Nuccio, Tampa's first Latin mayor, was elected as a city alderman from Ybor City in 1929, and became a Hillsborough County Commissioner in 1936, going on to serve seven terms. He first was elected mayor in 1956 and served two terms in that capacity. The Nuccio Parkway in Ybor City and the Lowry Park Zoo are two of his many achievements. For years he held court daily at Cuervo's Café, across from L'Unione Italiana club building.*

*The Ybor City of Chamber of Commerce installed its new slate of officers at the Columbia Restaurant in 1962. Standing, from left, are Ramon Alvarez, executive director; Raul Vega Jr., president; Dr. Henry Fernandez, past president; Joe Alonso, secretary, and Eddie Spoto, treasurer. La Gaceta.*

**Chapter 5 • Mixed Years and a Withering Town: 1950-1965**

*Attending this typical annual "Gala Celebration" at the Columbia Restaurant for members of the Ybor City Chamber of Commerce are (right front) Victor DiMaio, a past president of YCCC and active on many committees, seated across from his wife Mercy, who has chaired many Hispanic initiatives and civic activities in the Tampa community. Next to them are Judge Michael Kavouklis and his wife, Irene.* YBOR CITY CHAMBER OF COMMERCE.

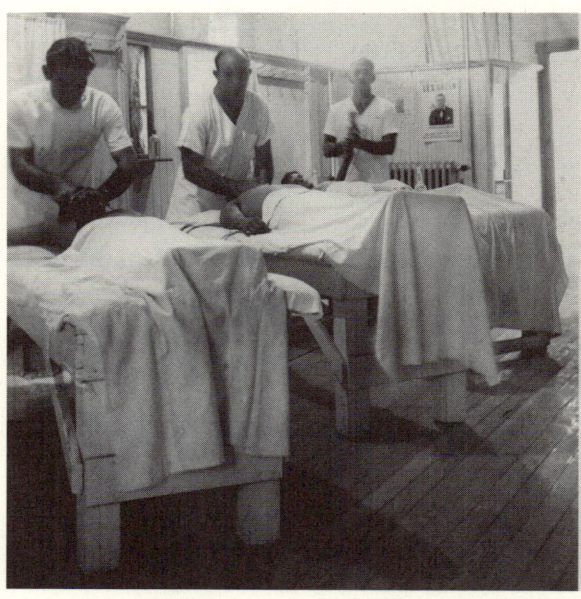

*Dr. Marcelino G. Arguelles, a Spaniard from Asturias, founded the Institute of Naturopathy at 15th Avenue and 17th Street in 1907, but it burned down in the great fire of 1908. He quickly rebuilt the new facility, shown above, at 1406 10th Avenue. It was named Arguelles Turkish Baths, but the town referred to it as "la Casa Cune." The word "Cune" is a reference to the hot baths. In the photo on the right masseurs Marcelino Arguelles, Benny Fidalgo, and Baby Burego, giving massages, about 1950. The building also housed a vegetarian restaurant and boarding rooms upstairs for young factory workers, foremen, and others.  The sedentary work of cigar workers—sitting all day in the factory and then playing cards, dominoes, and drinking coffee at the cafés and clubs—created body aches and pains that had to be treated. Dr. Arguelles introduced many specialized hot bath treatments, massages, and other cures. Some four years after he passed away, his son, Marcelino Jr., took over the business from his mother.  As women also went to work in the factories in increasing numbers, his wife Abdelia joined Marcelino Jr. in the profession. Both received physiotherapy certificates at The College of Swedish Massage in Chicago.  In the early 1960s a hot bath plus a massage cost six dollars. It was an Ybor City institution and very much a part of the town's folklore talked about in the cafés over coffee. I recall my father as a young man took many hot baths at "la Casa Cune." When Urban Renewal razed the building, Marcelino opened it again at Armenia, just north of Martin Luther King Jr. Boulevard, in the 1960s.  It was sold in 1987 after Marcelina Arguelles' son, Jose, passed away in 1986. Today Abdelia Arguelles carries the family torch and memories.* ABDELIA ARGUELLES.



**Ybor City: The Making of a Landmark Town**

*Fernandez & Garcia Store employees celebrate at a banquet in the 1955 photo. The store at the corner of La Setíma and 15th Street was a popular destination for shoppers for many years. "We were like family," former employee Josephine Varselona told a reporter. "Our main concern was to take care of the customers and to make sure they were satisfied." The longtime family business was eventually sold and became a Belk Lindsey store.* JOSEPHINE VARSELONA AND LA GACETA.

*Havana, Cuba, has long been near and dear to the hearts of many in Ybor City. This 1959 photograph of the Latin American Fiesta Court Goodwill Tour Group was taken at La Tropicana nightclub in Havana. Among thos pictured are Mr. and Mrs. Leon Cazin, Mr. and Mrs. Mario Cabrera, Mr. and Mrs. Hector Jimenez, Mr. and Mrs. Louis Salazar, Sam Marino, Al Cazin, Sam Rodante, and Frank Traina. Evidence of Fidel Castro's recent takeover can be seen in the presence of troops standing in back.* LOUIS SALAZAR AND LA GACETA.

**Chapter 5 • Mixed Years and a Withering Town: 1950-1965**

*Ybor Square was an ambitious part of early redevelopment efforts in Ybor City. Located at the historic Principe de Gales factory of Don Vicente Martínez Ybor, the Ybor Square shops and dining venues, shown here in a planning rendering, combined to form one of Ybor City's "must see" attractions after its completion in the 1970s. It adjoined parade routes and historic sites such as the José Martí Park, and was a popular location for arts and crafts exhibits and other outdoor festivities.* YBOR SQUARE.

# Empty Years and Early Redevelopment 1965-1970

## Our Disappearing Landmark: 1965-1967

In mid-1967 Urban Renewal reported that Phase One of the Ybor City project was moving even faster than the other projects in Tampa. However, there were still no completed plans for Phase Two. In other words, more quickly than anyone imagined, the historic fabric of Ybor City had been ripped apart, with no clear prospects for reweaving. Against the reality of an impending Richard Nixon presidential victory in early 1968, with an expected shrinkage and changing of federal spending objectives under a new Republican administration, an undercurrent of concern ran through Ybor. The possibility of local bank loans to support the renewal effort was a topic one heard discussed more often, and local banks declared themselves ready to cooperate with authorities and potential customers.

Then on June 11, 1967, African Americans rioted following the shooting of a 19-year-old black burglary suspect fleeing from Tampa police. Snipers fired on police from rooftops near downtown, a grocery store and other businesses were set aflame, and looters trashed and robbed some of the downtown establishments. Other than one young suspect killed by police, there was no loss of life, but there was substantial loss of property, including one entire block near downtown Tampa that was leveled by fire. Despite the fact that the damage was about a mile away from Ybor City, the event was reported prominently in the national press, tarnishing the entire area's image with this unrest reported in the "troubled" areas near Tampa's Ybor City. A cloud of gloom hung above the heads of Ybor's townspeople and civic leaders. Banks and insurance companies reportedly took a second, hard look at the stability of Ybor City and lost interest in financing development there. Urban Renewal was stopped dead in its tracks.[1]

However, in the wake of devastation created by Urban Renewal under the mostly non-Latin leadership of the Tampa program, a separate redevelopment effort did succeed. The Haciendas de Ybor project — an initiative of the Ybor City Chamber of Commerce to house displaced elderly residents — was successfully completed. Enabling legislation for the construction of the Haciendas was shepherded through the legislature by Congressman Sam Gibbons, and with dedicated commitment from city leaders, some of the residents who had been forced to leave discovered a way to move back home again. Today, at the beginning of a new millennium, The Haciendas complex

*Adalberto Ramírez, originally a superintendent in the Ybor factory, started his own company in the early 1900s and adopted the Jules Verne cigar label as a tribute to the French author who launched a space ship from Tampa in his 1865 novel* From the Earth to the Moon. *A real rocket launched from Florida's east coast, only about 127 miles from Tampa, took man to the moon in 1969.*

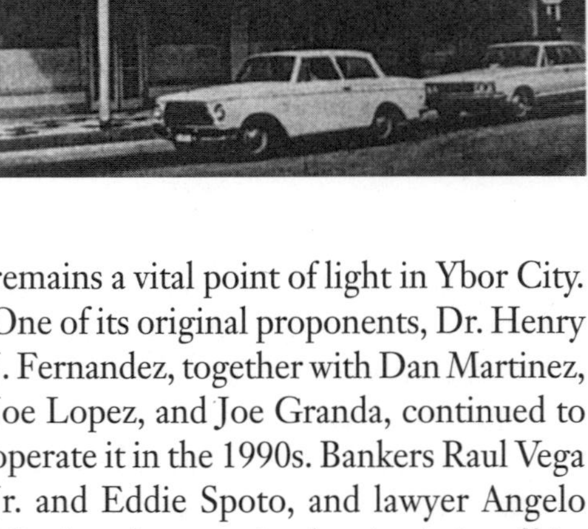

*Naviera Coffee Mills was opened by Carlos C. Menendez in 1921 at a location on the corner of 18th Avenue and 22nd Street that was demolished by Urban Renewal. They wanted to keep their Cuban coffee business in Ybor City and purchased a building at 2012 La Sétima, shown at the right in 1967 before and after renovation by owner Danilo Fernandez, grandson of the founder.* Urban Renewal News.

remains a vital point of light in Ybor City. One of its original proponents, Dr. Henry J. Fernandez, together with Dan Martinez, Joe Lopez, and Joe Granda, continued to operate it in the 1990s. Bankers Raul Vega Jr. and Eddie Spoto, and lawyer Angelo Martino also remained active in its affairs until they passed away. All of them were past presidents of the Ybor City Chamber of Commerce and they understood the city's needs and resources. Today, Haciendas still has a waiting list of prospective residents. All tenants pay rent. It has become a significant Ybor renewal success story—but it was not accomplished by the Urban Renewal program.

The Haciendas de Ybor project was begun by the Ybor Chamber of Commerce, and the project was overseen by the organization while it was run by the above-mentioned Latins. These men felt such deep commitment to the mothers and fathers of the town, and such profound appreciation for the great legacy they left, that they were determined this project would succeed. In addition, they understood the cultural history and the current needs of Ybor citizens; they themselves were full participants in the community's history and heritage. Thanks to this group, many displaced Latins were able to return to comfortable and convenient housing in the town they called their own.[2]

## Model City

Meanwhile, another new federal initiative known as "Model Cities" leapt to the forefront. On November 16, 1967, Tampa received a large federal boost toward redevelopment in the form of a Model Cities Planning Aid package. Its objective was to generate practical, city-specific plans to eliminate urban decay. This time responsibility for program administration was assigned to city mayors. In the case of Tampa, the leadership role fell to young Dick Greco, who became mayor just as the program began. Model Cities tried to include all aspects of community life and to assist with upgrading housing as one of many components designed to improve the nation's urban environments. In Tampa the program covered outer Ybor City and other areas. It worked piecemeal, using grant funding and public relations efforts to engage the community. Possibly because it tried to focus from the start on direct community involvement, it was substantially successful.

After only one term in office, Mayor Julian Lane had been defeated by former mayor Nick Nuccio in 1963 with solid support from the Latin community. Then in 1967 there had been the surprising choice between *two* Ybor Latin candidates for Tampa's highest office. Despite Nuccio's prior experience as mayor, political newcomer Dick Greco Jr., who spoke three languages and moved comfortably among Anglo and ethnic communities alike as a true inheritor of Ybor's multicultural past, was elected to become the youngest mayor of any major city in the U.S. While Nuccio had nurtured and

230

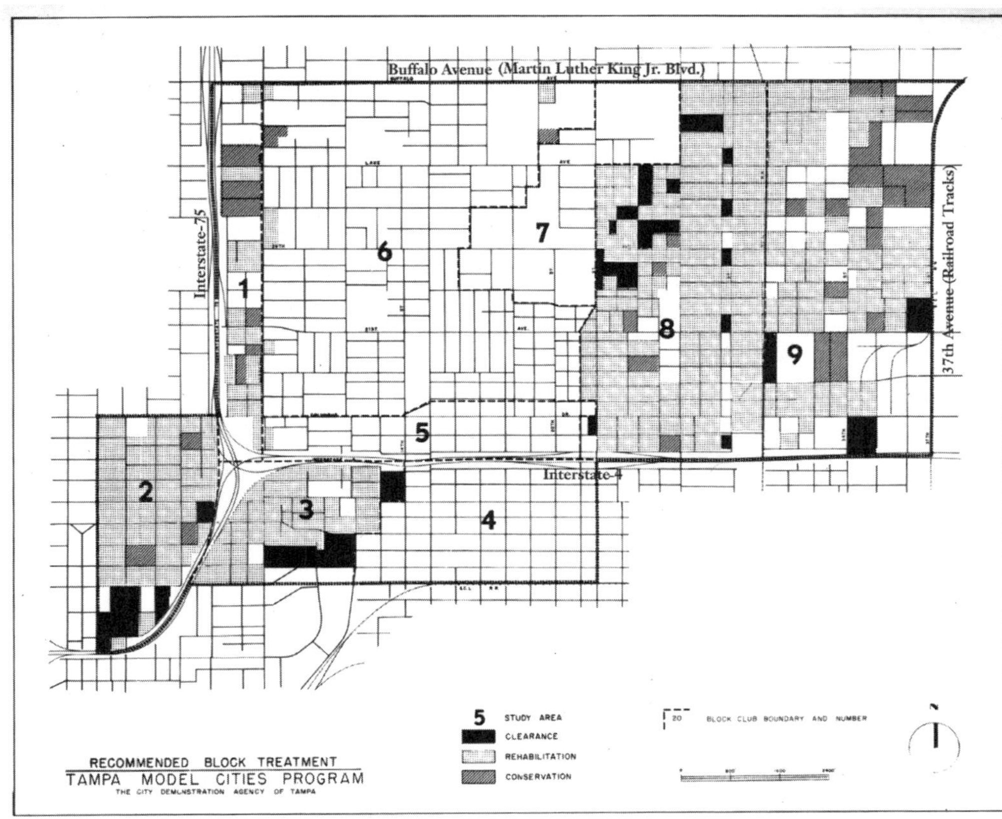



*This map from the Tampa Model Cities interim report prepared by the City Demonstration Agency (CDA) shows the designated boundaries for the project and the recommended treatment for specific blocks. Solid areas were marked for clearance; dotted areas were to be rehabilitated, and the areas marked with diagonal lines were slated for conservation.*

never abandoned the dreams of Ybor's rebirth, it was Tampa Mayor Greco who would be the chief city official during the planning phase of the Model Cities program. Working as project director with Greco was John Fernandez; assisting Fernandez was projects coordinator, alderman, and lead planner Cesar Gonzmart Jr. They in turn had twenty-five block committees coordinated by the Model Cities organization under the umbrella of an entity known as the City Demonstration Agency (CDA) with Fernandez as director, Gary Smith as assistant director, Alton White as assistant director for citizen participation, and Bobby L. Bowden as coordinator of citizen participation.[3]

The first round of planning grants went to sixty-three cities around the country. Tampa was one of two Florida cities chosen to receive one, thanks in part to the efforts of Florida congressman Sam Gibbons, who had been instrumental in promoting the Tampa program as part of the national, bipartisan urban redevelopment initiative. Tampa's Model City target area had a northern boundary of Buffalo Avenue (now Martin Luther King Jr. Blvd.), ran in a southerly direction along Interstate 275 to Columbus Drive, west to Florida Avenue, south to Interstate 4, eastward along Henderson, Sixth Avenue, and the railroad tracks to 22nd Street, north to Interstate 4, east to 37th Street, and north along 37th and the railroad tracks to Buffalo. Much of this area had already been the focus of considerable concern and effort within the Ybor City community, but now a more intense planning process began to try to find ways to make a dramatic improvement.

The Model Cities program ran somewhat parallel to other portions of the nationwide drive for urban renewal. A brochure from the Department of Health, Education, and Welfare described the program as "the first step in a realistic, massive effort to seek solutions to America's urban slum problems." It explained how the planning for Model Cities would connect with other national efforts to eradicate city blight: "Local officials and citizens are drawing up comprehensive neighborhood plans which will intermesh with existing programs and create new human and physical projects to fill the gaps. The goals are increased city government ability to deal with both physical and social problems, and substantial improvement in the lives and opportunities of those Americans now living in the slums."[4]

Model Cities officials would initially give undivided attention to the selected improverished neighborhood as representative of the worst parts of the city. The thinking was that if the most difficult problems could be solved in one representative neighborhood, then those solutions might also be applied to other similar areas. The program was designed to address various aspects of urban blight, including housing, transportation, communications, beautification, and a large number of related needs, such as education, health, employment, family living, and others. Planners sought to involve as many diverse groups and individuals as possible: local, state, and federal officials; business, professional, and private agencies and foundations; professional and cultural organizations; civic and social clubs; community and religious leaders; and others. In Tampa and Ybor City, local leaders tried to follow the spirit as well as the letter of the planning directives. They reached out to many constituencies, and as discussion got underway it raised both hopes and fears.

Within the first year after the award was announced, preliminary phases of outreach and consultation had begun. An editorial in the *Tribune* on June 29, 1969, posed a few of the many major questions which the program was raising: "Will Model Cities work? . . . Will Model Cities be a boom or boondoggle? Will high-salaried overseers and inept administration curdle the whole program?"[5] The writer pointed out that an executive council headed by Mayor Greco would recommend new projects, but before going forward the recommendations would need to be approved by the city council. Both the city and federal governments would then be required to evaluate all programs, so the "greatest concern is the overlapping and clashing of agencies. . . . It's a bureaucratic fact of life that Federal agencies—and local ones too—are jealous of their domains in public life."[6]

By the fall of 1969, the shape of the project was becoming clearer. During that year the Tampa redevelopment initiative was operating on a supplemental grant of some $4 million from the federal Housing and Urban Development program (HUD). Under the leadership of new national director George Romney, HUD seemed dedicated to breaking through bureaucratic walls. In Tampa John Fernandez was heading up a staff of one hundred workers in a group called the City Demonstration Agency (CDA), which in turn was a conduit for some additional funding from HUD and other U.S. agencies.[7]

During 1969 the program was administered with the participation of at least twenty-five citizens' block clubs. However, as far as the impact on historic Ybor City is concerned, it is important to note that the Model Cities program was not utilized in the core area. It was supposed to cover "blighted" areas. The boundaries for the overall scope included all of suburban or greater Ybor City, but the Latin areas within those boundaries were not blighted, nor were they particularly impoverished. Thus one must understand that the overall geographical designations used for the Model Cities planning was simply a matter of convenience to define the general parameters or extent of the project.

Model Cities, staffed by very competent and motivated men, was seemingly lost to

the general public in Ybor City. In this instance, city, county, and CDA functioned well. But their efforts were not always very visible. The Model Cities boundaries seemed far-flung and vague to many residents. The ongoing Urban Renewal meanwhile had captured the imagination of the public. It aroused stronger emotions. More was at stake: Ybor City itself. By now the Maryland Avenue project in the old Scrub area had been completed. Also, the Riverfront Project, a many-faceted one, was making strides. These all received press attention. But conflict always makes news, and failed promises fed conflict. Ybor was newsworthy! Its "contract with the people" was not fulfilled.

## Urban Renewal and Barrio Latino

Almost coinciding with the demise of the Latin Plaza Plan, Tampa's city council in December of 1959 had approved participation in the Urban Renewal program, based on enabling legislation approved in Tallahassee the previous year. The Urban Renewal Organization staff included A. R. Ragsdale, chairman; Joe Dalton, vice chairman; Thomas J. Fox, executive director; Marshall M. Tison, assistant executive director; James D. Marshall Jr., project manager; attorney Richard E. Leon, conservation officer; John D. Anderson Jr., relocation officer; A. William Benitez, conservation advisor (and editor of the *Urban Renewal News*); Richard Sargent, real estate officer; and Calvin Ellers, accountant, as well as other officers and office staff.[8]

Although the program was approved and an organization was named in response to the 1959 city council vote, the Urban Renewal office was not staffed until 1962. This three-year delay would later prove to have been a loss of invaluable lead time which the city could have used to great advantage. By the time the office got its feet on the ground and collected the staff, the funding, and the information it needed, the decade was half over.

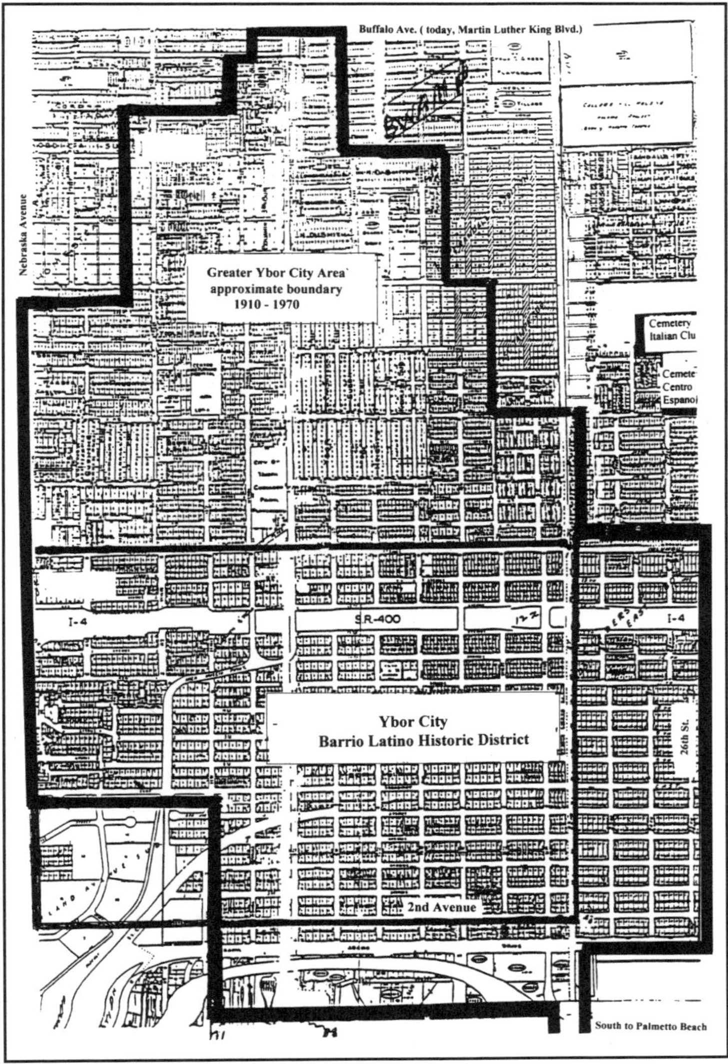


Ybor City community leaders observed that the town's business district was still functioning in the mid-60s, but just barely. With some notable exceptions, business was eroding fast. The older houses in the core area were deteriorating, lived in mostly by old cigar factory employees from the better days. Only a few major factories remained by 1965—Corral Wodiska, Perfecto Garcia, Villazon, Hav-A-Tampa, and a handful of others. Also still operating were various *chinchales.* These were small family-run "buckeyes," where production was low and promotion and marketing virtually nonexistent. With the Latin Plaza initiative sputtering out, the Model Cities funding directed else-

*This map indicates the greater Ybor City area that was the target for various Urban Renewal efforts. The precise configuration for each grant proposal would change, but this sketch shows the broad outlines as well as the Barrio Latino Historic District. For additional detail, please see the tables and exhibits at the back of the book.*

233

A. William Benitez

where at problems other than those in the old Ybor City core, and Urban Renewal efforts so slow to begin, confusion set in. Ybor civic leaders were in a quandary about how to remedy a growing, hopeless situation.

Against this background, even more conservative Ybor leaders, the Ybor Chamber of Commerce, active businessmen, and an occasional politician were beginning to consider the need for serious action to improve the area's future well-being. At the same time, a nucleus of Latin civic activists within the Chamber, Rotary Club, and other local organizations, began to call for swift measures, decisive action to assure that Ybor City would preserve its cherished and historical Latin character. Political leaders explored ways to assist with federal, state, and city programs in the Latin inner-city. This was the area bounded by Interstate 4 on the north, 6th Avenue on the south, Nuccio Parkway to the west, and 22nd Street to the east.

Concerning expected results, the 1967 quarterly *Urban Renewal News* published in Tampa offered news and information on the project's progress. A. William Benitez, conservation advisor and editor, wrote

(presumably trying to sound upbeat in a town seething with concern):

> In the midst of all the problems facing Ybor City, we still have many merchants who are willing to invest in the future of Ybor City . . . These merchants continue remodeling and repairing, even in some cases they are ridiculed by other merchants who have no feeling whatever for their community.
>
> The Ybor City Urban Renewal Project, (#Fla. R-13), is a unique type project in that we have combined clearance with rehabilitation of many old structures. Originally we had hoped to save 50% or more of the residential structures; however, after detailed structural surveys were made, 89% of the homes were considered not feasible for rehabilitation. We were then forced into complete clearance of residence[s] and partial clearance of business structures which were considered to[o] far gone for rehabilitation.
>
> In cooperation with the Barrio Latino Commission and the City of Tampa, the rehabilitation is following the Mediterranean or Latin Style architecture. Many commercial property owners and tenants have at their own expense done very fine work in this regard.[9]

Despite the sense of bustling activity, the positive involvement of businesses investing in their community, and the dedication to the spirit of the Latin style which Benitez's message contains, the bare fact at its heart was heartbreaking. This is the news that Urban Renewal officials had made the decision to destroy ("complete clearance") about 90 percent of the surviving historical residences in the city. Silence with respect to the specifics of costs, profits, and politics does not suffice to hush suspicions about how various vested interests may have played into the decision. Besides, from what perspective was the judgment made that the restoration of 89 percent of the homes was "not feasible"? Surely it was not based on a reasonable comparison with the feasibility and advantages of preserving historic buildings and the unique multicultural ambiance they contained. It could not have been made on any cost-benefit analysis that reasonably valued the humble origins of the Ybor City



**Ybor City: The Making of a Landmark Town**

experience in its full spectrum, from its original makeshift immigrant housing to its more prosperous residences. Through some skewed and partial valuation, the vast majority of properties had been judged as being beyond "rehabilitation," and their death sentence pronounced.

Meanwhile, Dr. Henry J. Fernandez, chairman of the Barrio Latino Commission, in the same issue of the newsletter, wrote an updated account of his commission's work:

> The Barrio Latino Commission Law has recently been amended by Ord. no. 4183 passed by the City Council . . . In this Ordinance the major change is that the Commission is now empowered by law to designate buildings and structures of architectural or historical value to the City. . . . The Commission is authorized to adopt and promulgate rules and regulations consistent with and relating to the appearance, colors of material, texture of material, and architectural design of the exterior of all private and semi-public buildings and structures including signs, and appurtenances erected on or abutting the public streets of the Barrio Latino Area, although they may not have been designated as having architectural or historical value.

Dr. Fernandez then went on to supply the rules governing lawfully classified historical structures, including signs and appurtenances, procedures for compliance, and punishment for violations:

> In order to obtain a building permit for any section of the Barrio Latino Area, plans must be submitted at the office of the Urban Renewal Agency, Ybor Site Office, after which time the plans will be submitted to the Design Review Committee. The aim of the committee is never to turn down a plan without offering some other methods whereby the work could be done to the satisfaction of the Barrio Latino Board."[10]

The conscientious manner in which the commission carried out its purposes is evidence that its members had the good of the community constantly in mind. In fact, it seems that every step ahead into Urban Renewal was taken with good intentions.

Writing an editorial for the newsletter was Oscar Aguayo, an Ybor Chamber of Commerce administrator, who briefly recounted the area's history, traced the deterioration of housing, mentioned the blessing of the Barrio Latino Commission, the faith of many merchants who were intent on carrying on, affirmed the right to disagree (and a few ways to minimize the differences), and emphasized the need for vision and courage.[11] His comments confirm that there was not unanimity regarding the best way to proceed with "renewal."

The most controversial aspect of the project was the decision to level and clear most of the existing housing. Not only did this mean a loss of neighborhoods, architecture, and history preserved in the creaking, dilapidated homes, it also meant the relocation of the residents themselves. James D. Marshall Jr. was the Ybor project manager, and he attempted to address the issue of relocation with a positive spin when he reflected on what had been done by fall of 1967:

The Ybor City Project, Fla., R-13, has moved faster than either of the other two projects in Tampa. We are approximately two years ahead of schedule. It might be comforting to Ybor Citizens to know that this project is the largest of the three Tampa projects. In August of 1965, we started making relocation payments in Ybor City. During the intervening 22 months, we have serviced 440 families, 138 more than the Riverfront Project, our second largest which is 50 months old. . . . When compared to Maryland Avenue, which has been operating for 57 months, Ybor City has taken 252 individuals into the workload against Maryland's 270. With the beginning of acquisition in Ybor City which started in January of 1966, 18 months ago, we entered into property management, which includes the mammoth jobs of maintenance, demolition and rent collecting. $35,557.00 have been collected compared to Maryland's $85,872.00.

Ybor City, our new baby, is certainly growing fast."[12]

From the bureaucratic point of view, the speed and numbers told the story. In hindsight it is easy to see that the numbers alone had little to do with the success of the undertaking. Marshall and others recognized this, of course, but because of the widespread participation by individuals, businesses, and community groups, nearly everyone seemed to assume that it would all work out for the best. Marshall's explanation of how the program was being implemented is interesting:

Urban Renewal is a locally planned and executed community-wide improvement program using public and private resources. Through it a city seeks to refashion and rebuild its physical plant along modern lines . . . . The members of the Site Office Staff are charged with the responsibility of working with the site occupants, whether they be families, individuals or businesses, on a daily basis. More specifically . . . our task [is] to explain and interpret the various pieces of federal legislation and agency resolutions that affect their relocation benefits—benefits that are 100 percent federal.

Marshall then went on to explain that in order to expedite the process, members of his staff had had to transport applicants to the central office, carry ill residents to

clinics, offer babysitting, and provide other services that otherwise would have lessened the rate of progress. Again, in hindsight, it is sad to contemplate the disintegration of the community caused by such juggling of people. The residents were carted back and forth from a central office and the social clubs and clinics that had once served nearby residents within walking distance were virtually out of the picture. The final phrase that refers to "benefits that are 100 percent federal" has an echoing ring of irony. What were the local benefits?

Coming forth on a positive note, Ybor City businessman, Sam Argintar, a highly respected merchant who still runs the store his family founded nearly a century ago, wrote about some positive economic aspects of the work as the Urban Renewal program, as well as some of the key merchants cooperating with it, began to assess the impact of their efforts:

The question which has been asked in Ybor City most this past year [1967] has been concerning the effect of Urban Renewal on the retail business. Has the removal of all the substandard homes, forcing the occupants to move out of the immediate Ybor City area hurt business? I can not speak for any merchant except myself; and I find, and happily so, that my business is on the increase. We have not only kept our old customers, but are adding new customers attracted to Ybor City because of the remodeling and revitalization of the area by the property owners, businessmen and Urban Renewal . . . a joint effort with a definite goal in mind.

I do not believe that Urban Renewal in itself will make any business better; only the business man himself can do that. . . .

Max Argintar's Men's Store has been in Ybor City for nearly a century and it is still doing well in 2000. It is the oldest store in the area and Argintar is committed to remaining. The remodeling of his store was an outstanding example of effective use of the opportunity. The interior was redesigned in a Mediterranean style by the nationally known wood craftsman



**Ybor City: The Making of a Landmark Town**

Jonathan Jones. The actual work was completed by Mario Lopez, and the result was an enduring, beautifully crafted interior that will be admired for years to come. When Argintar reflected in 1967 about the many changes that had come about over the decades, he concluded by stressing that he had never found the business prospects more promising: "We are proud to be a part of the redevelopment of Ybor City and we are optimistic and confident of the future."[13]

The perspective of this pioneering businessman is one gauge of the efforts to measure the impact and success of the urban renewal effort as the decade of the Sixties drew to a close. Perhaps it is not surprising that business would increase in the area, given the number of workers drawn to demolition and construction jobs and the amounts of money being invested in the renewal effort. Unfortunately, it seems that no one was keeping track of the sources of new business or counting the numbers of long-term customers who could be developed as a potential bread-and-butter base for the Ybor City economy.

A. R. Ragsdale, chairman of the Urban Renewal Board, seemed more focused on the legal and administrative structures of the agency and the leveling of slums than on building the basis for a neighborhood economy. His priorities also encompassed all projects for the City of Tampa, which enabled him to applaud former Ybor City businesses when they relocated to other areas of Tampa, even though the impact on Ybor City, taken by itself, was negative. In his assessment message, he explained that after the state's Urban Renewal enabling legislation in 1957 a test suit was instituted in 1959 in the Florida State Supreme Court, which resulted in a declaration that the Local Act was constitutional. Mr. Ragsdale continued:

The Local Act provides that the City of Tampa can carry out Urban Renewal, or by City Or-

dinance, the City may delegate their power to a separate agency. City Council and the Mayor wisely chose the latter course and created the Urban Renewal Agency of the City of Tampa, on May 20, 1958. The seven Board of Commissioners of the Agency are appointed by the Mayor with approval by City Council. To assure continuity appointments are staggered with four commissioners serving for three years and three serving two years . . .

The primary role of the Board of Commissioners is to establish policy for the Agency. The Board normally meets every other week . . . We are directly responsible to the Mayor who is briefed periodically on the progress of our program . . .

After ten years on the Board of Commissioners I am convinced that Urban Renewal is the only way to clear our slum areas and be certain of proper redevelopment. This is not a perfect program, but in spite of our problems I believe we have done a good job. The vast majority of the relocated families are, for the first time in their lives, in good housing which they can afford. Most of the relocated businesses have rebuilt elsewhere in Tampa and have considerably enlarged their operation. This in itself has helped the economy of Tampa. After redevelopment of the Urban Renewal areas we anticipate a major increase in the real estate tax revenue. Within just a few short years this increase will more than reimburse the City of Tampa for their investment in this program.[14]

While they were willing to accept almost any relocation as a success, the agency did single out those businesses relocating within Ybor City for special praise, and encouraged others to follow their example. Under the heading "Rehabilitation," Richard E. Leon, Attorney Conservation Officer, singled out twelve businesses that were successfully relocated

*A. R. Ragsdale (above left) was chairman of the Board of Commissioners of the Urban Renewal Agency of the City of Tampa. Seated at his desk (above right) is Thomas J. Fox, the agency's executive director.*

*After more than fifty years at its original location on La Setima and 18th Street (shown in photo at right), the Eagle Bicycle Shop relocated under Urban Renewal but remained in Ybor City. Its owner, Emilio Del Rio (above), was born at the site of Fort Brooke in Tampa on June 7, 1893. In addition to being a pioneer Ybor City businessman, he was the author of two books about the history of Ybor City and a novel, "The Love of Teresa."*

within the Ybor City Urban Renewal Area. Naviera Coffee Mills were able to change their status from tenants to owners and they also completely rehabilitated their building. Los Helados de Ybor, a fine restaurant with 40 years at the same location (they became famous for the sherbets they made and their name "Los Helados" translates as "the sherbets") moved to a rehabilitated building at the Ybor Mall on 8th Avenue.

The Eagle Bicycle Shop, another small business with over 40 years at the same location, moved just three blocks west of its original shop on La Setima. Its owner, Emilio Del Río, was the author of *Yo Fui Uno de los Fundadores de Ybor City* ("I Was One of the Founders of Ybor City") and *The Birth of a City: Ybor-Tampa in Pictures*, which were valuable historical references in preparing this history. Other neighborhood businesses that chose to remain in Ybor included Rudy's Barber Shop, Gallo's Shoe Repair, Frank Fort Tailor, Melchor's Sundries, Albert Alonzo Furniture, Fran's Wig Shop, La Caridad Del Cobre, and Tropicana Sandwich Shop.[15]

Project Manager Marshall reported:

Since the first building (1927-7th Avenue), was ceremoniously demolished September 1, 1966, 339 buildings have bitten the dust. Where structures stood yesterday, children are at play today. Where structures stood yesterday, cars are parked. Both play areas and parking areas have been very much needed in Ybor City. . . .

Our regulations provide for incurring expense to move families or individuals within the project area for reasons of health, safety, or Agency convenience. Several buildings are presently being used for such purposes. Families and individuals receiving such assistance are still entitled to their full relocation benefits, when they move permanently.

A total of 400 families have been permanently relocated. Since the first relocation payment was made in August 1965. 220 have purchased and 47 are in public housing projects.

In addition to the families that have moved, 230 individuals have moved also. This figure consists of those that were in self-contained housekeeping units as well as those that were in rooming houses and hotels.

Twenty-six individuals are in public housing projects. Some of the very first tenants to move into the 17-months-old Bethune High Rise for the elderly were from Ybor City.[16]

Finally, Raul Vega Jr., a descendant of the very respected family that had built its own successful business on La Sétima, wrote his evaluation:

238

*Photos taken in 1966 by the Florida Department of Commerce put the best face forward for business and commercial activities in Ybor City. The emphasis is on Cuban sandwiches, bean soup, and a Latin atmosphere. During this time, the true picture was much less rosey.* FSA.

*Photo shot near 15th Street looking east, shows 7th Avenue's "new" look in 1968. Before then La Sétima had a brick surface and streetcar rails. The bricks and rails were replaced with the asphalt that covers its surface today. Note that the W. T. Grant store, next to the Ritz Theatre, was still in business.* LA GACETA.

*At the corner of 12th Avenue and 19th Street, across from where the Ybor City Post Office is today, stood the Maximo Caras building, shown here in a 1920s photograph. It included Restaurant El Casin, the Cafe de Jesus, and a barber shop. None of the buildings in this photo remains standing today, and most of them were destroyed during Urban Renewal.* LA GACETA.

239

*The destruction during the 1960s was difficult to see as a sign of progress.* LA GACETA.

*The Labor Temple (right), built in the 1920s, served as a rallying point for workers. This photograph shows a mass meeting of cigar workers on November 28, 1931, protesting the removal of lectores from the factories. Urban Renewal destroyed the building in the late 1960s.*

240

**Ybor City: The Making of a Landmark Town**

What I have to say in the following article about Urban Renewal in Ybor City may be misconstrued as a pessimistic viewpoint; however, I actually don't wish to give this impression, since I have been a strong advocate of Urban Renewal and have worked for the redevelopment of Ybor City for many years. Even the strongest supporters of Urban Renewal will concede there are many problems which have to be solved and it's these problems I wish to discuss.

The greatest concern Ybor City Merchants have today is, "How long it will take?". . . [but] as Thomas J. Fox, Executive Director of Urban Renewal has stated, "The Ybor City Urban Renewal Project is two years ahead of schedule." This is true, but this project is so unique and it involves so many factors, it's difficult to predict a completion date.

In using the term, "Unknown Factors," I am referring to the reuse of land for housing and tourist attractions as the original plans are intended. Housing will not be a serious problem. The Federal Government has recently encouraged more housing projects with less red tape. Under these advantageous conditions, recently the Ybor City Chamber of Commerce applied to the Federal Government under section 202, of the Housing Act of 1959. This would permit the Chamber to build, under the sponsorship of a non-profit organization, Haciendas De Ybor, Inc., a 200-unit housing project for the elderly, of age 62 years and over. I have every reason to believe this project will be approved and it will be the first housing development in the Ybor City Urban Renewal Project.

Therefore, reuse of land for housing is not an immediate problem; however, the plan of creating tourist attractions is another matter of serious concern.

Several plans for tourist attractions have been offered . . . but I question the financial feasibility of some. Most of those plans suggest man made attractions which involve considerable money, which is hard to come by these days.

At a recent meeting . . . one of the best known men in the attraction field was our guest. He stated, "You should develop your natural historical environment in Ybor City." I agree with this theory wholeheartedly, and this could be done with less money, without acquisition of land, and without creating anything artificial. To accomplish this we must have assistance of government: City, County, State or Federal, which is not unusual. St. Augustine is a good example; Williamsburg is another. . . .

In conclusion I would like to express my optimism in the final result Urban Renewal will bring to Ybor City. It's not uncommon to hear someone say, "They should have done this 20 years ago, it's too late now." To these people I would reply, "It's not too late. Business is good in Ybor City and will get better. . . . These developments have been the salvation of Ybor City, and I am optimistic the future of Ybor City is brighter than most metropolitan business areas.[17]

While Urban Renewal officials and some key merchants were positive about the future of Ybor City, some of them agreed with Vega that the long-term approach should concentrate primarily on preserving and enhancing its historical charm and integrity. Many of the townspeople would have agreed completely with the importance of retaining the community's heritage, but they did not share his optimism about that possibility, especially the core families who were being moved. They were not impressed. They were the ones most impacted. Some did not know that the scribbled "X" on their wall meant they would be moved shortly.

In the fall 1967 edition of the *Urban Renewal News*, conservation advisor Benitez reported that after more than a year of waiting, the local agency had received funds to offer 3 percent financing for nonresidential remodeling in Ybor City. Low-interest loans of up to $50,000 would be available to property owners or tenants for terms of up to twenty years.[18]

Included in the same issue of the newsletter was an announcement of the dedication of the Nuccio Parkway:

. . .a brand new, beautifully landscaped drive, running thru the heart of the Maryland Avenue Urban Renewal Project . . . was dedicated on Saturday, August 19, 1967. . . . At a later date the Parkway will be extended through the Ybor City Urban Renewal Project to tie in with the new Palm Avenue which will also be landscaped and provide access to the new residential area of Ybor City.

This had been a largescale and controversial project, but the naming of it honored an important Latin political leader. In early July 1998, *La Gaceta* described Nuccio in anticipation of a statue to be built in his honor at Centennial Park: "Mayor Nuccio was a man of the people . . . [who] built sidewalks, benches, libraries, bridges, parks and piers." He left his stamp on the community in more than name only; he helped improve places and institutions that touched the daily lives of ordinary citizens. I often saw Mayor Nuccio at both Cuervo's and the Columbia Restaurant shaking hands and kissing children. Safety Village at Lowry Park, where many youngsters learn early lessons in traffic safety, is another of his legacies.

Phase I of Urban Renewal was colored by applications, review processes, endless paperwork, repayment schedules, notifications, bulldozing schedules, consent forms, availability of funds, appraisals, entitlements per room, moneys, offers, promises, releases, and more. A clumsy bureaucracy had been set in motion, with accompanying slippage of schedules, changes in management, and sliding program objectives. The result was a mess; a behemoth; a federal and local morass. Added to all of the above were an ever-increasing number of conflicting personal objectives, real estate interests and positioning, and private delays caused by these. Time was crucial. But Washington's priorities slipped. Conservatives in Congress were starting to turn skeptical eyes toward these programs and their attendant funds.

Meanwhile, the families already impacted shed many a tear. Others still in Ybor knew no other way of life. They were surrounded by a sea of friendliness, by an ambiance that was very warm and in which Spanish was heard from dawn to dusk.

They did not want their homes demolished or that ambiance destroyed.

Soon more than 600 families were relocated. Even though many residents still did not understand the program, let alone support it, they were moved out anyway. Meantime, with orders to proceed, bulldozer crews leveled some 90 percent of the housing in a brief period. The old central core of Ybor City was completely razed — but though it was a violation, it was not yet a complete rape, for there had been apparent civic consent. How widespread the actual consent was, no one will ever know. There were many who went along because their friends, neighbors, or leaders told them it would be a good thing; there were many who remained silent because they lacked the confidence to speak out; there were many who never knew what was about to happen. Soon only streets, curbs, and a few tropical trees were left in place, having escaped the bulldozers' angry wrath.

Nearby, the Cuyahoga Wrecking Company, with offices on-site in Ybor City, had a salvage yard nearby on 40th Street. Acres of salvage materials were on the ground: doors, plumbing, lumber, windows, and more. The arms and limbs of a community were stacked there still warm with life and spirit. If only inanimate objects could talk! (I visited that haunted yard during that period). Those who had ordered the wrecking were making way for renewal.

Phase 2 plans were not yet available. Nonetheless, banks in general, in both Tampa and Ybor City, declared support for the effort and announced that they were ready to receive proposals related to Urban Renewal.

By 1969, 380 low-cost houses in the African American, R-1, Maryland Avenue project had been completed. As it turned out, that was *all* that was completed. In Phase 2 of the Ybor City project, the residents were moved out and the town lev-



**Ybor City: The Making of a Landmark Town**

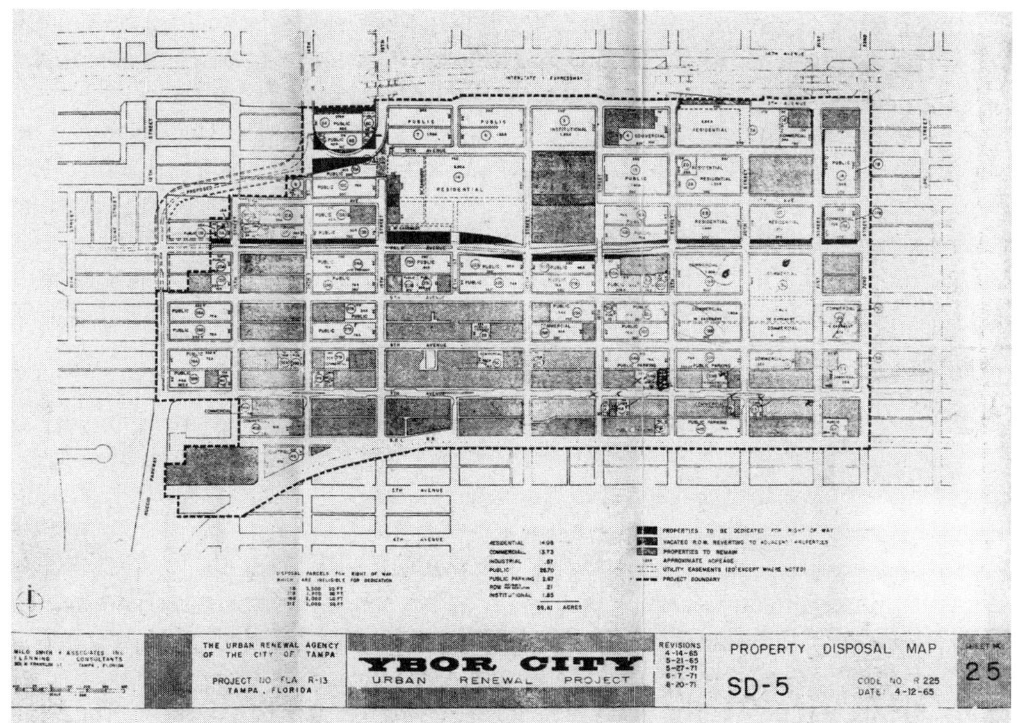



*This official "Property Disposal Map" was prepared originally in 1965 and revised multiple times by the administrative offices of Urban Renewal of the City of Tampa. This version is dated August 20, 1971, and shows properties to be dedicated to right of way, vacated, or preserved.*

eled. But there was no trace of a plan to complete the "contract" with the displaced townspeople of Ybor City.

Urban Renewal was besieged by more than just organizational and federal funding concern. Jeff Dunlap, *Tribune* staff writer, gave this account:

> Early in the evening of June 11, 1967, according to newspaper accounts, three black youths reportedly broke into a downtown camera store and stole several Polaroids.
>
> On-duty policemen spotted the youths, ordered them to stop, and when they didn't, the officers pulled service revolvers and opened fire, according to the old headlines.
>
> As the sun was going down, 19-year-old Martin Chambers fell dead on the sidewalk with a bullet in his back.
>
> Within hours, a grocery store, a restaurant and two other buildings near downtown were in flames. Snipers were on the roofs at Central Avenue and Harrison Street, shooting at cops and firemen. No one was killed (except Martin Chambers), but looting and racial unrest continued for nearly a week.
>
> When it was all over, dozens of people had been injured . . . and an entire block near downtown was burned to charcoal. As a result, Ybor City—even though it was more than a mile from the scorched, troubled neighborhood—was branded with the heavy nominative, "bad part of town."[20]

The 1968 presidential election propelled Richard Nixon into the White House, bringing with him a new, conservative philosophy. As the late '60s rolled by, the federal Urban Renewal Program floundered. Funding for housing and rehabilitation could no longer be taken for granted. Local problems and delays took their toll. HUD began to promote local bank financing as the best means to complete the renewal and renovation projects that were already underway. The untimely Tampa race riots in the summer of 1967 that had covered the front pages of Tampa newspapers and received national attention had branded many renewal areas as being in "the bad part of town." Banks that previously had declared themselves open to negotiate home or other loans took a hard look at the situation and backed off. Some insurance companies refused to insure properties from 1st Avenue to Buffalo Avenue and from Nebraska to 22nd Street. But more importantly, there were still no

*243*

Phase 2 completion plans announced to the townspeople.

Conversation with many of these old-timers revealed a town seemingly dazed by the reality of what had happened. The comments? They were troubled responses ranging from worry to anger: "The town has been betrayed." "Why didn't they use just a bit of the huge sums spent to help the owners to finance improvement—new utilities, a new roof, etc.—at a low interest rate?" "*Los hijos de putas . . . politicos!* (These political sons of b'—s !)." "What can you expect? They have sold us out!" "Look where they put so-and-so— out there three miles away—among gringos, and no way to communicate or walk to a grocery or to *la clinica*." "It is like a prison. We don't hear a word of Spanish to smooth things a little; and the Cuban club, those dances, they took our world away from us." These kinds of reactions and many more—very many more—permeated the town in the mid- and late-1960s.

The next days, weeks, months brought more of the same. At Alvarez Restaurant next door to La Norma Coffee Mill, at Valdes's Jewelry, on the sidewalk, leaning on the front wall of El Centro Espanol, or at Cuervos, at La Benefica, at Melchore Book and Sundry store, Gonzalez or Trelles clinics— wherever one went, the town buzzed with disdainful commentary. Some talked about starting a major law suit.

Armando Valdes, who was at the time President of the Ybor Chamber, displayed a map sent to him by the American Reserve Insurance Co. indicating the urban and suburban areas of Ybor City that would not now be insured by that company. The Valdes Jewelry Co. store at 1812 15th Street was then just around the corner from the later location of the Ybor Chamber offices on 8th Avenue, and Valdes was for many years a habitual walker of La Sétima. In the years of my affiliation with the Chamber, beginning in 1974, it was a pleasure to listen to him because of his detailed knowledge of the town. Sitting together at the Alvarez Restaurant, we would share stories, and he would lambaste the workings and results of Urban Renewal. "And the banks and insurance companies lost all interest in Ybor—and why not?" he would ask rhetorically.

Armando Valdes, arguably among the area's best and most sincere critics of Urban Renewal and the city government, ran in the 1980s for mayor of Tampa, but without success.[21]

## Haciendas de Ybor

One of the most successful concepts to emerge in the formative early days of construction related to Urban Renewal was a plan to build attractive and affordable housing for the elderly in Ybor City. The project was started by a group of dedicated sons of the area, called together by Dr. Henry J. Fernandez, who became President of the new Haciendas De Ybor, Inc.

Sponsoring the effort were the Ybor City Chamber of Commerce, the United Methodist Church, and the Latin American Baptist Church.

In the winter issue of *Urban Renewal News*, Dr. Fernandez called it "the most important news in Ybor City since our last issue," and wrote:

They have formed a non-profit corporation, which will be called Haciendas De Ybor, Inc. This will also be the name of the apartments.

There will be approximately 200 units. The units will be efficiencies and 1 bedroom units. They are expected to rent at approximately $50.00 to $60.00 for efficiencies and $65.00 to $75.00 for one bedroom. The rent will include all utilities and taxes.

All the units will have complete kitchens, including formica cabinets, oven and range, and refrigerator. All units will have complete bathrooms, all tile, and they will be carpeted and air conditioned.

The apartment complex will have a centralized administration department and recreation

*The Haciendas de Ybor apartment complex remains one of the few positive results of the Urban Renewal program. Today it offers affordable, attractive housing for the elderly within walking distance of the familiar historic businesses and buildings.* RM.

areas. There will also be coin operated laundries on every floor.

The impressive list of officers for the project included Fernandez, president; Daniel Martinez, vice president; Eddie Spoto, secretary-treasurer; and Raul Vega Jr., Joe Alfano, Joe Granda, Tom Ferraro, Frederick Eddows and Curtis Larmon, directors.[22] Oscar Bonis, also later served on this board.

By spring 1968, the Haciendas de Ybor project was moving steadily ahead. The Ybor Chamber had received approximately 80 applications for the 203 apartment structures and Fernandez reported that similar projects in other cities had received speedy approval when a large number of requests for residence were included in the application to HUD. The Haciendas directors were applying for 100 percent financing under Title 202 with preliminary estimates setting the total cost for the project at just $2,000,000, including land purchase. Preliminary drawings had also been prepared showing two-story Mediterranean-style buildings, with overhanging roofs of red Spanish barrel tile. the goal was to achieve an appropriate Mediterranean architectural style while still keeping the construction costs down.

After working with the budget and design details for several months, they were still projecting anticipated rents ranging from $55-$57 per month, and plans calling for 140 efficiencies and 63 one bedroom, apartments with five public areas, a pavilion, laundry and recreation rooms, elevators and inside corridors, carpeting, electric kitchen, air conditioning, heating and utility bills. The *Tampa Tribune* reported:

> The idea behind the Haciendas plan . . . is to provide close-in housing for longtime Spanish, Italian and Cuban residents of Ybor City displaced by Urban Renewal, which already had purchased 628 pieces of property.[23]

The construction and financing of this housing project was accomplished in two phases of about one hundred units each. The second phase would add a complementary unit to the west side of the earlier project, adjacent to one of Ybor City's historic spines, La Calle Quince (15th Street), with a second hundred for a total of 200 units for the entire complex accommodating elderly residents who could enjoy commendable, affordable housing that was competently supervised, clean, well-maintained, and very pleasant.

Despite the debacle created by Urban Renewal, the Haciendas de Ybor Project succeeded. It was an initiative geared to provide housing for Ybor City's displaced elderly in the face of Urban Renewal's failure. Fernandez and the officers working with him were among Ybor City's best sons at the time. Many had been past presidents of the Ybor Chamber of Commerce. Working closely with them was Congress-

245

man Sam Gibbons, who offered a strong hand of support in assisting and smoothing the way in Washington, D.C., to assure the success of the proposal.

Beyond the political battles for funding and the economic impact of community improvement, this project reflected the moral and personal commitment felt for the mothers and fathers of the town who had been displaced. Thanks to the responsible and dedicated men who served as leaders and directors for this effort, approximately a third of the elderly citizens that Urban Renewal had displaced were able to "come back home" to the town they had helped build.

It is a measure of the commitment of these sons of the founders that today this same group of men, with the exception of deceased members, still oversees the Haciendas. Dr. Fernandez, Dan Martinez, Joe Granda, and Tom Farraro are greatly deserving of recognition for their work as they continue to serve. By now as I write this chapter in the late 1990s, the Haciendas de Ybor complex has provided some four decades of excellent, clean, and orderly housing for the town's elderly citizens.

The Haciendas de Ybor units remain 100 percent full. There is a long waiting list of applicants.

This outstanding success story is a matter of great civic pride!

## The Walled City Project and Bullfights

Looking back to the Urban Renewal period a decade earlier, on Sunday, May 13, 1979, *Tampa Tribune* staff writer Jeff Dunlap described how one of Florida's most successful housing developers failed when it came to reconstructing Ybor City. His story ran under the headline ,"Walter's Walled City Idea Died with Bullfight Bill," and it presented a colorful chapter in the effort to revive and reinvent the town:

> The story goes like this . . .
> During Ybor City's Urban Renewal days, Tampa industrialist Jim Walter had an idea to turn five and a half vacant Ybor City acres into what would be called the "Walled City." The "Walled City," Walter asserted, would be a completely enclosed, Spanish-style tourist attraction, with dancers, singers, strolling guitarists, an arts and crafts complex, restaurants—you name it. It was supposed to provide the economic stimulus Ybor City needed to revitalize itself.

*The Haciendas de Ybor preserve welcome greenspace. With simple Latin touches to the architecture, shady live oak trees, and lovely landscaping, this recent addition "fits" the town, present and past.* RM.

In 1967 Walter financed a feasibility study for his "Walled City," but the report came back asserting that, in order to work, the project would need a strong "focal point" attraction. Walter then joined forces with restaurateur Cesar Gonzmart and Ybor Optometrist Dr. Henry J. Fernandez. The three agreed that "Portuguese bullfighting" should be the attraction's "focal point." [footnote Dunlap]

This was a novel and imaginative approach, but it certainly did not represent an organic part of Ybor City's past. Bullfighting was associated with Spain and Mexico in the popular mind, but it had never been central to the Cuban experience or to the unique Latin culture that had developed in Ybor City. To compound the oddly mismatched choice, and partially in an attempt to appease concerns about animal cruelty and "blood-sport," Walter had chosen a less violent Portuguese version of bullfighting. Unfortunately, this somewhat tamer version had its roots in Portugal, making the whole idea even less culturally appropriate for Tampa:

> Sometimes referred to as "bloodless bullfighting," the man-versus-bull maneuver revolved around the idea that the bull would wear shoulder pads, like a football player. Man and beast would enter a bull ring, parry with each other a while, and when the moment of truth came — the matador would plunge his sword not into the bull, but into the bull's shoulder pads. Walter, Gonzmart and Fernandez were positive the idea would appeal to thousands of people.
>
> The three investors secured the interest of yet more investors, including, according to Gonzmart, a Wall Street firm, the Columbia Broadcasting System and the Spanish government, which knew a good thing when it saw one.

Jeff Dunlap reported that the idea had support from Florida State Senator Louis de la Parte, who in Tallahassee advocated changing an anti-bullfighting law that had been enacted as a state statute. Billed as a $5 million project, Portuguese Bullfighting was promoted as the means to revitalize Ybor City.

To make matters difficult, the legislature in Tallahassee reasserted its anti-bull posture, with or without blood. A *Tribune* editorial weighed in on the opposite side to support the idea, and "the 'bull' kept rolling," Dunlap added. Then a different aspect of the proposal made its way into the news columns:

> The American Society for the Prevention of Cruelty to Animals began to howl . . . newspaper accounts reported about housewives in St. Petersburg . . . and their protests against the proposed "blood sport."

In May 1970, the *Tribune* reported that Cesar Gonzmart, Mayor Dick Greco, Jim Walter, and Fred Leary, then chairman of the Committee of 100, made a trip to the state capital to try "sweet-talking the legislation in Tallahassee."

> By this time, the project's cost was quoted at $10 million, and the annual revenue from it at $50 million. Gonzmart was seen strolling through the legislative offices, in full royal costume — ruffle cuffs and all — kissing the head of every secretary he saw. . . . It was said in one newspaper analysis that Gonzmart's charm was what finally swayed the ruling body into voting in the pro-bullfight law.
>
> Gonzmart said word of the issue reached Hollywood and Johnny Carson picked up on the conflict . . . It was tremendous business for Ybor City and the Columbia. People were lined up outside from all over, asking where the bullfighting was.

With the pro-bullfight legislation in place, and mere rumors of the innovation starting to swell the numbers of visitors to Ybor City, the promoters were tremendously encouraged. By the end of 1970 it looked as if Ybor City matadors might soon be attracting crowds to a new walled city. However, there were many state residents as well as Ybor City oldtimers who were less than enthusiastic about Tallahassee's approval of the scheme. And this episode had yet one more plot twist to unfold before its end.

> Then in February, 1971, a group unassociated with Walter and his friends staged a "bloodless" bullfight exhibition in Bradenton

with, as Gonzmart put it, "some untested Brahman bull they got from an Ocala farm" . . . The bull, perhaps angry at his shoulder pads, broke through the ring and charged the crowd. Two policeman put 12 bullets into the bull's brain before anyone was hurt.

As a result, the Florida legislature in May 1971, promptly and unanimously rescinded the pro-bullfight law it had approved a year before.[24]

"It was not to be," Dunlap concluded. This contrived attempt to fill the gap left by Urban Renewal looked good on paper and might have succeeded in purely economic terms. However, perhaps its failure was another instance where fate had intervened, for it would have taken Ybor City's history in a commercial direction somewhat out of character with its true nature.

## Urban Renewal Failure: How Did it Happen?

In reviewing the past decade, major questions beg to be asked. What really happened to defeat Urban Renewal in Ybor City? Why were the Maryland Avenue project and the Riverfront project in Tampa eventually completed, and rather successfully, while the Ybor City plan failed?

The critical loss of three years in staffing an organization named in 1959 but not fleshed-out until 1962, plus lack of complete and timely planning for Phase 2, are two important factors in the failure. The lawsuits filed in the late '50s seeking Supreme Court approval of the proceedings were sometimes given as a reason for the delay. Switching from HUD money to private bank financing and the general confusion attendant upon that major change, also helped to derail the program. More importantly, Phase 2 goals had steered away from the initial objective. Certainly the local organization had the benefit of the Maryland Avenue project's experience at apartment building, since that project had been completed on target just down the street, though Mediterranean architecture and other Latin requirements placed restrictions and demands that were different in many ways from less complicated constraints in the other target areas. Despite the differences, however, there were some striking similarities among the projects, too. Unfortunately, there seems to have been little organizational effort to apply lessons from prior experience to the needs of Ybor City.

In addition, real estate land speculation, growing personal objectives, and the rapidly changing area demographics, with implications at both the local and federal levels, introduced doubt into the process. This attracted attention to the area from local banks and insurance companies. But the downtown race riots, coming when they did, were especially negative in their impact. Finally, it is true that HUD funding was becoming difficult to obtain after the start of President Richard Nixon's administration in 1968. Ybor City's overall lack of dynamic forward momentum in the context of unrest and confusion locally and tightening federal purse strings only made Ybor's chances for success less likely.

Missing a window of opportunity during those three early years, when the objectives were new and fresh, had been costly. This, of course, leads one to re-evaluate the management philosophy and structure utilized in Tampa. Three major projects — the Maryland Avenue, Riverside, and Ybor City projects — were managed by one organization, staffed under one responsible head, with local council and city government intervention and with a choking tangle of federally mandated guidelines and approvals. Also, each project was scheduled to start on a different date. Obviously, any human, city, state, or national action that limited the time available would have an impact on the one scheduled last.

A decentralized project manager system would have opened the door to competitive performance between individual managers and their organizations. Central

248

posting of progress versus objectives would have been a natural competitive tool. Complaints and innuendoes of shortcomings could have been confirmed or dismissed if they could have been tested against actual results. The urge to compete, obtain results and recognition, and receive adequate compensation plays a vital role in American management. The organizational setup for Urban Renewal in Tampa and Ybor City should have been reviewed at the start of the program with an eye toward applying sound and tested American practices.

The "contract" with the people of the core area of Ybor City was to reconstruct their housing and then bring the residents back. This "contract" was not fulfilled, a shame against Urban Renewal, the federal government, the politicians, and those pursuing their own agendas, though there were many people simply doing their very best to meet the program objectives.

One has to wear the shoes of the dislocated townspeople to feel their wrath and bitterness. These displaced citizens were, in effect, evicted and exiled, unexpectedly deprived of the town they loved.

## What a Few Officials Said

Eventually, a few of the relocated merchants returned to La Sétima, improved their properties, and together with some key civic leaders reaffirmed their faith in the future and continued to toil for the town. Others, confident of the service they rendered, their long-time history on La Sétima, and their optimistic nature, stayed on and improved their properties. Among these Max Argintar and Raul Vega Jr. stand out.

"Urban Renewal officials who'd had their fingers crossed all the time, waxed eloquent with disappointment, as did the investors," wrote *Tampa Tribune* staff reporter Jeff Dulap.

Concerning the demise of HUD in Ybor City, one of the organization's own administrators, Marshall Tison, pointed to the huge scope and expense of the undertaking as one of the reasons so much remained unfinished — the fact that the core area project was gigantic and the work to be done required almost ten million dollars (in 1960s dollars). This was complicated by the need for the project to operate from a special category of grant funds. There was a nightmare of logistical problems and a required sequence of steps and reports due to Washington to detail goals, track progress, demolish buildings, determine building code and utility requirements, review process, and so on. Tison said that "meeting these primary requirements caused Urban Renewal to get bogged down with the applications and mandatory processes." Later he added, "We did a bang-up job on acquisition and clearance. We just didn't do a good job at all at keeping the program going."

Dunlap reported the facts as he was able to collect them for his 1979 series:

> Tison is telling the Urban Renewal story now because Tom Fox, the agency's executive director and Tison's former boss, apparently has become very forgetful of the years 1965-1972. . . . Fox , 51, bowed out of Urban Renewal in 1972 because, as he puts it, he received "a better offer." . . . His recollections of Urban Renewal's Ybor City operation are pockmarked with such declarations as "I don't recall. . ." and "I can't remember . . ." and he admits he finds no pleasure in discussing the Ybor City business.
>
> "I was the Executive Director and I was responsible for the entire Urban Renewal operation," says Fox. "But those things occurred many years ago, a long time ago. And I don't recall the facts. . . . But there were times that I was discouraged when the plans didn't materialize. It was disappointing to see . . . . but you just had to accept some of those things as facts of life."

When Dunlap interviewed the principal administrators, it was Tison who had the clearest understanding that after tearing down a considerable portion of the area's buildings, the HUD efforts seemed to hit a dead end. "Unfortunately," Tison said, "it became obvious that we were go-ing to have some difficulty attracting de-velopers and purchasers back into Ybor City." With the federal goverment unwill-ing or unable to staff and finance the long process of rebuilding, there seemed to be no alternative but to shut down the offices before the job was done. In winding up his comprehensive article, Dunlap quotes Tison once more: "You can't lay the fault on the doorstep of any single person." But he concludes, "in retrospect, it seems the difficulties in rebuilding Ybor manifestly intensified after Richard Nixon took the presidential oath and rechanneled the im-petus of government spending."

Another local perspective, closer to the events themselves, appeared ten years ear-lier in a story on March 13, 1969, by *Tampa Tribune* staff writer Mary Anne Corpin. As West Tampa prepared to cope with a new version of Urban Renewal in their neigh-borhood, the businessmen wanted be cer-tain they did not find themselves left with results similar to what they called "the Ybor City ghost town" and Thomas Fox was much more optimistic: "'We're in the very early stages," said UR executive director Fox. "This area can be enlarged or de-creased . . . . I realize we have our critics," said Fox, drawing a laugh as he added, "The Neighborhood Development Program is something entirely new . . . . It's Urban Renewal under a new name with different guidelines. The area to be rehabilitated is done at a much faster rate than in the past."

At that time it was John Fernandez, Model Cities director, who stepped in to explain that redevelopment had failed in Ybor City "because of problems on deci-sions that have to be made, and on amend-ments to the contract. It's no fault of the city. It is the federal government's fault."

## Hillsborough Community College and Ybor City

It was during the doldrum days of Ur-ban Renewal in the mid-to-late 1960s that the idea of a junior college campus in Ybor City became a subject for serious discussion. The county recognized the need for an accessible two-year college, and it appropriated $30,000 to begin the task.[25] My memories are not entirely clear, but as best I can recall the events and re-construct them from contemporary news-paper accounts and *A View from Inside*, Warren Johnson's informative his-tory of Hillsborough Community College (at that time called Hillsborough Junior College), the fledgling school first opened in space available in Hillsborough High School and a few adjoining houses, but that arrangement "left a world to be de-sired."[26]

Even before the junior college opened, at a meeting of the local school board on February 8, 1966, the executive secretary of the Florida Junior College Board, Dr. James L. Wattenbarger, stated for the record that the amount of money appropri-ated to get new junior college classes un-derway in Hillsborough County was clearly not enough. He pointed to the amounts that had been initially requested by other Florida counties, as well as the amounts intially awarded, and he argued forcefully that a much more significant financial com-mitment would have to be made.[27]

At the time there were some 20 junior colleges in the state system. Hillsborough County had identified the local need for more college classes for its large and un-der-served population, but neither space nor funds could be found to meet the need.

Plans for a proposed Hillsborough jun-ior college were discussed at a county school board meeting on July 14, 1967, and then moved forward rapidly. By Sep-tember 26, an advisory committee was ap-proved by the State Board of Education in Tallahassee for the purpose of investigat-ing the possibilities. This group officially became the HJC Board of Trustees on July 1, 1968. Today this date is considered the "birthday" of HCC.

Earlier that same year, a report by the McGuffey consulting group had recommended five potential campus sites. Ybor City was not among them.

In response, the Ybor City Chamber of Commerce resolved on June 18 "to take action to locate a campus in Ybor's Urban Renewal area."[88] The land they had in mind was the site that had previously been selected for the proposed "Spanish walled city and bullring" intended to attract tourists. However, Chamber President Joseph C. Granda believed the college was more important to Ybor City, economically and culturally, than another tourist attraction.

Tampa Mayor Dick Greco stepped into the discussion with his own suggestion of a different 33-acre site within the boundaries of the Urban Renewal project. However, it was already the location of the Hav-A-Tampa cigar corporation. The proposal to transform this area into a school despite the factory's interests "hit a raw nerve" because of the cigar industry's historical importance to Ybor City. The idea of placing the Hav-A-Tampa factory in jeopardy appalled many oldtimers.

Greco had earlier met with and talked to school superidentendent Dr. Raymond Shelton, who, in turn, discussed Greco's proposal with Dr. William Graham before the June 18 meeting. Graham had just been named as first president of the college-to-be by the HJC Board of Trustees. Graham responded to Greco's proposal by declaring that "he would not be stampeded into accepting any location for a permanent site that was not in the best interests of the college's future."[28]

However, the school board voted to purchase the thirty-three acres of Urban Renewal land as Greco had suggested. They borrowed $430,200 for the purpose, because "the Florida Department of Education had ruled the local [school] board must provide the first campus site."[29] The particulars of this land transaction had proven to be workable, and the trustees seemed convinced that taking this action was the most efficient and appropriate way to move ahead. It was evident that, whatever else was involved, the school board would have to pay for the site, and the members of the board were insisting that the campus be in Ybor City. Graham, however, would not be dictated to, which appeared to create a standoff. He and the HJC Board of Trustees faced only the choice of accepting the site proposed by the school board, or, if the two groups could not agree, the loan would be voided, leaving the future of the college in limbo.

The Ybor City Chamber and the Tampa Urban Renewal Agency feared that Ybor City could lose its college chances forever in the stubborn confrontation. A "vote to support the site was passed." However the *Tampa Tribune* editorialized against the Ybor City site, alleging that the selection had involved too much behind-the-scenes politicking. Mayor Greco responded at a Chamber meeting on July 25, 1968, when he "denied that politics were ever involved in the Ybor issue."[30]

Graham continued to resist all pressures to make an expedient decision. The Tampa Urban Renewal Agency argued that Graham was not even giving fair consideration to the Ybor proposal.

*Today the Ybor City campus of Hillsborough Community College forms an attractive and lively educational hub for young people and returning, nontraditional students. Its buildings and landscaping are contemporary, but already stand comfortably beside the architecture of the past in a community that values education.* RM.



**Chapter 6 • Empty Years and Early Redevelopment Efforts: 1965-1970**

While factions continued to argue over site selection, Hillsborough Junior College began operations temporarily at Hillsborough High School. On the first day of classes — September 30, 1968 — petitions circulated in Ybor City. Supporters believed that "by keeping the pressure up, they would get what they deserved," and the grassroots petition drive was a positive step in that direction.[31]

Local politics further complicated the issue when other interests became involved. Model City officials wanted an Ybor campus because they believed it would attract federal money. With an eye to the upcoming completion of Disney World in nearby Orlando, Model City "proponents wanted to ensure the campus, and perhaps combine it with a tourist attraction that would revitalize the Latin Quarter." On the other hand, Tampa Urban League officials now feared that they might lose support money if a campus was located in Ybor City, though they were assured that would not be the case.[32]

Despite the energetic efforts of the Ybor supporters, Ybor City did not make the list of nine "finalist" sites proposed by another consulting firm, Watson & Co., made public at the January 8, 1969, meeting of the Board of Trustees. Within weeks a State of Florida site inspection team was formed. It arrived in Tampa in March, and was met by pro-Ybor representatives. Mayor Greco told the team that an Ybor campus "would benefit both the school and the city" and that it "was important to him personally and to the revitalization of Ybor City." The team completed its inspection and was preparing its report when the process was preempted by other events.[33]

On April 18, 1969, the day of the HJC Board of Trustees meeting, Florida State Superintendant of Public Instruction Floyd Christian came to Tampa to "settle the issue of site selection." He announced that the first campus would be located on Dale Mabry, and that Ybor City would have a "branch campus." Planning began in 1970, and construction was soon underway.

This brief recap clearly indicates that the business of getting a community college in the Ybor City core area was complex and plagued by many issues.

The progress of the controversial initiative can be illustrated rather effectively simply by listing a few of the countless newspaper headlines on the subject. They show the complexity and seriousness of the task, and reveal the progress towards the realization of a community college campus in Ybor City:

"League Presses Ybor Junior College Site" (*Tampa Times*, March 1968)

"JC Officials Rapped On Urban Position" (*Tampa Tribune* or *Tampa Times*, March 21,1968)

"College Loan Approved if Site Okayed" (*Tampa Times*, July 10, 1968)

"HJC Site Selections Rejected — School Board Nixes Plan" (*Tampa Tribune*, 1968)

"Junior College Politics," (*Tampa Tribune*, July 14, 1968)

"Junior College Site Mired in Politics," (*Tampa Tribune*, July 14, 1968)

"New Junior College Looks For 1,000 Students in Month (*Tampa Tribune*, Aug. 11, 1968)

"Competition Is Keen For New Jr. College Campus," (*Tampa Tribune*, Oct. 1, 1968)

"College Site Dispute Grows," (*Tampa Tribune*, Oct. 16, 1968)

"Siteless HJC now has 'home'" (*Tampa Times*, Nov. 21, 1968)

"Locating the Junior College" (*Tampa Times*, Jan. 3, 1969)

"Ybor City Si, Ybor City No," (*Tampa Times* Jan. 9, 1969)

"College Snubs Sites in Ybor, Plant City," (Al West, *Tampa Tribune*, Jan. 9, 1969)

"HJC Site Choices Tied to Population," (*Tampa Tribune*, Jan. 19, 1969)

"Solon (Senator de la Parte) Gives Tip on HJC," (Tampa newspaper, Jan., 20, 1969)



**Ybor City: The Making of a Landmark Town**

"HJC Weighs Court Battle over Center," (*Tampa Times*, Jan. 24, 1969)

"HJC Drops Suit, Asks Center OK," (*Tampa Times*, Jan. 27, 1969)

"HJC Stand Attacked" (*Tampa Times* Jan. 30, 1969)

"Ybor, Plant City Fall to Criteria," (*Tampa Times*, Feb. 6, 1969)

"HJC Site Storms May End," (Tampa newspaper, c. March 1969)

"A Four-Campus Plan Worth Acceptance," (*Tampa Tribune*, April 5, 1969)

"White, Guyton Named To HJC Board," (*Tampa Tribune*, April 5, 1969)

"Cabinet Delays HJC Site Turnover at Kirk's Urging," (Frank Caperton, *Tampa Tribune*, Aug. 2, 1969)

"HJC Trustees Cold Shoulder Reporter," (Lowell Langford, *Tampa Times*, Aug. 19, 1969)

"HJC Gets Accredited Candidacy," (*Tampa Times*, Dec. 17, 1969)

## A Brief Commentary on HCC

If the birth of Hillsborough Community College had turned into a beehive of political intrigue, with bitter fights among community interests for its inclusion or exclusion that attracted regional and state support, the operation of the college once it opened proved to be equally contentious. Many of its presidents led a less-than-idyllic life in the course of their tenure. In other words, the unflattering and troubling headlines continued.

*Tampa Tribune* history columnist Leland Hawes encapsulated the some-times stormy fortunes of this new institutional neighbor in Ybor City in his "History and Heritage" feature for May 5, 1996.[34] The charter president's reluctance to act can be better understood in the context of strong support from the NAACP and other important groups for an Ybor City site. At the same time, Florida Governor Claude Kirk and his state cabinet brought their pressure to bear in favor of Ybor. There have been five presidents since the college opened. After Graham came Morton Shanberg, Frank Scaglione,

Ambrose Garner, and Andreas Paloumpis. Each of them felt the political heat.

Author Warren Johnson, a longtime HCC faculty member who has seen the development of the college from the inside, confirms its reputation as "the most political community college in Florida" as well as having "the most print attention of any public entity in Hillsborough County."[35]

Over the years the HCC conflicts have included issues involving racial and ethnic differences, claims of undue political influence and payoffs, sexual intimidation, mishandling of public funds, cronyism, and other issues involving purse strings.[36] By Johnson's account, all of the presidents seemed to run into criticism from board members critical of audits and consultants' reports, teachers' union representatives, NAACP leaders, ethnic groups, politicians, auditors, faculty committees, and consultants.

In spite of it all, the college made a great deal of progress and has brought innumerable benefits to Ybor City. The attractive and state-of-the-art campus provides courses for some 40,000 to 50,000 part-time students, or the equivalent of 10,000 to 12,000 full-time students.[37] Having personally talked to many young people attending classes there, I know they share an overall very positive impression of the school. Given the spiraling costs of tuition and fees at four-year public and private institutions, most of these students would simply be unable to pursue an advanced degree elsewhere. In other words, Hillsborough County Community College continues to offer education, advancement, and enrichment for a community that values learning and welcomes opportunity.[38]

*The first five presidents of Hillsborough Community College were (from top to bottom) R. William Graham, Morton Shanberg, Frank Scaglione, Ambrose Garner, and Andreas Paloumpis.*

253

*This photograph taken about 1970 at the corner of Palm Avenue and 15th Street, after Urban Renewal had cleared the neighborhood, affords a somewhat bleak and isolated view of La Benéfica medical building. Once a source of pride and unity for the Ybor City community, it stands alone amidst a wasteland as a melancholy reminder of bygone days.* USFSCL.

# Individual Initiatives, Continued Withering, & Hope: 1970-1980

## Renewed Efforts - the Dead Years - Flight of Artists

Ybor City was like a lovely woman who had been raped and abandoned. She would gather herself and try to regain her composure, her dignity, her self-confidence—but she would never be the same. Those who lived through the experience and felt its physical and emotional impact will never forgive the ravaging. If common suffering unites those people who survive hardship, then most Spaniards, Cubans, and Italians are united not only through their early years of struggle, which for many included the experience of emigration, but also through the desperate situation created by Urban Renewal.

No one in the core area was spared. The dispossessed townspeople were simply plucked out and told to wait—they would be brought back. They waited, waited. Eventually, they gave up waiting. Once again, Latins became mistrustful of state and local leaders in downtown Tampa. The real intentions of these "leaders," so heavily influenced by the affluent community to the south, were suspect. Even as Ybor City bled, entrepreneurs, politicians, Realtors, bankers, and opportunists surveyed the wasted terrain and the evolving demographics with avaricious eyes, reckoning the political implications and the profits.

On La Sétima, at the cafés, benches, and small, suitable corners of the avenue, one saw many groups of *Yborciteños* (Ybor citizens) whiling away the time discussing the encroaching blight that increased daily. They were among friends, for the most part. Here they could vent their anger; they shared the common misery and commiserated. Epithets spiced their conversations. What better way to express one's deepest feelings of anger and disgust than to damn and rail against the perpetrators.

The censuring commentary by the citizenry was no brief interlude. It lasted for a decade and only gradually subsided. One heard the men daily saying, "*Que se vayan al coño de su madre!*" (an obscene way of suggesting that the town-wreckers "get the hell back where they came from"—phrased in language that included the strongest invective the town offered); "*Esos hijos de putas!*" (those sons of bitches); and many other similar curses and complaints. On the morrow they would gather again to peruse the local *Tribune* and *Times* newspapers, hurl more epithets, and return home to face their unstable futures. Old-timers regularly dropped out of circulation, victims of Urban Renewal's continuing saga—the diaspora of Ybor citizens.

*This label from a factory established in 1910 echoes the name of the popular Cuban revolutionary hero, Carlos Manuel de Céspedes.*

*Toba and Louis Wohl (above, in 1907), born in Romania, opened Louis Wohl Household Supplies in Ybor City at 1520 La Sétima. They lived behind their shop and raised their family there. Over the years it became a family business—Louis Wohl & Sons—with its own building and warehouse at 1760 16th Street. The personnel were photographed there on Dec. 24, 1938, by Robertson & Fresch. It is one of many Ybor City successes lost to Urban Renewal.* MOSAIC COLLECTION/FSA.

On La Sétima increasing numbers of merchants arranged to leave. Many were the Jewish shopkeepers so much appreciated and then sorely missed by the remaining townspeople. Among the stores that departed were Rainbow Mens Wear, Louis Wohl & Sons restaurant supplies and furnishings, The Palace, Ida's Ladies Ready to Wear, Abe Wolfson's Men's Wear; Poller's Fashion Shoppe, and Louie's Department Store. Ybor City lost part of its history and character when these merchants and others closed their shops.

By 1969 it was apparent that Urban Renewal had completely failed in Ybor City. The town had been razed. The core residential area, so critical to the economic health of merchants on La Sétima, was nonexistent. By 1970 there was virtually nothing of the main spine left, though a few determined merchants kept their doors open. Woody García, a local Latin radio personality of the period, spoke with dismay about Ybor City's future. Day after day he repeated the words, *"Ybor, que serás?"* (Ybor City, what will become of it?). The question he spoke for all of us remained unanswered yet persistently asked for more than a full decade.

Then in the early 1980s I began to notice some concerted efforts to spruce up the buildings and restore the landscape. There was scattered tree planting, street improvements, a little fresh painting, and other signs of life. Still, only mowed grass covered the empty land. A very few of the old mango and avocado trees had somehow survived, and passing them, I would be filled with memories of the fruit trees that had once spilled over the fences and made the sidewalks such a delight when we strolled them in the evenings in my youth.

Not much remained of the many attempts to rejuvenate Ybor City. The Latin Plaza concept, an initiative of the Ybor City Chamber of Commerce, chaired by Dr. Henry Fernandez and covering much of the core area, had been widely approved, then reduced to a two-square-block concept. Money supposedly killed it. Out of the Latin Plaza initiatives, and based on a trip to New Orleans to study the Vieux Carre Commission, the Barrio Latino Commission had been founded by Dr. Fernandez and chaired by him for eight years. The Model Cities program had encompassed most of the greater Ybor City area minus the current historic district and three blocks south of Columbus drive to I-4. It was a relatively low-cost program aimed at stopping urban decay, and it had enjoyed modest success while federal funding was available. Operating under then-mayor Dick Greco, with John Fernandez as director and Cesar Gonzmart Jr. as head planner, it had nurtured twenty-five city-block clubs. It accomplished much, until with the election of Richard Nixon, the program gradually declined.

Sitting at Alvarez's restaurant on 15th Street near La Sétima, one heard many old-timers wonder why a Model Cities program had not been started in the inner areas. The beauty and warmth of the core area could have been salvaged, they thought. They also spoke of the beautiful mango, avocado, guava, and *fruta bombas* trees that could have still been around, their overhanging branches gracing the sidewalks, shading them so that a walk to the *panadería* (bakery) could be a cool and pleasant experience. It was a sharp and poignant longing for what might have been.



**Ybor City: The Making of a Landmark Town**

*This view looking southwest at 9th Avenue and 11th Street in July 1972, after the area had been cleared by Urban Renewal, reveals some of the numerous fruit and palm trees that were part of old Ybor City. Empty lots had gradually been covered by wild grass and weeds where neighborhoods once stood.* Tony Pizzo Collection, USFSCL.

The women, in turn, talked about their beautiful flowers, all with friendly Spanish names; the mere recitation of the syllables seemed to exalt both the spirit and the flowers as they spoke. They recalled the *claveles, campana, farolitos, cajigales, rosas, flor de Pascuas* (carnations, Turk caps, Zinnias, roses, and poinsettias). Mention these even today to Ybor City ladies and they will instantly smile with delight and great affection. Some vouched they would take their masonry pots that adorned the top of the masonry stairs leading into the front porch of the house, so common in Latins' homes.

Homes in the inner core were very old. Their utilities were outdated, but the pride of ownership was there, and it extended into the yards filled with favorite plants and trees, even though they were not landscaped in the modern sense. But it was home—safe, secure, friendly, and within walking distance of all a housewife needed at La Sétima or around the corner. Many would have preferred to update and paint these homes if only low interest loans had been available—if only jobs had once again become available in Ybor City.

It is ironic that years later—in the late 1990s—eager buyers are purchasing the few remaining older homes in greater Ybor City, and particularly in South Ybor. They are being encouraged to do so by city and local civic leaders. Many agree that incentives and special financing to preserve and restore these homes should be continued, though other nonresidential initiatives also want access to similar low-cost financing. The relative cost to the city is small for this residential improvement initiative, especially compared to the millions of dollars that other approaches take.

Three decades ago these homes in the core area, and others long ago destroyed, did not require as much work to set them right as those in South Ybor do today. Moreover, experience has shown that when dedicated homeowners are nearby, police costs go down and crime is kept in check. This is what many had wanted to do in the core area back in the '60s and '70s. Many old-timers just wanted to improve their homes, upgrade the utilities, perhaps add air conditioning in time, replace any damaged old wood, repaint the house, and perhaps repair the sidewalk.

Yes, there were more sensible, cost-effective options than the devastation wrought by Urban Renewal. The core area of old could have been saved, many still believe. Instead it was "raped," they say. Such strong adjectives best describe their feelings.

### Cesar Gonzmart and the Columbia Restaurant

The Columbia was ready for change six decades after its founding by Casimiro I. Under his son, Casimiro II, the restaurant had earned a national reputation. By 1970 its fine kitchens were equipped to cook world-class meals, prepared by chefs of international repute, and its dining rooms were decorated with handsome wall portraits, statues, and ornamentation. It had all the amenities befitting its status.

During the 1960s the Columbia Restaurant in Ybor City was embraced as a historic jewel. It became one of the three Florida restaurants joining one hundred from around the country in the National Restaurant Hall of Fame. Today it is one of the nation's oldest continuously operated Spanish restaurants of consequence. There can be no doubt that its decor, its numbers of valuable Spanish paintings, its unique ceramic tiles and priceless artifacts, and fabulous Spanish foods now vied for attention with Cesar's personal magnetism. One complemented the other. In fact, each needed the other.

The restaurant went through many physical improvements and additions. The huge Siboney Supper Club, finished in 1955, could seat up to three hundred people and featured a dance floor and raised bandstand. Visiting international dance groups sponsored by the Columbia entertained there. This was only one of many dining rooms, including El Café, La Fonda, El Patio, and El Don Quixote Room. The Siboney Room was the place where innumerable civic dinner meetings took place. Even in the years when Ybor City seemed to be disintegrating around it, the Columbia was a reassuring anchor for traditions and a sign of hope for the future. Today the restaurant has expanded to locations throughout Florida, including St. Augustine, Sarasota, St. Petersburg, and Disney World. The company is poised to keep growing, and much of the development can be traced to the dynamism of Cesar Gonzmart Sr.

In the trying years from the late 1950s through the 1980s, in the aftermath of the "rape" of the town, the Colombia Restaurant remained a steady point of confluence for Latin revitalization efforts in Ybor City. Many original thoughts were conceived there and much was discussed in that famous eating locale by the various organizations in the course of their meetings. Here dinner meetings by the Ybor City Chamber of Commerce, Rotary Club, and other civic groups took place, as well as innumerable regular business meetings, festive events, and annual celebrations. The Ybor City Chamber has, for decades, held its Annual Gala there. The Tony Pizzo Award for accomplishment in history and preservation has traditionally been presented there, and it has been the scene of many other awards and recognition banquets. A very elegantly attired staff delivers a first-class culinary experience, which has fed locals, tourists, international visitors, prominent politicians, and business personalities. The ambiance, which Cesar

*The Columbia Restaurant, gem of Spanish restaurants in America, was founded by Casimiro Hernandez I in 1905. This is how it looked in 1976. It served as a haven for Spanish, Italian, and Cuban cultural activities in the dismal post-Urban Renewal years.*



**Ybor City: The Making of a Landmark Town**

Gonzmart helped create, attracted all of these. There is no doubt that Cesar capitalized on these opportunities. The restaurant, its history, and its setting were ready-made for Cesar's personality.

Over the years the Columbia has served as an "extension" of many Ybor City civic organizations. Its continuing success was always inspiration for hope, and within its ambiance many initiatives were born. At the dinner meetings, discussions geared to reigniting the flame of Ybor City took place. Networking also went on there. People on opposite sides of an issue sometimes shook hands and even realigned their positions. Here Cesar would drop by to add his few words and offer encouragement or point the way, and sometimes even persuade a diner to change his adamant opinion over dessert and coffee.

Of particular importance was the fortuitous coming together there of several early personalities, all eventual presidents of the Ybor City Chamber of Commerce. These were Dr. Henry Fernandez, Dan Martinez, Joe Lopez, Joe Granda, Eddie Spoto, Raul Vega Jr., and Manuel Ballota. These were all business owners, professionals, and bankers. A common sympathy brought them together: their love of the town, their appreciation for the culture bequeathed to them by their fathers and mothers, and the realization that all this was in danger of being lost. Many other Latin leaders would follow, each projecting his program forward. All shared Cesar's vision and all were strong-willed individuals, dedicated through common heritage to the revival of Ybor City.

There can be little doubt that Cesar's personality and enterprising qualities helped inspire common action. Many positive decisions that helped Ybor City in the decades leading up to the 1980s were discussed at the Columbia and influenced by the caliber of civic, government and political personalities that gathered there.

Because it could claim the choicest

*The Columbia Restaurant helped preserve the cultural life of Ybor City by continuing to present live entertainers. Some performers are shown in this 1968 photograph.*

combination of dining, meeting, and festive rooms, and its dependable and respectful business climate, there was much opportunity for networking and sharing ideas. And one could count on its being a preferred venue for visiting local, state and national leaders.

Moreover, the Columbia had become a repository of artifacts, such as the portraits in the King's Room (photo on page 263) and the oil paintings throughout the restaurant, and a vehicle for affirming cultural traditions, such as the nightly Spanish dance performances, productions of the Ballet Folklorico and its predecessors, aged Spanish wines, and, of course, the authentic Columbia Restaurant cuisine. These, in turn, were orchestrated by immaculately dressed waiters serving in the stately dining rooms—and much more. For all these reasons, the Columbia Spanish Restaurant has attained the status of an "institution," and is not simply a well-known restaurant where people merely come to dine.

Yet, even the venerable and historic Columbia Restaurant was not immune to hard times in the days of Urban Renewal. The economic pressures were intense, and the Ybor City business community was in decline. Faced with these challenging realities, Cesar Gonzmart realized that the survival of the Columbia depended on the prosperity of Ybor City.

In 1966 when Republican Claude Kirk visited Gonzmart to ask for his support in

259

the upcoming gubernatorial election, Gonzmart overlooked their political differences. The two made a bargain, whereby Kirk, if elected, would support efforts to revitalize Ybor City. That meeting of minds eventually resulted in Kirk's support for the Ybor City campus of Hillsborough Community College. Cesar later said he felt that the campus "was the first spoke in the wheel" that turned things around.[1]

Some who knew Cesar attest that he was a man for his times. Having had the good fortune to work with him on a few occasions, I know he felt a calling and a responsibility to serve his community. I was occasionally well-positioned to evaluate his actions in Ybor City affairs, with the benefit of a little distance, and he showed many of the skills of a politician without actually holding an elected office.

His entry into the Columbia Restaurant organization was a great boon for the family.

### The Frank A. Weaner Gallery

In 1971, Cesar Gonzmart Sr. and banker Frank A. Weaner formed an organization to erect the upscale Frank A. Weaner Latin Quarter Gallery on 8th Avenue, next to the Ybor City Chamber of Commerce. With Weaner as the heaviest investor, the gallery was soon built. The

Chamber then, in addition to it normal activities, agreed to operate the gallery.

In the early years of operation, the gallery functioned reasonably well. It represented an important first step in the gradual rebirth of Ybor City, and at the time, as well as over the years, the Chamber expressed great appreciation to the donors, including, of course, Frank A. Weaner and Cesar Gonzmart, together with a number of supporting donors.

The Chamber managed many fine quality art events and scheduled many well-received gallery and street arts and crafts shows up until 1977. The Chamber administrator during those years was Oscar Aguayo, a talented and hard-working individual who had a wide acquaintance with artists and craftsmen, as well as good contacts in Tallahassee.

However, after a few years of expending considerable efforts to make it profitable, the Chamber discontinued its operation of the gallery. The small Chamber membership simply could not support it, nor could the office staff handle the extra work load. Moreover, the area's continuing, stubborn blight made it difficult to attract steady visitors to the gallery as hoped. The derelict condition of the many empty buildings on La Sétima made the area very unattractive, and there were no

**Ybor City: The Making of a Landmark Town**

prospects for improvement. The Chamber decided not continue operating the gallery at a loss.[2]

In 1977 the Chamber closed the gallery, moved its office into the former gallery space, and after leasing its old, vacated space for a time, sold the old location to attorney Bob Mitchum. With the Chamber now occupying the former gallery site, there arose, to everyone's regret, an unfortunate dispute with Frank A. Weaner over the gallery building's ownership. The Chamber's lawyer, Ed Rood Jr., declared that, in fact, the gallery building belonged to the Chamber.[3] This declaration was never legally contested.[4] The Chamber, nonetheless, was very appreciative of Weaner's early initiatives.

Then, as the result of negotiations between the Chamber and the State of Florida Parks Department, the organization determined to relocate once again, and moved to one of the old cigar-worker cottages (*casitas*) that were being restored with the help of state funds. The Chamber remains today in its *La Casita* building on the corner of 9th Avenue and 18th Street, having leased it from the State of Florida rent-free for a period of twenty-five years.[5] After the move, the Chamber leased out the former gallery building.

## The Krewe of the Knights of Sant' Yago

By the early 1970s the cigar industry in Ybor City was dead. Many Latin families had already moved out of the core and extended areas of the historic town, leaving few to carry on traditions and resulting in the disintegration of the social clubs and hospital. Most of the old-time merchants had closed up and departed. La Sétima had lost its vigor.

In light of this situation, an organization was needed that could add cohesiveness and spark to life for scattered Latins remaining in the town. Faced with a bleak prospect, an unswerving patriot of the

town, Dr. Henry J. Fernandez, convened a "Founding Group" to discuss this dreadful situation and begin to address it. He brought together men of known solid background and ones seriously interested in reversing Ybor City's downhill slide. This group consisted of Fernandez, the true "founder," with Cesar Gonzmart Sr., Daniel F. Martinez, Joe C. Granda, and Joseph R. Lopez. It met regularly at the Las Novedades Restaurant for a year researching and discussing many possibilities. Then came some unexpected international inpiration.

While in Spain on a fine-wine search for his restaurant, Cesar Gonzmart Sr. had met a respected vintner, owner of the "Yago" brand, and a man who had also been named as Spain's Baron of Sant' Yago, an honorary title awarded in a legendary organization. It was based on a theme born of Christianity, knighthood, and nobility.

The Krewe of the Knights of Sant' Yago is named in honor of Saint James, one of the twelve disciples. The early conversion of Spain to Christianity is based on the missionary zeal of a fisherman, who

*The State of Florida Parks Department has helped restore and maintain the historic "casitas" that were home to the early cigarworkers and their families in Ybor City. The Ybor City Chamber of Commerce maintains office space in La Casita building at the corner of 9th Avenue and 18th Street under a special lease arrangement.* SEAN DONNELLY.



**Chapter 7 • Individual Initiatives, Continued Withering, & Hope: 1970-1980**

like Peter, Andrew, and James, abandoned his livelihood in order to follow Jesus. After the crucifixion of Christ, Saint James, as did the other disciples, dispersed to rocky shores where even today fishermen claim their steps to be visible. He traveled to the far reaches of Spain, where he converted thousands from paganism to Christianity before he was killed by King Herod Agrippa I in Jerusalem in the year 44 A.D.

Some say that the followers of Saint James took his body to Spain, his adopted land, and buried him in Galicia, in northwest Spain, where his tomb was converted into the place for the early Christian missionaries to worship. Pilgrims came to the spot from many parts of Europe, defying all hazards and peril to render homage to Saint James. To this day one can travel "the way of Saint James," from France to Spain.

There are other refinements in the legend that vary somewhat, but the essential thing is that today, the body of Saint James is believed to rest in the Cathedral of Santiago de Compostela in Galicia, Spain. It is, today, the third most important place of Christian worship, after Jerusalem and Rome.

During the long centuries when the Spanish fought to rid themselves of invad-ing Moors, in one instance, at a time of possible defeat, legend has it that visions of Saint James (Sant' Yago), mounted on a white horse and carrying a flag with a cross on it, so uplifted and inspired the Spanish soldiers that they defeated the enemy. There are variations to this story, but over the years, Christian knights in Spain fought many battles to protect European missionaries from France, the Low Countries, Germany, and other areas on their pilgrimages to Santiago de Compostela in Galicia. Those who defended these religious pilgrims soon became famous, and they came to be known as the "Knights of Sant' Yago." The bravery and honor celebrated in the popular name was eventually formalized by the formation of the Knights of the Royal Order of Sant' Yago.

On his return to Ybor City from this visit to Spain, Cesar shared his interesting discovery with the "Founders Group" at Las Novedades—Fernandez, Martinez, Lopez, and Granda. He proposed that the high principles and traditions of the ancient Spanish order would be fitting inspiration for a local group of crusaders and defenders who would champion Ybor City and the heritage they loved. Cesar's idea was embraced by the others, and the



**Ybor City: The Making of a Landmark Town**

"Krewe of the Knights of Sant' Yago" was formed.

Today the Krewe of Sant' Yago functions as undoubtedly the most prestigious Latin social organization, composed of Spaniards, Cubans, Italians, and other interested citizens from all of Tampa. It holds many social functions and sponsors the annual Illuminated Night Parade on La Sétima. The King's Room at the Columbia Restaurant houses many of the key artifacts of the Krewe, including elegant portraits of the past kings and queens.

## Ybor Square and Harris Mullen

In 1972 Harris Mullen, a low-profile businessman and visionary, purchased the empty Vicente Martínez Ybor Factory and slowly converted it into a festive marketplace. He called the complex "Ybor Square." After total rehabilitation, the reconverted factory worked to attract tourist-related tenants offering everything from arts and crafts, antiques, books, and souvenirs to cigars and tobacco-related goods. Gradually the array of shopping opportunities grew, and they in turn brought in community, regional, and national visitors. By the 1990s the complex had some fifty-five tenants, which included offices, retail shops, and restaurants. This enterprise was a tremendous lift for the western end of Ybor City and served as a stable anchor for future growth.

However, Mullen was more than an absentee landlord. The owner, founder, and publisher of the prestigious *Florida Trend* business magazine, he moved his own publication into Ybor Square. The complex was the first major business initiative in Ybor City since Urban Renewal. Over the next twenty years, Mullen's positive influ-

*Phil LoCicero was elected first King of the Krewe of the Knights of Sant' Yago. He has been a leader in the Italian community, president of L' Unione Italiana, and a consistent supporter of common Latin objectives in Ybor City and West Tampa. A writer for La Gaceta, he is "The Story Teller of Ybor City."* SECOND ANNUAL PAOLO LONGO AWARD BOOK, 1989.

*This contemporary view of a portion of the King's Room upstairs at the Columbia Restaurant shows the continuing importance of the Krewe and affirms Ybor City's connections with the finest traditions of Latin art, architecture, culture, and belief. The elegant room displays portraits of past kings and queens of the Krewe of the Knights of Sant' Yago.*

263

*Kay and Harris Mullen both played active roles in the revitalization of Ybor City. Harris was the owner-publisher of Florida Trend business magazine and founder of Ybor Square, a festive marketplace in the former Don Vicente Martínez Ybor cigar factory building. He is greatly respected and was a leading factor in Ybor City's attainment of a "critical mass" of early infrastructure and development that led to an increase of commercial activity in the Historic Landmark District by 1990. A director and founding member of the Ybor City State Museum Society, Kay Mullen is remembered for her many civic and celebratory activities involving both the Ybor City Chamber of Commerce and the Museum Society.* 1996 YCCC GALA BROCHURE.

ence in Ybor City would spread. Moreover, he was and is a friend of preservation for the area's Latin cultural and architectural integrity. The investment by Mullen spoke louder than words. His example prompted a number of South Tampa investors to attempt Ybor City ventures, and this widening of interest injected new life into many activities. Suddenly there were Tampa business people who respected Ybor City's Latin history and who were interested in creating family-oriented festive events in the community, with a solid underpinning of law and order. This respect for law and order and wholesome local values resonated well with old-timers, for it was one of the historic values of Ybor City.

More specifically, Mullen was an articulate and energetic advocate for many projects, such as lighting the streets of the town, bringing in police protection, and having the city strengthen the Barrio Latino Commission. In the early '80s he served as vice president of the Ybor City Chamber of Commerce, chairman of Tampa Mayor Bob Martinez's Ybor City Development Advisory Commission, and chairman of the Ybor City Centennial Celebrations. This last initiative involved responsibility for arranging a year-long se-

ries of events, including a poster selection contest and commemorative gatherings to celebrate one hundred years of Ybor history. Mullen's connections with the downtown Tampa power base helped make the centennial a resounding success, and have been extremely beneficial to Ybor City.

Mullen had attended Plant High School, where he was a member of the 1942 All-State football team. He entered the Naval Officer Training program at Duke University in 1943 and graduated as an ensign, serving in the Navy until 1946. He then attended the University of Florida as a journalism student, and eventually worked for the *Tampa Tribune* as a reporter.

After his years of academic and practical experience as a journalist, he joined the family's printing and publishing business and became publisher of *The Florida Grower and Rancher* in 1950, a position he held for 14 years. He was perhaps best-known for his monthly column, "Florida Close-ups," which took strong views of business and political issues. The column was named best editorial column in the state five times by the Florida Magazine Association. In 1958 he founded *Florida Trend* magazine, which became the nation's largest state business magazine. (It

*Visitors to Ybor Square could browse in a variety of shops such as this Nostalgia Market, where these 1974 shoppers look at potted plants.* USFSCL.



**Ybor City: The Making of a Landmark Town**

*Another 1975 photo inside Ybor Square shows old-fashioned benches and the popular Chévere and Lucy O'Brien's Red Horse Book Stall.*

was purchased by the *St. Petersburg Times* in 1979.) When owned by Mullen, it was well-regarded in Tampa for its lucid articles on local and statewide industry, business innovations, personalities, problems, and challenges and, of course, was thought of as living up to its name in identifying important state trends.

The writer in Mullen never left. He now has two books to his credit on the American Civil War—*Ten Incredible Mistakes at Gettysburg* (High Water Press, 1995) and *Confederate Generals at Gettysburg: A Field Guide* (High Water Press, 1996)—and a Civil War novel, *God Bless General Early* (High Water Press, 1998), as well as other publications. Among his many awards are three important local honors: the D. B. McKay Award for contributions to local history, the Tony Pizzo Award, and the Cesar Gonzmart Award.

Mullen has been joined in his work by his respected wife, Kay, who has been involved in many civic and social affairs in Ybor City. She was a founding member of the Ybor City State Museum Society and has served on numerous cultural and historical committees for that society as well as for the Ybor City Chamber of Commerce. She has been a leader in organiz-

ing and supporting folkloric events and arts and craft exhibits within Ybor City, both on La Sétima and at Ybor Square, among others. These two committed individuals have made a difference, and their efforts helped change attitudes about Ybor City and its future.

Mullen sold his interest in Ybor Square in 2000, just as it was being converted primarily to office space.[7]

## An Artists' Colony in Ybor City

Latin culture has traditionally had an affinity for the arts. In the heyday of the cigar industry, fine craftsmanship was cultivated and rewarded. Aesthetics and skills were essential in crafting the handmade cigars, not to mention their importance in the graphic artistry and impressive fine lithography of the splendid cigar bands, labels, and the design and construction of the thin, wooden boxes, many of which are now collectors' items. This deeply rooted heritage was assuredly one of the factors that helped motivate the Chamber's efforts to launch its Weaner Gallery in Ybor City. Even though that particular endeavor failed to show a profit, it did communicate that there was an appreciation for the arts in Ybor City. Whether it was this tangible demonstration or simply some current in the air, there seemed to be a ripple effect within the Tampa Bay arts community. Soon the streets of Ybor City began to show signs of new, creative life as various artists arrived to establish themselves on or around the main spine.

Many studios and galleries opened. Rent was cheap, and the historic atmosphere was attractive. Two decades of blight had reduced the sales or rental prices of property considerably. Indeed, many buildings had been empty for over a decade. The extremely low prices attracted a few artists. These in turn passed the word on to others. What they saw they liked. The result was a steady stream of all kinds of artists into Ybor City.

265

*Sarah Romeo (left) and Jill Coville Wax both served as presidents of the Ybor City Chamber of Commerce.*

New presences along La Sétima included oil and water color painters, craftsmen in glass and wood, a portrait painter, suppliers of artistic wares, theatrical artists and producers, ceramic craftsmen, poster painters, and eventually Computer Assisted Design (CAD) operators and many more artists working in mixed media and genres.

Among the early artists with studios in the city were Roddy Reed, Rocky Kester, and Rikk Traweek. The artistic community blossomed virtually overnight, which led Traweek to explain that artists saw Ybor City as a desirable place to locate because it was "a community you can walk in" where the artists' "studios and galleries are virtually cheek by jowl—some 26 of them, within half an hour's hoofing distance."

By 1975 there was a core group of innovative and creative artists beginning to emerge. Jill Coville Wax, who now owns and operates La France on La Sétima, was an early artist to take up residence; others were Bruce Sargent, Sam Parker, Allen Sebring, David Audet, and Mike Turbe-

*Dancer and performance artist Susan Taylor dances in her third-floor studio at El Sama, circa 1980. The paintings leaning against the wall in the background hint at the range of artists working in the building at the time.* Susan Taylor Lennon.

ville. In a large studio adjacent to the Kress Building Joe Traina, a longtime Tampan, shared space with Claude Fiddler, from Trinidad, John Gurbacs, from Hungary, Bill McClellan, American realist painter and political activist, and Tom Kettner, Tampa avant garde artist also working with Robert Rauschenberg at his Captiva studio. Photographer Bud Lee arrived in 1976. The acclaimed modern artist James Rosenquist, who helped put the University of South Florida's Graphicstudio on the map, had a large studio on La Sétima. The British artist Malcolm Morley had an Ybor studio. Their presence attracted visits from those in the international art scene who would fly in for studio parties or to see a new Rosenquist work-in-progress.

One of the most energetic groups was a cooperative known as El Sama, a group of about twenty artists led by painter and sculptor Jerry Meatyard and housed in an old coffin factory on 22nd Street and 4th Avenue. Members included David Dye, Richard Santiago, Roberta Schofield, Bruce Sargent, Jill Wax, and dancer and performance artist Susan Taylor. In keeping with the coffins still in the basement, the group began a tradition of offbeat Halloween celebrations that established precedents for Guavaween and the Artists and Writers Balls to come

Jay Fechtel was chairman of the Ybor City Chamber of Commerce Arts and Commerce Committee, and he was an articulate champion for the arts in the community. He promoted the Ybor City heritage to artists who had enough imagination to see the possibilities in the sleeping town. "There is nothing like it in Florida," Fechtel said. "It's the only concentrated collection of old, ethnic buildings in the state . . . excepting St. Augustine and parts of Pensacola. Artists appreciate the atmosphere of such an environment."

Fechtel was instrumental in encouraging a collaboration of the Ybor City Centennial Committee, the Ybor City



**Ybor City: The Making of a Landmark Town**

*This t-shirt design by El Sama artists documents an Ybor City tradition that survives in the large street festivals of today.* JERRY MEATYARD.

Chamber of Commerce, the Tampa Arts Council, and the local arts community to launch a major sidewalk art show called Avenida de Arte and Fiesta, which would be a festive celebration of Ybor's ethnic history. Fechtel envisioned the arts as a means of Ybor development which could preserve the historic and cultural tone of the community and maintain the core area for pedestrians rather than encouraging automobile traffic.

At the same time, the counter-cultural and avant-garde artists of Ybor contributed to the festival atmosphere with gallery and studio openings as well as parties which became famous attractions in themselves. Musician and artist Gary Rexroad, poet Silvia Curbelo, and filmmaker Stuart Lippe joined others including Michael Kilgore, Mary & Charlie Greacen, Paul Wilborn, Ron Elliot, Stephen Roberts, and Ben Brown to organize the first Ybor City Artists and Writers Ball, Saturday, April 15, 1978. It was held at the Circulo Cubano, which was an empty and unrenovated building at the time. The first year it cost about $400 to put on, and had an attendance of about 200 people. Within four

years, the numbers had swelled to some 16,000, and those with their eyes open in Ybor City could sense the possibilities for an even more ambitious annual festival that could attract thousands of visitors.[1]

## In Search of New Direction

Cesar Gonzmart Sr., Dr. Henry Fernandez, and others had labored hard to reverse the decay that followed the rape of Ybor City's core area by Urban Renewal. Yet even in the face of many energetic attempts, there was no easy recovery from the shameful aftermath of human error and misdirection that had nearly eradicated the town. Despite good motives by many, Urban Renewal had left the Ybor City core in desperate condition. It lay prostrate, dormant, and virtually destroyed. Its land was cheap, and most of its buildings were still empty and in disrepair. Rent, of course, was also cheap—a circumstance that had presented favorable opportunities for some artists and craftsmen—yet there was no critical mass of retail or commercial tenants of consequence stepping forward to take advantage of the real estate bargains. The potential found in the creativity of projects like Ybor Square and the Artists and Writers Ball appeared to be a well-kept secret.

This was the atmosphere in the late 1970s when the town still struggled to wake itself from sleep. The difficulty of moving forward is illustrated by a memorable anecdote from my presidency of the Ybor City Chamber. In 1977, I attended a meeting of our Merchant Committee, which had taken as one of its primary goals the clean-up of many of the Ybor storefronts. Also invited to the meeting was Cesar Gonzmart Sr., a familiar leader of the town with whom I had only recently become personally acquainted. When I cited as an example of neglect a property across the street that badly needed some dressing-up, it turned out that, unknown to me, it was owned by the Gonzmart fam-

ily. Cesar jumped up and said, "Frank, I have just met you, and you have already insulted me. Is this the way to get my co-operation?"

Well, there had to be a start, and that meeting sparked Cesar's attention. Cesar liked candor. He respected it. Gradually, Cesar and a select few of the other Ybor merchants joined the clean-up effort—even though it meant investing time and money on the vacant and unproductive real estate. In defense of Cesar and the other merchants, it must be understood that after a decade of blight and largely empty buildings, no one was disposed to upgrade storefronts only to see them remain empty. Many buildings were up for sale, but there were no buyers; many were available for lease, with no prospective tenants in sight.

Many of us understood that it would take a major, favorable shift in the economic forces of supply and demand as well as aggressive promotion and marketing of the area's appeal as a historic and festive cultural center to cope with the problem. The Merchant Committee chairman, Jose Ourál, then owner of the Sherwin Williams paint store on the corner of 8th Avenue and 17th Street, was frustrated with the negativism he encountered, and his reports to me made that clear. We were in an uphill battle because free enterprise will not pour money into properties that can not be expected to show a reasonable return. Nonetheless, he and others helped to push improvement efforts forward.

It was a month or so after that meeting that I became aware of some of the persistent, imaginative thinking that had been going on behind the scenes. Cesar gave me a copy of a letter he had written to Busch Gardens officials years ago. In it he had proposed that the Busch organization buy much of the available Ybor City property and convert it to tourist-oriented historic and festive venues with a Latin theme. A substantial amount of real estate could have been acquired for a very modest cost, and it would have given the Busch Gardens complex a unique attraction in some ways comparable to colonial Williamsburg, where the organization successfully operated another park. And it could have benefitted from the thriving nearby Disney World complex and Orlando attractions. At the time he gave me the letter, he added that he had never received a reply.

What Cesar imagined was evidently too speculative a use of capital for the entertainment executives at Busch Gardens. True, Ybor City was a town with an enviable history, but any substantial investment in it in the late 1960s was still extremely risky. By the early '70s there had, indeed, been some tentative interest. Local investors, Realtors, artists, business people, sons and daughters of the old *tabaqueros*, and some dedicated preservationists were being attracted by the town. In spite of its mostly abandoned situation, its ambiance, its appealing grid design, and its treasured history and lore were still seductive and irresistible to individuals with taste and sensitivity. It might have been that fate decreed a narrow course: only through community and grassroots efforts, rather than through a valiant outside rescuer, would the town be truly reborn.

Activist Joan Jennewein, architect Stephanie Ferrell, and the dedicated members of Tampa Preservation Inc. had begun their work devoted to architectural preservation in 1973. By the end of the decade, the organization was gaining strength. Headed by Phil Wormley, it had located its offices in the old Ybor Chamber building at 1509 8th Avenue. When Wormley was promoted to head the state preservation effort, Ferrell, in turn, became the county's Director for Historic Preservation. I assume that her early residency in Ybor City had exposed her to its great potential, for she proved to be a tireless advocate.

Also devoted to the potential in the surviving buildings on La Sétima was Joyce

**Ybor City: The Making of a Landmark Town**

Schaffer, who headed her own construction company in south Tampa. She was assisted in this by her son, Jay Fechtel, who was equally motivated. In this era Schaffer, Jennewein, Tim Nugent, and Michael Shea—all of whom served terms as president of the Ybor City Chamber of Commerce—presided over many interim events, from administrative meetings to festive street celebrations and from preservation to relocation of the Chamber headquarters. Rendering consistent technical support was David Rigney of the Preservation office. And continuing to point the way—inspiring, without a doubt—was Harris Mullen with Ybor Square. By the mid-1970s, these leaders and a core of others became a viable force for future growth in Ybor City. They were possessed of professionalism and dedication. Some of them were, of course, pursuing their own business interests, but they labored with considerable love of Ybor City and its Latin history. Certainly, revitalization was a challenge but, fortunately, working together the preservationists had developed their own synergy. Slowly but surely the message was being heard: there was a slow but noticeable increase in the interest and demand for the unique combination of culture and history Ybor City had to offer; there was growth in the number of shops, festivals, sights, and tastes for visitors and customers to try. The unsteady scales of the free enterprise market forces that had for so long been swinging unbalanced between supply and demand were starting to tip in Ybor's favor—and Ybor Square became the epicenter of their dynamic movement.

## A Visionary Wish-List

In May 1977 as YCCC president, I appointed Emmett Clary to be Chairman of the Long Range Committee. We knew it would be impossible to reach our destination without a roadmap of sorts, so we set out to combine the practical and creative talents of the community to provide a wish-list of goals for Ybor City improvements. Clary's committee included Harris Mullen, representing the Barrio Latino Commission; Cesar Gonzmart Jr., head of the Grants Office at Hillsborough Community College; Dom Maggio, president of Ybor City Jaycees; Phil Wormley, president of Tampa Preservation Inc.; Phil Rosete, facilities coordinator at Hillsborough Community College; and me, by virtue of serving at that time as president of the Ybor City Chamber. On the basis of his "think tank," on June 1, 1977, Clary recorded the following thirty-two items that he and his committee felt the Ybor Chamber and the community should promote:

*Emmett Clary was the Chairman of the YCCC Long-Range Committee that produced a detailed "wish list" for the future.*

1. Reroute 13th Street into Ybor City from Tampa
2. Construct an Amtrak Station near 30th Street and I-4 (south side)
3. Convince Quality Inn or La Quinta Motor Inns or similar company to construct a Spanish-style motel in Ybor City
4. Diplomatic building for Latin-American Consuls, Casa España
5. A Utilities Building for City utilities collections (TECO, City utilities, GTE business, Dart Centers, etc.)
6. A combined Airlines Reservation Center (major airlines in Tampa are outgrowing their reservations space)
7. Spanish language Toastmasters Club in Ybor City
8. Yacht Club at the North end of Ybor Channel
9. Expand the Boundary of the Historic District to cover Ybor Channel on the south and the SCL Railroad on the East (natural boundaries)
10. Transportation Museum—Union Station restoration
11. Lozano Cigar Factory—Fine Arts Studios similar to Mt. Adams in Cincinnati
12. Maritime Museum including Submarine *Requin* and *Unicorn* at banana docks.
13. Law enforcement museum—new sheriff's complex.
14. Twenty-four-hour, seven-day Spanish language radio in Ybor City
15. Illuminate 9th Avenue from 13th Street to 19th Street
16. SCL Division Office move
17. Hexagonal pavers for sidewalks

*In this 1970s photo of a pedestrian area, the hexagonal pavers typical of many Ybor City sidewalks are clearly visible. The need to repair and preserve this distinctive sidewalk treatment was listed as item 17 on Clary's list. The costumed street performers recall the historic Latin roots of Ybor City culture, in keeping with the final item on the list.*

18. Balconies
19. McKay Bay Bird Sanctuary.
20. Park of the Americas (Plaza de las Americas, Plaza España)
21. HCC Land Improvement (grass)
22. Funding of an Ybor City Improvement Corporation
23. Creating an effective plan for promoting Ybor City
24. Landscaping public areas and making plans to maintain these
25. Creating a parking and transportation plan for Ybor City
26. Expanding boundaries of Historic buildings
27. Develop plans to create an Ybor City Museum Building
28. Improve relations with Miami's Havana Village, possibly as a " Sister City" concept
29. Create plans for a Farmers Market
30. Push private enterprise
31. Create plans to support traditional routes of egress and ingress to Ybor City
32. A deliberate attempt should be made to bring in and retain Latin culture

In his last paragraph to the report, Clary added the following words: "In no way are these plans firm and inflexible—there will be frequent additions and changes, even some deletion. They are not in priority order, so we may proceed in any order if the opportunity presents itself."

Clary held a public hearing on August 17, 1977, to present the list and invite support. It was well received, and by August we were also able to report our active steps to implement several of these items. We had already obtained Tampa Mayor Bill Poe's help with item fifteen on the list, the 9th Avenue lighting project.

With positive response from citizens in informal meetings, Clary turned the document over to consultants from Economic Research Associates (ERA), the private research group on urban revitalization and renewal selected by the City of Tampa, for possible use in their report. Some of the items from our wish list are recognizable in the recommendations of the final ERA report. Some of the other ideas were implemented during Mayor Poe's tenure, and the list also led to concepts that were addressed in Mayor Bob Martinez's administration.

## Attracting Attention to Ybor City

The need for accelerating outreach to attract tourists and residents to an increasingly appealing historic center remained a central focus. On June 2, 1977, as president of the Ybor Chamber of Commerce, I sent a letter to William C. Tatum, acting county administrator, asking that the county address the need for highway road signs at strategic locations on I-4 and I-75. I also asked that they install a tourist information booth at a key junction near Ybor City and assist the small Chamber in providing other services, such as monthly calendars of events, informational brochures, and other promotional literature. Harris Mullen, Manuel Blanco, and Emmett Clary joined the effort. A sum of $11,680 was requested for 1978. Eventually, a check for only $2,000 was received by the Ybor Chamber—far from what we hoped but better than nothing at all. In addition, two road signs were installed. Unfortunately, in those days the downtown Tampa mentality was lacking in appreciation for Ybor City. Many politicians from this area simply patted Ybor locals on the back. It was an empty and condescending gesture. Even Latin politicos would do nothing that might displease the Anglo community in South Tampa. Ironically, it took a non-Latin politician to help the area in those days, and we began to make for-



**Ybor City: The Making of a Landmark Town**

ward progress with the help of Mayor Bill Poe, who was elected in 1974. He seemed to recognize both residential and commercial needs in Ybor City, and he sensed that successful revitalization of the area would have benefits for the City of Tampa as a whole. (Fortunately, in the 1980s and forward, Bob Martinez and later Dick Greco would sense the mutual advantages even more clearly and would tend to give Ybor City its fair backing.)

Under the Poe administration, the first outreach efforts started to pay dividends. Visitors to Ybor were continuing to increase, and the improvements in appearance initiated by the Merchants Committee and others showed promise. However, there remained a need for a more substantial investment to highlight and sustain these improvements. One specific need that we had identified was for upgrading streetlights in the area. It was clear that attractive lighting would enhance the atmosphere, improve the safety, and help draw visitors at night.

Ybor City Chamber of Commerce minutes dated July 19, 1977, recorded that "a committee composed of Harris Mullen, Caesar Gonzmart Jr., and Emmett Clary and Frank Lastra spoke to Mayor Poe concerning the 9th Avenue lighting project. According to the project, decorative lampposts would be installed on 9th Avenue from HCC to the Ybor City State Museum. The committee was well received by Mayor Poe and has reason to believe the project will be approved." This lighting is today in place. Harris Mullen played a key role in this project. The wishes on Emmett Clary's list were being granted.

## Saving Our Historical Red Bricks

One item not on the list proved to be an important issue for the town. In the mid- to late-'70s, the red bricks that paved many if not most of our Ybor City streets began to disappear only to be replaced by asphalt, especially following public works projects

such as utilities improvements or repairs. Smatterings of antique red bricks turned up in people's yards as far as the northern end of town at the time that some streets in Ybor were being patched or repaved with asphalt. Work crews were reported to be replacing the red vitrified clay bricks, many of which bore the "Augusta Blocks" imprint, with asphalt for the sake of efficiency and cost reduction. These were pragmatic reasons, certainly, but the historical red brick streets in Ybor City were casually being dismantled and jeopardized. The warmth they conveyed was an integral part of the town's historical ambiance. In some cases, after Urban Renewal, the bricks of the streets were nearly all that was left of the original fabric of the community.

When residents learned their brick streets were being replaced by asphalt, they soon complained to the Ybor Chamber. As its president in early 1977, I asked Jan Platt, who was then a member of the Tampa City Council, to see if she would look into saving the red bricks of our historic town. Platt went to work energetically to obtain support for a more appropriate treatment of the brick streets that for so many years had been a part of Ybor City's visual charm. Helen Chavez of the City Council also defended the red bricks before that body.

We were fortunate to have such energetic and articulate representatives. In a letter to me dated June 24, 1977, Platt reported on results:

271

Attached are excerpts of a memo from Dale Twachtman regarding the city's position on brick streets. I know that you and the Chamber are delighted that the city is finally taking a positive stance toward preserving its beautiful brick streets. As Clay Resources Chairman for the Chamber, I urge the Chamber members to notify me immediately when it appears that any of the bricks are being threatened. Please pass this information on to the Chamber membership.

Platt also sent a copy of the memorandum issued by Dale Twachtman, Tampa's administrator of public works. His directive made it clear that convenience alone would no longer be a sufficient reason to destroy brick streets. Now preservation would be an important factor:

> Many citizens of Tampa have become increasingly aware in recent years of the benefits of preserving certain historic facilities. In this city one of the features considered worthy of such preservation are those brick streets that are still in reasonably good condition and/or have historic significance.
>
> The purpose of this memorandum is to make clear that policies which existed in the past—which allowed the use of asphalt patches and removal of the bricks after repairs of utilities—are no longer valid. We will endeavor to have our crews and other public and private utilities replace brick paving with brick paving whenever it is reasonable to do so . . . each department should do its best to preserve bricklaying skills with Department crews. If such skill does not exist, training can be conducted within or between departments to encourage the passing on of these skills from the older employees.

This message was not only reassuring in that it showed a willingness to act to maintain the basic historic fabric of the town; it was also a call to preserve the bricklaying skills that would be essential if the streets were to remain and be maintained in the future. The letter was sent by Dale Twachtman as administrator of water resources and public works to all supervisors. By including those workers who would be re-pairing the city's water lines as well as the streets themselves—and by mentioning also the private utilities workers who also would need to be fully involved in the preservation effort, Twachtman established a wide-reaching principle.[10]

This policy had not been enforced in the past. Jan Platt's stand closed the door on a bad practice and established a forward-looking guideline. For this the Chamber was deeply grateful.[11]

## Ybor City Banks

The Columbia Bank of Ybor City, founded in 1923 by Simon A. Grimaldi, was owned and directed by the highly respected Grimaldi family. In the 1990s it was operated by a nephew, Ray Grimaldi, who served as president, and by Rose Grimaldi, Ray's mother, who was chairman emeritus of the board of directors. Over the years it earned a reputation among Ybor citizens as a highly stable and dependable bank. It was the only bank in Ybor City to survive the 1929 stock market crash—which closed the doors of the Citizens Bank of Tampa. This speaks volumes for its prudent operation.

Under Ray Grimaldi's leadership, the bank expanded into the eastern areas of Hillsborough County. It received the "Blue Ribbon" commendation from the rating system of Veribanc, Inc., for financial safety and soundness during every quarter of its life. This award is the nation's oldest, and is considered a very prestigious form of national recognition. Grimaldi has been a big booster of Ybor City. He has helped many local businesses and has made many contributions in support of active projects sponsored by the Ybor City Chamber of Commerce. He has worked with the Centro Asturiano and Círculo Cubano in their building improvements. Another family member, A. J. Grimaldi, the bank's vice president in the 1990s, became president of the Ybor City Chamber of Commerce, chaired the Chamber's highly

*The decorative sign for the Columbia Bank in 1972. This Ybor City financial institution thrived under the direction of the Grimaldi family.* THCPLS.



272

successful business forum, and went on to serve on the board of directors. In August 1999 it was announced that the bank would be acquired by Southern Exchange, but the Columbia Bank and the Grimaldi family made a difference to the community.

Another important financial institution was the Broadway Bank of Ybor City. It too has earned a place in history and has performed countless services for its home community. Eddie Spoto, longtime president of the bank, is specifically remembered for his many civic activities in support of redevelopment projects, including the Haciendas de Ybor housing complex for the Latin elderly.[12]

## The Merchants

While artists were establishing a toehold in the area, merchants were assessing the current lack of business on La Sétima, and many were quietly making plans to leave. Most of the older Jewish merchants, so long a part of the Ybor City history, particularly on La Sétima, had left. Many of their buildings were up for sale.

Many of the original Jewish merchants in Ybor City had emigrated from Romania. Their numbers were relatively few in Florida before 1900, although some of those who were here accomplished great things. University of Florida history professor Samuel Proctor has identified the major Jewish population growth in the state as occurring during the real estate boom of the 1920s.[13]

There was a somewhat similar pattern in Ybor City. In the early years of the city's history, Jewish merchants began to trickle in. By the mid-20s there were approximately seventy Jewish merchants and businessmen with establishments throughout Ybor City, but principally on La Sétima. The names of some of their shops still ring in my ears and immediately come to mind when I think of the town: Max Argintar Clothing, Rainbow Mens Wear, Louis Wohl Household Sup-

*The Broadway Bank played an important part in community life. It was located at the corner of La Sétima and 17th Street.* USFSCL.

plies, The Palace, Sunshine Department Store, Louie's Department Store, Poller's Ladies Wear, Adam Katz Family Clothing, and Modern Home Furnishings. At the extreme ends of the town were American Pipe and Plumbing at the northeast corner of Nebraska and La Sétima, and Sol Walker and Co. Scrap Iron, to the far east.[14]

The loss of these merchants was part of the sad, slow death of the Ybor City I grew up in. A large reservoir of my memories of yesterday contains images of Saturday evenings and nights of shopping with our mothers and fathers, when we children dutifully followed behind them hurrying and sidestepping to avoid the heavy crowds. Much of the shopping was done in Jewish stores. (See the summary of Jewish merchants in the appendix to this book).

But of course, there were many other businesses. In Ybor's Golden Years the res-

*The shops along La Sétima were beginning to change, offering a spare selection of goods and slightly run-down appearance. This photograph shows some newer and struggling shops— Dorinda's Yarn Shop and Miami Jewelry, with Sam Argintar's sign visible at the far end of the block.*

273

taurants were mostly run by Spaniards, and the groceries by Italians, Spaniards, and Cubans. The grocery cooperatives during the depression years were primarily operated by Spaniards and two by Italians. After the 1970s Spanish restaurants declined, and Italians, particularly after the mid-80s, opened up many more eateries. While Las Novedades and the Spanish Park restaurants closed, the Columbia Restaurant gained in popularity and stature. It ranks as a national leader in its field.

### The "Rough Riders"

Another organization began in 1977 that served as an expression of and a catalyst for the revival of interest in Ybor City's history. A group convened in Tampa for the purpose of perpetuating a living memorial to the accomplishments of the members of the First U.S. Volunteer Cavalry Regiment, better known as the "Rough Riders." The historic troops were mounted soldiers who had served under the command of Lt. General Leonard Wood.

In the ultimate liberation of Cuba, "Teddy" Roosevelt had organized the First United States Volunteer Cavalry, known as the "Rough Riders," as the key contingent of U.S. troops in the Spanish-American War. He led the First Cavalry in Cuba in a storied charge up Kettle Hill during the battle of San Juan, and the accounts of his daring published in the U.S. papers made him a national hero. While the Rough Riders' stay in Tampa was brief—and, indeed, the actions of some of the members

of the unit were typical soldierly "doings"—the American population in general, as well as Cubans of the day, remembered their stay as historical. (See Chapter II for a more about their time in Tampa.)

The intent of the Tampa Rough Rider organization is to develop ways to celebrate this legendary episode in American history—and its Tampa connections—by such activities as an annual festival, the collection and display of artifacts of the era, the education and understanding for generations to come of the importance of this feat by U.S. military forces, and the creation of other memorials and activities that would be appropriate to serve these purposes from time to time.

This organization is largely the personal accomplishment of founder Charles Spicola Jr., who labored effectively throughout 1978 for its establishment and was dedicated to its formation. I recall sharing a plane ride to Tallahassee with him, on a different mission, when Spicola animatedly explained details of the plans he had for the Rough Riders. He started this organization with great thrust and spirit, and quickly engaged major participants such as Harris Mullen; James Covington, historian; H. L. Culbreath, president of Tampa Electric; and Hampton Dunn, historian. I also served on the first board. The organization has now enjoyed more than two decades of successful revelry, study, and representation of the history of its predecessor, the 1st United States Volunteer Cavalry Regiment. It holds annual events and participates with other groups in the celebration of Ybor City history. Many outstanding citizens have taken part in its activities and are supporting its mission today.[15]

### The Ybor City State Museum: A Decade of Milestones

While many individual initiatives and projects came and went during the 1970s

**Ybor City: The Making of a Landmark Town**

and '80s, those which looked toward the preservation of the town's history seemed most clearly tinged with hope. At the heart of these efforts lay groups of individuals who invested their time and talents in the endeavor to achieve state and national recognition for the historical architecture and cultural history of the town.

One crucial key to the endeavor was the concept of an Ybor City Historical Museum, which had the good fortune to be guided by Bettie Nelson, the Museum Society's first president.[16] She was witness to a steady unfolding of events that led to national recognition for the entire Ybor City district.

The formal sequence of events began in February 1971 when Cesar Gonzmart Jr., who was the acting director of development and urban studies at Hillsborough Junior College, made inquiries with the City Demonstration Agency regarding the historic significance of the old Ybor City Fire Station. The location was near the developing area where Hillsborough Community College was eventually to enlarge its Ybor campus. When a quick look at the fire station showed it to be of significant historic value, other queries followed, and just a year later, in February 1972, Gonzmart Jr. requested that several of the major locations in Ybor City be added to the map of Florida's "Bicentennial Trail" which was being planned for 1976 in celebration of the U.S. Bicentennial. He also contacted Dr. F. Blaire Reeves in the Department of Architecture at the University of Florida to explore the possibility of having Tampa—and especially Ybor City—surveyed in the Historic American Buildings Survey. Dr. Reeves had been influential in locating and preserving architecturally notable and historic buildings throughout the state and served on the executive committee of the National Trust for Historic Preservation.

Tampa City Councilman Joe Chillura Jr. also became interested in the prospects for documenting buildings of historical importance, and in January 1973 he arranged for Gonzmart and others who had expressed an interest to meet with John Poppeliers, chief of the Historic American Buildings Survey organization, to discuss local preservation. With the national Bicentennial celebration approaching, the climate for preserving American history was right. Florida State Senator David McClain had already pre-filed a legislative bill to set up a Historical Preservation Commission.

By June of 1973, Dr. Morton S. Shanberg, President of Hillsborough Community College, was advised that further consideration of the old Ybor City Fire Station had confirmed its historic importance for the community, and he suggested that renovation and reuse of the old fire station building, built between 1907 and 1918, would be a valuable addition to the Ybor City campus. Cesar recommended use of the phrase "Historic Ybor City" for all references to the location of that building, and for other structures that were being identified as candidates for preservation within the "Historic Ybor City" district.

By August of that year the Historic American Buildings Survey was completed in Ybor City under joint sponsorship of the Bicentennial Committee of Hillsborough County and the City of Tampa; by October, Ybor City had been nominated as a National Historic District.

With the nomination now formalized, there was the need to consider all of the potential development plans within Ybor City in a new light. When it was time for additional planning the following summer, a meeting on historic preservation was held in relation to the Ybor City Urban Renewal Project in August 1974. Among those attending were some familiar names: Dr. Morton Shanberg, president of Hillsborough Community College; Dr. Henry Fernandez, chairman of the Advi-

*Bettie Nelson.*

*Cesar Gonzmart Jr.*

sory Council of Historic Preservation in Ybor City; John McWhirter, attorney with HCC; Cesar Gonzmart Jr., chairman of the Hillsborough County Bicentennial; Harris Mullen, publisher of *Florida Trend* magazine; Ron Rotella, executive director of the Metropolitan Development Agency; and Raul Vega Jr., chairman of the Barrio Latino Commission. Dr. Fernandez commented that interested citizens had gone to Tallahassee in 1958 to help establish the Barrio Latino Commission (the founding ordinance was passed in August 1959, as detailed in Chapter V) hoping to stem the tide of deterioration in Ybor City by preserving architectural integrity. Now—nearly two decades after the start of that effort—it was beginning to seem like a real possibility that there would be wider support forthcoming for the preservation concerns which had been a long-standing interest of the commission. At the meeting, Robert Williams, director of the State of Florida Division of Archives and History, stated that his department recognized the unique historical value of Ybor City, and that it would contribute half of the cost of restoring another important Ybor building, the Ferlita Bakery, if the City of Tampa was willing to provide the other half. Meanwhile, the nomination of the Ybor City District to the National Register of Historic Places was expedited and the official designation as a Historic District was granted that same month—August 1974.

The Mayor's Advisory Commission on Historic Preservation of Ybor City recommended that the Ferlita Bakery be restored as a building of historical significance at an approximate cost of $70,000 in a cooperative venture with the State of Florida. It also recommended that an effort be made to save at least one of three houses located on 14th Street north of Hillsborough Community College in the path of a planned Nuccio Parkway interchange. One house of the three could be moved to available city property in the Barrio Latino area and restored with private funds.

Cesar Gonzmart Jr. went to Tallahassee in January of 1975 to discuss the possibilities for collaboration between the state and HCC for adapting the old bakery into a state museum devoted to the depiction of the ethnic origins of Ybor City and its cigar industry, and serving as a repository for many of the related papers and artifacts that were stored in Tallahassee at that time. By May 1975 the project had been approved by city council, mayor, and other appropriate local entities, and the proposal moved to the Florida Cabinet and Governor Reuben Askew for approval. Estimated cost was $200,000 with July 4, 1976, as the projected completion date. Architect Gilbert Flores was commended at the Ybor City Chamber of Commerce meeting for his work on renderings for the museum.

In August 1975 there was cause for celebration when the Florida Cabinet approved a $62,211 grant to purchase a 0.9 acre site, including the old Ferlita Bakery, to be used for a State Museum in Ybor City. The city owned the property, and planned to allocate $90,000 in grant funds from the U.S. Department of Housing and Urban Development for remodeling and improving the bakery building. Ney Landrum, director of the Division of Recreation and Parks, spoke at the September meeting of the Ybor City Chamber of Commerce stating the museum would be a part of the state park system. It looked unlikely, however,



**Ybor City: The Making of a Landmark Town**

*Ney Landrum.*

*Stanford Newman.*

*L. Glenn Westfall.*

that the plan would be ready for the Bicentennial July 4 celebration.

Unfortunately, that turned out to be the case. I was serving as president of the Ybor City Chamber of Commerce in May of 1977 when Cesar Gonzmart Jr. reported that final approval for the museum plans had at last been granted by Tampa City Council and that bids should be opened by June, with work to begin in late 1977. Mayor Bill Poe and Gonzmart Jr., as chairman of the new museum's board of advisors, joined HCC president Frank Scaglione and Ney Landrum for the official groundbreaking on June 28, 1977.

With work at last commencing, Gonzmart Jr. began additional steps to develop a truly outstanding facility. In October 1977, he wrote to Stanford Newman, president of the Standard Cigar Company and the Cigar Manufacturers Association, regarding Newman's long-standing interest in a cigar industry related museum. Among ideas suggested were a cigar-rolling artisan to demonstrate the hand-rolling technique; an audiovisual display portraying the cigar industry to consumers; a permanent exhibit of a selection of fine cigars; and a display of photographs, documents, labels, and other historically significant memorabilia.

Work on the museum progressed slowly but steadily. In February 1979, the Ybor City Chamber of Commerce presented a resolution donating its bronze bust of José Martí for permanent display at the Museum. Sam Leto was president of the Chamber at the time. Other donations were invited from businesses and individuals. On March 19, 1979, Elizabeth Ehrbar, the state's exhibit supervisor, wrote to thank Gonzmart Jr. and Tony Pizzo for donating historical artifacts. Among the items requested were cigar posters and signs, checkers, bolita balls, old cigar boxes and tins, and cigar workers' tools and molds.

By February 1980 the collection of artifacts and preparation of displays had come together. Gonzmart Jr., had taken over as Chamber president and announced that the only thing holding up the official opening of the museum was the completion of the gardens. A crescendo of interest was building and peaked in time for the dedication ceremony on Monday, October 13, 1980. That day marked completion of a dream. The Ybor City State Museum was officially dedicated in ceremonies conducted jointly by the Florida Department of Natural Resources and the Tampa Division of Recreation and Parks.[17] Gonzmart Jr. had provided leadership in the conceptualization, design, site acquisition, funding, construction, and even in the gathering of some of the display materials; he shepherded the early operation of the museum and had the privilege of serving as chairman of the Advisory Board until his departure from Tampa in 1980.[18]

277

# Some Leading Cigar Manufacturers

The Ybor City State Museum began the process of collecting, preserving, and presenting information about the history of cigar indusry workers and manufacturers, bringing to life many faces from the past.  Their collection now includes much more than space allows. However, here are portraits of some of the leaders.

*Vicente Martínez Ybor is best known as a cigar manufacturer, but he also demonstrated skill and vision as a developer who shaped the town that bears his name.*

*Eduardo Manrara, Ybor's partner, was vice president of the Ybor City Land and Improvement Company. Ybor and Manrara also purchased a controlling interest in the Tampa Street Railway Company in 1885.*

*Ignacio Haya immigrated from Spain to New York, where in partnership with another Spanish immigrant, Serafin Sanchez, their factory was the first in the country to make cigars from light Cuban tobacco known as "Clear Havana."*

*Salvador Rodriguez of Salvador Rodriguez, Inc., had a location at Palmetto Beach on 22nd Street and 3rd Avenue. They were known for the "Charles the Great" brand.*

*Emilio Pons, a factory partner of Candido Angel Martínez Ybor, son of Don Vicente Martínez Ybor. His factory was located at 17th Street and 10th Avenue.*

*Serafin Sanchez, partner of Ignacio Haya, had a factory located at 15th Street and La Sétima. Their Sanchez and Haya Factory No. 1 in Ybor City closed in 1976.*

*José Arango, owner of the Arango Cigar Company, located at 2112 15th Street.*

*Jerome Regensburg, owner of E. Regensburg & Sons, the "clock" factory, located at 16th Street and Michigan Avenue (today's Columbus Avenue). He later moved to Allentown, Pennsylvania. Today the factory is owned by the J. C. Newman Cigar Company.*

*Manuel Garcia, an owner of Perfecto Garcia Cigar Company ("El Paraiso"). Its best-known factory was located at 16th Street and 8th Avenue, and prior to that at other locations.*

*Enrique Pendas was a cigar pioneer active in the Ybor City community. The firm of Lozano, Pendas and Co. was based in New York before opening its Tampa factory. He also served as president of Centro Español. CENTRO ESPAÑOL DE TAMPA: BODAS DE ORO.*

*Manuel Corral, an owner of the Corral Wodiska Company factories at the northwest corner of 19th Street and 2nd Avenue, earlier at the southwest corner of 14th Street and Michigan and Avenue, and also at 1604 Cleveland in West Tampa.*

*Angel L. Cuesta, born in Asturias, Spain, moved to Tampa in 1893 and set up a factory in Port Tampa. In 1895 he joined with Peregrino Rey to form Cuesta-Rey and Co., eventually the largest factory in Tampa and the only U.S. factory with a royal appointment as "purveyors of Havana cigars to the Royal Court of Spain, granted by King Alfonso XIII in 1915. J. C. Newman Co. bought the Cuesta-Rey brand in 1959 and its sign crowned the old Regensberg Cigar "El Reloj" building in Ybor City.*



**Chapter 7 · Individual Initiatives, Continued Withering, & Hope: 1970-1980**

## The Historical Research Study for the Ybor City State Museum

An essential element required before formally opening the doors of the completed State Museum was the extensive historical compilation done by Dr. L. Glenn Westfall, the consultant hired by the Division of Archives, History, and Records to research the entire history of Ybor City, from its inception to the time the report was submitted in August 1978. Westfall began his work in December of 1975 when he started a systematic and extensive examination of primary and secondary sources, including study of places, artifacts, and resources such as oral history interviews. His final report is organized thematically, as suggested in the original research project proposal of 1975, with specific sections devoted to the founding of Ybor City; Ybor City as a planned industrial town in the South; Tampa's Cubans and the Spanish American War; the ethnic heritage of Ybor City; the economic impact of the cigar industry on Tampa and Florida; the conflicts between labor and management from 1887 to 1931; and the heyday, decline, and rebirth of Ybor City.

The final book-length report written by Dr. Westfall is a comprehensive study that defines the history of Ybor City and includes much detail. It was the first truly comprehensive and authoritative treatment of our past by a trained historian. To complete his research he visited such key related locations as New York City, Spain, and Key West. Of particular value is his research detailing the lives of the early key players: Vicente Martínez Ybor, Ignacio Haya, Serafin Sanchez, Eduardo Manrara, Gavino Gutierrez, and John Lesley (who sold the key parcel of land to Don Ybor). His study included recommendations to state museum technicians as to appropriate photographs, important dates and sequences of events, possible groupings for display materials, cigar-rolling manual artifacts to locate, interesting folklore by cultural groups, and other practical material. Westfall's extensive research provided the authenticity mandated by the great importance of this project.[19]

## The Empty Years

As it turned out, the "empty middle years" were really the building ground for the final rebirth that would take place in the early 1990s. These slow, disquieting years of the 1970s seemed to follow one another with constant hopes and expectations, but very little change to relieve the blight that enveloped Ybor City.

But the deep foundational supports for rebirth were being set in place in the early '70s. Some of the of these essential pillars were: La Benéfica improvements, the rejuvenation of the old El Pasaje Building, the Winery, the Environmental building, Sheriff's Operations Center, Centennial Park, El Parque Martí, the Ybor City State Museum, sidewalk tilescaping, Haciendas de Ybor, Ybor Square, Hillsborough Community College, and the Frank A. Weaner Latin Quarter Art Gallery.

Adding to an increasing community vitality were the continuing creativity of the artists, the appropriate 9th Avenue lighting from Ybor Square to the Museum building, the new enlarged U.S. Post Office, the Casitas project, and the ongoing beautification of La Sétima, including earlier island construction, night lights, treescaping,

**Ybor City: The Making of a Landmark Town**

landscaping, preservation and repair of the red brick pavements, the earlier Model Cities Program (impacting suburban Ybor), the slow rehabilitation of the social club buildings—so painfully slow—the Immigrant Statue, earlier street signage, and much more. On La Sétima the Joyce Schaffer properties were vastly improved and new quality office buildings evolved.

None of the accomplishments on this apparently lengthy list really seemed to bring in the wealth of tourism expected. These had been sought by the Ybor Chamber since 1931 when it was formed, with the cooperation of many other civic groups. Together these community stalwarts produced many Fiestas, museum events, craft shows, poster contests, bean soup days in Tallahassee, quality restaurants and festive places, Galas, El Carnaval, Avenida de Arte events, artist displays and walks, national Football Bowl, Super Bowl (though this was a miserable rainy day), Sant' Yago parades, and many others.

The infrastructure was there—the result of much civic and city effort, and organizations stemming from ERA and Associates of Boston, the consultants selected in the early 1980s, and the subsequent Redevelopment Agencies of the Bob Martinez years.

But the blight continued. Embarrassing for the Ybor Chamber was the act of scheduling a craft exhibit, art show, or festive event on the main spine when block after block of old, dirty, and visibly messy buildings were plainly visible. No long-term income equalled no money to spend—not a very realistic business equation.

The dismal years finally impacted the Las Novedades Restaurant, founded in 1890, and the Manuel Garcia family closed it in 1972. They succeeded significantly in fast food businesses throughout the state, including some key MacDonalds franchises. Also, the Spanish Park Restaurant, owned by the M. Valdez family, was bulldozed in the early 1990s. By the late 1990s,

*Performers in Latin costumes could be seen on the streets of Ybor in the early 1970s. A young tourist with his family takes a snapshot, but despite creative efforts by Ybor businesses, the tourists were relatively few in number.*

the Valdez family was once again entering the business after a few years of waiting

And the artists left. They had brought in many—but not enough—of the greater Tampa Bay area residents and out-of-town tourist visitors. Daytime interest in the town increased, but the visitors did not bring business adequate to exceed expenses. With the arrival of the larger, deep-pocketed wet bars, and a concomitant heavy increase in night life, many of the artists left, driven out by skyrocketing rents. With a few exceptions they all left.

At the time of the 9th Street lighting project, as we walked east towards 15th Street, Harris Mullen mentioned to me that we still didn't have a "critical mass" of attractions needed to keep tourist families in Ybor City for at least a full day—much less two. Though many substantial improvements had been and were being systematically completed, Ybor still appeared blighted. Many storefronts remained boarded through 1991. The bulldozed fields still stared out bleak and empty. Palm Avenue had not been streetscaped. New signs of life were visible, but so were the empty spaces between them. Despite all of the good work and solid progress, La Sétima still looked forlorn. Hardly a soul

frequented the main spines of the town for serious shopping. Only a few shops remained open, such as the indomitable Raul Vega Jr. and Max Argintar's Men's Clothing stores. Afternoon traffic saw minimal movement, and morning traffic was dismal. It was downright depressing.

If Ybor City's progress could not always be properly evaluated, perhaps one reason was that its historic district was not small. Indeed, it extended from Nebraska Avenue to 22nd Street, and from Columbus Drive to 4th Avenue. By comparison, the Church Street Station area in Orlando is equivalent to only several blocks of central Ybor. The sheer spread made it difficult to impress newcomers—there was so much to be done, over such a large area, that even valiant efforts could be overlooked and lost when measured in the context of the extensive work remaining. In the 1970s and mid '80s this situation was a strong negative. It scared investors. Only Ybor Square to the west, the Columbia Restaurant on the far east, and the oasis of a small park with the adjoining Ybor City State Museum and Patio on 8th Avenue were truly presentable historic points of interest. Most of the other venues were boarded up.

Much, much more was needed. Yet much of the infrastructure had actually been completed. A great deal of preparation and work had been done by the city fathers and civic leaders. And, most important, Ybor City's glorious history was there where it was being gathered so it could be seen and known—a history that will always set this town at the pinnacle—with America's other landmark cities, historic buildings, and national sites.

Even in these blighted years, the best leaders were taking steps to secure a most distinguished award for this most unique town: A National Historic Landmark award to the town's most historic building, and a National Historic Landmark District designation for a deserving town. This was in the making.

The blight would drag our spirits until the very end. But we were starting to hear faint whispers of hope! Unfortunately, the persistent feelings of despair in the last part of the 1970s continued painfully into the 1980s. It seemed to everyone involved in the slow and painful resuscitation that the near-fatal patient would never just sit up and get on with the business of living.[20]

**Ybor City: The Making of a Landmark Town**

An important sign of hope and renewal emerged in 1970 with the construction of the new La Tropicana. Built for Angel "Bebe" Menendez by his brother Joe. La Tropicana was the first new structure on La Sétima in forty years. The personality of Bebe Menendez—and the good food of La Tropicana—made it a success at a time when there was little traffic on the main spine and when other merchants were closing. This Ybor City institution attracted much local business and visits from state and national politicians. The photos above show the restaurant under construction in 1970 and the exterior shortly before completion. At left, Congressman Richard Gephardt, Bebe Menendez, and State Insurance Commissioner Bill Gunter at La Tropicana. LA GACETA.

(Below) The 1970 Model Cities Scholarship Program members speak with Mayor Dick Greco (far right). Those pictured are (left to right, seated) E. L. Crance, Hillsborough Community College; Mrs. Leroy Barco and Mrs. Rita Gerkins, Model Neighborhood residents; State Representative Elvin Martinez. Standing are Scholarship Director and Guidance Counselor Ralph Lazzara III and Model Cities Director John Fernandez. RALPH LAZZARO/LA GACETA.

**Chapter 7 · Individual Initiatives, Continued Withering, & Hope: 1970-1980**

*Along La Sétima in 1975 (left photo) Raul Vega still remained a prominent presence. A view of the street in 1976 (right photo) shows inceased traffic. Cuervo's Restaurant is in the foreground at the right of the 1976 photograph. USFSCL.*

*Catcher Al Lopez (left, with Casey Stengel) was inducted into the Baseball Hall of Fame in 1977. Born in Ybor City, son of an Asturian immigrant, Lopez was catcher for the Tampa Smokers*

*The Spanish Lyric Opera continued to attract audiences throughout the 1970s. Alma Phillips and Antonio Curbelo are shown center stage in the 1977 production of Luisa Fernanda.*

*many years in Cuscaden Park and went on to set a major league record of 1,918 games behind the plate in 19 seasons. As manager for the Cleveland Indians and the Chicago White Sox he held the record of most wins by a manager—1,381.*

*An aerial view of an outdoor art show in Ybor Square in the mid-1970s confirms signs of an increase in the number of visitors for special events.* TREND PUBLICATIONS.

**Ybor City: The Making of a Landmark Town**

*Joan Jennewein was the "point person" for many high-quality initiatives in Ybor City in the mid-Seventies and Eighties. Behind her in this photograph is one of the restored Casitas—a successful result of one of her pet projects in which she was assisted by Stephanie Ferrel, director of HT/CPB. Jennewein is a past president of the Florida Trust for Historic Preservation and was crucial to the state of Florida's purchase of the Centro Español. She worked with Harris Mullen and others for many achievements related to the Ybor City Centennial Park Celebration, including treescaping and lighting. She also served as president of the Tampa and Ybor City Street Railway Society and president of the Ybor City Museum Society. She was a driving force in helping Ybor City achieve its National Historic Landmark designation. Quiet in her ways, she is relentless in her initiatives.*

*Paolo Pupello Longo, born in 1889, was a distinuished man who served the Italian community as a leader from 1912 until his death in 1985. He held many offices and originated the Columbus Association in Ybor City. Today the Paolo Longo Award is presented annually in his honor at an awards dinner in tribute to his memory as a "benevolent and charitable humanitarian," and the annual Paolo Long Award publication is treasured.* Paolo Longo Awards, L' Unione Italiana.

*The old Sanatorio del Centro Asturiano, completed in 1927, received this modern addition in 1975 to become, once again, state-of-the-art. Built on the east side of the older hospital, the new facility and parking lot at 13th Street and 21st Avenue required removal of the huge water tank that had supplied water pressure and a fountain of memories for children who played in its shadow. Unfortunately, the facility had to be closed about 1990. It was a much-loved institution, and its loss was felt by the whole Latin community as the passing of an era.* USFSCL.



**Chapter 7 · Individual Initiatives, Continued Withering, & Hope: 1970-1980**

*Domino players in the cantina of the Italian Club in Ybor City, 1985.*

# Laying the New Foundations: 1980-1990

## New Faces and New Initiatives

There is no question but that the progress of the next two decades is due to the magnetic attraction of Ybor City itself. Newcomers to the town in the 21st Century will no doubt be overcome by the warm ambiance, the compact street grid, the beautiful social clubs, and the many other buildings with striking architectural features: La Benefica, at the corner of 15th Street and Palm Avenue; the Columbia Restaurant; El Pasaje; Las Novedades; and the Labor Temple.

Even just skimming the surfaces two decades ago, one sensed the town's old, authentic, and unusual history. It invited scrutiny. Built around its core were residential and commercial areas ripe for rehabilitation and expansion. There was wealth and potential in the land itself—empty land with paved streets, protected by the bay to the south and I-4 to the north. Much cried out to be done here. By the 1980s, that message was beginning to be heard.

History perhaps will record that this period brought the first mostly "Anglo" invasion of Ybor City—a friendly and productive one—one that would gradually break barriers. It represented an opening of the doors to all who could enhance the contemporary history of Ybor City. This "invasion," despite its Anglo angle, did much to orchestrate the Latin Landmark character of redevelopment and to highlight the need to sustain and articulate Ybor City history. The Anglo arrival was providential for Ybor City, for it brought new energies to a tired populace; it created and helped maintain synergy in civic and commercial activities—until that thrust, too, slipped into history as seemingly just another false start. Indeed, reawakening old Ybor City was to be no easy task.

As the decade of the 1980s began, we sensed that much had been accomplished following Harris Mullen's Ybor Square development, the recognition of the historic value of the city, and the agencies created to preserve it. Then, Ybor City revitalization seemed almost brought to fruition. But suddenly the forces of blight began to strike back with a vengeance. Decay appeared to be gaining the upper hand again, and even the artists left.

### The Ybor City Revitalization Consultant's Study

In July 1979, the Historic Tampa/Hillsborough County Preservation Board (HT/HCPB) applied for a grant from the Heritage, Conservation, and Recreation Service of the U.S. Department of the

*Tampa's status as the home of fine cigars added credibility to the Prince of Tampa label.*

Interior for the purpose of funding a market analysis, a financial analysis, and a development package for the Barrio Latino Historic District in Ybor City. The Preservation Board had completed a survey of cultural resources in Tampa which included Ybor City during its initial survey of cultural resources in Tampa. The estimated cost of the comprehensive follow-up study they proposed to commission under the Interior Department grant was $100,000. The Preservation Board voted tentatively to supply $40,000 toward the matching funds required for a federal grant application of $40,000. This meant that in order to carry out the comprehensive study, approximately $20,000 in additional funding would then need to be raised by the community. To choose the experts who would actually do the study, the Preservation Board appointed a selection committee that included Nelson Palermo, Gill Flores, Lee Menzies, Sharon Russell of the City of Tampa Planning Department, Joel Carlson of the planning commission, and three board members—Victor DiMaio, Dan Masters, and Sol Fleischman Jr. This selection committee, with the help of the Acting Director Stephanie Ferrell, would review proposals submitted by fifteen nationally recognized economic planning and architectural consulting teams.[1]

## Ybor City Development Task Force

On January 3, 1980, Ybor City Chamber of Commerce President Cesar Gonzmart Jr. called a meeting of a newly proposed Ybor City Task Force, listing senior advisory members and regular members. Chairman of the Task Force was Richard Salem, who immediately upon his appointment took the lead in detailing necessary action steps. The Task Force was asked to determine the most suitable organization for leading and implementing renewal efforts, with ideas ranging from a Redevelopment Corporation to a Devel-

opment Authority; to identify the necessary legislation and pave the road for its enactment; to direct attention toward funding and financing (it was doubtful that the City of Tampa would consider providing a budget for it); to prepare a preliminary Land-Use Plan; and then to present the findings before City Council for final adoption.

In addition, the Task Force would evaluate the existing traffic arteries and traffic patterns in relation to Ybor City (they had been altered during Urban Renewal) with the goal of creating an attractive and convenient main thoroughfare from downtown Tampa to Ybor City. It also would address the matter of the continuing demolition of structures, an apparently haphazard and ad hoc process that risked ruining our architectural heritage at the very time when it was finally beginning to gain state and national recognition for its historical value. Underlying all of these challenges remained a need to consider strategies for "repopulating," an essential consideration to provide a realistic consumer base for economic development of the area. The Task Force intended to emphasize the importance of residences in the area as a means of protecting the Latin culture and heritage and maintaining a balance between a continuing Latin populace and other ethnic populations coming in. Last but not least, the group would turn its attention to consideration of the waterfront area along McKay Bay and the Channel area.[2]

At the meeting on January 31, 1980, Chairman Richard Salem read the group's original charge from the City Council in its motion establishing the Task Force that was to explore the possibility of creating an Ybor City Development Authority. At the time, the Ybor City Task Force organization had not been endorsed by Mayor Bob Martínez due to an opposition argument that it might become an Authority, with legislative backing. This would give



**Ybor City: The Making of a Landmark Town**

it the power of taxation and other powers that the mayor deemed inappropriate for nonelected body. The opposition argument had been that an Authority would limit the City's own power, particularly its power to set taxes, and might result in its being at cross purposes with the City's objectives.

Nonetheless, the Task Force moved forward. Its next crucial meeting was held at the Columbia Restaurant. Upon receipt of and explanation of the Mayor's reservations, followed by a supporting vote of confidence from the directors of the Ybor City Chamber of Commerce who had initially created the Task Force concept, the Task Force chairman, Richard Salem, received a positive vote on a compromise proposition that called for the Ybor City Task Force to serve as the Advisory Council to the *Mayor's* Ybor City Task Force. With a subsequent Executive Order by the Mayor, this was given life. Nonetheless, both Cesar Gonzmart Jr's initiatives with respect to the independent Ybor City Task Force, and the Mayor's counterproposal, were viewed by insiders as indispensable to the ultimate outcome. One would not have happened without the other. The final configuration proved to be more inclusive and representative, with elements of independence and collaboration combined in a creative and potentially powerful manner.[3]

## Mayor's Ybor City Development Advisory Committee

On June 5, 1980, Bob Martinez launched the Mayor's Ybor City Development Advisory Committee, with Harris Mullen serving as chairman.[4]

Some of the essential elements of the structure of a major development endeavor had been summarized by the HT/HCPB in the federal application document for the $100,000 grant submitted in July 1979, while the Preservation Board voted to apply $40,000 towards the calculated $140,000.

The funding effort would be handled by the Mayor's Ybor City Development Advisory Committee.

On July 8, 1980, Mayor Bob Martinez addressed the Ybor Task Force and indicated that there were many alternatives for Ybor City including the use of Industrial Development Bonds, an Urban Development Action Grant, Tax Increment Financing, and other methods . . . the City would encourage private development through an upgrading of municipal services including water, sewer, streets, and lighting. The Mayor also indicated that he expected a five-year ripple effect from the downtown to affect Ybor City in a positive manner.

The Task Force found some useful parameters in a 1980 booklet of partial rules published by the Department of Community Affairs of the Division of Housing and Community Development. Entitled "An Enterprise Zone Incentive: a Community Contribution Tax Incentive Program," it outlined how programs could offer tax incentives to developers.

In time the Preservation Board appointed a Selection Committee to choose the planning consultants that included representatives from the Tampa Downtown Development Authority, the City of Tampa planning department, the Hillsborough County Planning Commission, and three Preservation Board members. The individuals serving were Chairman Phillip J. Clark, representing the local chapter of the American Institute of Architects (AIA); Gilbert Flores of the Barrio Latino Commission; Nassir Nagamia of the Hillsborough County City-County Planning Commission; George Pennington from the Mayor's Office; Daniel W. Masters, Sol Fleischman Jr., Victor DiMaio, and Stephanie E. Ferrell (ex officio) of HT/HCPB; and me, Frank Lastra, bringing my background as a trained engineer as well as a member of the Mayor's Ybor City Advisory Committee.[5] This group was to search for and select a top-notch, experienced professional urban redevelopment consulting firm to prepare a comprehensive and informed outside perspective on the issues at hand. The consultants would be asked to make a market analysis, complete an urban design study, prepare financial projections, and compile a redevelopment plan package including all pertinent information appropriate for attracting developers to execute the project.

On September 30, 1980, Selection Committee chairman Clark publicly commented on the excellence of all four qualified finalists under consideration as possible consultant teams and announced that the committee had selected Economic Research Associates (ERA), teamed with Benjamin Thompson Associates for the comprehensive survey and Arthur Ziegler as the consultant for the Ybor City Redevelopment Project. Other finalists that had been interviewed out of some thirty inquiries made, were Gladstone Associates with RTKL; Halcyon with Caesar Pelli and Rowe-Holmes; and Beyer-Blinder-Belle with Hammer-Siler-George.

Within a few months, a renewed sense of purpose and activity emerged within the town. At the December 9, 1980, meeting of the Mayor's Ybor City Advisory Committee on Development, Stephanie Ferrell stressed the importance of the fundraising effort, which at that time was $25,000 short of its goal. But there were signs of progress. Steve Michelini indicated that as of Jan 1, 1981, the city would be soliciting bids on the 9th Street lighting project and the Nebraska-Nuccio intersection improvement. Bob Morrison, representing the Mayor's Office, stated that the City Planning Office should be the planning arm for the project and that requests for planning, legal, or other assistance could be directed to the City.

At a December 19, 1980, meeting of the Mayor's Ybor City Advisory Committee on Development, Cesar Gonzmart Jr. reported that "business is beginning to grow in Ybor City, especially at night at the cafes. The young professionals are coming back and this is a good sign," he said.

## Ybor City Historic District 1983 Revitalization Plan

In May 1983, an Ybor City Historic District Revitalization Plan had been prepared for the Ybor Redevelopment Agency by ERA Associates. The result of a two-year study, the plan recommended development of the district as a high-quality, mixed-use environment, promoting preservation, festive marketing, and tourism, while reinforcing Ybor City's cultural heritage. To those of us who had been long involved in the Ybor City revitalization effort, it had a familiar but appropriate sound. The consulting fee was $130,000. Perhaps the concepts we had been advocating would stand a better chance of being heard with the authority of a long-term study and high price tag behind the report. The ERA representatives made several visits to the area and multiple presentations of work done by their staff. The plans were well-received and much enthusiasm prevailed.

Unfortunately, the plan stalled initially. Bank financing was not available. In the ERA plan, *7th Avenue was recognized as the high quality retail spine*. The plan promoted housing along 7th Avenue between 16th and 19th Streets. It had projected 1,400 residents and the residential component was considered a priority because it would support other retail redevelopment.

**ERA—Partial Recommendations**

| Housing | |
|---|---|
| | 700 D.U. |
| Rehab | 65,000 S.F. |
| New Construction | 635,000 S.F. |
| Parking | 700 cars |
| **Retail** | |
| Units | 300,000 S.F. |
| Rehab | 218,000 S.F |

| | |
|---|---|
| Existing, as is | 42,000 S.F. |
| New Const. | 70,000 S. F. |
| Parking (3/1000) | 990 cars |

**<u>Office</u>**

| | |
|---|---|
| Units | 300,000 S.F. |
| Rehab | 140,000 S.F. |
| Existing, as is | 25,000 S.F. |
| New Const. | 165,000 S.F. |
| Parking ( 2/100) | 660 cars |

**<u>Hotel</u>**

| | |
|---|---|
| Units | 200 Rooms |
| Rehab | 25,000 S. F. |
| New Const. | 170,000 S. F. |
| Parking | 200 cars |

**<u>Parking for Retail
and Office Uses</u>**

| | |
|---|---|
| Surface | 935 cars |
| Structures | 715 cars |

Among other ERA recommendations were the following

**Latin Plaza** site at 16th Street and Seventh Avenue is already developed as a public space at the center on the Seventh Avenue retail district. **The Plaza should be expanded to the east, along Seventh Avenue, by removal of the small freestanding building.** Landscaping, paving, lighting and street furniture comparable with that already in place should be provided in this expanded area to create a substantial cohesive Central Park.

Independent of the ERA plan, this location became home to the *Centro Español Plaza* and was a site for various festive events such as the "City Marketplace" sponsored by Ybor's Entertainment and Arts Association.[6]

## New Support for Revitalization

After Harris Mullen converted Don Vicente's old Principe de Gales factory into the festive warehouse known as Ybor Square in the 1970s, a number of new personalities began to enter the civic and business arenas in Ybor City. Among these was Mullen's son-in-law, Mike Shea. Shea eventually served as president of the Ybor City Chamber of Commerce. He is prob-

ably best remembered for his promotion of a variety of festive entertainments, and particularly for his leading role in originating Guavaween as an annual festival and parade. This colorful and innovative event, now sponsored annually by the Ybor City Chamber of Commerce, is an afternoon and night activity that by 1997 had grown to entertain just under 100,000 people, with the crowds swelling impressively each year. Its popular parade is called the "Mama Guava Stumble."

Joyce Schaffer, developer and contractor, was Shea's principal assistant in establishing Guavaween. She also served as president of the Ybor Chamber in 1985-86 and joined the members of the Chamber's Board of Directors with her son, Jay Fechtel. Both Fechtel and Schaffer were instrumental in the move to rebuild and restore office buildings in Ybor City. In the early 1980s Schaffer purchased two old buildings located on the north side of La Sétima between 17th and 18th Streets, virtually across from L'Unione Italiana. She rehabilitated the second floors to create an elegant cluster of offices featuring attractive archtectural amenities. The bottom floors were renovated as retail shops, art

*Guavaween has grown in size each year from the spirited and colorful but less crowded early parades. The name is an inventive reference to Halloween and to the exotic guava fruit that once indirectly brought the Ybor City location to the attention of the early cigar factory owners.*

studios, and other commercial uses. When completed, the open house received prominent billing by the Ybor Chamber and the preservationists.

Joyce Schaffer's business office was located at the site until the building sold. Her rehabilitation there began the first wave of building updating, which later slowed up somewhat in the late '80s when the continued blight on the Avenue together with other forces, such as artists leaving, became a strong negative. Those days, also, saw the beginning of the contest to select the poster painting that best exemplified the historic area. The first winning poster was presented at Joyce Schaffer's revitalized building, and the event was an upbeat occasion attended by many people interested in Ybor City's rebirth.[7]

Schaffer is, additionally, remembered for her practical and commonsense treatment of the topics of the day. She fostered celebrations, including a memorable one devoted to the historical games of Ybor City, often staging them on the patio of the Ybor City State Museum. There were other poster events, Latin food tastings, and folkloric festivals, some of them ambitiously planned for the main spine of La Sétima. Much of her work for these events occurred behind the scenes. Her more public work in Ybor City in addition to her Chamber leadership was a brief stint chairing the independent and nonprofit Ybor City Redevelopment Corporation, formed in 1987 during the administration of Tampa Mayor Sandy Freedman. Freedman helped finance this grassroots initiative of Ybor business people and property owners with proceeds from Ybor City's designation as a Tax Increment Financing (TIF) district.

Tim Nugent, another Ybor Chamber president (1986-87), continued much of the Chamber's normal civic and Latin entertainment format. Tim is best remembered for his performance as chairman of the Redevelopment Corporation's predecessor, the governmental entity called the Ybor City Redevelopment Agency in 1985. Henry Gonzalez had served as first chairman of the Agency, created by Mayor Bob Martinez in 1983, and was succeeded by Nugent, and then Santos Rodriguez. Both the Ybor City Redevelopment Agency and the Redevelopment Corporation involved significant energy and effort, and will be discussed in greater detail later in this chapter. I was present at most of the Agency meetings and remember that they were well-attended by many interested civic and business leaders. The efforts to attract major investors were often very promising and ably led. The results were limited not by community or city support, but by scarce and insufficient funding. In fact, the major reason solid results were not obtained during the decades of the 1970s and '80s was that the large private developers, after making significant housing presentations, did not deliver when it came time to actually make the investment required.

Each time a significant plan for renewal started to come into focus, talk of troubling new demographics, lack of banking support, and unsettling business realities simply caused these proposed projects to evaporate. Several impressive concepts for community development in Ybor City met this type of fate. Certainly the downtown blight at the core of the town was a factor, but so, too, was an insufficient understanding of the importance of the city's history and its potential importance for future generations.

Among newcomers to Ybor City, Joan Jennewein was one of the few who seemed to grasp both its past and future significance. A soft-spoken person, she was and is nonetheless an extraordinarily effective leader who is known for her persistent and productive efforts to make preservation not only an ideal, but a reality. She facilitated one of the most important success



**Ybor City: The Making of a Landmark Town**

stories of the 1980s, the establishment of Ybor City's "Casita Complex" to save and display for future generations a cluster of the simple little houses called "Casitas" that were the heart of life for the average cigar workers in the early days. (Today their importance in preserving the history of the early days can almost not be overstated, and I have given them special attention on page 299 and in Chapter 10). Jennewein was an ally for the Centennial Celebration, with its many phases and accompanying projects on La Sétima, and she assumed leadership roles in the Ybor Chamber and in the Museum Society, which she served as its second president. She made use of her position as a trustee of the State Preservation Board to assist a variety of Ybor City preservation efforts. Her ties with and knowledge of county, state, and national agencies were highly beneficial to the community's ultimate success in reversing its deterioration. Among her main achievements would be the fight she helped win as champion for the nomination of the Centro Español building as a National Historic Landmark and the even more ambitious effort to designate Ybor City itself as a National Historic Landmark District.

Stephanie Ferrell, the long-term director of the Historic Tampa/ Hillsborough County Preservation Board (see Chapter VII) who had succeeded its first director Phil Wormley when he advanced to do organizational work at the state level, also proved to be a great asset to Ybor City. In particular, her office's technical support (and especially the help of David Rigney) was tremendously useful in enabling Jennewein to proceed successfully with the acquisition and location of the Casita complex buildings in the early 1980s. Her work as a director of the Chamber's board, her management of its business activities, and her numerous supporting activities during the process of initiating the complex application process to qualify for National Historic Landmark District classification were invaluable. Other individuals who were of significant assistance were Bettie Nelson, Pat R. Carter, James R. Turner, Kay Mullen, and Sylvia Vega Smith, past president of the Ybor City Museum Society. They had been principal organizers of the Ybor City Museum Society organization in its earliest days.

## The Cuban Boat Lift and Cesar Gonzmart Sr.

Diplomatic relations between Cuba and the U.S. had not improved since the disastrous Bay of Pigs and the Cuban Missile Crisis in the 1960s. As the 1980s began, many Ybor City Cubans with friends and relatives in Castro's Cuba were desperate to help their suffering compatriots. Most Cuban residents of the Ybor community lived not only with their feelings of helplessness for those who remained in Cuba, they also suffered their lack of success in reviving the fortunes of their own adopted town. However, there remained the conspicuous success of the Columbia Restaurant, and its owner, Cesar Gonzmart Sr., expressed his allegiance to the community. An interview in the *Tampa Times* preserves one of his basic tenets: "The only way the Columbia Restaurant will survive is for Ybor City to survive."[8]

Gonzmart decided to apply his leadership skills in response to the Cuban situation, made worse by the fact that the U.S. government under President Jimmy Carter had tightened restrictions on the Cuban refugee flow. Gonzmart's idea was that not only could he help lift the morale of Ybor City Cubans and improve the lives of captive friends and relatives on the island, he would also recruit a new wave of immigrant energy, hopes, and vitality to help revive the spirit of Ybor City. He determined to sponsor a cruise ship to rescue relatives of Cuban Americans.[9] The project attracted national attention, and soon Cubans from as far away as Alaska, New York, and California were gathered at the Columbia to plan for the trip.[10] Families from around the country, it turned out, were willing to help sponsor the effort, and many of them paid deposits to help cover the monumental expense of the undertaking.

Thus motivated, Gonzmart threw himself into the campaign to bring Cuban refugees to this country. In his various initiatives, he worked with three ships at various times, among them a banana boat called the *Anagua* and a Panamanian ship named the *Rio Indio*. But soon things began to unravel.

The first thing that went wrong occurred on May 9, 1980, as his first ship was to make its way to Tampa. Suddenly the news began to spread that the Sunshine Skyway bridge had fallen after being hit by a freighter, which the Cuban passengers set to depart on the Gonzmart-sponsored ship did not at first believe. Soon enough, however, the catastrophe was confirmed. A 609-foot phosphate freighter called the *Summit Venture* had entered the mouth of Tampa Bay amidst a rainstorm that obscured visibility, and the ship had crashed into one of the major bridge supports, dropping approximately a quarter-mile of the span into the bay. Thirty-five people lost their lives, and the shipping lanes were blocked. The port of Tampa was in chaos. Those circumstances forced the Captain of Gonzmart's ship to change his mind and not make the trip.

Disturbed by the mounting flow of Cuban refugees into cities unprepared to deal with waves of immigrants, President Jimmy Carter issued an edict that called for all vessels unlawfully carrying Cubans to this country to be stopped and turned back. Suddenly prohibited from bringing Cuban nationals to the U.S., Gonzmart offered to take them to any country in the Caribbean or South America which would open its doors to them.

Then, in addition to coping with the operational and governmental restrictions that were plaguing his efforts, Gonzmart found himself facing a monetary crisis due to the large amounts of money advanced by families who were sponsoring Cuban relatives to make the trip. The adverse situations that had stopped the project created some legal problems for Gonzmart when one particular family abruptly filed suit to recover its investment.

The trip, canceled by the Panamanian vessel because Panama had asked the Cuban government to ensure that the ship left empty, cost the project $300,000, of which sum Gonzmart was the trustee. Copies of the checks paid in good faith to the ship's managing corporation were in the court's custody. In the end, a final court ruling relieved the mounting tensions of the situation, and cleared Gonzmart of monetary blame as well as putting to rest any doubts about his personal integrity or governmental opposition.

Those who knew Cesar never questioned his motives. This was perhaps the most important initiative he had ever attempted. His restaurant had been the scene of many Cuban gatherings, with groups of people attempting to hear personal words of encouragement from Gonzmart himself. His efforts had placed him in charge of an endeavor that had become more intricate with each passing day. Finally, though the effort failed through no fault of his own, it was still a serious blow to Gonzmart, who had put himself on the line because of his belief in and dedication to this project. He had seen this as a chance to help the Cuban people and the town he loved. Like presidents, diplomats, and patriots before him, he ended his venture into Cuban-American problem-solving frustrated and disheartened.

There were a few cynics who uttered unappreciative words in those days, but those who knew Cesar never questioned his integrity or the depth of his convictions.[11]

## Environmental Building

In the early 1970s the empty land that then lay dormant in Ybor City offered Hillsborough County government a rare chance to open or relocate municipal offices and agencies from Tampa's central core or distant suburbs to a more convenient site. A new building for the Environmental Protection Agency of Hillsborough County, built on 19th Street and Palm Avenue, was one such early success story. Construction of the new facility brought new people and economic energy to the area. When the Roger P. Stewart Environmental Center opened, employees offered much-needed support to the remaining eating houses. In particular, La Tropicana benefited, for suddenly the restaurant had a steady and dependable stream of daily diners.

The decision to redevelop land in Ybor City for the Environmental Agency building—and additional property for the nearby Sheriff's Operations Center at 2008 8th Avenue—would in years to come be blamed for preventing the construction of much-needed upscale housing and additional businesses in the core area, but for the interim two or three decades, their presence proved to be a blessing for daytime merchants. They brought much-needed stability at a time of change.

The new Hillsborough County Sheriff's Operations Center served more than one good civic cause. It doubled the amount of usable space that was available to that essential department while drawing much-needed financial and human re-

*Today the Roger P. Stewart Environmental Center is a hub for coordination of the county's work to monitor and protect the environment. Appropriate landscaping and lighting has given the building a natural look that helps it blend into the community and avoids a sterile, institutional image. RM.*

**Chapter 8 · Laying the New Foundations: 1980-1990**

The Hillsborough County Sheriff's Operations Center combines law enforcement functions that were once spread out in three cramped and outdated locations in downtown Tampa. RM.

sources into the area. It was paid for through a $6.3 million bond issue. The operations center had been budgeted as a $2 million project, with an additional $4.3 million in bonds slated for an expansion of the county jail in Tampa. As design work moved forward, however, it became clear that the county's needs already had exceeded the first estimates, and with population growing by leaps and bounds, it became clear that a much larger facility would be needed. Planners and architects went back to their drawing boards, and county administrators reconsidered bond fund allocation. Originally scheduled to open in mid-August of 1978, the Operations Center was not occupied until late January of 1979. Major David Parish of the Sheriff's administrative division was quoted at the time as saying that the staff was "stepping on each others' toes" as they eagerly awaited the move.[12] The Ybor office consolidated sheriff's operations that had been spread among three different buildings—the Hillsborough County jail, the Stovall building, and the county courthouse annex. The decision to move the center to the Ybor site not only "made sense because of its proximity to the courthouse and major traffic arteries," Parish said, "it made sense from a monetary perspective, also."[13]

The plans hit a stumbling block, however, when Ybor City's architectural review board—the Barrio Latino Commission, the body from which final approval had to come for all the planned construction in the Latin district—disapproved a 300-foot communication tower that had been slated to sit atop the facility. After about four months of disagreement and deliberation, a compromise was agreed upon and Barrio Latino[14] finally approved a small microwave transmitting dish in lieu of the tower.[15]

While this building, like the Environmental Center, tied up very valuable Ybor City land, its construction not only gave the area a visible symbol of the law and order values long-time residents believed in, but just as the Environmental building had done, it arrived upon the scene during the preliminary phase of Ybor City revival, at a time when restaurants and other Ybor City businesses were deperately in need of reasons for hanging on. Many of the Sheriff's Department employees today fill the nearby coffee shops and dining rooms each day. Though originally much debated by the locals as to their suitability for Ybor City, these two agencies proved to be congenial neighbors, and the majority opinion today seems to be that they made great additions to the area. Looking back, it is difficult to imagine how many of the key merchants would have survived without them.

In the late 1970s and early 1980s, informal and preliminary planning had been taking place to revitalize Ybor City. The Historic Tampa/Hillsborough County Preservation Board, the Barrio Latino Commission, the Ybor City Chamber of Commerce, and the City of Tampa all joined to convince private developers that now was the time to build in Ybor City.

"Ybor City has not received much attention compared to downtown or Hyde Park," said Stephanie Ferrell, head of the Preservation Board and, at the time, also

296

serving as chair of the Barrio Latino Commission. "Scarce housing close to downtown Tampa makes Ybor City a prime target for residential and commercial development."[16]

The truth of the matter was, however, that private investors and developers were slow to step forward. As part of the effort to promote development, a University of Florida Department of Architecture project began the task of photographing and sketching important historic buildings, completing a booklet, drawing, and models that highlighted preservation, appropriate new uses for old buildings, and possible new construction styles that would complement and enhance the old. The purpose of this was to suggest ideas that would lead to proposals for housing, businesses, and transportation in the historic area. Some thirty students spent ten weeks doing the project. The students' work cost $1,300, of which the Preservation Board paid $1,000, with Ybor Square owner Harris Mullen contributing the additional $300.

One proposal included construction of a railroad depot that would connect Ybor City with downtown Tampa. The whole project envisioned by the student architects stressed "mixed use" zoning where residential and commercial uses would be combined.[17]

Models and drawings from the project were displayed at the Frank A. Weaner Latin Quarter Gallery, which at that time was the new home of the Ybor City Chamber of Commerce. The presentation was imaginative and professional. It conveyed a very impressive vision, and it energized many of the civic leaders at the time. Little came directly out of this initiative, though the various three-dimensional displays helped others begin to see new possibilities. And for many who had worked tirelessly to reverse the town's decay, such a tangible, three-dimensional rendering made the dream seem not so remote and out of reach. In fact, some components of

this project, such as the railroad depot concept, continued to be discussed and helped shape future agendas.

## The Ybor City Museum Society

At the Ybor City Museum's dedication ceremony in 1980, Bettie Nelson, who had served two years as president of the Tampa Historical Society and was active in community affairs, suggested to Stanford Newman, the president of Standard Cigar Company and the Cigar Manufacturers Association, that an auxiliary group would be helpful to the museum. He agreed. In this informal way, the Ybor City Museum Society began.[13] First there was a small organizational steering committee formed by Newman that met at the Columbia Restaurant on January 29, 1981, and recommended a slate of officers: Bettie Nelson, president; Dr. Glenn Westfall, historian; Jim Turner, secretary; and Stan Newman, vice president. When the group had its first board meeting at Nelson's home on February 17, Alice Bustelo was named treasurer, and the board was complete. This was the group that actually launched the society.

Over the next two years they talked and planned. Their ideas culminated in a charter membership reception on March 18, 1983, in the beautiful Museum Patio. Mayor Bob Martinez was named the First

*The Ferlita Bakery Building is an Ybor City landmark that not only speaks to history through its distinctive architecture, but continues to deliver a nourishing feast of history and culture to the community and its tourists through the Ybor City State Museum now housed there. RM.*

297

Honorary Member. He, in turn, presented the society with a resolution declaring 1986 as the Centennial Year for Ybor City. Ney C. Landrum came from Tallahassee for the occasion to report the exciting news of a possible addition to the Museum. Soon there was work for the Society to do. The restoration of a cigar worker's house had been a popular idea for some years, and Elizabeth Ehrbar, the exhibits supervisor for the museum, wrote Nelson to ask if the Society would be interested in endorsing such a project. The board promptly returned a positive vote, and Nelson arranged an initial meeting on July 27, 1983, calling together interested groups who could work together to make it happen. Landrum came from Tallahassee for the meeting. The movement that resulted in the Casitas complex previously discussed was off to an ambitious start. The remaining available *casitas*—the narrow cigarworkers' houses that had once been so typical of Ybor City—were discussed, identified, and looked at. The idea took root more deeply, and it grew. One house alone would not convey the feeling of the history. The group would try for something more.

At a general membership meeting on July 28, Stephanie Ferrell, director of the Historic Tampa/Hillsborough County Preservation Board, spoke about tax credits for historic preservation. Her discussion underscored the advantages of a sponsoring organization having formal nonprofit status. Following that talk the membership voted to amend its incorporation articles to comply with IRS requirements so that the society would be exempt from federal income tax.

The pace of Society activities increased. The first two issues of its newsletter, Volume 1, were written and mailed using a new nonprofit bulk mail permit #3472. Catherine Healy and Nootchie Smith were named co-chairs of a Museum Planning Committee to focus on long-range planning. Membership co-chairs,

Kay Mullen and Stan Newman provided the Society with an excellent roster. Tony Pizzo agreed to serve as chairman of the promotional committee and Calvin Carter became creative consultant.

Nelson had another goal close to her heart in addition to the restoration of the workers' houses, and that was to initiate steps that could provide the Society an appropriate place to "hang its hat," as she had done with the acquisition of the historic Peter O. Knight House in Hyde Park for the Tampa Historical Society. A cigar worker's house seemed to be an appropriate spot for an Ybor City historical support group, and this became a way of expanding the initial idea of restoring a single house.

Thus the Society began the ambitious goal of relocating some of Ybor City's original workers' houses to a spot where they could be restored, appreciated, and used. The effort was called Ybor City Preservation Park, and a site plan (reproduced at right) showed it in relation to the museum courtyard and what became known as Ybor Centennial Park. Great credit for the success of this imaginative venture goes to the quick, visionary grasp of Ney C. Landrum, Director of the Florida Park Service, in cooperation with City of Tampa's Parks and Recreation Department, working with a coalition of diverse groups from the city, county, and state. Great credit also goes to Mayor Bob Martinez and the progressive philosophy of his administration in providing the necessary linkage to make it all happen with a renewed vigor expressing the unique cultural, historical, and architectural heritage that is the keystone of Ybor City.

On October 26, 1983, at the first Annual Banquet, a new president took the helm of the Ybor City Museum Society. Joan Jennewein, former president of Tampa Preservation, Inc., and a board member of the National Trust for Historic Preservation, was named president for 1983-84.

*A view of typical housing in Ybor City in the 1890s. The streets were not yet paved, and the identical homes in this factory town were known as "canones casitas."* THCPLS.

*Photographer Brian Koepnick took this documentary photograph (left) of an Ybor City casita at 1416 East 14th Avenue as it looked in the 1970s. His work is part of the Historic American Buildings Survey that began in 1933 as a WPA program and continues as a collaborative project of the American Institute of Architects, the National Park Service, and the Library of Congress.* LOC.

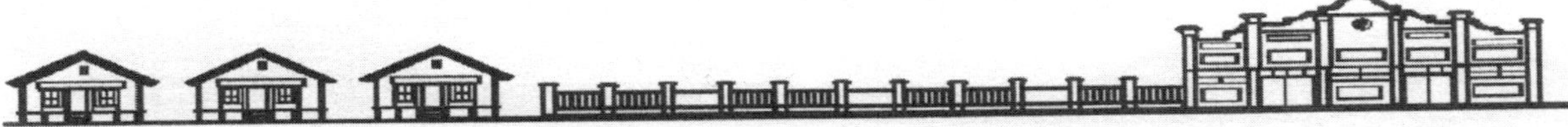

*The architect's rendering of the Ybor City State Museum and its three adjacent casitas down the block has become the Museum's logo on the newsletter from the Ybor City Museum Society and even on paper bags from the gift shop.* YCSM/GIL FLORES, ARCHITECT.

*Today the restored casitas at 1800 East 9th Avenue allow visitors to experience the scale and features of the shotgun houses constructed for workers. They had no electricity or plumbing, but featured good cross ventilation, shutters for privacy, and porches where families spent considerable time visiting with one another and with neighbors from porch to porch.* RM.

*Tampa Mayor Bob Martinez (left) created the Ybor City Redevelopment Agency in 1983. He is shown here with Henry Gonzalez Jr., whom he named as first chairman of the agency. Gonzalez was succeeded by Tim S. Nugent and Santos Rodriguez who served successively to chair the agency during the administration of Mayor Sandy Freedman.*

*Celebrating the Ybor City Fiesta (above) are, from left, Braulio Alonso, the 1986 Latin Fiesta Princess Yamel Moralejo, Governor Bob Martinez, and Italian Club President Vince Pardo.*

*Guy St. Paul (left) was elected first President of the "new" Ybor City Round Table, Inc., in the centennial year of 1986. He convened representatives from some 20 civic organizations in the Siboney Room to propose they unite and speak with one voice for Ybor City's future and the preservation of its heritage. His efforts received continuing support from Floyd Head and Steve Lester, who became second and third presidents of the group, and from the colorful Ybor City Alcalde Sam Leto, who followed them to serve as president in 1993-94.*

300

*Members of the Ybor City Centennial Committee at a party in 1986. Left to right are Harris Mullen, Mercedes Ybor, unidentified, Fernando Mesa, Maria Julia Ybor, and Angel Bustelo.*

**Ybor City: The Making of a Landmark Town**

Joan's administration placed emphasis on promotion of Ybor City—promoting tourism, community awareness, and Ybor City's heritage through the development of Ybor City Preservation Park and the initiation of an impressive array of Centennial activities. As with many promotional activities, simple and almost obvious steps can make a tremendous difference. Directional signs requested by the Society were installed and helped to more than double attendance at festival events. And the "Bay Area Museums and Galleries Guide" was published, helping to make the historic and cultural treasures of Ybor City much more visible and accessible.

On October 17, 1984, the Society hosted a patron reception, beautifully organized by Kay Mullen, for three hundred people attending the Southeastern Museum Conference. Secretary of State George Firestone was delighted by our "jewel of a museum." From this "jewel" there radiated an energy that helped put the shine on many other aspects of the area.

Working together, the Department of Natural Resources, the Historic Tampa/Hillsborough County Preservation Board, the City of Tampa, and the Ybor City Museum Society set about recreating a typical turn-of-the century streetscape adjacent to the museum patio. The result was the Casitas Complex previously discussed, and worth mentioning again here in its chronological context, for the tremendous effort and logistical planning necessary to bring this about started in the 1980s and became a reality as the decade progresseed.

Tampa Preservation, Inc., (TPI) moved six endangered 1890s cigar workers' houses to this site. The TPI Board, which had leased the back half of the block, renovated three of the houses relocated there as offices for the Barrio Latino Commission and itself. The Department of Natural Resources completely restored one of three houses facing 9th Avenue as a "Casita" museum and restored the exteriors of the other two. The interior of one was renovated to become the Ybor City Museum Society's headquarters, providing additional exhibit space and a museum shop. Programs outlining the goals and progress of the project were given at meetings of the Ybor City Chamber of Commerce and the Ybor Redevelopment Agency. This was (and is) a work in progress that is recreating clear glimpses of the past. Preservation Park and the adjacent state/city park and marketplace, are becoming centers of major tourist activity.

Cigar House researcher Dr. Pat Waterman of the University of South Florida Anthropology Department worked with Junior League volunteers to provide detailed cultural and historic information that could serve as the research foundation for the whole Preservation Park. Local historian Bettie Nelson and Maria Julia Martinez-Ybor were asked to co-chair this committee.

The Museum's membership committee, chaired by Kay Mullen, assisted by Maria Pasetti and Alice Bustelo, began ambitious efforts to expand participation and involvement. The goal was to have six membership functions by 1986, three of them social and three educational. The first three were held in 1984: the kick-off to Preservation Park on March 14, the Spring membership party on May 17, and the annual meeting on November 19.

On November 19, 1984, the third roster of Ybor City Museum Society officers was introduced. Officers installed at the event, held in Ybor Square due to rain, were Mrs. Calvin W. Carter, president; James R. Turner, president elect; Rafael Martinez-Ybor, second vice president; Mrs. Vance Smith, secretary; and Mrs. Angel Bustelo, treasurer. Harris Mullen received the first annual Ybor City Museum Society Outstanding Citizen Award, and Ney Landrum received an award from the Society expressing sincere appreciation for his great help. Other awards of appreciation were given to Tampa Mayor Bob Martinez, Frances Kruse, of Tampa Preservation, Inc.; Hampton Dunn and David Rigney, of the Historic Tampa/Hillsborough County Preservation Board; and, B. J. Altschul.

It was decided at the first board meeting of these officers that a written history of the Ybor City Museum Society was essential, and Bettie Nelson was asked to compile and write the story (from which my summary of its progress has been gathered).

One of the most successful fundraisers as well as one of the most popular events undertaken by the Society was reviving the Matinee Tea Dance on December 2, 1984, at the historic Centro Español Club building. Tea Dances had been an age-old tradition of the city, but had been lost in the dislocations and disruptions of Ybor City life. The Society's revival afforded a warm, inviting connection with the past. It was repeated in the Spring of 1985 at the Centro Asturiano Club building. Beautifully organized by Chair Alice Bustelo, it was a sell-out not only as a fundraiser, but a smash hit with both members and residents. Dr. Dennis Pupello donated his wonderful and appropriate music with his band, the "Heart Beats," and Jack Espinosa was pulled from the audience to repeat his ever-popular role as a stand-up comedian.

A formal coalition of Tampa Preservation Inc., the Junior League of Tampa, HT/HCPB, Florida Department of Natural Resources, and the Ybor City Museum Society, was formed to exchange information and execute action in a more coordinated manner as the last of the cigar workers' houses had been moved to Preservation Park.

With Carole Guyton (Mrs. John Guyton) serving as Chairman, the Society began initial plans to renovate the second house, and Rafael Martinez-Ybor kicked off a drive in September 1985 to raise funds to renovate and reimburse TPI for moving expenses. Kay Mullen served as chairman to establish a new program. Volunteers began to serve as hostesses at the Museum, allowing the Rangers to care for additional duties.

And so . . . under the excellent leadership of Pat R. Carter and her officers and board the adopted logo of the architectural drawing of the Museum, loaned by Gil Flores, Architect, has become widely known and immediately recognizable on letters, brochures, and even the paper bags the tourists carry away filled with mementos of their visit to this historic site.

On September 18, 1985, a new slate of officers would be installed. Bettie Nelson, first Ybor City Museum Society President, ended her committee's report with the following beautiful words: "Quo Vadis, Ybor City! The Ybor City Museum Society walks beside you, and wishes you always, all ways, the very best!"[18]

## Ybor City Centennial Celebrations

In the early 1980s Harris Mullen and Tony Pizzo organized a steering committee representing Ybor City organizations and related interests to begin planning for the 1986 Ybor City Centennial. Officers of the committee were Harris Mullen, chairman; Tim Nugent, vice chairman; Joan Jennewein, secretary-director; and Rafael Martinez Ybor, treasurer.

The celebration of the founding of Ybor City by Don Vicente Martínez Ybor in 1886 would be a two-year event: 1985 and 1986. Below is a summary of the activities that took place throughout these two festive years. Point person was Joan Jennewein.

"The Hillsborough County Commissioners provided the committee with $47,000 in resort tax money to prepare for the event," Committee Chairman Harris Mullen told a small group at the museum at 1818 Ninth Avenue.[19] Though this initial funding was quite modest, it raised the spirits and sparked the imagination of those involved. Led by Joan Jennewein and others, a team of dedicated volunteers arranged an inspiring series of events for these two festive years.

## 1985

A poster contest was held for the artistic poster that best captured the history, architecture, and spirit of Ybor City. Local civic and social organizations arranged events and attractions for residents and visitors alike: an Arts and Crafts Fiesta at Ybor Square, repeated many weekends; inauguration of a bus service from downtown Tampa to Ybor City; a birthday celebration for Ybor City's founding father, Don Vicente Martínez Ybor; continuous improvements along La Sétima; a balcony-reconstruction program; Hispanic Heritage Week, with a Columbus Day Celebration; an art show and 80th birthday festivities for the Columbia Restaurant; a Halloween Parade and Ball; the premiere of a Lightfoot Films documentary on Ybor City at the Ritz Theatre; publication of a special double issue of *Tampa Bay History* devoted to Ybor City; a Christmas Tea Dance; and the Ybor City Museum Society's Ybor City Christmas *Pascuas.*

## 1986

Highlights of the year included a Grand Centennial kickoff; a Hispanic Heritage Festival; an Ybor City Exhibit; and the opening of the Mascotte Room at City Hall. Organizations and businesses continued their implementation of facade improvements and balcony-restoration programs. There was a Special Centennial Edition of *Tampa Tribune-Times*; a Centennial Gala (an invitational fundraiser); a Maria Benitez Dance Troupes event; a birthday celebration for José Marti, the "George Washington of Cuba;" an Ybor City Marathon; and the official opening of Preservation Park and the Cigar Maker's House Museum.

Events that were fast becoming important new Ybor City traditions included a Gasparilla Festival Fiesta Day; "Ybor City Carnivale/ Krewe of Sant' Yago Night Parade; a "Night in Olde Ybor;" a Seafood Festival; an "Imagination Festival" of the J. F. Kennedy Center for Performing Arts; a Children's Art Festival emphasizing the Latin heritage of Ybor City presented with a "Music Under the Stars" series of concerts; Ybor City Family Weekend; Artist in the Schools Program; and an Ybor City traditional Folk Art Festival followed by a "Concert in the Park" by the Florida Orchestra. One of the most memorable events was an International Festival sponsored jointly by the Embassy of Spain, the Tampa Museum of Art, the Tampa Bay Performing Arts Center, and Ybor City, at which the Spanish Ambassador from Washington, D.C., was present for a beautiful and memorable occasion at the Museum Patio.

Unquestionably the team of Harris Mullen, Rafael Martinez Ybor, Tim Nugent, and Joan Jennewein succeeded in awakening justified pride about Ybor City. Participating were many sponsors, money raisers, promoters, event chairpersons, and support personnel throughout the community.[20]

### The Ybor Redevelopment Agency

In early 1983, the Ybor Redevelopment Agency was created by Mayor Bob Martinez to gradually implement the consultants' recommendations. Established as an independent unit with its own board members and chairman, its home office was the old Broadway Bank building at La Sétima and 17th Street. It pursued a free enterprise approach, seeking investors and scheduling presentations by serious developers, while coordinating their work with various city departments and keeping the pertinent civic organizations apprised of plans and opportunities. Also, it kept the official running score on progress in the core area. The group featured some of the more animated civic and business leaders in the area as members of its board. The first three chairmen, in order of their service, were Henry Gonzalez, Tim Nugent, and Santos Rodriguez. Building on its thorough background study, Economics Research Associates was engaged to write a "Technical Memorandum" entitled "Ybor Historic District Revitalization Plan."[21]

By 1983 the recommendations were being made public, including a call for more than $90 million in investments for projects such as a 200-room hotel, townhouses, specialty stores, an old-fashioned square and an outdoor food market. The report envisioned a trolley shuttling between Ybor and downtown Tampa, plus new or renovated stores and offices with jobs for 3,000 workers and new housing for 1,400 residents.[22]

Newspaper coverage and construction records show that both private and public efforts soon began showing results. "Private Projects Give a Boost to Ybor City Redevelopment," proclaimed a *Tampa Tribune* headline. The story reported more than $3 million dollars in private projects with two new restaurants just opening and a winery in the planning stages. Carmine's Restaurant relocated from Buffalo Avenue in Tampa to La Sétima at 19th Street "in a building bought and renovated for about $350,000."[23]

The newspaper report reviewed details of the redevelopment effort:

> The private enterprise projects are the biggest developments since the announcement this past winter of a $175,000 consultant's study that recommended $80 million private investment and $10 million public improvements over a 10 year revitalization period," according to Tim Nugent, then director of the Ybor Redevelopment Agency.
>
> Agency board chairman, Henry Gonzalez said he hopes the restaurants and winery will spur residential construction in Ybor. The winery will employ about 20 persons, said Edward V. Gogel, president of the Wines of St. Augustine. While a "shell" in which the wine will be produced should be ready in July 7, Gobel projected a September or October completion for the Latin-style complex that will include a wine tasting room, offices and space for several shops. Tours of the winery are expected to draw visitors to Ybor.[24]

Two years later some of the momentum had been lost. On March 25, 1985, the *Tribune* reported:

> "The Ybor Park and Farmers' Market has been delayed by differences on how to build it," says the Ybor Redevelopment Agency Director.
>
> The city of Tampa is dragging its feet in vital redevelopment projects in Ybor City, some area leaders are saying ...and a historic district ordinance that would provide redevelopment guidelines and ban businesses such as X-rated theaters and plasma centers has become a point of contention between Ybor boosters and municipal officials. . . . The Ybor land-use plan is part of a city wide zoning update that is complicated and may take several more months to complete . . . . Nugent and the zoning officials disagree about the very nature of the zoning staff's revision dealing with building setbacks, new parking and where to build single and multifamily housing . . . . The city currently is negotiating with one developer to build about 300 condominiums and apartments on vacant land near the Ybor City State Museum.[25]

Nonetheless, by the end of March 1985, during Bob Martinez's watch, some $12 million in new buildings and area restorations had been made, and the city had invested $2.6 million to restore sidewalks and lampposts, and proceed with planning.

At the Redevelopment Agency board meetings, many individual development plans were presented by various companies, including serious housing projects, generally in keeping with the area's original ERA consulting plans.[26] But in several instances, lack of bank financing and continued blight in the area discouraged the developers and finally, the Agency itself. Demographics may have been of concern for developers.

Finally, the Agency was put on hold.

By this time, during my many trips to Ybor City, I noticed a large improvement in the overall look of the still vacant areas, attesting to the large amount of work done by the city. The incoming view approaching Ybor City was now more impressive than driving into the Tampa approaches. This was especially true as one drove eastward on Palm Avenue (10th Street) into Ybor. This could not be said of the areas generally surrounding downtown Tampa, most of which remained blighted into the very early '90's, a comparison the writer made on purposeful drives along various approaches to downtown Tampa from different directions. It definitely showcased considerable land, streets, lighting, trees, and other improvements that had been made. And it lifted the spirit. One could sense that the potential for a great town was slowly in the making. Much of the essential infrastructure was visible.

## Zoning Ordinance

In 1986 a zoning ordinance plan was approved. The plan was adopted via the creation of special zonings for Ybor City then underway. The ordinance provided for the division of the Ybor District into six zones. Included in this ordinance were incentive tools or financial incentives, such as tax increment financing, exclusion from city-wide transportation impact fees, tax credits, and federal tax advantages for rehabilitation of buildings. Other incentives were added through the start of the forthcoming Ybor City Development Corporation, and its fabric is still essentially in place. Gradually, some of the last remaining impediments to redevelopment were thus removed.[27]

## Ybor City Round Table, Inc.

Coordination of improvements efforts is never a simple matter, and often issues become tangled in hierarchy of authorities. What emerged eventually in Ybor City was an altogether different model, allowing a convening of equals united by a common purpose. It seems altogether appropriate that the group's name held an allusion to Arthur's round table in Camelot.

Steve D. Lester, former Ybor City Round Table president, sent me a letter to explain the history of this key group, and my account is based largely on his information. In the Ybor City festive Centennial year of 1986, Guy St. Paul was elected President of the colorful Alcalde Association. Sam D. Leto, in turn, was elected Alcalde (Honorary Mayor) for a record of three terms.

Some three hundred special guests attended the installation banquet held in the Siboney Room of the historic Columbia Restaurant. At the podium, both Guy St. Paul and Sam Leto spoke eloquently of the urgent need for all organizations to keep the city's glorious history factual, preserve its tri-ethnic heritage, and continue Ybor City's restoration and growth to become the South's major "Latin Quarter." Guy St. Paul recalled that in 1940 Rogelio Berdeal had formed The Ybor City Round Table to speak for all Ybor City in one voice. And from him, Guy St. Paul procured many notes and ideas for launching of a new organization to reaffirm this ideal.

Lester commented in his letter that at the numerous meetings following the 1986 installation, many presidents "lamented the fact that Ybor City's progress was now on such an accelerated basis that instead of Ybor City developing into what it should be, it might develop into what those in charge today wanted it to be. A chief complaint was that the present spokesmen had in the last few years fallen into the hands of aggressive influential persons who often were new to the area and speedily strove for progress at any cost. As an example they pointed out that too much emphasis was being placed on late-night liquor bars instead of slowly promoting a well-balanced housing and business mix. They predicted that liquor bars would eventually discourage your better class of people from investing in the area and definitely kill tourism." There is no doubt that such a trend violated the historic values of the town and could, if not restrained and balanced, alter the flavor of the community beyond recovery.

During Guy St. Paul's first year in office the Round Table was incorporated for the first time, including a constitution with democratic input by all clubs. In one of its first actions, Sam Leto was appointed to head the Special Committee for an Ybor City Immigrant Statue, which today stands in Centennial Park across from the Ybor City State Museum. This statue is emblematic of the essential values of the past. Its image bespeaks the depth and diversity of the town's culture and the determination of those who have appreciated it and affirmed it to see that this history not be lost in the glitter of contemporary clubs and merchandise. Family, determination, unity, dignity, and hard work are part of the picture, along with wholesome fun— and to that end, the Round Table organization is the sponsor of the annual Alcalde Association event, with all its revelry.[28]

### The Casita Complex (1980-85)

By the mid-1980s the work of Joan Jennewein, the Ybor City Chamber of Commerce, the Museum Society, and Stephanie Ferrell, director of the Preservation Board had accomplished the development of the Casita Complex. It was envisioned as a "streetscape" of preserved historic buildings that would be a Preservation Park. Three cottages that had originally been located next to each other in the 1500 block of 5th Avenue had been relocated to the northeast corner of 9th Avenue and 18th Street. In front of them now stood Ybor Park (later renamed "Centennial Park") with its Immigrant Statue. One of the houses was fully restored as a cigar worker's house museum with furnishings dating from 1895 to 1920. The second or third casita housed the Ybor City State Museum office and the demonstration casita, respectively. Soon after, the first, or corner casita, was occupied by the Ybor City Chamber of Commerce.

Now volunteers led visitors on a walk into the past through a cottage typical of residences built throughout Ybor City by the cigar manufacturers for their workers between 1885 and 1915. Now guides were heard explaining that the frame cottages were often referred to as "cañones" (cannon houses), because was said that one could fire a cannon down the central hallway, front to rear, without hitting anyone. The rooms were on either side.

There was an advantage in the fact that these homes had stood next to one another, for a visitor could gain a correct sense of scale and size while walking through or pausing for a few minutes on a porch. Originally the homes lacked heat, electricity, or running water. There was no insulation, and shutters provided protection from the heat of the day. Cheese cloth was often used to protect against mosquitoes. Water, at first, came from springs and rain barrels, later from hand pumps by the back door or inside. Also, there were no septic tanks then. Among the daily household chores was the emptying of chamber pots. Early bathroom facilities in Ybor City were outdoors. Italians referred to them as "backahous," meaning the toilets were in the back of the housse. And the roofs of many homes were covered with galvanized metal sheets after the 1908 fire destroyed entire blocks in the town as the fire jumped from house to house from cinders and sparks igniting neighboring unprotected foortops. Many of the original homes in the historic areas and in the suburbs still have tin roofs today.

Other landowners and investors later continued the pattern, varying in the design. These houses are not representative of

the second or last wave of housing that took place in the late 1910s to early and later 1920s. These later houses were the result of the normal evolutionary process where those that could moved out of the barrio and built new modern wood housing.[29]

The Casita Complex had come to life and was working, passing on the oral history of the town through trained volunteers to new generations of residents as well as visitors. Thanks to vision and practical hard work, we had created a community complex that could serve Ybor City at relatively low cost to the city and the public. It has provided a hub around which much Ybor City civic life revolves.

This complex has worked well for going on two decades, and must continue to be strengthened and developed for the future. In 1997, Mary Alvarez, president of the Ybor City Museum Society, submitted a proposal to add more casitas on land owned by the Sheriff's Operation Center facing Centennial Park. The specific houses were selected and in due time were moved into place.

### Tony Pizzo: Historian

Tampa and Ybor City were blessed by the presence of a local son with the talent and vision to record and preserve what he valued in the past. He was a man possessed of a great love of the history of Tampa and of the town he grew up in. His passing in 1994 left a great void in Tampa.

Pizzo became Hillsborough County's official historian in 1984 after having made innumerable contributions to historical research and preservation. He was born on September 22, 1912, the grandson of Sicilian immigrants. His parents, Paul and Rosalia Pizzolato Pizzo, ran a grocery store in Ybor City, and Tony grew up right in Ybor. As a lifelong member of the community, he witnessed many of the historical changes he wrote about in his books, including *Tampa Town, 1824-86: The Cracker Village with a Latin Accent* (1968)

and *Tampa's Italian Heritage* (1978) and he co-authored *Tampa: The Treasure City* in 1983 with Gary Mormino, eminent history professor of the University of South Florida.

In 1971 Pizzo founded the Tampa Historical Society, now with some six hundred members. He was responsible for the placement of more than eighty historical markers in Tampa and Ybor City. After graduating from Stetson University in Deland, Florida, Tony went into business. He mastered the wholesale liquor business, and imported wines from Spain and Italy with Tampa Wholesale Liquor, the House of Midulla, where he held a range of executive titles including general manager, vice president, and president.

He travelled in Spain and Sicily, where he gathered much historical material that he later used to develop his understanding of Tampa's heritage. His persistent personal interest and curiosity drove him deeper and deeper into history. His steadfastness at finding the elusive threads of Tampa and Ybor City legacies led him early on to meetings with Cuban President Fulgencio Batista, Col. Manuel Quevedo of the Cuban Army, and Blas O'Halloran (son of West Tampa Cuban patriot and

*Tony and Josephine Pizzo were both active promoters of historic preservation. Tony was acclaimed as Hillsborough County's official historian. A ceaseless worker for preservation, he founded the Tampa Historical Society and initiated its Historical Plaques project that now has placed more than a hundred permanent markers to identify important historical locations throughout the county. He also was important in the establishment of José Martí Park and in undertaking many other initiatives, some of them in connection with the Ybor City Rotary Club. The annual Tony Pizzo Award commemorates his memory as it honors the efforts of others to promote knowledge and preservation of local history. La Gaceta.*

307

*Historical markers like these now help visitors and area residents alike to know and remember the area's history. Tony Pizzo established the format and began the project of placing them throughout the county. RM.*

*Today this statue of historian Tony Pizzo stands in the southwest corner of Ybor City Centennial Park to commemorate his many contributions to Ybor City and his work on behalf of preserving and sharing its history. RM.*

*Santos Rodriguez became the third director of the Ybor City Redevelopment Agency, appointed by Mayor Sandy Freedman. He fostered major public/private parternships in revitalization. TEDCO.*

*Part of the challenge for social clubs in the late twentieth century was to preserve and restore their buildings. During a coffee reception in 1987, L'Unione Italiana was presented with a restoration grant of $250,000 from the state Historic Preservation Board. From the left in this photo are Rep. Elvin Martinez, Secretary of State Jim Smith, Rep. James Hargrett Jr., Vince Pardo, and Senator Malcolm Beard. L'UNIONE ITALIANA.*

**Ybor City: The Making of a Landmark Town**

factory owner who rolled the famous cigar that carried the call of war to the Cuban Insurgent General—all intrinsic parts of Cuban history.

Urged on by his unwavering and inquisitive nature, and supported faithfully by his loving wife, Josephine Villazon Acosta, a Tampa native, Tony captured much of Tampa's history in his writings, in numerous speeches, and in a television series called "Tony Pizzo's Tampa," that won two national awards. He had been honored with the Order of Carlos Manuel de Cespedes, Cuba's highest award, in 1952; he was named Tampa's Outstanding Citizen in 1956, the city's most prestigious award; he was named Knight Officer of the Order of Merit by the Italian government in 1974 for contributions to the Italian traditions in Tampa; he received the D. B. McKay Award from the Florida Historical Society in 1980 for extraordinary contributions to the cause of Florida history; and the Liberty Bell Award in 1990 from the Hillsborough County Bar Association.

Tony Pizzo died on a Sunday in January, 1994. He was 81 years of age. A beautiful life-size statue of him is located at the southwest corner of Centennial Park, across the street from where his father and mother owned and operated their grocery store, one of the earliest in Ybor City.[30]

Tony was a kind, mild-mannered, and extremely cooperative individual. He encouraged other people who attempted to write or research history. It was my good fortune to get to know him, to serve with him on Bettie Nelson's Museum Committee, and to meet with him both at his home and in the coffee houses of Ybor City. His advice was never taken lightly.

## José Martí Park

Among his many campaigns for local history, Tony led the preservation efforts that resulted in the construction of *Parque Amigos de José Martí*. Today José Martí

Park is a completely fenced piece of Cuban soil in America. In a 1979 interview, Tony explained how it came about:

I never will forget an elderly Negro man, a Cuban Negro, coming to me and pointing to the old shack and saying, "That's where José Martí lived. That's where . . . Paulina Pedroso had her boarding house . . . ." When I heard all of this, I did some investigation to make sure that the old gentleman was right. And so I went before the Rotary Club and we formed a committee to preserve the building—but the building was too far gone. . . . We made many trips to Cuba seeking help. . . . Finally, on one of our trips we saw President Batista. The committee was composed of Mayor Curtis Hixon, Doyle Carlton, the former governor of Florida, Earl Mullen, director of the Pan-American Commission, Tony Grimaldi, and Johnny Diaz. We have a photograph taken with Batista, the president of Cuba, at the meeting. . . . And he said, "I will give you $25,000." Batista sent architects from Cuba to inspect the old frame house. The building was filled with termites. It was so far gone that you really would have had to rebuild it. It couldn't be preserved.

So they said, "Why don't we make a little park?" And they came up with plans—I have them—the original plans of what the park was supposed to look like. . . . So we waited about two or three months and nothing happened. And in the meantime the building caught fire, and the fire department saved it.

So we took a picture of the building, partially burned, and sent it to Cuba. Every newspaper in Cuba ran stories and the picture of the house . . . . And things got so hot in Cuba over that picture that, believe it or not, President Batista called a special session of Con-

*This expressive statue of José Martí graces the José Martí Park on the southeast corner of 8th Avenue and 13th Street, site of the home of Ruperto and Paulina Pedroso, who sheltered Martí on his visits to Tampa. The park was developed in 1960 as a tribute to the Cuban patriot and to his friendship with the Ybor City Cuban-American community. The park is technically Cuban property, and Cuban soil was brought there at its inception. Its development occurred due largely to the efforts of Tampa historian Tony Pizzo. Sculptor Alberto Sabas, who also created a statue of Christopher Columbus that stands on Tampa's Bayshore Boulevard, donated his talents for the Martí statue. Today care of this park is under the auspices of the Heritage Club Consortium.* RM.

gress, and the money was appropriated for the house.

Tony worked with Cuban Col. Manuel Quevedo, Homer Hesterly, and real estate agent Leslie Blank to complete the project. The land was bought and the title deeded to the government of Cuba. Soil from each of the Cuban provinces was placed there, so it is literally and legally Cuban soil in Ybor City. It is a sacred place for many Cubans, dedicated to their great patriot and writer José Martí. Many visiting Cubans arrive intent on finding this site, where José Martí composed some of his most famous revolutionary speeches; they consider it a shrine commemorating their history. Here, also, many of the post-Fidel Castro exiled Cuban groups pay homage to Cuba's Supreme Patriot.[31]

## Historical Markers and Monuments

Ybor City has some fifty-three historical markers, just over 25 percent of the total markers shown on the list of official Historical Markers and Monuments in Tampa and Hillsborough County. The others are in downtown Tampa, Plant Park/University of Tampa, South Tampa, West Tampa, the University of South Florida, Hillsborough County, and other Tampa areas. These, too, are part of the legacy of Tony Pizzo. His own colorful account says it best:

> The first marker was erected in front of the Ybor factory. It is a beautiful stone put up by the Ybor City Rotary Club. I think it was in 1949. That was the first one . . . At that time there was a foundry on the Hillsborough River near the site of Interstate 75. I talked to the owner, and he said, "Tony, I'll make those markers for $75 apiece." I went out and raised the money. I went to about twenty-five major corporations and nobody turned me down. So I was able to raise the money and had the plaques put up. We made it an official project of the Ybor City Rotary Club. . . .The city cooperated in putting up the markers. The markers were made at $75 apiece, but after the first ten markers were made the price went up to $100. So we paid $100. Later they went to

$150. Today they're being made in Ohio at a cost of $450 a plaque. And we're still putting up markers. I guess I personally have been involved in putting up more than forty historical markers not only in Ybor City but all over Tampa.[32]

A very active fellow Rotarian, and first president of the Ybor City Rotary Club, Tony found that organization receptive to historical preservation and it served as a springboard for many of his projects. In 1994, after his death, *Tampa Bay History* recognized the importance and impact of his life's work by publishing a special edition dedicated to him.[33]

## The Ybor City Redevelopment Post Office Task Force

This task force first met at the Ybor City Development Agency in the old Broadway Bank building, on December 17, 1985, to determine the future site of the U.S. Post Office, then located on 18th Street and 8th Avenue, one building west of the southwest corner. Task force members present were, Chairman Herbert Fisher, Cesar Medina, Joan Jennewein, Stephanie Ferrell, Alan Kahana, Frank Lastra, Tony Huesca, Thomas Sounders, and Marshall Tison. Warren Johnson attended representing Dr. Andreas Paloumpis of Hillsborough Community College. The Redevelopment Agency staff was represented by Santos Rodriguez (Perry Harvey was out of town).

The U.S. Post Office was an integral part of the Ybor City scenery, and given the number of immigrants and the mobility of workers, it formed a focal point for families and friends. In the 1930s it was located on the southwest corner of La Sétima at 15th Street, where in 1886 La Flor de Sanchez y Haya cigar factory was first built. At some point in the late 1930s or early '40s it was moved to the northeast corner of 14th Street and 6th Avenue, and in the 1950s had been relocated to the 8th Avenue and 18th Street site.

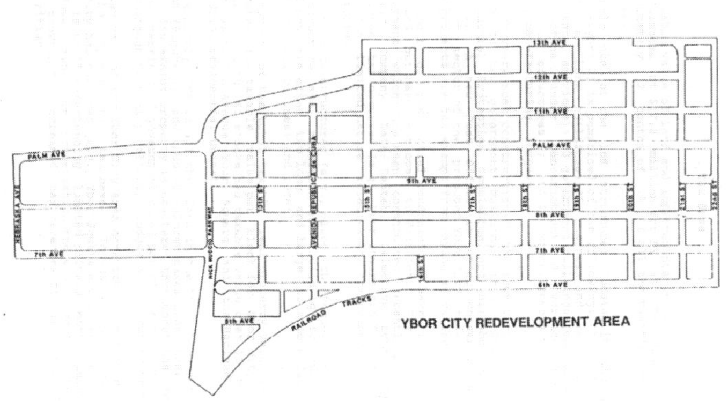


*A document entitled "YBOR CITY: Factors Determining 'Slum' and/or 'Blighted' Conditions" was issued in booklet form by Tampa City Planning May 26, 1988. It included the legal description of the redevelopment area, as well as maps that noted existing types of structures by use, tax exempt blocks, total taxable property value, and other measures. The first figure in the booklet, shown above, identified the "Ybor City Redevelopment Area." UT MERL KELCE LIBRARY SPECIAL COLLECTIONS.*

*The Ybor City Redevelopment Agency produced a booklet in the 1980s to convey plans for the historic district and to celebrate improvements in the area. In his introduction, Mayor Bob Martinez wrote, "Ybor City is now undergoing a renaissance." The publication featured the Historic District logo on the cover, superimposed on a tobacco leaf. It included a foldout map, reproduced below, to illustrate plans for the future.*

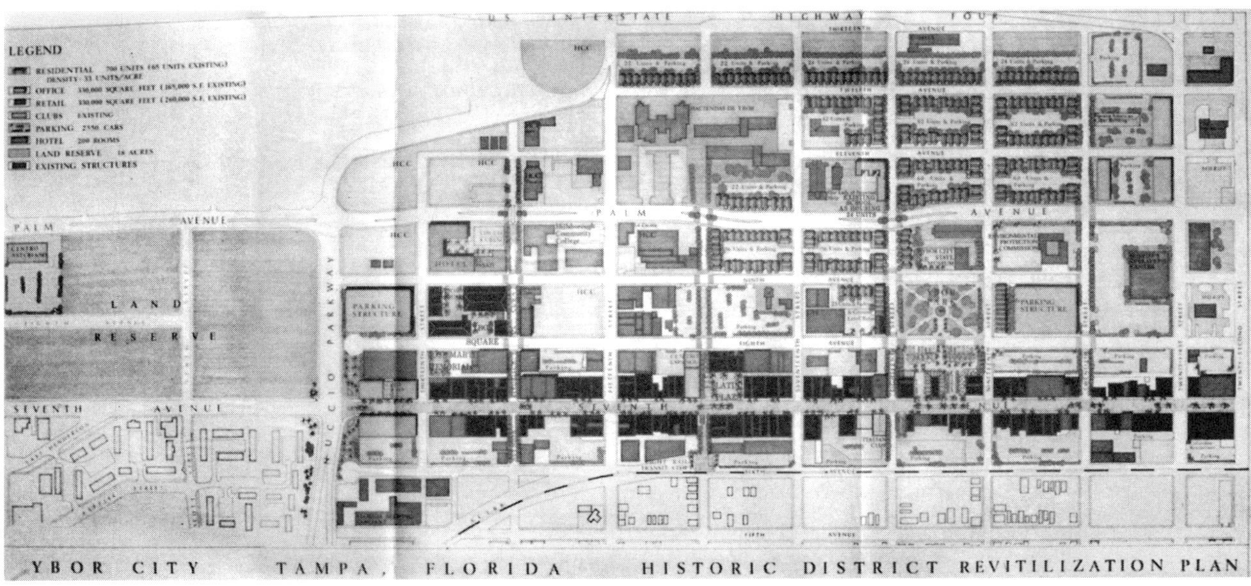

**Chapter 8 · Laying the New Foundations: 1980-1990**

No decision was made during the first meeting, but at a later one the post office staff indicated their preferred new location was the southeast corner of 19th Street and 13th Avenue. This was strongly contested because that land had been designated for housing in the Economic Research Associates consultant plan. However, it was pointed out that Ybor citizens, both in the core area and the suburbs had historically depended on the post office, and its removal from central Ybor City would deprive citizens coming into town for commerce or residence of a vital service. The post office personnel had signaled that they would leave the area if they could not have the site. The task force voted narrowly to allow the post office to possess it. Much questioning occurred in a final meeting to ensure that necessary amenities and Barrio Latino guidelines were met.

A letter from Chairman Fisher dated March 11, 1986, was directed to all participants in the last crucial meeting. Its reference to a compromise proposal suggests something of the difficulty we faced in choosing to deviate from our comprehensive plan:

> Enclosed for your review is a "Summary" of the meeting we had on approval of a site for the Ybor City Station of the U.S. Post Office. . . . Basically, the Huesca/Lastra recommendation appearing on page four is the one I will be taking to the Ybor Redevelopment Agency Board meeting . . . March 19, for their consideration. If accepted by the Board, the recommendation will be forwarded to Mayor Bob Martinez for his consideration . . . [signed,] Herbert Fisher, Task Force Meeting Chair

In due course the proposed post office site was approved by Mayor Bob Martinez. Now, as I write this in the late 1990s, the Ybor City Post Office is serving large numbers of new and old businesses on the Avenue and is large enough to accommodate much more growth. Parking is very adequate and the facility is easily accessible. It anchors that area without ob-structing other proposed housing projects, or constricting future venues.[34]

## The Ybor City Trolley: "No More Back Burners for Ybor"

In a letter to the editor, Monday, February 15, 1988, under the heading "No More Back Burners for Ybor," respected Ybor City and Tampa personality Harris Mullen stressed the urgent need for Tampa officials to act on a long-discussed plan for a trolley that would join Tampa and Ybor City:

> The downtown-Ybor trolley plan is a simple one using low intensity traffic routes. Its existence would not be likely to conflict with any major mass transit system.
>
> Ybor City cries now for the rehabilitation that can make Tampa a great city . . . a city that badly needs urban excitement to offer visitors and home folks. You failed to mention Ybor City's appeal in your editorial, including only the delights of Harbour Island.
>
> I suggest that the downtown-Ybor City system should be on a front burner as something we can easily accomplish by Super Bowl XXV, 1991. We can build a downtown Ybor link for less than $5 million . . . A trolley car is just that—a car, small and simple enough to relate to people, particularly appealing to people seeking a meal, shopping, sightseeing, or a good time . . .
>
> It's time for Tampa to recognize what it has in Ybor City . . . . Please, no more back burners for Ybor City. [ signed ] Harris H. Mullen, Tampa.[35]

Of course, the trolley was not a new idea. *El Carrito Eléctrico* first appeared on our streets in the mid-1890s, and the streetcars had been in operation through the mid-1940s in Ybor City. Originally built by C. W. Chapin, who owned the streetcar line, it was later sold to the Tampa Electric Company when Mr. Chapin left town following the dynamiting of the dam he constructed on the Hillsborough River.

*El Carrito Eléctrico*, the electric streetcar or trolley, was a necessary part of daily life, a widely used and much-loved method of transportation in Ybor City. Even at the

*La Sétima bustled with activity when this photograph was taken, about 1910, and the trolley's comfortable and central place in the life of the street can be read in this scene. It fostered interaction between people, as can be seen from the driver who stands proudly at the front, and the pedestrian who knows he will have time to walk safely across the street, the boy who is safe enough to bend over and turn his back, knowing it will remain safely on its track, and the vendors and cyclists who also share the street.* H. B. PLANT MUSEUM.

313

**Chapter 8 · Laying the New Foundations: 1980-1990**

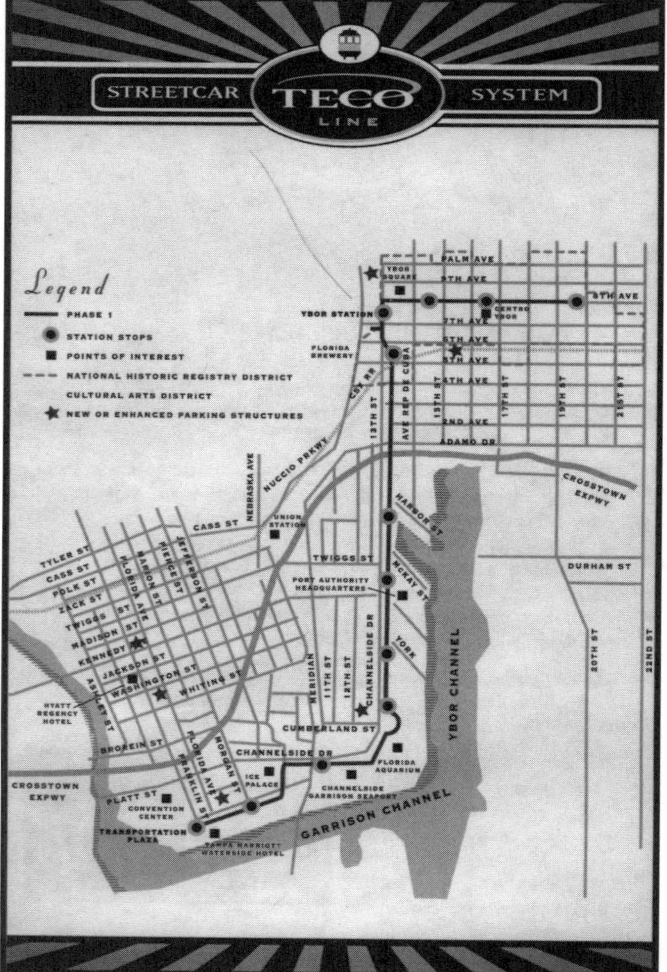


*Ybor's historic streetcar system is now much more than a memory. Construction of the system was a sometimes inconvenient feature of Ybor City revitalization. But as the rails slowly reappeared along the streets, the reality of how much has been accomplished raised the spirits of many of the friends and families of the Ybor City "originals."*

*The City of Tampa's "TECO Line Streetcar System" opened with eight cars operating on a track 2.3 miles long. Powered by a suspended overhead electric line, the cars link Ybor City and downtown Tampa with stops at the Convention Center, Ice Palace, Garrison Seaport, Florida Aquarium, in addition to five Ybor City stops, from the first one on the Avenue de Republic de Cuba, just inside the National Historic District, to "Ybor Station" and Centro Ybor.* RM.

*The new streetcars are charming and true to the vintage Ybor cars—and the new ones are appropriately painted yellow.* TECO.

**Ybor City: The Making of a Landmark Town**

turn to the 21st century, there are still many Ybor and Tampa natives living who enjoyed this form of transportation long ago. Relatively few cigar workers owned a *chivolocos* or *fotingos*, so the streetcars were *their* cars

The streetcars I recall were painted a soft yellow and their presence gliding through the streets seemed inviting, reassuring, and exciting—like the visit of a friend. The entire family rode on them. Children loved them, and many mothers and fathers rode them daily to get to their distant factories, though within the core area most walked to the local factories. Their slow operating speed was perfectly suited to Ybor City's small grid. Due to the closing of cigar factories and other reasons, the lines became unprofitable and were discontinued. By 1946 Tampa Electric shut down its trolley system in Tampa.

The principal streets served by the trolley system in the Ybor area were 7th Avenue, Nebraska Avenue, Columbus Drive (then Michigan), 29th Street to Hillsborough Avenue, 12th Avenue, 22nd Street and Palmetto Beach to the south. Serving the above were the Michigan, the Ross Avenue, West Tampa, Tampa Heights, the Fair Oaks, the Nebraska, and the Union Station-Gary cars. The streetcars began service at 5:30 a.m. and ceased operation between midnight and 1 a.m.

Through a system of ticket exchanges, one could hop a car on La Sétima and go to many places in greater Tampa. These included: Port Tampa, Hyde Park, West Tampa, Grand Central (now Kennedy), Tampa Heights, Seminole Heights to Sulphur Springs, Jackson Heights up to Hillsborough Avenue, Cass, Port Tampa City, Palmetto Beach, and DeSoto Park.[3]

## Tampa & Ybor City Trolley Society

In the early 1980s many interested civic leaders, particularly in the Ybor City area, began a gradually accelerating dialogue on the need to bring back the historic electric trolley. By August 11, 1985, a fourth revision of the "Concept Paper" of the Tampa and Ybor City Street Railway Society had been produced. Leading the dialog was trolley advocate and society founder, Tom Ruddel. He stimulated enthusiasm and created such mutually supportive synergy that it seemed not merely possible but likely that the Society would achieve a steel-wheeled trolley replica to operate in historical Ybor City.

With the coming of the administration of Mayor Sandy Freedman in 1986, the steel-wheel trolley concept was challenged, as well as its proposed route. After considerable discussion, a compromise rubber-wheeled tire trolley bus was given the go-ahead and a reduced route—between Garrison Channel and downtown —was agreed upon to begin operation in late 1995.

While progress on the project had stalled after 1986, the society continued to keep alive its plans to restore an authentic steel-rail trolley. In January 1990, the Tampa & Ybor City Street Railway Society, then chaired by Joan Jennewein, issued its first newsletter with some good news to report:

> Supporters of a trolley link between Ybor City and downtown Tampa packed Cherokee Club on November 9 to launch a founding membership drive. Fifty-one founders with more memberships promised to join.

Authentic conductor hats were issued to those who attended, and the hope of reviving the town's traditional trolley sparked anew. At this dinner Jim Amdal, who guided the Riverfront Trolley in New Orleans from a dream to an astounding success, was the main speaker.

On June, 5,1996, the *Tribune* carried some favorable news:

> By shuffling money, the county's transportation planning board may have found a way to revive the city's electric streetcar system . . . The MPO unanimously agreed to shift $14.9 million from other projects to build the 2.27 mile sys-

tem linking downtown Tampa with Ybor City .
. . . With other grants and promise of $5 million
from Mayor Dick Greco, MPO members said
the system soon should become a reality.[37]

### Farmers' Market

The Evans Development Company of
Baltimore, a nationally acclaimed consulting firm, was selected by Tampa officials
to plan a farmers' market and park for
Ybor City. Bruce Dudley, *Tribune* Staff
writer in a May 30, 1984, article quotes
Tim Nugent, then chairman of the Redevelopment Agency, as saying, "The farmers' market . . . will be a centerpiece of
Ybor City redevelopment plans, with construction possibly starting before the end
of the year. . . . This will be the festival
market where people will gather, and we
will have produce for sale. But we will also
have entertainment and other things."

Dudley reported that about $600,000
dollars had been earmarked for the combined marketplace and park project at that
time, and he expected additional funds to
be allocated in 1985. The city had budgeted
$353,000—$200,000 for the market place
and $153,000 for the park to be combined
with $250,000 from the state Department
of Natural Resources for the park.

Plans called for the park to fill the
block bordered by 18th Street on the west
and 19th Street on the east, and 8th and
9th Avenues on the south and north. The
festival market would then be situated
along 8th Avenue behind existing businesses such as the La Tropicana Café.[38]

Plans for the project included an impressive red brick structure on the 8th Avenue side of the park where up to sixteen
vendors could sell fresh fruits and vegetables. The market would face a terraced,
landscaped park with a fountain and plenty
of benches for shoppers or sightseers to
rest and sample their purchases.

Diana Kyle, deputy director of the
Tampa Parks Department who helped
plan and coordinate the park's gala dedication, expressed the hopes of many of us
when she said, "We expect this park to be
a real people generator . . . . We think
people will come down here to buy produce in the farmers' market, enjoy the artists in the park and then decide to wander
through other sections of Ybor and have
lunch or dinner." Although the Farmers'
Market was not planned to begin operating until the late spring, Ybor Park's dedication took place at 11 a.m., Saturday,
January 18, 1986, kicking off the Ybor City
centennial year. Mayor Bob Martinez,
Florida Commissioner of Agriculture
Doyle Connor, and Ney C. Landrum, director of the Florida Department of Natural Resources were on hand for the
ceremony.

Ceremony aside, accomplishing the
goals of the Ybor Park and Farmers' Market was quite a challenge. It was being developed under the auspices of the Ybor
City State Museum, with the active help
and cooperation of numerous local civic
and historical organizations.[39]

As late as 1985, not much progress had
been made. Referring to the Economic
Research Associates' recommendation of
two years earlier, Daniel Alarcon reported
in the *Tampa Tribune* on March 25, 1985:

> The city of Tampa is dragging its feet in
> vital redevelopment projects in Ybor City,
> some area leaders say . . . . Groundbreaking has
> not yet been set for the Ybor Park and Farm-
> ers' Market. . . . And a historic district ordi-
> nance that would provide redevelopment
> guidelines and ban businesses such as X-rated
> theaters and plasma centers has become a point
> of contention between Ybor boosters and mu-
> nicipal officials.
>
> Henry Gonzalez, Chairman of the munici-
> pal Ybor Redevelopment Agency, said that the
> contrast between Ybor's redevelopment and
> that of downtown Tampa and Harbour Island
> prompts people to ask: "Is Ybor City really on
> the back burner? Why is downtown moving so
> rapidly and Ybor is not off the starting block?"

Alarcon quotes development agency
Director Tim Nugent as saying that despite a projected cost of some $814,000, it
was not the cost that slowed the project:

"The park has been delayed because of differing opinion on how to build it, the death of an architect, and the normal slow pace of government."

"Everyone is on the same sheet of music now," Nugent said, "They weren't there before.

The preparation of the historic district ordinance was on schedule until city zoning staffers, who helped draft it, decided to change it, departing from the recommendations of a 1983 consultant's report that cost the city $175,000.

Alarcon added, "The city last year paid another consulting firm, Robert M. Leary and Associates of Raleigh, N.C., $38,000 to draft the ordinance with the help of the zoning staff, Nugent's agency and other involved parties."

On February 24, 1986, letters appointing the Farmers' Market Advisory Commissioners were mailed out. Joe Abraham, Ross Ferlita, and Terry Johnson of the Parks Department were included in the early orders sent by Mayor Bob Martinez. Several other commissioners were appointed.

This Advisory Commission met many times to deliberate the manner, timing and scope of operations. Considerable advice was given by state agricultural and farm personnel, county, city, and local civic leaders as well as Hillsborough Farmers' Market officials. With the city's support and blessing, the market opened up that year and operated on weekends. There was a great deal of publicity, but public attendance was only modest. The market, in turn, appeared to operate with less than enthusiastic zest.

Much effort went into improving the scheduling of dedicated and responsible vendors, who parked around the roofed, opened stall on the west side. Curiosity seekers abounded in the early weeks. Attempts were made by the Park Commission, (which met monthly, as scheduled) to ensure that there was proper clean-up and

disposal of trash as well as careful scheduling and on-going publicity.

Enthusiasm for the project began to wane after only a few short months of operation. In addition, Tampa Mayor Bob Martinez became Governor of Florida. Sandy Freedman succeeded him as Mayor.

For whatever reason, city support for the Farmers' Market came to an abrupt halt in the late 1980s. The citizens had never turned out in great numbers, and it was not a money-making project for the city. A chief reason for this was the lack of a nearby residential base. Urban Renewal had taken care of that. There were few people living within walking distance for shopping. Nor did housewives from the relatively poor, more distant suburbs have cars to drive to the market to shop. Their own shopping areas were sufficient for them. Very modest numbers of buyers drove in from distant areas, but these were casual visitors and tourists, not repeat customers.

Finally, the original Farmers' Market closed. Many questions were left unanswered when it did. The market had not failed for lack of city support. Bob Martinez's staff gave it good initial leadership and backing. Key members of the state and county agricultural community were represented. Indeed, the commissioners



*Planning the design for a permanent Open Air Market resulted in these handsome brick facilities in the Ybor Centennial Park. Even though the market operates primarily on weekends and during festive events, the covered areas are also proving to be practical and attractive for a variety of activities and displays. RM.*



**Chapter 8 • Laying the New Foundations: 1980-1990**

had been carefully selected. The city also had promised to nurture it through its infancy, and civic organizations supported it. Still, the lack of customers posed a difficult hurtle and the change in city government was another factor. New administrations bring their own agendas. Funds dried up quickly. The clock was ticking for the Farmers' Market, despite the continuing celebration in honor of the founding of Ybor City by Don Vicente Martínez Ybor, but Centennial Park would be a center for future activities.

The last two meetings of the Farmers' Market Commission witnessed fewer key personalities and a somber setting. Others had stopped attending. Suddenly it was over. Communications with the Commissioners ceased.

The first attempt to operate the Farmers' Market failed like so many prior lurching revitalization efforts in Ybor City. It might have been a predictable consequence of the free market system. Free enterprise moves quickly to force businesses to change and adapt. The owner-operator shows his skills and talents as he decides when to open and close, what to stock, and when to sprinkle the fruits and vegetables. Most successful markets open early and cater to customers who live nearby—preferably within walking distance, especially if parking is a problem. Some of the essential flexibility was missing in the publicly supported pseudo-enterprise guided by bureaucracy and the Commmission.

However, time has brought its changes. Today a new apartment complex with some 450 owners has opened nearby, and the plans to develop "Ybor South" (see next section) will increase the potential customer base. A second attempt to revive the market started—then stalled. As I write this, there is a good possibility that the third time's the charm. Rick Jansen opened the not-for-profit Ybor City Fresh Market, Inc., in April 2000. Today it continues each weekend and opens for festivals and special occasions in Centennial Park. With support from the City of Tampa, Tampa Parks Department, Ybor City Chamber of Commerce, Ybor City State Museum, Centro Ybor, and Ybor City Development Corp, its future looks bright. Jansen brought a touch of the new—a state-of-the-art Web site to the timeless appeal of an open-air market, and his dedication and energy seemed to have brought the right spark to the enterprise at last.

## Ybor City Redevelopment Corp., Inc.

Early in 1988 Tampa began implementation of a plan by Mayor Sandy Freedman to stimulate more private development in the historic district. The idea was to establish a new agency, the Ybor City Redevelopment Corp., Inc. It began work in 1988 even though chairman Craig Campbell and the board members were not sure where the funds would come from.

Financial aspects were soon given a boost as important in symbolic approval as in the actual dollars involved when members of the State Historic Preservation Advisory Council recommended approval for two local grant proposals. One provided $4,000 to prepare urban design and economic planning for "Ybor South" in the southern part of Ybor City and the other secured $3,100 to create a brochure on preservation and the Historic Tampa/Hillsborough County Preservation Board. The planning and design document was to be especially important. According to Suzanne Walker, chief of the Bureau of Historic Preservation under the Department of State, ninety to one hundred locations were targeted for surveying in an area bounded by Adamo Drive (State Road 60) on the south, an alleyway behind La Sétima on the north, Nuccio Parkway on the west, and 30th Street on the east. Here at last was a solid start at embracing some of the extended Ybor community.[41]

On November 17, 1988, the Tampa City Council passed a resolution giving

the Ybor City Development Corp. Inc. $100,000 from the city's operating budget. With the selection of directors the city established its own nonprofit agency specifically devoted to the redevelopment of Ybor City.[42]

Fortunately, the new group could benefit from important groundwork and initiatives already in place. The Ybor City Historic District Revitalization Plan completed in 1983 was a two-year planning study done by the consulting firm from Boston called Economic Research Associates that has figured prominently in the Ybor City story. The ERA Plan had recommended promotion of the district as a high-quality, mixed-use environment fostering preservation and tourism while reinforcing Ybor City's cultural heritage. In the 1983 plan, La Sétima had been recognized as the retail spine, and renewal efforts were envisioned as related to it. The plan stated that it was logical that community housing needs should be met by residential development north of La Sétima, and the report proceeded to propose much detail.

In 1986 partial implementation of the ERA plan was begun through the creation of special zoning for Ybor City. The City of Tampa's zoning ordinances made unique provisions for Ybor City to allow mixed-use development by dividing the Historic District into six zones. The Central Core area, YC-1, contains 71 acres representing 15 percent of the Historic District's 462 acres. The areas designated YC-2 and YC-4, containing a total of 215 acres and representing 47 percent of the land in the Historic District, are designated for primary use residential districts. District YC-3 is designated for college use, and Y-5 and Y-6 are commercial districts serving primarily as transitional zones into an area with more intense land uses.

Since its inception, the Ybor City Redevelopment Corporation has worked to

*At the microphone is Dr. Mark Barnes of the National Park Service as he presents Florida Governor Bob Martinez with the official citation designating Ybor City's Centro Español building a National Historic Landmark.*
LA GACETA.

create additional incentives. These now include an exemption of the Tampa requirements for on-site storm water retention and an allowance for outdoor cafes on the city right-of-way (sidewalks) of Ybor City. A tax deferral for renovation of historic buildings is in place, and other incentives have also been negotiated.[43]

## Ybor City designated a National Historic Landmark District.

In January of 1988 a historian from the National Park Service was scheduled to visit Ybor City to evaluate it for possible recognition as a National Historic Landmark District by the U.S. Department of the Interior. A study in the late 1970s by the Association for State and Local History had identified Ybor City as one of 40 "very significant ethnic communities' in the United States" which community leaders had hoped might result in additional recognition. However, according to Joan Jennewein, who had been seeking the recognition, "the study went no further, and Ybor City was not designated as a National Historic Landmark District."

A spokesman for the National Park Service, Duncan Morrow, explained the purpose of the historian's visit: "Basically, he would be looking to see if the general area has been maintained reasonably intact with its historic character."



**Chapter 8 · Laying the New Foundations: 1980-1990**

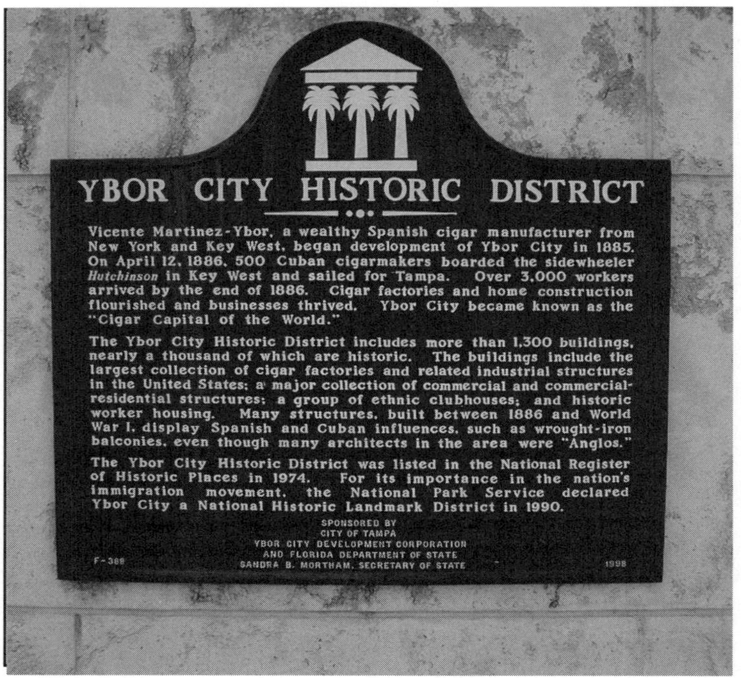


*This historic marker mounted on the base of an arched entrance to Ybor City commemorates its 1990 designation by the National Park Service as a National Historic Landmark District. RM.*

After the damage to the community caused by Urban Renewal there were concerns that too much of the fabric of history might already have been destroyed. In addition, lack of funding was delaying current preservation efforts. The National Historic Landmark designation could make property owners in Ybor City eligible for federal preservation grants and tax credits to carry out appropriate restoration of remaining structures. The hopes of many in the community were riding on this avenue for saving the town.

Joan Jennewein, president of the Ybor City Chamber of Commerce, had initiated the request for an evaluation after attending a National Preservation Conference in previous October.[44] In addition to being president of the Ybor Chamber of Commerce, Jennewein was a trustee of the National Trust for Historic Preservation and owner of Historic Ybor Marketing, Inc. She had successfully led significant preservation efforts in Ybor City for more than a decade, some of which have already been described.

James H. Charleton, National Park Service historian, toured the area and viewed a film, *100 Years of Ybor City*, produced with the backing of Florida state grants for cable television in Atlanta.[45] Before leaving Tampa he told a reporter that he would like to see the historic Ybor boundaries expanded from those that the National Register of Historic Places had previously established.

"The National Historic Landmark is the highest rating that a property can receive," Charleton said. "It is applied to properties that represent broad patterns of American history, while the National Register of Historic Places concentrates more on properties of state and local importance, some of which have national significance as well."[46]

This was a most welcome and authoritative external confirmation of the high value so many of us had believed to be found in Ybor City for long years of effort. Its designation became official on December 14, 1990. *Tampa Tribune* staff writer Ivan J. Hathaway said it beautifully in a story in January 1991 that was accompanied by Joan Jenewein's photograph:

> For this long-standing part of Tampa and the preservationists who toil to save every red brick and slab of marble in it. Monday was rather like the wedding after a prolonged engagement.
>
> Word came in December 1990 that Ybor City was being designated as a national landmark district by the U.S. Department of Interior.
>
> "Ybor City's day has finally come," Ybor preservationist Joan Jennewein announced to a noontime crowd gathered in the courtyard of the historic Centro Español building on Seventh Avenue. It [the designation] puts the final mark on Ybor City as being a very special place."
>
> The ceremony coincided with a week-long visit to Tampa by members of the National Trust for Historic Preservation and an appearance by Jerry L. Rogers, the associate director of the National Park Service, who presented a plaque to local officials.
>
> "There are 60,000 places listed on the national register, but a scant 1,900 are designated as national historic landmarks," Rogers said. "We select only the cream."

*One of the challenges of maintaining the hard-won National Landmark District status for Ybor City will be seeking appropriate and harmonious ways for the old and new to complement one another. This recent photograph of a Hillsborough Community College building adjacent to the historic El Pasaje Building shows that there are appropriate and complementary uses. Students on the campus Ybor City campus are surrounded by a living history museum. And even the divergent architectural styles can peacefully coexist with the help of appropriate landscaping and an indoor/outdoor cafe atmosphere. RM.*

"Ybor City's historic significance comes from the early stages of self-help among minorities in the United States—a mutual aid to pull their economies together," Rogers continued. "With Cuban, Spanish and Italian immigrants joining forces in the late 1800s, Ybor City's factories put Tampa on the map as a cigar city."

It had to be a special place just to be here today. It has faced down serious threats from urban renewal. Ybor City was threatened by the construction of Interstate-4 and still may be affected by plans to widen the interstate where it runs along the northern part of the district.[47]

Following years of work, Ybor City became Florida's third National Historic District, joining the nation's oldest city in St. Augustine's "Old Town," and the Pensacola Naval Air Station. Harris Mullen was among the many longtime supporters celebrating the achievement, and in his thinking it was not only good for the historic preservation; he saw it would bring the possibility of economic preservation as well, since Ybor's landmark designation would inevitably mean increased tourism.

"It's a handle; it's like getting on the map," he said. "There are a limited number of those landmarks. It increases your notoriety as a place of history and you will have more visitors."[48]

Being named a Historic District means that an area has a *collection* of historically significant buildings. Today the National Park Service points out on its Web site that Ybor City contains the largest collection of cigar-related buildings in the United States—and probably in the world. A total of 1,349 buildings—cigar factories, worker houses, and ethnic clubs—were deemed to meet that criterion in the city.

Yet more than the buildings, it preserved a tribute to cigar manufacturing, the first major industry in the state, and the reason thousands of immigrants came to this country. While the buildings are tangible evidence of the cultural past, it was also the unique blend of ethnic groups that composed Ybor City—Cuban, Spanish, Italian, Jewish, and German—that gave rise to the culture they reflect.[49]

Certain facts now emerge as one reflects on the significance of this coveted designation:

First, Jerry L. Rogers, associate director of the National Park Service, alerts all



**Chapter 8 · Laying the New Foundations: 1980-1990**

*The new flag of Ybor City incorporates the design of the city's original flag with the Ybor City seal designed by Tony Pizzo. The flag's history can be viewed on the facing page.* RM.

*The flag and seal images appear on many festive and promotional items and printed materials.*

when he adds, "National historic landmarks are as important as the national parks, but the park service doesn't own this and it won't. *Its future is up to the people who are here.*" And earlier in this work, Jeff Mangum, *Tribune* writer, cites National Park Service spokesman Duncan Morrow, when he states that future historians reviewing the worthiness of a district to retain the conveted National Historic Landmark District status will *"be looking to see if the general area has been maintained reasonably intact with its historic character."*

He suggest that one must never take this designation for granted—a trumpet call to responsible civic organizations such as the Ybor City Chamber of Commerce and the Ybor City Museum Society—groups that already have accomplished so much—to make defense of this National

Historic Landmark District designation a very high priority.

Despite the feelings of frustration involved in watching the efforts at rebirth fall short of the mark, a lot of the work accomplished resulted in major portions of the area's necessary infrastructure being completed. Final success could not have been achieved without the underpinning which developed over many years when little progress could be seen. And here, one must acknowledge the essential support and initiative of the Bob Martinez staff and organization. Staff aide Bob Morrison, for example, was a consistently well-organized and convincing personality when it came to structuring the various redevelopment agencies. Nearly two decades later, he could reflect on the outcome of the efforts he helped organize. At the Ybor Chamber's monthly luncheon meeting in January 1998—over a decade after the various redevelopment agencies closed—Morrison, as an invited speaker, pointed out, "Today's progress and upbeat mood rest squarely on the work done by the redevelopment agencies of the early '80s." And then he added, "And Frank Lastra, sitting there, can attest to it."

Morrison was referring to the enormous amount of invisible work done by the many agencies, and I can, indeed, bear witness to the tremendous efforts and tenacity of many good people who accomplished this. They have left an example, traced a path, and preserved a story that others must now learn and repeat . . . that others must now tell and complete.

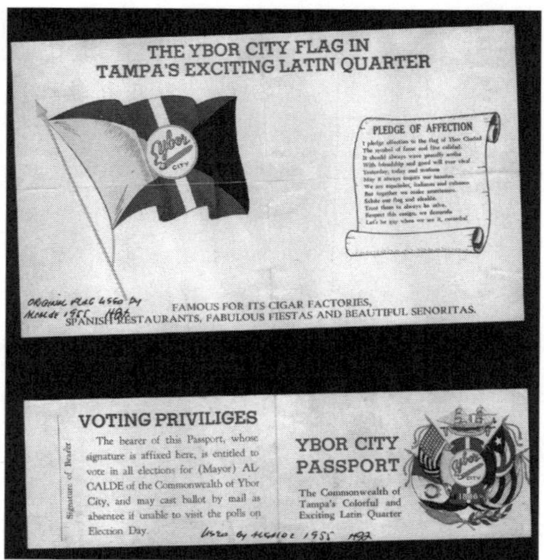




**Ybor City: The Making of a Landmark Town**

*Rafael Martinez-Ybor (left), senior vice president of the Bank of Tampa, past president of the Rotary Club, and great-grandson of Vicente Martínez Ybor, celebrates the thirty-seventh anniversary of the Ybor City flag at a ceremony at the TECO Energy Building on 8th Avenue and 12th Street in 1989. Holding the flag are (left to right) Frank Llaneza and Tino C. Gonzalez, executives of the pioneer cigar firm of Villazon & Company, who also represent the Tampa Cigar Manufacturers Association.  Standing at right are Gregory A. Ehlers, vice president and chief information officer of TECO Energy, Inc., and Tony Pizzo, Hillsborough County Historian and the original designer of the flag and seal of Ybor City. Rafael Martinez-Ybor concluded the flag-raising ceremony with the words, "May the Ybor flag ever wave over this tobacco land of history." USFSCL, Tony Pizzo Collection.*

*The original flag of Ybor City was designed by Tony Pizzo, first Ybor City Alcalde Association President, 1952-53, and was declared "official" by that organization. This original cloth flag was provided courtesy of Sam D. Leto. RM.*

*The 1950s Ybor City seal, also designed by Tony Pizzo. The central element and lettering match the flag.  USFSCL.*

**Chapter 8 · Laying the New Foundations: 1980-1990**

*The Gonzmart family poses for a photograph at their Columbia Restaurant. Left to right are Cesar, Casey, Adela, and Richard.*

# Building and Renewing: 1990-1995

The draw of Ybor City was now contagious. In 1989 the Ybor City Development Corporation (YCDC) was headed by President Rebecca Gagalis—and the group began to find receptive ears. Many accomplished business people were brought on board. As the YCDC pursued its energetic search for investors, businesses, and tenants for Ybor City, landlords, finally, began to see a growing interest in their properties—and deservedly so. Many had carried empty buildings for as long as two decades! With the underpinnings and infrastructure finally in place—though utilities, sewers, and signage updates were not yet complete—the YCDC at last saw major redevelopment occur. Between 1988 and and 1995, approximately $45 million was invested to create more than 150 new businesses. These businesses have added some 1,200 new job opportunities to the economy and have redeveloped and added 360,000 square feet of productive space to the Ybor City area.

*This label includes Tampa's skyline, complete with the H. B. Plant Hotel.*

As of an inventory in late May 1996 some 23 residential units had been built on La Sétima, with 14 more in the planning stages or under construction. A consortium of developers was planning the construction of 50 bed-and-breakfast units. Also, between 1990 and 1996 there were 45 new retail merchants, 52 offices, six restaurants, 14 wet-zoned clubs, 28 wet-zoned restaurants, and one micro brewery that opened in the Ybor City historic district.[1]

## The Passing of a Legend—Cesar Gonzmart Sr.

Cesar Gonzmart Sr., a practical and visionary Ybor City leader for decades, died on Wednesday, December 9, 1992. His charisma and drive had been exactly what the Columbia Restaurant needed to move forward vigorously. Yes, his wife Adela and her family's resources allowed for considerable forward motion, but move the restaurant forward he did! Together, he and Adela made a great team. Adela promoted Spanish culture and Cesar added his engaging leadership. With his magnetic personality, his great inspirational qualities, and his daring enterprises, he influenced other individuals to step forward and do their very best. Many Ybor City civic leaders were inspired by him. Ybor City owes a profound debt to his great interest in promoting the town.

*Adela and Cesar at home with their young sons, Casey, and Richard. Music was always an important part of their lives.* ADELA GONZMART.

## The Passing of a Legend

Whatever else history will say, it must first declare that Cesar Gonzmart Sr. was dedicated to his new profession — the restaurant business. Indeed, he had left his musical world for his wife Adela, her family, and the Columbia Restaurant. There at the restaurant, too, he dazzled diners nightly with his beautiful violin over many years. With Adela he raised his family on Davis Islands, and Adela and sons ran a whole chain of restaurants. He prepared them well, and he seems to have passed along both his culinary professionalism and his an immense flair for music, showmanship, and business acumen.

Cesar was infatuated with Ybor City—with its history, its culture, and its people. The Columbia Restaurant served as his platform to project his persona and enthusiasm. The synergy he created both brought into the fold many real sons of

*Decorative tiles adorn the exterior as well as interior of the Columbia Restaurant.* RM.

the town, and, perhaps even repelled unworthy promoters and ideas. The "Columbia institution" he bequeathed Ybor City took root under his watch! Many of his ideas were bigger than the town — or even the larger community - could accept or digest. But his largeness of vision and imagination helped create an atmosphere and attitude where other imaginations and dreams could flourish. The Ybor City Chamber and other major Ybor civic clubs relied on the Columbia Restaurant as the locale of choice for many of their business meetings and festivities.

The last time I saw Cesar was at a strikingly beautiful performance of the Ballet Folklorico de Ybor in that majestic Tampa Theater I recall so fondly from my youth. I turned around to see Cesar sitting by himself, Adela having left to tend to some of the ballet needs. She had founded the organization, and she continued to nurture it. As I walked over, Cesar smiled at me and held my hands with both of his.

"Frank, it was a good ride," he said, a weak but beautiful gleam in his eyes.

"Yes," I said, "and you were the driver!"

Cesar was a frail man at that time, a shadow of himself. I walked back to my seat. It was the last time I would see this truly influential and historic personality alive.

Upon Cesar's death in the last decade of the last century, Adela Gonzmart and family had a small but very elegant statue of him sculpted and erected for posterity. It is located in front of the restaurant that blossomed to its current height during his lifetime. The statue is a remarkable likeness of him and his violin. It is a fitting place to locate it—there, by the entrance where the endless diners drawn to this famous location enter the splendid restaurant.

When Cesar died, Roland Manteiga, publisher of Ybor City's outstanding newspaper *La Gaceta*, said of him, "The legendary Cesar Gonzmart of Columbia



**Ybor City: The Making of a Landmark Town**

Restaurant fame passed away. Ybor City and Tampa have lost an outstanding and distinguished citizen. He will be missed."

The Hispanic Advisory Council sponsored a dedication ceremony for the Cesar Gonzmart statue at the Columbia Restaurant, at 10 a.m. on November 6, 1993, almost one year after he died. Adela, the entire Gonzmart family, and many civic leaders, friends, and admirers from the general public were present. The following words graced both the front cover of the brochure, and the statue itself:

" Cesar Gonzmart . . . He lived . . . He reigned . . . He cared . . ."

## Adela Hernandez Gonzmart, Ybor City's First Lady of Culture

Cesar's role was not over until the late '80s. Adela's seemed to catch the coming wind in the early part of that decade. By the end of the decade of the 1980s, Adela would be recognized as Ybor City's unofficial First Lady. Her romance with Ybor City was not late in coming. But once unleashed, her passion for maintaining and enhancing Ybor City's Latin culture grew unabated.

*Adela as a child with her mother, Carmen, and father, Casimiro Hernandez II in 1921.* YCSM.

Born a few blocks from the Columbia Restaurant, with many of her close relatives nearby, this young lady was steeped in Spanish and Cuban culture. Her grandfather, Casimiro Hernandez I, had started the restaurant and eventually her father, Casimiro II, inherited it.

Relatively few people remember Adela from her early youth, but she was in many ways part of the traditional heritage of Ybor City. She received a strict upbringing. Music was a part of her life from the earliest years, and she gave her first piano recital when she was six years old. After receiving a typical high school education, she was whisked away to the Juilliard School of Music in New York, where she became an accomplished and select pianist.

After a movie-like romance and marriage to the incomparable Cesar Gonzmart Sr., a superb violinist and band leader, the couple hit the road in a musical interlude that took them to both North and South America, and to local venues such as the Sapphire Room of Tampa's Floridian Hotel. When Cesar began work at Casimiro Hernandez's restaurant, the Columbia, Adela began her childbearing and housekeeping years. During this time she devoted herself to raising her children, Casey and Richard,



327

who today run the Columbia as chairman and president, respectively.

To say that Adela's marriage to Cesar Gonzmart Sr. was providential for Ybor City's Latin culture and the promotion of its history is to think carefully, view the facts calmly, and draw the inevitable conclusion.

Cesar entered the mainstream of Ybor City civic life early, and his accomplishments were many. Adela's entry would come much later. Adela had listened to her father speak of events in earlier years, and over the years she had listened to Cesar as he related the events of the day, the endless happenings and problems of the town, and the nightly cultural offerings by the Columbia. She learned of the financial impact that the economic highs and lows of the period had on the restaurant. Interlaced through all this were acquaintances with many of the interesting personalities of the day, including nationally known baseball players, congressional representatives and senators, boxing champions, famed artists, musicians, theatrical players and movie idols, nobility, national reporters, and of course, the local, regional and state political leaders of the day. That was quite an exposure. Cesar, of course, had been there in most cases.

Adela grew in stature and prestige. When it seemed that perhaps Cesar's star occasionally flickered, Adela's seemed constantly to brighten and help carry the heavy momentum he had generated.

Soon Adela was at the epicenter of many activities in Ybor City. This included heading the Damas of the Knights of the Krewe of Sant Yago, serving three terms as president of the Ybor City Chamber of Commerce, where she left an unmatched record of financial and cultural accomplishment, and, then becoming president of the Ybor City Museum Society. She also shared presidencies and committees with many of Ybor's better-known personalities and became a coveted member of the Rotary Club of Ybor City.

In her position as owner of the Columbia Restaurant she constantly offers its resources toward the enhancement of Latin culture, festivities and prime civic events, making that institution a vital part of the daily events in the city.

With both Cesar's and Adela's backing, the Columbia has been a long-term major participant in community activities including Fiesta Day, A Taste of Ybor City, and Bean Soup Day in Tallahassee. Food, such as Spanish garbanzo bean soup from the Columbia, is often donated, for these special events. The Columbia participates annually in the dispensing of this soup at the State Capitol, along with other Ybor products contributed by the Naviera Coffee Mill, More's Segunda Central Bakery, and various cigar factories. The Columbia Restaurant also often sends singers and dancers to accompany the mostly Spanish themes.

Many of these events have been achieved by Adela in joint effort with the Ybor City Museum Society, Ybor City Chamber of Commerce, Centro Asturiano, L'Unione Italiana, and the Círculo Cubano. Personally chairing or co-chairing many of these events with Adela have been Mary Alvarez, Eva Ciaccio, and shared co-presidencies of the Ybor City Museum society with Adrienne García. (Shared leadership roles such as co-president or co-chair are common in Ybor City, perhaps reflecting a deep-



*El Ballet Folklorico de Ybor was founded and chaired by Adela Gonzmart, with Adrienne Garcia as president. The organization played an important role in bringing the musical and dance culture of Spain, Cuba, Sicily, Mexico, and South America to Tampa. This photograph includes fifteen of the principal dancers.*

328

**Ybor City: The Making of a Landmark Town**

*Dancers from El Ballet Folklorico de Ybor strike a dramatic pose for a program cover design.*

*Clemente Ochoa of Madrid (center) sang at the Columbia Restaurant. Here he delights in the company of Blanca Lionarons (left) and Mary González. They were three of the talented and popular singers of the Spanish Lyric Theater of Tampa in the mid 1970s when the photograph was taken.* LA GACETA.

*This 1962 Spanish Lyric Theater production of "Bohemios" featured Alma Phillips, Gerardo Valdes, and Joyce Fernandez in the central roles.*

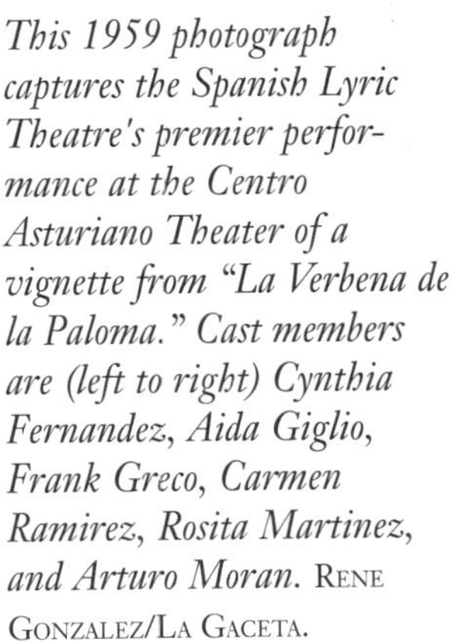

*This 1959 photograph captures the Spanish Lyric Theatre's premier performance at the Centro Asturiano Theater of a vignette from "La Verbena de la Paloma." Cast members are (left to right) Cynthia Fernandez, Aida Giglio, Frank Greco, Carmen Ramirez, Rosita Martinez, and Arturo Moran.* RENE GONZALEZ/LA GACETA.

In the early and mid 1990s these leaders, actively supported the cultural and social life of the town and made Ybor City run faster. Left to right are (seated) Adela Gonzmart, Mary Alvarez, and Eva Ciaccio; standing are Enrique Woodroffe, Lisa Harris, Cookie Ellis, Jill Wax, Donna Parrino, Terri Bishop, Angeles Ferlita, Tish Bohner, Lori Smith, Rosann Garcia, and Vince Pardo.

Rene Gonzalez, founder and director of the Spanish Little Theater, now the Spanish Lyric Theater, has directed productions there for the past thirty-eight years. His shows have included zarzuelas, Cuban and South American musicals, operettas, Broadway shows, and musical reviews. Today the Spanish Lyric Theater performs regularly on the stage of the Playhouse at the Tampa Bay Performing Arts Center. It continues to grow and regularly fills the hall. Its repertoire is now strong on American Broadway musicals and among its most successful productions have been its versions of The Sound of Music, Gigi, Oklahoma, and Camelot. It has received international recognition, including a coveted award from Her Majesty, Queen Sofia of Spain.

The popular theater in the Centro Asturiano featured a handsome painted proscenium curtain from the Zapata Studio in Havana. It portrayed the cathedral and grotto of Our Lady of Covadonga, the patron saint of Asturias, and was used in the theater from 1914 until it was finally replaced in 1972. RENE GONZALEZ/SPANISH LYRIC THEATER.

**Ybor City: The Making of a Landmark Town**

seated social inclination toward mutual support.)

Adela founded the Ballet Folklorico de Ybor. Today it is a major dispenser of much of the best of Spanish, Cuban, Italian, Mexican, and South American dance. All the above enhanced Ybor City's Latin culture. That phase of Latin culture had been gradually disappearing in Tampa.

The restaurant participates to this day in the Annual Illuminated Night Parade. This event is sponsored by the Krewe of the Knights of Sant' Yago. As previously reported, their artifacts are housed in the King's room at the Columbia Restaurant, along with portraits and other items of that social organization.

Among the artistic troupes that have performed at the Columbia's Siboney and Patio Rooms have been the Don Quixote orchestra, Jose Molina troupe, Amparo Garrido, and *Los Chavales de España*. More recently, the restaurant has featured an outstanding flamenco troupe led by Gisela Sotomayor, artistic director, with daughter, Gisela Antognelli, first dancer and partner, and principal dancer Oscar Trevino. Today the Columbia Restaurant Dance Troupe performs two 45-minute flamenco shows nightly, except Sundays, under the direction of Artistic Director Faustino Rios.

In the 1980s and 1990s Adela's influence in the cultural world of Ybor City was large and much solicited. Her personal star led her to prominence thoughout Tampa. Nonetheless, though today her light spills over Ybor City's "borders," her star still shines most brightly over Ybor City. She is a tireless worker. She remains closely supportive of an entourage of personal friends who still head the many functions she is affiliated with. Adela is a remarkably intelligent person, and one unfailingly in tune with the happenings in the town. Her knowledge of the Spanish, Cuban, Sicilian, and Mexican heritage of artistic folklore is extensive.

Adela received many awards and frequent recognition in both Ybor City and the wider Tampa community. There are simply too many to itemize. Perhaps epitomizing the scope of her accomplishments is the *Hispanic Woman of the Year* award given her by the national Hispanic magazine *Vista*. The award presented at the National Press Club in Washington, D.C., in early 1997 was given to the thirteen top Hispanic women in the country in recognition of contributions to the Hispanic community. Accompanying Adela on that trip was Adrienne Garcia, director of the H. Lee Moffit Cancer Center and Research Institute Foundation, Inc., and an emerging prominent Tampa Hispanic civic leader in her own right.

Late in life, Adela added a new dimension to her outstanding career. Over the years she had become known as a superb connoisseur of Spanish cuisine, having been exposed to a lifetime of fine Spanish culinary excellence. In 1995 she coauthored *The Columbia Restaurant Spanish Cookbook* with artist and writer Ferdie Pacheco, a popular Ybor City personality known as "The Fight Doctor" as a result of his having served as a physician for professional boxers and as a personal physician for Mohammed Ali. The popularity of the cookbook led to a number of printings, and it became one of the all-time bestsellers for the University Press of Florida.

In the May/June 1997 issue of the elite *Tampa Bay Magazine*, Marie Hamm's article "Adela Gonzmart, A Lady of Legend" opened with the following words:

> At 77 years of age, Adela Gonzmart is widely perceived as the matriarch of Ybor City. In Tampa Bay, when she enters a room, Adela naturally commands the respect and acknowledgment of all present. This woman, who has contributed so much to the growth of many of Tampa Bay's cultural organizations, is a dynamo . . .

Adela Gonzmart was Ybor City's unrivaled "First Lady."

*331*

### Ballet Folklorico de Ybor

In December 1989, Ballet Folklorico de Ybor, Inc., was established to preserve and promote a vital and important dimension of the folklore and history of the Spanish, Cuban, Afro Cuban, Italian, and other cultures that settled Ybor City at the turn of the century. The founder of the organization was Adela Gonzmart, but grant funding from the Hillsborough County Board of County Commissioners and the Ybor City Chamber of Commerce made possible this superb folkloric organization. The idealistic mission of the group was brought within reach with the leadership of Adela Gonzmart, chair; Adrienne Garcia, president; Maria Pasetti, secretary; and Sylvia Fernandez, treasurer. A very successful premiere performance on September 23, 1990, at the Centro Asturiano Theater was undoubtedly a forecast of a brilliant future for a group whose dance repertoire embraced classical Spanish, Italian, Afro Cuban and Cuban, and Spanish flamenco suites. Included in the classical Spanish suite at the premier was the beginning number, the formidable *La Boda de Luis Alonso.*

Thanks to Adela's leadership, the Ballet Folklorico de Ybor began years of successful performances. Since its opening, a Mexican suite and some South American numbers were added to its repertoire and further strengthen its impact on audiences.

The reputation and resources of the Columbia Restaurant contributed much to the group's success. At a time when social club cultural performances declined in Ybor City, the existence of the Ballet Folklorico aided greatly in maintaining a bit of Latin culture.

### The Social Clubs in the Last Half of the Twentieth Century

The role of social clubs in the Golden Age of Ybor City was unprecedented. Nothing unified those within a given ethnic culture—especially the Cubans, the Spaniards, and the Italians—as much as having their own clubs. The benefits of their homegrown HMO medical programs and the excellence of their facilities assured the highest level of membership available in the Latin community.

Greatly facilitating their cohesiveness were the clubhouses that each group possessed. They were magnificent buildings. They offered amenities that were nearly unimaginably fine for the modest families who enjoyed them, and they were essential in an era when few facilities were available to the cigar workers. Because the social buildings included quality theaters, beautiful dance halls, cantinas, and recreation rooms complete with bars, coffee and snack areas, large meeting rooms, offices, exercise rooms, and libraries, the community benefited from truly rich cultural and social resources. Entertainment included local and foreign artists, singers, movies, and folkloric troupes.

The clubs gave neighbors a chance to dwell on and appreciate their own forebears, their history and struggles as well as the great and beautiful cultures they each wanted to retain at all cost. Cubans, Italians, and Spaniards not only had impressive buildings; their medical facilities included the state-of-the-art sanatoriums, cemeteries, and eventually mausoleums. The cost in 1940 had remained only $1.50 per month per family, collected by a "cobrador" and still including cradle-to-grave health coverage. But the numbers were harder and harder to add up.

The loss of a viable cigar industry, the impact of Urban Renewal, the departure of many Spaniards, Cubans, and Italians, and the mammoth rise in cost of the new medical technologies—all these and more resulted in the withering of the social clubs. Centro Español de Ybor moved its club to West Tampa, and eventually had to close its doors. The Ybor building was sold to the State of Florida. Its hospital on far-off Bayshore Boulevard closed also, after an

In the winter of 1992, Fernando Noriega (center) received the Outstanding Citizen Award presented at the Ybor City State Museum. Celebrating the ceremony with him are Elvira Garcia (left), president of the Damas de Centro Asturiano, and Sonya Ziegler, three-term president of the Ybor City Museum Society.

Fernando Noriega and his wife with Mary and Manuel Alvarez.

L'Unione Italiana Mausoleum.

Centro Español Mausoleum.

Centro Asturiano de Tampa Mausoleum.

"Cradle to grave" care offered by the social clubs in Ybor City included not only medical facilities, but cemeteries. These photographs taken in 1995 show the well-maintained facilities with flowers recently deposited by family members. Cemeteries cover three to five acres. Here many of the founding mothers and fathers or Ybor City are buried, many in simple plots, but many in tombs handsomely decorated with engraved marble. Both the old Centro Español and the current L'Unione Italiana cemeteries are located at 21st Avenue and 26th Street. The newer Centro Español cemetery is located on Lake Avenue at about 46th Street. The Centro Asturiano cemetery is on Martin Luther King Boulevard at 54th Street. Its mausoleum is being enlarged. The older cemetery on Ola Avenue and Indiana Avenue is closed, but is still maintained. Weekends find much visitation by family members carrying flowers to honor their loved ones. The Colón Cemetery is widely used by Cubans, Italians, and Spaniards in the West Tampa area. It is centrally located on Columbus Drive and MacDill Avenue and is very well maintained.



**Chapter 9 · Building and Renewing: 1990-1995**

*Centro Español in the centennial year of 1986.*

*This view of Hillsborough Community College shows a side of campus familiar to commuting students. The Círculo Cubano is visible in the background at the right.*

*Members of the Ybor City Chamber of Commerce present a scholarship check to Dr. Lois Gaston of Hillsborough Community College (seated at desk) in 1997. Left to right (standing) are Annette DeLisle, YCCC executive director; Dr. Gwen Stevenson, HCC president; Mike Rabaut of HCC; and Gil Hernandez, YCCC president. YCCC.*

*Four past Ybor City Chamber of Commerce presidents posed together with the chamber's secretary for a photograph in 1992. They are (left to right) Vince Pardo, Henry Woodroffe, Gill Hernandez, Neida De LaParte (secretary) and Scott Rolston. La Gaceta.*

*The officers and directors of the Ybor City Chamber of Commerce for 1990 included many individuals who assumed leadership roles in the Ybor City renaissance. They are (left to right) Jim Serina, Marilyn Perry, Frank Lastra, Dan De La Cruz, Adela Gonzmart (president), Al Kurzenhauser, Braulio Alonso, Rafael Martinez-Ybor, Joan Jennewein, Vic DiMaio, Max Traina, Henry Woodroffe, Michael Bobo, Al Fernandez, Scott Rolston, Stephanie Ferrell, Mary Alvarez, Eva Ciacco, Audrey Perez, Mario Garcia, and Bill Cadrecha. La Gaceta.*

**Ybor City: The Making of a Landmark Town**

unsuccessful attempt to keep offering services by relocating them near West Tampa. With these moves, the La Benefica facility on Palm and 15th Street was closed. Finally, the Centro Asturiano Hospital shut down. El Bien Publico and the Trelles Clinics had already ceased operations.

With the loss of the club hospitals, a very large portion of the glue that bound the members into a particular club is now gone. Latins were very proud of their large and modern hospitals and clinics. The memories from earlier years are still shared, and the clubs, today, still maintain their various cemeteries and mausoleums in excellent condition. In 1997 the Centro Asturiano began adding a new wing to theirs. This is a great testimony to the quality of the sons and daughters the original Latins of the town raised. Aside from their clubhouses, unity still comes among the various clubs through a common heritage, family ties woven through intermarriages, and a mutual love and respect for the forebears and the town they grew in—Ybor City. Today, though most descendents live throughout Tampa, they still have much in common.

The mechanism that unites and draws Latins together is today less clear, but it still exists. Aside from their cultural history and heritage, and some purely individual club activities, they are still united by their memories and family stories, reinforced by new successful interactions in programs and celebrations in conjunction with the Ybor City Chamber of Commerce, the Ybor City Museum Society, the Rotary Club, Round Table, and other town organizations. Much of the Taste of Ybor City, Fiesta Day, Tallahassee Bean Soup Day, special events at Centennial Park, El Ballet Folklorico de Ybor, and other groups, are often jointly arranged through the various Latin club societies.

New initiatives are being taken by officers and members of each organization. Since 1994, the Centro Asturiano has leased its large Cantina Room to owners of the Latam Restaurant. Recently it added a modern elevator. The Cuban Club sponsored a very successful business convention for Ybor City and outside businesses at its large patio, and much of the basement floor. L'Unione Italiana continues to operate its many activities; the Martí-Macéo club has supported student art displays and history events; and the community radio station WMNF-FM has presented live contemporary music performances—including Latin, South American, Salsa, and Zydeco groups—at a variety of venues in Ybor City.[2]

The Heritage Structures of Ybor City was organized in the late 1980s to provide an overall umbrella for the work of maintaining the historic "Social Palaces" and other places. The Heritage Structures Collection of Ybor City includes the Centro Asturiano, Circulo Cubano, Deutsche Amerikanisher, El Centro Español, La Union Martí-Macéo, L'Unione Italiana, and the Parque Amigos de José Marti. During the early 1990s their mission was clarified and the results began to be seen. Recognizing the need not only to restore but also to maintain and preserve the unusual architecture and cultural contributions found in the fabric of these ethnic structures, the community has undertaken redevelopment of the area through the joint efforts of private citizens and businesses working with numerous local, state, and national entities; and, significantly, they have been joined by family members who trace their American beginnings to Ybor City, wishing to preserve the heritage that has stood the test of time.[3]

Thanks to their work, today a unified organization supports the complete Heritage Structures Collection of Ybor City. This organization is dedicated to the redevelopment of the area. Renewed historical interest from tourists has helped to encourage their efforts.[4]

There is today a feeling of reawakening. It can be sensed not only within the daily rhythms of the community, but also in activities reaching out to strengthen ties beyond the city limits. The Sister Cities relationship with Oviedo, Spain, Agrigento, Sicily, and Barranquilla, Colombia, have supplied needed synergy.

Very much needed is a new generation of young American grandchildren who value dearly the heritage of values left them by their grandparents. Undoubtedly, many of the grandchildren have been raised on grandmothers' and grandfathers' foods, stories of old, pictures of long ago, heirlooms, artifacts, and games. Some have even made a trip to the old country with their parents or grandparents. There they have been inspired by all they see and have linked this experience with their feelings for the past, thus extending the family dreams. Once again they will be inspired by the songs and music they often heard at home. They will help assure a living heritage for generations to come.

Fortunately, the decendants of the original Yborciteños are being joined by surprising numbers of unrelated Americans with a sensitivity for history who see the values and resources available in Ybor City. They are the ones whose interest, action, and support will assure that this landmark town will be maintained and enhanced. One hopes they will lead others to action. They will be tomorrow's guardians of the Ybor City history.

## The Final Withering of the Vine: William E. Field & the Ritz Theatre

Unfortunately, part of the saga of Ybor City includes stories of unsuccessful attempts by potential guardians or nurturers to preserve historic venues. In January 1984, businessman William E. Field took it upon himself to reopen what he believed to be the oldest movie house in the South. He reported that Ybor City's Ritz Theatre had served as a silent movie theater in 1917

and he planned a grand re-launching of the landmark to coincide with Tampa's hosting of the 1984 Super Bowl. Disappointed by a lack of backing from what he referred to in a letter to the *Tampa Tribune* as "the Tampa establishment," Field abandoned the project. His letter lamented that "what happened was financial disaster for me and others" but it went on to point out the community's potential, wishing it well:

> The Latin Quarter of Ybor City and the French Quarter in New Orleans were the only immigrant enclaves in the South. In the first decade of this century, Ybor had the largest theater district in the South and the great stars like Enrico Caruso and Lily Pons, appeared there. Today the French Quarter is internationally known, and Ybor City languishes in slumber and past glory . . . I hope that good people stay involved in the promotion of Ybor City.[5]

W. E. Field was a dynamic personality and his leaving represented a great loss to Ybor City. I felt privileged to have talked to this outstanding gentle person on several occasions about his project. It could have been an important step forward if his efforts had succeeded.

## The Playmakers & the Ritz Theatre

Within a few years, however, the appeal of the historic theater led to another chance at its revival. In November 1988 the marquee of the vacant Ritz proclaimed: *"The New Home of Playmakers Theater."* Freedom Savings of Tampa had foreclosed on the property in 1987, and the building was bought by Joe Capitano, his father Nick, and his brother-in-law, Al Garcia, all respected, stable businessmen. Joe Capitano, who hailed from Ybor City, said in newspaper reports that he and his partners were delighted with a chance to help both Ybor City and The Playmakers, who had been performing since the early 1980s in the Cuban Club.

The new owners signed a lease with the theater company, and according to Steve Bragin, president of The Playmakers' board

of directors, they "turned our dreams into reality practically overnight." But, unfortunately, within a short time the dream had faded. The company's artistic director since 1981, Mark Hunter, resigned and is now a professor in the theater department at Cornell. The theater group's new artistic director announced they would have to leave the Ritz location. The space was more than they could afford, and they had never been able to draw the consistently large audiences they needed, in part because "a lot of people said they had problems with Ybor City at night . . . when you're talking about getting out of a play at 11 p.m."[6]

The effort of the talented Playmakers and their failure to make the Ritz a functioning live theater in Ybor City is indicative of the lack of support for many types of artistic ventures in the last years of the 1980s and through the early 1990s. Many outstanding artists left as casualties of persistent blight, increasing rents, and seemingly unappreciative landlords. Some said these changes were merely the result of free enterprise as landlords who had weathered up to twenty years of empty and run-down buildings with no income attempted to make up for lost time. Others said that allowing the departure of many artists represented a lack of vision on the part of some landlords who lost patience with the artists whose presence had seen them through some of the worst of times. Whatever the reasons, the outflux of many artists and artistic ventures was a loss for the city.

Nonetheless, the Ritz had been remodeled, and I still recall scrutinizing the graceful entrance hall and the building's attractive amenities. It was all there, again, as it had looked in the 1930s. It was so near to being reborn . . . but the theater once again closed its doors.

## Tampa Sister City Initiatives: Agrigento and Oviedo

In January 1990 the Sister Cities Committee of Tampa announced plans to

*Vince Pardo, who helped spearhead the Italian Sister City effort on behalf of the Italian Club and as President of the Ybor City Chamber of Commerce, stands with Rebecca Gagalis, past president of the Ybor City Development Commission, and Enrique Woodroffe, another YCCC past president.*

add two new European affiliates. Both of them had special significance for Ybor City. James R. Turner, president and director of the Tampa committee and former president of the Ybor City Museum Society, said his group had approval from Sister Cities International to join forces with Oviedo, Spain, and Agrigento, Italy, in a program to help communities learn more about one another and "develop friendly and meaningful exchanges."[7]

The Sister Cities program had been launched in 1956 by President Dwight D. Eisenhower, when he called for massive exchanges between Americans and people from other countries. Tampa's new Sister Cities were especially appealing in light of the strong Spanish and Italian roots in Ybor City and the extended Tampa community.

## Tampa–Agrigento Sister Cities

Alfonso Belluccia, chairman of the Sister Cities Tampa-Agrigento Committee, reported that it took six years of work to establish Tampa's first European Sister City relationship with Agrigento, Sicily. On July 15,1991, Tampa Mayor Sandra W. Freedman met with Agrigento's Mayor, Giovanni Roberto DiMauro to sign a Sister City agreement between the



337

two cities. L'Unione Italiana had been chiefly responsible for fostering the Tampa-Agrigento relationship. During Vince Pardo's presidency of the Italian Club the quest for an Italian Sister City had emerged as a pirority. Twenty Italian Sister City members were selected with Sandra Alfieri acting as liaison between the Sister City Committee of Tampa and L'Unione Italiana. At the time they estimated that there were more than 40,000 Italian Americans living in Tampa, and many of them were descendants from families from Agrigento and its surrounding towns of Alessandria della Rocca, Santo Stefano Quisquina, Cianciana, and Contessa Entellina.[8]

In 1991 Vince Pardo, as president of the Ybor City Chamber of Commerce, made the trip with Mayor Freedman and Sister City Committee representatives, to Agrigento, Sicily, for the official signing of formal ties with Tampa. Later, Pardo was also point man in arranging a formal reception for the Agrigento Mayor and his delegation. This beautiful and widely attended reception was held in the formidable Tower Club, situated on top of the First Florida Bank building. Mayor Freedman, the Sister City Committee, and an Italian delegation from Tampa, and a Sicilian delegation were present to formalize the Agrigento-Tampa Twin City agreement. The Sicilian delegation's dancing troupe put on a dazzling display of folk dancing to climax the evening.

The link continued to thrive in 1993 when the Ybor City's *Festa della Madonna* celebration became a joint project between the Italian Club's Ladies Auxiliary and the Tampa-Agrigento Sister City Committee. A visit by Agrigento's folklore dance troupe *Compagina Folclorica Trinacria* coincided with the Italian Club's annual festival honoring the patron saint of Alessandria della Rocca. Volunteer Mary Frances Granell coordinated host families for the visiting company.[9]

Then during May 19-24, 1996, Mayor Dick Greco and Hillsborough County Commissioner Joe Chillura led a Tampa delegation to Sicily. They carried gifts, including a replica of the immigrant statue that stands in Ybor City. While in Agrigento, Ken Ferlita, another past Ybor City Chamber of Commerce president who was part of the delegation, gathered a considerable amount of family tree data in the neighboring towns of Alessandria della Rocca and Santo Stefano, which had been the starting point for many of Ybor's and West Tampa's Sicilians. The formal renewal of ties to our immigrant heritage marked an important step in historical awareness for new generations and was another milestone for historic preservation.[10]

## Reception for Oviedo and the Christopher Columbus Anniversary

In the meantime, similar efforts affirmed Ybor City's roots in Spain. In 1985-86, Rafael Martinez-Ybor, then President of the Ybor City Rotary Club, led the Sister Cities initiative. His pursuits were sustained by subsequent presidents of this club. Jose Pando, a native of Oviedo, joined Rafael Martinez Ybor, attorney E. J. Salcines, and others in the effort to seek Oviedo as the Sister City of Ybor. City Councilman Lee Duncan helped make it a reality.

By 1992, the planning had led to a stunning event: the observance of the 500th anniversary of the voyages of Christopher Columbus coincided with our Tampa Bay area connections with our Sister Cities. The ceremonies were made more unforgettable by the arrival in Tampa Bay of full-scale replicas of Columbus's vessels, *La Niña*, *La Pinta*, and *La Santa Maria*. They sailed into Tampa as part of the national celebration tour of the fifth centennial anniversary of the discovery of America just a few days before the official reception for the Oviedo delegation.

A dual event of this historical magnitude had not been seen in Tampa before. The colorful, historic antique ships were docked at the foot of the elegant Tampa Convention Center. Present at the Sister-Cities program were many of the crew of the fleet and its elegantly attired, Comandante, Capitan de Corbeta (Commander of the Fleet, Lieutenant Commander). Don Santiago Bolibar Pineiro, from Galicia, Spain, did an impressive job of representing Cristobal Colon, Genoves (Christopher Columbus, Genoese). Standing in white uniforms as honorary guards were four Asturian sailors of the squadron.[11]

For the Sister City Program, this event was prologue to the official signing of the protocol joining the cities of Tampa and Oviedo, which would take place that night at the University Club. Many city officials were there, led by Tampa Mayor Sandy Freedman and her aide, Margarita Gonzalez. Also present were the main participants from the Ybor City Rotary Club, the Tampa Sister Cities Committee, the Bank of Tampa, and the delegation from Oviedo, numbering approximately 30 and led by Mayor Don Gavino de Lorenzo Ferrera, and E. J. Salcines, the Honorary Spanish Consul in Tampa. Also present was the Mayor of Barranquilla, Colombia, who was in Tampa to attend an international Tampa Sister Cities Committee meeting with representatives from Cordova, Argentina; Agrigento, Sicily; and now, Oviedo, Spain.

With Salcines acting as Master of Ceremonies, Mayor Sandy Freedman handed to Mayor Gavino de Lorenzo Ferrera the flag of the city of Tampa. In turn, Don Gavino presented the official gift from the city and people of Oviedo to the city of Tampa and its Tampa-Oviedo Sister City Committee. It was the hand-carved official seal of the city of Oviedo, commonly referred as "The Cross of the Angels."

*Judge E. J. Salcines helped to arrange and host the Tampa visit of a Sister City delegation from Ovideo, Spain, during Tampa's observance of the 500th anniversary of Columbus's voyage to the New World.*
E. J. SALCINES.

The University Club's top floor pamoramic view of brilliantly lit Tampa and the Tampa Bay was exhilarating. One looked towards the bay to attempt to see the Columbus flotilla below. Following the signing of the official documents, E. J. Salcines led the singing of "*Asturias, Patria Querida,*" the beloved anthem of that province. Much dancing followed the jotas and paso dobles, provided by the incomparable Margot and Augustine Freire, who two days earlier, at the private reception for Columbus fleet commandante Don Santiago, had wowed the select group with *Valencia* and *La Violetera*.[12] The evening was tuly memorable and meaningful to me as it renewed, affirmed, and celebrated the cultural foundations that immigrant generations had brought to our local history through Ybor City.

The modern awareness of this legacy was further strengthened and affirmed in June of 1996 when Tampa Mayor Dick Greco headed a delegation from Tampa to Oviedo, Spain, which included Fernando Noriega, Director of Community and Business Services Department, and others. Among the great reception

*339*

activities offered the Tampa delegation was a visit to the seven-thousand-member Centro Asturiano de Oviedo club building, a beautiful thing to behold. The club was the forerunner of the Centro Asturiano Club in Havana, which in turn was the sponsor of its counterpart in Tampa.

Today Tampa continues to enjoy affiliation with the Sister Cities of Oviedo and Agrigento, and as well as our newer "Sisters" of Barranquilla, Colombia; Cordoba, Argentina; Izmir, Turkey; Le Havre, France; Granada, Nicaragua; and Camerines, South Philippines.[13]

## Spanish Lyric Theater

As of the late 1990s the Spanish Lyric Theater remained the principal Spanish musical theater in Tampa and one of the finest in the nation. I know of no other Spanish or Hispanic theater in the country with the same degree of maturity and repertoire. What Rene Gonzalez had started as the Spanish Little Theater had evolved over four decades to include an astounding repertoire of fine Spanish music and theater. Its performances have included most of the classical Spanish *zarzuelas* such as *Verbena de La Paloma*, *La Revoltosa*, *Agua Azucarillo y Agua Ardiente*, *La Del Manojo de Rosas*, *Luisa Fernanda*, *Los Gavilanes*, and many others; Viennese operettas like *La Viuda Alegre*, *The Merry Widow*, *El Conde de Luxemburgo*, and *La Duquesa Del Bal Tabaran*, *Viena*; Cuban *zarzuelas* and musicals such as Ernesto Lecuona's *Maria La O* and *Cecilia Valdez*; and, in increasing numbers, Broadway musicals like *The King and I*, *Fiddler on the Roof*, *Camelot*, *Gigi*, *Oklahoma*, *West Side Story*, and others. This list is but a small sample of the prodigious number of works persented by the theater.

On February 14, 1989, on the occasion of the theater's 30th anniversary, Her Majesty, Queen Sofia of Spain, honored Rene Gonzalez, in which, among other exquisite praises, she mentioned that the Spanish Lyric Theater deserved special words of appreciation from the Spanish world of culture. Gonzalez and the Spanish Lyric Theater company have deservedly received other international recognition, including a reception with the Duque de Cadiz at the Columbia Restaurant in 1981.

Present on several occasions, also, was the General Consul of Spain, Carlos M. Fernandez-Shaw. Don Carlos was personally associated with the world of *zarzuela* theater in Spain. His father left a brilliant record in the early part of the century, particularly in his composition of one of the leading *zarzuelas*, *Luisa Fernanda*.

The Spanish Lyric Theater, from the doldrum years following its beginning in 1959, to the near present, brought to mind much that was select and beautiful of Spain, which the town's fathers and mothers needed to compensate for the gradually receding culture.

Tampa in general, and Latins in particular, owe a great debt of gratitude to Gonzalez as its brilliant musical and theatrical director. Many question what Ybor's culture would have been in these last decades without a night out to his theater. He has directed, played in the casts, warehoused costumes, inspired a board of directors, and fostered a Damas organization while expressing the brilliance of his musical mind. His casts have included many Cubans, Italians, Spaniards, and now, more than ever, many of South's and Greater Tampa's best players and singers.[14]

## Renewal of the Centro Español Building in Ybor City

In a significant achievement for Ybor City's historic future, the State of Florida agreed to purchase the Centro Español building in 1990, a necessary step in the preservation of this National Historic Landmark building. Florida Governor Bob Martinez and the Florida Cabinet

**Ybor City: The Making of a Landmark Town**

*The brick building of Centro Español had withstood years of neglect, but was in need of major restoration funds. Private investment creatively adapted it for new life as the centerpiece of a new Centro Ybor project. This photo from the 1940s shows the original architectural features. The decorative ironwork on the front and the covered sidewalk on the right are evidence of Ybor City craftsmanship and attention to detail. Compare this to the building of today. the centerpiece of Centro Ybor.* USFSCL.

voted to buy the building described as "the oldest and 'brightest jewel' among Tampa's ethnic, social and mutual-aid clubs" from the Trust for Public Land, which had purchased the building to save it from a foreclosure auction in 1989.

Florida placed the building on its purchase list in 1988, planning to acquire it with funds through the Conservation and Recreational Lands program (CARL). Fortunately, the Trust had saved the building from the auction block, spent some $700,000 to bring the exterior up to standards, and officially delivered it, in better shape, to the state in 1990.

Florida, in turn, spent about $12 million to stabilize it and make it safe and agreed to lease it for fifty years to the Historic Tampa-Hillsborough County Preservation Board, which began to seek private partners to restore it to life.

Stephanie Ferrell, director of the preservation board, was quoted in the *St. Petersburg Times* as saying, "It's going to make a major difference to Ybor City." And Rebecca Chittum, executive director of the Ybor City Development Corporation at the time, declared that it was "excellent news," as she worked to revitalize what was still a largely vacant and rundown neighborhood.

Her colleague Wayne Garcia added that, "Ybor redevelopers place a high priority on rebuilding business and life along East 7th Avenue. The vacant two-story Centro Español with its theater, cantina and ballroom could play a vital role in making the Avenue as lively as it was before federal urban renewal in the 1960s sparked the decline of Tampa's Latin Quarter."[15]

The building then remained in a sort of "holding pattern" until Steiner and Associates of Columbus, Ohio, in collaboration with the Sembler Company of St. Petersburg proposed to preserve the building as the centerpiece of their Centro Ybor development. They spent another $5 million renovating it to include ground-floor shopping, a resturant, and an improvisational comedy club. Ground-breaking for the $40 million

*This photograph by Robertson and Fresh captures the grand architectural features of the Cuban Club building that have drawn new generations to work for its restoration and preservation.* USFSCL.

Centro Ybor project was in 1998, and soon the Centro Español landmark structure lived again at the heart of Ybor City.

To the delight of residents and businesses alike, the stunning building had begun its return to glory. With the support of the State of Florida and the long-standing affection of Spanish families and the greater community of Ybor City descendants, the club became a physical symbol of how the great achievements of the past could continue to inspire the present. Although there had been clear signs of renewal prior to this important anchor of historic preservation, the saving and restoration of this Ybor City monument marked a clear turning of the tide. A new vitality embracing history could be felt and seen along La Setíma, and the impulse for renewal was rapidly advancing.

### El Círculo Cubano Renovation

Another influential and inspiring project emerged as the old El Círculo Cubano worked with determination to achieve its necessary structural renovation and exterior facelift. The historic Hispanic building at 10th Avenue and 14th Street had long been in need of repairs.

In 1992 it, too, faced foreclosure. The Cuban Club Foundation managed to keep it alive thanks to cash contributions of $127,000. By 1994 the foundation had obtained a $250,000 grant from the State of Florida to begin major restoration.

This was a major beginning, but there was still much to be done. Ray Grimaldi organized the first annual Tropicana Night fundraiser in 1994 at the Hyatt Regency in downtown Tampa with WFLA-TV news anchor Yolanda Fernandez as mistress of ceremonies and actor Cameron Diaz as a special guest. The $100-a-plate benefit raised about $35,000, and Grimaldi announced, "We're going to bring in everything it takes to restore all four stories. We expect to be able to make this up in five or six years."[16]

With determination and community support, combined efforts began to pay

off. In May of 1995, Rep. Elvin Martinez presented the foundation with the last installment of its $250,000 state grant. Cuban Club President Angelo Perez spoke for the members and the community when he said, "This is really a dream come true."

Work was impressively underway by the fall of 1995, with the first goal being the major renovation of the first floor, where over the years the Cuban Club at various times had operated a gymnasium, boxing hall, baskeball court, and indoor track. With the backing of its foundation, the Cuban Club undertook a $400,000 project to remove termite damge and to convert the two-level cantina into three levels, with a sunken dance floor, a bar, and a table level.

Cristino Perez, treasurer of the Cuban Club Foundation, reported that they expected to complete the cantina by December of 1995. Once it was finished, the cantina and patio would comply with codes and with the federal Americans with Disability Act guidelines for accessibility. These areas could become part of future fundraising, since they could be rented for special events. But much remained to accomplish, including repairs to the fourth-floor ballroom, the plumbing system, fire escape, and restrooms.

With special events, concerts, and fundraisers happening there, the Ballet Folkloric de Ybor practicing regularly in the club's second-floor theater, and plans for an additional $2 million in restoration ahead, there was a new vitality in the air as 1995 drew to a close. Then, on New Year's Day of 1996, a worker who stopped by the building discovered that part of the ballroom's ceiling had fallen, crashing to the floor and destroying a large section of the 70-year-old ceiling mural executed by Cuban painter Juan Aciego.

"The mural is kind of the showpiece of that building and of the ballroom itself," said Joan Jennewein, who had worked

*The Greco sisters, Mary (left) and Theresa, had lived in the same Ybor City house for 82 years when this photograph was taken in 1998. At the time Mary was 87 and Theresa was 82. They became visible treasures of Ybor City's past, continuing to live in their tight, well-kept wooden house in the center of town and walking to local venues. Their father, Francisco, emigrated from Sicily about 1905. He worked as a manual laborer, and his wife, Sebastiana, worked as a tobacco stripper. The Greco sisters attend civic functions like royalty and are recognized as living symbols of Ybor City's heritage.*

tirelessly for Ybor preservation and served on the Heritage Structure Consortium. "It's a real gem."

The ceiling collapse was not the work of vandals or criminals, but the result of time and decay. In fact, it was one of the single worst incidents of decay that preservationists could recall. Fortunately, much of the 30-by-60-foot mural remained, including Aciego's rendering of the Greek muse of dance, Terpsichore. The Cuban Club Foundation had accomplished much, but despite its tremendous dedication, they had been unable to repair things quickly enough. It was not clear where the necessary funds would be found to move forward. "There are just so many areas of need," said Cuban Club President Rolando Perez-Pedrero. "The irony is that 1996 started with the cantina almost being finished, at the same time that a priceless piece of art and history was lost in the ballroom."[17]

Building and renewing in Ybor City has meant construction of a new entrance to the National Historic Landmark District. The design makes use of wrought iron appropriate to the historical style of the Latin area, but workers in the cigar town would never have seen such a sight on their way home. RM.

*Mary Alvarez (left) received the Vicente Martínez Ybor Award from the Ybor City Museum Society in 1994 for her outstanding contributions to cultural preservation of the Ybor City community. With her in this photograph at the reception are U.S. Representative Sam Gibbons and Tampa Mayor Sandra Freeman. The award was presented in conjunction with the 176th birthday celebration of Ybor City's founder, held in the courtyard of the Ybor City State Museum.*

*Joyce Schaffer's purchase and rebuilding of two old buildings on north side of La Sétima between 17th and 18th streets in the early 1980s encouraged others to join her unwavering initiatives. A builder and developer throughout the Tampa region, Joyce brought enthusiasm and experience to the presidency of the Ybor City Chamber of Commerce in 1985-86. Her son, Jay Fechtel, participated heavily in Chamber activities.*

*Delia P. Sanchez and Angeles Marti, active volunteers with the Ybor City Museum, discuss plans in this 1994 snapshot. Delia Sanchez received a Tony Pizzo Award in 2002.*

*Salha and Ralph Bobo, shown above with six of their children, owned and ran the Blue Ribbon Grocery at 1431 La Sétima. Salha Levy Bobo, shown at right working at her desk in 1993, was born in Aleppo, Syria, immigrating to the U.S. in 1921 and then to Ybor City in 1947, where she and her husband Ralph opened the Blue Ribbon. After Ralph died in 1949, Salha and her children carried on managing the market, and it became a neighborhood landmark, active through the 1990s.*



**Ybor City: The Making of a Landmark Town**

# The Memorable Schools of Ybor City

*Education has always been one of the strongest family values in the Ybor City community. Generations of parents supported their children not only through years of homework and activities in the public schools, but also supported their educational dreams of attaining higher education. Both public and private local institutions have had a role, but the public schools on this page played and especially important part in the lives of many.*

*The Vicente Martínez Ybor School, as it appeared in 1921 (left) and as it looked in the late 1990s, when it was no longer in use as a school. The windows have been boarded-up and the surrounding trees and shrubs appear untrimmed.*

*Ybor City elementary education was available at Philip Shore Elementary (left), shown shortly after its construction. On the right is a recent photo of Orange Grove Elementary, serving a new generation of Ybor City children in the 1990s as a magnet school and now as a middle school.*

*George Washington Junior High School. The building was demolished to make room of the widening of the highway on its south and east side.*

*Hillsborough High School, in a building dating from 1927, continues as an educational leader. Today it is home to the International Baccalaureate program.*

St. Joseph's Academy, on the southwest corner of 11th Avenue and 18th Street, was one of the oldest parochial schools in the diocese. When a Redemptorist priest took over the parish, which was originally named "Our Lady of Mercy" after Mercedes Ybor, wife of Vicente Martinez Ybor, the parish and school were renamed Our Lady of Perpetual Help. The school became known as O.L.P.H. and offered classes from Kindergarten through high school—elementary classes on the first and second floors and secondary classes on the third. The high school was closed in the 1970s and other classes gradually phased out. The building was torn down in the 1980s.

Roland Marcelo Manteiga, eminent publisher and editor of La Gaceta, passed away in September 1998. Son of the newspaper's founder, he began his journalism career working at the paper as a youngster and assumed the role of editor and publisher upon his father's death. Under his direction, the weekly trilingual paper increased its local, state, and national stature. Roland left a legacy of memories unique to his reserved nature as well as his manner of capturing and reporting the news. Not a noted public speaker, he is famous for a five-word "talk" at the Ybor City State Museum patio when presented with an award: "Thank you for this recognition." Still, La Gaceta was awaited weekly, especially for Roland's column "As We Heard It." And Latins with roots in Ybor City looked forward to the historic photos, so dear to our past, published weekly on its front page. Now Roland's son, Patrick, has stepped to the plate fighting vigorously and effectively for the town's historic landmark values and the paper's tradition of strong political values.

Meeting at La Tropicana, an Ybor City mecca for café con leche, are (above, left to right) Patrick Manteiga, associate editor of La Gaceta; Roland Manteiga, editor and publisher; Bill Nelson, State of Florida Insurance Commissioner; and Jim Shimberg Jr., attorney. Roland for many years conducted interviews with local, state, and national leaders at this table, especially reserved for him. He could be seen there virtually every weekday morning. For instant reporting, a red telephone graced the table.

Roland's father, founding editor/publisher Victoriano Manteiga (below, seated) was a former lector known as El Intelectual ("The Intellectual One"). Shown here in his senior years being presented with a YCCC award by representatives of the Chamber (from left) President Frank Lastra, and Board Members Mary Sachs and Angel Rañon. La Gaceta.

**Ybor City: The Making of a Landmark Town**

*In 1992 Armando P. Valdes Jr., 77, closed Valdes Jewelry on La Sétima at 15th Street 45 years after he opened it there. The son of cigar workers, Valdes was a dynamic leader, past president of Ybor City Chamber of Commerce and Ybor City Lions Club, Ybor's Outstanding Citizen in 1962, Alcade of Ybor City, and three-time candidate for Mayor of Tampa. Former Tampa Mayor Dick Greco said, "I've known the man all my life. There isn't a thing he wouldn't do for his friends . . . or community."*

*Joe Capitano Sr. has been a timely blessing to Italians of the Tampa Bay area and to L'Unione Italiana in particular. He has not only served as the club's president, but also presided over much fundraising, helping the Italian Club attract a $600,000 grant from the state, as well as many coporate donations. A philanthropist himself, he has been one of the club's largest donors. Today the Italian Club building is once again fully functional, with the second and third floors beautifully restored. He has also worked to restore the Ritz Theatre, Las Novedades, and the former Corral Wodiska Cigar Factory building on 2nd Avenue and 19th Street, which houses his family business, Radiant Oil. Moreover, he has used his talents to bolster educational initiatives for children lacking in means and for those with severe learning disabilities.* Paul Guzzo/ La Gaceta.

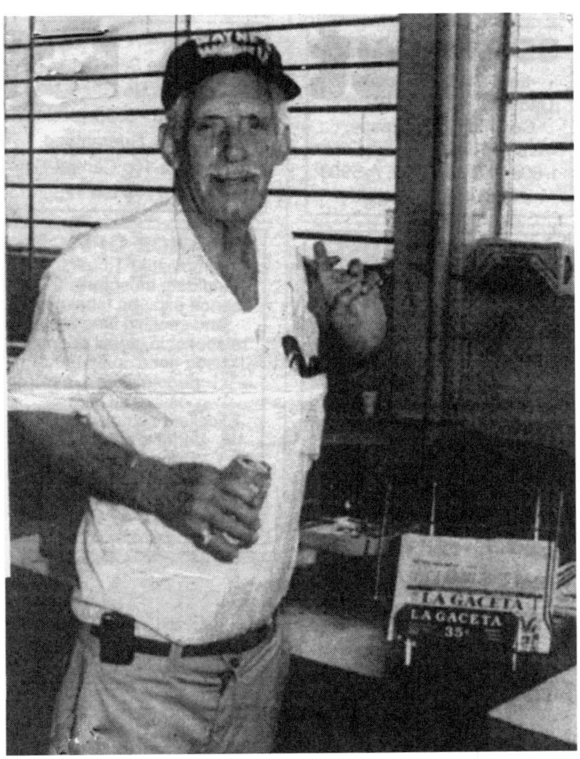

*Caesar Romero is an authentic figure of the fast-vanishing Ybor City world. Born here in the 1920s, he attended Orange Grove Grammar School in north Ybor City (where we shared a home room). In earlier years he sold crab cakes on a motor bike. Humble, unassuming, honest, and law-abiding, he lives today at the Haciendas de Ybor on Palm Avenue, built for the town's residents whose homes were taken away by Urban Renewal. He continues to walk to town for shopping and social events and says he will never leave this beautiful town. He is our living past, caught with a smile in this photo at the Blue Ribbon Grocery on La Setima next to a rack with the latest issue of Manteiga's historic Ybor City newspaper.* La Gaceta



**Chapter 9 · Building and Renewing: 1990-1995**

*The corner of La Sétima and 17th Street brims with life during Fiesta Day in Ybor City in the 1990s. Bernini's Restaurant, a popular new Ybor City landmark owned by attorney Frank de la Grana, is now located on the northeast corner in a building that once housed the Ybor City Broadway Bank.*

# Rebirth and Responsibility: Preserving Ybor's Heritage into the Third Millenium

By the mid-1990s, Ybor City was a whirlwind of activity. While remaining Latins now residing in the wider Tampa community attempted to maintain some of their key institutions and cultural connections in Ybor City, they now found allies among energetic newcomers—professionals, planners, activists, speculators, and landowners—who were energetically attempting to carry the town forward, often along directions matching their personal interests or focuses. The many prior years of efforts at redevelopment and the town's elevation to National Landmark status had made the mechanism and process for accomplishing renewal clearer. Despite challenges and set-backs, in the late 1990s the prior signs of hope were looking more and more like definite rebirth.[1]

*This post-1950s label from the Ybor City Cigar Company celebrates a heritage of fine cigars in a unique community.*

## Some New Entrepreneurs and Advocates

Tampa developer Alan Kahana was one of the new converts who stepped forward as a champion for Ybor City. A former physics major, Kahana seemed to have the ability to read trends accurately in charts and graphs, and he even used the language of physics to describe improvements in the historic district, when he spoke of economic development as "achieving critical mass."[2] Another investor beginning to make his mark on Ybor City was Joe Capitano, young son of a prominent Italian industrial family headed by Nick Capitano.

Developer Jack Shiver negotiated an $850,000 agreement to purchase the Kress Building and Kress Annex on the north side of La Sétima and planned to spend at least half a million to restore those 70-year-old Ybor landmarks and convert them for use as retail shops, offices, a restaurant, and even apartments on the third floor.[3] Another of his projects, "Shiver's B and B" (Bed and Breakfast) in the 1600 block of La Sétima was scheduled for 1995 opening, after about $1.4 million in renovation costs.[4] It became the Don Vicente Ybor Hotel.

Meantime, Dick Greco, a politician with family roots in Ybor City, returned to office as Tampa's mayor. He understood the historical importance of the community and imagined the potential positive impact for both the city and the state if its revitalization succeeded. In recognition of the exceptional support for Ybor City by Mayor Greco, the Ybor City Chamber of Commerce voted unanimously to award him a

*Born in 1943 in Gary, Florida, just outside of east Ybor City, Jack Shiver became one of the influential promoters of Ybor City beginning in the 1980s. Among his many endeavors was the rebuilding of much of the old Kress Building block into offices, businesses, and apartments. In the late 1990s he converted the former Gonzalez Clinic building into the elite Don Vicente Ybor Hotel. Jack is highly regarded as one of the developers who had faith in the town's potential and served as chairman of the Ybor City Development Corporation.*

Certificate of Appreciation in late spring of 1996. It was presented to him by President Jill Wax.

Greco brought in four full-time staff people to work on Ybor City projects, where none had previously been allocated. This offered the capacity for sustained strategic planning and initiatives. The Chamber also expressed appreciation for the leadership of Fernando Noriega Jr. in Tampa's new Department of Business and Community Services and of Rebecca Gagalis, newly appointed president of Ybor City Development Corporation.[5]

Another energetic leader in the entrepreneurial ranks was Richard Gonzmart, who became president of the Columbia Restaurant enterprises. Gonzmart has represented Ybor City well in many statewide activities, and he expanded his new theme eatery, "Cha Cha Coconuts," based on the success of that format in Ybor City. The popular Ybor club occupied virtually a block on land already owned by the family.

## Development with YCDC Leadership

As a result of efforts by the Ybor City Development Corporation in cooperation with Noriega and his staff at the Tampa Department of Business and Community Services, Curts Gaines Hall Architects Planners, Inc., and December Design, a comprehensive report and long-range plan entitled "Tampa-Ybor Revitalization Strategy" was released in May 1996 by Mayor Greco's office. In it for the first time, the major goals of Ybor City renewal

*"Made in Ybor City" is a phrase applied to the tobacco products that first made the city famous. Today it also applies to other products, to an economic renaissance, and to the people who made it happen. Two of those key individuals are Ybor City native sons Dick Greco, former mayor of Tampa (left), and Fernando Noriega, former director of business and community services. Their vision and concern for the present and near future development of the Ybor City historic district had resulted in major accomplishments by the time of this 1998 photograph. Underway in the heart of Ybor City and designed to bolster its basic infrastructure are Centro Ybor projects by Steiner and Associates, the Tampa/Ybor Hilton Garden Inn, and the Camden Subsidiary upscale apartment complex of more than 450 units. Complementing these are the Ybor City Trolley, the South Ybor City upgrade, and other developments that result in an investment of nearly $200 million in Ybor City alone. At the groundbreaking for the Ybor Hilton Garden Inn, Mayor Greco described the overall vision as one that "will honor the fathers and mothers of the town."*

**Ybor City: The Making of a Landmark Town**

were envisioned as being accomplished by proper linkages between the Ybor City Historic District, the Central Business District, and the Channel District.

The master plan outlined a systematic approach in three phases:

### Phase I — Infrastructure

This phase will build fundamental and underlying improvements to enhance all areas. The specific items to be addressed include

> Gateway Enhancements
> Signage Program
> 7th Avenue Street-scaping
> Solid Waste Enclosures
> Centennial Park Improvements
> Water/Fire Protection
> Alley Improvements
> Security and Decorative Lighting
> 6th Avenue Road Construction
> 7th Ave. Video Surveillance
> Surface Parking under Crosstown

### Phase II — Tourism

This phase will concentrate on commercial redevelopment and promotion of tourism establishments in the Channel District.

### Phase III — Expansion

This phase will address additional expansion of the Community Redevelopment Area boundaries to the north to 17th Avenue between Nebraska and 26th Street and to the east to 26th Street between Adamo and I-4.

In June 1997 Gagalis announced that the YCDC had won the first major federal grant for the historic Latin business district since redevelopment efforts began in 1989. It nearly doubled the resources which the city of Tampa was committing to the project. The U.S. Department of Commerce's Economic Development Administration had awarded $750,000, and the federal dollars would be mixed with just over $1 million in city infrastructure improvement funds.[6] Gagalis estimated it would bring about 850 more jobs to Ybor City at the same time that many of the improvements would finally be accomplished.

In addition, the major grant enabled the planners and visionaries to "think big." Mayor Greco indicated he expected even more ambitious announcements, and soon there were many new doors opening.

### Proposed Development Projects

Among the most important new development targets to emerge from these discussions were:

> Proposed Ybor Hotel Development
> Major Office and Retail Development
>   (150,000 sq. ft.)
> Streetcar Project
> Five-Block Development Scenario
>   (North of Palm Avenue)
>     1. International Outdoor Marketplace
>      (Interim Use of City Property)
>     2. Mixed Use Project (Office, Retail,
>      Bed and Breakfast)
> Identification of Interim Parking and
> Future Parking Garage Sites

Potential sites for these projects included the block south of the Ybor City Brewing Co., the Sheriff's block, and the block north of 6th Avenue at Nuccio Parkway. This visionary thinking also included a variety of incentives to help attract investors. The creation and marketing of redevelopment incentives were primary considerations for Phase I, and remained important to each stage of the process.

Fortunately, the efforts began showing results quickly. One especially important one, as an example, was the opening of the new Hilton Hotel in Ybor City, which marked the first new hotel opening there in a century. With the plans enjoying success, there has been a gradual expansion of the original Community Redevelopment Area. One important expansion model envisions the creation of Ybor City

cused on land from Nebraska Avenue on the east to North Boulevard on the west, and from the city center to the south to Columbus Drive on the north. In the early- to mid-1900s Tampa Heights was home to many elite Ybor City cigar manufacturers and other prominent Latins.[7]

Of particular importance to Ybor City, this $84 million project to be completed over five years would include a finger of land extending roughly from east of Nebraska to 15th Street and from I-4 to 7th Avenue on the west. Included within these boundaries are single-family homes from I-4 to Palm Avenue, and planned townhouses and mixed-use construction from Nebraska to the west side of the Tampa Electric property on the east and Palm Avenue to La Sétima on the south. As Joe Hoyden, president of the Historic Ybor Neighborhood Civic Association, has emphasized, new homes and apartments are the major component needed to make Ybor more than a night-time attraction Hoyden and his group have given their whole-hearted support to the residential redevelopment goals because "no area develops as well as an area where

South, an area bounded by the CSX railroad on the north, 22nd Street on the east, Adamo Drive on the south, and Nuccio Parkway and Channelside Drive on the west. Proposed uses for enhancement are residential, office, light commercial, and eclectic elements. Present heavy industry section plans have not yet been finalized.

Linkages to redevelopment of other parts of the city have also started to pay off. Mayor Greco's residential redevelopment plans in 1997 called for renovation of at least a thousand homes and apartments in the once-prominent neighborhood of Tampa Heights. The project fo-

**Ybor City: The Making of a Landmark Town**

people live."[8] The improvements west and east of Nebraska will particularly impact Ybor City.

## The Sixtieth Year Anniversary of the Spanish Civil War

Of high historical significance for Ybor City was the late fall of 1997 celebration in Tampa of the 60th year since the beginning of the Spanish Civil War. This three-month-long observance, in addition to the many months of planning, was a culmination of the personal work of Ana Varela-Lago, a history graduate student at the University of South Florida, whose research and presentations on this event helped earn her a Master's degree in history. Varela is a native of Vigo in the Spanish province of Galicia, Spain. Her research on Tampa focused on the Spanish Civil War between 1936 and 1939 for a thesis entitled "La Retaguardia de Tampa" ("The Rearguard of Tampa"). She studied the major aspects of the Spanish Civil War as it related to the Spanish immigrant colony in Tampa, which was the largest such group in the U.S. at that time.

The historical anniversary program in Tampa featured daily events in a variety of locations, including the Centro Asturiano Club Covadonga Room, the USF Special Collections meeting room and other USF sites, and venues as far away as a St. Petersburg Beach theater. Among the many and varied forms of the observance were posters, videos, informal talks and discussons, printed literature, and lectures—both multi-lingual and multi-media. Retired educator and theatrical producer Ron Mussleman, for example, lectured at the USF St. Petersburg campus on "*España en el Corazón* (Spain in my Heart)" and "The Disappearance of Garcia Lorca," a discussion of the famed Spanish poet killed by Genralissimo Francisco Franco's Fascist soldiers. Ana Varela-Lago, author of several works on Ybor City, also gave a number of presentations.

Her article, "From Patriotism to Mutualism," covers the early turn-of-the-century struggles within the Centro Español Club and its Galician and Asturian members with reference to Cuba's War of Independence and the Spanish-American War at the turn of the century.[9]

## The Ybor City Chamber of Commerce in 1998

As I bring the history of our Landmark Town up to the start of the new millennium, it is proper to note the continuing vigor exemplified by the Ybor City Chamber of Commerce, led by chairman Gil Hernandez and by Annette Gonzalez DeLisle, president of the reorganized Chamber organization. Their efforts are enhanced by the work of the Chamber's publications editor/designer, Rosalie Guarino Simms, and by an office staff strengthened by experienced professionals.

Other organizations are working with the Chamber in presenting a variety of events, exhibits, and activities that enhance awareness of the historical fabric of the town and nurture the continuing and growing attention of tourists and visitors. It collaborates frequently with the Ybor City Museum Society and the Ybor City State Museum, the Round Table, and the Alcalde Association; the Centro Asturiano, L'Unione Italiana, and Círculo Cubano clubs; the Tampa Hispanic Heritage Council; the Lion's Club and Rotary Club of Ybor City; La Sociedad Union Marti Macéo; the Jewish and German organizations; the Columbia Restaurant; the Ballet Folklorico de Ybor; the Spanish Lyric Theater; the joint Rotary-Tampa Sister City initiatives with Oviedo, Spain; Agrigento, Sicily; Córdova, Argentina; and Barranquilla, Columbia; educational initiatives and programs sponsored by the University of South Florida, University of Tampa, and Hillsborough Community College; and the USF Tampa Hispanic Heritage Celebration, Inc.; the Henry B.

Plant Museum; and the Tampa Bay History Center. The many separate arms and activities of these organizations and others are helping to perpetuate Latin history and to maintain its spirit.

Selected items from its list of accomplishments in 1997 will give an idea of the accelerated pace of the Chamber: purchase of updated office computer software; creation of a database and of an Internet Web Page; founding of a bi-monthly *El Boletín*. a monthly published *Calendar*—and the expansion of the main newsletter, *La Sétima*, now incorporated once a month into our tri-lingual newspaper *La Gaceta*. It has recently awarded a $15,000 grant to the Consortium of Historic Clubs and now has sponsored an invaluable First Annual Business Expo. Now it has also assumed the responsibility for operating the Official Visitor Information Center for the Historic District while the number of visitors stopping there is steadily increasing. It continues to arrange many annual festive events in Centennial Park and other venues.[10]

As the decade of the 1990s ended, incoming YCCC Chair Sarah Romeo brought new synergy to Chamber outreach efforts through her many friends and contacts she has built over many years of service with civic and cultural groups. Other recent presidents who each led the Chamber to new heights of achievement include Vincent Pardo, Ken Ferlita, Enrique Woodruff, and Gil Hernandez.[11]

By 1998 it had become quite clear that the work of Mayor Greco and his Business and Community Director, Fernando Noriega, would leave a significant and enviable record of improvements for Ybor City, including approximately $100 million of "in-ground" legacies. These two native sons brought great drive, initiative, and ingenuity in seeking ways to preserve and enhance the community. Through their efforts the face of housing in greater Ybor City, as in Tampa Heights, has changed greatly for the better. New paint, architectural repairs, and innumerable small restorations abound, and steady upgrades to the infrastructure are being implemented and closely administered. The work of the Ybor City Redevelopment Agency headed by Jack Shiver now



**Ybor City: The Making of a Landmark Town**

*This view from 18th Street provides another angle on the restored casitas making up an Ybor City "streetscape" in the Preservation Park casita complex. Each house was originally separate, but several have been unobtrusively joined together to create more flexible space for the Ybor City Museum Society.* RM.

more than ever also seems to be closely attuned to civic needs and to the betterment of the entire Historic District.

### The Ybor City Strategic Committee

In April of 1998, the Chamber's Strategic Committee, appointed by President Gil Hernandez and chaired by Al Kurzenhauser, completed its rewrite of the Chamber's Constitution and By-laws. Joseph Amin, Anthony J. Perrone, Lois Gaston, Jim Serina, Rafael Martínez-Ybor, and I were working with Kursenhauser. Within Article II, we set forth two purposes that will continue to guide the efforts of this important leadership group in the years to come. First, there is the goal: "to perpetuate, enhance, and promote the proud Latin heritage and culture of Ybor City and its immigrant citizens." Since Spaniards, Cubans, and Italians were the significant historical majority, and the town revolved around their culture, clubs, hospitals, and factories, perpetuation of this heritage will form a significant dimension of this community for future generations and future histori-

ans. And, second, the Chamber's Constitution pledges that the group will work "to preserve, protect, market, and cherish the honor of the Ybor City National Historic Landmark District designation," as it also honors those who brought hope, foresight, vigor, and vitality from their origins to create a unique ethos in America.[12]

Ybor City is a fortunate town—one whose National Historic Landmark history places it approximately within the top 3 percent of the nation's 60,000 places listed on the National Register. This national honor must be effectively maintained and carried forward in the centuries ahead—just as the nation's other landmark cities maintain their heritage. As Jerry L. Rogers, associate director of the National Park Service, clearly stated, "Its future is up to the people who are here."

### The Ybor City Museum Society

The energetic work of President Sonya Ziegler is recognized by the fact that the museum matured substantially under her disciplined leadership. Much outstanding and serious planning took



**Chapter 10 · Rebirth and Responsibility**

place during her three-term service in office. It led the way to substantial achievements under her successors, Sonya Ziegler and Mary Alvarez. The Society has been blessed with a Board that is not only highly educated but is also composed mostly of daughters and sons of Ybor City. Their vision, dedication, and professionalism have proven to be efficient, admirable, and often inspiring. Much has been accomplished because of them.

Leading the Society into the new millenium, president Mary Alvarez had prepared herself in earlier years as she co-chaired many activities with Adela Gonzmart and Iva Ciaccio, including the Taste of Ybor City, a highly successful event held in the old cantina room of the Centro Asturiano, and other programs in the museum patio and the Columbia Restaurant.

Alvarez, also a three-term president, pursued several major projects, among them the complete repair and upgrade of the museum building and the complex task of installing additional casita houses on the east side of Centennial Park. This undertaking (in progress as I complete this manuscript) has received the city's blessing. As of 2002, the casitas have been singled out and relocated and restoration work will soon bring increased activity as the new Casita Complex site takes shape. A resource center, library, and even a trained historian to staff it, are also in the works. A paid executive administrator position was created and profesionally filled by Melinda Chavez and her successor, Chris Harp. Negotiations with the city and county regarding new usage for the casita houses formerly occupied by the Tampa-Hillsborough County Preservation Board offices were satisfactorily completed in January 1998, providing an additional 3,000 square feet for Museum Society activities.

Among its many programs, the museum sponsors the annual Tony Pizzo Award brunch at Ybor City's Columbia Restaurant, holds coffees at several venues, such as the Centro Español Plaza in 1994, and annually celebrates the birthday of the town's founder, Don Vicente Martínez Ybor. The Ybor City State Museum is blessed with a beautiful patio that grows better with time. A new stage is currently being built there; it is the site of frequent memorable events that sustain the Ybor City traditions of social events in the open air.

This subject of the Ybor Museum Society cannot be concluded without mentioning the outstanding work and effort of

**Ybor City: The Making of a Landmark Town**

some 100 or more Museum Volunteers in a support group originally founded by Providence Velasco in 1988. They work on all phases of the museum operation. They are a fountain of history through first-hand knowledge, oral traditions and anecdotes, and their own research and learning. And who could better be entrusted to convey the historical facts and feelings of this special place, for the majority of the volunteers are ladies born and raised in Ybor City. Many of them live today at the historic Haciendas de Ybor.

Current president of the Museum Volunteers is Violetta Lombardia, who was for many years the president of the Tampa chapter of the American Red Cross and a volunteer with that organization for decades. The museum is blessed to have this accomplished community leader and the invaluable gifts of time and talents by an extraordinarily dedicated volunteer staff.

Another person who has made a difference is Providence Velasco, the immediate past president of the Museum Volunteers. The Velasco Student Service Center building is named in recognition and appreciation for this truly great lady. Her early docent work in education was done at a time when women were hardly able to enter universities. She has shared her love for learning with others and has done much for the Ybor Museum.

Accolades for Museum work must also go to Laura Andrade. She works in the patio garden for hours—alone. Her life is devoted to nurturing the simple, natural beauty of the world—assuring that the flowers and trees of yesterday in Ybor City can still flourish there today—*los cajigales* (zinnias), *las margaritas* (daisies), *los claveles* (carnations), *las rosas* (roses), *el platano* (banana tree), and *el árbol de mora* (mulberry tree).[13]

The Museum Society continues to seek a variety of creative opportunities to pass along Ybor City's historic heritage into the new millenium. Rosann Garcia has assumed the presidency of the Museum Society and has already proven she is equal to the task. Her priorities include the completion of *La Casita* complex, the complete updating and refurbishing of the museum exhibits, and the firm anchoring of the Botanical Gardens, so ably led by Gus Jimenez in the last year and a half.

Preservation in Ybor City is succeeding not simply because of the dollars keeping the old buildings from falling apart, but because these immensely talented, creative, generous sons and daughters of Ybor City, and others like them, have dedicated themselves as caretakers who will pass to future generations a vital and living inheritance.

## La Sétima

In mid-1996 I introduced to the Board of the Ybor City Chamber of Commerce and the Ybor City Museum Society a reso-


*The Ybor City State Museum has been an active preserver of history, offering a wealth of programs and information. Providence Velasco (left photo) is founder and past president of the Museum Volunteers. In the center photo, standing, is Melinda Chavez, former executive director of the Ybor City Museum Society, and seated in front of her are Rosann Garcia, vice president (left) and Mary Alvarez, president (right). Violeta Murgado Lombardia (right photo) was head of the Museum Volunteers as of the writing of this book.*

lution asking the City of Tampa to append *La Sétima* to the signage on the city's main spine, 7th Avenue, sometimes also known as Broadway. Both bodies approved it unanimously and recommended it to the City of Tampa. On April 2, 1998, the City Council, with prior approval from Mayor Dick Greco and Director of Business and Community Services Fernando Noriega, passed a resolution to implement the change. A resolution to this effect was prepared by the City's legal department.

The *tabaqueros* of Ybor City—the fathers and mothers of the town—had called 7th Avenue "La Sétima." The Royal Academy of the Spanish Language, and major dictionaries in Spain, define both *sétima* and *séptima* as meaning "seventh." Whatever the origins of their choice, the tabaqueros unanimously used *sétima* as the standard name for their main street. Our perpetuation of this unique word form seems appropriate to the distinctive National Historic Landmark District character of the Ybor City area. It was by far the most widely used street name in Ybor City.

This action by the Ybor City Chamber of Commerce, the Ybor City Museum Society, the City of Tampa, and Mayor Dick Greco honors the *tabaqueros* of yesterday as it honors and affirms the ordinary language used for so many years in the daily oral life of the community.[14] Those who promenade along Ybor City's main spine in the next decades and centuries will now see on the town's street signs the actual name that the the Cubans, Spaniards, and Italians bestowed on their beloved avenue, *La Sétima*.

## The Future

In late 1996 two current developments received much praise. The first was the Centro Ybor project, with the Centro Español Plaza and Mall concept—an approximately $40 million venture which includes some 400 apartments in the heart of Ybor City—and a new hotel located between the above Centro project and the Chamber's office building. Both efforts are being coordinated through the Office of Business and Community Services headed by Noriega on behalf of Mayor Greco's administration. City land was made available to developers for $300,000. Plans called for a four-story, 50,000-square-foot, 90-room Hilton Garden Inn. Groundbreaking took place in October 1997.

As the hotel was being built, work on the renovation of the Centro Español building proceeded, and plans for the Centro Español Plaza also moved along. In the Hispanic section of the *Tribune*, titled "Que Pasa," Chloe Cabrera, *Tribune* Hispanic staff writer, devoted a portion of her page to Gil Hernandez, new president of the Ybor City Chamber of Commerce. In this article Gil alluded to the need to continue growth and development as well as to protect the historic values of the town. In his comments he also spoke very positively of the need to see the Centro Español and the Centro Español Plaza move forward.

*The Ybor City State Museum Patio is a popular area for cultural events. Celebrating a Garden Fiesta are (left to right) Maria Pasetti, Margaret Hobbs, and Bobbie Ward, wearing costumes from the Yucatan Peninsula, Spain, and northern Italy.* YBOR CITY STATE MUSEUM SOCIETY.

**Ybor City: The Making of a Landmark Town**

*Dr. Adrienne Garcia was president of Ballet Folklorico de Ybor while serving as director of H. Lee Moffitt Center and Research Institute.*

*Contributing creative energy to the Ybor City Chamber of Commerce are (left to right) Rosalie Guarino Simms, editor and designer; Annette G. Delisle, president; and Anna Ramos, events associate.*

*Sonya Ziegler was three-term president of Ybor City Museum Society.*

*Ybor City Museum volunteers welcome guests at a volunteer recruitment coffee. Left to right are Vi Conte, Delia Sanchez, Laura Lopez, and Lily Kendrick.* Ybor City Museum Society.

*Museum volunteers (from left) Hope Orihuela, Magdalena Perez, Aida de Ros, and Mary Dominguez receive recognition at a Volunteer Recognition Coffee.* Ybor City Museum Society.

*Helping serve coffee to volunteers are Mary Caltagirone, Yoli Fernandez, and Florence Perotti.* Ybor City Museum Society.

*Violet Torres, Olga Fernandez, and Angeles Marti demonstrate that museum volunteer work includes moments of fun and friendly companionship.* Ybor City Museum Society.

**Chapter 10 · Rebirth and Responsibility**

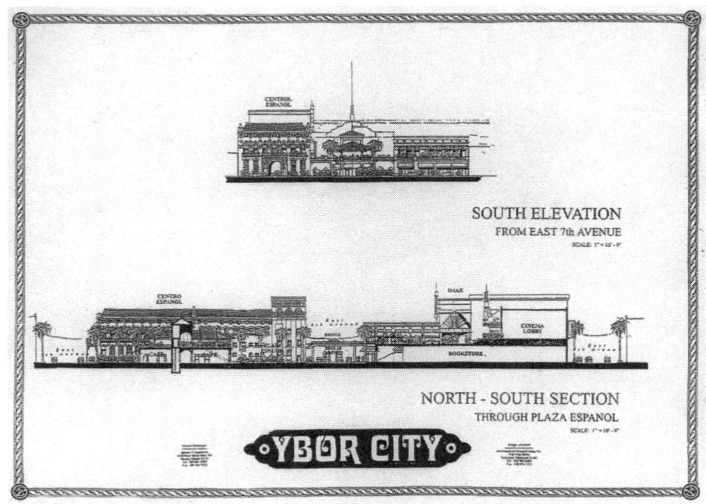

*Innovative thinking resulted in plans to save and restore the Centro Español Building as part of the restaurants and shops of the Centro Ybor development.*

*Tony Moré, Al Piazza, and Raymond Moré prepare fresh sandwiches at La Segunda Central Bakery on 15th Street in 1994. Catalán Spaniard Juan Moré first used the Cuban bread formula in Cuba and then brought it to Ybor City, where it became a staple of his bakery. In the 1920s the bakery was located on 15th Street just south of I-4. Shortly after Urban Renewal buldozed the town, the bakery moved to its present site on the southwest corner of 15th Street and 15th Avenue. Today it is still known for its magnificnet Cuban bread and Latin pastries. In addition, La Segunda makes a superb Cuban sandwich.* La Gaceta.

*As rapid development continues in Ybor City, there is more of the past to be saved. Members of the Ybor City Chamber of Commerce, the Ybor City Development Corporation, the Florida Department of Transportation, and others celebrate the relocation of five more historic casitas from the corner of 13th Avenue and 14th Street to the block between 8th and 9th Avenues, across from Centennial Park. They will be restored there and deeded to the City of Tampa for the use of the Ybor City State Museum.* La Gaceta.

**Ybor City: The Making of a Landmark Town**

A new, fresh idea surfaced in the town on April 3, 1997. On that date, the Ybor City Chamber of Commerce sponsored the first Annual Business Expo and Food Fair at the Cuban Club building and patio. The event was chaired by A. J. Grimaldi, vice president of the Columbia Bank. The ample and ideal space at the Cuban Club—both in the building and outside on the patio—served the event's needs well. It was a chance for everyone involved to recognize the major success of the Cuban Club and Cuban Club Foundation in advancing restoration. This Expo was widely attended. Over 60 businesses from Ybor and nearby areas participated. The success of this venture bodes well for the town and for the beautiful Cuban Club building.

The German-American Club building was beautifully renovated in 1997 to preserve its neoclassical style and Romanesque columns. Joe Panda, a Spanish-born architect based in Palma Ceia, won the contract to restore the two-story buiilding and convert it to offices for City of Tampa employees. Mayor Greco had championed the project, which was achieved with private funding.

Meantime, the Cuban Club Foundation and Centro Asturiano received additional restoration funding from the state. Senator James Hargrett delivered checks to both groups in September 1997, calling Centro Asturiano "one of the great treasures of this part of the world—a living monument to history." The state funding supported installation of fire sprinklers in the Centro Asturiano building. And with matching funding from the Cuban Club Foundation, $300,000 from the state supported fire extinguishers, fire alarms, and an elevator at the Cuban Club, while it also carried forward work on the fourth floor ballroom, including repair of the damaged ceiling mural and chandelier.

The Italian Club continued also to raise money for restoration. As of 1998, it had raised about $900,000 in private funds and state grants, but its goal was to raise nearly twice that to make basic repairs. According to Joseph Capitano Sr., president of the Italian Club, "We need $2 million to do a good job." The good news, however, was that the work ahead no longer seemed impossible. With the passing of each year, there was clearer evidence of progress.

The indomitable Jack Shiver continued to make major contributions. In 1999 he announced plans to develop the historic A. A. Gonzalez Clinic into a grand bed-and-breakfast to reopen as the Don Vicente de Ybor Inn.

By the late 1990s Ybor City's renewed infrastructure was virtually complete. Still to be finished are the full objectives of the Tampa-Ybor Revitalization Strategies. But the critical mass Harris Mullen and others worked hard for in the 1980s and earlier is now assured by so many interesting venues and initiatives in town. Tourists could well elect to spend two full days in Ybor City, if they so wished, and not have to cover the same venues twice.

One must be grateful to the impartial role of the Consortium organization for the objective way in which it is dispensing and managing funds for the historic buildings. Much early work was done in this regard by Vince Pardo of the City of Tampa Planning Department, a well-known son of Ybor City who has served as a past YCCC president.

*Fiesta Day has become a popular annual event in Ybor City. When this photoraph was taken in 1994 an estimated 60,000 people turned out for the daylight festivities, and more that 200,000 lined the streets for the Illuminated Night Parade.* La Gaceta.



**Chapter 10 · Rebirth and Responsibility**

Now we can answer radio personality Woody Garcia's question from the late 1960s stemming from Urban Renewal's bulldozing of the town, "Ybor City, *Que Serás?*" ("Ybor City, what will you become?"). Today's old-timers might answer: "Woody, it will become the best town one could hope for, given the absence of new immigration of Cubans, Spaniards, and Italians, the founding cultures, and the virtual shut-down of the cigar industry that brought them here."

But it will become so because the founding fathers and mothers left a wealth of resources. These include the beautiful social club buildings, the red brick streets, the tight town grid, and the civic organizations that are dedicated to carrying the town's history forward. And they also left a beautiful folklore that needs to be highlighted and promoted. Their legacy includes Ybor City's Latin foods, music, festive entertainment, and lively street events. Much of this is being continued today.

The town was founded on strong and traditional family values. These must be revered as shining examples. That inheritance is the underpinning for today's and tomorrow's revitalization. However, competing cultural values threaten some of this tradition, and even the town's unique musical heritage is under assault by the onslaught of non-representative music pouring from the shops and clubs. In some ways this is a good and healthy thing, a way of carrying on the innovative, multicultural atmosphere that allowed immigrants from many lands to succeed here in the first place. Still, more emphasis by civic organizations is needed to maintain the musical and theatrical flavor that make this a landmark town. The area is blessed with two outstanding professional groups: the Spanish Lyric Theater and the Ballet Folklorico

*The 1996 Ybor City Chamber of Commerce Board of Directors included, left to right: (front row) Jill Wax, Rosann Garcia, Eva Ciaccio, Mary Alvarez, Ruben Alfaras, Kris Fernandez, Ileana Devin, Rebecca Gagalis, Joe Capitano, and Gary Gsell; (second row) John Suarez, Kathleen Bambery, Enrique Woodroffe, Kerri Post, Lois Gaston, Victor DiMaio, Sarah Romeo, Joan Jennewein, Frank Lastra, Ron Rampollo, and Michael Mann; and (third row) Steve Hayes, Michael Cruz, Steve Parker, Jim Serina, Jack Shiver, and Bill White.* RICHARD STEINMETZ.

**Ybor City: The Making of a Landmark Town**

of Ybor. The *Tabláos*, general Latin dance numbers, Spanish *zarzuelas*, and Italian folk dances such as Tarantelas, must be continued. They are irreplaceable treasures of this place. As to the food: it is mostly still here, although other foods have been introduced along the main spine.

Responsible organizations such as the Ybor City Chamber of Commerce, the Ybor City State Museum Society, the State Museum itself, and the historians and civic leaders who have embraced our town must insist that the *history* of Ybor City continue to be the centerpiece that ensures the town's future. It is necessary that the City of Tampa sound this theme in its development activities and at side activities during convention center events. Guidance and selection of interesting, appropriate venues should help—placing the emphasis on those that would faithfully convey the history of our National Historic Landmark District.

The free market with its supply-and-demand economics is one of the pillars on which America rests, but amidst improving econmic energies, special care and vigiliance must be directed to preserving the physical, cultural, and spiritual values of Ybor City. Preservation of the Historic Landmark classification is the way. It is the only true way! But as I conclude this history, the Ybor City story I have told is currently in danger of being overwhelmed by new wet venues, clubs, and concepts foreign to the historical fabric of the area. There is a real threat here. Some would prefer that Ybor City become Tampa's wet zone while Hyde Park Village continues to cater to higher-class shopping tastes. There is work to be done in this area. Ybor must be true to itself.

Written history alone cannot suffice to convey its story. It needs dimension, spirit, duration, and soul. The more observant tourists will be able to sense light wafts of the culture. These emanate from the architecture of the club houses, the old La Benéfica and El Pasaje buildings, the remaining red brick factories, the side streets, wood houses, and the few lingering scents of fresh tobacco, baked bread, and coffee. Impacting the senses also are the overall walkable scale, the tight streets, the unrepaired houses and half-uncovered tracks where a restored Ybor trolley will soon run once again.

However the main spine's eclectic look today is bound to stagger the tourist's imagination. A post-modern club or contemporary art gallery adjoins a hand-rolled cigar shop or antique clothes emporium. But here, also, there is a need for the visionary civic artist who can improve the imagery with his finest brush, finding the opportunities for harmony, balance, and blending—including, for example, using the wasted space above existing one- and two-story rooftops. Capturing this vertical space is vitally important as horizontal space becomes increasingly scarce. A greater number of three-story buildings could add much to the main spine, as well as foster many more verandas to celebrate events from. The YC-1 classification for the historic district allows 45 feet of height, and my engineering background leads my future thinking toward these and other as yet unused dimensions.

One sees an overwhelming number of buildings in Europe that are three and four stories high. How could an owner go wrong? Operate his business on the first floor, live on the second floor, and sell (not rent) the next one or two floors. Not only would such architectural additions bring added income that could guarantee long-range success to building owners, but the town would benefit from apartment residents on the avenue who would foster law and order around their property, and perhaps even expand shopping in the morning—so soothing to visitors. Madrid shops, for example, open at 7 a.m. The city is a beehive of activity by 8 in the morning—bread, fruit, coffee, services—and much

*Ybor City's unique and historic newspaper continues to affirm the present and the past of our National Historic Landmark town. In keeping with our heritage, it publishes in English, Italian, and Spanish.*

more. Much less policing is needed. Why? Those who are truly *invested* in the community abound. The apartments are *owned*, not rented. In Madrid the streets are filled with the apartment owners' families, those who live above the many first-floor shops. As the sun sets, their evening walks guarantee that the cafes remain full—or at least have business enough to meet their expenses. Tourists provide the profit.

Add, now, even more of the historical roast coffee smells and the delicious aroma of fresh baked goods and pastries. Add, too, a small fruit market here and there, a Latin grocery, another bakery that specializes in the town's distinctive Cuban bread, and other early morning services, such as Cuban coffee outlets. Then Ybor downtown will project a warm and vibrant ambiance. The cafes and other businesses will fill up in the early hours, almost as in the old, early days. Now throw in many quality gift shops, general retail shops, professional venues, and specialty shops, along with an appealing variety of ethnic foods and beverages, and the basic elements for rebirth *and* preservation are in place. Tourists with money in their pockets will flood the area.

In addition to the many cultural exhibits in the club houses—El Centro Asturiano, L'Unione Italiana, El Centro Español, and El Circulo Cubano—that complement the draw of the Ybor Museum, Ybor Square, the Columbia Restaurant, and the intermittent Chamber and museum cultural and festive events. A small, standing band performing daily at the Centro Español Plaza and at Centennial Park playing Spanish, Cuban, and Italian songs would significantly boost the area. Eventually each club could assemble its own band. Other menus are already offered in the wet or food bars, but more moderation in the numbers of party crowds and taste would increase evening visitations by families and tourists.

What is missing? Missing is the assurance of safety, of adequate parking, of pleasant sounds, shade trees for hot summer months, interesting plazas or nooks and corners with benches for families or couples to sit, for children to feed pigeons. Adequate bathroom facilities properly maintained are a must. These are now about to be completed. A look and feeling provided by a clean ambiance is necessary, along with medium decibels of noise. Certainly, this last is needed in the day and evening hours.

The future of Ybor City depends very heavily on the ability of the Ybor City Chamber of Commerce to ensure the survival of the character of the National Historic Landmark District. Aside from the day-to-day activities which give real meaning to the historic values of the town. The history cannot and must not be allowed to be diluted.

364

**Ybor City: The Making of a Landmark Town**

The Strategic Planning Committee of the Ybor City Chamber of Commerce, appointed in mid-1997 by president Gill Hernandez is concluding its activities. These included studying the Chamber's mission, developing a new vision for the next five years, and recommending such organizational changes as will allow successful completion of its mission. It has also rewritten the Chamber's by -laws and Constitution. The organizational changes were approved by the Executive Committee on January 2, 1998, the Board on January 8, and the general membership on February 17. It includes the upgrading of the position of the Executive Director position to that of President of the Chamber, and, upgrading the current position of Chamber President, to the position of Chairman of the Board. The Chairman of the Strategic Planning committee at the time was Al Kurzenhouser, and the committee consisted of Joe Amon, Lois Gaston, Jim Serina, and me.

One of the most significant actions taken by the Chamber's Strategic Planning Committee is the insertion in the Constitution the statement that *"it is in the highest interest of Ybor City Chamber of Commerce to promote and defend the National Landmark Historic District Classification."* It should come as no surprise for me to admit that I was point man for this initiative. I believe as a matter of faith that the heritage of our landmark town must be loved well and preserved.

### Ybor City is no ordinary town.

Many towns in America would move mountains to have such a history. Not lightly did the national government designate this town a National Historic Landmark District. The future of Ybor City greatly depends on the defense of this classification. It must not be taken for granted. It must be jealously guarded. This town needs men and women dedicated to its landmark heritage. Beware of personal agendas. Ybor City is at a crucial point in its existence, and this will remain true in the years ahead. Strong, resolute leaders are needed. And when they fail, whistle-blowers will be needed.

Finally, it is my hope that this sequential and detailed history, with its notes, bibliography, and index will serve to explode interest in the town's history. Combined with Web sites, support from nearby universities and historic societies with their invaluable publications, and the ever-increasing ordinary visitors who always have new questions of their own to raise—I hope that all of these will attract wide student interest in this most intriguing town. Thousands of articles can be written on the subject of Ybor City's past, and many new historic findings will only serve to enhance our admiration—and provoke creative and appropriate visions for her future.

Aside from my desire to faithfully preserve what is known of the town's history, I hope that setting down the story on these pages will inspire greater interest by future students and historians. The lively play of creative, inquisitive, and open minds upon the history of this special place, and the dreams and future possibilities that new generations can imagine and achieve— these will keep the past and future of Ybor City meaningful and alive. The dust of time has not yet settled on this town that *patrones* and *tabaqueros* built.

**Chapter 10 · Rebirth and Responsibility**

*Dr. Lois J. Gaston has served as president of the Hillsborough Community College Ybor City Campus since May 1992 and has played a key role in its growth and development. She was a member of the prestigious Ybor City Chamber of Commerce Strategic Committee.*

*The Ybor City Campus of Hillsborough Community College dedicated its Public Service Technology Building at the corner of Palm and 9th Avenue in 1999. It offers training academies for police, fire, and corrections professions. Here at the ribbon-cutting ceremony are (left to right) Thomas Huggins; Nancy Watkins; Dr. Gwendolyn Stephenson, president of HCC; Dr. Ed Gonzalez, chairman of the HCC District Board of Trustees; and Lois Gaston, president of the HCC Ybor Campus.* La Gaceta.

*Ybor City's Nick C. Nuccio, Tampa's first mayor of Latin heritage, joined other historic leaders memorialized in Centennial Park when this life-size bronze sculpture by artist Steve Dickey was dedicated in October 1999. The son of Sicilian immigrants, Nuccio served two terms on Tampa City Council, eight terms on the Hillsborough County Commission, and was twice elected mayor.  He is portrayed with his ever-present hand-rolled cigar and trademark hat in hand.* RM.

*Dr. Henry J. Fernandez was undoubtedly Ybor City's greatest patriot in the second half of the 20th century. He founded the Barrio Latino Commission in 1959 to protect our historical architecture; the Haciendas de Ybor in 1962 to bring our townspeople back after a failed Urban Renewal uprooted them; and in 1972 he founded the organization that formed the Knights of the Krewe of Sant' Yago, the most influential and prestigious Spanish social group, open to all Latins and Americans in general. In addition to serving on five occasions as president of the Ybor City Chamber of Commerce, he had been involved in development, beautification, art, cultural clubs, and civic of activities of all kinds. His is a life full of service to his beloved community.*

*The Don Vicente de Ybor Historic Inn is located across from the Principe de Gales cigar factory built by Ybor at 9th Avenue and 14th Street. Once the site of the Ybor City Land and Development Company building, El Bien Publico, and the Gonzalez Clinic, the Inn has been totally renewed and refurbished. Today it contains an elegant lobby with period furnishings, a restaurant serving Italian and ethnic Ybor City cuisine in attractive dining rooms, and comfortable accommodations.* Lou Segade/Don Vicente de Ybor Historic Inn.

*The Centro Español building today stands as the centerpiece of Centro Ybor. The National Historic Landmark building was the anchor and beacon for preservation and renewal in Ybor City. It was chartered by the State of Florida in 1891 and was designated a National Historic Landmark in 1988.* RM.

*These interior views of Centro Español today are eloquent reminders of a beautiful and inspiring Ybor City history. Although the building no longer functions as a traditional social club, it continues as a central focus of social activities. Its doors are open to visitors, diners, and shoppers as part of the Centro Ybor development; its architecture link contemporary life to the past.* SD/RM.



**Chapter 10 · Rebirth and Responsibility**

*Al Kurzenhauser, who served many years as governor and vice president of the Southeast Region of the American Society of Mechanical Engineers, is an 18-year member of YCCC and an eight-year director. He has served as leader of the Fiesta Day Parade, YCCC Retreat speaker, and chairman of the Chamber's Strategic Planning Committee (1997-2000). Under his tutelage two important strategies evolved: First, the redesign of the Chamber organization, with President becoming Chairman, Executive Director becoming President, and others; and, second, the addition written into the YCCC's by-laws of the prime purpose of promoting Ybor City's economic growth while defending the National Historic Landmark District status.*

*Emiliano J. Salcines, associate justice of the Florida Second District Court of Appeals, installs officers of Centro Asturiano a century after its founding in 1902. In the first row, from left, are Director Hope Orihuela, Eva Ciaccio, and Margaret Garcia; and in the back row, Director Paul Vincent, Second Vice President Phil LoCicero, and Director Roland Rodriguez.* La Gaceta.

*This relatively new U.S. Post Office also went up in flames in the Ybor City fire of 2000. It was the biggest fire in Ybor City history since 1908. The post office was destroyed in less than an hour.*

*Smoke and flames begin to engulf the nearly completed 434-unit luxury apartment complex called "The Park at Ybor City" on Friday morning, May 19, 2000.* Patrick Mantiega/La Gaceta.

**Ybor City: The Making of a Landmark Town**

*Ybor City's bronze Immigrant Statue was dedicated in 1992. Local artist Anthony Cardoso drew the original portrait; sculptor Steve Dickey of Tampa created the clay model, and eventually carried out the bronze casting. The project began under the administration of Guy St. Paul, who, with Sam D. Leto, selected the marble on a trip to Elberton, Georgia, marble and granite capital of the Southeast. The names of some 1,000 original immigrants and their children are inscribed on the marble and granite wall surrounding the monument. According to Leto, Alice Bustelo first proposed the idea of honoring the immigrants: "a stone . . . something . . . to say that the immigrants were here!" The statue was dedicated in 1992 under the presidency of Steve Lester.*

*Honoree Sam D. Leto (left) receives an award in 1992 from Guy St. Paul, president of the Ybor City Round Table, as a tribute to his successful leadership of the effort to erect the Immigrant Statue in Centennial Park.*

*U. S. Congressman Sam M. Gibbons helped Ybor City redevelopment efforts over many years. His support of the Barrio Latino Commission, the Haciendas de Ybor housing for elderly, and other projects was invaluable. Always available, he could be reached quickly by phone in Washington, D.C.*

*Gathered at the Ybor memorial in Oaklawn Cemetery in tribute on the 100th Anniversary of the birth of Don Vicente Martínez Ybor are (from left) John T. Lesley Jr.; his father, John T. Lesley, son of Capt. John Thomas Lesley who sold the crucial first 40 acres of land to Don Vicente; and Rafael Martinez Ybor. The event was coordinated by Arsenio Sanchez of the Tampa Historical Society, with distinguished attorney and respected local historian Judge E. J. Salcines (right), acting as master of ceremonies.*

369

**Chapter 10 · Rebirth and Responsibility**

*Frank Lastra and Rafael Martinez Ybor discuss today's Ybor City at the base of a statue of Don Vicente Martínez Ybor. Dedicated on July 11, 2001, the statue faces southwest, overlooking La Sétima, at the entrance to Centro Ybor. It is the work of sculptor Steve Dickey and was made possible by some sixty civic, corporate, and individual donors who contributed to a fund-raising effort led by great-grandson Rafael.* SD.

# fterword

*Ybor City: The Making of a Landmark Town* has much that deserves
acclai°m. Many other excellent books and articles have been written about
this special place, and they deserve many compliments,  but few authors
have penetrated the heart of each period the way Frank Lastra does, from
the early days to the present day, to touch, in a sequential way, the spirit
and making of this town.

Frank has covered many of the most important events, cultural influences, initiatives, and people, including my great-grandfather, Vicente
Martinez Ybor, and other leading personalities of the early days. And he
has also recorded the contributions of so very many outstanding business
and civic leaders of the middle and late periods. His book preserves a
strong, representative sample of those who have helped to make the more
recent history of the town. Unquestionably, in the middle and current
years, as in the past, many individuals have devoted their best years to the
betterment of Ybor City, and it is only fitting that their achievements be
celebrated, together with the better-known accomplishments of the early
founders.

## The Current Years

Frank tells us that the late 1980s were very depressing years for Ybor
City, and the exit of most of the artists during that decade revealed, without doubt, that the market forces of supply and demand are alive. The
survival indexes of businesses are not all the same. Many factors determine the survivability of a worthy enterprise.  Artists as a rule need a relatively large studio space available at low rent, an ingredient not common
to a resurgent district. Ironically, as the gradual resurgence of Ybor City
began, nurtured in part by the artists who had found the supply of low-
cost studio spaces and aesthetic atmosphere attractive, increased demand
for rental space and commercial property slowly but surely raised the going rates beyond the reach of "starving artists."

The process has built steadily from the 1980s to the present. From
Rebecca Gagalis, president of the Ybor City Development Corporation, I

learned that dramatically increased activities in her office have coincided with a flurry of recent commercial activities along Ybor City's main spine. Also, from the office of Fernando Noriega, Director of Business and Community services for the city of Tampa, I found that there is an approximate 50 percent increase in the number of businesses on the avenue since 1990. Of this increase in business, some 33 percent has been in new bars, restaurants, and night spots. Many civic and community leaders are now working with the city and its redevelopment arm to attempt to create a unique, complementary set of venues that will balance daytime and nighttime visitations and traffic. And civic and city planners are attempting to "tame" the venues that are thriving in the town. Currently, some 40,000 young people visit the historic district each weekend, most of them arriving in the late afternoon or evening, with many remaining into the small hours of the morning.

What, indeed, does the future hold? The recent explosion of redevelopment and re-furbishing on *La Sétima* and 8th Avenue, a new focus on Ybor South, a new mall, hotel, and more—these are all worth waiting for. There is no question that supply and demand can fill the space—or empty it. As new directions and developments occur, an active role by a knowledgeable community will be greatly needed.

One of the promising concepts is a major venue that has been proposed for Ybor City to be called *Centro Ybor*. It will be approximately a $40 million project to refurbish and reinvigorate another landmark building. It is only proper that the Centro Español be recognized. The need for remodeling and utilizing this national historic landmark building—our first structure bearing the auspicious National Landmark title—must be supported. The proposed use of the land it fronts as a public plaza is also fitting. Plazas are traditionally spaces with suitable amenities where people can sit a while on shaded benches, relax, meet and chat with friends, and perhaps enjoy the fruits of the nearby merchants' products. Both elderly and young people enjoy these types of public facilities. The whole family will be comfortable in such a surrounding.

City organizations should take a look at the greater use of plazas, though space is limited. An Ybor South is being contemplated. in the land south of 6th Avenue. Already several of the old houses are being renewed—buildings that originally housed cigar workers and other early pioneers. Town rumors for their use tease the imagination with the ideas of family dwellings, offices, apartments, and light commercial uses. Some eclectic venues are being considered. Naturally, government must be assured that all this is to the benefit of the community. Properly zoned and maintained, and with law and order as one of its strongest attributes, it will be a great assistance to Ybor City.

If there is anything this festive district needs, it is people—a community of its own residents. Ybor City's ground space was truncated when US HWY I-4 crisscrossed it. It behooves us now to consider picking up vertical space—perhaps no higher than three or four stories near La Sétima. Increasing the number of owner- occupied apartments would add much greater security and stability to the neighborhood, at a savings of police protection cost. And owners, more so than renters, guarantee a safer environment. Moreover, of vital importance is the fact that residents living in proximity to La Sétima greatly increase local purchasing.



**Ybor City: The Making of a Landmark Town**

Also, with time a hotel or two may be required for overnight or short stays. Hospitable guest accommodations are a necessity for a festive and historic town. One such noted investor is on the scene. Officials hope that the finish of a proposed hotel will trigger the attraction of non-alcohol-related businesses.

What requires much consideration and effort is the question of what type of town our future Ybor City will be. Recently a flurry of excitement and uncertainty was raised when it was rumored that the area's designation of a National Historic Landmark District might be in jeopardy. Supposedly so, because it is believed by many that its main draw had dropped to that of a night and late-night district only —one littered with sleazy bars, semi-nudity, and many businesses incompatible with its historic designation. This is not entirely correct. This is a betrayal of all the values the Latins stood for. Yet, it is a warning signal that our community leaders must carefully evaluate the current and future directions of commercial development. The impact of single-dimensional development, no matter how financially successful, could be decisive. Financial gain alone must not be allowed to jeopardize the history nor the prospects for this unique and dynamic place.

One cannot return Cuban, Spanish, or Italian tabaqueros to factories that don't exist, though an unexpected rebirth of tobacco smoking has been recorded lately. Nor can the immigrant cigar workers of old be replicated, especially not in the old, unexpected, successful mix— Cuban, Spaniards, and Sicilians—with their historic values and industriousness. Nor will the common Castilian language, with lectores and highly successful Latin clubhouses and hospitals and cafes be here to maintain its purity. That world is history. Our duty now is to honor and preserve all that we can.

What can be done, then, to retain the historic legacy of the multicultural Latin, Jewish, Afro Cuban, and German presence in Ybor City? One way that the town could help restore its historic, multi-ethnic image is by creating events, attractions, and shops that draw family, regional, national, and international tourism to enjoy the festive types of social gatherings, foods, music, theatrical entertainment, and folkloric features of the Latin culture that once existed. Contemporary Ybor City life can be enriched by ethnic pageantry, visiting artists, cultural artifacts, historical reviews, foreign language films, and more. In fact, what is needed is a renaissance of cultural offerings, combined with the excitement needed to cause whole families to come to see them—to *participate*—to spend a day or two in the area. Whatever is festive, colorful, proper, and reasonable is what works. Tourists want to take safety as a given. The area must be clean-looking and orderly; the flow of traffic must be organized; and baths and other public facilities must be clean and sanitary. Above all, our community must look interesting and alive. Here colors, smells, and musical sounds can play prominent roles in bringing children out. Frank has written vividly of his childhood memories that include the colorful, bustling streets, the sounds of song and conversation, and the smells of coffee, fresh-baked bread, savory foods, and tobacco. Ybor City in its heyday was a feast for all the senses, and the delightful appeal can be revived today for new generations of young people. Imagination is needed to accomplish this.

A museum within the area is a strong necessity. It must display the landmark his-

tory of this area. It must not be diluted!. Savannah has its mansions; San Antonio has its Alamo and its Mercado. Nashville maintains its musical history and New Orleans protects its Cajun , Creole, and  musical past. The South protects its battlefields and monuments, and the country protects and projects our Constitution—the guiding force of this democracy. Through these and other cultural artifacts the living history of our nation and our neighborhoods are passed down to the young. Throughout America there are many memorable cities and towns known for their peculiar history because they have nurtured, preserved, and celebrated their past in the present day. Some peculiar-sounding names are virtually household names throughout America because of their history. They do not allow the real identity of these places to shift or be diluted in the name of "bringing them up to date"!. But yes, festive supports and appealing new venues must be provided here. However, Ybor City must be vigilant to protect its history.  A fragile town like ours that shifts too much with the times will lose its way—and its history.

The future of Ybor City rests with our city and civic leaders.  And our informed citizenry can exercise their thoughts to effect changes if needed.  Free enterprise and supply and demand  alone must not be allowed to dictate the future.  Our Constitution would become  an empty document if the country's founding fathers had not built safeguards to assure the survival of basic principles, values, and beliefs.  No, without safeguards even our national history would be forsaken or betrayed

The history of Ybor should be monitored by highly motivated Tampans with a historic sense or tie to this town. Some whistle-blowers will be needed if ever the history or the town is about to be abused. It is up to the historic societies in Tampa, particularly the Ybor City State Museum, with technical assistance  and know-how of  the universities nearby,  to study and improve, but not change the basic history to suit selfish interests. It should behoove the state and these institutions of learning to monitor fidelity to the facts and cultures which built our fascinating and dynamic town.  Fidelity to and respect of its history are imperative.

Modestly, but dutifully, I thank my great-grandfather, Vicente Martinez Ybor, for his labor and dedication in founding this Landmark town. I have faith that the year 3000 will see the history of Ybor City's birth, golden years, middle and late years—and perhaps even an unwritten renaissance millennium—still being honored, though there may be good and bad times in-between. And I trust that in the near future an adequate, permanent and well-located public statue will be dedicated to Ybor City's founder, who put Tampa on the world map. This is, indeed, a landmark town.  Please—let us not ever forsake or loose this cherished designation!  I trust the future of our town to the many new generations ahead.  Never forget that the longer we have this history, the more precious it will become!  God bless Ybor City.

My appreciation to Frank Trebín Lastra, a personal friend, for the many years he has devoted to this insightful and affectionate written account of a delightful and beloved place.

–Rafael Martinez Ybor

**Ybor City: The Making of a Landmark Town**

# TABLES & EXHIBITS

# Tampa Population and Cigar Production: 1880-1940

| Year | Tampa Population[2] | Total Export of[2]<br>Tobacco Products<br>(millions of pounds) | High<br>Quality | Low<br>Quality |
|---|---|---|---|---|
| 1880 | 720 | | | |
| 1881 | | | | |
| 1882 | | | | |
| 1883 | | | | |
| 1884 | | | | |
| 1885 | c. 3000 | 175.9 | 76.2 | 97.5 |
| 1886 | | 157.9 | 79.8 | 108.8 |
| 1887 | | 162.7 | 83.0 | 118.3 |
| 1888 | | 220.0 | — | — |
| 1889 | | 226.2 | 101.7 | 134.4 |
| 1890 | 5,532 | 223.5 | 95.1 | 169.2 |
| 1891 | | 182.1 | 52.2 | 160.6 |
| 1892 | | 154.9 | 54.1 | 184.3 |
| 1893 | | 147.4 | 46.0 | 216.9 |
| 1894 | | 134.2 | 40.0 | 145.8 |
| 1895 | | 158.6 | 39.5 | 201.8 |
| 1896 | | 185.9 | 40.6 | 267.7 |
| 1897 | | 123.4 | 34.0 | 44.1 |
| 1898 | | 91.6 | 29.0 | 44.0 |
| 1899 | | 193.2 | 39.0 | 78.0 |
| 1900 | 15,839 | 205.0 | 41.6 | 128.4 |
| 1905 | | | | |
| 1910 | 37,782 | | | |
| 1915 | | | | |
| 1920 | | | | |
| 1925 | | | | |
| 1930 | 101,161 | | | |
| 1935 | | | | |
| 1940 | 108,391 | | | |

| YEARS | TOTAL CIGARS<br>PRODUCED IN TAMPA | PERCENT OF PREVIOUS<br>PRODUCTION | POPULATION OF<br>TAMPA | PERCENT OF PREVIOUS<br>POUPLATION |
|---|---|---|---|---|
| 1900 | 147,545,000 | 174%[2] | 15,839 | 101% |
| 1905 | 220,430,000 | 149% | 22,823 | 144% |
| 1910 | 201,405,000[3] | 91% | 37,722 | 165% |
| 1915 | 295,936,000 | 142% | 43,150 | 127% |
| 1920 | 227,732,000[1] | 80% | 51,808 | 107% |
| 1925 | 413,502,000 | 212% | 94,743 | 184% |
| 1930 | 453,223,000[4] | 94% | 101,161 | 107% |
| 1935 | 321,345,000 | 69% | 100,181 | 99% |

[1] Ten Months Strike; 1919 production: 410,745,000. [2] Estimated. [3] Six Months Strike; 1909 production: 257, 059. [4] Peak production, 1929: 504, 755,000

# Tampa Cigar Production: 1897-1918

| 1897 | 90,480,000 |
| 1898 | 85,144,000 |
| 1899 | 111,679,000 |
| 1900 | 197,848,000 |
| 1901 | 147,333,000 |
| 1902 | 141,905,000 |
| 1903 | 220,430,000 |
| 1904 | 196,961,000 |
| 1905 | 220,430,000 |
| 1906 | 277,662,000 |
| 1907 | 285,660,000 |
| 1908 | 236,681,000 |
| 1909 | 287,059,000 |
| 1910 | 201, 405,000 |
| 1911 | 293,360,000 |
| 1912 | 273,485,000 |
| 1913 | 284,991,000 |
| 1914 | 260,800,000 |
| 1915 | 285,836,000 |
| 1916 | 312,456,376 |
| 1017 | 356,690,194 |
| 1918 | 365,062,928 |



**Tables and Exhibits**

# Pioneer Cigar Firms of Tampa, 1886-1905

| Firm | Location Prior to Tampa |
|---|---|
| Ybor and Manrara | Havana and Key West |
| Sanchez and Haya | New York |
| Lozano, Pendas and Co. | New York |
| Y. Pendas and Alvarez | |
| F. Lozano, Son and Co. | |
| R. Monne and Co. | New York |
| Emilio Pons and Co. | Tampa (origin) |
| Seidenberg and Co. | Key West |
| O'Halloran and Co. | Key West |
| Teodoro Perez and Co. | Key West |
| S. and F. Fleitas and Co. | Key West |
| Julius Ellinger and Co. | Key West |
| A. Del Pino | Key West |
| Bustillo Bros. and Diaz | Key West |
| Creagh, Gudnecht and Co. | Chicago |
| V. Guerra, Diaz and Co. | New York |
| Juan La Paz and Co. | Key West |
| Bonifacio Garcia and Co. (Port Tampa) | Chicago |
| Jose Morales and Co. (Port Tampa) | Key West |
| Menendez Bros. and Verplanck | New York and Cuba |
| Gonzalez, Mora and Co. | New York |
| Arguellas, Lopez and Bros. | New York |
| Cuesta, Ballard and Co. | Atlanta |
| Cuesta, Rey and Co. | |
| A. B. Ballard and Co. | |
| Trujillo and Benemelis | Chicago and Key West |
| Fernandez and Saxby | Chicago |
| F. Garcia and Bros. | New York |
| M. Perez and Co. | Key West |
| Jose M. Diaz and Bros. | New York |
| Amo, Ortiz and Co. | New York |
| Jose Lovera and Co. | Tampa (origin) |
| Clarkson Bros. | Tampa (origin) |
| P. San Martin and Co. | Tampa (origin) |
| Salvador Rodriguez | New York |
| M.  Stachelberg and Co. | New York |
| A. Santaella and Co. | New York |
| Berriman Bros. | Chicago |
| Val M. Antuono | Tampa (origin) |
| V. M. Ybor Sons and Co. | Tampa (origin) |

Source: A. Stuart Campbell, *The Cigar Industry of Tampa, Florida*

# Ybor City Cigar Factories, 1926-1950

| | |
|---|---|
| D. Acosta & Sons | 952  La Sétima [1926] |
| José D. Alvarez & Sons | 1918 12th Avenue [1926] |
| Alvarez & Rogers | 102 E. Scott Street [1932] |
| American Cigarette & Cigar Co. | 1916 14th Avenue [1926] |
| American Cigar Co. | 1916 14th Avenue [1932] |
| Andrieu Frank | 1906 Nebraska Avenue [1932] |
| Anna Cigar Factory | 1716 9th Avenue [1950] |
| Anna Cigar Factory | 2601 17th Street [1950] |
| Arango & Arango | 2502 12th Street [1932] |
| José Arango & Co. | 2112 15th Street [1926, 1932] |
| Vincent Baltar Cigar Co. | 1601 22nd Street [1950] |
| Berriman Brothers | 2311 North 18th Street [1926] |
| Berriman Brothers | 402 S. 22nd Street [1932, 1950] |
| M. Bustillo & Merriam | 1410 21st Street [1932] |
| Capitano,  Francisco & Co. | 3rd Avenue and 24th Street [1926] |
| Capitano,  Francisco & Co. | 1403 24th Street [1932, 1950] |
| Célso Cigar Co. | 2108 La Sétima [1926] |
| Corral, Wodiska (# 2 ) | NW corner, 19th Street & 2nd Avenue [1929, 1932] |
| Felix Cruz & Co. | 2605 17th Street |
| Diaz Havana Co. | 2311 18th Street [1950] |
| H. C. Diaz Cigar Factory | 1809 14th Street [1926] |
| José Diaz | 1008 8th Avenue [1932] |
| Rafael Diaz & Co. (#395) | Corner of 12th Street & 15th Avenue |
| The House of Delmage | 405 22nd Street [1926] |
| El Puro Cigar Co. | 1808 4th Avenue [1932] |
| José Escalante & Co. | 202 S. 22nd Street [1932, 1950] |
| F and F Cigar Factory | 1518 15th Street [1926] |
| Famous Cigar Factory | 1608 29th Avenue [1950] |
| Fernandez and Co. | 2302 14th Street [1926] |
| José Fernandez and Sons | 1318 12th Ave. [1926] |
| José Fernandez | 2910A 22nd Street [1932] |
| John B. Fernandez | 2113 1/2 22nd Street [1950] |
| Fernandez and Ruilova Cigar Co. | 1601-12 22nd Street [1926] |
| Flor de America Cigar Co. | 2309 14th Avenue [1932] |
| Flor de Valdez & Penichett | 1801 Central Avenue [1932] |
| Gallo Cigar Factory | 906 17th Avenue [1950] |
| Gonzalez y Sánchez Cigar Co. | (Sign on narrow mansard reads "Havana Cigars") [1926] |
| Gradiaz-Annis and Co. | 2311 North 18th Street [1926, 1950] |
| V. Guerieri Cigar Co. | 2935 21st Street [1926, 1950] |
| Hav-A-Tampa Cigar Co. | 2007 21st Street (entry on 22nd Street) [1926, 1932, 1950] |
| Happy G. Ligar Co. | 1602 9th Avenue [1926] |
| Antonio Hernandez Cigar Co. | 1406 12th Avenue [1926] |
| Oscar Hernandez | 2708 Mitchell Avenue [1932] |
| M. E. Hernandez | 1318 12th Avenue [1950] |
| K-5 Cigar Factory | 1903 Nebraska Avenue (rear) [1950] |
| La Flor de Cuba | 20th Street and 12th Avenue [1926] |
| La Floridiana Cigar Factory | 1607 17th Street [1950] |
| La Invasion Cigar Factory | 4901 12th Street [1932] |
| La Integridad Cigar Co. | 1607 17th Street [1926, 1932] |

| | |
|---|---|
| La Integridal Cigar Co. | 2406 17th Street [1950] |
| La Palma Cigar Co. | 1411 14th Avenue [1926] |
| Alvarez Lopez & Co. | 2008 19th Street [1950] |
| Carlos Loredo | 1607 4th Avenue [1932] |
| Silvo Lufriu Factory | 1009 1/2 14th Avenue [1950] |
| Martinez Demetrio Cigar Co. | 1804 12th Avenue [1926] |
| Aurelio Mascuñana | 1506 10th Avenue [1932] |
| Melrose Cigar Co. | 601 22nd Street [1926] |
| Benjamin J. Mills | 3101 29th Avenue [1932] |
| MiRey Cigar Factory | 2308 19th Street [1950] |
| Vicente Nieto & Bros. | 2708 18th Street [1932] |
| Nordac Cigar Co. | 1006 1/2 Central Avenue [1932] |
| Martin Nordase | 1719 5th Avenue [1932] |
| Luis Parra | 2226 8th Avenue [1932, 1950] |
| Oscar M. Pedrazas | 1601 22nd Avenue [1932] |
| V. Pereira Cigar Factory | 2607 10th Street [1950] |
| Aurelio Pérez | 1805 20th Street [1932] |
| Marcelino Pérez & Co. | 2008 19th Street [1932] |
| Pedro Pérez Cigar Co. | 1607 22nd Street [1926] |
| Pedro Pérez Cigar Co. | 1609 22nd Street [1832, 1950] |
| Perfecto Garcia ( El Paraiso ) | SW corner, 16th Street & 18th Avenue [1926] |
| Perfecto Garcia & Bros. | 2808 16th Street [1932, 1950] |
| Regensburg & Sons | NE corner 16th St. & Michigan Avenue [1926] |
| E. Regensburg & Sons | 2701 16th Street [1932, 1950] |
| Richard Roche | 2212-14 16th Street [1950] |
| Salvador Rodriguez, Inc. | 1310 22nd Street [1926, 1932, 1950] |
| Armando Romaella | 2204 Mitchell Avenue [1932] |
| Armando Romaella | 2408 15th Street [1950] |
| Ramon Sanchez | 2104 13th Street [1932] |
| Sánchez y Haya (#1) | Corner of La Sétima & 15th Street |
| Sánchez y Haya Co. (#2) | 2311 18th Street [1926, 1932] |
| Waldo Salas Cigar Co. | 2302 16th Avenue [1926] |
| Schwab-Davis & Co. | 2406 17th Street [1932] |
| Star Thompson Tobacco Co. | 1607 17th Street [1926, 1932, |
| Star Thompson Tobacco Co. | 201 N. 26th Street [1926, 1950] |
| A. Suarez. & Co | 2605 15th Street [1926] |
| G. Suarez & Son | 1814 1/2 9th Avenue [1950] |
| Tampa Cigar Co. | 2502 12th Avenue [1926, 1950] |
| Tampa Havana Industrial Co. | 1414 13th Avenue [1950] |
| Tampa Have It Cigar Co. | 1918 9th Avenue [1926] |
| Tampa-Vana Cigar Co. | 2007 11th Street [1926, 1950] |
| Tampa-Vana Cigar Co. | 912 11th Avenue [1932] |
| Thompson & Co., Inc. | 2411 21st Street [1932] |
| Leopoldo Toribio | 2909 12th Street [1950] |
| Try-A-Tampa Cigar Co. | 2401 21st Street [1926] |
| Andres Vallina | 1414 13th Avenue [1932] |
| Villazon  & Co. | 2511 21st Street [1926, 1932, 1950] |
| Vincent-Baltar Cigar Co. | 1019 1/2 19th Avenue [1950] |
| Wengler & Mandell, Inc. | 2311 18th Street [1932, |

Notes: The factories listed are compiled from annual editions of the *Tampa Classified Business Directory* and other sources. Conspicuously missing is Principe de Gales, 1886, located on the southwest corner of 14th Street and 9th Avenue. Many small *Chinchales* ("Buckeyes") are not included. These occasionally changed addresses or later closed. Duplication of names and addresses reflects shifting business names and locations over the years. In the case of changing or multiple locations for a single factory, the first address given is the earliest found; additional locations are followed by a listing year in square brackets when a year is known.  Source: *Tampa Classified Business Directory*, USFSPCL.

**Table 4**

# Major Ybor City Strikes and Labor Actions: 1886-1931

**1886**  Don Vicente Martíinez Ybor's Principe de Gales factory is the subject of worker action as Cubans object to the hiring of a Spanish bookkeeper and walk out, delaying completion of construction. As a result, La Flor de Sanchez y Haya factory owned by Ignacio Haya was able to obtain factory permit Number 1 to produce cigars. The Spaniard was let go.[1]

**1887**  January 17, the official first strike is declared by the members of the *Caballeros del Trabajo* union against the Principe de Gales factory. The workers wanted increased wages.[2]

**1887**  Between 1887 and 1894 there were 23 walkouts, but no effective organization claimed leadership.[3]

**1891**  Protesters in Ybor City demonstrate publicly against the November 1887 hanging of four anarchists convicted for instigating the Haymarket Square riots in Chicago in May 1886. Petitions for release of the three remaining instigators eventually led to their pardon by the Illinois governor in 1893.[4] In May, two Cuban labor clubs are formed to protest against Spaniards. These are the *Los Independientes* and the *Ignacio Agramonte Revolutionary* clubs.

**1897**  Italians are still not allowed to work in a majority of factories. Latin workers believed that Italians would work for less pay and hurt their own wages.[5] In April, Spanish factory *patrones* urge Spaniards not to obstruct Cuban worker efforts in order not to hurt production.[6]

**1899**  Spaniards join *La Resistencia*, a local union, and are placed alongside Cubans. This was intended to counter the ICCU of America. (8) This is the year of "The Weight Strike" (*La Huelga de la Pesa*). In July some 4,000 *tabaqueros* go on strike protesting the introduction of weight scales in the Principe de Gales factory. It reflected on the integrity of the workers. Also, workers wanted a *Cartabon*, a uniform wage scale. Owners replied with a "lockout," but by August conceded both requests. (9)

**1901**  The first general strike occurs. A feud erupts between *La Resistencia* and the ICM. *La Resistencia* wants Cuesta Rey and Co. (of West Tampa) to close its low-wage factory in Jacksonville. Strike is settled. (10)

**1902**  Cigar workers strike the Bustillo Brothers and Díaz factory in West Tampa. They wish to have a *lector* installed. *Patron* agrees but wants *El Presidente de Lectura* to collect outside factory. *Lector* Milian resigns. A strike follows. Assailants kidnap Milian, strip and beat him, then order him to leave for Havana or be hanged. Milian returns to a huge welcoming crowd. The Bustillo *patrón* gives in and Milian returns to work.

**1910**  June 23. The second general strike begins, known as the Seven Months Strike (*Huelga de los 7 meses*). The cause of the strike was the fact that various factories had not carried out the promise to abide by the pay scales agreed upon (managers were experiencing a price war, with attendant heavy competition), which made the *tabaqueros* innocent victims. The American bookkeeper at Bustillo Brothers and Diaz factory is shot. The next morning the bullet-riddled bodies of Angelo Albano and Castrense Ficarrotta are found hanging from a tree, believed to be the work of militants from South Tampa. It was believed this action would instill terror in the workers and force them to return to work, a thing manufacturers wanted badly, but not as much as the downtown establishment, who by now depended on regular factory dollars for its welfare. Workers in Cuba sent help. The Seven Months Strike ends on January 6. (11)

**1912**  September 2. Some 4,500 cigar makers celebrate in Labor Day parade. (12)

**1920**  April 14. The third general strike begins. It lasts 10 months (but is called, *Huelga de Nueve meses*). It paralyzes the industry. Some 6,400 *tabaqueros* walk out of 27 factories. *Patrones* won. They got rid of uniform wage scale, and *lectores* were dismissed. (13) "The question at issue was whether the owner should run the factory or whether that power should be delegated to the Joint Advisory Board of the Cigarmakers Union....The issue was joined, and the bulk of the 15,000 cigarmakers of Tampa have been out of employment for the past eight months..." (13a)

**1931**  A final strike results in the dismissal of certain *lectores* that had been allowed to come back, provided they read what was required by *patrones*. (14) By now the depression had eliminated any remaining power the *tabaqueros* had. Most were without a job.

*383*

# Major Fires in Ybor City History

**April 1, 1886.** A fire rages through Key West, destroying Don Vicente's cigar factory. He decides to transfer his entire operation to Tampa. In the aftermath, some of the cigar workers left unemployed by the devastation seek work in Ybor City.

**November 12, 1891.** A fire breaks out in the Aurelio Campos restaurant on 7th Avenue, between 14th and 15th Streets. It destroys two and a half city blocks. The fire causes the cigar manufacturers to reconsider the use of vulnerable materials like wood in the construction of their factories. Ybor and others turn to brick, creating the distinctive look that the city has today.

**March 1, 1908.** The great Ybor City fire burns five cigar factories and over 250 homes across 55 acres, spreading over almost 13 city blocks, from roughly 16th to 20th Streets and from 12th Avenue to Michigan Avenue (today's Columbus Drive). Some of the headlines of the "Fire-Extra" edition of *The Tribune-News* dated March 1, 1908, read:

> "The Most Disastrous Fire in Tampa's History Raged for Four Hours in Densely Populated District. Almost Panic Prevails. . . . Five Cigar Factories and Over 250 Homes are Consumed in Insatiable Maw of Flames. . . . Over a Thousand Workmen Thrown Out of Employment."

**June 8, 1912.** Fire destroys the main building of Centro Asturiano. A new one is built at the current site in 1914. Upon completion of the building on May 15, 1914, it is considered the state's most elegant social building.

**1914.** The first L'Unione Italiana building burns.

**April 30, 1916.** El Círculo Cubano is destroyed by fire. Spaniards and Italians immediately place their club at the disposal of the Cuban members. Construction of a new building begins on February 25, 1917; it is dedicated in 1918.

**January 8, 1994.** A fire breaks out at 4:15 p.m. at the E. H. Steinberg building. Until recently the building had been occupied by the Louis Wohl Restaurant Supply Co. The fire enveloped the Tradition Store, burning much men's clothing. Loss was estimated at $49,000, based on tax records. One sprinkler head went off. The fire in the two-story building at 1613-1617D 7th Avenue jeopardized all of the buildings on the block. A loss of $49,500 was estimated. Serious impact on merchandise was incurred by rented stores.

**May 19, 2000.** The passing of the years and the replacement of the town's vulnerable wooden structures didn't immunize Ybor City against its oldest enemy. A fire sparked by a construction worker who severed a power line with his forklift is fanned by winds and destroys the nearly completed 454-unit apartment complex known as The Park at Ybor City (now named the Camden Ybor City). In addition to the destruction of the $40-million urban housing development, flames gutted the 12-year-old, $3 million U. S. Post Office and damaged Oliva Tobacco, the U-Haul Center, and Our Lady of Perpetual Help church on North 18th Street. All of the buildings were repaired or rebuilt.

**Table 6**

# Unions and Cigar Manufacturers

## Workers' Organizations

**1886**  *La Noble Orden de los Caballeros de Trabajo* (The Noble Order of the Knights of Labor). A Cuban order that was mostly comprised of hauling and freight business employees.

**1886**  *Los Caballeros del Trabajo* (Knights of Labor). The Cuban branch of the above order aimed at attracting cigar makers as members.

**1891**  *Los Independientes*. An early Cuban organization formed to respond to Spanish anarchists who paraded in Ybor City and yelled "Long live Spain" in front of Cuban houses (this following the hanging of four anarchists in Haymarket Square, Chicago, in November 1887).

**1891**  Ignacio Agramonte Cuban Revolutionary Club. Principle objective: to gather funds for the coming war against Spain. Founders, Eligio Carbonell Manta  and José Gomez Santoyo. First met May 10, 1891 at the Liceo Cubano.

**1892**  Cuban Federation of Labor. Formed by the Cuban, Ramon Rubiera de Armos. This federation disappeared when the union *La Resistencia* came into being.

**1911**  IWW, local 102. Organized in 1906. Its official organ was *El Obrero Industrial*.

**1899**  *La Resistencia (La Sociedad de Torcederos de Tampa)*. The first major union.

**1901**  Cigar Makers International Union of America, local of AFL-CIO (CMIU).  This was the strongest union.

**1931**  Tobacco Workers International Union (TWIU).


## Manufacturers' Organization

The Clear Havana Cigar Manufacturers Association. Also often referred to as The Trust, this group included the owners of the cigar factories *(los Patrones)*.

## References:

*The Ybor City Story* by José Rivero Muñíz, translated by Dr. Eustasio Fernandez and Henry Beltran.
*The Immigrant World of Ybor City* by G. R. Mormino and G. E. Pozzetta.

**Table 7**

# Clubs, Hospitals, Clinics

*La Sociedad Benéfica*. A Cuban medical organization founded in latter part of 1886. Members sent to hospitals or clinics in Key West or Havana.

*El Porvenír*. An early Spanish medical organization in latter part of 1886. In time physicians from Key West or Havana were enticed to relocate in Ybor City.

*Centro Español*. The Spanish social club that built its first club house in 1902 at 16th Street and La Sétima. It was rebuilt in 1912, at which time it concurrently built a second club house in West Tampa, both elegant "palaces." At the same time it also built the *Sanatorio del Centro Español* on Bayshore Boulevard. This hospital was opened in 1904. It was a three story, state-of-the-art hospital, with a magnificent view of Tampa Bay. The Club offered an HMO-style medical service, cradle to grave. The Centro Español had two cemeteries and a mausoleum. In 1940 the dues were still $1.50 per month. The old cemetery, which is still open, is located at 26th Street and 21st Avenue. The newer cemetery and mausoleum is located on the extension of Lake Avenue at approximately 46th Street.

*La Benéfica*. Affiliated with the Centro Español. It was the city arm of the hospital. It was located on the second floor of 10th Avenue and 15th Street on the southeast corner. (The beautiful building still stands). Medical consulting took place there, and minor sicknesses were treated. Patients were sent to Centro Español Sanatorium on Bayshore Boulevard, if the doctors requested it. When that hospital was closed, a long, two story modern hospital was opened in the vicinity of Armenia and Hillsborough. This hospital, in turn, was sold in the late 1970's.

*El Centro Asturiano*. In 1902, after 11 years with the Centro Español, the Asturians organized as a branch of the Havana Centro Asturiano. Operating out of several locations, it took the lead in mutual aid and built the first major Latin medical facility, the Covadonga Sanitarium, the best facility in Tampa at the time.

  The Centro Asturiano club house was built in 1907. After the original burned, a new building was erected in 1915. It is located at Nebraska and Palm Ave., and remains very active. In 1926 it opened the elegant *Sanatorio del Centro Asturiano*. It was located on 21st. Avenue, its front entrance overlooking 13th street to the south. The Club offered a **cradle to grave** HMO hospitalization plan. In 1997 it still operates a cemetery and mausoleum. It also maintains the **old cemetery** at Ola Avenue north of Columbus Drive. The newer cemetery is just east of 56th St. on Martin Luther King Jr. Boulevard. The sanatarium closed in the late 1980's.

*L'Unione Italiana*. "The first club house was built in November 1911 at 1724 7th Avenue at a cost of $60,000, and had 900 members. This building was destroyed by fire in May of 1914," according to Tony Pizzo, article, "The Italians in Tampa" (date unknown). The current building was built in 1918.at the corner of 7th Ave and 18th street   Also, *La Societa di Mutuo Soccorso* erected a wooden building on 19th St. and 8th Ave. It was later removed by Urban Renewal. L'Unione Italiana offers HMO care, cradle to grave service. Originally, Lobato's pharmacy was located next door, 1st floor, #1 and #3 space. Many Italians were hospitalized at the Centro Español or the Centro Asturiano Sanatorium. The cemetery and beautiful mausoleum has an entry on 26th street, located aside of the Centro Español cemetery on 21 St. Ave.

  In West Tampa the local Sicilians founded **La Societa Sicilia,** a beautiful building on Howard Ave. This organization was later merged into the greater *L'Unione Italiana.* Sons of Italy of America has a building in West Tampa. An affiliate lodge is over 70 years old.

*El Círculo Cubano*. The original club house was built in 1907, and was then called Club National Cubano. It later burned and was replaced in 1918 by the current very elegant "palace" on the same site, corner of Palm Ave and 14th street. The club members used a small clinic in the Club house for members, and these used El Bien Publico, while others used the Centro Español's *La Benefica*, through arrangement with that Spanish facility. Some also used Trelles Clinic. All three were within blocks of their club house.

*Sociedad Union Martí-Maceo*. It is a black Cuban society and honors Jose Marti and the Black General, Antonio Maceo, both supreme patriots. It first operated a two story building on 6th Ave and 12th street. Later it built its present club building 13th and La Setima. It is still active. Its medical services were available at the Cuban and Spanish clinics or hospitals. Black Cubans worked side by side with Latins in the factories. The Club provided recreational and meeting services to black Cubans. These numbered under a thousand at its peak.

*El Bien Público*. Served the Cuban Club community. It was located at the corner of 14th St. and 9th Avenue. It combined consulting and hospital care on the 2nd floor. It was originally owned by Dr. Jose Ramon Avellanal who, in turn, sold it to Dr. Gonzalez. Until its closing following Urban Renewal it was known as the Gonzalez Clinic.

*Trelles Clinic*. Founded in 1926, was formally inaugurated in 1930. It was referred to as *la nueva Clinica de Sociedad de Socorros (La Populár)* by Dr. Jorge A. Trelles. Consulting was done in the 1st floor and the hospital was in the 2nd floor. A pharmacy was located in the first floor.

**Table 8**

# Centro Español Presidents, 1891-1941

| | |
|---|---|
| Ignacio Haya | 1891-1892 (First President of Centro Español) |
| Enrique Pendás | 1893 |
| Ignacio Haya | 1894-1895 |
| Vicente Guerra | 1896 |
| Adalberto Ramirez | 1897-1898 |
| Vicente Guerra | 1899-1900 |
| Alejandrino Nistal | 1901 |
| Jaime Pendás | 1902 |
| Ignacio Haya | 1903 |
| Vicente Guerra | 1904-1906 |
| Alejandrino Nistal | 1907 |
| Enrique Pendás | 1908-1910 |
| Celestino Vega | 1911-1915 |
| Angel L. Cuesta | 1916 |
| Ambrosio Torres | 1917-1918 |
| Laureano Torres | 1919-1920 |
| Ramon Fernandez Rey | 1921-1928 ( Honorary President) |
| Domingo Quintana | 1929-1932 |
| Ramon Fernandez Rey | 1933-1941 |

NOTE: Many of those who served as president—including Ignacio Haya, Angel Cuesta, and Celestino Vega—were prominent cigar manufacturers. Most *Yborciteños* addressed them with the honorofic "Don"—"Don Ignacio," "Don Angel," "Don Celestino." This is a Spanish social custom that acknowledges significant accomplishments, influence, and social status.

**Table 9**

# Sanatorio del Centro Español Bayshore Boulevard Medical Services Rendered: 1939-1941

The following data represents the number of members served by the medical doctors of the *Sanatorio del Centro Español* so that readers can appreciate the extent of their service.

Members consulted during 1939

| | |
|---|---|
| At the Ybor City Clinic | 11,088 |
| At the  West Tampa Clinic | 6,771 |
| Total | 17,859 |

Members consulted during 1940

| | |
|---|---|
| At the Ybor City Clinic | 13,586 |
| At the West Tampa clinic | 8,692 |
| Total | 22,278 |

Members consulted during first six months of 1941:

| | |
|---|---|
| At the Ybor City Clinic | 8,080 |
| At the W. Tampa Clinic | 5,101 |
| Total | 13,181 |

Clinic assistance by  Dr. Carlos Barbas

| | |
|---|---|
| A monthly average of emergencies | 25 |
| A monthy average of consulting and cures | 1,500 |
| General radiography (La Benéfica and Sanatorio) | 2,620 |
| Treatments, Radiography (La Benéfica and Sanatorio) | 1,492 |

(since the acquisition of the radiography equipment in 1938)



**Tables and Exhibits**

# Doctors  Serving Centro Español de Tampa

| <u>Doctors</u> | <u>Function</u> |
| --- | --- |
| Dr. Jose Ramon Avellanál | First Director of Sanatorium  (c. Feb. 1906 to Aug. 13, 1913) |
| Dr. Moat | Intern |
| Dr. Pezuela | Assisting |
| Dr. Serafín Loredo | |
| Dr. Guillermo Molinet | Interim Director. |
| Dr. Alfonso Sánchez | Director |
| Dr. Duke | Faculty |
| Dr. L. Hull Pierce | Faculty |
| Dr. R. R. Myers | Dentist |
| Dr. Rafael Ortega | Director |
| Dr. Santiago Paniello | Faculty, then Director |
| Dr. Parsons M. García | Faculty |
| Dr. William Howsley | Faculty |
| Dr. Lancaster | Surgeon |
| Dr. M. R. Winton | Surgeon ("Illustrious") |
| Dr. George Cook | Head Surgeon |
| Dr. L. Forbes | Consultation |
| Dr. Angel Solano Grimál | Consultation |
| Dr. J. A.  Domingues | Faculty |
| Dr. Gustavo Porro | Radiologist |
| Dr. Abelardo Martorell | |
| Dr. Ismael Angulo | |
| Dr. Anthony P. Perzia | |
| Dr. Manuel A. Pérez | |
| Dr. J. A. Minardi | |
| Dr. J. R. Porta | Bacteriologist |
| Dr. M. J. Rodes | |
| Dr. Carlos F. Arroyo | |
| Dr. Blackburn W. Lowry | |
| Dr. William Patterson | |
| Dr. Adrian Bustillo | |
| Dr. Giuseppe Di Gaetani | |
| Dr. Ricardo Fina | |
| Dr. S. A. Scuderi | |
| Dr. Amado Mas | |
| Dr. Joseph N. Torretta | |
| Dr. Luis Rey | |
| Dr. M. Garcia Gutierrez | |

On January 19, 1906, the social cost of belonging to the hospital was set at $1.50 per month, per family, "with rights of benefits provided by La Benéfica."

On Sept. 7, 1909, an agreement was made so that the patients of two sister associations, Circulo Cubano and El Porvenír, could receive hospital service.

# Sección Benéfica del Centro Español

**Su cuerpo facultativo (Faculty):**

Dr. Santiago Paniello
Dr. Parsons M. García
Dr. Abelardo Martoréll
Dr. Joseph Torretta
Dr. Amado Mas
Dr. Julio Gavilla

Reference: Ad placed by Sección Benéfica del Centro Español in the
*Album de la Orden Caballeros del Águila de Oro, Capítulo Cristobal Colón, No. 7,* dated August 1930.

Table 12

# Doctors Serving El Bien Público Clinic

Dr. José Ramon Avellanál   (Founder of El Bien Público Clinic)
Dr. N. A. Portocarrera, Director
Dr. Santiago Paniello
Dr.  Rafael Ortega
Dr. Amado Mas
Dr. M. J. Rodes
Dr. Parsons M. García

*Comadronas* (Midwives)
*Relacion de las que prestan sus servicios*
*profesionales a la Sociedad,  El Bien Público.*
Sra. Maria Bonino
Sra. Rita C de Garcia
Sra. G. Pendino
Sra. Olga Naranjo
Sra. Ercolini Premori
Sra. Dannie Ciccarello
Sra. Mariana Ciccarello
Sra. Luisa Gutierrez
Sra. Lucrecia Arredondo

*Dentistas* (Dentists)
De la Sociedad, El Bien Público
Dr. A. J. Kohly
Dr. R. D. Whiteside
Dr. R. E. Myers
Dr. L. A. Jowell

Table 13

# Doctors Serving Trelles Clinic (founded 1926)

Dr. Jorge A. Trelles (Director of "Instituto de Dr. Arguelles" and doctor of *La Benéfica*)

Supplying services:
Dr. Ricardo Fina
Dr. G. H. Altree
Dr. Aurelio Sust

# Doctors Serving Sanatorio Centro Asturiano de Tampa

| | |
|---|---|
| Acosta, Abelardo P., MD | Anesthesiology |
| Bajo, Pedro T., MD | Bone and Joint Surgery |
| Cernuda, Chas. E., MD | Pulmonary Diseases-Internal Medicine |
| Cohen, Richard D., MD | Pulmonary Diseases and Internal Medicine |
| Fernandez, Luis E., MD | Internal Medicine-Gastroenterology |
| Henderson, Robert C., MD | Bone and Joint Surgery |
| Lorenzo, Marcos F., MD | |
| Mallea, Victor A., MD | General Practice |
| Myers, W. Mahon, MD | Fellow of American College of Surgeons |
| Palacios, Gerardo F., MD | Internal Medicine & Gastroenterology |
| Patel, Kiran C., MD | Cardiovascular Diseases |
| Pérez, Hilda W., MD | General Practice-Gynecology |
| Tejedor, Antonio, MD | |
| Toledo, Florentino H., MD | Gynecology-Obstetrics-Fertility |
| Valdés, Julio C., MD | Family Practice |
| Vizzi, Fernando, MD | Internal Medicine |
| Yarnoz, Michael D., MD | Cardiac Thoracic and Vascular Surgery |

# Cultural and Social Activities of El Centro Español: 1912-1940

Selected cultural activities of the **Centro Español de Tampa** and the sources that reported on them.

### *Tampa Ilustrado*

October 12, 1912: "The Board of Directors has contracted the excellent Vienese Operatta Co. , now in Habana, Cuba, to appear at the Centro for its inauguaration celebration."

Feb. 10, 1913: Señora Emilia Rico, first soprano of the Compañia Opera appeared in "El Gran Teatro Español." An article with picture appeared on page 184.

Carmen Ramirez, the celebrated singer, was great in her role in the unforgettable "Carmen".

March 12, 1913: Gran Theater de El Centro Español, fine operas were presented, including five marvelous presentations of *Rigoleto, Aida, Lucia, La Traviata*, and *Il Travatore!* La Compañia Opera Co. was an excellent group from Europe.

April 28, 1913, His Excellency Don Juan Riano Gayanos, the Spanish Ambassador to the U.S., visited the Centro Español. Alicia, his wife, was given a tea party at the Club.

### *La Gaceta*

May 22, 1929: Centro Español Theater ran a popular Spanish play, *En un Burro, Tres Baturros.* This was a comedy punctuated with jokes; Spanish actors participated.

1929: Eugenio Noel, a famous Spanish journalist, spoke before 500 members on "La Raza Española" ("The Spanish Race").

Nov. 28, 1934: Former Cuban President, Ramón Grau San Martin, visited Centro Español.

Nov. 21, 1936: Centro Español gives grand reception for Don Fernando de los Ríos, Spanish Ambassador to the United States.

August 27, 1938. Don Ramon Gonzalez Peña, Spanish Minister of Justice honored by the Centro Español.

Oct. 29, 1938: Don Fernando de los Ríos, Spanish Ambassador, visits Tampa. (Awards a prestigious medal to the committee raising funds for ambulances to be used in the Spanish Civil War).

Victoriano Manteiga, editor and publisher of *La Gaceta* and Ybor City's most illustrious intellectual of the day, writes:

> El Centro Español, the dean of mutual aid societies, is a prestigious organization, owning two social palaces, a Sanatorium on Bayshore Boulevard, and a modern clinic known as La Benéfica.
>
> The Centro Español's great club house, erected primarily by cigar rollers, assisted by industrialists and merchants, has a beautiful theatre, ball room a gymnasium and a cantina for the enjoyment of the members. A first class library with classical reading material was also part of the offerings.
>
> In the late 1920's the Centro Español Theatre became known as El Casino. It began showing classic movies. . . . In the Thirties the theatre became the first movie house in Florida to show [Hispanic] movie stars of the time. The movies were imported from Argentina, Spain, Mexico and Cuba. On many occasions the celebrities made personal appearances on the stage. One of the greatest was Libertad Lamarque of Buenos Aires.

# Centro Asturiano Presidents: 1902-2000

| | | |
|---|---|---|
| 1. | Antonio Gonzalez Prado (Founder) | 1902 (served two months: Feb. 20-April 14) |
| 2. | Enrique Fernandez Quesada | 1902-1904 |
| 3. | Jose Fernandez Vega | 1904-1907 |
| 4. | Ramon Fernandez Valdés | 1907-1911 |
| 5. | Joaquin Lopez Díaz | 1911-1914 |
| 6. | Laureano Torres López | 1914-1915 |
| 7. | Jaime Pendas Trelles | 1915-1919 |
| 8. | Manuel Corrál Collado | 1919-1921 |
| 9. | Francisco Sánchez Sánchez | 1921-1923 |
| 10 | Laureano Torres Lopez | 1923-1929 |
| 11. | Francisco Gonzalez Longo | 1929-1931 |
| 12. | Carlos Menendez Campo | 1932-1934 |
| 13. | Luis Lopez Gestedo | 1934-1936 |
| 14. | Carlos Menendez Campo | 1936-1938 |
| 15. | Justo Rodriguez Fernandez | 1938-1940 |
| 16. | Francisco Gonzalez  Longo | 1940 (served five months) |
| 17. | Juan Fernandez Gonzalez | 1940-1941 |
| 18. | José Gonzalez Álvarez | 1941-1945 |
| 19. | Prudencio M. Gonzalez | 1945-1947 |
| 20. | Francisco Gonzalez Longo | 1947-1948 |
| 21. | Carlos Menendez Campo | 1948-1951 |
| 22. | Manuel Alonso y San Miguel | 1951-1960 |
| 23. | Joe Moran Trelles, Esq. | 1960-1964 |
| 24. | José Martinez Martinez | 1964-1966 |
| 25. | Fernando Hevia Gonzalez | 1966-1969 |
| 26. | José Martinez Martinez | 1969-1970, |
| 27. | Emilio Rodriguez Álvarez | 1970-1971 |
| 28. | Frank A. Gonzalez Baez | 1971-1977 |
| 29. | Joe Martinez Martinez | 1977-1980 |
| 30. | Manuel Tamargo Fernandez | 1980-1983 |
| 31. | Joe M. Garcia | 1983-1986 |
| 32. | Andres Faza Diaz | 1986-1989 |
| 33. | Braulio Lombardia Martinez | 1989-1991 |
| 34. | Juan Fernandez Martinez | 1991-1994 |
| 35. | Jose Manuel Sanchez Coviella | 1994-1995 |
| 36. | Elvira Tamargo Garcia | 1996-2000 |

Reference:
*Centro Asturiano de Tampa, Inc., Souvenir Book, 1902-1985.*

**Table 17**

# L'Unione Italiana Presidents, 1894-2000

| | | |
|---|---|---|
| 1. | Bartolomeo Filogamo | 1894-1900 |
| 2. | Gaetano Ciccarello | 1901-1906 |
| 3. | Phillip Licata | 1907-1924 |
| 4. | Joseph Bacellona | 1925-1926 |
| 5. | Antonio Reina | 1927 |
| 6. | Antonio Dibona | 1928 |
| 7. | Vincenzo Cannella | 1929-1930 |
| 8. | Paolo Longo | 1931-1934 |
| 9. | Peter Maniscalco | 1935-1936 |
| 10. | Vincenzo Guastella | 1937-1940 |
| 11. | E. O. Henry Palermo | 1941-1944 |
| 12. | Paolo Longo | 1945-1946 |
| 13. | Giulio Cacciatore | 1947-1948 |
| 14. | Paolo Longo | 1949-1950 |
| 15. | Stefano G. Spoto | 1951-1954 |
| 16. | Joe P. Maniscalco | 1955-1956 |
| 17. | Phil LoCicero | 1957-1960 |
| 18. | Jimmy Pardo | 1961-1962 |
| 19. | Frank P. Settecasi | 1963-1964 |
| 20. | Phillip V. Valenti | 1965-1966 |
| 21. | Peter Maniscalco | January 1967 |
| 22. | Sam C. Zummo | February 1967-1968 |
| 23. | Phil LoCicero | 1969-1970 |
| 24. | Vincent LoScalzo | 1970-1973 |
| 25. | Lorenzo Lorenzano | 1974 |
| 26. | Nelson J. Palermo | 1975-1978 |
| 27. | Bennie Barbiera | 1979-1980 |
| 28. | Nelson Palermo | 1981-1982 |
| 29. | Vincent LoScalzo | 1983-1984 |
| 30. | Vincent J. Pardo | 1985-1987 |
| 31. | Charles Spicola, Jr. | 1988-January 1989 |
| 32. | Phyllis L. Traina | February 1989-1990 |
| 33. | Dennis Diecidue | 1990-1992 |
| 34. | James J. Granell | 1992-1994 |
| 35. | Domenic P. Cammarata | 1994-1996 |
| 36. | Joe Capitano, Sr. | 1996-1998 |
| 37. | Joe Capitano, Sr. | 1998-2000 |

The L' Unione Italiana was founded as the *Societa Italiana Di Mutuo Soccorso L'Unione* on April 4, 1894, with 127 members.

Reference:
"Paolo Longo Awards" booklet, November 7, 1992.

# El Círculo Cubano Presidents: 1902-2000

*A continuación, nos honramos en dedicar este espacio a nuestros pasados presidentes, cuyos esfuerzos en la dirección de esta institución, se han hecho patente en el trascurso de los años, y hoy podemos disfrutar de muchos beneficios realizados con la magnifica labor de estos distinquidos senores.*

*A aquellos que han desaparecido, ofrecimos la memoria de todos los socios del Círculo Cubano, y para los que aun tenenmos la dicha de tener entre nosotros, tenemos un saludo cordial y nuestra eterna gratitud por una labor bien hecha.*

| | | |
|---|---|---|
| 1. | Eladio Paula | 1902-1906 |
| 2. | Alfredo J. Kohly | 1907-1917 |
| 3 | Salvador M. Ybor | 1918-1920 |
| 4. | Ricardo Cabarrouy | 1921-1928 |
| 5. | Eduardo Valdez Generique | 1929-1930 |
| 6. | José S. Franco | 1931-1932 |
| 7. | Eduardo Valdez Generique | 1933-1934 |
| 8. | Juan Quesada | 1935-1936 |
| 9. | Francisco García | 1937-1946 |
| 10. | Rogelio Berdeal | 1947-1948 |
| 11. | Armando Dorta | 1949-1952 |
| 12. | Francisco Fernandez de la Nuez | 1953-1954 |
| 13. | Armando Dorta | 1955-1956 |
| 14. | Emilio Almendares | 1957-1958 |
| 15. | Francisco Fernandez de la Nuez | 1959-1960 |
| 16. | Sántos Rodriguez | 1961-1962 |
| 17. | Henry Gonzalez | 1963-1964 |
| 18. | Evelio Alvarez | 1965-1970 |
| 19. | Roberto M. Viana | 1971-1974 |
| 20. | Enrique Quesada | 1975-1976 |
| 21. | Evelio Alvarez | 1977-1978 |
| 22. | Silvio Vega | 1979-1981 |
| 23. | Frank Valdez | 1981-1987 |
| 24. | Ventura Perot | 1987-1988 |
| 25. | Mike Pedriñan | 1988-1989 |
| 26. | Ramon Hernandez | 1989-1989 |
| 27. | Hortensia Morales | 1989-1991 |
| 28. | Ventura Perot | 1991-1994 |
| 29. | Rolando Perez Pedrero | 1994-1998 |
| 30. | Paul Dosal | 1998-2000 |

COURTESY OF ROLANDO PEREZ PEDRERO AND DR. PAUL DOSAL.

# Sociedad la Union Martí-Maceo Presidents: 1904-2000

Exact years of service were not available, but members provided this chronological list.

1. Manuel Baños
2. Ruperto Pedroso
3. Lorenzo Rodriguez
4. Domingo Pérez
5. Diego Caballero
6. Jacinto San Martín
7. Santiago Jacquez
8. Bernardo Velasquez
9. José Ramos
10. Tomas Cuervas
11. Alejo Palomino
12. Facundo Accion
13. Angel Noriega
14. Francisco Flores
15. Juan Casellas
16. Eugenio Felipe
17. Francisco Rodriguez
18. Juan Franco
19. Florentino Mallea
20. Rogelio Alfonso
21. Laureando Díaz
22. Enrique Bermudez
23. Eugenio Felipe
24. Frank Jimenez
25. Aurelio O'Reilly
26. Rene García
27. Pedro Millét
28. Juan Mallea
29. Jerry Govantes
30. Manuel Alfonso
31. Mrs. Clara Maldonado
32. Victoriano Valdés
33. Rigoberto M. Garcia
34. Miguel Torres

# Ybor City Chamber of Commerce Presidents 1930-2000

| # | Name | Years | | # | Name | Years |
|---|------|-------|---|---|------|-------|
| 1. | James Fernandez | 1930-32 | | 33. | Daniel F. Martinez | 1967-68 |
| 2. | Charles G. Spicola | 1932-33 | | 34. | Joseph C. Granda | 1968-69 |
| 3. | Harry Wilderman | 1933-34 | | 35. | H. Frey | 1969-70 |
| 4. | Joseph E. Chamoun | 1934-35 | | 36. | A. William Benitez | 1970-71 |
| 5. | R. B. Díaz | 1935-36 | | 37. | Charles W. Cadrecha | 1971-72 |
| 6. | Raul Vega, Sr. | 1936-37 | | 38. | James L. Ghiotto | 1972-73 |
| 7. | Joseph E. Chamoun | 1937-38 | | 39. | Alvaro Fernandez | 1973-74 |
| 8. | M. K. Hudson | 1938-39 | | 40. | Manuel G. Álvarez, Jr. | 1974-75 |
| 9. | John A. Díaz, Sr. | 1939-40 | | 41. | Arthur M. Dosál | 1975-76 |
| 10. | Dick A. Greco, Sr. | 1940-41 | | 42. | Antonio Huesca | 1976-77 |
| 11. | John Fernandez | 1941-42 | | 43. | Frank T. Lastra | 1977-78 |
| 12. | Sam Ferreri | 1942-43 | | 44. | Daniel Lásso | 1978 |
| 13. | John Adamo | 1943-44 | | 45. | Sam D. Leto | 1978-79 |
| 14. | G. C. Spicola | 1944-45 | | 46. | Cesar Gonzmart, Jr. | 1979-80 |
| 15. | George Spoto | 1945-46 | | 47. | Dr. Henry J. Fernandez | 1980-81 |
| 16. | Manuel García, Jr. | 1946-47 | | 48. | Richard Gonzmart | 1981-82 |
| 17. | Edward C. Spoto | 1947-48 | | 49. | Victor E. Dimaio | 1982-83 |
| 18. | Dick Reina | 1948-49 | | 50. | Frank de la Grana | 1983-84 |
| 19. | Joe A. Bua | 1949-50 | | 51. | Michael L. Shea | 1984-85 |
| 20. | J. L. Hart | 1950-51 | | 52. | Joyce C. Schaffer | 1985-86 |
| 21. | Max Goodrich | 1951-52 | | 53. | Timothy S. Nugent | 1986-87 |
| 22. | Joseph F. DiBona | 1952-53 | | 54. | Joan W. Jennewein | 1987-88 |
| 23. | Aristo Pérez | 1953-54 | | 55. | Adela Gonzmart | 1988-91 |
| 24. | Angelo C. Martino | 1954-55 | | 56. | Vince J. Pardo | 1991-92 |
| 25. | Cesar Gonzmart, Sr. | 1955-56 | | 57. | Enrique A. Woodroffe | 1992-93 |
| 26. | Manuel J. Buchman | 1956-57 | | 58. | Kenneth C. Ferlita | 1993-94 |
| 27. | Dr. Henry J. Fernandez | 1957-59 | | 59. | Scott Rolston | 1994-95 |
| 28. | Joseph R. López | 1959-60 | | 60. | Jill Wax | 1995-96 |
| 29. | Dr. Henry J. Fernandez | 1960-62 | | 61 | Kristopher Fernandez | 1996-97 |
| 30. | Raul Vega, Jr. | 1962-64 | | 62. | Gil Hernandez | 1997-98 |
| 31. | Manuel Ballota | 1964-66 | | 63. | Sarah Romeo | 1998-99 |
| 32. | Armando P. Valdés, Jr. | 1966-67 | | 64. | E. J. Grimaldi | 1999-2000 |

# Rotary Club of Ybor City Presidents: 1948-2000

| | | | |
|---|---|---|---|
| Anthony P. Pizzo | 1948-49 | David W. Martin | 1972-73 |
| Joseph E. Chamoun | 1949-50 | Heywood A. Turner | 1973-74 |
| Homer E. Hesterly | 1950-51 | Frank G. Pascual | 1974-75 |
| Charles G. Spicola | 1951-52 | José A. Álvarez | 1975-76 |
| Al Chiaramonte | 1952-53 | Brian W. Longbottom | 1976-77 |
| Evelio Cernuda | 1953-54 | Daniel F. Martinez | 1977-78 |
| Henry Scaglione | 1954-55 | Gene Shearer | 1978-79 |
| William A. Krusen | 1955-56 | Álvaro Fernandez | 1979-80 |
| Joe Alonso | 1956-57 | Dr. Hernán Leon | 1980-81 |
| Anthony J. Grimaldi | 1957-58 | Armando Dorta, Jr. | 1981-82 |
| Francis J. Davis | 1958-59 | D. Keith Hensley | 1982-83 |
| Bonifacio Valero | 1959-60 | Rene Huesca | 1983-84 |
| Frank V. Giunta | 1960-61 | Mario Garcia | 1984-85 |
| Fred R. Church Jr | 1961-62 | Rafael Martinez Ybor | 1985-86 |
| Dr. Mariano Paniello | 1962-63 | Vincent I. Antolín | 1986-87 |
| Angelo G. Spicola | 1963-64 | Lew W. Kaminga | 1987-88 |
| Kendrick Hardcastle, III | 1964-65 | José E. Valiente | 1988-89 |
| Frank Suarez | 1965-66 | James J. Moohan | 1989-90 |
| Robert E. Guyton | 1968-67 | Gilbert J. Hernandez | 1990-91 |
| Julius C. DeLotto | 1967-68 | Manuel A. Lopez, Jr. | 1991-92 |
| Jackson Parmer | 1968-69 | Jack E. Fernandez, Sr. | 1992-93 |
| Cesar P. Alfonso | 1969-70 | John A. Rañon | 1993-94 |
| Harold H. Davis | 1970-71 | Anders W. Johnson | 1994-95 |
| Danilo V. Fernandez | 1971-72 | Jack E. Fernandez, Sr. | 1995-96 |
| Dennis J. Alfonso | 1996-97 | Dennis D. Fusileir | 1997-98 |
| Klaus D. Eastridge | 1998-99 | J. Costa | 1999-2000 |

Chartered October 20, 1948

UPDATED OFFICERS COURTESY OF AL FERNANDEZ

# Ybor City Museum Society Presidents 1982-2000

| | |
|---|---|
| Bettie Nelson | 1982-83 |
| Joan W. Jennewein | 1983-84 |
| Pat R. Carter | 1984-85 |
| James R. Turner | 1985-86 |
| Sylvia Vega Smith | 1986-87 |
| Donna Parrino | 1987-88 |
| Joan Jennewein | 1988-89 |
| Joan Jennewein | 1989-90 |
| Adela Gonzmart /Adrienne García | 1990-91 (co-Presidents) |
| Adela Gonzmart /Adrienne García | 1991-92 (co-Presidents) |
| Sonya Ziegler | 1992-93 |
| Sonya Ziegler | 1993-94 |
| Sonya Ziegler | 1994-95 |
| Mary Álvarez | 1995-97 |
| Rosanne Garcia | 1998-2000 |

**Table 23**

# Ybor City Lion's Club Presidents

| | |
|---|---|
| Sam Cannella | Feliz Cannella |
| Frank Cannella | Ginny Jones |
| John Lazzara | Jerry Vazquez |
| Paul Di Pietra | Angelo Spicola |
| Joe Di Stefano | Stanley Moss |
| Henry Ayo | Harry Moradiellos |
| Cecil Henriquez | Michael Spoto |
| Sam Martino | Dr. Luciano Martinez |
| Dr. Anthony Martino | Angeloa Martino |
| Tony Cutrono | Phil O'Hara |
| Sal Caravella | Ben Underberg |
| Tom Spicola | Tony Huesca |
| Floyd Head | Dr. Henry J. Fernandez |
| Pete Leto | Armando Valdez |
| Frank Puppello | Joe Bua |
| Jack Guida | Joe Ligouri |
| Phil Provenzano | Victor E. DiMaio |

398

The Lion's Club of Ybor City was chartered at the Cuban Club on April 11, 1951. It was sponsored by the downtown Tampa Lion's Club. It has since been meeting twice a month at the Columbia Restaurant in Ybor City. (Information courtesy of Vic DiMaio)

# Alcaldes & Alcaldesas of Ybor City: 1953-2000

| | | | | |
|---|---|---|---|---|
| Anthony Pizzo | 1953 | | Sam D. Leto | 1977 |
| John A. Díaz | 1954 | | Sam D. Leto | 1978 |
| Molly Ferrara | 1955 | | James Wackerle | 1979 |
| Dr. Henry J. Fernandez | 1956 | | Gladys Levy | 1980 |
| Frank Cannella | 1957 | | Bobbie Rizzi | 1981 |
| Armando Gonzalez | 1958 | | Victor Marrero | 1982 |
| A. L. ("Mac") Traina | 1959 | | Genia P. Ward | 1983 |
| Braulio Alonso | 1960 | | Clinton Oaks | 1984 |
| Joe Bua | 1961 | | Lucy Thomas | 1985 |
| Armando P. Valdés, Jr. | 1962 | | Sam D. Leto | 1986 |
| Charles Tucker | 1962 | | Lamar Rankin | 1987 |
| Marcelo Maseda | 1964 | | Branndon Barszcz | 1988 |
| Peter D. Leto | 1965 | | Dalia (Dee) Sanchez | 1989 |
| Marcelo Maseda | 1966 | | Marilyn Joyce Perry | 1990 |
| Angelo Traina | 1967 | | Amanda Stephens | 1991 |
| Guy St. Paul | 1968 | | Ernestine Dodson | 1992 |
| Hilda White | 1969 | | Bob Sánchez | 1993 |
| Charlie Miranda | 1970 | | Edna G. Miller | 1994 |
| Sal Ciaravella | 1971 | | Anthony O. Ciucio | 1995 |
| Phillip Provenzano | 1972 | | Edith Pandiella | 1996 |
| Arthur M. Dosál | 1973 | | Bob Parrado | 1997 |
| Phillip Provenzano | 1974 | | Bob Parrado | 1998 |
| Carlos Estrada | 1975 | | Johnny P. Sims | 1999 |
| Casey Gonzalez | 1976 | | Jack Harris | 2000 |



# Ybor City Round Table Presidents: 1986-2000

| | |
|---|---|
| Guy St. Paul | 1986 |
| Floyd Head | 1987 |
| Floyd Head | 1988 |
| Floyd Head | 1989 |
| Guy St. Paul | 1990 |
| Steve Lester | 1991-92 |
| Sam Leto | 1993-94 |
| Bob Sánchez | 1995-96 |
| Bob Sánchez | 1996-97 |
| Angelo Spicola | 1998-99 |
| Bob Parrado | 2000 |

# Pilot Club of Ybor City Presidents: 1954-2000

| | | | |
|---|---|---|---|
| Molly Ferrara | 1954-55 | Jeanne Walker | 1976-77 |
| Dorothy Leet | 1955-56 | Blanche De La Cruz | 1977-78 |
| Rose Palermo | 1956-57 | Blanche De La Cruz | 1978-79 |
| Margaret Monaco | 1957-58 | Evelyn Fernandez | 1979-80 |
| Mary Galan | 1958-59 | Jean O'Neal | 1980-81 |
| Josephine Jordan | 1959-60 | Ida Sacoco | 1981-82 |
| Adrienne Griffin | 1960--61 | Linda Trimble | 1982-83 |
| Mimi Benet | 1961-62 | Nuri Ayres | 1983-84 |
| Delphine Rodriguez | 1962-63 | Adella Arguelles | 1984-85 |
| Hortense Rubio | 1963-64 | Blanche De La Cruz | 1985-86 |
| Ruth Rosner | 1964-65 | Carolyn Duke | 1986-87 |
| Gloria Rubin | 1965-66 | Dorinda Smith | 1987-88 |
| Adella Arguelles | 1966-67 | Martha Benitez | 1988-89 |
| Antionette Maggio | 1967-68 | Carolyn Duke | 1989-90 |
| Rose Antinori | 1968-69 | Dorinda Smith | 1990-91 |
| Clara Britton | 1969-70 | Adella Arguelles | 1991-92 |
| Adella Arguelles | 1970-71 | Stephanie Lorilla | 1992-93 |
| Ruth Salsbury | 1971-72 | Blanche De La Cruz | 1993-94 |
| Adella Arguelles | 1972-73 | Carolyn Duke | 1995-96 |
| Pamela Price | 1973-74 | Dorinda Smith | 1997-98 |
| Dian Taylor | 1974-75 | Stephanie Olinoski | 1998-99 |
| Doris Oman | 1975-76 | Dana Pines | 1999-2000 |

COURTESY OF ADELLA ARGUELLES. THE PILOT CLUB WAS DISBANDED AFTER 2001.

**Table 27**

# Popular Ybor City Names and Expressions

| Ybor City Expression | Translation | Meaning |
|---|---|---|
| *Báckahous* | Anglicized Italian bathroom | Outhouse |
| *Baqueár* | Anglicized: To back up | Same |
| *Aroeira* | Brazilian Pepper | Mockingbirds got drunk on the berries |
| *Cachúmbambéy* | A children's swing game. | Same |
| *El maricón* | He is a gay person | Same |
| *Es un culo cagao* | His butt is dirty | He's really a nobody |
| *Es un tinglao* | It is a platform, shed | Its a set-up; a tangled mess |
| *Eso es un timbeque* | That's a wretched hovel | Same |
| *La mariquita* | Mama's little boy | A "Mama's boy"; overly protected |
| *La Trocha* | A Spanish fort in Cuba | The Arango factory nickname |
| *Le dio mucha lata* | He gave him a lot of cans | He talked and talked |
| *Le tiró la cuchilla* | He threw the knife at her | He flirted with her |
| *Le chifla el mono!* | The monkey whistled | It's very cold |
| *Le ronca el coco* | The coconut snored | It's a strange or unusually grave situation. |
| *Lo que se te ve!* | You can see the unmentionable | Whoa! |
| *Mas lejos que San Quintín* | Further than San Quintín | Very far; see below |
| *Me cago en diez!* | I poop on ten (of them) | Sh—t on him!  I'll be damned! |
| *Metele caña!* | Add sugar cane! | Hurry! |
| *palmacristi* | Castor oil | Same; bad taste |
| *Patica pa que te quiero?* | Legs, why do I need you? | Run fast! |
| *Que maleta es* | What a suitcase he is. | He was bad at it |
| *Que me la tiren de flai* | May they throw a high ball at me | I don't care. |
| *Que timbeque ni timbeque!* | | What the  devil! |
| *Se coló!* | He filtered or strained through | He slipped through |
| *Se hace el bobito* | He makes a fool of himself. | He's faking it |
| *Tinguiriche* | | Paper kite |
| *Un chivoloco* | A Chevrolet | Same |
| *Un fotingo* | A Ford | Same |

## Common Expressions

The following expressions were supplied by Estevan Orestano (next door neighbor and writer)

| | | |
|---|---|---|
| *Patica paque the quiero* | Why do I need you, feet? | Fast get-a-way! |
| *Pagó los platos roto* | He paid for the broken dishes | He paid his just dues |
| *Es un come mierda* | He is a manure eater. | He's no good |
| *Es un maricon* | He is a sissy. | Same |
| *Esta que—* | She is—!! | Implies she is ripe to eat! |
| *Es un come fango* | He is a mud eater. | He's a nobody, trashy, a zero |
| *Le pican las pulgas* | The fleas itch him. | He's  fit to be tied |

# Ybor City Barrios

***El Bataclan.*** This was the area from 14th to 15th Streets and 13th to 11th Avenues in Ybor City, approximately. Three cement houses facing west on 14th St. pinpointed the area. These were lived in by low-income Cuban families, most of whom in those days were highly mobile and rented rather than owned. The three landmark cement houses were leveled by Urban Renewal.

***La Draga.*** In the early days of Ybor City a huge dredge was stationed in the channel waters to dredge and deepen the port. It was based at the 13th Street estuary. As a result the broad area in that vicinity was referred to loosely as *la draga* ("the dredge") by the *Yborciteños* (Ybor citizens).

The state once set a mandatory requirement on cow owners that their cattle be dipped periodically to prevent the spread of ticks and other infectious bugs. The site of the state-mandated cow dipping was broadly described as being *arriba de la draga* ("above the dredge site"). The treatment area was in an open field immediately above the channel waters, east of 13th Street. The cows had to be dipped into a long, slender concrete vat and swim the length of it. Then they were tied and walked home.

The term *"la draga"* was used by many to route people to the channel area or around it, along 13th Street heading downtown. One knew right away where a given event was located or in what direction to head. To direct one around the 13th Street channel area towards downtown Tampa, one would say, *vete alrededor de la draga!* ("go around the dredge!").

***Los Cien.*** In the early years of the cigar industry in West Tampa, a developer built one hundred homes. One hundred Spaniards signed up for them, as the saying goes. The area thus became known as *los cien* with reference to the hundred Spaniards. An alternate form also heard was *"las cien,"* with reference to the hundred houses. In Ybor City, in order to describe the great distance to "Los Cien" one used another expression, mainly, *Estaban mas lejos que San Quintin* ("They were further than San Quintin"). This expression was born in Spain from Castillian peasants who were saddled with huge taxes imposed by the kings to maintain possession of the Low Countries, Belgium, and Holland. Over time, this expression evolved: "They were further than San Quintin!" In spite of the victory at San Quintin, peasants didn't see the need to pay taxes on it, and the expression became popular. In Ybor one said, *Los Cien estaban mas lejos que San Quintín!*

***La Asturias Pequena.*** *La Asturias Pequena* (Little Asturias) referred to a small stretch of 12th Avenue between 16th and 19th Streets. The houses in this area were mainly owned by Asturianos. Mostly white in color, these appeared very much like the homes in the greater Spanish neighborhood north of Michigan Avenue (today's Columbus Drive), west of 15th St. to Nebraska Avenue, which were larger and modern. With rare exceptions, these were among the better of the houses in the 20's, in the core area of Ybor City. This area was very centrally located. One could easily walk to many factories, bakeries, fondas, Cafés, groceries, pharmacies (as Máximos) and La Sétima. There was a Methodist Church between 16th and 17th where fathers and mothers often left their children during work hours (as this writer's father did). While flat, the level of the land was high, as Ybor City goes, and had excellent drainage southward, due to its slope towards the bay. One assumes this is one of many reasons Gabino Gutierrez, Civil Engineer, must have considered in recommending it to Don Vicente. Ybor City has excellent drainage. If one stands at the far side of the parking lot back of El Centro Español, and looks north at the Haciendas de Ybor and OLPH church next to it, one will see that the land rises. With a Civil Engineer to advise him, it is understandable why Don Vicente Martínez Ybor located his *quinta*, or country home, there.

402

***Little Italy.*** Tony Pizzo, author of the work, *The Italians in Tampa*, describes *Little Italy* as follows: "Little Italy in the 1890s extended from 17th Street on the west to about 26th Street on the east. The south boundary was 4th Avenue and at 22nd Street the boundary line veered south and included 2nd and 3rd Avenues. The north boundary was Michigan Avenue—today's Columbus Drive. In the beginning, their small wood frame houses dotted this area of wilderness.

***La Pachata.*** Tony Pizzo, in the work cited above, continued: "Some of the Italians moved into rental cottages while others made purchases from Mr. Ybor on the installment plan. The Italian quarters became known as *La Pachata*, after a Cuban rent collector."

***Little Sicily.*** Little Sicily dates back to the turn of the century, if not earlier. Italians in those days preferred the nearby area between 17th and 19th Streets and 8th to 9th Avenues. This was convenient to the first L'Unione Italiana Club building and to the later, large wooden building that housed *La Societa di Mutuo Soccorso* erected on 19th Street and 8th Avenue. (I entered it on several occasions.) As more and more Italians came into Ybor City, they pushed south, east, and north, into the greater Ybor City areas.

***Barrio Candamo.*** Many Asturianos from the Candamo region of Asturias, which encompassed the villages of Aces and Granelos, lived in Ybor City. This Candamo barrio in Ybor stretched from 21st Avenue to 19th Avenue and 15th to 17th Streets, just east of Cuscaden Park.

***El toro de Balboa.*** On the southeast corner of Lake Avenue (30th Avenue and 18th Street) Señor "Balboa" had a bull — *el toro*. One referred to it as the area of *el toro de Balboa*. The bull serviced most of the community cows. In the early Depression years, Spaniards and Italians pastured many cows for milk. The bull was kept behind a six-foot fence. Little boys were not allowed inside the fence. Families with cows knew where to find the bull.

**Table 29**

# Familiar Personalities, Vendors, & Nicknames

**El Afilador.**  The knife sharpener and umbrella fixer was another familiar character on the Ybor City streets.  He also sharpened the cigar worker's *chavetas* (blades for cutting tobacco leaves).  He blew his *apito*— a whistle locally called *el pito*—to announce his presence. Benito Blanco and Julio were the main *afiladores* in Ybor City, though other Blancos and transients came through.  Benito Blanco had a shop on 7th Avenue, between 12th and 13th Street on 7th Avenue. Julio came a little later and became a well-known personality—comical and carefree. To find, perhaps, a certain unknown afilador's wheel who had come in and tried to occupy the same territory, one would have to begin by dredging *La Draga* (the bay along 13th Street). Established *afiladores* tolerated no new competition once the area was staked out.* Julio stayed until the Spanish Civil War ended. He never practiced his profession after returning. In Ybor City he was comical to the extent of being foolish. When he left for Spain he was broke. It was said that he squandered his modest earnings on the numbers game, bolita, and such. But he was entertaining. He would push his *rueda* (wheel), blowing his *apita* to announce himself to the housewives so they would bring their knives to be sharpened or their umbrellas to be fixed. He was known to dance a *Jota* (a Spanish folk dance) at the Cuban Club, where it is said he was in love with a Cuban female entertainer.

**Pepe.** Pepe was an admirable and memorable person. He had contracted meningitis as a child, and most people greatly admired him for his determination to work in spite of his disability.  He was as dependable and timely as the community's  Regensberg factory clock.  His father, a World War I veteran, died after the war. Pepe sold newspapers and turned his paycheck over to his mother, which along with those of his brothers and sisters in this large and hardworking family, supported the home and assured the family's survival during the Great Depression. His brother Benny was my first close friend, and I became friends with his entire family. I remember as a little boy often drinking black coffee with Benny, Pepe, and the family. They lived around the corner—in the shadows of the huge water tank next to Centro Asturiano Sanatorium—in those early Depression days. Their old-fashioned player piano was one of the most fascinating musical instruments I ever heard. Rolls of perforated musical paper guided the piano's musical output. I remember Benny's father's WWI motorcycle and rifle. Pepe is not deserving of a common but misinformed name that was sometimes used around town but will not be used here. He has always been simply "Pepe" to this writer. The whole town seemed to know this great man. He is fondly remembered for his high-pitched voice and his strange ways of keeping score and giving change. He immediately scribbled on a piece of paper, but it was just that—a scribble—and he saved it in his left shirt pocket. Pepe had never gone to school, and he had a mental defect, but he knew what he did. You could not fool him. His gestures were beautiful! He was very savvy, and he worked hard selling newspapers, often on the street corner near the old Spanish Park Restaurant on 34th Street and La Sétima or at the Columbia Restaurant corner. After peddling his papers, he would walk to a distant market to bring his mother fruit and vegetables, and then walk back home, several miles away. The whole town knew Pepe, including the policemen, who would sometimes give him a ride home. When they did, he would tell his mother that they were his friends, just as the trainmen on 6th Avenue were when they would wave to him and he would tell his mother about that. He was an intelligent man who coped amazingly well with his medical limitations—a beautiful and real legend!

**El Pirulero.**  The pirulí man sold pirulís, cone-shaped hard candy, four to five inches long, with a round stick in it. The individual pirulís were inserted into the holes in a long pole with many arms which he carried as he walked. He sold the candies for a penny or a soap coupon. He blew a whistle that announced his coming.

**El Polaco.**  El Polaco was a true original. In the earliest days of the cigar industry he operated a café on the south side of the Sanchez y Haya factory, located on the southwest corner of La Setima and 15th Street. It faced south, overlooking today's railroad tracks. El Polaco also ran a small store located on Rocky Point. Here he stocked refreshments, cigarettes, cigars, and other items for picnickers who crowded the primitive beach. His daughter's name was Margarita.

### Other Familiar Tradesmen's Names from the Streets of Old Ybor



**Cobrador.** The Centro Español's medical bill collector was El Cobrador. The monthly bill for treatment a La Benéfica clinic or at the Centro Español Sanatorium on Bayshore Boulevard was $1.50 per month, per family in 1906. El Cobrador was oneof the more respected men in the community at the time. He was often treated as a friend and frequently referred to with a respectful *El Señor* preceding his name.

**Ybor City: The Making of a Landmark Town**

**Jaivero.**  This unusual vendor sold *croquetas de jaivas* (deviled crabs). Miranda and Cesar were among the best-known *jaiveros* in Ybor City.

**Mantecadero.**  A vendor who sold *mantecadas* (ice creams). Some of the popular flavors were Mamey, Sapote, Mango, Vanilla, and Chocolate. In the early days his ice cream wagon was pulled by a horse, as were those of other vendors, so the street often had a few horse residues in those days.

**Nevero.**  An essential and hard-working tradesman who delivered blocks of ice, often carrying them to second-floor homes. Luigi (Louis) was possibly the only *nevero* serving much Ybor City.  He was Pepe and Benny Frisco's brother. It was scary to watch Luigi grab a great block of ice (not the much smaller household size) and walk up one of the very narrow and steep stairways at one of the two-story buildings, as he could just barely manage it with that load on his back. I watched him go up once and still remember it. He told me not to stand in the bottom steps.

**Panadero.**  A home delivery person bringing fresh bread daily. The *panadero* would usually stick the long loaf on a nail by the door.

**Pescador.**  A fish vendor, who sold fresh seafood. Bay fish was a given.

**Verdurero.**  The *verduro* carried a large variety of vegetables, fruits, platanos, and other fresh products through the streets in an open truck.

## Nicknames and Other Memories

Nicknames hold many memories for those who grew up in Ybor City. One group of friends who gather regularly at the Pacific Café informally compiled a list of nicknames very much in use years ago by the Latin population of Tampa. The nicknames gained such popularity that often the real name of the person was not known. Participants included Indy Cuesta, Tony García, Julio Orta, Frank Barcena, Willie Martinez, Julian Fabian, Jack Espinosa, Mario Castro, and Al Fernandez.

The nicknames they collected, together with English equivalent in parenthesis, are given alphabetically below. The real names of the individuals were not provided.

*Aguila, Bon Bon, Boniato, Boca Chivo* (billy goat's mouth), *Bombero* (fireman), *Bombillo* (lightbulb), *Bisco* (crosseyed), *Bigote* (mustache), *Barilla* (stick), *Carreton* (wagon), *Cara Papaya* (the face of a Papaya fruit), *Cabezón* (hardheaded), *Chambelona, Chocolate, Chancleta* (sandals), *Chinaco* (cash and carry), *Cabeza melon* (melon head), *Cien Pesos* (one hundred dollars), *Diente Frio* (cold teeth), *Diabilito* (little devil), *Escaparate* (wardrobe), *Mono* (monkey), *El Sapo* (the frog), *El Baboso* (scummy), *El Manco* ( handless ), *Chivo* (goat), *El Gaitero* (bagpipe player), *Flaco* ( skinny) , *Pirulero* ( *pirulí* candy man), *Fosforito* ( small match), *Frankestein Gambáo* (bowlegged), *Grillo* (cricket), *Gasolina, Guampi, Huevo Frito Huele Bicho* (fried eggs smells like bugs), *Killigra, Melena* (hair), *Mosquito, Macago, Manga Mocha, Mosquito de la Drága* ( dredge site mosquito), *Maleta, Martillito*( small hammer ), *Manguera* (water hose), *Mundito* (worldly), *Mondonquera, Mala Madera or mala pulga* (bad wood, bad flea both implying bad blood), *Masinguilla,* Now or Never, *Pina Chica, Pisi y Corre* (step on it; or a vehicle), *Picadillo* (ground beef), *Pichon* (youngster), *Piti Feo, Pàta Sucia* (dirty feet), *Picadura* (cigar filler), *Parachu, Pan con Chincha* (bread with bed bugs), *Pirucho, Pepe Lubabo* (a beloved personality who sold newspapers), *Pasta Electrica , Poquen Bin* (pork and beans), *Panque* (cake), *Pesi Cola* (Pepsi Cola), *Pepe Tranca, Raton* (rat or mouse), *Rober Talo* (Robert Taylor [actor]), *Rompe Hueso* (bone crusher), *Sapatico* (little shoes), *Speedy Brown, Sapo Tuerto* (twisted or warped mind), *Tornillo* (screw).

*See *The Knife Sharpener and His Wheel* by Manuel Blanco and Frank T. Lastra.

405

These recollections were originally printed in an article in *La Gaceta* in July 1992. The list may have originated from *"El Club Unico"* (Key Club) in West Tampa, according to Al Fernandez, who co1nfirms that these names were used by many cigar factory workers in both West Tampa and Ybor City. I personally remember hearing many of them.

# Some Cafés and Restaurants in Ybor City

The foods and beverages of Ybor City have rightly won acclaim. This table offers a snapshot of food businesses in 1905 and 1930 as a way of indicating historical names and places, and as a way of showing the growth in such gathering spots over the years.

## Ybor City Cafés in 1905

| | | | |
|---|---|---|---|
| Álvarez, José | 2202 20th St. | Perose, Joseph | 1702 14th St. |
| Álvarez, J. F. | 1709 15th St. | Riera & Herrera | 2206 20th St. |
| Benitez, N. & Co. | 1908 14th St. | Sague, Joaquín | 1316 7th Ave. |
| Checo, Gabriel | 1913 14th St. | La Florida Restaurant | 1901 14th St. |
| Cueto, Vega M. | 1703 15th St. | Sans, Camilo | 1909 14th St. |
| Lopez, José | 1429 7th Ave. | La Marina Restaurant | 1907 Nebraska Ave. |
| Molina, Carlos | 1400 9th Ave. | Silverio Patrocinio | 1711 14th St. |

## Ybor City Restaurants in 1930

| | | | |
|---|---|---|---|
| Angelo, Gus | 1605 15th St. | La América Café | 1901 1715 E. 7th Ave. |
| Arias, José | 1401 21st St. | Ladrillo Café | 1822 12th Ave. |
| Black Cat, The | 2205 12th Ave. | Las Novedades Café | 1416-1418 E. 7th Ave. |
| Blue Ridge Sandwich Shop | 2104 22nd St. | HCT Public Library - Cafe/Rest. | |
| Cacciatore, Pasquale | 2118 7th Ave. | Leto, Felippo | 1904 20th St. |
| Castro, Manuel | 1802 12th Ave. | Leto, Phillip | 1906 16th St. |
| Chicago Restaurant | 2202 15th St. | Llano, Faustino | 2513 21st St. |
| Collier, Carl | 1916 22nd St. | Lopez, Gumersindo | 802 E. Michigan Ave. |
| Columbia Restaurant | 2117 E. 7th Ave | Lopez & LLano | 1402 19 th. St. |
| Cuervo, Máximo | 2413 17th St. | Los Helados de Ybor Café | 1806 14th St. |
| Cusmano Giuseppe | 2101 E. Michigan Ave. | Maniachi Biaggio | 2115 E. 7th Ave. |
| El Aséo Café | 2102 14th St. | Mecca Café | 1701 7th Ave. |
| El Dorado Café | 1815 14th St. | Mendez, Jesús | 1901 12th Ave. |
| El Casino Restaurant | 1905 12th Ave. | Pérez, Antonio | 2701 15th Ave. |
| El Pasaje Restaurant | 1319 9th Ave. | Pérez, Antonio M. | 1702 Nebraska |
| El Príncipe de Gales | 1812 14th St. | Portee, Leon | 1415 Nebraska |
| Farfante, Raymond C. | 2303 18th St. | Pote, Café | 1400 9th Ave. |
| Fernandez, Francisco | 102 15th St. | Rightway Café | 2100 10th Ave. |
| Fernandez, José | 2115 22nd St. | Rubiera, Celestino | 1402 22nd St. |
| Flamingo Café | 1722 8th Ave. | Sánchez y Vega | 2807 16th St. |
| Garcia, Arturo | 2011 14th St. | Seaboard Restaurant | 1902 2nd Ave. |
| Garcia, Celestino R. | 821 12th Ave. | Ship, Curtis L. | 2102 22nd Ave. |
| Gonzalez, Baldomero | 1702 12th Ave. | Spanish Park Restaurant | 3519 E. Broadway |
| Gonzalez, Fructuoso | 1520 15th Ave." | Suarez, José | 1405 21st St. |
| Gonzalez, Máximo (Café) | 1702 1601 E. Michigan | Valdez, Lawrence | 2705 22nd St. |
| Hatfield, Harry | 2110 E. 7th Ave. | Valentine Restaurant | 105 12th Ave. |
| Italiano, Joseph | 1901 E. 7th Ave. | Vega, Casimiro | 910 E. 7th Ave. |

# Principal Food Cooperatives in Ybor City: 1927-1940

Mutual aid has been an enduring value in Ybor City history, applying to everything from medical treatment and social activities to food. The following Cooperative Grocery Stores existed in Ybor City.

|  | 1927 | 1931 | 1940 |
|---|---|---|---|
| El Futuro Obrero, 1226 11th Ave. |  | x | x |
| El Segundo Progreso Grocery, 2501 17th St. |  | x |  |
| El Segundo Progreso Grocery, 2212 15th St . |  | x |  |
| Eureka Grocery, Co., 2614 21st St. | x |  |  |
| La Legada, 1704 12th St. | x | x |  |
| Premier Progress Grocery, 1919 14th St. |  | x |  |
| El Progreso Grocery, 1520 9th Ave. |  | x |  |
| El Recurso, 2931 15th St. | x | x | x |
| La Epoca Grocery and Market, 2013 15th St. |  |  | x |

Source: Tampa City Directories, 1927, 1931, and 1940.

# Ybor City Bakeries: 1910-1930

## 1910

C. Anastasie Co., 1904 7th Ave.
Antonio Colom, 916 7th Ave.
Columbia Bakery, 2118 7th Ave.
J. Diaz Brothers, 1320 7th Ave.
Rosario Ferlita, 2416 15th Ave.
Diaz and Medina, 2101 7th Ave.
Serafin Garcia, 1714 Nebraska Ave.
Pietro Georgianni, 2704 Nebraska Ave.

H. E. Joyce, 1322 7th Ave.
Pardo and Gonzalez, 2101
Enrique Rodriguez, 1505 8th Ave.
Mrs. Nila Testasecca, 1907 11th Ave.
Ybor Steam Bakery, 2516 15th Ave.
Guiseppi La Barbera, 2605 15th St.
Los Hermanos, 2101 7th Ave.

## 1920

C. Anastasie Co., 1904 7th Ave.
John Fernandez, 2020 7th Ave.
J. Diaz and Brother, 1320 7th Ave.
Rosario Ferlita, 2516 15th Ave.
Diaz and Medina, 2101 7th Ave.
Esteba Gianes, 2804 16th St.
Fernandez Gonzalo, 1311 12th Ave.
Guiseppi La Barbera, 2605 15th St.
La Paloma Bakery, 1810 Nebraska & 2202 12th Ave.

La Segunda Central, 2411 15th St.
Mrs. Nila Testasecca, 1907 11th Ave.
La Siciliana Bakery, 2201 9th Ave.
La Union Bakery, 1506 9th Ave.
Lewis Bakery, 2708 Nebraska Ave.
Palm Bakery, 207 22nd St.
Thurston S. Risher, 270 E. Broadway
Stevens Brothers, 930 7th Ave.
Two Brothers Bakery, 1805 22nd St.

## 1930

Anthony Alfieri, 2201 _____ Ave.
C. Anastasie Co., 1904 7th Ave.
John Fernandez, 2020 7th Ave.
Italian Bakery, 1916 7th Ave.
La Caoba Bakery, 1916 7th Ave.

Royal Palm Bakery, 2008 7th Ave.
Guiseppi La Barbera, 2605 15th St.
La Segunda Central, 2411 15th St.
Stevens Brothers, 930 7th Ave.
Mrs. Nila Testasecca, 1907 11th Ave.

# Ybor City Buildings & Districts
# on the National Register of Historic Places


**Centro Asturiano de Tampa**
1913 Nebraska Avenue
Built in 1913
Designed by architect M. Leo Elliot
Added to the NR in 1974


**Centro Español de Tampa**
1526-1536 E. 7th Avenue
Built 1911-1912
Designed by architect Francis J. Kennard
Added to the NR in 1988
(Replaced original structure erected in June 1892)


**Circulo Cubano de Tampa**
10th Avenue and 14th Street
Built in 1907
Designed by architects Bonfoey and Elliott
Added to the NR in 1972


**El Pasaje**
14th St. and Palm Ave.
Built in 1886
Added to the NR in 1972


**Ybor Factory Building**
La Sétima, between 13th and 14th Streets
Built in 1886
Designed by architect C. E. Parcell
Added to the NR in 1972


**Ybor City Historic District**
Added to the NR in 1974

**Table 34**

# Principal Schools Attended by Ybor City Students

## Early Schools

**[First School].** Name unknown. Founded by the Cuban, Carlos Zequira, an old Cuban immigrant and teacher from Baltimore, Maryland, when he heard from fellow Cuban patriots that they could not give their children an adequate education. No names are recorded and it is believed by Jose Rivero Muniz that it was started in late 1886. (1)

**[Second School].** Name unknown. Mrs. Inez Sainz de la Pena, a Cuban, inaugurated a new school in Tampa. She taught children of cigar workers in her home. This was toward the end of 1886, according to Jose Rivero Muniz. (2)

**V. M. Ybor Free School.** Founded circa 1903-04. A grammar school located on the south side of Michigan Ave. (now Columbus Dr.), between 14th and 15th St.

**"First Italian School."** According to Tony Pizzo it was located at 13th Ave. and 17th St. during the first decade of the 20th century. Ralph A. Scorzzo (later Scozzi) was the teacher.

**St. Benedict's School.** Founded circa 1906-07. Located at the southwest corner of 20th St. and 15th Ave.

**Italian Schools.** Founded circa 1909. According to Tony Pizzo, Lorenzo Panipinto, a native of Santo Stefano, an educator and an ardent Socialists (while in Ybor City) organized three Italian Schools. ("Panipinto died a martyr's death in his home village when he defended the cause of the share croppers against the land barons.")

**Most Holy Name Church.** A school was operated by the church, located at the SE corner of 8th Ave. and 23rd St. The Rt. Rev. Vincent M. Dente, S.J., was the pastor of the Italian Church.

## Later schools that exist today

**DeSoto Elementary School.** Founded circa 1915. Located in Palmetto Beach, on the north side of DeSoto Park.

**Philip Shore Elementary.** Founded circa 1920. Located on 2nd Ave. between 19th and 20th Streets.

Orange Grove Grammar School. Founded circa 1920. Located on 17th St. between 26th and 28th street in north east greater Ybor.

**Jefferson High School.** Founded circa 1920. It was located one block north of Michigan, between Highland and ala St. It was originally Hillsborough Senior High School until that school moved to Central and Osborne Ave. in Tampa. In 1970 Jefferson High School moved to a new modern facility on West Shore and one block north of I-4.

**George Washington Jr. High School.** Circa 1918 to 1960. Located on the south side of Michigan Ave., NE block west of Nebraska. Mr. Leto was principal in 1937.

**Hillsborough Senior High School.** 1927 to circa 1980. Mr. Vivian Gaither was a principal. The Gaither Senior High School on north Dale Mabry was named after him when built in early 1980. He was over 80 years at the time of dedication. The author graduated from Hillsborough High School in 1939.

References:  (I) Jose Rivero Muniz. *Los Cubanos en Tampa.* (2) Jose Rivero Muniz. *The Ybor City Story, 1885-1954.*

Note: In his work, "The Italians in Ybor City," Tony Pizzo tells us: "At one time there were five Italian schools in Ybor City. Among those in existence in the early 1920's were the school] on 8th Ave and 19th St., SE corner, with Don Ernesto as School-Master; and, also" the school on 6th Ave and 19th St. ( more research would be needed to firm all of these.. Perhaps that figure includes the three (3) that Panipinto founded - writer.) An Italian school on 7th Ave. at 23rd to 24th St. has been sited, but not verified by this writer. However, as a young lad, in riding with father, this writer remembers an early type church building on 8th Ave, which occupied the same space cited above as being on 7th Ave. It fronted 8th Avenue,  not 7th Ave. It might also have been used as a school.

**Ybor City: The Making of a Landmark Town**

# Popular *Ybor* City Newspapers

Some of the best-known Ybor City newspapers:

*Tampa Guardian* (1886). An independent newspaper.

*El Yara* (1886). Ybor City's first newspaper. Published by Jose Dolores Poyo. He was also the first *lector* at V. M. Ybor's factory. *El Yara* was based upon "EI Grito de Yara" a Cuban battle cry in 1868 when the first rebellion against Spanish rule took place. It was founded in Key West in 1869.

*Heraldo de Tampa* (1887). It was published by a group of Spanish workers. Constantino Diaz was the editor.

*Cuba* (1887). Ramon Rivero published the first Cuban Revolutionary newspapers after Jose Dolores Poyo discontinued *El Yara*.

*El Mosquito*. Detail unavailable

*La Contienda* (1890). Started by Nestor Leonardo Carbone.

*El Patriota* (1890). Founded by E. Planas.

Note: To keep the Cubans happy the  manufacturers allowed the Cuban revolutionary newspapers in the factories.

*La Revista* (1901). Published by Rafael Martinez Ybor, Don Vicente's son.

*La Traduccion* (1915). First published by Ramon Valdespino. (In an article by J. R. Sanfeliz, in the 1930 edition of the
*Extra-Almanac,*_there is considerable references to much earlier efforts by others leading to its takeover by Ramon Valdespino.) He translated the *Tampa Tribune* and the *Tampa Journal* beginning in 1886. It circulated in all the Tampa factories and was very successful. Curiously, in the 1930 special issue of *Extra-Almanac*, there is the caption, "Fundada en 1903" (founded in 1903).

*La Gaceta*
(1922). A tri-lingual (English, Spanish, and Italian) weekly newspaper. Founded by Victoriano Monteiga, "EI Intelectual," ultimate voice of the interests of the Latin community, as demonstrated by his defense of the concerns of the Spanish citizens of Tampa against the heavy bombing of Guernica, Spain during the Spanish Civil War. Upon his death he was succeeded by son, Roland Monteiga. Roland is a long time employee of the paper and is now Editor and Publisher of *La Gaceta*. He was a staunch supporter of El Circulo Cubano in its hour of need. He is widely known in political circles for his column, "As We Heard It," and is a powerful voice in Tampa and state-wide. He is supported in his work by the very talented and able, Patrick Monteiga, Associate Publisher, and a host of highly skilled staff.

# Greater Ybor City Area, 1910-1970

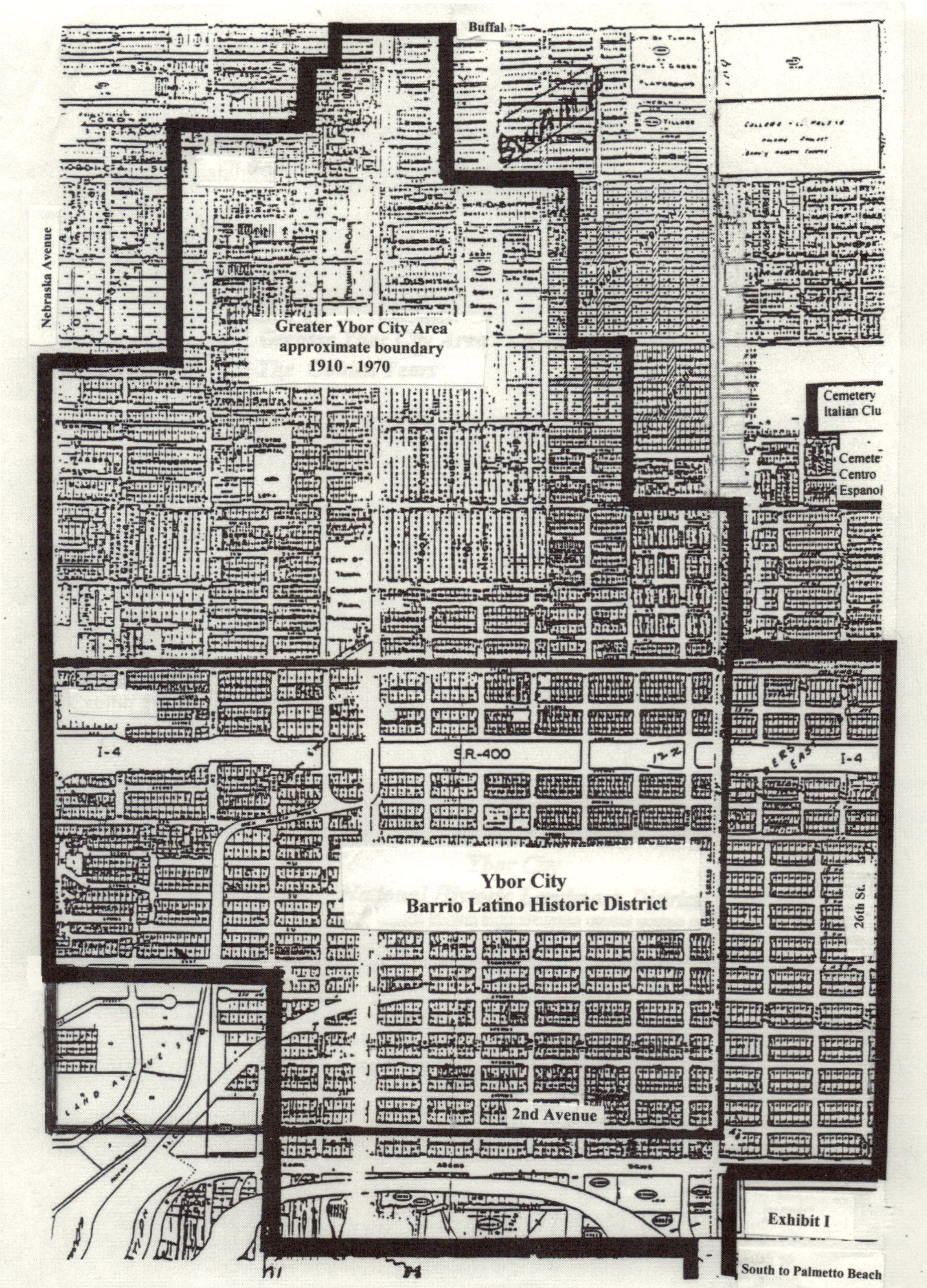

412

**Ybor City: The Making of a Landmark Town**

# Cultural Districts in Ybor City

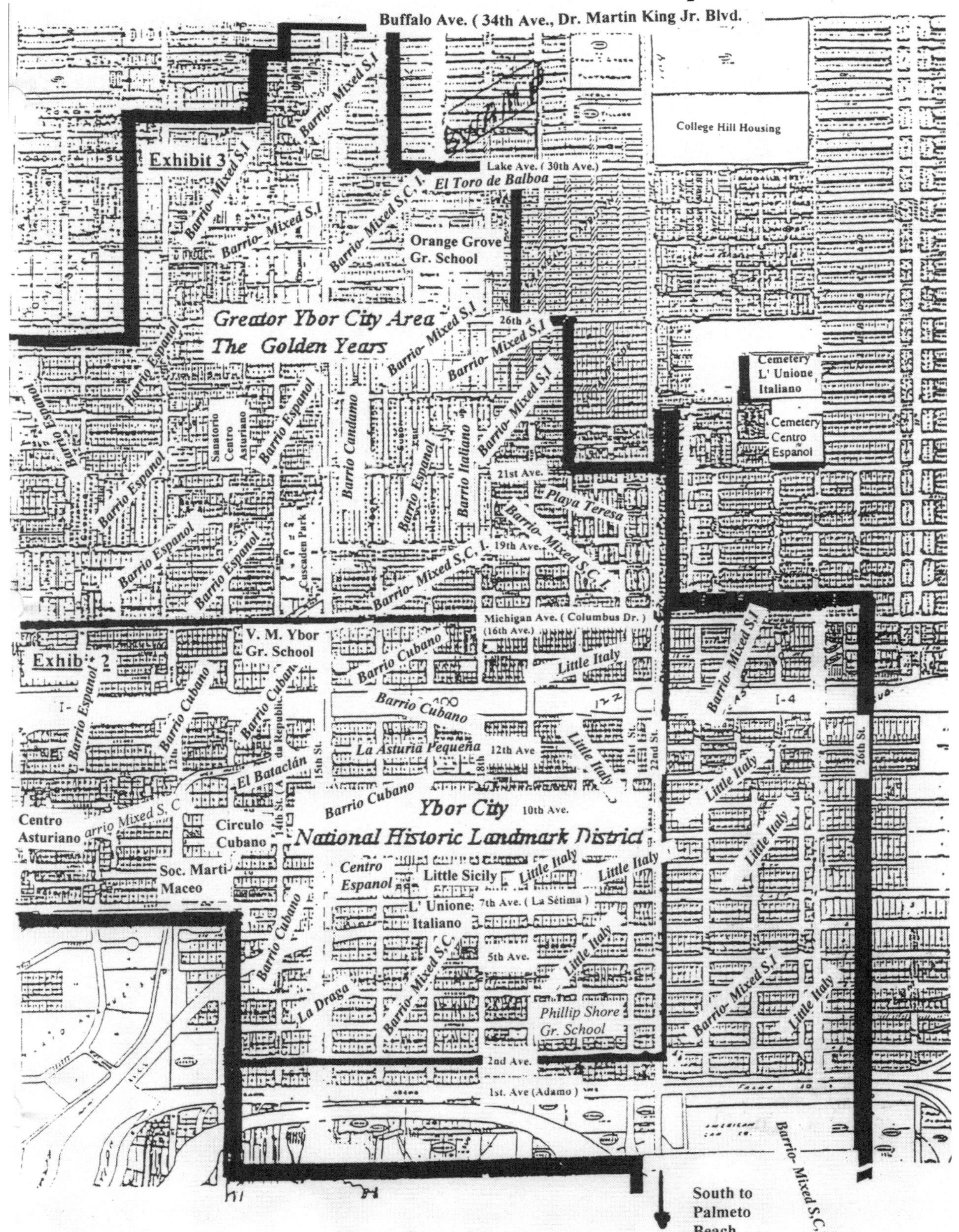

# Ybor City Historic Districts

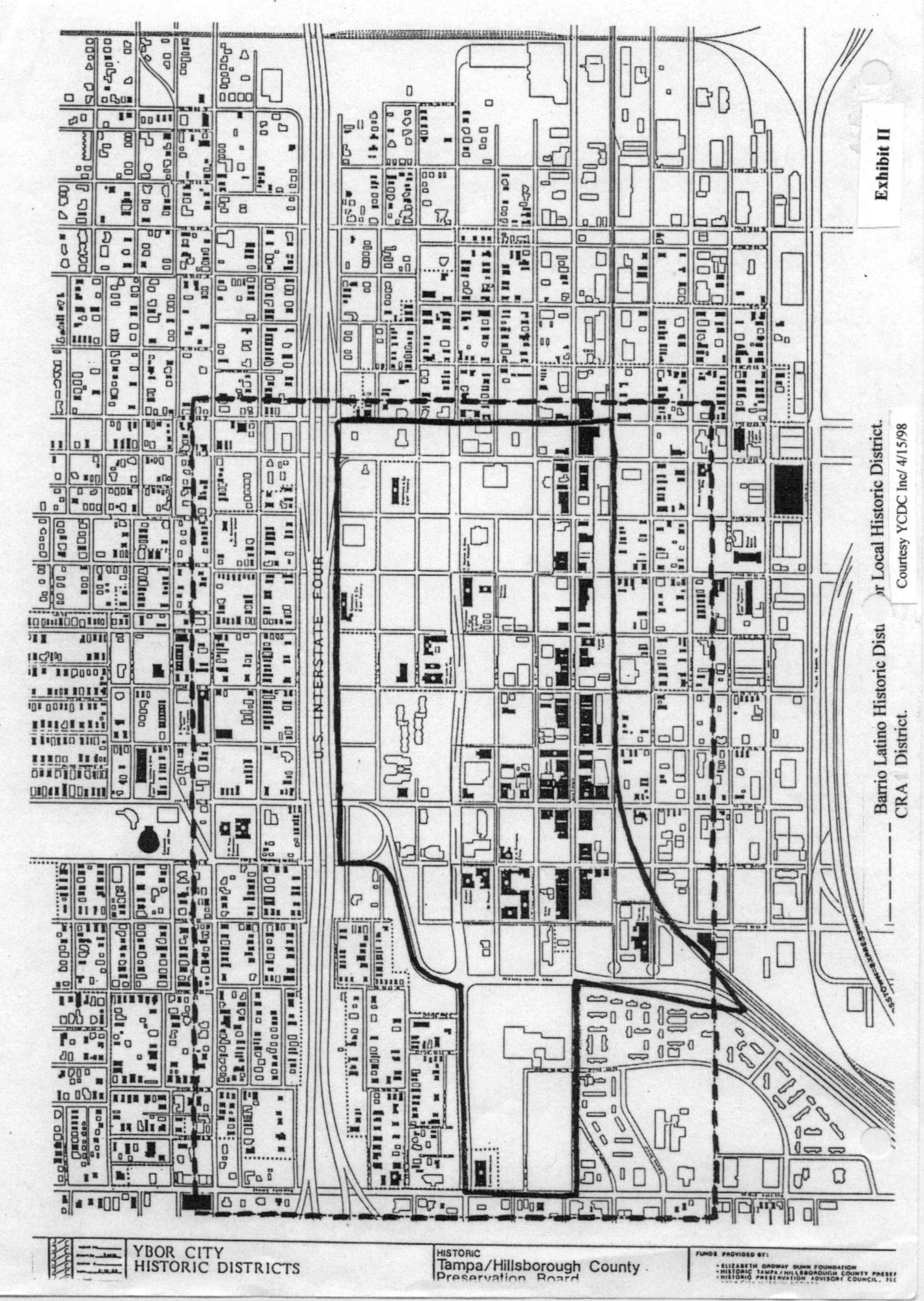





**Ybor City: The Making of a Landmark Town**

# Ybor City National Historic Landmark Boundary

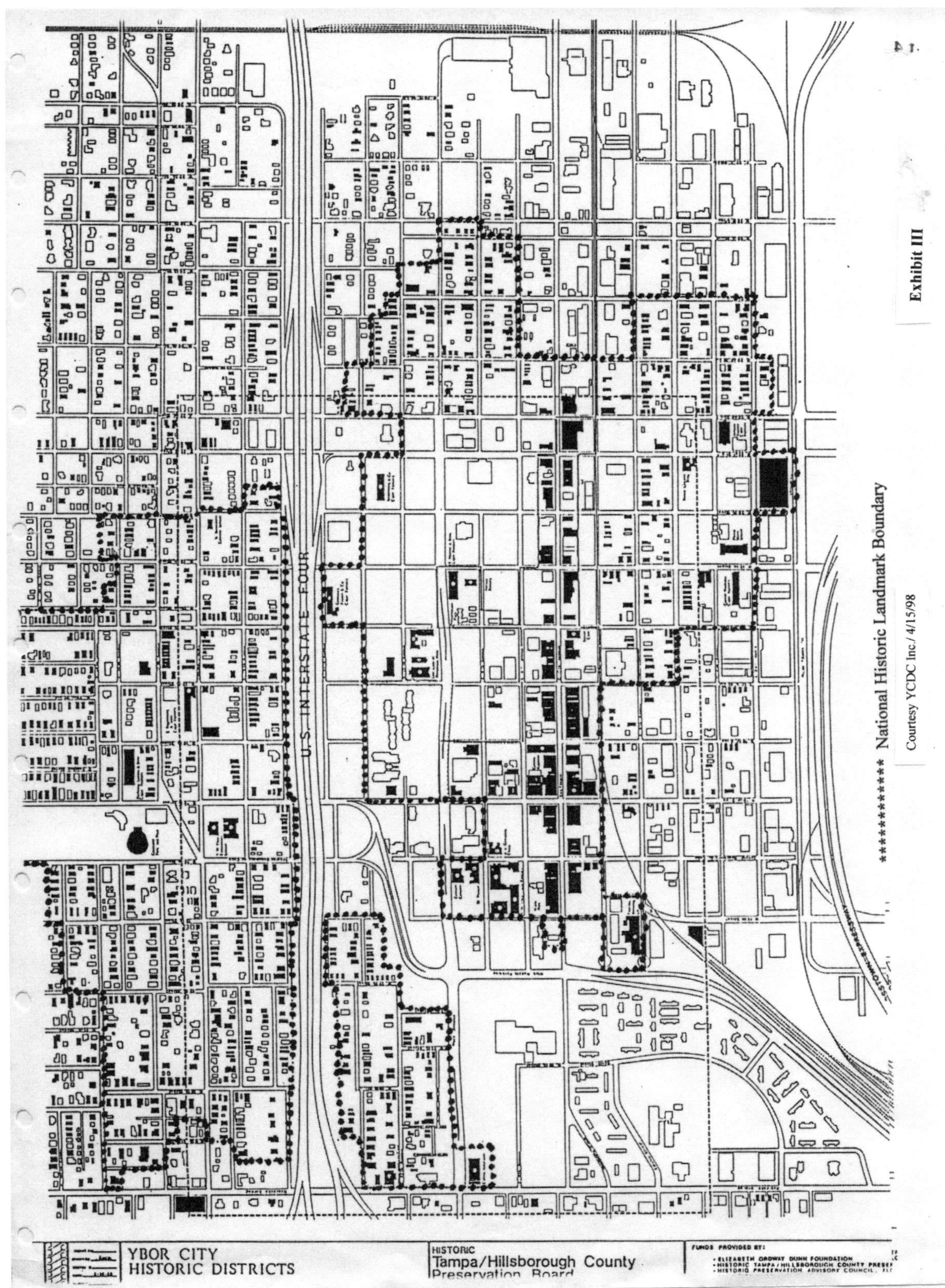


415

# Tampa's Historic Streetcar Lines

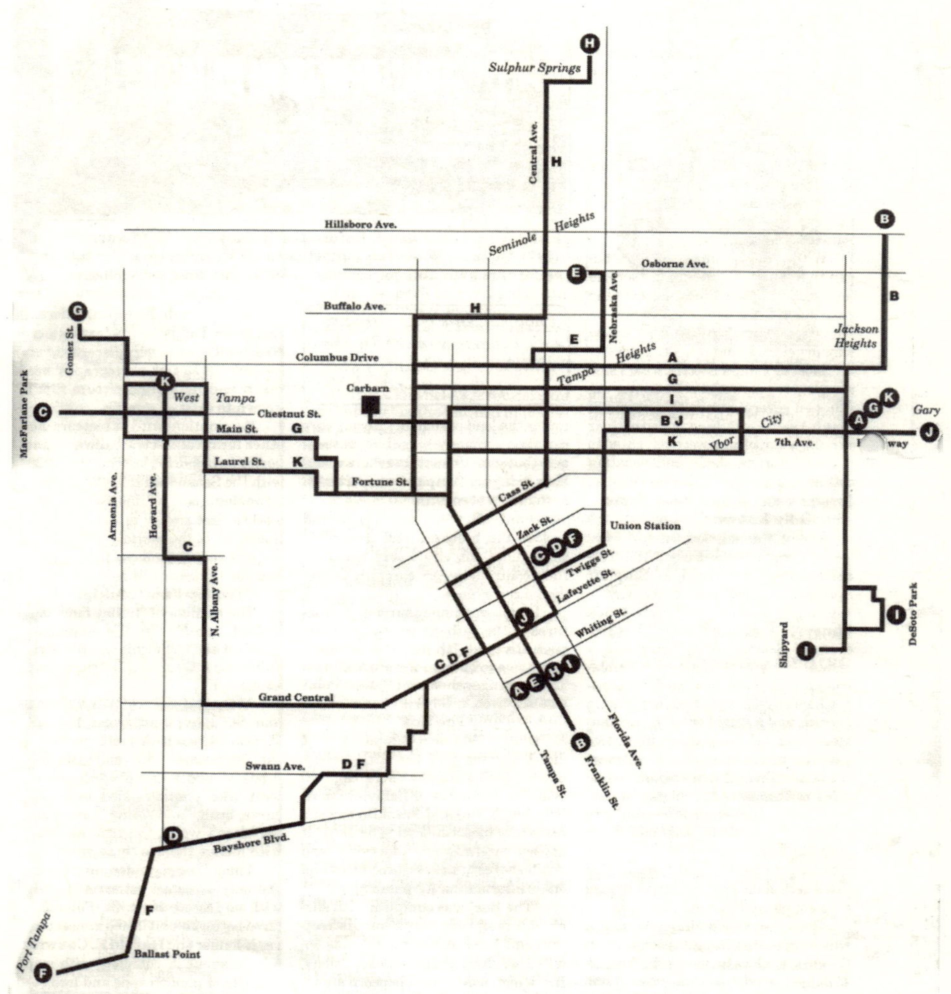






**Ybor City: The Making of a Landmark Town**

# Tampa's Projected Streetcar Lines

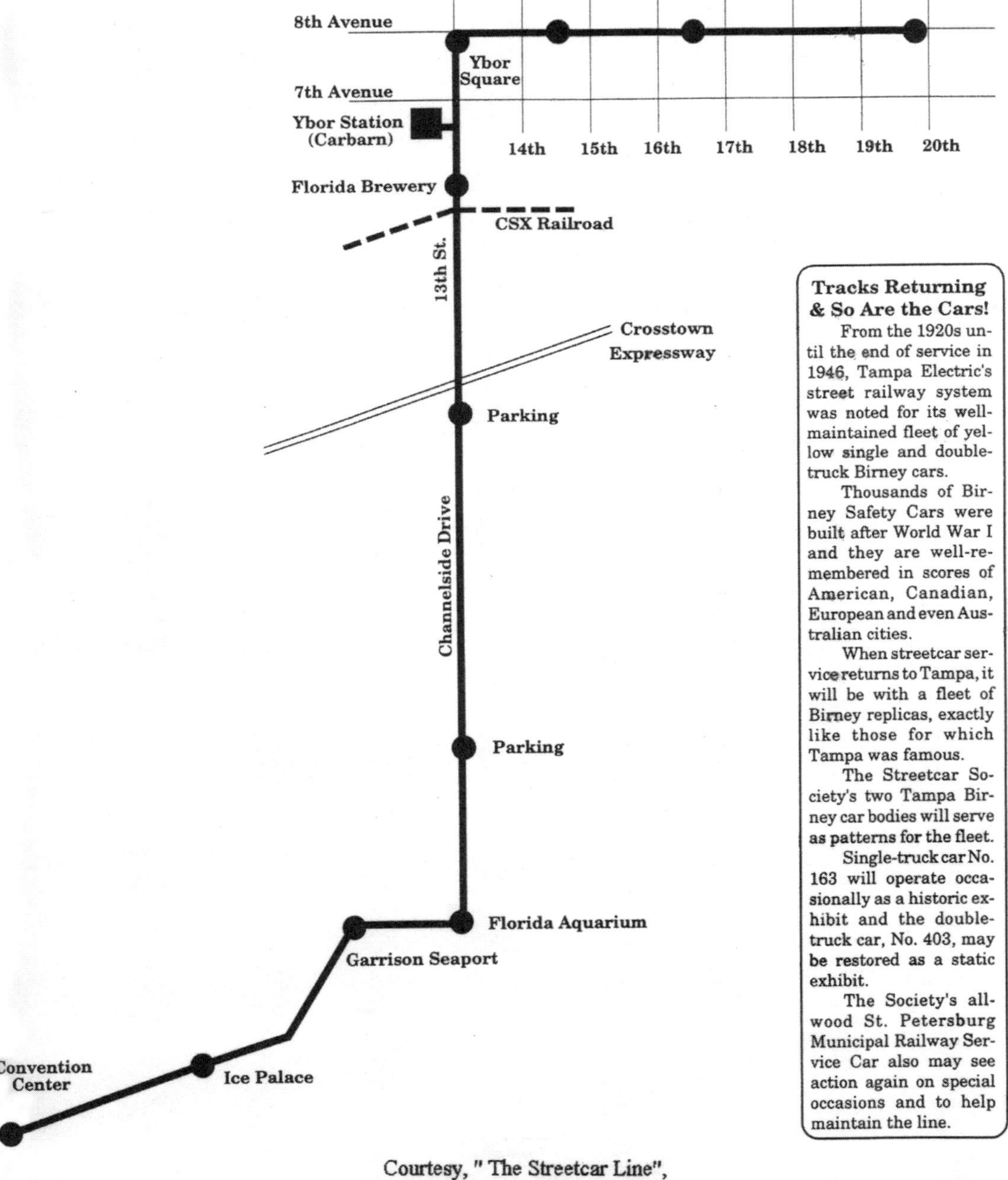


**Tracks Returning & So Are the Cars!**

From the 1920s until the end of service in 1946, Tampa Electric's street railway system was noted for its well-maintained fleet of yellow single and double-truck Birney cars.

Thousands of Birney Safety Cars were built after World War I and they are well-remembered in scores of American, Canadian, European and even Australian cities.

When streetcar service returns to Tampa, it will be with a fleet of Birney replicas, exactly like those for which Tampa was famous.

The Streetcar Society's two Tampa Birney car bodies will serve as patterns for the fleet.

Single-truck car No. 163 will operate occasionally as a historic exhibit and the double-truck car, No. 403, may be restored as a static exhibit.

The Society's all-wood St. Petersburg Municipal Railway Service Car also may see action again on special occasions and to help maintain the line.

Courtesy, "The Streetcar Line", July, 1996, Vol. 7 No. 3., Tampa and Ybor City Street Railway Society

417

# Map of Ybor City Jewish Business and Cultural Sites

1. Rodeph Sholom Synagogue
2. Knesses Yisroale Synagogue
3. (Meyer) Kisler Pharmacy
4. YMHA
5. American Pipe & Plumbing (Irv & Roy Salsbury)
6. House of a Million Auto Parts (Phil Grubstein & George Ichill)
7. Milchman Kosher Deli [2]
8. William Bass Scrap Metals
9. Grocery (front) Printing (rear) (Julius Silverman)
10. Finman Kosher Market
11. Elozory Furniture Store
12. Blue Ribbon Supermarket (Bobo Families) [1]
13. Tick/Reznick Bags & Drums
14. (2nd Ybor Post Office) Hallmark Emblems (Klein, Weissmans, etc.)
15. West Coast Army Store (became Fremacs Mens Wear) (Fred & Mack Perlman and Sam, Alex, & Milton Bokor)
16. (Max) Star Grocery
17. Max Argintar Pawn & Clothing [1]/ Martin's Uniforms [4]
18. Adam Katz Family Clothing (Harry Wilderman)
19. Liberty Mens Store (Abe Herscovitz)
20. Curtis Gimpel, Office Machines
21. Dr. I. Einbinder, Dentist (upstairs)
22. Blue Ribbon Supermarket [2]
23. Isadore Davis Department Store
24. Rophies Mens Wear [3]
25. Style Hat Shop (Alma Fleischman)
26. Rainbow Mens Wear (Abe & Sam Verkauf)
27. Adorable Hat Store (Tillye Simovitz/Waltzer/Freedman)
28. Isadore Segall Ladies Wear
29. Russells Ladies Wear (Russell & Jean Bernheim)

30. David Kasriel Dept. Store/The Jewel Box (Buddy Levine; then Dave Kartt)
31. Louis Wohl Household Supplies [1]/ The Palace (Louis & Mark Shine)[1]
32. Max (& Sam) Argintar Mens Wear [2]
33. Rophies Linens [1 & 2]
34. Joseph Kasriels Ladies Dept. Store
35. Louis Wohl & Sons Restaurant Supply [2]
36. Silver's 5-10¢ and $1.00 Stores
37. Bond Shoe Store (Jack Woolfe)
38. Weber Ladies Uniform Dress Mfg.
39. United Shoe Store (Leon Woolfe)
40. Rippa Ladies Wear (Bob Rippa's Grandfather)
41. Haber's Ladies Wear (Bob Rippa's Grandfather)
42. Ida's Ladies Ready to Wear (Max & Ida Goodrich) The Palace [2]
43. Economy Ladies Wear (Oscar Poller)
44. David Stein Furniture Co.
45. Abe Wolfson Mens Wear
46. Pollers Ladies Wear (Nathan Poller)
47. Wolfson's Trimming Store (Adam Wolfson & Son, William)
48. Modern Home Furnishings (Louis Buchman & Son "Booky")
49. Manuel Aronovitz Store
50. Herman Aronovitz Clothing Store/ (Buddy) Arnold's Shoes & Art Supply
51. Dayan Linens (Victor Dayan) [2]
52. Dayan Linens (Nissam Day) [1]
53. Little Katz Fabrics (Fannie Katz & nephew Irving) Edwards Childrens Store (Morris Weisman & Son, Edward)
54. Steinbergs
55. Ike Weiss Department Store/Sunshine Department Store [2] (Manuel Leibovitz & Sons)
56. Milton Schwartz Tire Co.
57. Sunshine Department Store [1]
58. Philip Weissman Clothing [2]

59. Philip Weissman Clothing [1]
60. Louie's Department Store (Soloman Simovitz & Sons)
61. Buchman's Department Store & Royal Palm Window Shades (Jacob Buchman Family) [1]
62. Martin's Uniforms (Spicola) [6B]
63. Red Globe Store (Joseph Weissman) Martin Uniforms (Howard & Irving Weissman) [2 & 6A]
64. Royal Palm Window Shades [2]/ Martin's Uniforms [5]
65. Leader Dry Goods & Notions (Toba Margolis & Daughter Cecelia) Milchman Watch & Jewelry Repair
66. Red Globe Store [1]/ A & Z Restaurant Supply (Anton & Zack) [2]
67. Julius & Fannie Buckman Store
68. Sam Hartzman (2nd Hand Suits)
69. Weissman Clothing Store [3]; then to Martins Uniforms [1]
70. Charles Haimovitz Mens Store (Barney Haimes' Father)
71. The Leader Clothing Store (Hyman Golden)
72. Corona Brush Co. (Gregory & David Waksman)
73. Louis Markovitz Clothing
74. Ozias Meerovitz Mens Store
75. Tampa Typewriter Service (Martin Haas)
76. Southern Iron & Bag (Louis Gordon)
77. Zack Restaurant Supply [3A]
78. Peretzman Scrap Iron & Metal
79. Hillsborough Plumbing Supply (William & Bootsie Oster)
80. Anton Restaurant Supply [3B]
81. (Leo) Chardkoff Bag Co.
82. A & Z Restaurant Supply [1]
83. West Coast Salvage & Iron [1] (Sidney Bernstein)
84. West Coast Salvage & Iron [2] (Sol Walker & Co. Scrap Iron)

Notes: Approximate locations for these businesses were identified as an oral history memory project by longtime Ybor City residents walking the streets and comparing memories. Their compilations and records have been preserved and provided for this edition by Dorothy P. (Dolly) Wllliams of Tampa. Numbers is square brackets indicate sequential locations. Earlier versions of the map were prepared as part of the MOSAIC local history project and included in *Florida Jewish Heritage Trail* by Rachel B. Heimovics and Marcia Zerivitz (Florida Department of State, Division of Historical Resources, 2000).

**Ybor City: The Making of a Landmark Town**

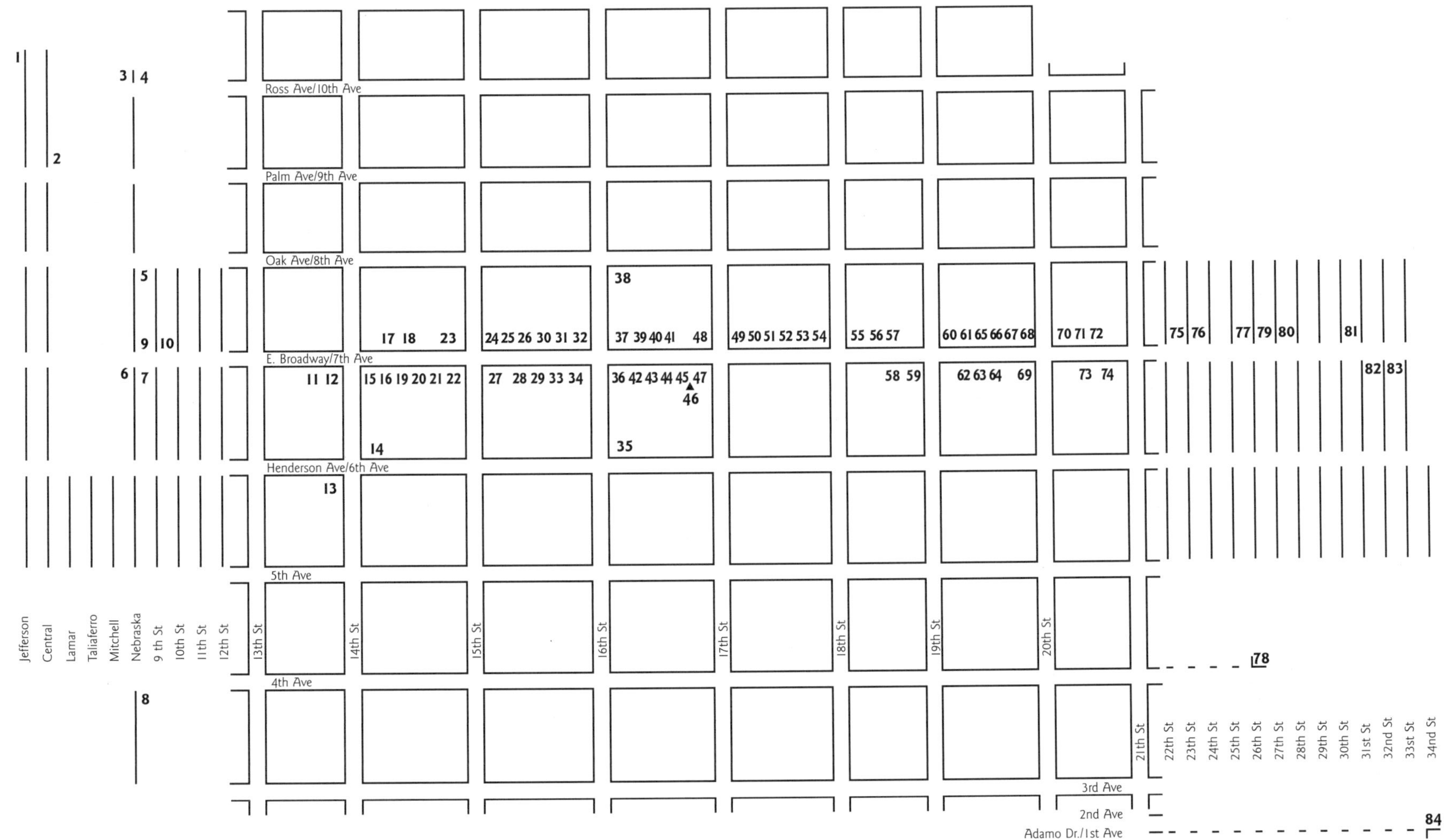


**Tables and Exhibits**

419

# Historic American Buildings Survey: Ybor City

This exhibit reproduces the first page (and an enlarged detail, left) from the report of the Historic American Buildings Survey (HABS) jointly undertaken by the National Parks Service, the Florida Bicentennial Commission, and the City of Tampa, measured and drawn under the direction of John Poppilier, Chief, Historic American Buildings Survey.

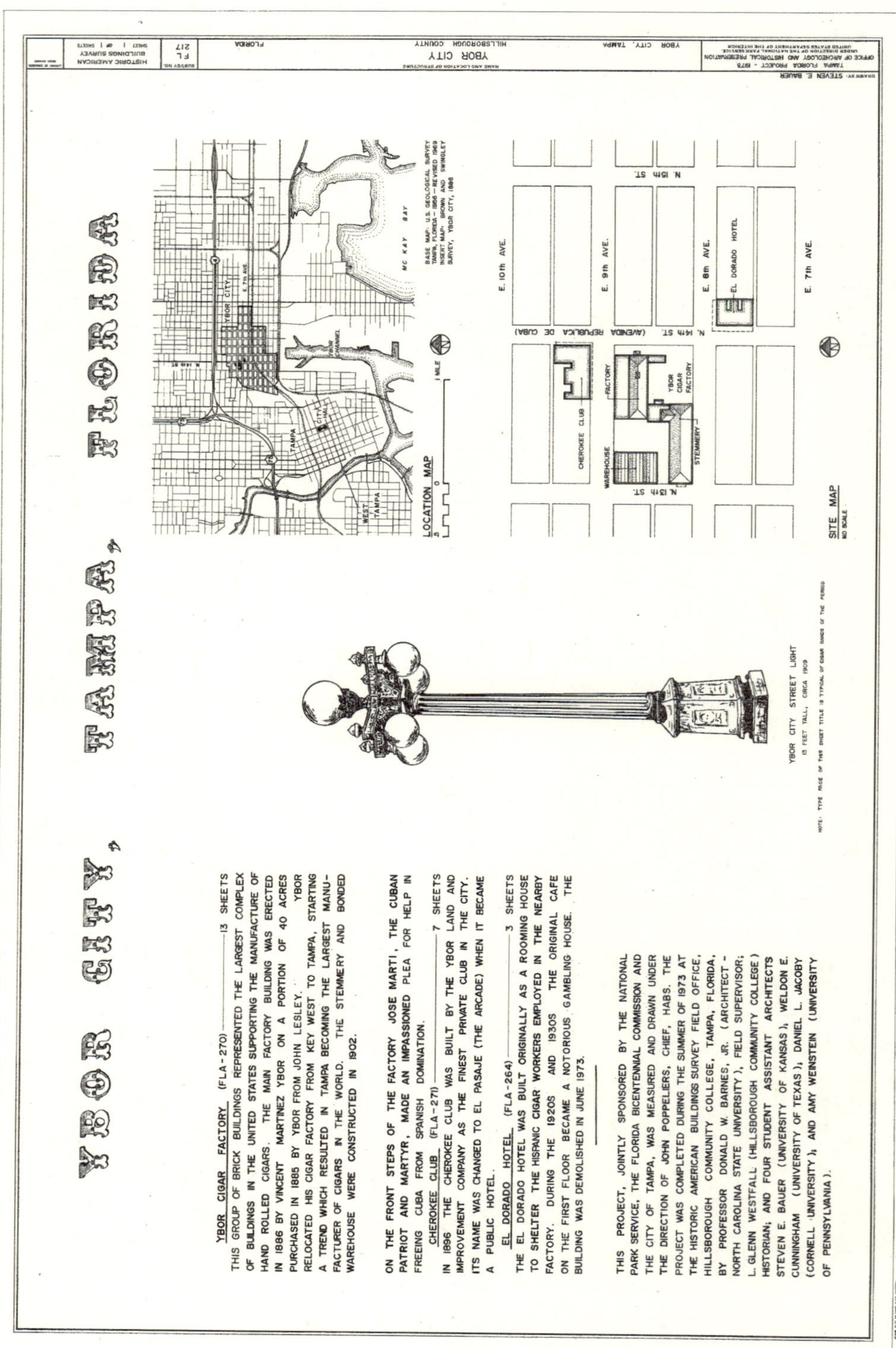




**Ybor City: The Making of a Landmark Town**

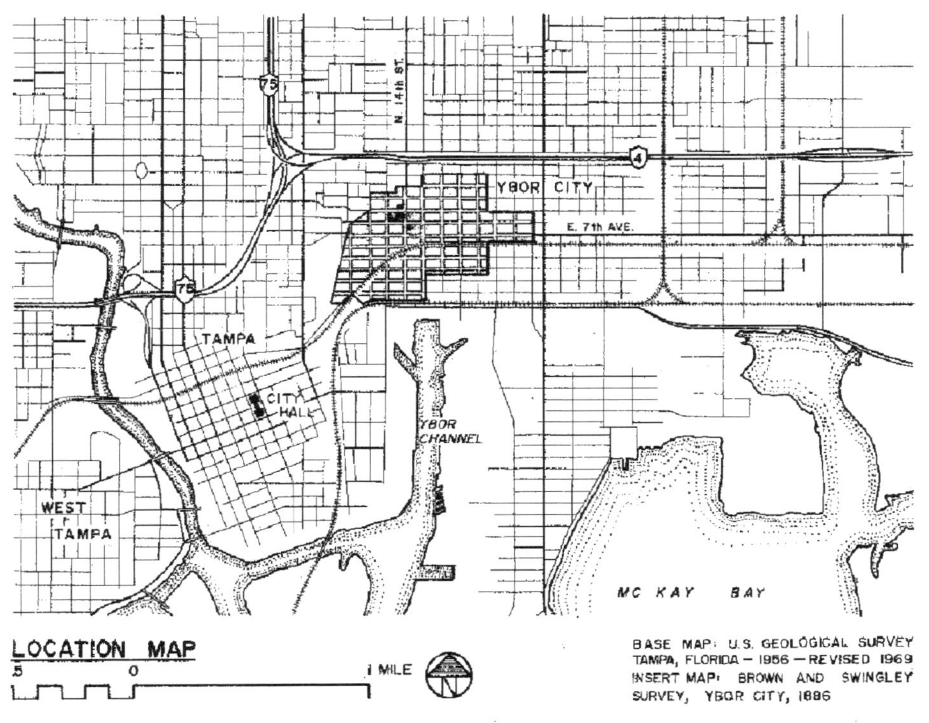


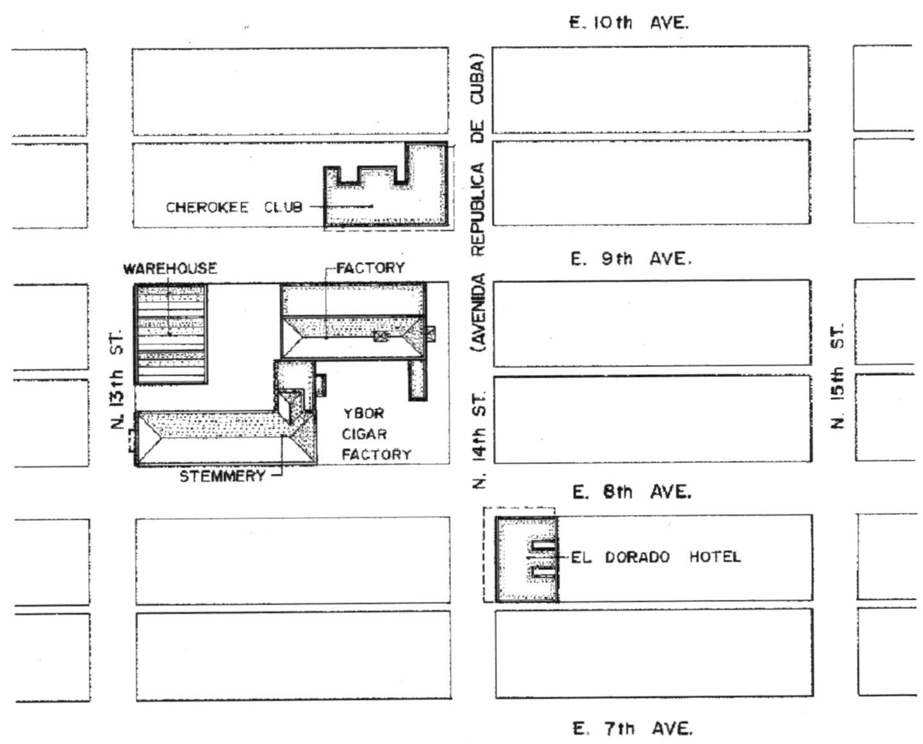




**Tables and Exhibits**

# Popular Ybor City Games

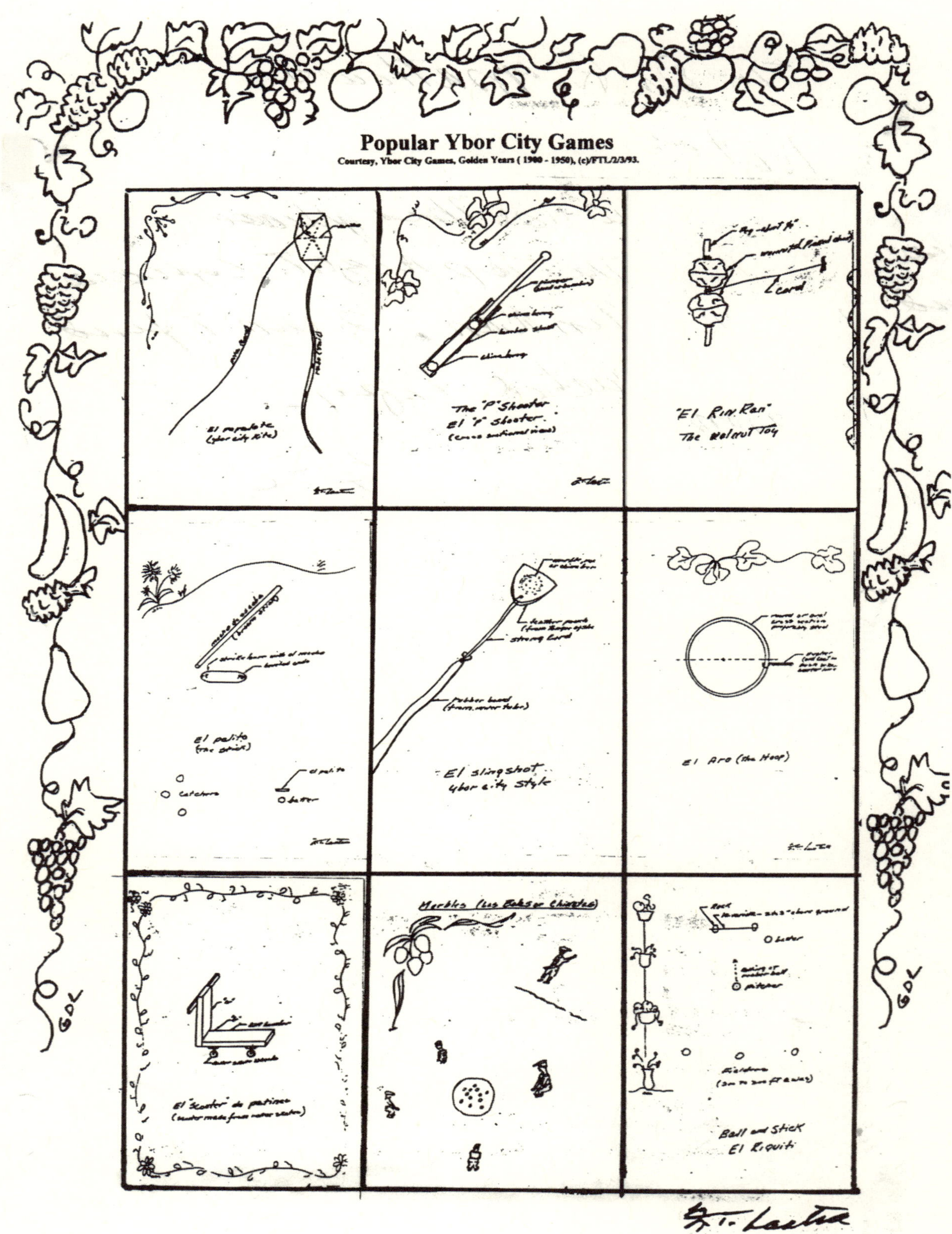



**Ybor City: The Making of a Landmark Town**

# NOTES & BIBLIOGRAPHY

# Notes

## Chapter 1

1  For a good discussion of the Spanish backgrounds, see Luis Zalamea, *Spain Omnipresent in Florida: A Historical-Literary Essay* (Miami, Fla.: Ediciones Universal, 1978) 75-76; and José Terrero, *Historia de España* (Barcelona: R. Sopena, 1977) 196-206.

2  Ibid.

3  Ibid.

4  Charles Gibson, *Spain in America* (NY: Harper and Row, 1966) 182-204.

5  Carlos M. Fernandez-Shaw, *Presencia Español en los Estados Unidos* (Madrid: Instituto de Cooperación Iberoamericana, Ediciones Cultura Hispánica, 1987) 40-46.

6  Jose Rivero Muniz, *The Ybor City Story, 1885-1954*, trans. Eustasio Fernandez and Henry Beltran (Tampa: [no publisher], 1976) 3-4.

7  Muniz 12-14; Gary R. Mormino and George E. Pozzetta, *The Immigrant World of Ybor City*, 55, Table 4.

8  L. Glenn Westfall, *Key West: Cigar City, U.S.A.* (Key West: Key West Preservation Board, 1984) 22-24.

9  Ibid.

10  Ibid.

11  Ibid.

12  Ibid.

13  Muniz 5-6.

14  Hillsborough County Real Estate Agency, *Descriptive Pamphlet of Hillsborough County, Florida* (Tampa: The Hillsborough County Real Estates Agency, 1885) 37.

15  Muniz 7.

16  One of his sons, Hamilton Disston, owned the St. Cloud sugar plantation in Florida where many Italians worked in 1882 and later migrated to Tampa. He and his brother Jacob were instrumental in the development of Pinellas County.

## Chapter 2

*  The May 30, 1998, performance of *You Are There* at the Círculo Cubano in Ybor City dramatizedthe fight for Cuban Independence and included a reminder of the contributions made by black American soldiers. In *The War to Free Cuba*, author Brigadier General S.L.A. Marshall, U.S.A.R. (Ret) refers to "elements of two Negro regiments, the Ninth and Tenth Cavalry, [who] figured conspicuously in the charge which finally cleared out the topmost work on the San Juan crests. Lieutenant John J. Pershing helped nudge them along. So did Colonel Roosevelt and some of his Rough Riders. Teddy Roosevelt was always in the thick of battle, waving his hat to the troopers to follow him." The black Americans who fought in the  Spanish-American War are also known as "Buffalo Soldiers."

1  Gary R. Mormino and Anthony P. Pizzo, *Tampa: The Treasure City* (Tulsa: Continental Heritage, 1983) 45; Grismer 54-60 and 301.

2  Karl Grismer 301.

3  Joseph Hipp, "What Happened in Tampa on July 15, 1887, or Thereabouts," *The Sunland Tribune* VI, 1 (Nov. 1980) 82-94; Grismer 116-117; Mormino and Pizzo, 45.

4  For a brief discussion of Tampa in the Civil War years see Mormino and Pizzo 60-67; also Canter Brown Jr., *Tampa in Civil War and Reconstruction* (Tampa: University of Tampa Press, 2000).

5  Hampton Dunn, "Turn to Greatness," *Sunland Tribune*, October 1984, 12-14.

6  Dunn, 12-14.

7  Hipp, 82-94.

8  Hipp, 82-94.

9  Hipp, 82-94.

10  Qtd. in Hipp, 82-94.

11  L. Glenn Westfall, "Latin Entrepreneurs and the Birth of Ybor City," *Tampa Bay History* Fall/Winter 1985, 11-12.

12  Durward Long, "The Historical Beginnings of Ybor City and Modern Tampa," *Florida Historical Quarterly* 45 (July 1966) 34.

13  *Tampa Guardian*, October 27, 1886

14  Quoted in Henry A. Cawston, ed., *History of Hillsborough County, Florida: 1986 Centennial Guide* (Harris Mullen, Chairman) (Tampa: Committee Festive Publication, 1986) 61.

15  Durward Long, "The Historical Beginnings of Ybor City and Modern Tampa," *Journal of Southern History*, *31*, November 1965, 34.

16  Cawston 37.

17  Cawston 38.

18  Jose Rivero Muniz, *The Ybor City Story: 1885-1954*, Eustasio Fernandez and Henry Beltran, trans. (Tampa: n.p., 1976) 27.

19  Emilio Del Rió, *Yo Fui Uno de los Fundadores de Ybor City*. (Tampa: [no publisher], 1950) 11.

20  Ibid.

21  Ibid. Also see Glenn Westfall, *Research Study*, 103.

22  Ibid, 31-32.

23  Ibid, 11.

24  Ibid.

25  Ibid, 20-24.

26  Ibid.

27  Arsenio M. Sánchez, "Incentives Helped Build West Tampa," *The Sunland Tribune*, December 1985, 9-12.

28 Armando Méndez, *Ciudád de Cigars, West Tampa* (Tampa: Florida Historical Society, 1994) 2.

29 Ibid, 3.

30 Muniz 65-66.

31 Muniz 43-44

32 Mormino & Pozzetta 55.

33 My father, Evaristo Trebín Lastra, came to Ybor City from Galicia, Spain, via Cuba, and could report the immigrant experience firsthand.

34 *Florida Cuban Heritage Trail* 4.

35 Victoriano Manteiga, *Centro Español de Tampa Bodas de Oro, 1891-1941* (Tampa: [no publisher], 1941) 8; *Centro Asturiano, Album de Recuerdos 1902-1985*.

36 These terms and attitudes are based on the conversations I heard often in the streets and cafés of Ybor City. The author's father worked at Corral-Wodiska and Perfecto Garcia factories and was also a Realtor. Tales of the factory workers, staff, and management were told over meals at home.

37 R. G. Dunn provides a "List of Cigar Manufacturers Extant in the State of Florida" in his *Booklet of Business Enterprises, 1919-1920*, the forerunner to reports later to be issued by his famous firm of Dunn & Bradstreet, New York.

37a Unfortunately I can offer no more detail about this source. The clipping from my files does not have a reporter's name, and the source and date are written on the side as "*Tampa Tribune* 1894."

38 Del Rio 32.

39 A. G. Rodriguez Morejon, *Raices de la Repblica de Cuba* 31, 33, 123-24. See also, Jorge Mañach, *Martí: Apostle of Freedom* trans. by Coley Taylor (Devon 1950).

40 Muñiz 64-65.

41 I am familiar with Tony Pizzo's extensive article from an undated manuscript, assumed to have been written in 1983, now in the Midulla Collection at the University of South Florida. Another account, "The Italian Heritage in Tampa," appears as a chapter in *Little Italies in North America*, Robert Harney and Vincenza Scarpaci, eds. (Toronto: Multicultural Society of Ontario, 1981).

42 Pizzo manuscript 3.

43 ibid.

44 ibid.

45 My mother began working in the factory when she was fourteen or fifteen years old, sitting alongside her skilled father (*de los laargos*), Felice Leto, who supervised her by special permission of *El Capataz* (the general foreman). The factory was Corral Wodiska #8, then at 14th Street and Michigan Avenue (called Columbus Drive today).

46 Mormino and Pozzetta 17-18.

47 Mormino and Pozzetta 78.

48 Muniz 18.

49 Ibid.

50 John A. Crow, *Spain: The Root and the Flower.* Berkeley: University of California Press, 1985. 302.

51 These accounts are verified by many family stories, as well as the experiences of our immediate neighbors, Asturianos and Gallegos, in the shadows of the Centro Asturiano Sanatorio in the late Boom and Depression years.

52 *Bodas de Oro–Centro Español de Tampa: 1891-1941* 10 ff.

53 Ibid.

54 Ana M. Varela-Lagos, "From Patriotism to Mutualism: The Early Years of the Centro Español de Tampa, 1891-1903," *Tampa Bay History* Fall-Winter, 93; pp. 5-23; also see esp. 17-18.

55 A. G. Rodriguez Morejón, *Raíces de la Republica de Cuba* 5-15, 61-62.

56 See John M. Kirk, *Jose Martí: Mentor of the Cuban Nation* (Gainesville: University of Florida Presses, 1983) 3-39.

57 E. J. Salcines emphasized this connection in his lecture "José Martí" at the University of South Florida Library Special Collections, June 27, 1997.

58 Muñiz 48.

59 Ibid.

60 Muñiz 49-50.

61 Muñiz 50.

62 Muñiz 51-52.

63 Muñiz 52-53; Mañach is author of *Martí, El Apóstol* [*Martí: Apostle of Freedom* (New York: O'Toole, 1984)].

64 Muñiz 54.

65 Muñiz 54-55.

66 Muñiz 56.

67 Muñiz 56.

68 Muñiz 56-57.

69 Muñiz 59.

70 Salcines at USF, June 27, 1997.

71 Muñiz 63-64.

72 John M. Kirk, *Jose Martí: Mentor of the Cuban Nation* (Gainesville: University of Florida Presses, 1983) 161.

73 Anthony Pizzo, "The Historic Cigar," *La Gaceta* (date uncertain) 1952. See also Pizzo's "The Cigar That Sparked a Revolution," *Sunland Tribune* 6/1 (November 1980) 32-35.

74 Morejón 124.

75 Ibid

76 Ibid

77 The article by Nydia Sarabia is entitled "*Aquel tabaquero amigo de Martí*" and was presumably written after December 13, 1896, the date on which Don Vicente Martínez Ybor died. A copy



**Ybor City: The Making of a Landmark Town**

of the newspaper clipping was given to me Nov. 28, 1996, by Rafael Martínez-Ybor, great-grandson of Don Vicente. The newspaper in which the article appeared is unknown, but a *Tampa Daily Times* nameplate and headline placed graphically adjacent to the article is dated Dec. 14, 1896. For purposes of quotation I have provided my own English translation of the original Spanish article.

[78] Ibid.

[79] *Tampa Daily Times*, 17 December 1896, p. 1.

[80] Ibid.

[81] Ibid.

[82] Ibid.

[83] At an Ybor City Museum Society meeting in early 1997, with Mary Alvarez presiding, I was present when a question was raised concerning the role of Ignacia Haya in the founding of Ybor City. Following that discussion, Rafael Martínez-Ybor sent me the *Tampa Weekly Times* articles which form the basis for this chapter. (I was unable to locate any other contemporary accounts of the funeral.) A detailed summary of the funeral and related events, based on the articles cited, has now been given to the Ybor Museum Society for archiving.

[84] The complexities of Spanish history are beyond the scope of this book, but no history of Ybor City would be complete without deep consideration of multicultural impact. I have summarized some of the key elements culled primarily from my reading of two works, which I recommend for greater insight: J. Terrero, *Historia de Espagña* (Barcelona: Editorial Ramon Sopena, S.A., 1977) and John A. Crow, *Spain: The Root and the Flower* (Berkeley: University of California Press, 1985).

[85] Louis A. Pérez Jr., *Cuba Between Empires, 1878-1902* (Pittsburgh: University of Pittsburgh Press, 1983) 73-87.

[86] Ibid.

[87] Tererro 526-563.

[88] Archie Blount, "Immigrants Created a New World," *The Tampa Tribune* Sept. 25, 1994, p. 5.

[89] Leland Hawes, "Figueredo Sought Cuban Independence," *The Tampa Tribune*, April 8, 1990, H6.

[90] Ibid.

[91] Muñiz 87-89.

[92] C. Verdejo, *Carlos V* (Barcelona, Spain: Editorial Ramon Sopena, S.A., 1968); V. Vazquez de Prada, *Felipe II* (Barcelona, Spain: Editorial Ramon Sopena, S.A., 1978).

[93] Terrero 542.

[94] Ibid.

[95] Perez 151-153.

[96] Parez 148-167.

[97] Gil Klein, "Remembering the Maine," *The Tampa Tribune*, Feb. 15, 1998, 1.

[98] Quoted in Klein, 1.

[99] Leland Hawes, "A Chance to Shine or Shame," *The Tampa Tribune* Feb. 15, 1998, Nation/World 1. Paul Eugen Camp of the University of South Florida Library Special Collections places the date of arrival as June 3, 1898.

[100] Ibid.

[101] Mormino and Pizzo 125.

[102] Klein 1. See also Admiral Hyman Rickover's book *How the Battleship Maine Was Destroyed* (Washington, D.C.: Naval History Division, Department of the Navy, 1976).

[103] Thomas B. Allen, "Remember the *Maine*?" in *National Geographic*, February 1998.

[104] Muñiz 117-118.

[105] *Bodas de Oro–Centro Español de Tampa* 20.

[106] Archie Blount, *Tampa Tribune* Sept. 25, 1994, Special Centennial issue.

[107] Andy Smith, "The Old Tribune Told News Stories in Different Ways," *Tampa Tribune* Sept. 25, 1994, Special Centennial, 6.

[108] Ibid.

[109] Ibid.

[110] For this quotation and information in the following paragraphs, see Perez, 28, 118, 178, 330, 376.

[111] Ibid.

[112] Klein 1.

[113] In their march to capture San Juan, U.S. troops successfully charged up Kettle Hill, which was popularly romanticized with the help of drawings by artist Frederic Remington and American journalists into Col. Teddy Roosevelt and his "Rough Riders" winning the Battle of San Juan Hill. Most historians now agree that Roosevelt's role was exaggerated.

**Chapter 3**

[1] Archie Blount, "Immigrants Created New World in Tampa, *Tampa Tribune*, Sept. 25, 1994, Special Centennial 5.

[2] Muñiz 131.

[3] Blount 5.

[4] Bodas de Oro, 19-21.

[5] Varela-Lago, Ana M. "From Patriotism to Mutualism, The Early Years of the Centro Espanol de Tampa, 1891-1903." *Tampa Bay History* (Fall/Winter 1993)

[6] Souvenir Book, 1902-1985, Centro Asturiano de Tampa, Inc., 9-10.

[7] Mormino and Pozzetta 115.

[8] Robert P. Ingalls, "Strikes and Vigilante Violence in Tampa's Cigar Industry," *Tampa Bay History* Fall/Winter 1985, 123.

[9] Leland Hawes, "Kidnappings Squelched Strike," *Tampa Tribune*, Nov. 6, 1994, Metro section 4.

[10] Ibid.



**Notes and Bibliography**

<sup>11</sup> Ibid.

<sup>12</sup> Ingalls 123.

<sup>13</sup> Ingalls 124.

<sup>14</sup> The terms "Black Cuban," "person of color," or "mestizo" are considered proper use among Cubans, and these are the primary terms I have tried to use consistently in this book. In general usage "Afro-Cuban" refers to a musical and artistic genre from the Cuban nation, but is not often used to describe personal ethnicity. This distinction was confirmed to me in 1990 by Marta Mulén Romero, a writer for *La Gaceta* in Tampa. However, in recent years "Afro-Cuban" has become a common term used by historians, and most notably by anthropologist Susan D. Greenbaum in her book *More Than Black: Afro-Cubans in Tampa* (University Press of Florida, 2002). As a result, you will find the occasional use of "Afro-Cuban" in this book used as a general designation of cultural identity and background rather than referring to a specific musical style.

<sup>15</sup> Writer Mara Mulén Romero also contributed many useful insights to this discussion of Black Cubans.

<sup>16</sup> Muñiz 35.

<sup>17</sup> Mormino and Pozzetta, 102, 123, 148-51; 164-69.

<sup>18</sup> My observations on the factory environment are based on my 25 years of industrial engineering experience in large U.S. factories, where I observed the characteristics first-hand in many different locations. The knowledge of factory issues was widespread and much discussed and debated. Working conditions and management styles were virtually daily conversation at the coffee houses and *fondas* (small restaurants near factories).

<sup>19</sup> Dirk Lammers, [title unknown]. *Tampa Tribune*, May 5, 1995, University section, 1 & 5.

<sup>20</sup> "Florida Mosaic: Jewish Geography of Ybor City, 1920s-1970s." Although no author or publisher is listed for the publication, this map was largely coordinated and compiled by Dorothy P. (Dolly) Williams of Tampa, who also met with the editor to share updated information for inclusion in the revised map of Jewish businesses presented on pages 418-19. See also Leland Hawes, "Romanian Jews' Exodus to Tampa Was a Long Trip," *Tampa Tribune*, June 7, 1992, Baylife 4. Page 1 of the same section carries an anonymous article titled "Mosaic Details Jewish History."

<sup>21</sup> See Exhibit 7, pages 418-19.

<sup>22</sup> L. Glenn Westfall, "Research Study for the Development of the Ybor City State Museum." University of South Florida Special Collections, Misc. Project Series #435, August 1978, 1.

<sup>23</sup> Julius J. Gordon, *German American Influence in Florida, 1840-1900*, (Tampa, Florida: n.p., 1991) 11. This work, not widely distributed, is available at the Special Collections Library, University of South Florida. No publisher is stated, but it bears the address 215 W. Grand Central Avenue, #708, Tampa, Fla. 33606, and is dated 12/10/1991.

<sup>24</sup> Gordon 6.

<sup>25</sup> This I know from personal observation, having spent almost two-thirds of my life in or around Ybor City.

<sup>26</sup> Susan D. Greenbaum, "Afro-Cubans in Exile: Tampa, Florida, 1886-1984," *Tampa Bay History* Fall/Winter 1985, 80. Dr. Greenbaum found this statement in the society's "Minutes of Meeting" for October 26, 1900, which are now in the Special Collections Library at the University of South Florida.

<sup>27</sup> Greenbaum 79-80.

<sup>28</sup> Greenbaum 80. See also Durward Long, "An Immigrant Co-operative Medicine Program in the South, 1887-1963," *The Journal of Southern History*, November 1965, 417-34.

<sup>29</sup> An excellent account of the struggle, including the special legislation that validates the club's historic contributions and the importance of perserving its current home for the future is found in Dr. Susan Greenbaum's *More Than Black*, 315-324. The Heritage Club Consortium is apparently no longer in existence; however, its principles of cooperative portrayal of Ybor City heritage are very much alive.

<sup>30</sup> My comments are based mostly on personal experience, during the time I first knew a number of the Black Cubans in Ybor in the years from about 1920 into the 1940s. I once again appreciated a shared sense of the enjoyment of games when I fielded a booth exhibiting games one played in the early days of Ybor City at the Museum Patio during the Ybor City Museum's Folk Fair in the 1980s. I have written a manuscript on this subject, "Games and Pastimes We Played in the Golden Years of Ybor City," which is in the University of South Florida Special Collections.

<sup>31</sup> Mormino and Pozzetta 114.

<sup>32</sup> Robert P. Ingalls, "Strikes and Vigilante Violence in Tampa's Cigar Industry," *Tampa Bay History* Fall/Winter 1985, 122.

<sup>33</sup> Mormino and Pozzetta 115-116.

<sup>34</sup> Ibid. 119-120.

<sup>35</sup> Leland Hawes, "Strike of 1910 Turned Violent," *Tampa Tribune*, Nov. 22, 1992, Baylife section 4. Hawes based his column on an article by Joe Scaglione, "City in Turmoil, Tampa and the Strike of 1910", *The Sunland Tribune*, November 1992, 32 ff.

<sup>36</sup> Ibid.

<sup>37</sup> From a letter dated October 10, 1910, in the Records of the Department of State now in the National Archives in Washington, D.C. Quoted in Ingalls 125.

[38] Ingalls 125.

[39] *El International* January 20, 1911; quoted in Ingalls 126.

[40] Muñiz .

[41] A. Stuart Campbell, with W. Porter McLendon, *The Cigar Industry of Tampa, Florida*, n.p., 1939.Note especially Table 45. Also see Joe Scaglioni, "City in Turmoil: Tampa and the Strike of 1910" in *Sunland Tribune*, November 1992, 29-36.

[42] Lago

[43] Cawston

[44] Frank T. Lastra's recollections

[45] *Tampa Electric Street Railway System* (1892-1946). Courtesy of W. Curtis Welch, Assistant City Archivist.

[46] Arsenio Sanchez, "Tampa's Early Lighting and Transportation" in *The Sunland Tribune*, November 1991.

[47] Frank T. Lastra's recollections.

[47] Ibid.

[48] Mormino and Pozzetta.

[49] Various articles in *Tampa Illustrado*, 1913.

[50] Frank T. Lastra.

[51] *Grimaldi's Official Guide Book* 3-8

[52] *Mechanization and Productivity of Labor in the Cigar Manufacturing Industry. Bulletin 600.* Bureau of Labor Statistics, September 1938. Table 6.

[53] Ibid. Table 17.

[54] Ibid. Table 17. Elizabeth Dunham of the Tampa Bay History Center confirmed many anecdotal statements from those who were working during that period when she reported in a personal note that total cigar "production was up in the '20s and down after 1930" and enclosed a photocopied chart of "Tampa's Growth in Figures" that showed the 1929 peak total of 504,753,265.

[55] Grun, *Time Tables of History.*

[56] *Mechanization and Productivity of Labor in the Cigar Manufacturing Industry. Bulletin 600.* Bureau of Labor Statistics, September 1938. Table 21, "Number of Concerns Manufacturing Cigars Exclusively by Principal States, 1929-1937."

[57] Information provided to author by Angel Garcia, son of Perfecto Garcia, who was one of the owners of Perfecto Garcia Brothers Cigar Factory in Ybor City.

[58] Frank T. Lastra.

[59] Thomas H. Meyer, "Davis Islands: The Booming Two Month Transformation of Tampa's Mudflats into Tampa's Dreamscape" in *Sunland Tribune* 18 (November 1992), 45-57.

[60] Ibid.

[61] Charles A. and Mary J. Brown, *The Bayshore: Boulevard of Dreams* (Tampa Historical Society, 1995).

[62] Frank T. Lastra. The author grew up less than a block away from the Centro Asturiano Sanitarium and recalls from his boyhood the sound of the hammers during its construction.

[63] *Mechanization and Productivity of Labor in the Cigar Manufacturing Industry. Bulletin 600.* Bureau of Labor Statistics, September 1938. Table 29, "Per Capital Consumption of Cigars and Cigarettes in the U.S., 1900-1938."

[64] Brown, 23-26.

[61] Ibid.

## Chapter 4

[1] Alistaire Cooke. *America.* (New York: Alfred A. Knopf, 1973).

[2] Frank T. Lastra.

[3] Bill Moyers. *The Roaring 20s.*

[4] Frank T. Lastra personal memory

[5] Ibid.

[6] Ibid.

[7] This custom was practiced by the author's family.

[8] Without television the people looked to the newspapers and the radio for news. Cuban stations offered a change from the standard fare heard on American stations.

[9] This was common knowledge among Ybor City citizens.

[10] Thomas H. Meyer.

[11] Ibid.

[12] Two years or so following Mr. Davis's death, tall grass grew in the unfinished areas of the project. The author cut the grass with his father for a haystack to feed the family's cattle.

[13] Grun.

[14] Moyers.

[15] Frank T. Lastra's recollections.

[16] The author prepared and ate the sandwiches at Orange Grove; and also got sick on them at George Washington Jr. High.

[17] The author milked cows for nine years, planted gardens, delivered newspapers, sold milk and limes, helped with honey bees, made haystacks from grass reaped on Davis Island, and raised chickens.

[18] The author's mother shopped there regularly.

[19] i.e. the TWIU.

[20] Author's observations.

[21] In 1929 or 1930, the author noted a free magazine on Russia available at the Labor Temple. Word on the street had it that a communist meeting had been allowed to take place.

[22] Lee Landenberger, "Playing Numbers," *Tampa Tribune* (January 14, 1990).

[23] It was common knowledge about the town's citizens where tickets could be bought.



**Notes and Bibliography**

<sup>24</sup> Frank Alduino, "The Smugglers' Blues and Alien Traffic in Tampa During the 1920s," in *Tampa Bay History* (Fall/Winter 1991).

<sup>25</sup> Mormino and Pozzetta, "Organized Crime," in *La Gaceta.*

<sup>26</sup> Mormino and Pizzo.

<sup>27</sup> Ibid.

<sup>28</sup> Grun.

<sup>29</sup> Mormino and Pozzetta 284.

<sup>30</sup> Author's recollections.

<sup>31</sup> The author served in the Signal Corps on island of Adak. Little alcohol was available from the mainland. Moonshine, however, was available. A remote Quonset hut on the island was used by soldiers who were making it from potatoes.

<sup>32</sup> The author's Spanish father and mother's Italian uncle made wine together. The author served as assistant.

<sup>33</sup> The Spaniards mentioned were neighbor's of the author during his childhood who lived on 14th Street and 21st Avenue. The author reveres the memory of those Spaniards and their proprieties.

<sup>34</sup> The author and his father listened to Madrid stations on a short wave radio.

<sup>35</sup> Hugh Thomas, *The Spanish Civil War.*

<sup>36</sup> Jose Terrero, *Historia de Espana* (Provenza: Editorial Ramon Sopen, 1977).

<sup>37</sup> Ibid.

<sup>38</sup> John A. Crow, *Spain: The Flower and the Root* (Berkeley: University of California Press, 1985).

<sup>39</sup> Ibid. Also see Miguel de Unamuno, *Essays and Soliloquies* (New York: Knopf, 1925).

<sup>40</sup> Jose Ortega y Gasset, *Espana Invertebrada* (Madrid, 1921) and Jose Ferrater Mora, *Ortega y Gasset* (New Haven: Yale University Press, 1957).

<sup>41</sup> Crow 308-314.

<sup>42</sup> Terrero; Crow 314-317.

<sup>43</sup> Ibid.

<sup>44</sup> Crow.

<sup>45</sup> Ibid.

<sup>46</sup> Ronald Fraser, *Blood of Spain: An Oral History of the Spanish Civil War* (NY: Pantheon Books, 1979).

<sup>47</sup> Crow.

<sup>48</sup> Ibid.

<sup>49</sup> The author was 14 years old when the war started. He listed to La Voz de Madrid nightly to follow the latest news. And he waited with his father for the early morning paper at the Columbia Restaurant. He listened to his father and Spanish friends discuss the war; all of them were Loyalists who supported the Popular Front. In 1930 and 1931 the author saw a lot of Leftist literature passed out around town.

<sup>50</sup> Ibid.

<sup>51</sup> Ibid.

<sup>52</sup> The author remembers several occasions when he waited on the steps of the cigar factory while his father made his weekly donation to the Loyalist war effort.

<sup>53</sup> Copies of the song, *No Parasan,* were passed out at Centro Asturiano in commemoration of the Spanish Civil War's 60th anniversary.

<sup>54</sup> See Table 4.

<sup>55</sup> see note 49.

<sup>56</sup> Leland M. Hawes Jr., "Solidarity Failed to Save Spain," *Tampa Tribune* (July 29, 1990).

<sup>57</sup> Peter N. Carroll, *The Odyssey of the Abraham Lincoln Brigade* (Stanford, Ca.: Stanford University Press, 1994).

<sup>58</sup> Ibid.

<sup>59</sup> Grun.

<sup>60</sup> The author's neighbor, Estevan Orestano, and his father attended Marcelino Domingo's appearance at Centro Asturiano. Orestano related the recital of a story, "Un Duro Por Ano," by Domingo.

<sup>61</sup> Crow.

<sup>62</sup> The author and his father heard Don Fernando de Los Rios at Centro Asturiano.

<sup>63</sup> The author's recollections.

<sup>64</sup> Ibid.

<sup>65</sup> Ibid.

<sup>66</sup> Confirmed by trips to Spain the author made with his family in 1975 and 1995.

<sup>67</sup> Ibid.

<sup>68</sup> Crow.

<sup>69</sup> The author's personal observations.

<sup>70</sup> The author's own memories.

<sup>71</sup> Ibid.

<sup>72</sup> *El Pais,* the newspaper founded by Ortega y Gasset, is the largest liberal newspaper, while *ABC* is Spain's largest conservative newspaper.

<sup>73</sup> Crow.

<sup>74</sup> Ibid.

<sup>75</sup> Cooke; Philip and Amitai Etzioni, *Anatomies of America.*

<sup>76</sup> The author and his father went to the Columbia daily.

<sup>77</sup> The author's recollections.

<sup>78</sup> The author's recollections, 1941-43.

<sup>79</sup> While in the Signal Corps in Alaska and on the Aleutian Islands the author received homemade food from his mother.

<sup>80</sup> Grun.

<sup>81</sup> The author's recollections of his father's friends' conversations.

<sup>82</sup> Harry Crumpacker.

<sup>83</sup> The author's recollections, 1941-43.

<sup>84</sup> Crumpacker.



**Ybor City: The Making of a Landmark Town**

85 The author lived in the area. Tony Fernandez, Buck Fernandez, and Joe Aizpuru attended Georgia Tech at about the same time as the author.

86 Account given by Dom Maggio, a mutual friend of the author and Lopez. The author attended the 46th anniversary of Lopez's death, which was marked at Centro Asturiano Cemetery in September 1996.

87 Crumpacker.

88 Remark made during a White House ceremony in 1995.

89 The author's recollections.

90 Ibid.

91 Information found in a Rotary Club brochure.

## Chapter 5

1 Information supplied by Marcelino Huerta Jr.

2 Most of the sports information is from the author's memories. He lived next to Cuscaden Park and knew a few of the personalities. Others are names that were talked about or that he read about in *La Gaceta* or *The Tampa Tribune*.

3 During the early years of this period the author was working at Continental Can Company as an industrial engineer. He married in Tampa in 1952, and he and his wife lived temporarily in a West Tampa apartment. This was a typical pattern for many sons and daughters of Ybor City. As much as possible the author met with his father to drink café con leche at the Columbia, and visited his parents in Ybor City on weekends. The author would shop on La Sétima, stop by Centro Español, visit friends, and maintain close connections there even though he no longer lived in the town.

4 Adela Hernandez Gonzmart and Ferdie Pecheco. *The Columbia Restaurant Spanish Cookbook* (Gainesville: University Press of Florida, 1995) 56.

5 The author has been a regular customer of the restaurant for many years. He is familiar with Casimiro II, having seen him at his favorite table during many visits to the Café, and remembers other members of the family, including Lawrence and Casimiro I. Details of its history have been verified with Adela Gonzmart and through reference to the book she wrote with Ferdie Pacheco (see note 4).

6 The author knew Cesar Gonzmart Sr., having worked with him on several occasions (during the author's presidency of the Ybor City Chamber of Commerce, and during service on the board of directors). The author and Gonzmart were also acquainted as knights of the Krewe of Sant' Yago. Cesar Sr. wasthe Krewe's King and key founder, and a most influential member of that social organization. The author's memory was refreshed by an article entitled "A Tradition of Excellence" and a testimonial given to Adela and Cesar Gonzmart on March 3, 1990, in ceremonies sponsored by the City of Tampa and at the dedication ceremony in conjunction with the unveiling of Cesar Gonzmart's statue in Ybor City Nov. 6, 1993.

7 Mormino and Pozzetta 302-303.

8 Dr. Fernandez gave the author a copy of this letter, which was presented to the Ybor City Chamber of Commerce by its president in 1957 and distributed widely to other groups and organizations. It dates from 1957.

9 The text is from a letter by Louis de la Parte to Dr. Henry F. Fernandez, dated October 8, 1958. The letter was loaned to the author in 1995 by Dr. Fernandez together with other clippings, notes, and letters which were invaluable in writing this portion of the story.

10 Mormino and Pizzo 176.

11 This clipping was among materials obtained from Dr. Fernandez. There is no page number.

12 Various Latin groups wrote letters of complaint regarding the city officials' decision to kill the Plaza Latino Plan. This example is from the Italian Club and was signed by its president, Phil LoCicero.

13 Ibid.

14 This clipping was among materials obtained from Dr. Fernandez. There is no page number.

15 Information from undated newspaper clippings from the local press in Dr. Fernandez's files.

16 From Dr. Fernandez's personal notes on the Vieux Carre Commission, undated.

17 *Tampa Times*, December 19, 1958.

18 Fernandez, personal notes on the Vieux Carre Commission, undated.

19 Ibid.

20 From an article, "Barrio Latino Seen As Tourist Trade Booster," late 1959.

21 From an address by Dr. Fernandez to the Rotary Club of Ybor City.

22 *Tampa Times*, "Mayor Gets Plans for Redevelopment," April 8, 1960.

23 From brochures by Dr. Fernandez on trip to New Orleans to investigate tourism.

24 Article dated April 8, 1960.

25 *Tampa Times*, "Council Legalizes Use of Balconies in Latin Quarter," author and date unknown.

26 Jeff Dunlap, "Broken Promises, Broken Hearts," *The Tampa Tribune* (May 13, 1979).

27 Ibid.

28 Ibid.

29 The author's personal observations.

30 Keith Coulbourn, "Many Ybor City Streets Blocked as Thruway Cuts Wide Strip," *The Tampa Tribune*, June 3, 1962.

31 *Urban Renewal News*, Fall and Winter 1967.

32 Ibid.

33 Author's reading of the Fernandez papers in 1995.



**Notes and Bibliography**

34 Bill Cox, "Tampa Gets Model Cities Planning Aid," *The Tampa Tribune*, Nov. 17, 1967, 8B.

35 The author's observations.

## Chapter 6

1 The information on this announcement was reported in *The Tampa Tribune* on Nov. 17, 1967, in a story by Bill Cox, "Tampa Gets Model Cities Planning Aid," editorial section, 8B.

2 Ibid.

3 U. S. Government, Department of Health, Education and Welfare, "The Model Cities and HEW: Guidelines for Model Cities," [brochure], 1967, 1-2.

4 Ibid.

5 "Sound Management for the War on Urban Decay," *The Tampa Tribune*, June 29, 1969, editorial page.

6 Ibid.

7 *Urban Renewal News*, staff listings (partial) July-September 1967, 9.

8 Ibid.

9 A. W. Benitez, "We Believe in Ybor," *Urban Renewal News* July-September 1967, 7.

10 Henry J. Fernandez, "Barrio Latino Commission," *Urban Renewal News* July-September 1967, 4.

11 Oscar Aguayo, column in editorial section, *Urban Renewal News*, July-September 1967, 2.

12 James D. Marshall Jr., "Relocation," *Urban Renewal News*, July-September 1967, 3.

13 Sam Argintar, "An Ybor Merchant Speaks," *Urban Renewal News*, July-September 1967, 5.

14 The author became personally acquainted with Armando Valdez's discerning observations about the undesirable changes and the desirable ones for Ybor City's future during many hours of conversation. He was a perceptive witness to the Urban Renewal fiasco, and had much to contribute to the author's understanding of the issues.

15 Richard E. Leon, "Rehabilitation," *Urban Renewal News*, Winter 1967.

16 J. D. Marshall, "Relocation," *Urban Renewal News*, Winter 1967.

17 Raul Vega Jr., "An Ybor Merchant Speaks," *Urban Renewal News*, Winter 1967.

18 A. William Benitez, "We Believe in Ybor," *Urban Renewal News*, Winter 1967.

19 A. William Benitez, "Nuncio Parkway Dedicated," *Urban Renewal News*, Winter 1967.

20 Jeff Dunlap, "Riot and Red Tape Snarled Ybor Revival," *Tampa Tribune* (May 14, 1979) D-1.

21 The author spent many hours talking with Armando Valdes.

22 *Urban Renewal News*, Winter 1967.

23 "Ybor Apartment Plans Progress," *The Tampa Tribune* (March 3, 1968).

24 Jeff Dunlap, "Walter's Walled City Idea Died With Bullfight Bill," *The Tampa Tribune* (May 13, 1979).

25 Norma J. Hill, *Tampa Tribune* (February 9, 1968).

26 Lowell Angford, *Tampa Times* (January 1968).

27 Norma J. Hill, *Tampa Tribune* (February 9, 1968).

28 Gary Braddock, *Tampa Times* (July 10, 1968).

29 Carol Neef, *Tampa Tribune* (June 6, 1969).

30 Ibid.

31 Ibid.

32 Ibid.

33 Ibid.

34 Leland M. Hawes Jr., "H.C.C. Presiding Over Institutional Turmoil," *The Tampa Tribune* (May 6, 1996).

35 Ibid.

36 Ibid.

37 Ibid.

38 The author's personal observations.

## Chapter 7

1 Linda Goldstein, *Tampa Times* (July 20, 1981).

2 The author took part in negotiations with Frank Weaner.

3 Daniel Alarcon, "Weaner Wants Chamber Out of Gallery," *Tampa Tribune* (April 28, 1983).

4 Daniel Alarcon, "Ybor Chamber Owns Land," *Tampa Tribune* (May 5, 1983).

5 The author and Joan Jennewein, YCCC Directors, negotiated the 25-year free lease with Ney Landrum.

6 The author was a member of the Krewe of Sant' Yago.

7 The author and Harris Mullen served together on several committees; as Nominating Committee Chairman, the author brought Mullen into the Chamber as Vice President.

8 Ted Hoffman, *Tampa Tribune* (1985).

9 Ibid.

10 The author, as President of the YCCC in 1977, appointed Jan Platt to head the "Save the Red Bricks Committee." Letter from Platt to the author dated June 24, 1977, with policy memorandum to all departments by Dale Twatchman dated February 22, 1977. Letter from author to Platt dated July 5, 1977.

11 According to Stephanie Ferrell, who was present at the City Council meeting where Helen Chavez defended the red bricks.

12 The author has worked with Ray Grimaldi and Eddie Spoto.



**Ybor City: The Making of a Landmark Town**

[13] Leland M. Hawes Jr., *The Tampa Tribune* (September 1993), quoting Samuel Proctor.

[14] Leland M. Hawes Jr., "Exhibit Traces Jewish Roots in Florida," *Tampa Tribune* (early 1990s).

[15] Based on brochure, *Rough Riders: First U.S. Volunteer Cavalry Regiment*, courtesy of Charles Spicola Jr.

[16] Report prepared by committee composed of Bettie Nelson (first Museum Society President), Stan Newman, Tony Pizzo, Joan Jennewein, and the author, dated September 18, 1985. Distributed at the Columbia Restaurant at the Third Annual Banquet.

[17] Based on letters, documents, etc., given to the author by Gonzmart.

[18] Ibid.

[19] Westfall's book is titled *Research Study for the Development of the Ybor City State Museum* (August 1978). He has been involved in Historic Preservation in Tampa since 1971.

[20] The author was actively engaged in local affairs as a Director of the YCCC and YCMS during those years.

**Chapter 8**

[1] HT/HCPB. *Goals of the Ybor City Revitalization Consultant Study.* July 1979.

[2] Cesar Gonzmart Jr., remarks made during special meeting of the Board of Directors, Senior Advisors.

[3] Minutes of the Ybor City Development Task Force meeting, January 31, 1980.

[4] Record of author's appointment to the Ybor City Development Advisory Committee, in author's possession.

[5] Minutes of the Selection Committee meeting, September 30, 1980.

[6] Technical Memorandum, ERA and Associates, report prepared for Ybor City, May 1983.

[7] Author's recollections. Joyce Shaffer was a respected member of the YCCC board and was President in 1985-86. Her son Jay Fechtel made valuable contributions.

[8] Linda Goldstein, "Renaissance man Cesar Gonzmart still hopes for a rebirth of Ybor City," *The Tampa Tribune* (July 22, 1981).

[9] Doron Levin, "Tampa restauranteur firm on project to rescue Cubans," *The Tampa Tribune* (May 16, 1980).

[10] Rosemary Frawley, "The Restauranteur Strives to Complete the Boatlift," *The Tampa Tribune* (May 21, 1980).

[11] Author's opinion.

[12] Jeff Wittle, "Offices nearly set," *Tampa Times* (February 18, 1978)

[13] Ibid.

[14] Joe Nice, article, *Tampa Times* (May 1978).

[15] Wittle.

[16] John Meynard, "Revitalization Drive Planned for Ybor City, *The Tampa Tribune* (March 27, 1980).

[17] Wittle.

[18] Bettie Nelson, first president of the Ybor City Museum Society, chaired the History Committee in 1985. Other members were Stan Newman, Tony Pizzo, Joan Jennewein, and the author. Nelson published the *Historical Synopsis, 1971-1985*, which was distributed on September 18, 1985 at the 2nd Annual Banquet.

[19] aniel Alarcon, "Ybor Centennial promotion under way," *Tampa Tribune* (January 15, 1985).

[20] Ybor City Centennial Committee's publication.

[21] Technical Memorandum, ERA and Associates, report prepared for Ybor City, May 1983.

[22] David Alarcon, "$90,000 Ybor City revitalization plan proffered," *Tampa Tribune* (May 5, 1983).

[23] David Alarcon, "Private projects give a boost to Ybor City redevelopment," *Tampa Tribune.*

[24] Ibid.

[25] David Alarcon, "Ybor City renewal is lagging," *Tampa Tribune* March 25, 1985).

[26] David Alarcon, "New Townhouses to add dimension to Ybor City life," *Tampa Tribune* (date unknown).

[27] *Tampa-Ybor Revitalization Strategy*, report dated 1996, addressed to Mayor Dick Greco, based on the Lincoln Property Company recommendations and approved by CRA and the YCDC.

[28] From the copy of a letter from Guy St. Paul, dated August 23, 1996.

[29] Plan package of the Casita complex, including Ybor City Preservation Park, HT/HCPB and Barrio Latino Commission, with description of the cigar workers' houses.

[30] Tom McEwen, "Tony Pizzo," *Tampa Tribune* (October 27, 1993).

[31] Ibid.

[32] "Tony Pizzo's Ybor City: An Interview with Tony Pizzo, " *Tampa Bay History*, Vol. 7, No. 2 (Fall/Winter 1985) 150; see also, *Historical Markers and Monuments in Tampa and Hillsborough County* (Tampa Historical Society, 1994).

[33] Ibid. The interview with Tony Pizzo cited above was also reprinted in the 1994 tribute volume accompanied by different photographs; see *Tampa Bay History*, Vol. 16, No. 4.

[34] Letters to the author from H. Fisher, Task Force Chairman, dated December 17, 1985 and March 3, 1986.

[35] Harris Mullen, "No More Back Burners," *Tampa Tribune* (February 15, 1988).

[36] "Tampa Electric Street (Railway System): 1892-1946," brochure with schedule.

[37] Tom Brennon, article, *The Tampa Tribune* (June 5, 1996).

[38] Bruce Dudley, "Firm Selected to Design Ybor's Farmers Market," *Tampa Tribune*, May 3, 1984.

[39] Author's recollections.

[40] Panky Snow, article [on city council resolution giving the YCDC, Inc., $100,000 from the city operating budget] in *The Tampa Tribune*, date omitted from clipping.

[41] Ibid.

[42] Author's recollections based on his personal papers.

[43] Jeff Magnum, "Historian to look at Ybor City," *Tampa Tribune* (January 27, 1988).

[44] [no author] "Historian to Scope Ybor City," *Tampa Tribune* (January 28, 1988).

[45] Panky Snow, "Federal Historian likes what he sees during Ybor City tour," *The Tampa Tribune* (February 4, 1988).

[46] Ivan J. Hathaway, "Ybor City gets National Landmark Honor," *Tampa Tribune* (January 1991).

[47] Michele Drayton and Leland M. Hawes Jr., "Ybor City gets national honor," *Tampa Tribune* (January 1991).

[48] *Ybor Square Shooter* (Spring-Summer 1992).


## Chapter 9

[1] Based on material obtained from the YCDC, Inc., by the courtesy of President Rebecca Gagalis.

[2] The author was an active YCCC Director for most of the period in question and so a witness to the activities and events discussed here.

[3] Booklet, "The Heritage Structures of Ybor City," (circa 1990).

[4] Ibid.

[5] William E. Fields, letter to the editor, *Tampa Tribune* (1985).

[6] Marty Clear, "Playmakers' Curtain Rises," (January 5, 1991).

[7] Pamela Lessard, article, *Tampa Tribune*, (January 20, 1990).

[8] Alfonso Belluccia, "Tampa and Agrigento Sister Cities," in brochure for 1991 Paolo Longo Awards.

[9] Ibid.

[10] Based on a conversation the author had with Ken Ferlita.

[11] Frank T. Lastra, "A Night to Remember— Oviedo and Ybor" (1996) in *Select Works on Ybor City* (Tampa: FTL, 2004) 145-153.

[12] The author was present at the celebration for the visiting commander.

[13] Mira I. Olivo, "Alcalde de Oviedo, España, de visita en Tampa," *La Gaceta*, February 13, 1998.

[14] The author has attended more than half of the Spanish Lyric Theater performances since its opening.

[15] Karen Dukess, "State Agrees to Buy Ybor City Building." *St. Petersburg Times*, Feb 8, 1990; Steven Girardi, "Centro Espanol's renewal 'A Very Happy Solution' to Disrepair," *Tampa Tribune*, Oct. 7, 2000.

[16] Richard Danielson, "Cuban Club Struggles to Defy Age," *St. Petersburg Times*, January 5, 1996.

[17] Ibid. See also Susan Clary, "A Night to Cherish Cuban Club," *St. Petersburg Times*, Sept. 26, 1994.


## Chapter 10

[1] Author's recollections.

Specifically, the January 20, 1998, YCCC luncheon featured speaker Tom Sullivan, President of the Hillsborough Hotel Association, and General Manager of the local Hyatt Regency hotel. Accompanying him was Bob Morrison, attorney, now Executive Director of the Association. In the 1879 through 1986 years, Morrison was Mayor Bob Martinez's staff coordinator for Ybor City development initiatives. While introducing Tom Sullivan, and on hearing the Chamber's report on progress being made in 1998, Morrison then called my name for confirmation of what he would say. He grinned and said, gracefully: "The progress of the current period (early '90s on ) rests heavily on the work done in the early and mid 1980s." This was music to the ears of the very few of us present from earlier years.

Morrison did not list the details, but he was referring to the many essential activities that had built a foundation. These had to be in place before the progress of the early 1990s could be realized. They included the acquisition of early financial support by Stephanie Ferrel's Preservation Board; the adoption of the Mayor's Ybor City Development Advisory Committee, with Harris Mullen as Chairman; Cesar Gonzmart Jr. and Richard Salem's effort at an Ybor City Development Task Force, that then became the Advisory Council to the Mayor's Ybor City Task Force; selection of ERA as the consulting group; the Ybor City Historic District Revitalization Plan (1983); founding of The Ybor Redevelopment Agency, led by chairmen, Henry Gonzalez, Tim Nugent, and Santos Rodriquez, sequentially; the city's adoption of a Zoning Ordinance in 1986, carried in the ERA consultant report and still utilized today. Morrison continued the progress, carrying out some effective coordinating sessions at YCCC's



**Ybor City: The Making of a Landmark Town**

office, which was then the Weaner's Art Gallery office building.

2 Ivan J. Hathaway, "Ybor near takeoff velocity," *The Tampa Tribune* (1994).

3 Ibid.

3 Katherine Smith, "Shiver's B and B (Bed and Breakfast) is expected to open in six months," *Tampa Tribune* (1994).

4 "Ybor Revitalization Strategy" (May 1996). Prepared by YCDC and the department of Business and Community Services.

5 Ivan J. Hathaway, "Improvements, 850 more jobs slated for Ybor," *The Tampa Tribune* (June 1997).

6 David Pedreira, "Mayor Wants to rebuild a tattered neighborhood," *The Tampa Tribune*, November 15, 1997.

7 Statement made by Joe Hoyden, president of the Historic Ybor Neighborhood group.

8 Author's recollections of events.

9 The author was an advisor to the YCCC and a member of the Strategic Committee.

10 The author was appointed by Mayor Bob Martinez to several committees; and familiar with Bob Morrison.

11 The author insisted that the Constitution have a clause that stressed the importance of the National Historic Landmark classification.

12 Author's recollections as a YCMS advisor.

13 The author presented the original resolution to both the YCCC and YCMS in late 1996.

# Illustration Credits

FSA – Florida State Archives

FTL – Frank Trebín Lastra

RM – Richard Mathews

SD – Sean Donnelly

TBH  – *Tampa Bay History*

THCPLS – Tampa Hillsborough County Public Library System

USFSCL – University of South Florida Special Collections Library

# Bibliography

## Books

*Album de la Orden Caballeros del Aguila de Oro, Castillo Cristobal Colon no. 7 dedicado al la inauguracion de su hermoso edificio social.* Tampa: [No publisher], [1930].

Barzini, Luigi, *The Italians.* New York: Atheneum, 1983.

*Bodas de Oro, 1891-1941, Centro Español de Tampa.* Tampa: The Tribune Press, Inc., 1941.

Brown, Charles A. and Mary J. *The Bayshore: Boulevard of Dreams.* Tampa: Tampa Historical Society, 1995.

Campbell, Archer Steward and McLendon, W. Porter. *The Cigar Industry of Tampa, Florida.* Gainesville: [No publisher], 1939.

*Centenario, [1885-1955], La Tampa de Ayer.* [Tampa]: [No publisher], [1955].

Centro Asturiano de Tampa, Inc. *Souvenir Book: 1902-1985.*

Clark, James Hyde. *Cuba and the Fight for Freedom.* Philadelphia: The Globe Bible Publishing Co., [1896].

Cooke, Alistair. *America.* NY: Alfred A. Knopf, 1973.

Crow, John Armstrong. *Spain: The Root and the Flower.* Berkeley: University of California Press, 1985.

de Quesada, A. M. *Images of America: Ybor City.* Charleston: Arcadia, 1999.

Del Río, Emilio. *The Birth of a City: Ybor-Tampa in Pictures.* [No place]: [No publisher], [no date].

Del Río, Emilio. *Yo Fui Uno de los Fundadores de Ybor.* Tampa: [No publisher,] 1972.

Ehrensaft, Philip and Amitai Etzioni. *Anatomies of America: Sociological Perspectives.* NY: Macmillan, 1969.

*Extra-Almanaque.* [Tampa: La Traduccion, 1930].

Fernandez-Shaw, Carlos M. *Presencia Española en los Estados Unidos.* Madrid: Institutio de Cooperacion Iberoamericana, Ediciones Cultura Hispanica, 1987. (Published in English translation by Facts on File.)

Ferrater Mora, Jose. *Ortega y Gasset.* New Haven: Yale University Press, 1957.

Fink, Gary and Merl E. Reed. "Radicals and Vigilantes: The 1931Strike of Tampa Cigar Workers." In *Southern Workers and Their Unions, 1880-1975: Selected Papers. The Second Southern Labor History Conference*, edited by Merl E. Reed, Leslie S. Hough, and Gary M. Fink. Westport: Greenwood Press, 1981.

Fountain, Anne. *Jose Marti and U.S. Writers.* Gainesville: University Press of Florida, 2003.

"Strike of Tampa Cigar Workers." In *Southern Workers and Their Unions, 1880-1975: Selected Papers. The Second Southern Labor History Conference*, edited by Merl E. Reed, Leslie S. Hough, and Gary M. Fink. Westport: Greenwood Press, 1981.

Frank, Waldo. *Cuba: Prophetic Island.* New York: Marzan & Munsell, 1961.

Fraser, Ronald. *Blood of Spain: An Oral History of the Spanish Civil War.* New York: Pantheon Books, 1979.

Gannon, Michael, ed. *The New History of Florida.* Gainesville:University Press of Florida, 1996.

Gibson, Charles. *Spain in America.* New York: Harper & Row, 1966.

Gonzmart, Adela Hernandez and Ferdie Pacheco. *The Columbia Restaurant Spanish Cookbook.* Gainesville: University Press of Florida, 1995.

Gordon, Julius J. *German-American Influence in Florida, 1840-1900.* Tampa: J. J. Gordon, 1991.

Greenbaum, Susan D. *More Than Black: Afro-Cubans in Tampa.* Gainesville: University Press of Florida, 2002.

Grismer, Karl H. *A History of the City of Tampa and Tampa Bay Region of Florida.* St. Petersburg: St. Petersburg Printing Office Co., 1950.

Grun, Bernard. *Time Tables of History.* New York: Simon & Schuster, 1982.

Harner, Charles E. *A Pictorial History of Ybor City.* Tampa: Trend Publications, 1975.

Harvey, Paul. *The Rest of the Story.* New York: William Morrow & Co., 1983.

Ingalls, Robert P. and Louis A. Perez, Jr. *Tampa Cigar Workers: A Pictorial History.* Gainesville: University Press of Florida, 2003.

Kirk, John M. *Jose Martí: Mentor of the Cuban Nation.* Tampa: University Press of Florida, 1982.

*L'Unione Italiana: Annual Paolo Longo Awards, Dec. 6, 1987.* [Tampa]: L'Unione Italiana, 1987.

Mañach, Jorge. *Martí: Apostle of Freedom*, trans. by Coley Taylor. New York: O'Toole, 1984.

Méndez, Armando. *Ciudad de Cigars: West Tampa*. Tampa: Florida Historical Society, 1994.

Mormino, Gary R. *Hillsborough County Goes to War: The Home Front, 1940-1950*. Tampa: Tampa Bay History Center, 2001.

Mormino, Gary R. and Ann L. Henderson, eds. *Spanish Pathways in Florida: 1492-1992*. Sarasota: Pineapple Press, 1991.

Mormino, Gary R. and George E. Pozzetta. *The Immigrant World of Ybor City: Italians and Their Latin Neighbors in Tampa, 1885-1985*. Urbana: University of Illinois Press, 1987.

Mormino, Gary R. and Anthony P. Pizzo, *Tampa, the Treasure City*. Tulsa: Continental Heritage Press, 1983.

Muñiz, Jose Rivero (translated by Eustasio Fernandez and Henry Beltran). *The Ybor City Story, 1885-1954*. Tampa: No publisher, 1976.

Muñiz, Jose Rivero. La Lectura en las Tabaquerias, May 1, 1948.

Ortega y Gasset, Jose. *España Invertebrada*. Madrid, 1921.

Pacheco, Ferdie. *Ybor City Chronicles: A Memoir*. Gainesville: University Press of Florida, 1994.

Pérez, Louis A., Jr., *Cuba Between Empires, 1878-1902*. Pittsburgh: University of Pittsburgh Press, 1983.

Pizzo, Anthony P. *Tampa Town: The Cracker Village with a Latin Accent, 1824-1886*. Miami: Hurricane House, 1968.

Ragano, Frank and Selwyn Raab. *Mob Lawyer*. New York: Macmillan Publishing Co., 1994.

Rickover, Admiral Hyman. *How the Battleship Maine Was Destroyed*. Washington, D.C.: Naval History Division, Department of the Navy, 1976.

*Rinaldi's Guide Book* (see Williams, Walter C., ed.; Van Horn, Charles Vincent, ed.)

Rodriguez Morejón, A. G. *Raíces de la República de Cuba*. Miami: Editorial Omega, 1964.

* Rowan, A.S. and M.M. Ramsey. *The Island of Cuba*. 1886.

Sanchez, Arsenio M. *West Florida: A Short History*. [No publisher, no date].

Snyder, Robert E. and Jack B. Moore. *Pioneer Commercial Photography: The Burgert Brothers, Tampa, Florida*. Gainesville: University Press of Florida, 1992.

*Souvenir Book, 1902-1985*. [Tampa]: Centro Asturiano de Tampa, [1985].

Terrero, J. *Historia de España*. Barcelona: Editorial Ramon Sopena, S.A., 1977.

Ugarte, Francisco. *España Y Su Civilizacion*. NY: The Odyssey Press, Inc., 1952.

Unamuno, Miguel de. *Essays and Soliloquies* (NY: Knopf, 1925).

Van Horn, Charles Vincent, ed. *Rinaldi's Official Guide Book of Tampa and South Florida*. Tampa: Rinaldi Printing Co., 1920.

Vazquez de Prada, V. *Felipe II*. Barcelona: Editorial Ramon Sopena, S.A., 1978.

Verdejo, C. *Carlos V*. Barcelona: Editorial Ramon Sopena, S.A., 1968.

Westfall, L. Glenn. *Key West: Cigar City U.S.A.* Key West: Historic Key West Preservation Board, 1984.

Westfall, L. Glenn. *Research Study for the Development of the Ybor City State Museum*. Special Collections, USF, Misc. project series, # 435, August 1978.

Williams, Walter C., ed. *Rinaldi's Guide Book to the City of Tampa*.

Zalamea, Luis. *Spain Omnipresent in Florida: A Historical-Literary Essay*. Miami: Ediciones Universal, 1978.

## Brochures and Pamphlets

*Back to Ybor City Day: Sunday, November 7, 1976*. [Optimist Club of Ybor City, 1976].

Cawston, Henry A., managing editor. *History of Hillsborough County*. 1986 Centennial Guide, a Committee Festive publication, Harris Mullen, Chairman.

"Descriptive Pamphlet of Hillsborough County, Florida." Tampa: Hillsborough County Real Estate Agency, 1885. (USF-Sp. Collections.)

Fernandez, Henry J., brochure on trip to Havana for tourism.

"Florida Mosaic Business Listings," courtesy of the Florida Mosaic of Jewish Geography in Ybor City, published circa 1990, Table 25 of this work.

Greco, Mayor Dick. *City of Tampa*, presented by YCDC and BCS, City of Tampa, footnoted. Revitalization Strategy, May 1996. Provided by YCCC staff.

"The Heritage Structures of Ybor City," Vince Pardo, Coordinator. City of Tampa, Community Planning, W. Curtis Welch. booklet, early 1990s.

Hillsborough/ Tampa Preservation Board Studies/Releases/Activities, Reports. Tampa-Ybor Revitalization Strategy Reports.

"Historical Markers and Monuments in Tampa and Hillsborough County," published in 1994 by the Tampa Historical Society, dedicated to the memory of Tony Pizzo, Special edition book.

"Rough Riders," 1st US Volunteer Cavalry Regiment Rough Riders, Inc., Valrico, Florida, courtesy of Charles Spicola Jr., May 21, 1997; The author was on the first Board of the organization.

"Tampa Electric Street Railway System (1892 through 1946)." Courtesy, Assist. City Archivist. Donor, courtesy of Estevan Orestano, 1408 Holmes Ave., Tampa (Ybor City)."Tampa Ilustrado," published many cultural articles taking place at El Centro Español circa 1913.

"Tampa Model Cities Program. City of Tampa, Florida. Part I: Interim Report."

"Ybor City: Factors Determining 'Slum' and/ or 'Blighted' Conditions." Prepared by Tampa City Planning. May 26, 1988.

## Articles

Alarcon, Daniel. "Weaner Wants Chamber Out of Gallery," *Tampa Tribune* (April 28, 1983).

Alarcon, Daniel. "Ybor Chamber Owns Land," *Tampa Tribune* (May 5, 1983).

Alduino, Frank. "The Damnedest Town This Side of Hell: Tampa, 1920-29 (part 1)," *The Sunland Tribune* 16 (November 1990): 13-17.

Alduino, Frank. "The Damnedest Town This Side of Hell: Tampa, 1920-29 (part 2)," *The Sunland Tribune* 17 (November 1991): 43-46.

Alduino, Frank. "The Smugglers' Blues and Alien Traffic in Tampa During the 1920s," *Tampa Bay History* (Fall/Winter 1991).

Blount, Archie. "Immigrants Created a New World," *Tampa Tribune* (Sept. 25, 1994).

Coulbourn, Keith. "Many Ybor City Streets Blocked as Thruway Cuts Wide Strip," *Tampa Tribune* (June 3, 1962).

Cox, Bill. "Tampa Gets Model Cities Planning Aid," *Tampa Tribune* (Nov. 17, 1967): 8B.

Culp, Susan O'Brien. "For the Duration: Women's Roles in St. Petersburg and Tampa During World War II," *Tampa Bay History*, 17:1 (Spring/Summer 1995).

Danielson, Richard. "Cuban Club Struggles to Defy Age," *St. Petersburg Times*, January 5, 1996.

Dudley, Bruce. "Firm Selected to Design Ybor's Farmers Market," *Tampa Tribune* (May 3, 1984).

Dukess, Karen. "State Agrees to Buy Ybor City Building," *St. Petersburg Times* (Feb 8, 1990).

Dunlap, Jeff. "Broken Promises, Broken Hearts," *Tampa Tribune* (May 13, 1979).

Dunlap, Jeff. "Riot and Red Tape Snarled Ybor Revival," *Tampa Tribune* (May 14, 1979): D-1.

Dunlap, Jeff. "Walter's Walled City Idea Died With Bullfight Bill," *Tampa Tribune* (May 13, 1979).

Dunn, Hampton. "Turn to Greatness." *Sunland Tribune* (October 1,1984): 82-86.

Frawley, Rosemary. "The Restauranteur Strives to Complete the Boatlift," *Tampa Tribune* (May 21, 1980).

Goldstein, Linda. "Renaissance man Cesar Gonzmart still hopes for a rebirth of Ybor City," *Tampa Tribune* (July 22, 1981).

Hathaway, Ivan J. "Ybor City gets National Landmark Honor," *Tampa Tribune*, (January 1991).

Hauptman, O. E. "Spanish Folklore from Tampa," *Southern Folklore Quarterly* (March 1938).

Hawes, Leland M., Jr. "A Chance to Shine or Shame," *Tampa Tribune* (Feb. 15, 1998).

Hawes, Leland M., Jr. "Figueredo Sought Cuban Independence," *Tampa Tribune* (April 8, 1990).

Hawes, Leland M., Jr. "H.C.C. Presiding Over Institutional Turmoil," *Tampa Tribune* (May 6, 1996).

Hawes, Leland M., Jr. "Kidnappings Squelched Strike," *Tampa Tribune* (November 6, 1994).

Hawes, Leland M., Jr. "Romanian Jews' Exodus to Tampa Was a Long Trip," *Tampa Tribune* (June 7, 1992): Baylife 4.

Hawes, Leland M., Jr. "Solidarity Failed to Save Spain," *Tampa Tribune* (July 29, 1990).

Hipp, Joseph. "What Happened in Tampa on July 15, 1887 or thereabouts," *The Sunland Tribune* 6 (November 1980): 82-94.

Ingalls, Robert P. "Strikes and Vigilante Violence in Tampa's Cigar Industry," *Tampa Bay History*, Fall/Winter 1985, 123.

Keene, Jesse L. "Gavino Gutierrez and His Contributions to Tampa, Fla." *Florida Historical Quarterly* (July 1957): 36.

Klein, Gil. "Remembering the Maine," *Tampa Tribune* (Feb. 15, 1998).

Kolinski, Charles J. "El tabaquero en la Historia de Cuba, Islas," *Florida Historical Quarterly* (July 1963): 93-312.

Landenberger, Lee. "Playing Numbers," *Tampa Tribune* (January 14, 1990).

Levin, Doron. "Tampa restauranteur firm on project to rescue Cubans," *Tampa Tribune*, May 16, 1980.

Long, Durward. "An Immigrant Co-operative Medicine Program in the South, 1887-1963," *The Journal of Southern History*, November 1965, 417-34.

Long, Durward. "The Open-Closed Shop Battle in Tampa's Cigar Industry 1919-21," *Florida Historical Quarterly* 47 (October 1968).

Long, Durward. "Labor Relations in the Tampa Cigar Industry, 1885-1911," *Labor History* 12 (Fall 1971): 551.

Meyer, Thomas H. "Davis Islands: The Booming Two Month Transformation of Tampa's Mudflats Into Tampa's Dreamscape," *The Sunland Tribune* (November 1992): 45-57.

Meynard, John. "Revitalization Drive Planned for Ybor City," *Tampa Tribune* (March 27, 1980).

Middleton, De Wight. "The Organization of Ethnicity in Tampa Ethnic Groups," *Florida Historical Quarterly* (March 1981): 281-306.

Mormino, Gary R. "The Summer of '46," *The Sunland Tribune* (November 1996): 79-86.

Mullen, Harris, "Charlie Wall." *Florida Trend*, (March 8, 1966): 20-22.

Mullen, Harris. "No More Back Burners," *Tampa Tribune*, February 15, 1988.

Olivo, Mira I. "Alcalde de Oviedo, España, de visita en Tampa," *La Gaceta*, February 13, 1998.

Paleveda, Joe. "Silhouettes." *La Gaceta* (March 13, 1992).

Pedreira, David. "Mayor Wants to rebuild a tattered neighborhood," *Tampa Tribune* (November 15, 1997).

Perez, Louis A., Jr. "Cubans in Tampa: From Exiles to Immigrants, 1892-1901," *Tampa Bay History* 7:2 (Fall/Winter 1985).

Pérez, Louis A., Jr. "Reminiscences of a Lector: Cuban Cigar Workers in Tampa," *Florida Historical Quarterly* 53 (April 1975): 137.

[Pizzo, Tony]. "Tony Pizzo's Ybor City: An Interview with Tony Pizzo, " *Tampa Bay History* 7:2 (Fall/Winter 1985): 150.

Rodriguez Morejón, A. G. "Historic Cigar." *La Gaceta* [Tampa: date unknown].

Sánchez, Arsenio M. "Incentives Helped Build West Tampa," *The Sunland Tribune* (December 1985): 9-12.

Sánchez, Arsenio M. "Tampa's Early Lighting and Transportation," *The Sunland Tribune* 17 (November 1991): 27-38.

Scaglione, Joe. "City in Turmoil: Tampa and the Strike of 1910," *The Sunland Tribune* 18 (November 1992): 29-36.

Scherr, Abraham. "Tampa's MacDill Field During WW II," *Tampa Bay History* 17:1 (Spring/Summer 1995).

Sharpe, Clifford C. "Kip." "The Tampa Fla. Brewery, Inc., Florida's First Brewery," *The Sunland Tribune* 18 (November 1992).

Smith, Andy. "The Old Tribune Told News Stories in Different Ways," *Tampa Tribune* (Sept. 25, 1994): Special Centennial, 6.

Snow, Panky. "Federal Historian likes what he sees during Ybor City tour," *Tampa Tribune* (February 4, 1988).

Tignor, Lisa. "La Colonia Latina: The Response of Tampa's Immigrant Community to the Spanish Civil War," *Tampa Bay History* 12: 1 (Spring/Summer 1990).

Yglesias, José. "The Depression Years in Ybor City," "La Nochebuena: The Best of Nights," "Un Buen Obrero, A Short Story," "The Bittersweet Legacy of La Madre Patria," "José Martí in Ybor City," "The Radical Latino Island in the South," "I Am a Gallego," "Ybor City and the Social Vision," *Tampa Bay History*, (Spring/Summer, 1996) Vol. 18, No. 1.

Varela-Lago, Ana M. "From Patriotism to Mutualism, The Early Years of the Centro Espanol de Tampa, 1891-1903," *Tampa Bay History* (Fall/Winter 1993).

Varela-Lago, Ana M. "The Immigrant Women in Tampa, The Italian Experiences, 1890-1930," *Tampa Bay History*, Fall/Winter 1985, 36-58.

**Notes and Bibliography**

# Index

A page number set in bold italics indicates a reference to either visual or factual information provided in a caption. In some cases, additional information may also exist within the running text on that page.

For purposes of clarity and consistency, this book uses a standard spelling of "Ybor" and indexes it as the family name. Some members of the family have rendered the spelling as "Ibor" in English; some have preferred a hyphenated name—"Martínez-Ybor" or "Martínez-Ibor"—and some have retained an accent in "Martínez" while others have dropped it.

## A

A. Del Pino and Company *21*
A. Mortellaro & Co. *54*
*ABC* (newspaper) 166
Abe Wolfson Men's Wear 256
Abraham, Joe 317
Abraham Lincoln Battalion. *See* Abraham Lincoln Brigade
Abraham Lincoln Brigade 163
Abraham Lincoln Brigade Archives *163*
Aces (Asturian village) 112
Acosta, Alberto *152*
Acosta, Juan Pérez *170*
Acosta, Josephine Villazon 309
Adam Katz Furnishing Family Clothing 84
Adamo Drive *190*, 318, 352
Adamo, Frank 175, *190*
Adorable Hat Shop *171*
Advisory Commission on Historic Preservation. *See* Historic Preservation Commission
aerial view *188*
Afanador, Dr. José O. *181*
afilador *194*, 195
AFL (American Federation of Labor) 164
African Americans 207, 214, 219
    riots in 1967 229
    and Urban Renewal 217
Afro-Cubans 88, 91
    dance 332
Agliano's fish market 200
Agramonte, Ignacio (club) 21
Agramonte y Loynaz, Ignacio 21

Agrigento, Sicily 336-39, 353
Agrigento-Tampa Twin City agreement 338
Aguayo, Oscar 235, 260
Airlines Reservation Center 269
Aizpuru, Joe 175, *190*
Alafia River 6
Alarcon, Daniel 316
Albano, Angelo 94
Albert Alonzo Furniture 238
Alcalde Association 208, 305, 306, *323*
Alcalde of Ybor City *200,* 213
Alchidiak, Hilda 105
Alduino, Frank 147
Alea, Raymond *173*
Alessandria della Rocca *64*, 76, 338
Alfano, Joe 245
Alfaras, Ruben *362*
Alfieri, Sandra 338
Alfonso XII (of Spain) 40
Alfonso XIII (of Spain) 41, 156, 202
Ali, Mohammed 331
Almendares, Emilio 201
Alonso, Angel 200
Alonso, Braulio *300, 334*
Alonso, Claudio *67*
Alonso, Joe *225*
Alpizar, Justa *68*
Altree, G. H. *71*
Altschul, B. J. 302
Alvarez, Allento *170*
Alvarez, Angelita Gonzales *182*
Alvarez, Cesario *173*
Alvarez, Daniel *134*
Alvarez, Evelio 201
Alvarez, Helen *197*
Alvarez, Manuel *333*
Alvarez, Mariano *170*
Alvarez, Mary 307, 328, *330, 334, 344*, 356, *357, 362*
Alvarez, Oscar "Chino" *189*, 190
Alvarez, Ramon *169, 197*, 200, *225, 234*
Alvarez, Rudolfo "Cuti" *173*
Alvarez, Tony *179*
Alvarez, Violeta *134*
Alvarez's Restaurant 244, 256
Amdal, Jim 315
American Federation of Labor 8
American Institute of Architects (AIA) 289, 299
American Pipe and Plumbing 273
American Red Cross 357
American Reserve Insurance Co. 244
American Society for the Prevention of Cruelty to Animals (ASPCA)
    opposition to bullfighting 247
American Tobacco Company 93
Americh, Ida *169*

Amin, Joseph 355
Amtrak 269
*Anagua* (ship) 294
anarchists
    in Spanish Civil War 160
Andalucia 158
Anderson, John D. Jr. 233
Andrade, Laura 357
Andrés (Father's friend) 153, 167
Anglo community
    in 1977 270
    development in Ybor City 287
Angulo, Dr. I. *181*
antiques 263
Antognelli, Gisela 331
Antonio Diaz boarding house *82*
Antonio Maceo Free Thinkers of Santa Clara 89
apartments 304
Arango Cigar Company *279. See Also* Pancho Arango cigar factory
Arango, José *51, 279*
Arcade Building *24*
architects *24*, 361
architecture *263*, 268, 275, 276, 287-88, *297*, 303, *321*
Arcuri, Josephine *169*
Argintar, Max *84*, 85, *116*, 221
    and Urban Renewal 236, 249
Argintar, Sam 200, 236, *273*
Argintar, Sender *84*
Arguelles, Abdelia *226*
Arguelles, Dr. Marcelino G. *226*
Arguelles, Lopez, and Brothers *3, 118*
Arguelles, Marcelino Jr. *226*
Arguelles Turkish Baths *226*
Armory 189, 200
Arnavat, Frederico *67*
Artist in the Schools Program 303
artists 265, *266, 267*, 268, 280, 337
    attracted in 1970s by low rents 265
    departure from Ybor City 281, 337
    in 1970s 266
    leaving Ybor City 292
Artists and Writers Ball 266, 267
arts *263*
    in 1970s 266
    exhibits 265
arts and crafts *228*, 263, 281
Arts and Crafts Fiesta 303
Askew, Reuben
    museum approval 276
asphalt
    replaces brick streets 271
Asturianitos *62*
Asturians
    in Ybor City 69, 70, 112, *188*
    sailors 339
Asturias (province of Spain) 23, 32, 40, *60, 62*, 158, *71*, 166, 176, *226*

442

**Ybor City: The Making of a Landmark Town**

**Ybor City: The Making of a Landmark Town**

448

**Ybor City: The Making of a Landmark Town**

454

**Ybor City: The Making of a Landmark Town**

**Ybor City: The Making of a Landmark Town**

**Ybor City: The Making of a Landmark Town**

**Index**

**Ybor City: The Making of a Landmark Town**

*463*

**Ybor City: The Making of a Landmark Town**

**Ybor City: The Making of a Landmark Town**

## About the Author

Frank Trebín Lastra is a native son of Ybor City, born there on Ybor Street in 1922. He has written that his early life was influenced heavily by his father's Spanish culture and his Sicilian mother's great love. His father was Evaristo Trebín Lastra, of the province of Galicia in Spain, and his mother was Ana Leto Lastra, granddaughter of Guiseppe Cacciatore, pioneer shopkeeper of a famous Ybor City grocery. Growing up, Frank was immersed in the Latin culture of Ybor City in unforgettable ways.

He later served in World War Two, attended one year at the Massachusetts Institute of Technology (M.I.T.), and graduated in industrial engineering from the Georgia Institute of Technology (Georgia Tech).

In the late 1960s, Lastra made a decision to return to the Tampa Bay area to be near his ailing father. He accepted an entry-level job at Honeywell Aeronautical Manufacturing Division in St. Petersburg, rising quickly to head his department there. After some seven years as Supervisor of Industrial Engineering, he dropped engineering for good, doing only some occasional consulting. His father's condition had deteriorated due to a disease not well understood in those years. (It was Alzheimer's.) He opened a small hardware store in Lutz, adding building supplies and lumber and expanding it many times before eventually retiring from it.

Beginning in 1974, Frank joined the Ybor City Chamber of Commerce, and gradually he found himself increasingly involved in the life of his hometown. He served as president and as a long-term director of the Ybor City Chamber of Commerce and the Ybor City Museum Society, and he worked on behalf of preservation and revitalization in many ways.

Frank's love for Ybor City is deep. He cherishes its old ways and traditions and has written a variety of literary works using it as the setting, including many stories and articles that have been published in Ybor City's tri-lingual newspaper *La Gaceta*. His books include *Select Works on Ybor City* and *The Knife Sharpener and His Wheel*, written with Manuel Blanco.